SATURN | VUE
2002-07 REPAIR MANUAL

CHILTON'S

CHILTON'S

Covers U.S. and Canadian models of Saturn VUE
2002 through 2007

Does not include information specific to hybrid models

by Tim Imhoff

CHILTON *Automotive Books*

PUBLISHED BY **HAYNES NORTH AMERICA, Inc.**

Manufactured in USA
©2009 Haynes North America, Inc.
ISBN-13: 978-1-56392-772-0
ISBN-10: 1-56392-772-1
Library of Congress Control Number 2009928139

Haynes Publishing Group
Sparkford Nr Yeovil
Somerset BA22 7JJ England

Haynes North America, Inc
861 Lawrence Drive
Newbury Park
California 91320 USA

ABCDE
FGHIJ
KLMNO
PQRST

D1209542

Contents

Photograper and mechanic with a 2005 Saturn VUE

ACKNOWLEDGEMENTS

Wiring diagrams originated exclusively for Haynes North America, Inc. by Valley Forge Technical Information Services.

About this manual

ITS PURPOSE

The purpose of this manual is to help you get the best value from your vehicle. It can do so in several ways. It can help you decide what work must be done, even if you choose to have it done by a dealer service department or a repair shop; it provides information and procedures for routine maintenance and servicing; and it offers diagnostic and repair procedures to follow when trouble occurs.

We hope you use the manual to tackle the work yourself. For many simpler jobs, doing it yourself may be quicker than arranging an appointment to get the vehicle into a shop and making the trips to leave it and pick it up. More importantly, a lot of money can be saved by avoiding the expense the shop must pass on to you to cover its labor and overhead costs. An added benefit is the sense of satisfaction and accomplishment that you feel after doing the job yourself.

USING THE MANUAL

The manual is divided into Chapters. Each Chapter is divided into numbered Sections, which are headed in bold type between horizontal lines. Each Section consists of consecutively numbered paragraphs.

At the beginning of each numbered Section you will be referred to any illustrations which apply to the procedures in that Section. The reference numbers used in illustration captions pinpoint the pertinent Section and the Step within that Section. That is, illustration 3.2 means the illustration refers to Section 3 and Step (or paragraph) 2 within that Section.

Procedures, once described in the text, are not normally repeated. When it's necessary to refer to another Chapter, the reference will be given as Chapter and Section number. Cross references given without use of the word "Chapter" apply to Sections and/or paragraphs in the same Chapter. For example, "see Section 8" means in the same Chapter.

References to the left or right side of the vehicle assume you are sitting in the driver's seat, facing forward.

Even though we have prepared this manual with extreme care, neither the publisher nor the author can accept responsibility for any errors in, or omissions from, the information given.

➡NOTE

A *Note* provides information necessary to properly complete a procedure or information which will make the procedure easier to understand.

✳✳ CAUTION

A *Caution* provides a special procedure or special steps which must be taken while completing the procedure where the Caution is found. Not heeding a Caution can result in damage to the assembly being worked on.

✳✳ WARNING

A *Warning* provides a special procedure or special steps which must be taken while completing the procedure where the Warning is found. Not heeding a Warning can result in personal injury.

Introduction

This manual covers the Saturn VUE. These vehicles feature either an in-line four-cylinder engine or a V6 engine. The engine drives the front wheels via independent driveaxles. On AWD models, the rear wheels are also propelled by way of a transfer case, driveshaft, rear differential and two rear driveaxles.

Transaxles are either a five-speed manual or a four or five speed automatic. In addition, early four-cylinder models may be equipped with a continuously-variable transaxle that doesn't use shifting functions.

Suspension is independent at all four wheels, MacPherson struts being used at the front and coil springs with shock absorbers at the rear. The rack-and-pinion steering unit is mounted on the subframe.

The brakes are disc at the front and drums at the rear, with power assist standard. Some models are equipped with an Anti-Lock Brake System (ABS).

Vehicle identification numbers

Modifications are a continuing and unpublicized process in vehicle manufacturing. Since spare parts manuals and lists are compiled on a numerical basis, the individual vehicle numbers are essential to correctly identify the component required.

VEHICLE IDENTIFICATION NUMBER (VIN)

This very important identification number is stamped on a plate attached to the dashboard inside the windshield on the driver's side of the vehicle (see illustration). It can also be found on the certification label located on the driver's side door post. The VIN also appears on the Vehicle Certificate of Title and Registration. It contains information such as where and when the vehicle was manufactured, the model year and the body style.

CERTIFICATION LABEL

The certification label is attached to the driver's door post (see illustration). The plate contains the name of the manufacturer, the month and year of production, the Gross Vehicle Weight Rating (GVWR), the Gross Axle Weight Rating (GAWR) and the certification statement.

ENGINE NUMBER

On four-cylinder models, the engine identification number is found on a sticker on the right end of the valve cover, and through a partial VIN etched into the bowl around the oil filter (see illustrations). On 3.0L V6 engines, the number is stamped near the oil pan rail on the rear of the engine. On 3.5L V6 engines, it's stamped near the transaxle on the radiator side of the engine.

TRANSAXLE NUMBER

There are four transaxles used on these models. All have important information, such as the transaxle type and build date, on a metal tag that is attached near the center top of the unit. Some models also have a prominent sticker that gives similar information.

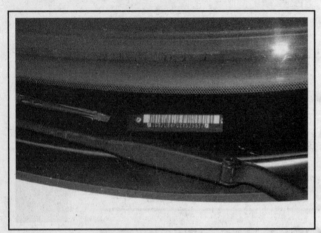

The Vehicle Identification Number (VIN) is located on a plate (arrow) on top of the dash (visible through the windshield)

The vehicle certification label is located at the driver's door pillar

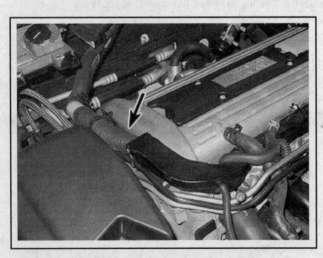

The engine ID label is attached to the valve cover (four-cylinder engine)

The engine unit number and build code date can be found on the side of the engine block, on the oil filter housing (four-cylinder engine)

Recall information

Vehicle recalls are carried out by the manufacturer in the rare event of a possible safety-related defect. The vehicle's registered owner is contacted at the address on file at the Department of Motor Vehicles and given the details of the recall. Remedial work is carried out free of charge at a dealer service department.

If you are the new owner of a used vehicle which was subject to a recall and you want to be sure that the work has been carried out, it's best to contact a dealer service department and ask about your individual vehicle - you'll need to furnish them your Vehicle Identification Number (VIN).

The table below is based on information provided by the National Highway Traffic Safety Administration (NHTSA), the body which oversees vehicle recalls in the United States. The recall database is updated constantly. For the latest information on vehicle recalls, check the NHTSA website at www.nhtsa.gov, www.safecar.gov, or call the NHTSA hotline at 1-888-327-4236.

Recall date	Recall campaign number	Model(s) affected	Concern
Dec 18, 2001	01V386000	2002 Saturn VUE	Certain models fail to comply with the requirements of FMVSS no. 210, "Seat Belt Assembly Anchorages." Some vehicles were produced with rear outer seat belt shoulder guide anchor bolts that were incorrectly installed. If these bolts were incorrectly installed, they would not withstand the load requirements of the standard. If an anchorage failed in a crash, the occupant would not be properly restrained and could have an increased risk of injury.
Dec 10, 2003	03V519000	2004 Saturn VUE	Certain models equipped with 3.5L V6 (L66) engines fail to conform to the requirements of Federal Motor Vehicle Safety standard no. 120, tire selection and rims for vehicles other than passenger cars. The front and rear wheel rim size specifications on the tire/certification label are not correct. The printed wheel rim designation specified a 16-inch wheel when a 17-inch wheel designation was required. If the wheel rim size is incorrectly printed on a tire/certification label, a service technician who solely uses the tire/certification label for service information may attempt to replace a damaged wheel with an incorrect wheel.

Buying parts

Replacement parts are available from many sources, which generally fall into one of two categories - authorized dealer parts departments and independent retail auto parts stores. Our advice concerning these parts is as follows:

Retail auto parts stores: Good auto parts stores will stock frequently needed components which wear out relatively fast, such as clutch components, exhaust systems, brake parts, tune-up parts, etc. These stores often supply new or reconditioned parts on an exchange basis, which can save a considerable amount of money. Discount auto parts stores are often very good places to buy materials and parts needed for general vehicle maintenance such as oil, grease, filters, spark plugs, belts, touch-up paint, bulbs, etc. They also usually sell

tools and general accessories, have convenient hours, charge lower prices and can often be found not far from home.

Authorized dealer parts department: This is the best source for parts which are unique to the vehicle and not generally available elsewhere (such as major engine parts, transmission parts, trim pieces, etc.).

Warranty information: If the vehicle is still covered under warranty, be sure that any replacement parts purchased - regardless of the source - do not invalidate the warranty!

To be sure of obtaining the correct parts, have engine and chassis numbers available and, if possible, take the old parts along for positive identification.

MAINTENANCE TECHNIQUES

There are a number of techniques involved in maintenance and repair that will be referred to throughout this manual. Application of these techniques will enable the home mechanic to be more efficient, better organized and capable of performing the various tasks properly, which will ensure that the repair job is thorough and complete.

Fasteners

Fasteners are nuts, bolts, studs and screws used to hold two or more parts together. There are a few things to keep in mind when working with fasteners. Almost all of them use a locking device of some type, either a lockwasher, locknut, locking tab or thread adhesive. All threaded fasteners should be clean and straight, with undamaged threads and undamaged corners on the hex head where the wrench fits. Develop the habit of replacing all damaged nuts and bolts with new ones. Special locknuts with nylon or fiber inserts can only be used once. If they are removed, they lose their locking ability and must be replaced with new ones.

Rusted nuts and bolts should be treated with a penetrating fluid to ease removal and prevent breakage. Some mechanics use turpentine in a spout-type oil can, which works quite well. After applying the rust penetrant, let it work for a few minutes before trying to loosen the nut or bolt. Badly rusted fasteners may have to be chiseled or sawed off or removed with a special nut breaker, available at tool stores.

If a bolt or stud breaks off in an assembly, it can be drilled and removed with a special tool commonly available for this purpose. Most automotive machine shops can perform this task, as well as other repair procedures, such as the repair of threaded holes that have been stripped out.

Flat washers and lockwashers, when removed from an assembly, should always be replaced exactly as removed. Replace any damaged washers with new ones. Never use a lockwasher on any soft metal surface (such as aluminum), thin sheet metal or plastic.

Fastener sizes

For a number of reasons, automobile manufacturers are making wider and wider use of metric fasteners. Therefore, it is important to be able to tell the difference between standard (sometimes called U.S. or SAE) and metric hardware, since they cannot be interchanged.

All bolts, whether standard or metric, are sized according to diameter, thread pitch and length. For example, a standard 1/2 - 13 x 1 bolt is 1/2 inch in diameter, has 13 threads per inch and is 1 inch long. An M12 - 1.75 x 25 metric bolt is 12 mm in diameter, has a thread pitch of 1.75 mm (the distance between threads) and is 25 mm long. The two bolts are nearly identical, and easily confused, but they are not interchangeable.

In addition to the differences in diameter, thread pitch and length, metric and standard bolts can also be distinguished by examining the bolt heads. To begin with, the distance across the flats on a standard bolt head is measured in inches, while the same dimension on a metric bolt is sized in millimeters (the same is true for nuts). As a result, a standard wrench should not be used on a metric bolt and a metric wrench should not be used on a standard bolt. Also, most standard bolts have slashes

radiating out from the center of the head to denote the grade or strength of the bolt, which is an indication of the amount of torque that can be applied to it. The greater the number of slashes, the greater the strength of the bolt. Grades 0 through 5 are commonly used on automobiles. Metric bolts have a property class (grade) number, rather than a slash, molded into their heads to indicate bolt strength. In this case, the higher the number, the stronger the bolt. Property class numbers 8.8, 9.8 and 10.9 are commonly used on automobiles.

Strength markings can also be used to distinguish standard hex nuts from metric hex nuts. Many standard nuts have dots stamped into one side, while metric nuts are marked with a number. The greater the number of dots, or the higher the number, the greater the strength of the nut.

Metric studs are also marked on their ends according to property class (grade). Larger studs are numbered (the same as metric bolts), while smaller studs carry a geometric code to denote grade.

It should be noted that many fasteners, especially Grades 0 through 2, have no distinguishing marks on them. When such is the case, the only way to determine whether it is standard or metric is to measure the thread pitch or compare it to a known fastener of the same size.

Standard fasteners are often referred to as SAE, as opposed to metric. However, it should be noted that SAE technically refers to a non-metric fine thread fastener only. Coarse thread non-metric fasteners are referred to as USS sizes.

Since fasteners of the same size (both standard and metric) may have different strength ratings, be sure to reinstall any bolts, studs or nuts removed from your vehicle in their original locations. Also, when replacing a fastener with a new one, make sure that the new one has a strength rating equal to or greater than the original.

Tightening sequences and procedures

Most threaded fasteners should be tightened to a specific torque value (torque is the twisting force applied to a threaded component such as a nut or bolt). Overtightening the fastener can weaken it and cause it to break, while undertightening can cause it to eventually come loose. Bolts, screws and studs, depending on the material they are made of and their thread diameters, have specific torque values, many of which are noted in the Specifications at the end of each Chapter. Be sure to follow the torque recommendations closely. For fasteners not assigned a specific torque, a general torque value chart is presented here as a guide. These torque values are for dry (unlubricated) fasteners threaded into steel or cast iron (not aluminum). As was previously mentioned, the size and grade of a fastener determine the amount of torque that can safely be applied to it. The figures listed here are approximate for Grade 2 and Grade 3 fasteners. Higher grades can tolerate higher torque values.

Fasteners laid out in a pattern, such as cylinder head bolts, oil pan bolts, differential cover bolts, etc., must be loosened or tightened in sequence to avoid warping the component. This sequence will normally be shown in the appropriate Chapter. If a specific pattern is not given, the following procedures can be used to prevent warping.

Initially, the bolts or nuts should be assembled finger-tight only. Next, they should be tightened one full turn each, in a criss-cross or diagonal pattern. After each one has been tightened one full turn, return to the first one and tighten them all one-half turn, following the same

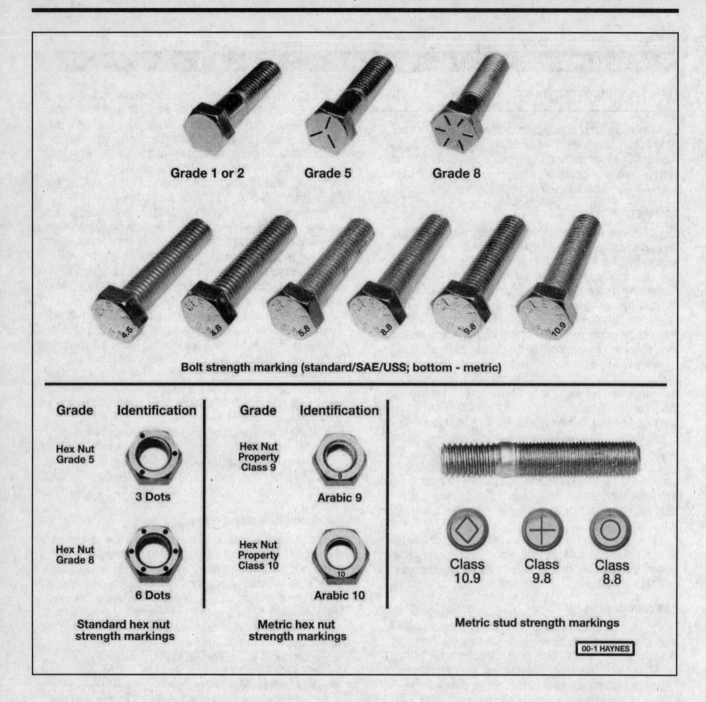

Grade 1 or 2   Grade 5   Grade 8

Bolt strength marking (standard/SAE/USS; bottom - metric)

Grade	Identification
Hex Nut Grade 5	3 Dots
Hex Nut Grade 8	6 Dots

Standard hex nut strength markings

Grade	Identification
Hex Nut Property Class 9	Arabic 9
Hex Nut Property Class 10	Arabic 10

Metric hex nut strength markings

Class 10.9   Class 9.8   Class 8.8

Metric stud strength markings

00-1 HAYNES

pattern. Finally, tighten each of them one-quarter turn at a time until each fastener has been tightened to the proper torque. To loosen and remove the fasteners, the procedure would be reversed.

Component disassembly

Component disassembly should be done with care and purpose to help ensure that the parts go back together properly. Always keep track of the sequence in which parts are removed. Make note of special characteristics or marks on parts that can be installed more than one way, such as a grooved thrust washer on a shaft. It is a good idea to lay the

disassembled parts out on a clean surface in the order that they were removed. It may also be helpful to make sketches or take instant photos of components before removal.

When removing fasteners from a component, keep track of their locations. Sometimes threading a bolt back in a part, or putting the washers and nut back on a stud, can prevent mix-ups later. If nuts and bolts cannot be returned to their original locations, they should be kept in a compartmented box or a series of small boxes. A cupcake or muffin tin is ideal for this purpose, since each cavity can hold the bolts and nuts from a particular area (i.e. oil pan bolts, valve cover bolts, engine

Metric thread sizes

	Ft-lbs	Nm
M-6	6 to 9	9 to 12
M-8	14 to 21	19 to 28
M-10	28 to 40	38 to 54
M-12	50 to 71	68 to 96
M-14	80 to 140	109 to 154

Pipe thread sizes

	Ft-lbs	Nm
1/8	5 to 8	7 to 10
1/4	12 to 18	17 to 24
3/8	22 to 33	30 to 44
1/2	25 to 35	34 to 47

U.S. thread sizes

	Ft-lbs	Nm
1/4 - 20	6 to 9	9 to 12
5/16 - 18	12 to 18	17 to 24
5/16 - 24	14 to 20	19 to 27
3/8 - 16	22 to 32	30 to 43
3/8 - 24	27 to 38	37 to 51
7/16 - 14	40 to 55	55 to 74
7/16 - 20	40 to 60	55 to 81
1/2 - 13	55 to 80	75 to 108

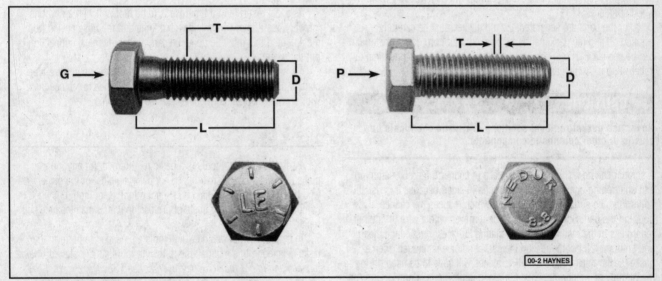

00-2 HAYNES

Standard (SAE and USS) bolt dimensions/grade marks

G   Grade marks (bolt strength)
L   Length (in inches)
T   Thread pitch (number of threads per inch)
D   Nominal diameter (in inches)

Metric bolt dimensions/grade marks

P   Property class (bolt strength)
L   Length (in millimeters)
T   Thread pitch (distance between threads in millimeters)
D   Diameter

mount bolts, etc.). A pan of this type is especially helpful when working on assemblies with very small parts, such as the carburetor, alternator, valve train or interior dash and trim pieces. The cavities can be marked with paint or tape to identify the contents.

Whenever wiring looms, harnesses or connectors are separated, it is a good idea to identify the two halves with numbered pieces of masking tape so they can be easily reconnected.

Gasket sealing surfaces

Throughout any vehicle, gaskets are used to seal the mating surfaces between two parts and keep lubricants, fluids, vacuum or pressure contained in an assembly.

Many times these gaskets are coated with a liquid or paste-type gasket sealing compound before assembly. Age, heat and pressure can sometimes cause the two parts to stick together so tightly that they are very difficult to separate. Often, the assembly can be loosened by striking it with a soft-face hammer near the mating surfaces. A regular hammer can be used if a block of wood is placed between the hammer and the part. Do not hammer on cast parts or parts that could be easily damaged. With any particularly stubborn part, always recheck to make sure that every fastener has been removed.

Avoid using a screwdriver or bar to pry apart an assembly, as they

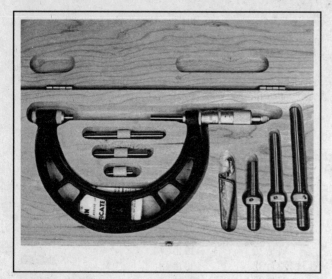

Micrometer set

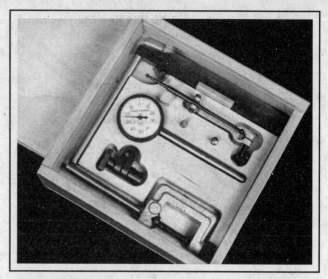

Dial indicator set

can easily mar the gasket sealing surfaces of the parts, which must remain smooth. If prying is absolutely necessary, use an old broom handle, but keep in mind that extra clean up will be necessary if the wood splinters.

After the parts are separated, the old gasket must be carefully scraped off and the gasket surfaces cleaned. Stubborn gasket material can be soaked with rust penetrant or treated with a special chemical to soften it so it can be easily scraped off.

✳✳ CAUTION:

Never use gasket removal solutions or caustic chemicals on plastic or other composite components.

A scraper can be fashioned from a piece of copper tubing by flattening and sharpening one end. Copper is recommended because it is usually softer than the surfaces to be scraped, which reduces the chance of gouging the part. Some gaskets can be removed with a wire brush, but regardless of the method used, the mating surfaces must be left clean and smooth. If for some reason the gasket surface is gouged, then a gasket sealer thick enough to fill scratches will have to be used during reassembly of the components. For most applications, a non-drying (or semi-drying) gasket sealer should be used.

Hose removal tips

✳✳ WARNING:

If the vehicle is equipped with air conditioning, do not disconnect any of the A/C hoses without first having the system depressurized by a dealer service department or a service station.

Hose removal precautions closely parallel gasket removal precautions. Avoid scratching or gouging the surface that the hose mates against or the connection may leak. This is especially true for radiator hoses. Because of various chemical reactions, the rubber in hoses can bond itself to the metal spigot that the hose fits over. To remove a hose, first loosen the hose clamps that secure it to the spigot. Then, with slip-joint pliers, grab the hose at the clamp and rotate it around the spigot. Work it back and forth until it is completely free, then pull it off. Silicone or other lubricants will ease removal if they can be applied between the hose and the outside of the spigot. Apply the same lubricant to the inside of the hose and the outside of the spigot to simplify installation.

As a last resort (and if the hose is to be replaced with a new one anyway), the rubber can be slit with a knife and the hose peeled from the spigot. If this must be done, be careful that the metal connection is not damaged.

If a hose clamp is broken or damaged, do not reuse it. Wire-type clamps usually weaken with age, so it is a good idea to replace them with screw-type clamps whenever a hose is removed.

TOOLS

A selection of good tools is a basic requirement for anyone who plans to maintain and repair his or her own vehicle. For the owner who has few tools, the initial investment might seem high, but when compared to the spiraling costs of professional auto maintenance and repair, it is a wise one.

To help the owner decide which tools are needed to perform the tasks detailed in this manual, the following tool lists are offered: *Maintenance and minor repair, Repair/overhaul and Special.*

The newcomer to practical mechanics should start off with the *maintenance and minor repair* tool kit, which is adequate for the simpler jobs performed on a vehicle. Then, as confidence and experience grow, the owner can tackle more difficult tasks, buying additional tools as they are needed. Eventually the basic kit will be expanded into the *repair and overhaul* tool set. Over a period of time, the experienced do-it-yourselfer will assemble a tool set complete enough for most repair and overhaul procedures and will add tools from the special category when it is felt that the expense is justified by the frequency of use.

Maintenance and minor repair tool kit

The tools in this list should be considered the minimum required for performance of routine maintenance, servicing and minor repair work. We recommend the purchase of combination wrenches (box-end and open-end combined in one wrench). While more expensive than open end wrenches, they offer the advantages of both types of wrench.

Combination wrench set (1/4-inch to 1 inch or 6 mm to 19 mm)
Adjustable wrench, 8 inch
Spark plug wrench with rubber insert

Spark plug gap adjusting tool
Feeler gauge set
Brake bleeder wrench
Standard screwdriver (5/16-inch x 6 inch)
Phillips screwdriver (No. 2 x 6 inch)
Combination pliers - 6 inch
Hacksaw and assortment of blades
Tire pressure gauge
Grease gun

Oil can
Fine emery cloth
Wire brush
Battery post and cable cleaning tool
Oil filter wrench
Funnel (medium size)
Safety goggles
Jackstands (2)
Drain pan

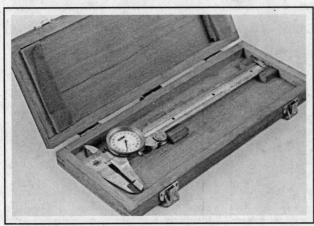

Dial caliper

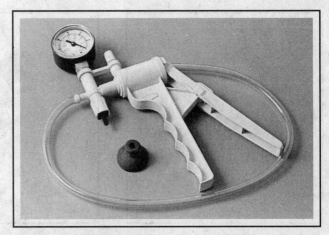

Hand-operated vacuum pump

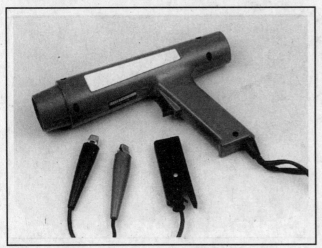

Timing light

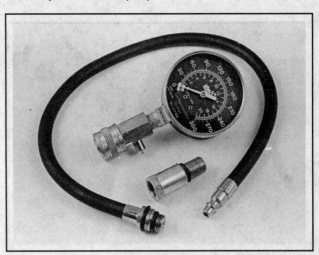

Compression gauge with spark plug hole adapter

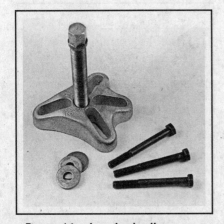

Damper/steering wheel puller

General purpose puller

Hydraulic lifter removal tool

➡**Note:** If basic tune-ups are going to be part of routine maintenance, it will be necessary to purchase a good quality stroboscopic timing light and combination tachometer/dwell meter. Although they are included in the list of special tools, it is mentioned here because they are absolutely necessary for tuning most vehicles properly.

Repair and overhaul tool set

These tools are essential for anyone who plans to perform major repairs and are in addition to those in the maintenance and minor repair tool kit. Included is a comprehensive set of sockets which, though expensive, are invaluable because of their versatility, especially when various extensions and drives are available. We recommend the 1/2-inch drive over the 3/8-inch drive. Although the larger drive is bulky and more expensive, it has the capacity of accepting a very wide range of large sockets. Ideally, however, the mechanic should have a 3/8-inch drive set and a 1/2-inch drive set.

Valve spring compressor

Valve spring compressor

Ridge reamer

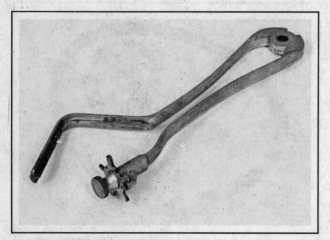
Piston ring groove cleaning tool

Ring removal/installation tool

Ring compressor

Cylinder hone

Brake hold-down spring tool

Torque angle gauge

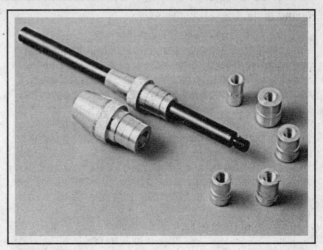

Clutch plate alignment tool

Socket set(s)
Reversible ratchet
Extension - 10 inch
Universal joint
Torque wrench (same size drive as sockets)
Ball peen hammer - 8 ounce
Soft-face hammer (plastic/rubber)
Standard screwdriver (1/4-inch x 6 inch)
Standard screwdriver (stubby - 5/16-inch)
Phillips screwdriver (No. 3 x 8 inch)
Phillips screwdriver (stubby - No. 2)
Pliers - vise grip
Pliers - lineman's
Pliers - needle nose
Pliers - snap-ring (internal and external)
Cold chisel - 1/2-inch
Scribe
Scraper (made from flattened copper tubing)
Centerpunch
Pin punches (1/16, 1/8, 3/16-inch)
Steel rule/straightedge - 12 inch
Allen wrench set (1/8 to 3/8-inch or 4 mm to 10 mm)
A selection of files
Wire brush (large)
Jackstands (second set)
Jack (scissor or hydraulic type)

→**Note: Another tool which is often useful is an electric drill with a chuck capacity of 3/8-inch and a set of good quality drill bits.**

Special tools

The tools in this list include those which are not used regularly, are expensive to buy, or which need to be used in accordance with their manufacturer's instructions. Unless these tools will be used frequently, it is not very economical to purchase many of them. A consideration would be to split the cost and use between yourself and a friend or friends. In addition, most of these tools can be obtained from a tool rental shop on a temporary basis.

This list primarily contains only those tools and instruments widely available to the public, and not those special tools produced by the vehicle manufacturer for distribution to dealer service departments. Occasionally, references to the manufacturer's special tools are included in the text of this manual. Generally, an alternative method of doing the job without the special tool is offered. However, sometimes there is no alternative to their use. Where this is the case, and the tool cannot be purchased or borrowed, the work should be turned over to the dealer service department or an automotive repair shop.

Valve spring compressor
Piston ring groove cleaning tool
Piston ring compressor
Piston ring installation tool
Cylinder compression gauge
Cylinder ridge reamer
Cylinder surfacing hone
Cylinder bore gauge
Micrometers and/or dial calipers
Hydraulic lifter removal tool
Balljoint separator
Universal-type puller
Impact screwdriver
Dial indicator set
Stroboscopic timing light (inductive pick-up)
Hand operated vacuum/pressure pump
Tachometer/dwell meter
Universal electrical multimeter
Cable hoist
Brake spring removal and installation tools
Floor jack

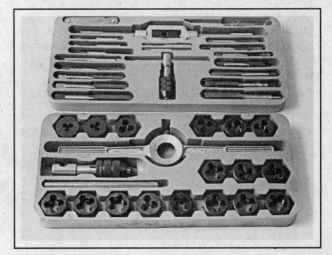

Tap and die set

Buying tools

For the do-it-yourselfer who is just starting to get involved in vehicle maintenance and repair, there are a number of options available when purchasing tools. If maintenance and minor repair is the extent of the work to be done, the purchase of individual tools is satisfactory. If, on the other hand, extensive work is planned, it would be a good idea to purchase a modest tool set from one of the large retail chain stores. A set can usually be bought at a substantial savings over the individual tool prices, and they often come with a tool box. As additional tools are needed, add-on sets, individual tools and a larger tool box can be purchased to expand the tool selection. Building a tool set gradually allows the cost of the tools to be spread over a longer period of time and gives the mechanic the freedom to choose only those tools that will actually be used.

Tool stores will often be the only source of some of the special tools that are needed, but regardless of where tools are bought, try to avoid cheap ones, especially when buying screwdrivers and sockets, because they won't last very long. The expense involved in replacing cheap tools will eventually be greater than the initial cost of quality tools.

Care and maintenance of tools

Good tools are expensive, so it makes sense to treat them with respect. Keep them clean and in usable condition and store them properly when not in use. Always wipe off any dirt, grease or metal chips before putting them away. Never leave tools lying around in the work area. Upon completion of a job, always check closely under the hood for tools that may have been left there so they won't get lost during a test drive.

Some tools, such as screwdrivers, pliers, wrenches and sockets, can be hung on a panel mounted on the garage or workshop wall, while others should be kept in a tool box or tray. Measuring instruments, gauges, meters, etc. must be carefully stored where they cannot be damaged by weather or impact from other tools.

When tools are used with care and stored properly, they will last a very long time. Even with the best of care, though, tools will wear out if used frequently. When a tool is damaged or worn out, replace it. Subsequent jobs will be safer and more enjoyable if you do.

HOW TO REPAIR DAMAGED THREADS

Sometimes, the internal threads of a nut or bolt hole can become stripped, usually from overtightening. Stripping threads is an all-too-common occurrence, especially when working with aluminum parts, because aluminum is so soft that it easily strips out.

Usually, external or internal threads are only partially stripped. After they've been cleaned up with a tap or die, they'll still work. Sometimes, however, threads are badly damaged. When this happens, you've got three choices:

1) *Drill and tap the hole to the next suitable oversize and install a larger diameter bolt, screw or stud.*

2) *Drill and tap the hole to accept a threaded plug, then drill and tap the plug to the original screw size. You can also buy a plug already threaded to the original size. Then you simply drill a hole to the specified size, then run the threaded plug into the hole with a bolt and jam nut. Once the plug is fully seated, remove the jam nut and bolt.*

3) *The third method uses a patented thread repair kit like Heli-Coil or Slimsert. These easy-to-use kits are designed to repair damaged threads in straight-through holes and blind holes. Both are available as kits which can handle a variety of sizes and thread patterns. Drill the hole, then tap it with the special included tap. Install the Heli-Coil and the hole is back to its original diameter and thread pitch.*

Regardless of which method you use, be sure to proceed calmly and carefully. A little impatience or carelessness during one of these relatively simple procedures can ruin your whole day's work and cost you a bundle if you wreck an expensive part.

WORKING FACILITIES

Not to be overlooked when discussing tools is the workshop. If anything more than routine maintenance is to be carried out, some sort of suitable work area is essential.

It is understood, and appreciated, that many home mechanics do not have a good workshop or garage available, and end up removing an engine or doing major repairs outside. It is recommended, however, that the overhaul or repair be completed under the cover of a roof.

A clean, flat workbench or table of comfortable working height is an absolute necessity. The workbench should be equipped with a vise that has a jaw opening of at least four inches.

As mentioned previously, some clean, dry storage space is also required for tools, as well as the lubricants, fluids, cleaning solvents, etc. which soon become necessary.

Sometimes waste oil and fluids, drained from the engine or cooling system during normal maintenance or repairs, present a disposal problem. To avoid pouring them on the ground or into a sewage system, pour the used fluids into large containers, seal them with caps and take them to an authorized disposal site or recycling center. Plastic jugs, such as old antifreeze containers, are ideal for this purpose.

Always keep a supply of old newspapers and clean rags available. Old towels are excellent for mopping up spills. Many mechanics use rolls of paper towels for most work because they are readily available and disposable. To help keep the area under the vehicle clean, a large cardboard box can be cut open and flattened to protect the garage or shop floor.

Whenever working over a painted surface, such as when leaning over a fender to service something under the hood, always cover it with an old blanket or bedspread to protect the finish. Vinyl covered pads, made especially for this purpose, are available at auto parts stores.

Jacking and towing

JACKING

The jack supplied with the vehicle should only be used for raising the vehicle for changing a tire or placing jackstands under the frame.

✳✳ WARNING:

Never crawl under the vehicle or start the engine when the jack is being used as the only means of support.

All vehicles are supplied with a scissors-type jack. When jacking the vehicle, it should be engaged with the rocker panel flange. Some models have notches that the jack head engages with (see illustration).

The vehicle should be on level ground with the wheels blocked and the transmission in Park (automatic). Pry off the hub cap (if equipped) using the tapered end of the lug wrench. Loosen the lug nuts one-half turn and leave them in place until the wheel is raised off the ground.

Place the jack under the side of the vehicle in the indicated position. Use the supplied wrench to turn the jackscrew clockwise until the wheel is raised off the ground. Remove the lug nuts, pull off the wheel and replace it with the spare.

With the beveled side in, reinstall the lug nuts and tighten them until snug. Lower the vehicle by turning the jackscrew counterclockwise. Remove the jack and tighten the nuts in a diagonal pattern to the torque listed in the Chapter 1 Specifications. If a torque wrench is not available, have the torque checked by a service station as soon as possible. Replace the hubcap by placing it in position and using the heel of your hand or a rubber mallet to seat it.

TOWING

Two-wheel drive models can be towed from the front with the front wheels off the ground, using a wheel lift type tow truck. If towed from the rear, the front wheels must be placed on a dolly. All-wheel drive models must be towed with all four wheels off the ground. A sling-type tow truck cannot be used, as body damage will result. The best way to tow the vehicle is with a flat-bed car carrier.

In an emergency the vehicle can be towed a short distance with a cable or chain attached to one of the towing eyelets located under the front or rear bumpers. The driver must remain in the vehicle to operate the steering and brakes (remember that power steering and power brakes will not work with the engine off).

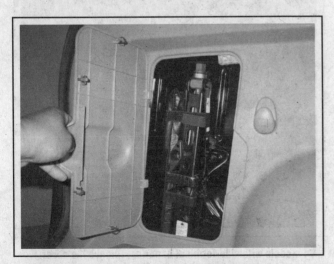

The jack is located behind this door in the left rear quarter panel

The jack fits over the rocker panel flange (there are two jacking points on each side of the vehicle)

Booster battery (jump) starting

Observe these precautions when using a booster battery to start a vehicle:

a) *Before connecting the booster battery, make sure the ignition switch is in the Off position.*

b) *Turn off the lights, heater and other electrical loads.*

c) *Your eyes should be shielded. Safety goggles are a good idea.*

d) *Make sure the booster battery is the same voltage as the dead one in the vehicle.*

e) *The two vehicles MUST NOT TOUCH each other!*

f) *Make sure the transaxle is in Park (automatic).*

g) *If the booster battery is not a maintenance-free type, remove the vent caps and lay a cloth over the vent holes.*

Connect the red jumper cable to the positive (+) terminals of each battery (see illustration).

➥**Note: On models with side-terminal batteries, a remote positive terminal is provided that makes it easier to connect the jumper cable; it's located under the fuse/relay box cover (see illustration).**

Connect one end of the black jumper cable to the negative (-) terminal of the booster battery. The other end of this cable should be connected to a good ground on the vehicle to be started, such as a bolt or bracket on the body.

Start the engine using the booster battery, then, with the engine running at idle speed, disconnect the jumper cables in the reverse order of connection.

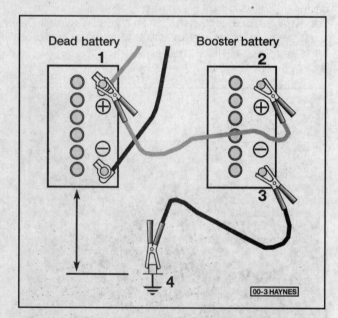

Make the booster battery cable connections in the numerical order shown (note that the negative cable of the booster battery is NOT attached to the negative terminal of the dead battery)

On models with side-terminal batteries, remove the cover from the underhood fuse/relay box to access the remote positive terminal

Automotive chemicals and lubricants

A number of automotive chemicals and lubricants are available for use during vehicle maintenance and repair. They include a wide variety of products ranging from cleaning solvents and degreasers to lubricants and protective sprays for rubber, plastic and vinyl.

CLEANERS

Carburetor cleaner and choke cleaner is a strong solvent for gum, varnish and carbon. Most carburetor cleaners leave a dry-type lubricant film which will not harden or gum up. Because of this film it is not recommended for use on electrical components.

Brake system cleaner is used to remove brake dust, grease and brake fluid from the brake system, where clean surfaces are absolutely necessary. It leaves no residue and often eliminates brake squeal caused by contaminants.

Electrical cleaner removes oxidation, corrosion and carbon deposits from electrical contacts, restoring full current flow. It can also be used to clean spark plugs, carburetor jets, voltage regulators and other parts where an oil-free surface is desired.

Demoisturants remove water and moisture from electrical components such as alternators, voltage regulators, electrical connectors and fuse blocks. They are non-conductive and non-corrosive.

Degreasers are heavy-duty solvents used to remove grease from the outside of the engine and from chassis components. They can be sprayed or brushed on and, depending on the type, are rinsed off either with water or solvent.

LUBRICANTS

Motor oil is the lubricant formulated for use in engines. It normally contains a wide variety of additives to prevent corrosion and reduce foaming and wear. Motor oil comes in various weights (viscosity ratings) from 0 to 50. The recommended weight of the oil depends on the season, temperature and the demands on the engine. Light oil is used in cold climates and under light load conditions. Heavy oil is used in hot climates and where high loads are encountered. Multi-viscosity oils are designed to have characteristics of both light and heavy oils and are available in a number of weights from 0W-20 to 20W-50.

Gear oil is designed to be used in differentials, manual transmissions and other areas where high-temperature lubrication is required.

Chassis and wheel bearing grease is a heavy grease used where increased loads and friction are encountered, such as for wheel bearings, ball-joints, tie-rod ends and universal joints.

High-temperature wheel bearing grease is designed to withstand the extreme temperatures encountered by wheel bearings in disc brake equipped vehicles. It usually contains molybdenum disulfide (moly), which is a dry-type lubricant.

White grease is a heavy grease for metal-to-metal applications where water is a problem. White grease stays soft under both low and high temperatures (usually from -100 to +190-degrees F), and will not wash off or dilute in the presence of water.

Assembly lube is a special extreme pressure lubricant, usually containing moly, used to lubricate high-load parts (such as main and rod bearings and cam lobes) for initial start-up of a new engine. The assembly lube lubricates the parts without being squeezed out or washed away until the engine oiling system begins to function.

Silicone lubricants are used to protect rubber, plastic, vinyl and nylon parts.

Graphite lubricants are used where oils cannot be used due to contamination problems, such as in locks. The dry graphite will lubricate metal parts while remaining uncontaminated by dirt, water, oil or acids. It is electrically conductive and will not foul electrical contacts in locks such as the ignition switch.

Moly penetrants loosen and lubricate frozen, rusted and corroded fasteners and prevent future rusting or freezing.

Heat-sink grease is a special electrically non-conductive grease that is used for mounting electronic ignition modules where it is essential that heat is transferred away from the module.

SEALANTS

RTV sealant is one of the most widely used gasket compounds. Made from silicone, RTV is air curing, it seals, bonds, waterproofs, fills surface irregularities, remains flexible, doesn't shrink, is relatively easy to remove, and is used as a supplementary sealer with almost all low and medium temperature gaskets.

Anaerobic sealant is much like RTV in that it can be used either to seal gaskets or to form gaskets by itself. It remains flexible, is solvent resistant and fills surface imperfections. The difference between an anaerobic sealant and an RTV-type sealant is in the curing. RTV cures when exposed to air, while an anaerobic sealant cures only in the absence of air. This means that an anaerobic sealant cures only after the assembly of parts, sealing them together.

Thread and pipe sealant is used for sealing hydraulic and pneumatic fittings and vacuum lines. It is usually made from a Teflon compound, and comes in a spray, a paint-on liquid and as a wrap-around tape.

CHEMICALS

Anti-seize compound prevents seizing, galling, cold welding, rust and corrosion in fasteners. High-temperature anti-seize, usually made with copper and graphite lubricants, is used for exhaust system and exhaust manifold bolts.

Anaerobic locking compounds are used to keep fasteners from vibrating or working loose and cure only after installation, in the absence of air. Medium strength locking compound is used for small nuts, bolts and screws that may be removed later. High-strength locking compound is for large nuts, bolts and studs which aren't removed on a regular basis.

Oil additives range from viscosity index improvers to chemical treatments that claim to reduce internal engine friction. It should be noted that most oil manufacturers caution against using additives with their oils.

Gas additives perform several functions, depending on their chemical makeup. They usually contain solvents that help dissolve gum and varnish that build up on carburetor, fuel injection and intake parts. They also serve to break down carbon deposits that form on the inside surfaces of the combustion chambers. Some additives contain upper cylinder lubricants for valves and piston rings, and others contain chemicals to remove condensation from the gas tank.

MISCELLANEOUS

Brake fluid is specially formulated hydraulic fluid that can withstand the heat and pressure encountered in brake systems. Care must be taken so this fluid does not come in contact with painted surfaces or plastics. An opened container should always be resealed to prevent contamination by water or dirt.

Weatherstrip adhesive is used to bond weatherstripping around doors, windows and trunk lids. It is sometimes used to attach trim pieces.

Undercoating is a petroleum-based, tar-like substance that is designed to protect metal surfaces on the underside of the vehicle from corrosion. It also acts as a sound-deadening agent by insulating the bottom of the vehicle.

Waxes and polishes are used to help protect painted and plated surfaces from the weather. Different types of paint may require the use of different types of wax and polish. Some polishes utilize a chemical or abrasive cleaner to help remove the top layer of oxidized (dull) paint on older vehicles. In recent years many non-wax polishes that contain a wide variety of chemicals such as polymers and silicones have been introduced. These non-wax polishes are usually easier to apply and last longer than conventional waxes and polishes.

CONVERSION FACTORS

LENGTH (distance)

Inches (in)	X 25.4	= Millimeters (mm)	X 0.0394	= Inches (in)
Feet (ft)	X 0.305	= Meters (m)	X 3.281	= Feet (ft)
Miles	X 1.609	= Kilometers (km)	X 0.621	= Miles

VOLUME (capacity)

Cubic inches (cu in; in^3)	X 16.387	= Cubic centimeters (cc; cm^3)	X 0.061	= Cubic inches (cu in; in^3)
Imperial pints (Imp pt)	X 0.568	= Liters (l)	X 1.76	= Imperial pints (Imp pt)
Imperial quarts (Imp qt)	X 1.137	= Liters (l)	X 0.88	= Imperial quarts (Imp qt)
Imperial quarts (Imp qt)	X 1.201	= US quarts (US qt)	X 0.833	= Imperial quarts (Imp qt)
US quarts (US qt)	X 0.946	= Liters (l)	X 1.057	= US quarts (US qt)
Imperial gallons (Imp gal)	X 4.546	= Liters (l)	X 0.22	= Imperial gallons (Imp gal)
Imperial gallons (Imp gal)	X 1.201	= US gallons (US gal)	X 0.833	= Imperial gallons (Imp gal)
US gallons (US gal)	X 3.785	= Liters (l)	X 0.264	= US gallons (US gal)

MASS (weight)

Ounces (oz)	X 28.35	= Grams (g)	X 0.035	= Ounces (oz)
Pounds (lb)	X 0.454	= Kilograms (kg)	X 2.205	= Pounds (lb)

FORCE

Ounces-force (ozf; oz)	X 0.278	= Newtons (N)	X 3.6	= Ounces-force (ozf; oz)
Pounds-force (lbf; lb)	X 4.448	= Newtons (N)	X 0.225	= Pounds-force (lbf; lb)
Newtons (N)	X 0.1	= Kilograms-force (kgf; kg)	X 9.81	= Newtons (N)

PRESSURE

Pounds-force per square inch (psi; lbf/in^2; lb/in^2)	X 0.070	= Kilograms-force per square centimeter (kgf/cm^2; kg/cm^2)	X 14.223	= Pounds-force per square inch (psi; lbf/in^2; lb/in^2)
Pounds-force per square inch (psi; lbf/in^2; lb/in^2)	X 0.068	= Atmospheres (atm)	X 14.696	= Pounds-force per square inch (psi; lbf/in^2; lb/in^2)
Pounds-force per square inch (psi; lbf/in^2; lb/in^2)	X 0.069	= Bars	X 14.5	= Pounds-force per square inch (psi; lbf/in^2; lb/in^2)
Pounds-force per square inch (psi; lbf/in^2; lb/in^2)	X 6.895	= Kilopascals (kPa)	X 0.145	= Pounds-force per square inch (psi; lbf/in^2; lb/in^2)
Kilopascals (kPa)	X 0.01	= Kilograms-force per square centimeter (kgf/cm^2; kg/cm^2)	X 98.1	= Kilopascals (kPa)

TORQUE (moment of force)

Pounds-force inches (lbf in; lb in)	X 1.152	= Kilograms-force centimeter (kgf cm; kg cm)	X 0.868	= Pounds-force inches (lbf in; lb in)
Pounds-force inches (lbf in; lb in)	X 0.113	= Newton meters (Nm)	X 8.85	= Pounds-force inches (lbf in; lb in)
Pounds-force inches (lbf in; lb in)	X 0.083	= Pounds-force feet (lbf ft; lb ft)	X 12	= Pounds-force inches (lbf in; lb in)
Pounds-force feet (lbf ft; lb ft)	X 0.138	= Kilograms-force meters (kgf m; kg m)	X 7.233	= Pounds-force feet (lbf ft; lb ft)
Pounds-force feet (lbf ft; lb ft)	X 1.356	= Newton meters (Nm)	X 0.738	= Pounds-force feet (lbf ft; lb ft)
Newton meters (Nm)	X 0.102	= Kilograms-force meters (kgf m; kg m)	X 9.804	= Newton meters (Nm)

VACUUM

Inches mercury (in. Hg)	X 3.377	= Kilopascals (kPa)	X 0.2961	= Inches mercury
Inches mercury (in. Hg)	X 25.4	= Millimeters mercury (mm Hg)	X 0.0394	= Inches mercury

POWER

Horsepower (hp)	X 745.7	= Watts (W)	X 0.0013	= Horsepower (hp)

VELOCITY (speed)

Miles per hour (miles/hr; mph)	X 1.609	= Kilometers per hour (km/hr; kph)	X 0.621	= Miles per hour (miles/hr; mph)

FUEL CONSUMPTION *

Miles per gallon, Imperial (mpg)	X 0.354	= Kilometers per liter (km/l)	X 2.825	= Miles per gallon, Imperial (mpg)
Miles per gallon, US (mpg)	X 0.425	= Kilometers per liter (km/l)	X 2.352	= Miles per gallon, US (mpg)

TEMPERATURE

Degrees Fahrenheit = (°C x 1.8) + 32   Degrees Celsius (Degrees Centigrade; °C) = (°F - 32) x 0.56

*It is common practice to convert from miles per gallon (mpg) to liters/100 kilometers (l/100km),
where mpg (Imperial) x l/100 km = 282 and mpg (US) x l/100 km = 235

FRACTION/DECIMAL/MILLIMETER EQUIVALENTS

DECIMALS TO MILLIMETERS

Decimal	mm	Decimal	mm
0.001	0.0254	0.500	12.7000
0.002	0.0508	0.510	12.9540
0.003	0.0762	0.520	13.2080
0.004	0.1016	0.530	13.4620
0.005	0.1270	0.540	13.7160
0.006	0.1524	0.550	13.9700
0.007	0.1778	0.560	14.2240
0.008	0.2032	0.570	14.4780
0.009	0.2286	0.580	14.7320
		0.590	14.9860
0.010	0.2540		
0.020	0.5080		
0.030	0.7620		
0.040	1.0160	0.600	15.2400
0.050	1.2700	0.610	15.4940
0.060	1.5240	0.620	15.7480
0.070	1.7780	0.630	16.0020
0.080	2.0320	0.640	16.2560
0.090	2.2860	0.650	16.5100
		0.660	16.7640
0.100	2.5400	0.670	17.0180
0.110	2.7940	0.680	17.2720
0.120	3.0480	0.690	17.5260
0.130	3.3020		
0.140	3.5560		
0.150	3.8100		
0.160	4.0640	0.700	17.7800
0.170	4.3180	0.710	18.0340
0.180	4.5720	0.720	18.2880
0.190	4.8260	0.730	18.5420
		0.740	18.7960
0.200	5.0800	0.750	19.0500
0.210	5.3340	0.760	19.3040
0.220	5.5880	0.770	19.5580
0.230	5.8420	0.780	19.8120
0.240	6.0960	0.790	20.0660
0.250	6.3500		
0.260	6.6040		
0.270	6.8580	0.800	20.3200
0.280	7.1120	0.810	20.5740
0.290	7.3660	0.820	21.8280
		0.830	21.0820
0.300	7.6200	0.840	21.3360
0.310	7.8740	0.850	21.5900
0.320	8.1280	0.860	21.8440
0.330	8.3820	0.870	22.0980
0.340	8.6360	0.880	22.3520
0.350	8.8900	0.890	22.6060
0.360	9.1440		
0.370	9.3980		
0.380	9.6520		
0.390	9.9060		
		0.900	22.8600
0.400	10.1600	0.910	23.1140
0.410	10.4140	0.920	23.3680
0.420	10.6680	0.930	23.6220
0.430	10.9220	0.940	23.8760
0.440	11.1760	0.950	24.1300
0.450	11.4300	0.960	24.3840
0.460	11.6840	0.970	24.6380
0.470	11.9380	0.980	24.8920
0.480	12.1920	0.990	25.1460
0.490	12.4460	1.000	25.4000

FRACTIONS TO DECIMALS TO MILLIMETERS

Fraction	Decimal	mm	Fraction	Decimal	mm
1/64	0.0156	0.3969	33/64	0.5156	13.0969
1/32	0.0312	0.7938	17/32	0.5312	13.4938
3/64	0.0469	1.1906	35/64	0.5469	13.8906
1/16	0.0625	1.5875	9/16	0.5625	14.2875
5/64	0.0781	1.9844	37/64	0.5781	14.6844
3/32	0.0938	2.3812	19/32	0.5938	15.0812
7/64	0.1094	2.7781	39/64	0.6094	15.4781
1/8	0.1250	3.1750	5/8	0.6250	15.8750
9/64	0.1406	3.5719	41/64	0.6406	16.2719
5/32	0.1562	3.9688	21/32	0.6562	16.6688
11/64	0.1719	4.3656	43/64	0.6719	17.0656
3/16	0.1875	4.7625	11/16	0.6875	17.4625
13/64	0.2031	5.1594	45/64	0.7031	17.8594
7/32	0.2188	5.5562	23/32	0.7188	18.2562
15/64	0.2344	5.9531	47/64	0.7344	18.6531
1/4	0.2500	6.3500	3/4	0.7500	19.0500
17/64	0.2656	6.7469	49/64	0.7656	19.4469
9/32	0.2812	7.1438	25/32	0.7812	19.8438
19/64	0.2969	7.5406	51/64	0.7969	20.2406
5/16	0.3125	7.9375	13/16	0.8125	20.6375
21/64	0.3281	8.3344	53/64	0.8281	21.0344
11/32	0.3438	8.7312	27/32	0.8438	21.4312
23/64	0.3594	9.1281	55/64	0.8594	21.8281
3/8	0.3750	9.5250	7/8	0.8750	22.2250
25/64	0.3906	9.9219	57/64	0.8906	22.6219
13/32	0.4062	10.3188	29/32	0.9062	23.0188
27/64	0.4219	10.7156	59/64	0.9219	23.4156
7/16	0.4375	11.1125	15/16	0.9375	23.8125
29/64	0.4531	11.5094	61/64	0.9531	24.2094
15/32	0.4688	11.9062	31/32	0.9688	24.6062
31/64	0.4844	12.3031	63/64	0.9844	25.0031
1/2	0.5000	12.7000	1	1.0000	25.4000

Safety first!

Regardless of how enthusiastic you may be about getting on with the job at hand, take the time to ensure that your safety is not jeopardized. A moment's lack of attention can result in an accident, as can failure to observe certain simple safety precautions. The possibility of an accident will always exist, and the following points should not be considered a comprehensive list of all dangers. Rather, they are intended to make you aware of the risks and to encourage a safety conscious approach to all work you carry out on your vehicle.

ESSENTIAL DOS AND DON'TS

DON'T rely on a jack when working under the vehicle. Always use approved jackstands to support the weight of the vehicle and place them under the recommended lift or support points.

DON'T attempt to loosen extremely tight fasteners (i.e. wheel lug nuts) while the vehicle is on a jack - it may fall.

DON'T start the engine without first making sure that the transmission is in Neutral (or Park where applicable) and the parking brake is set.

DON'T remove the radiator cap from a hot cooling system - let it cool or cover it with a cloth and release the pressure gradually.

DON'T attempt to drain the engine oil until you are sure it has cooled to the point that it will not burn you.

DON'T touch any part of the engine or exhaust system until it has cooled sufficiently to avoid burns.

DON'T siphon toxic liquids such as gasoline, antifreeze and brake fluid by mouth, or allow them to remain on your skin.

DON'T inhale brake lining dust - it is potentially hazardous (see Asbestos below).

DON'T allow spilled oil or grease to remain on the floor - wipe it up before someone slips on it.

DON'T use loose fitting wrenches or other tools which may slip and cause injury.

DON'T push on wrenches when loosening or tightening nuts or bolts. Always try to pull the wrench toward you. If the situation calls for pushing the wrench away, push with an open hand to avoid scraped knuckles if the wrench should slip.

DON'T attempt to lift a heavy component alone - get someone to help you.

DON'T rush or take unsafe shortcuts to finish a job.

DON'T allow children or animals in or around the vehicle while you are working on it.

DO wear eye protection when using power tools such as a drill, sander, bench grinder, etc. and when working under a vehicle.

DO keep loose clothing and long hair well out of the way of moving parts.

DO make sure that any hoist used has a safe working load rating adequate for the job.

DO get someone to check on you periodically when working alone on a vehicle.

DO carry out work in a logical sequence and make sure that everything is correctly assembled and tightened.

DO keep chemicals and fluids tightly capped and out of the reach of children and pets.

DO remember that your vehicle's safety affects that of yourself and others. If in doubt on any point, get professional advice.

STEERING, SUSPENSION AND BRAKES

These systems are essential to driving safety, so make sure you have a qualified shop or individual check your work. Also, compressed suspension springs can cause injury if released suddenly - be sure to use a spring compressor.

AIRBAGS

Airbags are explosive devices that can CAUSE injury if they deploy while you're working on the vehicle. Follow the manufacturer's instructions to disable the airbag whenever you're working in the vicinity of airbag components.

ASBESTOS

Certain friction, insulating, sealing, and other products - such as brake linings, brake bands, clutch linings, torque converters, gaskets, etc. - may contain asbestos or other hazardous friction material. Extreme care must be taken to avoid inhalation of dust from such products, since it is hazardous to health. If in doubt, assume that they do contain asbestos.

FIRE

Remember at all times that gasoline is highly flammable. Never smoke or have any kind of open flame around when working on a vehicle. But the risk does not end there. A spark caused by an electrical short circuit, by two metal surfaces contacting each other, or even by static electricity built up in your body under certain conditions, can ignite gasoline vapors, which in a confined space are highly explosive. Do not, under any circumstances, use gasoline for cleaning parts. Use an approved safety solvent.

Always disconnect the battery ground (-) cable at the battery before working on any part of the fuel system or electrical system. Never risk spilling fuel on a hot engine or exhaust component. It is strongly recommended that a fire extinguisher suitable for use on fuel and electrical fires be kept handy in the garage or workshop at all times. Never try to extinguish a fuel or electrical fire with water.

FUMES

Certain fumes are highly toxic and can quickly cause unconsciousness and even death if inhaled to any extent. Gasoline vapor falls into this category, as do the vapors from some cleaning solvents. Any draining or pouring of such volatile fluids should be done in a well ventilated area.

When using cleaning fluids and solvents, read the instructions on the container carefully. Never use materials from unmarked containers.

Never run the engine in an enclosed space, such as a garage. Exhaust fumes contain carbon monoxide, which is extremely poisonous. If you need to run the engine, always do so in the open air, or at least have the rear of the vehicle outside the work area.

THE BATTERY

Never create a spark or allow a bare light bulb near a battery. They normally give off a certain amount of hydrogen gas, which is highly explosive.

Always disconnect the battery ground (-) cable at the battery before working on the fuel or electrical systems.

If possible, loosen the filler caps or cover when charging the battery from an external source (this does not apply to sealed or maintenance-free batteries). Do not charge at an excessive rate or the battery may burst.

Take care when adding water to a non maintenance-free battery and when carrying a battery. The electrolyte, even when diluted, is very corrosive and should not be allowed to contact clothing or skin.

Always wear eye protection when cleaning the battery to prevent the caustic deposits from entering your eyes.

HOUSEHOLD CURRENT

When using an electric power tool, inspection light, etc., which operates on household current, always make sure that the tool is correctly connected to its plug and that, where necessary, it is properly grounded. Do not use such items in damp conditions and, again, do not create a spark or apply excessive heat in the vicinity of fuel or fuel vapor.

SECONDARY IGNITION SYSTEM VOLTAGE

A severe electric shock can result from touching certain parts of the ignition system (such as the spark plug wires) when the engine is running or being cranked, particularly if components are damp or the insulation is defective. In the case of an electronic ignition system, the secondary system voltage is much higher and could prove fatal.

HYDROFLUORIC ACID

This extremely corrosive acid is formed when certain types of synthetic rubber, found in some O-rings, oil seals, fuel hoses, etc. are exposed to temperatures above 750-degrees F (400-degrees C). The rubber changes into a charred or sticky substance containing the acid. *Once formed, the acid remains dangerous for years. If it gets onto the skin, it may be necessary to amputate the limb concerned.*

When dealing with a vehicle which has suffered a fire, or with components salvaged from such a vehicle, wear protective gloves and discard them after use.

Troubleshooting

CONTENTS

This section provides an easy reference guide to the more common problems which may occur during the operation of your vehicle. These problems and their possible causes are grouped under headings denoting various components or systems, such as Engine, Cooling system, etc. They also refer you to the chapter and/or section which deals with the problem.

Remember that successful troubleshooting is not a mysterious black art practiced only by professional mechanics. It is simply the result of the right knowledge combined with an intelligent, systematic approach to the problem. Always work by a process of elimination, starting with the simplest solution and working through to the most complex - and never overlook the obvious. Anyone can run the gas tank dry or leave the lights on overnight, so don't assume that you are exempt from such oversights.

Finally, always establish a clear idea of why a problem has occurred and take steps to ensure that it doesn't happen again. If the electrical system fails because of a poor connection, check the other connections in the system to make sure that they don't fail as well. If a particular fuse continues to blow, find out why - don't just replace one fuse after another. Remember, failure of a small component can often be indicative of potential failure or incorrect functioning of a more important component or system.

ENGINE

1   Engine will not rotate when attempting to start

1   Battery terminal connections loose or corroded (Chapter 1).
2   Battery discharged or faulty (Chapters 1 and 5).
3   Automatic transaxle not completely engaged in Park (Chapter 7) or clutch pedal not completely depressed/faulty clutch pedal position switch (Chapter 8).
4   Broken, loose or disconnected wiring in the starting circuit (Chapters 5 and 12).
5   Starter motor pinion jammed in flywheel ring gear (Chapter 5).
6   Starter solenoid faulty (Chapter 5).
7   Starter motor faulty (Chapter 5).
8   Ignition switch faulty (Chapter 12).
9   Starter pinion or flywheel teeth worn or broken (Chapter 5).

2   Engine rotates but will not start

1   Fuel tank empty.
2   Battery discharged (engine rotates slowly) (Chapter 5).
3   Battery terminal connections loose or corroded (Chapter 1).
4   Leaking fuel injector(s), faulty fuel pump, pressure regulator, etc. (Chapter 4).
5   Broken or stripped timing belt or broken timing chain (Chapter 2).
6   Ignition components damp or damaged (Chapter 5).
7   Worn, faulty or incorrectly gapped spark plugs (Chapter 1).
8   Broken, loose or disconnected wires at the ignition coil or faulty coil (Chapter 5).
9   Defective crankshaft or camshaft sensor (Chapter 6).

3   Engine hard to start when cold

1   Battery discharged or low (Chapter 1).
2   Malfunctioning fuel system (Chapter 4).
3   Faulty coolant temperature sensor or intake air temperature sensor (Chapter 6).
4   Faulty ignition system (Chapter 5).

4   Engine hard to start when hot

1   Air filter clogged (Chapter 1).
2   Fuel not reaching the fuel injection system (Chapter 4).
3   Corroded battery connections, especially ground (Chapter 1).

4   Faulty coolant temperature sensor or intake air temperature sensor (Chapter 6).

5   Starter motor noisy or excessively rough in engagement

1   Pinion or flywheel gear teeth worn or broken (Chapter 5).
2   Starter motor mounting bolts loose or missing (Chapter 5).

6   Engine starts but stops immediately

1   Loose or faulty electrical connections at ignition coil or alternator (Chapter 5).
2   Insufficient fuel reaching the fuel injector(s) (Chapters 1 and 4).
3   Vacuum leak at the gasket between the intake manifold/plenum and throttle body (Chapter 4).

7   Oil puddle under engine

1   Oil pan gasket and/or oil pan drain bolt washer leaking (Chapter 2).
2   Oil pressure sending unit leaking (Chapter 2D).
3   Valve cover leaking (Chapter 2).
4   Engine oil seals leaking (Chapter 2).
5   Oil pump housing leaking (Chapter 2).

8   Engine lopes while idling or idles erratically

1   Vacuum leakage (Chapters 2 and 4).
2   Leaking EGR valve (Chapter 6).
3   Air filter clogged (Chapter 1).
4   Malfunction in the fuel injection or engine control system (Chapters 4 and 6).
5   Leaking head gasket (Chapter 2).
6   Timing belt or chain and/or sprockets worn (Chapter 2).
7   Camshaft lobes worn (Chapter 2).

9   Engine misses at idle speed

1   Spark plugs worn or not gapped properly (Chapter 1).
2   Vacuum leaks (Chapter 1).
3   Uneven or low compression (Chapter 2D).
4   Problem with the fuel injection system (Chapter 4).

10 Engine misses throughout driving speed range

1 Fuel filter clogged and/or impurities in the fuel system (Chapters 1 and 4).
2 Low fuel pressure (Chapter 4).
3 Faulty or incorrectly gapped spark plugs (Chapter 1).
4 Faulty emission system components (Chapter 6).
5 Low or uneven cylinder compression pressures (Chapter 2).
6 Weak or faulty ignition system (Chap-ter 5).
7 Vacuum leak in fuel injection system, intake manifold, or vacuum hoses (Chapters 2, 4 and 6).

11 Engine stumbles on acceleration

1 Spark plugs fouled (Chapter 1).
2 Problem with fuel injection or engine control system (Chapters 4 and 6).
3 Fuel filter clogged (Chapters 1 and 4).
4 Intake manifold air leak (Chapters 2 and 4).
5 Problem with the emissions control system (Chapter 6).

12 Engine surges while holding accelerator steady

1 Intake air leak (Chapters 4 and 6).
2 Fuel pump or fuel pressure regulator faulty (Chapter 4).
3 Problem with the fuel injection system (Chapter 4).
4 Problem with the emissions control system (Chapter 6).

13 Engine stalls

1 Idle speed incorrect (Chapter 1).
2 Fuel filter clogged and/or water and impurities in the fuel system (Chapters 1 and 4).
3 Faulty emissions system components (Chapter 6).
4 Faulty or incorrectly gapped spark plugs (Chapter 1).
5 Vacuum leak in the fuel injection system, intake manifold or vacuum hoses (Chapters 2 and 4).

14 Engine lacks power

1 Obstructed exhaust system (Chapter 4).
2 Faulty coil (Chapter 5).
3 Faulty or incorrectly gapped spark plugs (Chapter 1).
4 Problem with the fuel injection system (Chapter 4).
5 Plugged air filter (Chapter 1).
6 Brakes binding (Chapter 9).
7 Automatic transaxle fluid level incorrect (Chapter 1).
8 Clutch slipping (Chapter 8).
9 Fuel filter clogged and/or impurities in the fuel system (Chapters 1 and 4).
10 Emission control system not functioning properly (Chapter 6).
11 Low or uneven cylinder compression pressures (Chapter 2).

15 Engine backfires

1 Emission control system not functioning properly (Chapter 6).
2 Problem with the fuel injection system (Chapter 4).
3 Vacuum leak at fuel injector(s), intake manifold, air control valve or vacuum hoses (Chapters 2 and 4).

4 Valve clearances incorrectly set and/or valves sticking (Chapter 2).

16 Pinging or knocking engine sounds during acceleration or uphill

1 Incorrect grade of fuel.
2 Fuel injection system faulty (Chapter 4).
3 Improper or damaged spark plugs or wires (Chapter 1).
4 Knock sensor defective (Chapter 6).
5 EGR valve not functioning (Chapter 6).
6 Vacuum leak (Chapters 2 and 4).

17 Engine runs with oil pressure light on

1 Low oil level (Chapter 1).
2 Idle rpm below specification (Chapter 1).
3 Short in wiring circuit (Chapter 12).
4 Faulty oil pressure sender (Chapter 2D).
5 Worn engine bearings and/or oil pump (Chapter 2).

18 Engine continues to run after switching off

Faulty ignition switch (Chapter 12).

ENGINE ELECTRICAL SYSTEMS

19 Battery will not hold a charge

1 Alternator drivebelt defective or not adjusted properly (Chapter 1).
2 Battery electrolyte level low (Chapter 1).
3 Battery terminals loose or corroded (Chapter 1).
4 Alternator not charging properly (Chapter 5).
5 Loose, broken or faulty wiring in the charging circuit (Chapter 5).
6 Short in vehicle wiring (Chapter 12).
7 Internally defective battery (Chapters 1 and 5).

20 Alternator light fails to go out

1 Faulty alternator or charging circuit (Chapter 5).
2 Drivebelt defective (Chapter 1).
3 Alternator voltage regulator inoperative (Chapter 5).

21 Alternator light fails to come on when key is turned on

1 Warning light bulb defective (Chapter 12).
2 Fault in the dash wiring or bulb holder (Chapter 12).

FUEL SYSTEM

22 Excessive fuel consumption

1 Dirty or clogged air filter element (Chapter 1).
2 Emissions system not functioning properly (Chapter 6).
3 Fuel injection system not functioning properly (Chapter 4).
4 Low tire pressure or incorrect tire size (Chapter 1).

23 Fuel leakage and/or fuel odor

1 Leaking fuel line (Chapter 4).
2 Tank overfilled.
3 Problem with EVAP system (Chapter 6).
4 Problem with the fuel injection system (Chapter 4).

COOLING SYSTEM

24 Overheating

1 Insufficient coolant in system (Chapter 1).
2 Drivebelt defective (Chapter 1).
3 Radiator core blocked or grille restricted (Chapter 3).
4 Thermostat faulty (Chapter 3).
5 Electric coolant fan inoperative or blades broken (Chapter 3).
6 Expansion tank cap not maintaining proper pressure (Chapter 3).

25 Overcooling

1 Faulty thermostat (Chapter 3).
2 Inaccurate temperature gauge sending unit (Chapter 3).

26 External coolant leakage

1 Deteriorated/damaged hoses; loose clamps (Chapters 1 and 3).
2 Water pump defective (Chapter 3).
3 Leakage from radiator core or coolant reservoir (Chapter 3).
4 Engine drain or water jacket core plugs leaking (Chapter 2).

27 Internal coolant leakage

1 Leaking cylinder head gasket (Chapter 2).
2 Cracked cylinder bore or cylinder head (Chapter 2).

28 Coolant loss

1 Too much coolant in reservoir (Chapter 1).
2 Coolant boiling away because of overheating (Chapter 3).
3 Internal or external leakage (Chapter 3).
4 Faulty radiator cap (Chapter 3).

29 Poor coolant circulation

1 Inoperative water pump (Chapter 3).
2 Restriction in cooling system (Chapters 1 and 3).
3 Drivebelt defective (Chapter 1).
4 Thermostat sticking (Chapter 3).

CLUTCH

30 Pedal travels to floor - no pressure or very little resistance

1 Master or release cylinder faulty (Chapter 8).
2 Hose/pipe burst or leaking.

3 Connections leaking.
4 No fluid in reservoir.
5 If there is fluid on dust seal at master cylinder, piston primary seal is leaking (Chapter 8).
6 Faulty pressure plate diaphragm spring (Chapter 8).

31 Fluid in area of master cylinder dust cover and on pedal

Rear seal failure in master cylinder (Chapter 8).

32 Fluid leaking from bellhousing

Release cylinder plunger seal faulty (Chapter 8).

33 Pedal feels spongy when depressed

Air in system (Chapter 8).

34 Unable to select gears

1 Faulty transaxle (Chapter 7).
2 Faulty clutch disc or pressure plate (Chapter 8).
3 Faulty release bearing (Chapter 8).
4 Faulty shift lever assembly or control cables (Chapter 8).

35 Clutch slips (engine speed increases with no increase in vehicle speed)

1 Clutch plate worn (Chapter 8).
2 Clutch plate is oil soaked by leaking rear main seal (Chapters 2 and 8).
3 Warped pressure plate or flywheel (Chapter 8).
4 Weak diaphragm springs (Chapter 8).
5 Clutch plate overheated. Allow to cool.

36 Grabbing (chattering) as clutch is engaged

1 Oil on clutch plate lining, burned or glazed facings (Chapter 8).
2 Worn or loose engine or transaxle mounts (Chapter 2).
3 Worn splines on clutch plate hub (Chapter 8).
4 Warped pressure plate or flywheel (Chapter 8).
5 Burned or smeared resin on flywheel or pressure plate (Chapter 8).

37 Transaxle rattling (clicking)

Clutch plate damper spring failure (Chapter 8).

38 Noise in clutch area

Faulty release bearing (Chapter 8).

39 Clutch pedal stays on floor

1 Clutch master cylinder piston binding in bore (Chapter 8).
2 Defective release bearing (Chapter 8).

40 High pedal effort

1 Piston binding in bore (Chapter 8).
2 Pressure plate faulty (Chapter 8).
3 Incorrect size master or release cylinder (Chapter 8).

MANUAL TRANSAXLE

41 Knocking noise at low speeds

1 Worn driveaxle constant velocity (CV) joints (Chapter 8).
2 Worn side gear shaft counterbore in differential case (Chapter 7A).*

42 Noise most pronounced when turning

Differential gear noise (Chapter 7A).*

43 Clunk on acceleration or deceleration

1 Loose engine or transaxle mounts (Chapter 2).
2 Worn differential pinion shaft in case.*
3 Worn side gear shaft counterbore in differential case (Chapter 7A).*
4 Worn or damaged driveaxle inboard CV joints (Chapter 8).

44 Clicking noise in turns

Worn or damaged outboard CV joint (Chapter 8).

45 Vibration

1 Rough wheel bearing (Chapter 10).
2 Damaged driveaxle (Chapter 8).
3 Out-of-round tires (Chapter 1).
4 Tire out of balance (Chapters 1 and 10).
5 Worn CV joint (Chapter 8).

46 Noisy in neutral with engine running

1 Damaged input gear bearing (Chapter 7A).*
2 Damaged clutch release bearing (Chapter 8).

47 Noisy in one particular gear

1 Damaged or worn constant mesh gears (Chapter 7A).*
2 Damaged or worn synchronizers (Chapter 7A).*
3 Bent reverse fork (Chapter 7A).*
4 Damaged fourth speed gear or output gear (Chapter 7A).*
5 Worn or damaged reverse idler gear or idler bushing (Chapter 7A).*

48 Noisy in all gears

1 Insufficient lubricant (Chapter 7A).
2 Damaged or worn bearings (Chapter 7A).*
3 Worn or damaged input gear shaft and/or output gear shaft (Chapter 7A).*

49 Slips out of gear

1 Worn or improperly adjusted linkage (Chapter 7A).
2 Shift linkage does not work freely, binds (Chapter 7A).
3 Input gear bearing retainer broken or loose.*
4 Worn shift fork (Chapter 7A).*

50 Leaks lubricant

1 Side gear shaft seals worn (Chapter 7).
2 Excessive amount of lubricant in transaxle (Chapter 1).
3 Input shaft seal damaged (Chapter 7A).*

51 Locked in gear

Lock pin or interlock pin missing.*

Although the corrective action necessary to remedy the symptoms described is beyond the scope of this manual, the above information should be helpful in isolating the cause of the condition so that the owner can communicate clearly with a professional mechanic.

AUTOMATIC TRANSAXLE

➡**Note: Due to the complexity of the automatic transaxle, it is difficult for the home mechanic to properly diagnose and service this component. For problems other than the following, the vehicle should be taken to a dealer or transmission shop.**

52 Fluid leakage

1 Automatic transaxle fluid is a deep red color. Fluid leaks should not be confused with engine oil, which can easily be blown onto the transaxle by air flow.
2 To pinpoint a leak, first remove all built-up dirt and grime from the transaxle housing with degreasing agents and/or steam cleaning. Then drive the vehicle at low speeds so air flow will not blow the leak far from its source. Raise the vehicle and determine where the leak is coming from. Common areas of leakage are:

    a) *Dipstick tube (Chapters 1 and 7)*
    b) *Transaxle oil lines (Chapter 7*
    c) *Speed sensor (Chapter 6*
    d) *Driveaxle oil seals (Chapter 7).*

53 Transaxle fluid brown or has a burned smell

Transaxle fluid overheated (Chapter 1).

54 General shift mechanism problems

1 Chapter 7, Part B, deals with checking and adjusting the shift cable on automatic transaxles. Common problems which may be attributed to poorly adjusted cable are:

    a) *Engine starting in gears other than Park or Neutral.*
    b) *Indicator on shifter pointing to a gear other than the one actually being used.*
    c) *Vehicle moves when in Park.*

2 Refer to Chapter 7B for the shift cable adjustment procedure.

55 Transaxle slips, shifts roughly, is noisy or has no drive in forward or reverse gears

There are many probable causes for the above problems, but the home mechanic should be concerned with only one possibility - fluid level. Before taking the vehicle to a repair shop, check the level and condition of the fluid as described in Chapter 1. Correct the fluid level as necessary or change the fluid and filter if needed. If the problem persists, have a professional diagnose the cause.

DRIVEAXLES

56 Clicking noise in turns

Worn or damaged outboard CV joint (Chapter 8).

57 Shudder or vibration during acceleration

1 Excessive toe-in (Chapter 10).
2 Worn or damaged inboard or outboard CV joints (Chapter 8).
3 Sticking inboard CV joint assembly (Chapter 8).

58 Vibration at highway speeds

1 Out-of-balance front wheels and/or tires.
2 Out-of-round front tires.
3 Worn CV joint(s) (Chapter 8).

BRAKES

➡Note: Before assuming that a brake problem exists, make sure that:

  a) The tires are in good condition and properly inflated (Chapter 1).
  b) The front end alignment is correct.
  c) The vehicle is not loaded with weight in an unequal manner.

59 Vehicle pulls to one side during braking

1 Incorrect tire pressures (Chapter 1).
2 Front end out of alignment (have the front end aligned).
3 Restricted brake lines or hoses (Chapter 9).
4 Malfunctioning drum brake or caliper assembly (Chapter 9).
5 Loose suspension parts (Chapter 10).
6 Excessive wear of brake shoe or pad material or disc/drum on one side (Chapter 9).
7 Contamination (grease or brake fluid) of brake shoe or pad material or disc/drum on one side (Chapter 9).

60 Noise (high-pitched squeal when the brakes are applied)

Front brake pads worn out. Replace pads with new ones immediately (Chapter 9).

61 Brake roughness or chatter (pedal pulsates)

1 Excessive lateral runout (Chapter 9).
2 Uneven pad wear (Chapter 9).
3 Defective disc (Chapter 9).

62 Excessive brake pedal effort required to stop vehicle

1 Malfunctioning power brake booster (Chapter 9).
2 Partial system failure (Chapter 9).
3 Excessively worn pads or shoes (Chapter 9).
4 Piston in caliper or wheel cylinder stuck or sluggish (Chapter 9).
5 Brake pads or shoes contaminated with oil or grease (Chapter 9).
6 Brake disc grooved and/or glazed (Chapter 9).
7 New pads or shoes installed and not yet seated. It will take a while for the new material to seat against the disc or drum.

63 Excessive brake pedal travel

1 Partial brake system failure (Chapter 9).
2 Insufficient fluid in master cylinder (Chapters 1 and 9).
3 Air trapped in system (Chapter 9).

64 Dragging brakes

1 Master cylinder pistons not returning correctly (Chapter 9).
2 Restricted brakes lines or hoses (Chapter 9).
3 Incorrect parking brake adjustment (Chapter 9).

65 Grabbing or uneven braking action

1 Malfunction of proportioning valve (Chapter 9).
2 Binding brake pedal mechanism (Chapter 9).
3 Contaminated brake linings (Chapter 9).

66 Brake pedal feels spongy when depressed

1 Air in hydraulic lines (Chapter 9).
2 Master cylinder mounting nuts loose (Chapter 9).
3 Master cylinder defective (Chapter 9).

67 Brake pedal travels to the floor with little resistance

1 Little or no fluid in the master cylinder reservoir caused by leaking caliper or wheel cylinder piston(s) (Chapter 9).
2 Loose, damaged or disconnected brake lines (Chapter 9).

68 Parking brake does not hold

Parking brake improperly adjusted (Chapter 9).

SUSPENSION AND STEERING SYSTEMS

➡Note: Before attempting to diagnose the suspension and steering systems, perform the following preliminary checks:

a) Tires for wrong pressure and uneven wear.
b) Steering universal joints from the column to the rack and pinion for loose connectors or wear.
c) Front and rear suspension and the rack and pinion assembly for loose or damaged parts.
d) Out-of-round or out-of-balance tires, bent rims and loose and/or rough wheel bearings.

69 Vehicle pulls to one side

1 Mismatched or uneven tires (Chapter 10).
2 Broken or sagging springs (Chapter 10).
3 Wheel alignment incorrect. Have the wheels professionally aligned.
4 Front brake dragging (Chapter 9).

70 Abnormal or excessive tire wear

1 Wheel alignment out-of-specification. Have the wheels aligned.
2 Sagging or broken springs (Chapter 10).
3 Tire out-of-balance (Chapter 10).
4 Worn strut damper (Chapter 10).
5 Overloaded vehicle.
6 Tires not rotated regularly.

71 Wheel makes a thumping noise

1 Blister or bump on tire (Chapter 10).
2 Worn strut or shock absorber (Chapter 10).

72 Shimmy, shake or vibration

1 Tire or wheel out-of-balance or out-of-round (Chapter 10).
2 Loose or worn wheel bearings (Chapter 10).
3 Worn tie-rod ends (Chapter 10).
4 Worn balljoints (Chapters 1 and 10).
5 Excessive wheel runout (Chapter 10).
6 Blister or bump on tire (Chapter 10).

73 Hard steering

1 Balljoints and/or tie-rod ends worn out (Chapter 10).
2 Wheel alignment out-of-specifications. Have the wheels professionally aligned.
3 Low tire pressure(s) (Chapter 1).
4 Worn steering gear (Chapter 10).
5 Power assist motor on steering column defective (Chapter 10).

74 Poor returnability of steering to center

1 Balljoints and/or tie-rod ends worn (Chapter 10).
2 Binding in balljoints (Chapter 10).
3 Binding in steering column (Chapter 10).
4 Lack of lubricant in steering gear assembly (Chapter 10).
5 Wheel alignment out-of-specifications. Have the wheels professionally aligned.

75 Abnormal noise at the front end

1 Balljoints and/or tie-rod ends worn (Chapters 1 and 10).
2 Damaged strut mounting (Chapter 10).
3 Worn control arm bushings or tie-rod ends (Chapter 10).
4 Loose stabilizer bar (Chapter 10).
5 Loose wheel nuts (Chapter 1).
6 Loose suspension bolts (Chapter 10).

76 Wander or poor steering stability

1 Mismatched or uneven tires (Chapter 10).
2 Balljoints and/or tie-rod ends worn (Chapters 1 and 10).
3 Worn strut assemblies (Chapter 10).
4 Loose stabilizer bar (Chapter 10).
5 Broken or sagging springs (Chapter 10).
6 Wheels out of alignment. Have the wheels professionally aligned.

77 Erratic steering when braking

1 Wheel bearings worn (Chapter 10).
2 Broken or sagging springs (Chapter 10).
3 Leaking wheel cylinder or caliper (Chapter 10).
4 Warped discs or drums (Chapter 10).

78 Excessive pitching and/or rolling around corners or during braking

1 Loose stabilizer bar (Chapter 10).
2 Worn struts or shock absorbers (Chapter 10).
3 Broken or sagging springs (Chapter 10).
4 Overloaded vehicle.

79 Suspension bottoms

1 Overloaded vehicle.
2 Sagging springs (Chapter 10).

80 Cupped tires

1 Front wheel or rear wheel alignment out-of-specifications. Have the wheels professionally aligned.
2 Worn strut dampers or shock absorbers (Chapter 10).
3 Wheel bearings worn (Chapter 10).
4 Excessive tire or wheel runout (Chapter 10).
5 Worn balljoints (Chapter 10).

81 Excessive tire wear on outside edge

1 Inflation pressures incorrect (Chapter 1).
2 Excessive speed in turns.
3 Wheel alignment incorrect (excessive toe-in). Have professionally aligned.
4 Suspension arm bent or twisted (Chapter 10).

82 Excessive tire wear on inside edge

1 Inflation pressures incorrect (Chapter 1).
2 Wheel alignment incorrect (toe-out). Have professionally aligned.
3 Loose or damaged steering components (Chapter 10).

83   Tire tread worn in one place

1   Tires out-of-balance.
2   Damaged or buckled wheel. Inspect and replace if necessary.
3   Defective tire (Chapter 1).

84   Excessive play or looseness in steering system

1   Wheel bearing(s) worn (Chapter 10).
2   Tie-rod end loose (Chapter 10).
3   Steering gear loose (Chapter 10).
4   Worn or loose steering intermediate shaft U-joint (Chapter 10).

85   Rattling or clicking noise in steering gear

1   Steering gear loose (Chapter 10).
2   Steering gear defective.

Section

Reference to other Chapters

Timing belt replacement - See Chapter 2

Valve clearance check and adjustment - 3.5L V6 engine - See Chapter 2C

1

TUNE-UP AND MAINTENANCE

Typical four-cylinder engine compartment

1	Air filter housing	4	Windshield washer fluid reservoir	7	Fuse and relay center
2	Engine oil dipstick	5	Coolant expansion tank	8	Brake fluid reservoir
3	Engine oil filler cap	6	Battery housing		

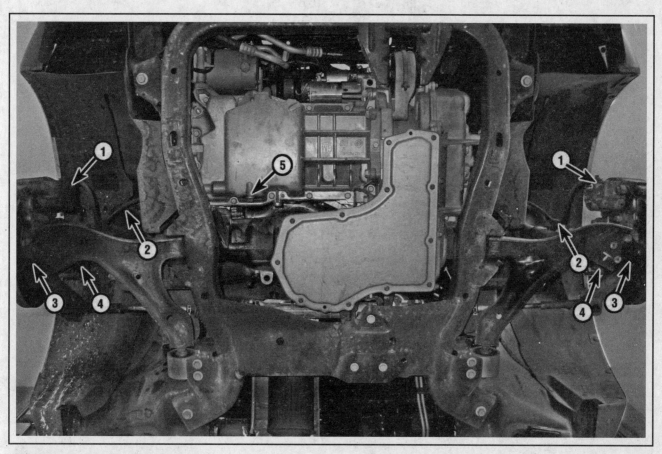

Typical front underside components

1	Front brake calipers	3	Balljoints	5	Engine oil drain plug
2	Brake hoses	4	Outer driveaxle boots		

Typical rear underside components

1   Muffler
2   Coil spring
3   Shock absorber
4   Brake drums
5   Fuel tank
6   Exhaust pipe

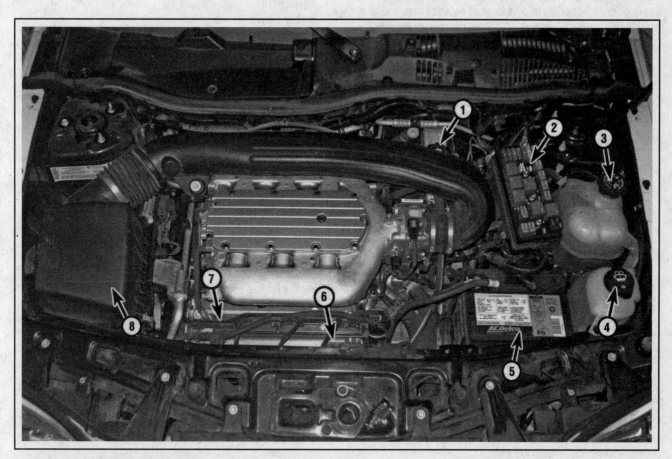

Typical 3.5L V6 engine compartment

1   Brake fluid reservoir
2   Fuse and relay center
3   Coolant expansion tank
4   Windshield washer fluid reservoir
5   Battery
6   Engine oil filler cap (not visible; location given)
7   Engine oil dipstick (not visible; location given)
8   Air filter housing

1   Saturn VUE maintenance schedule

The maintenance intervals in this manual are provided with the assumption that you, not the dealer, will be doing the work. These are the minimum maintenance intervals recommended by the factory for vehicles that are driven daily. If you wish to keep your vehicle in peak condition at all times, you may wish to perform some of these procedures even more often. Because frequent maintenance enhances the efficiency, performance and resale value of your car, we encourage you to do so. If you drive in dusty areas, tow a trailer, idle or drive at low speeds for extended periods or drive for short distances (less than four miles) in below freezing temperatures, shorter intervals are also recommended.

When your vehicle is new, it should be serviced by a factory authorized dealer service department to protect the factory warranty. In many cases, the initial maintenance check is done at no cost to the owner.

EVERY 250 MILES (400 KM) OR WEEKLY, WHICHEVER COMES FIRST

Check the engine oil level (Section 4)
Check the engine coolant level (Section 4)
Check the windshield washer fluid level (Section 4)
Check the brake fluid level (Section 4)
Check the power steering fluid level (Section 4)
Check the automatic transaxle fluid level (Section 4)
Check the tires and tire pressures (Section 5)

EVERY 3000 MILES (4,800 KM) OR 3 MONTHS, WHICHEVER COMES FIRST

All items listed above plus:
Change the engine oil and oil filter (Section 6)

EVERY 5000 MILES (8000 KM) OR 6 MONTHS, WHICHEVER COMES FIRST

All items listed above plus:
Check and service the battery (Section 7)
Rotate the tires (Section 8)
Inspect and replace if necessary the windshield wiper blades (Section 9)
Inspect and replace if necessary all underhood hoses (Section 10)
Check the cooling system (Section 11)
Inspect the brake system (Section 12)

EVERY 15,000 MILES (24,000 KM) OR 18 MONTHS, WHICHEVER COMES FIRST

All items listed above plus:
Inspect the suspension, steering components and driveaxle boots (Section 13)*
Inspect the exhaust system (Section 14)

EVERY 25,000 MILES (40,000 KM) OR 36 MONTHS, WHICHEVER COMES FIRST

All items listed above plus:
Change the automatic transaxle lubricant (Section 15)**
Change the transfer case lubricant (AWD models) (Section 16)**
Replace the air filter (Section 17)*
Inspect the fuel system (Section 18)
Replace interior ventilation filter (Section 19)*
Change the brake fluid (Section 20)

EVERY 50,000 MILES (80,000KM) OR 60 MONTHS, WHICHEVER COMES FIRST

Check the engine drivebelts (Section 21) (after the initial 60,000-mile [96,000 km] or 72-month check)
Change the rear differential lubricant (AWD models) (Section 22)**
Service the cooling system (drain, flush and refill) (Section 24) (after the initial 100,000-mile [160,000 km] or 120-month service)
Replace the timing belt (four-cylinder and 3.5L V6 engines) (Chapter 2) ***

EVERY 60,000 MILES (96,000 KM) OR 72 MONTHS, WHICHEVER COMES FIRST

Replace the fuel filter (2002 and 2003 models) (Section 23)

100,000 MILES (160,000 KM) OR 120 MONTHS, WHICHEVER COMES FIRST - THEREAFTER EVERY 50,000 MILES (80,000 KM) OR 60 MONTHS, WHICHEVER COMES FIRST

Service the cooling system (drain, flush and refill) (Section 24)
Replace the spark plugs (Section 25)
Check and adjust, if necessary, the valve clearance (3.5L V6 engine) (Chapter 2C)

*   *This item is affected by "severe" operating conditions as described below. If your vehicle is operated under "severe" conditions, inspect all maintenance indicated with an asterisk (*) at 3000 mile/3 month intervals and perform maintenance or replace parts as necessary. Severe conditions are indicated if you mainly operate your vehicle under one or more of the following conditions:*
Operating in dusty areas
Idling for extended periods and/or low speed operation
Operating when outside temperatures remain below freezing and when most trips are less than 4 miles

** *If used for trailer towing, change the automatic transaxle and transfer case fluid lubricant every 25,000 miles. Likewise, change the rear differential fluid every 50,000 miles. Under normal conditions, change these fluids every 100,000 miles (160,000 km).*

*** *If normal operating conditions are extremely hot or cold (over 110 degrees F or under -10 degrees F), the timing belt should be replaced every 50,000 miles - otherwise every 100,000 miles.*

2 Introduction

This Chapter is designed to help the home mechanic maintain his vehicle for peak performance, economy, safety and long life.

Included is a master maintenance schedule, followed by sections dealing specifically with each item on the schedule. Visual checks, adjustments, component replacement and other helpful items are included. Refer to the accompanying illustrations of the engine compartment and the underside of the vehicle for the location of various components.

Servicing your vehicle in accordance with the mileage/time maintenance schedule and the following Sections will provide it with a planned maintenance program that should result in a long and reliable service life. This is a comprehensive plan, so maintaining some items but not others at the specified service intervals won't produce the same results.

As you service your vehicle, you will discover that many of the procedures can - and should - be grouped together because of the nature of the particular procedure you're performing or because of the close proximity of two otherwise unrelated components to one another.

For example, if the vehicle is raised for any reason, you should inspect the exhaust, suspension, steering and fuel systems while you're under the vehicle. When you're rotating the tires, it makes good sense to check the brakes and wheel bearings since the wheels are already removed.

Finally, let's suppose you have to borrow or rent a torque wrench. Even if you only need to tighten the spark plugs, you might as well check the torque of as many critical fasteners as time allows.

The first step of this maintenance program is to prepare yourself before the actual work begins. Read through all sections pertinent to the procedures you're planning to do, then make a list of and gather together all the parts and tools you will need to do the job. If it looks as if you might run into problems during a particular segment of some procedure, seek advice from your local parts man or dealer service department.

3 Tune-up general information

The term tune-up is used in this manual to represent a combination of individual operations rather than one specific procedure.

If, from the time the vehicle is new, the routine maintenance schedule is followed closely and frequent checks are made of fluid levels and high wear items, as suggested throughout this manual, the engine will be kept in relatively good running condition and the need for additional work will be minimized.

More likely than not, however, there will be times when the engine is running poorly due to lack of regular maintenance. This is even more likely if a used vehicle, which has not received regular and frequent maintenance checks, is purchased. In such cases, an engine tune-up will be needed outside of the regular routine maintenance intervals.

The first step in any tune-up or engine diagnosis to help correct a poor running engine would be a cylinder compression check. A check of the engine compression (see Chapter 2C) will give valuable information regarding the overall performance of many internal components and should be used as a basis for tune-up and repair procedures. If, for instance, a compression check indicates serious internal engine wear, a conventional tune-up will not help the running condition of the engine and would be a waste of time and money. Also in Chapter 2C is information on checking engine vacuum, which also gives information on the engine's state-of-tune and condition.

The following series of operations are those most often needed to bring a generally poor-running engine back into a proper state of tune.

MINOR TUNE-UP

Check all engine related fluids (Section 4)
Clean, inspect and test the battery (Section 7)
Check all underhood hoses (Section 10)
Check the cooling system (Section 11)
Check the air filter (Section 17)
Check the drivebelt (Section 21)

MAJOR TUNE-UP

All items listed under Minor tune-up, plus . . .
Replace the air filter (Section 17)
Check the fuel system (Section 18)
Replace the spark plugs (Section 25)
Check the charging system (Chapter 5)

4 Fluid level checks (every 250 miles [400km] or weekly)

1 Fluids are an essential part of the lubrication, cooling, brake, clutch and other systems. Because these fluids gradually become depleted and/or contaminated during normal operation of the vehicle, they must be periodically replenished. See *Recommended lubricants* *and fluids* and *Capacities* in this Chapter's Specifications before adding fluid to any of the following components.

➡**Note: The vehicle must be on level ground before fluid levels can be checked.**

4.2 The engine oil dipstick is mounted on the front (radiator) side of the engine (four-cylinder model shown)

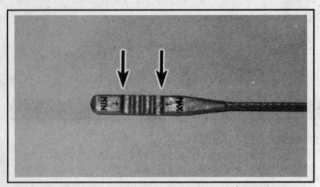

4.4 The oil level should be at or near the upper mark on the dipstick - if it isn't, add enough oil to bring the level to or near the upper mark (it takes one quart to raise the level from the lower mark to the upper mark)

ENGINE OIL

▶ **Refer to illustrations 4.2, 4.4 and 4.6**

2   The engine oil level is checked with a dipstick located at the front of the engine (see illustration). The dipstick extends through a metal tube from which it protrudes down into the engine oil pan.

3   The oil level should be checked before the vehicle has been driven, or about 5 minutes after the engine has been shut off. If the oil is checked immediately after driving the vehicle, some of the oil will remain in the upper engine components, producing an inaccurate reading on the dipstick.

4   Pull the dipstick from the tube and wipe all the oil from the end with a clean rag or paper towel. Insert the clean dipstick all the way back into its metal tube and pull it out again. Observe the oil at the end of the dipstick. At its highest point, the level should be between the lower and upper marks (see illustration).

5   It takes one quart of oil to raise the level from the lower mark to the upper mark on the dipstick. Do not allow the level to drop below the lower mark or oil starvation may cause engine damage. Conversely, overfilling the engine (adding oil above the upper mark) may cause oil-fouled spark plugs, oil leaks or oil seal failures.

6   Remove the threaded cap from the valve cover to add oil (see illustration). Use a funnel to prevent spills. After adding the oil, install the filler cap hand tight. Start the engine and look carefully for any small

leaks around the oil filter or drain plug. Stop the engine and check the oil level again after it has had sufficient time to drain from the upper block and cylinder head galleys.

7   Checking the oil level is an important preventive maintenance step. A continually dropping oil level indicates oil leakage through damaged seals, from loose connections, or past worn rings or valve guides. If the oil looks milky in color or has water droplets in it, a cylinder head gasket may be blown. The engine should be checked immediately. The condition of the oil should also be checked. Each time you check the oil level, slide your thumb and index finger up the dipstick before wiping off the oil. If you see small dirt or metal particles clinging to the dipstick, the oil should be changed (see Section 6).

ENGINE COOLANT

▶ **Refer to illustrations 4.8 and 4.9**

✳✳ WARNING:

Do not allow antifreeze to come in contact with your skin or painted surfaces of the vehicle. Flush contaminated areas immediately with plenty of water. Don't store new coolant or leave old coolant lying around where it's accessible to children or pets - they're attracted by its sweet smell. Ingestion of even a small amount of coolant can be fatal! Wipe up garage floor and drip pan spills immediately. Keep antifreeze containers covered and repair cooling system leaks as soon as they're noticed.

8   All models covered by this manual are equipped with a coolant reservoir. The coolant expansion tank is connected by hoses to the radiator and the engine (see illustration). The coolant circulates through the tank while the engine is running. As it becomes heated, it expands and its level in the tank rises.

9   The coolant level should be checked regularly. The level will vary with the temperature of the engine. When the engine is cold, the coolant level should be at the Cold Fill mark on the tank (see illustration). Once the engine has warmed up, the level should be slightly above the Cold Fill mark. If it isn't, allow the coolant in the tank to cool, then remove the cap from the tank and add coolant to bring the level up to the Fill line. Use only the type of coolant listed in this Chapter's Specifications or in your owner's manual. Do not use supplemental inhibitors or additives. If only a small amount of coolant is required to bring the system up to the proper level, water can be used. However, repeated additions of water will dilute the recommended antifreeze and water solution. In order to maintain the proper ratio of antifreeze and water, it is advisable to top up the coolant level with the correct mixture.

10   If the coolant level drops within a short time after replenishment, there may be a leak in the system. Inspect the radiator, hoses, expansion tank cap, drain plugs and water pump. If no leak is evident, have the expansion tank cap pressure tested.

✳✳ WARNING:

Never remove the cap when the engine is running or has just been shut down, because the cooling system is hot. Escaping steam and scalding liquid could cause serious injury.

11   If it is necessary to remove the cap, wait until the system has cooled completely, then wrap a thick cloth around the cap and slowly unscrew it. If any steam escapes, wait until the system has cooled fur-

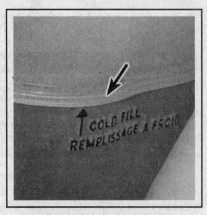

4.6 The threaded oil filler cap is located on the valve cover - to prevent dirt from contaminating the engine, always make sure the area around this opening is clean before removing the cap

4.8 The coolant expansion tank is located at the left side of the engine compartment

4.9 When the engine is cold, the coolant level should be at the Cold Fill mark on the tank

ther, then remove the cap.

12 When checking the coolant level, always note its condition. It should be relatively clear. If it is brown or rust colored, the system should be drained, flushed and refilled. Even if the coolant appears to be normal, the corrosion inhibitors wear out with use, so it must be replaced at the specified intervals.

13 Do not allow antifreeze to come in contact with your skin or painted surfaces of the vehicle. Flush contacted areas immediately with plenty of water.

WINDSHIELD WASHER FLUID

▶ **Refer to illustration 4.14**

14 Fluid for the windshield washer system is stored in a plastic reservoir which is located at the left side of the engine compartment (see illustration). In milder climates, plain water can be used to top up the reservoir, but the reservoir should be kept no more than two-thirds full to allow for expansion should the water freeze. In colder climates, the use of a specially designed windshield washer fluid, available at your dealer and any auto parts store, will help lower the freezing point of the fluid. Mix the solution with water in accordance with the manufacturer's

directions on the container. Do not use regular antifreeze. It will damage the vehicle's paint.

BRAKE FLUID/CLUTCH FLUID

▶ **Refer to illustration 4.16**

15 The brake and clutch fluid reservoir is mounted near the brake power booster unit in the engine compartment.

➡**Note: On some vehicles equipped with a manual transaxle, this reservoir also supplies fluid to the clutch system. On other models, a separate reservoir supplies fluid to the clutch release system.**

16 To check the fluid level of the reservoir, simply look at the MAX and MIN marks on the reservoir (see illustration). The level should be within the specified distance from the maximum fill line.

17 If the level is low, wipe the top of the reservoir cover with a clean rag to prevent contamination of the brake system before lifting the cover.

18 Add only the specified brake fluid to the brake reservoir (refer to *Recommended lubricants and fluids* in this Chapter's Specifications or your owner's manual). Mixing different types of brake fluid can damage the system. Fill the brake master cylinder reservoir only to the dotted

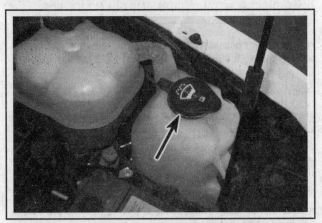

4.14 The windshield washer fluid reservoir is located at the left front corner of the engine compartment

4.16 The brake fluid should be kept between the Min and Max marks on the reservoir

line - this brings the fluid to the correct level when you put the cover back on.

✳✳ WARNING:

Use caution when filling the reservoir - brake fluid can harm your eyes and damage painted surfaces. Do not use brake fluid that has been opened for more than one year or has been left open. Brake fluid absorbs moisture from the air. Excess moisture can cause a dangerous loss of braking.

19 While the reservoir cap is removed, inspect the reservoir for contamination. If deposits, dirt particles or water droplets are present, the system should be drained and refilled (see Chapter 9 for information on flushing the brake system).

20 After filling the reservoir to the proper level, make sure the lid is properly seated to prevent fluid leakage and/or system pressure loss.

21 The fluid in the reservoir will drop slightly as the brake pads at each wheel wear down during normal operation. If the master cylinder requires repeated replenishing to keep it at the proper level, this is an indication of leakage in the brake system, which should be corrected immediately. Check all brake lines and connections, along with the wheel cylinders and booster (see Section 12 for more information).

22 If, upon checking the master cylinder fluid level, you discover the reservoir empty or nearly empty, the brake (and clutch, if equipped) system should be thoroughly inspected for leaks (see Chapter 9 for more information on the brake system).

AUTOMATIC TRANSAXLE FLUID

➡Note: Only vehicles with AF33-5 and 5-AT transaxles are equipped with dipsticks. The manufacturer states that transaxle fluid level checks are not usually necessary. Refer to Section 15 for additional transaxle maintenance information.

23 The level of the automatic transaxle fluid should be carefully maintained. Low fluid level can lead to slipping or loss of drive, while overfilling can cause foaming, loss of fluid and transaxle damage.

24 The transaxle fluid level should only be checked when the transaxle is hot (at its normal operating temperature). If the vehicle has just been driven over 10 miles (15 miles in a frigid climate), and the fluid temperature is 160 to 175-degrees F, the transaxle is hot.

✳✳ CAUTION:

If the vehicle has just been driven for a long time at high speed or in city traffic in hot weather, or if it has been pulling a trailer, an accurate fluid level reading cannot be obtained. Allow the fluid to cool down for about 30 minutes.

25 If the vehicle has not just been driven, park the vehicle on level ground, set the parking brake and start the engine. While the engine is idling, depress the brake pedal and move the selector lever through all the gear ranges, beginning and ending in Park.

26 With the engine still idling, remove the dipstick from its tube. Check the level of the fluid on the dipstick and note its condition.

27 Wipe the fluid from the dipstick with a clean rag and reinsert it back into the filler tube until the cap seats.

28 Pull the dipstick out again and note the fluid level. If the transaxle is cold, the level should be in the COLD or COOL range on the dipstick. If it is hot, the fluid level should be in the HOT range. If the level is at the low side of either range, add the specified automatic transaxle fluid through the dipstick tube with a funnel.

29 Add just enough of the recommended fluid to fill the transaxle to the proper level. It takes about one pint to raise the level from the low mark to the high mark when the fluid is hot, so add the fluid a little at a time and keep checking the level until it is correct.

30 The condition of the fluid should also be checked along with the level. If the fluid at the end of the dipstick is black or a dark reddish brown color, or if it emits a burned smell, the fluid should be changed (see Section 15). If you are in doubt about the condition of the fluid, purchase some new fluid and compare the two for color and smell.

MANUAL TRANSAXLE FLUID

➡Note: It isn't necessary to check the manual transaxle fluid weekly; every 15,000 miles (24,000 km) or 12 months is sufficient (unless a leak is noticed).

31 Raise the vehicle and support it securely on jackstands.

32 Remove the fluid check plug on the side of the transaxle.

➡Note: The lower of the two plugs is for draining the unit. Remove only the upper plug.

33 Check that the fluid is near the bottom of the hole. If it isn't, remove the fill cap from the top of the transaxle and add fluid using a funnel until it begins to run out of the check hole.

34 Install the check plug. If the transaxle required fluid, determine the cause of the leak.

TRANSFER CASE LUBRICANT (AWD MODELS)

➡Note: It isn't necessary to check the transfer case lubricant weekly; every 15,000 miles (24,000 km) or 12 months is sufficient (unless a leak is noticed).

35 To check the fluid level, raise the vehicle and support it securely on jackstands. On the back side of the transfer case housing, you will see a plug - remove it. If the lubricant level is correct, it should be up to the lower edge of the hole.

36 If the transaxle needs more lubricant (if the level is not up to the hole), use a syringe or a gear oil pump to add more. Stop filling the transaxle when the lubricant begins to run out the hole.

37 Install the plug and tighten it securely. Drive the vehicle a short distance, then check for leaks.

REAR DIFFERENTIAL LUBRICANT (AWD MODELS)

➡Note: It isn't necessary to check the rear differential lubricant weekly; every 15,000 miles (24,000 km) or 12 months is sufficient (unless a leak is noticed).

38 Raise the vehicle and support it securely on jackstands.

39 Unscrew the plug from the extreme front of the rear differential.

40 Use your little finger to reach inside the housing to feel the lubricant level. The level should be at or near the bottom of the plug hole. If it isn't, add the recommended lubricant through the plug hole with a syringe or squeeze bottle.

41 Install the plug and tighten it securely. Check for leaks after the first few miles of driving.

➡Note: It may take several miles of driving to allow the fluid to establish its normal level.

5   Tire and tire pressure checks (every 250 miles [400 km] or weekly)

▶ Refer to illustrations 5.2, 5.3, 5.4a, 5.4b and 5.8

1   Periodic inspection of the tires may spare you from the inconvenience of being stranded with a flat tire. It can also provide you with vital information regarding possible problems in the steering and suspension systems before major damage occurs.

2   Normal tread wear can be monitored with a simple, inexpensive device known as a tread depth indicator (see illustration). When the tread depth reaches approximately 1/16-inch, replace the tire(s) (preferably long before that).

3   Note any abnormal tread wear (see illustration). Tread pattern irregularities such as cupping, flat spots and more wear on one side than the other are indications of front end alignment and/or balance problems. If any of these conditions are noted, take the vehicle to a tire shop or service station to correct the problem.

4   Look closely for cuts, punctures and embedded nails or tacks. Sometimes a tire will hold its air pressure for a short time or leak down very slowly even after a nail has embedded itself into the tread. If a slow leak persists, check the valve stem core to make sure it is tight

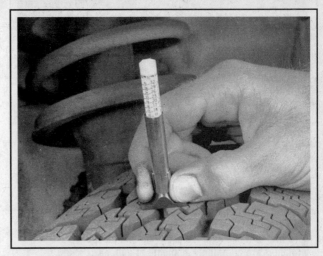

5.2 Use a tire tread depth gauge to monitor tire wear - they are available at auto parts stores and cost very little

UNDERINFLATION

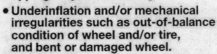

CUPPING

Cupping may be caused by:
- Underinflation and/or mechanical irregularities such as out-of-balance condition of wheel and/or tire, and bent or damaged wheel.
- Loose or worn steering tie-rod or steering idler arm.
- Loose, damaged or worn front suspension parts.

OVERINFLATION

INCORRECT TOE-IN OR EXTREME CAMBER

FEATHERING DUE TO MISALIGNMENT

5.3 This chart will help you determine the condition of your tires, the probable cause(s) of abnormal wear and the corrective action necessary

5.4a If a tire loses air on a steady basis, check the valve core first to make sure it's snug (special inexpensive wrenches are commonly available at auto parts stores)

5.4b If the valve core is tight, raise the corner of the vehicle with the low tire and spray a soapy water solution onto the tread as the tire is turned slowly - slow leaks will cause small bubbles to appear

(see illustration). Examine the tread for an object that may have embedded itself into the tire or for a plug that may have begun to leak (radial tire punctures are repaired with a plug that is fitted in a puncture). If a puncture is suspected, it can be easily verified by spraying a solution of soapy water onto the puncture area (see illustration). The soapy solution will bubble if there is a leak. Unless the puncture is inordinately large, a tire shop or gas station can usually repair the punctured tire.

5 Carefully inspect the inner sidewall of each tire for evidence of brake fluid leakage. If you see any, inspect the brakes immediately.

6 Correct tire air pressure adds miles to the lifespan of the tires, improves mileage and enhances overall ride quality. Tire pressure cannot be accurately estimated by looking at a tire, particularly if it is a radial. A tire pressure gauge is therefore essential. Keep an accurate gauge in the glove box. The pressure gauges fitted to the nozzles of air hoses at gas stations are often inaccurate.

7 Always check tire pressure when the tires are cold. "Cold," in this case, means the vehicle has not been driven over a mile in the three hours preceding a tire pressure check. A pressure rise of four to eight pounds is not uncommon once the tires are warm.

8 Unscrew the valve cap protruding from the wheel or hubcap and push the gauge firmly onto the valve (see illustration). Note the reading on the gauge and compare this figure to the recommended tire pressure shown on the tire placard in the glove box. Be sure to reinstall the valve cap to keep dirt and moisture out of the valve stem mechanism. Check all four tires and, if necessary, add enough air to bring them up to the recommended pressure levels.

9 Don't forget to keep the spare tire inflated to the specified pressure (consult your owner's manual). Note that the air pressure specified for a compact spare is significantly higher than the pressure of the regular tires.

5.8 To extend the life of your tires, check the air pressure at least once a week with an accurate gauge (don't forget the spare!)

6 Engine oil and oil filter change (every 3000 miles [4,800 km] or 3 months)

▶ Refer to illustrations 6.2 and 6.7

➡Note: These vehicles are equipped with an oil life indicator system that illuminates a light or message on the instrument panel when the system deems it necessary to change the oil. A number of factors are taken into consideration to determine when the oil should be called out worn out. Generally this system will allow the vehicle to accumulate more than the traditional 3000-mile interval, but we believe that frequent oil changes are cheap insurance and will prolong engine life. If you decide not to change your oil every 3000 miles and rely on the oil life indicator instead, make sure you don't exceed 7,500 miles (12,500 km) or 6 months (whichever comes first) before the oil is changed, regardless of what the oil life indicator shows.

1 Frequent oil changes are the best preventive maintenance the home mechanic can give the engine, because aging oil becomes diluted

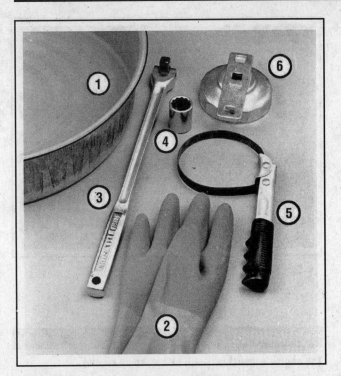

6.2 These tools are required when changing the engine oil and filter

1 **Drain pan** - It should be fairly shallow in depth, but wide in order to prevent spills

2 **Rubber gloves** - When removing the drain plug and filter, it is inevitable that you will get oil on your hands (the gloves will prevent burns)

3 **Breaker bar** - Sometimes the oil drain plug is pretty tight and a long breaker bar is needed to loosen it

4 **Socket** - To be used with the breaker bar or a ratchet (must be the correct size to fit the drain plug)

5 **Filter wrench** - This is a metal band-type wrench, which requires clearance around the filter to be effective

6 **Filter wrench** - This type fits on the bottom of the filter and can be turned with a ratchet or beaker bar (different size wrenches are available for different types of filters)

and contaminated, which leads to premature engine wear.

2 Make sure that you have all the necessary tools before you begin this procedure (see illustration). You should also have plenty of rags or newspapers handy for mopping up any spills.

3 Access to the underside of the vehicle is greatly improved if the vehicle can be lifted on a hoist, driven onto ramps or supported by jackstands.

※※ **WARNING:**

Do not work under a vehicle which is supported only by a bumper, hydraulic or scissors-type jack.

4 If this is your first oil change, get under the vehicle and familiarize yourself with the location of the oil drain plug. The engine and exhaust components will be warm during the actual work, so try to anticipate any potential problems before the engine and accessories are hot.

6.7 Use the proper size box-end wrench or socket to remove the oil drain plug without rounding off the corners

5 Park the vehicle on a level spot. Start the engine and allow it to reach its normal operating temperature (the needle on the temperature gauge should be at least above the bottom mark). Warm oil and sludge will flow out more easily. Turn off the engine when it's warmed up. Remove the filler cap.

6 Raise the vehicle and support it securely on jackstands.

※※ **WARNING:**

To avoid personal injury, never get beneath a vehicle when it is supported only by a jack. The jack provided with your vehicle is designed solely for raising the vehicle to remove and replace the wheels. Always use jackstands to support the vehicle when it becomes necessary to place your body underneath the vehicle.

7 Being careful not to touch the hot exhaust components, place the drain pan under the drain plug in the bottom of the pan and remove the plug (see illustration). You may want to wear gloves while unscrewing the plug the final few turns if the engine is really hot.

8 Allow the old oil to drain into the pan. It may be necessary to move the pan farther under the engine as the oil flow slows to a trickle. Inspect the old oil for the presence of metal particles.

9 After all the oil has drained, wipe off the drain plug with a clean rag. Even minute metal particles clinging to the plug would immediately contaminate the new oil.

10 Clean the area around the drain plug opening, reinstall the plug and tighten it securely, but do not strip the threads.

11 Move the drain pan into position under the oil filter.

12 If you're working on a four-cylinder model, remove all tools, rags, etc. from under the vehicle, being careful not to spill the oil in the drain pan, then lower the vehicle.

FOUR-CYLINDER AND 2002 AND 2003 3.0L V6 MODELS

◆ **Refer to illustrations 6.14a, 6.14b and 6.14c**

13 On four-cylinder models the canister-type oil filter is at the front left side of the engine and is accessible from the top. On the 2002/2003 V6 engine the canister-type filter is also located at the front of the

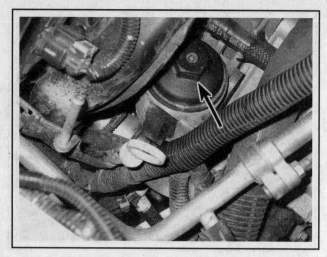

6.14a Unscrew the cap to access the oil filter

6.14b Remove the oil filter cartridge . . .

engine, but is accessed from under the vehicle.

14 Unscrew the oil filter cap using a special large socket and a ratchet (see illustrations). Withdraw the cap and the filter together. Make sure that the O-ring comes out of the housing.

15 Clean the oil filter housing and the cap with a clean rag.

16 Install a new O-ring in the groove of the cap, then install the new filter element in the cap and insert them both into the filter housing. Screw on the cap and tighten it securely.

2004 AND LATER 3.5L V6 MODELS

▶ **Refer to illustrations 6.17 and 6.19**

17 Loosen the oil filter by turning it counterclockwise with an oil fil-ter wrench (see illustration). Once the filter is loose, use your hands to unscrew it from the block. Just as the filter is detached from the block, immediately tilt the open end up to prevent the oil inside the filter from spilling out.

✳✳ WARNING:

The engine exhaust may still be hot, so be careful.

18 With a clean rag, wipe off the mounting surface on the block. If a residue of old oil is allowed to remain, it will smoke when the block is heated up. It will also prevent the new filter from seating properly. Also make sure that none of the old gasket remains stuck to the mounting surface. It can be removed with a scraper if necessary.

19 Compare the old filter with the new one to make sure they are the same type. Smear some engine oil on the rubber gasket of the new filter and screw it into place (see illustration). Overtightening the filter will damage the gasket, so don't use a filter wrench. Most filter manufactur-ers recommend tightening the filter by hand only. Normally they should be tightened 3/4-turn after the gasket contacts the block, but be sure to follow the directions on the filter or container.

6.14c . . . then separate the element from the cap

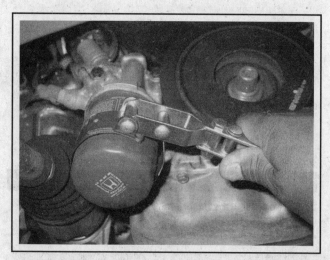

6.17 Use an oil filter wrench to remove the filter from 3.5L V6 models

ALL MODELS

20 If you're working on V6 model, lower the vehicle.

21 Add new oil to the engine through the oil filler cap in the valve cover. Use a funnel to prevent oil from spilling onto the top of the engine. Pour three quarts of fresh oil into the engine. Wait a few minutes to allow the oil to drain into the pan, then check the level on the oil dipstick (see Section 4 if necessary). If the oil level is at or near the F mark, install the filler cap hand tight, start the engine and allow the new oil to circulate.

22 Allow the engine to run for about a minute. While the engine is running, look under the vehicle and check for leaks at the oil pan drain plug and around the oil filter. If either is leaking, stop the engine and tighten the plug or filter slightly.

23 Wait a few minutes to allow the oil to trickle down into the pan, then recheck the level on the dipstick and, if necessary, add enough oil to bring the level to the F mark.

24 During the first few trips after an oil change, make it a point to check frequently for leaks and proper oil level.

25 The old oil drained from the engine cannot be reused in its present state and should be disposed of. Check with your local auto parts store, disposal facility or environmental agency to see if they will accept the oil for recycling. After the oil has cooled it can be drained into a container (capped plastic jugs, topped bottles, milk cartons, etc.) for transport to one of these disposal sites. Don't dispose of the oil by pouring it on the ground or down a drain!

RESETTING THE OIL CHANGE REMINDER LIGHT

2002 and 2003 models

26 Turn the key ignition ON but don't start the engine.

6.19 Lubricate the filter gasket with clean engine oil before installing it

27 Open the hood and remove the cover from the underhood fuse and relay box.

28 Hold down the red RESET button for at least five seconds. The oil change reminder light should be flashing if the system is reset. The light should not come on the next time the vehicle is started.

2004 and later models

29 Turn the key ignition ON but don't start the engine.

30 Press the accelerator pedal to the floor three times within five seconds. The oil change reminder light should be flashing if the system is reset. The light should not come on the next time the vehicle is started.

---

7   Battery check, maintenance and charging (every 5000 miles [8000 km] or 6 months)

❈❈ WARNING:

Certain precautions must be followed when checking and servicing the battery. Hydrogen gas, which is highly flammable, is always present in the battery cells, so keep lighted tobacco and all other open flames and sparks away from the battery. The electrolyte inside the battery is actually dilute sulfuric acid, which will cause injury if splashed on your skin or in your eyes. It will also ruin clothes and painted surfaces. When removing the battery cables, always detach the negative cable first and hook it up last!

MAINTENANCE

▶ **Refer to illustrations 7.1, 7.5, 7.7a, 7.7b and 7.7c**

1   A routine preventive maintenance program for the battery in your vehicle is the only way to ensure quick and reliable starts. But before performing any battery maintenance, make sure that you have the proper equipment necessary to work safely around the battery (see illustration).

2   There are also several precautions that should be taken whenever battery maintenance is performed. Before servicing the battery, always

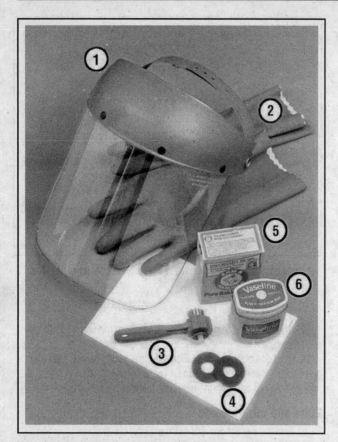

7.1 Tools and materials required for side-terminal type battery maintenance

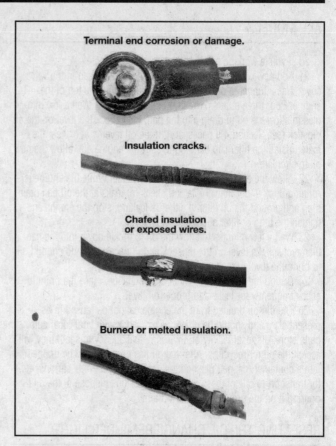

7.5 Inspect the battery cables carefully for problems like these

1 *Face shield/safety goggles* - *When removing corrosion with a brush, the acidic particles can easily fly up into your eyes*
2 *Rubber gloves* - *Another safety item to consider when servicing the battery; remember that's acid inside the battery*
3 *Battery post/cable cleaner* - *This wire brush cleaning tool will remove all traces of corrosion from the battery terminals and cable clamp*
4 *Treated felt washers* - *Placing one of these on each post, directly under the cable clamps, will help prevent corrosion - generally used on top-post batteries*
5 *Baking soda* - *A solution of baking soda and water can be used to neutralize corrosion*
6 *Petroleum jelly* - *A layer of this on the battery terminals will help prevent corrosion*

turn the engine and all accessories off and disconnect the cable from the negative terminal of the battery.

3 The battery produces hydrogen gas, which is both flammable and explosive. Never create a spark, smoke or light a match around the battery. Always charge the battery in a ventilated area.

4 Electrolyte contains poisonous and corrosive sulfuric acid. Do not allow it to get in your eyes, on your skin on your clothes. Never ingest it. Wear protective safety glasses when working near the battery. Keep children away from the battery.

5 Note the external condition of the battery. Look for any corroded or loose connections, cracks in the case or cover or loose hold-down clamps. Also check the entire length of each cable for cracks and frayed conductors (see illustration).

6 If corrosion, which looks like white, fluffy deposits is evident, particularly around the terminals, the battery should be removed for cleaning. Disconnect the negative battery cable first, followed by the positive. Then disconnect the hold-down bolt, remove the terminal and lift the battery from the engine compartment.

7 Clean the cable ends thoroughly with a battery brush or a terminal cleaner and a solution of warm water and baking soda (see illustrations). Wash the terminals and the top of the battery case with the same solution but make sure that the solution doesn't get into the battery. When cleaning the cables, terminals and battery top, wear safety goggles and rubber gloves to prevent any solution from coming in contact with your eyes or hands. Wear old clothes too - even diluted, sulfuric acid splashed onto clothes will burn holes in them. If the terminals have been extensively corroded, clean them up with a terminal cleaner. Thoroughly wash all cleaned areas with plain water.

8 Make sure that the battery tray is in good condition and the hold-down clamp bolts are tight. If the battery is removed from the tray, make sure no parts remain in the bottom of the tray when the battery is reinstalled. When reinstalling the hold-down bolts, do not overtighten them.

9 Any metal parts of the vehicle damaged by corrosion should be covered with a zinc-based primer, then painted.

10 Information on removing and installing the battery can be found in Chapter 5. Information on jump starting can be found at the front of this manual.

7.7a Use a clean wire brush to remove debris from the threaded holes . . .

7.7b . . . as well as the terminal outer surfaces

CHARGING

✱✱ WARNING:

When batteries are being charged, hydrogen gas, which is very explosive and flammable, is produced. Do not smoke or allow open flames near a battery. Wear eye protection when near the battery during charging. Also, make sure the charger is unplugged before connecting or disconnecting the battery from the charger.

➡Note: The manufacturer recommends the battery be removed from the vehicle for charging because the gas that escapes during this procedure can damage the paint. Fast charging with the battery cables connected can result in damage to the electrical system.

11 Slow-rate charging is the best way to restore a battery that's discharged to the point where it will not start the engine. It's also a good way to maintain the battery charge in a vehicle that's only driven a few miles between starts. Maintaining the battery charge is particularly important in the winter when the battery must work harder to start the engine and electrical accessories that drain the battery are in greater use.

12 It's best to use a one or two-amp battery charger (sometimes called a "trickle" charger). They are the safest and put the least strain on the battery. They are also the least expensive. For a faster charge, you can use a higher amperage charger, but don't use one rated more than 1/10 the amp/hour rating of the battery. Rapid boost charges that claim to restore the power of the battery in one to two hours are hardest on the battery and can damage batteries not in good condition. This type of charging should only be used in emergency situations.

13 The average time necessary to charge a battery should be listed in the instructions that come with the charger. As a general rule, a trickle charger will charge a battery in 12 to 16 hours.

14 Remove all the cell caps (if equipped) and cover the holes with a clean cloth to prevent spattering electrolyte. Disconnect the negative battery cable and hook the battery charger cable clamps up to the battery posts (positive to positive, negative to negative), then plug in the charger. Make sure it is set at 12-volts if it has a selector switch.

15 If you're using a charger with a rate higher than two amps, check the battery regularly during charging to make sure it doesn't overheat.

7.7c Regardless of the type of tool used to clean the battery terminals, a clean, shiny surface should be the result

If you're using a trickle charger, you can safely let the battery charge overnight after you've checked it regularly for the first couple of hours.

16 If the battery has removable cell caps, measure the specific gravity with a hydrometer every hour during the last few hours of the charging cycle. Hydrometers are available inexpensively from auto parts stores - follow the instructions that come with the hydrometer. Consider the battery charged when there's no change in the specific gravity reading for two hours and the electrolyte in the cells is gassing (bubbling) freely. The specific gravity reading from each cell should be very close to the others. If not, the battery probably has a bad cell(s).

17 Some batteries with sealed tops have built-in hydrometers on the top that indicate the state of charge by the color displayed in the hydrometer window. Normally, a bright-colored hydrometer indicates a full charge and a dark hydrometer indicates the battery still needs charging.

18 If the battery has a sealed top and no built-in hydrometer, you can hook up a voltmeter across the battery terminals to check the charge. A fully charged battery should read 12.6 volts or higher after the surface charge has been removed.

19 Further information on the battery and jump starting can be found in Chapter 5 and at the front of this manual.

8 Tire rotation (every 5000 miles [8000 km] or 6 months)

◆ **Refer to illustration 8.2**

1   The tires should be rotated at the specified intervals and whenever uneven wear is noticed. Since the vehicle will be raised and the
tires removed anyway, check the brakes (see Section 12) at this time.

2   Radial tires must be rotated in a specific pattern (see illustration).

3   Refer to the information in *Jacking and towing* at the front of this
manual for the proper procedures to follow when raising the vehicle
and changing a tire. If the brakes are to be checked, do not apply the
parking brake as stated. Make sure the tires are blocked to prevent the
vehicle from rolling.

4   Preferably, the entire vehicle should be raised at the same time.
This can be done on a hoist or by jacking up each corner and lowering
the vehicle onto jackstands placed under the frame rails. Always use
four jackstands and make sure the vehicle is firmly supported.

5   After rotation, check and adjust the tire pressures as necessary
and be sure to check the lug nut tightness.

6   For further information on the wheels and tires, refer to Chapter 10.

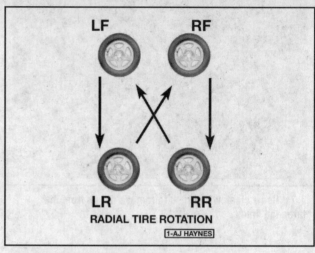

8.2 Four-tire rotation pattern

9 Windshield wiper blade inspection and replacement (every 5000 miles [8000 km] or 6 months)

◆ **Refer to illustrations 9.5a and 9.5b**

1   The windshield wiper and blade assembly should be inspected
periodically for damage, loose components and cracked or worn blade
elements.

2   Road film can build up on the wiper blades and affect their efficiency, so they should be washed regularly with a mild detergent solution.

3   The action of the wiping mechanism can loosen bolts, nuts and
fasteners, so they should be checked and tightened, as necessary, at the
same time the wiper blades are checked.

4   If the wiper blade elements are cracked, worn or warped, or no
longer clean adequately, they should be replaced with new ones.

5   Lift the arm assembly away from the glass for clearance, press
the release lever, then slide the wiper blade assembly out of the hook at
the end of the arm (see illustrations).

6   Attach the new wiper to the arm. Connection can be confirmed by
an audible click.

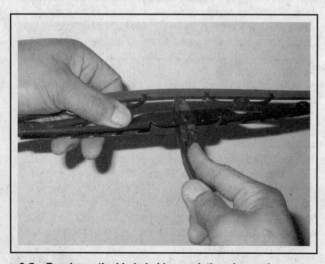

9.5a To release the blade holder, push the release pin . . .

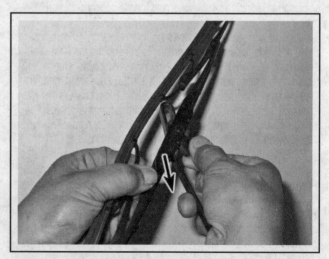

9.5b . . . and pull the wiper blade in the direction of the
arrow to separate it from the arm

10 Underhood hose check and replacement (every 5000 miles [8000 km] or 6 months)

☀☀ WARNING:

Replacement of air conditioning hoses must be left to a dealer service department or air conditioning shop that has the equipment to depressurize the system safely. Never remove air conditioning components or hoses until the system has been evacuated and the refrigerant recovered by a dealer service department or air conditioning shop.

GENERAL

1 High temperatures in the engine compartment can cause the deterioration of the rubber and plastic hoses used for engine, accessory and emission systems operation. Periodic inspection should be made for cracks, loose clamps, material hardening and leaks.

2 Information specific to the cooling system hoses can be found in Section 11.

3 Some, but not all, hoses are secured to the fittings with clamps. Where clamps are used, check to be sure they haven't lost their tension, allowing the hose to leak. If clamps aren't used, make sure the hose has not expanded and/or hardened where it slips over the fitting, allowing it to leak.

VACUUM HOSES

4 It's quite common for vacuum hoses, especially those in the emissions system, to be color coded or identified by colored stripes molded into them. Various systems require hoses with different wall thickness, collapse resistance and temperature resistance. When replacing hoses, be sure the new ones are made of the same material.

5 Often the only effective way to check a hose is to remove it completely from the vehicle. If more than one hose is removed, be sure to label the hoses and fittings to ensure correct installation.

6 When checking vacuum hoses, be sure to include any plastic T-fittings in the check. Inspect the fittings for cracks and the hose where it fits over the fitting for distortion, which could cause leakage.

7 A small piece of vacuum hose (1/4-inch inside diameter) can be used as a stethoscope to detect vacuum leaks. Hold one end of the hose to your ear and probe around vacuum hoses and fittings, listening for the hissing sound characteristic of a vacuum leak.

☀☀ WARNING:

When probing with the vacuum hose stethoscope, be very careful not to come into contact with moving engine components such as the drivebelts, cooling fan, etc.

FUEL HOSE

☀☀ WARNING:

Gasoline is extremely flammable, so take extra precautions when you work on any part of the fuel system. Don't smoke or allow open flames or bare light bulbs near the work area, and don't work in a garage where a gas-type appliance (such as a water heater or a clothes dryer) is present. Since gasoline is carcinogenic, wear fuel resistant gloves when there's a possibility of being exposed to fuel, and, if you spill any fuel on your skin, rinse it off immediately with soap and water. Mop up any spills immediately and do not store fuel-soaked rags where they could ignite. The fuel system is under constant pressure, so, if any fuel lines are to be disconnected, the fuel pressure in the system must be relieved first. When you perform any kind of work on the fuel system, wear safety glasses and have a Class B type fire extinguisher on hand.

8 Check all rubber fuel lines for deterioration and chafing. Check especially for cracks in areas where the hose bends and just before fittings, such as where a hose attaches to the fuel filter.

9 High quality fuel line should be used for fuel line replacement. Never, under any circumstances, use unreinforced vacuum line, clear plastic tubing or water hose for fuel lines.

10 Spring-type clamps are sometimes used on fuel lines. These clamps often lose their tension over a period of time, and can be sprung during removal. Replace all spring-type clamps with screw clamps whenever a hose is replaced.

METAL LINES

11 Sections of metal line are often used for fuel line between the fuel pump and fuel injection unit. Check carefully to be sure the line has not been bent or crimped and that cracks have not started in the line.

12 If a section of metal fuel line must be replaced, only seamless steel tubing should be used, since copper and aluminum tubing don't have the strength necessary to withstand normal engine vibration.

13 Check the metal brake lines where they enter the master cylinder and brake proportioning unit (if used) for cracks in the lines or loose fittings. Any sign of brake fluid leakage calls for an immediate thorough inspection of the brake system.

11 Cooling system check (every 5000 miles [8000 km] or 6 months)

▶ Refer to illustration 11.4

1 Many major engine failures can be attributed to a faulty cooling system. If the vehicle is equipped with an automatic transaxle, the cooling system also cools the transaxle fluid and thus plays an important role in prolonging transaxle life.

2 The cooling system should be checked with the engine cold. Do this before the vehicle is driven for the day or after the engine has been shut off for at least three hours.

Never remove the reservoir pressure cap when the engine is running or has just been shut down, because the cooling system is hot. Escaping steam and scalding liquid could cause serious injury.

3   Remove the reservoir pressure cap by turning it to the counter-clockwise until it reaches a stop. If you hear a hissing sound (indicating there is still pressure in the system), wait until it stops. Press down on the cap with the palm of your hand and continue turning to the left until the cap can be removed. Thoroughly clean the cap, inside and out, with clean water. Also clean the filler neck on the radiator. All traces of corrosion should be removed. The coolant inside the reservoir should be relatively transparent. If it's rust colored, the system should be drained and refilled (see Section 24). If the coolant level isn't up to the top, add additional antifreeze/coolant mixture (see Section 4).

4   Carefully check the large upper and lower radiator hoses along with the smaller diameter heater hoses which run from the engine to the firewall. Inspect each hose along its entire length, replacing any hose which is cracked, swollen or shows signs of deterioration. Cracks may become more apparent if the hose is squeezed (see illustration). Regardless of condition, it's a good idea to replace hoses with new ones every two years.

5   Make sure that all hose connections are tight. A leak in the cooling system will usually show up as white or rust colored deposits on the areas adjoining the leak. If wire-type clamps are used at the ends of the hoses, it may be a good idea to replace them with more secure screw-type clamps.

6   Use compressed air or a soft brush to remove bugs, leaves, etc. from the front of the radiator or air conditioning condenser. Be careful not to damage the delicate cooling fins or cut yourself on them.

7   Every other inspection, or at the first indication of cooling system problems, have the cap and system pressure tested. If you don't have a pressure tester, most gas stations and garages will do this for a minimal charge.

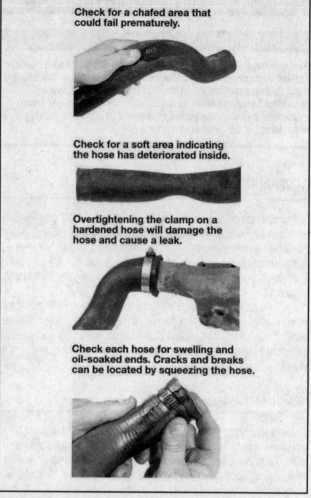

Check for a chafed area that could fail prematurely.

Check for a soft area indicating the hose has deteriorated inside.

Overtightening the clamp on a hardened hose will damage the hose and cause a leak.

Check each hose for swelling and oil-soaked ends. Cracks and breaks can be located by squeezing the hose.

11.4 Hoses, like drivebelts, have a habit of failing at the worst possible time - to prevent the inconvenience of a blown radiator or heater hose, inspect them carefully as shown here

12   Brake check (every 5000 miles [8000 km] or 6 months)

The dust created by the brake system is harmful to your health. Never blow it out with compressed air and don't inhale any of it. An approved filtering mask should be worn when working on the brakes. Do not, under any circumstances, use petroleum-based solvents to clean brake parts. Use brake system cleaner only!

➡Note: For detailed photographs of the brake system, refer to Chapter 9.

1   In addition to the specified intervals, the brakes should be inspected every time the wheels are removed or whenever a defect is suspected.

2   Any of the following symptoms could indicate a potential brake system defect: The vehicle pulls to one side when the brake pedal is depressed; the brakes make squealing or dragging noises when applied; brake pedal travel is excessive; the pedal pulsates; or brake fluid leaks, usually onto the inside of the tire or wheel.

3   Loosen the wheel lug nuts.

4   Raise the vehicle and place it securely on jackstands.

5   Remove the wheels (see *Jacking and towing* at the front of this book, or your owner's manual, if necessary).

DISC BRAKES

◗ **Refer to illustrations 12.7a and 12.7b**

6   There are two pads (an outer and an inner) in each caliper. The pads are visible with the wheels removed. The vehicles covered by this manual have disc brakes in front only.

12.7a You'll find an inspection hole like this in each caliper through which you can view the inner brake pad lining

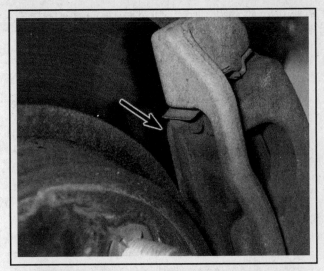

12.7b The outer pad is more easily checked at the edge of the caliper

7   Check the pad thickness by looking at each end of the caliper and through the inspection window in the caliper body (see illustrations). If the lining material is less than the thickness listed in this Chapter's Specifications, replace the pads.

➡Note: Keep in mind that the lining material is riveted or bonded to a metal backing plate and the metal portion is not included in this measurement.

8   If it is difficult to determine the exact thickness of the remaining pad material by the above method, or if you are at all concerned about the condition of the pads, remove the caliper(s), then remove the pads from the calipers for further inspection (see Chapter 9).

9   Once the pads are removed from the calipers, clean them with brake cleaner and re-measure them with a ruler or a vernier caliper.

10 Measure the disc thickness with a micrometer to make sure that it still has service life remaining. If any disc is thinner than the specified minimum thickness, replace it (see Chapter 9). Even if the disc has service life remaining, check its condition. Look for scoring, gouging and burned spots. If these conditions exist, remove the disc and have it resurfaced (see Chapter 9).

11 Before installing the wheels, check all brake lines and hoses for damage, wear, deformation, cracks, corrosion, leakage, bends and twists, particularly in the vicinity of the rubber hoses at the calipers. Check the clamps for tightness and the connections for leakage. Make sure that all hoses and lines are clear of sharp edges, moving parts and the exhaust system. If any of the above conditions are noted, repair, reroute or replace the lines and/or fittings as necessary (see Chapter 9).

DRUM BRAKES

▶ **Refer to illustrations 12.15 and 12.17**

12 All models have rear drum brakes. With the rear wheels removed, make sure the parking brake is off and tap on the outside of the brake drums with a mallet to loosen them.

13 Remove the brake drums. If they won't come off, refer to Chapter 9.

14 Carefully clean the brake assemblies with brake system cleaner.

✳✳ WARNING:

Don't blow the dust out with compressed air and don't inhale any of it it's harmful to your health).

15 Note the thickness of the lining material on both front and rear shoes (see illustration). Compare the measurement with the limit given in this Chapter's Specifications; if any lining is thinner than specified, then all of the brake shoes must be replaced (see Chapter 9). They should also be replaced if they're cracked, glazed with shiny areas or soaked with brake fluid.

16 Make sure that all of the brake springs are connected and in good condition.

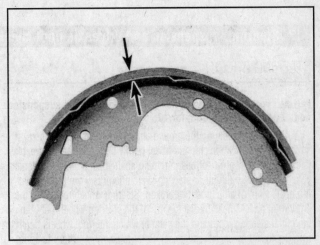

12.15 If the lining is bonded to the brake shoe, measure it's thickness from the outer surface to the steel shoe, as shown here; if the lining is riveted to the shoe, measure from the lining outer surface to the rivet head

17 Check the wheel cylinders for fluid leakage. Carefully pry back the wheel cylinder rubber cups with your fingers or a small screwdriver (see illustration). Any leakage is an indication that the wheel cylinders should be replaced at once (see Chapter 9). Also check all hoses and connections for signs of leakage.

18 Wipe the inside of the brake drums with a clean rag and brake cleaner or alcohol. Again, be careful no to breathe the dangerous brake dust.

19 Check the inside of the drum for score marks, deep scratches and hard spots that appear as small discolored areas. If imperfections can't be removed with fine emery cloth, the drum must be taken to an automotive machine shop for machining.

20 If your inspection reveals that all parts are in good condition, install the drums, install the wheels and lower the vehicle.

BRAKE BOOSTER CHECK

21 Sit in the driver's seat and perform the following sequence of tests.

22 With the brake fully depressed, start the engine - the pedal should move down a little when the engine starts.

23 With the engine running, depress the brake pedal several times - the travel distance should not change.

24 Depress the brake, stop the engine and hold the pedal in for about 30 seconds - the pedal should neither sink nor rise.

25 Restart the engine, run it for about a minute and turn it off. Then firmly depress the brake several times - the pedal travel should decrease with each application.

26 If your brakes do not operate as described, the brake booster has failed. Refer to Chapter 9 for the replacement procedure.

PARKING BRAKE

27 One method of checking the parking brake is to park the vehicle on a steep hill with the parking brake set and the transmission in Neutral (be sure to stay in the vehicle for this check). If the parking brake cannot prevent the vehicle from rolling, it's in need of attention (see Chapter 9).

12.17 Carefully peel back the wheel cylinder boot and check for leaking fluid, indicating that the cylinder must be rebuilt

13 Steering, suspension and driveaxle boot check (every 15,000 miles [24,000 km] or 18 months)

STEERING CHECK

➡Note: For detailed illustrations of the steering and suspension components, refer to Chapter 10.

1 With the vehicle on the ground and the front wheels pointed straight ahead, rock the steering wheel gently back and forth. If freeplay is excessive, a front wheel bearing, main shaft yoke, intermediate shaft yoke, lower arm balljoint or steering system joint is worn or the steering gear is out of adjustment or broken. Steering wheel freeplay is the amount of travel (measured at the rim of the steering wheel) between the initial steering input and the point at which the front wheels begin to turn (indicated by slight resistance). Refer to Chapter 10 for the appropriate repair procedure.

2 Other symptoms, such as excessive vehicle body movement over rough roads, swaying (leaning) around corners and binding as the steering wheel is turned, may indicate faulty steering and/or suspension components.

SUSPENSION CHECK

▶ Refer to illustrations 13.7 and 13.8

3 Check the shock absorbers by pushing down and releasing the vehicle several times at each corner. If the vehicle does not come back to a level position within one or two bounces, the shocks/struts are worn and must be replaced. When bouncing the vehicle up and down, listen for squeaks and noises from the suspension components. Additional information on suspension components can be found in Chapter 10.

4 Raise the vehicle with a floor jack and support it securely on jackstands. See *Jacking and towing* at the front of this book for the proper jacking points.

5 Check the tires for irregular wear patterns and proper inflation. See Section 5 in this Chapter for information regarding tire wear and Chapter 10 for the wheel bearing replacement procedures.

6 Inspect the universal joint between the steering shaft and the

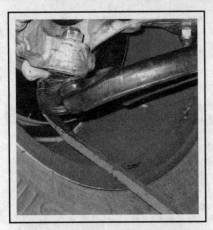

13.7 To check the balljoints, attempt to move the lower arm up and down with a prybar to make sure here is no play in the balljoint (if there is, replace it)

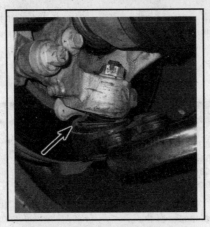

13.8 Push on the balljoint boot to check for tears and grease leaks

13.10 Flex the driveaxle boots by hand to check for tears, cracks and leaking grease

steering gear housing. Check the steering gear housing for lubricant leakage or oozing. Make sure that the dust seals and boots are not damaged and that the boot clamps are not loose. Check the steering linkage for looseness or damage. Check the track rod ends for excessive play. Look for loose bolts, broken or disconnected parts and deteriorated rubber bushings on all suspension and steering components. While an assistant turns the steering wheel from side to side, check the steering components for free movement, chafing and binding. If the steering components do not seem to be reacting with the movement of the steering wheel, try to determine where the slack is located.

7   Check the balljoints for wear by trying to move each lower arm up and down with a prybar (see illustration) to ensure that its balljoint has no play. If any balljoint does have play, replace it. See Chapter 10 for the front balljoint replacement procedure.

8   Inspect the balljoint boots for damage and leaking grease (see illustration). Replace the balljoints with new ones if they are damaged (see Chapter 10).

DRIVEAXLE BOOT CHECK

▶ **Refer to illustration 13.10**

9   The driveaxle boots are very important because they prevent dirt, water and foreign material from entering and damaging the constant velocity (CV) joints.

10 Inspect the boots for tears and cracks as well as loose clamps (see illustration). If there is any evidence of cracks or leaking lubricant, they must be replaced as described in Chapter 8.

---

14 Exhaust system check (every 15,000 miles [24,000 km] or 18 months)

▶ **Refer to illustration 14.2**

➡**Note: All transaxles have identification tags. Refer to "Vehicle Identification Numbers" at the front of this manual for information about their locations.**

1   With the engine cold (at least three hours after the vehicle has been driven), check the complete exhaust system from its starting point at the engine to the end of the tailpipe. This should be done on a hoist where unrestricted access is available.

2   Check the pipes and connections for evidence of leaks, severe corrosion or damage. Make sure that all brackets and hangers are in good condition and tight (see illustration).

3   At the same time, inspect the underside of the body for holes, corrosion, open seams, etc. which may allow exhaust gases to enter the passenger compartment. Seal all body openings with silicone or body putty.

4   Rattles and other noises can often be traced to the exhaust system, especially the mounts and hangers. Try to move the pipes, silencer and catalytic converter. If the components can come in contact with the body or suspension parts, secure the exhaust system with new mounts.

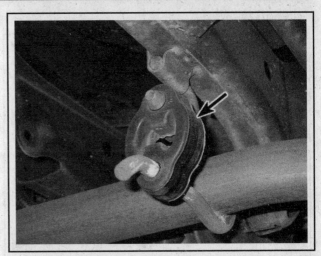

14.2 Check the exhaust system for damage, or worn rubber hangers

5   Check the running condition of the engine by inspecting inside the end of the tailpipe. The exhaust deposits here are an indication of engine state-of-tune. If the pipe is black and sooty or coated with white deposits, the engine is in need of a tune-up; including a thorough fuel system inspection.

15   Automatic transaxle fluid change (25,000 miles [40,000 km] or 36 months)

➡**Note 1: There are four transaxles used on these models. All have important information such as the transaxle type and build date on a metal tag that is attached near the center top of the unit. Some models also have a prominent sticker that gives similar information.**

➡**Note 2: The manufacturer states that routine checks of the automatic transaxle fluid are not necessary. Low fluid level can lead to slipping or loss of drive, while overfilling can cause foaming and loss of fluid.**

➡**Note 3: The mileage interval given is only for vehicles used in severe service conditions. Refer to the notes in the "Maintenance Schedule" at the beginning of this Chapter for information about severe service.**

1   At the specified time intervals, the transaxle fluid should be drained and replaced. Since the fluid will remain hot long after driving, perform this procedure only after everything has cooled down completely.

2   Before beginning work, purchase the specified transaxle fluid (see *Recommended lubricants and fluids* in this Chapter's Specifications) and a new filter.

3   Other tools necessary for this job include jackstands to support the vehicle in a raised position, a drain pan capable of holding several quarts, newspapers and clean rags.

4   Raise and support the vehicle on jackstands.

4T40-E/4T45-E TRANSAXLES

▶ **Refer to illustrations 15.10a, 15.10b and 15.12**

5   With a drain pan in place, remove the front and side transaxle pan mounting bolts.

6   Loosen the rear pan bolts one turn.

7   Carefully pry the transaxle pan loose with a screwdriver, allowing the fluid to drain.

8   Remove the remaining bolts, pan and gasket. Carefully clean the gasket surface of the transaxle to remove all traces of the old gasket and sealant.

9   Drain the fluid from the transaxle pan, clean the pan with solvent and dry it with compressed air. Be careful not to lose the magnet.

10 Remove the filter and pry out the seal (see illustrations).

11 Push a new filter seal fully into its bore, then install the new filter.

12 Make sure the gasket surface on the transaxle pan is clean, then install the new gasket (see illustration). Put the pan in place against the transaxle and install the bolts.

13 Working around the pan, tighten each bolt a little at a time until

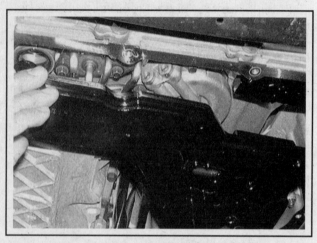

15.10a Pull the filter downward to remove it - it has no fasteners

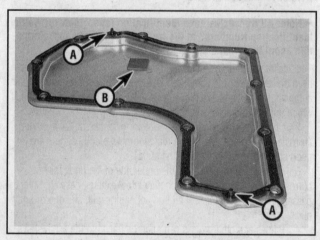

15.12 Check the pan rail for straightness and install a new gasket (A) after you clean the magnet (B)

15.10b Make sure to remove the old filter O-ring

the final torque figure is reached.

14 Lower the vehicle and add the specified amount of automatic transmission fluid through the vent/fill cap and check the fluid level (see Steps 15 through 21).

Fluid level check

▶ **Refer to illustrations 15.17a and 15.17b**

15 The manufacturer states that routine checks of the automatic transaxle fluid are not necessary; this procedure should only be used when refilling the transaxle after the fluid has been drained, unless an obvious leak has been detected. Low fluid level can lead to slipping or loss of drive, while overfilling can cause foaming and loss of fluid.

※※ WARNING:

This procedure is potentially dangerous and is best left to a professional shop with a safe lifting apparatus. The vehicle must be kept level while being safely raised high enough for access to the check plug on the transaxle.

16 With the vehicle raised and safely supported, start the engine, then move the shift lever through all the gear ranges, ending in Park.

➡**Note: Incorrect fluid level readings will result if the vehicle has just been driven at high speeds for an extended period, in hot weather in city traffic, or if it has been pulling a trailer. If any of these conditions apply, wait until the fluid has cooled (about 30 minutes).**

17 Remove the vent/fill cap (see illustration). With the engine running and the transaxle at normal operating temperature (having idled for 3 to 5 minutes), locate the check plug on the transaxle. The check plug is located near the pan, adjacent to the engine oil drain plug (see illustration).

18 Place a container under the check plug and remove it. Observe the fluid as it drips into the pan, indicating correct fluid level.

19 The fluid level should be at the bottom of the check hole. If fluid pours out excessively, the transaxle may have been overfilled. Double-check to make sure the vehicle is level. If no fluid drips from the check hole, add small amounts of fluid through the vent/fill cap at the top of the transaxle until the level is at the bottom of the check hole. A long-

necked funnel will be necessary to add fluid (through the vent/fill opening).

20 The condition of the fluid should also be checked along with the level. If the fluid in the drain pan is a dark reddish-brown color, or if the fluid has a burned smell, the fluid should be changed (see Steps 1 through 14). If you're in doubt about the condition of the fluid, purchase some new fluid and compare the two for color and smell.

21 Be sure to install the check plug and tighten it securely when you're done.

AF33-5 AND 5-AT TRANSAXLE

➡**Note: The use of a scan tool is recommended for monitoring transmission fluid temperature when checking the transaxle fluid level.**

22 Place a drain pan under the transaxle. Remove the transaxle drain plug allowing the transaxle fluid to drain. The transaxle drain plug is located at the bottom of the transaxle, below and forward of the right (passenger's side) driveaxle, facing the right side of the vehicle. Discard the sealing washer (a new one should be used when reinstalling the plug).

23 Install the drain plug (using a new sealing washer) and tighten it to the torque listed in this Chapter's Specifications.

24 Lower the vehicle and remove the bolt securing the fluid level gauge, then pull out the gauge.

➡**Note: The fluid level gauge is located on the front side of the transaxle, between the pressed-metal pan on the front of the transaxle and the bellhousing.**

※※ CAUTION:

Don't remove the bolt for the third gear anchor bolt band, which is located at the top of the transaxle. If this bolt is removed, the transaxle will have to be removed and disassembled to put the parts back in place.

25 Fill the transaxle with approximately 3.3 quarts (3.1 liters) of the proper automatic transmission fluid (see *Recommended lubricants and fluids* in this Chapter's Specifications) through the hole left by the level gauge.

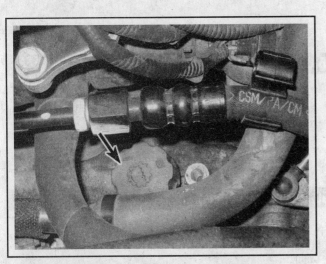

15.17a The fluid add cap is on the top of the transaxle

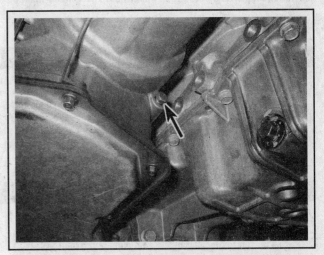

15.17b The transaxle level plug (4T40-E/4T45-E transaxles)

26 Start the engine and run it until the transmission fluid reaches approximately 140 to 158-degrees F (60 to 70-degrees C).

27 With the engine running, push the brake pedal and shift the transmission into each gear range, pausing for a few seconds in each position, then shift into Park.

28 Install the fluid level gauge into its tube until it seats completely, then pull it out and check the fluid level.

29 If necessary, add fluid a little at a time, repeating Steps 27 and 28, until the fluid level is correct.

➡Note: The 5-AT transaxle has a fill cap. Remove the air intake duct for access (see Chapter 4).

30 Reinstall the fluid level gauge and hold-down bolt, tightening it securely.

VT25-E (CVT OR CONTINUOUSLY VARIABLE TRANSAXLE)

➡Note: The use of a scan tool is required for monitoring transmission fluid temperature when refilling the transaxle with fluid.

31 Place a drain pan under the transaxle. Unscrew the drain plug; it's the smaller plug in the center of a larger one at the bottom of the transaxle (the larger one is known as the "lower tube").

32 Unscrew the lower tube and allow the fluid to drain.

33 Reinstall the lower tube and tighten it to the torque listed in this Chapter's Specifications.

34 Install the drain plug in the lower tube, but don't tighten it completely, then lower the vehicle.

35 Fill the transaxle with 6 to 7 quarts (6 to 6.5 liters) of the proper automatic transmission fluid (see *Recommended lubricants and fluids* in this Chapter's Specifications).

36 Connect a scan tool to the diagnostic connector, then start the engine.

37 Shift the transmission into Reverse for ten seconds, then into Drive for ten seconds, then back into Park (don't turn the engine off).

38 Raise the vehicle and support it securely on jackstands.

✳✳ WARNING:

This procedure is potentially dangerous and is best left to a professional shop with a safe lifting apparatus. The vehicle must be kept level while being safely raised high enough for access to the drain/check plug on the transaxle.

39 Place a container under the transaxle, then unscrew the check/drain plug.

a) If fluid flows out, let it drain until it stops.

b) If no fluid flows out (or just a very small amount), add fluid to the transaxle until fluid does begin to flow out, then let it drain until it stops.

40 Install a new drain plug and tighten it to the torque listed in this Chapter's Specifications.

41 Lower the vehicle and, using the scan tool, measure the temperature of the transaxle fluid:

a) If the temperature of the fluid is 68-degrees F (20-degrees C) or less, add 1/2-quart (0.47 liter) of the proper transmission fluid to the transaxle.

b) If the temperature of the fluid is 104-degrees F (40-degrees C), add 3/4-quart (0.71 liter) of the proper transmission fluid to the transaxle.

c) If the temperature of the fluid is 140-degrees F (60-degrees C), add 1-quart (0.95 liter) of the proper transmission fluid to the transaxle.

d) If the temperature of the fluid is 176-degrees F (80-degrees C), add 1-1/4 quarts (1.2 liters) of the proper transmission fluid to the transaxle.

42 Turn off the engine and add DEX-CVT fluid additive to the transaxle (use all of the contents in the applicator).

ALL MODELS

43 Check under the vehicle for leaks after the first few trips.

44 The old fluid drained from the transaxle cannot be reused in its present state and should be disposed of. Check with your local auto parts store, disposal facility or environmental agency to see if they will accept the fluid for recycling. After the fluid has cooled it can be drained into a container (capped plastic jugs, topped bottles, milk cartons, etc.) for transport to one of these disposal sites. Don't dispose of the fluid by pouring it on the ground or down a drain!

16 Transfer case lubricant change (AWD models) (25,000 miles [40,000 km] or 36 months)

1 Raise the vehicle and support it securely on jackstands.

2 Remove the check/fill plug, then remove the drain plug and drain the lubricant.

3 Reinstall the drain plug and tighten it securely.

4 Add new lubricant until it is even with the lower edge of the filler hole. See *Recommended lubricants and fluids* for the specified lubricant type.

5 Reinstall the check/fill plug and tighten it securely.

17 Air filter replacement (every 30,000 miles [48,000 km] or 36 months)

▸ **Refer to illustrations 17.1, 17.4 and 17.5**

1 The air filter is located inside a housing at the left (driver's) side of the engine compartment. To remove the air filter, first loosen the clamp and disconnect the air outlet duct from the filter housing (see illustration).

2 On 2002 and 2003 3.0L V6 engines, disconnect the MAF sensor wiring.

3 Release the filter housing clips (see illustration 17.1).

17.1 Loosen the air duct clamp and release the filter housing clips (arrows)

17.4 Lift the cover up and remove it

17.5 Remove the air filter element

4   Rotate the lid on its hinges until it can be lifted off (see illustration). Remove the lid.

5   Take out the air filter (see illustration).

6   Inspect the outer surface of the filter element. If it is dirty, replace it. If it is only moderately dusty, it can be reused by blowing it clean from the back to the front surface with compressed air.

❋❋ WARNING:

Always wear eye protection when using compressed air! Because it is a pleated paper type filter, it cannot be washed or oiled. If it cannot be cleaned satisfactorily with compressed air, discard and replace it.

❋❋ CAUTION:

Never drive the vehicle with the air cleaner removed. Excessive engine wear could result and backfiring could even cause a fire under the hood.

7   Installation is the reverse of removal. Make sure the hinge tabs on the housing cover engage properly with the lower part of the housing before snapping the clips into place.

18 Fuel system check (every 30,000 miles [48,000 km] or 36 months)

❋❋ WARNING:

Gasoline is extremely flammable, so take extra precautions when you work on any part of the fuel system. Don't smoke or allow open flames or bare light bulbs near the work area, and don't work in a garage where a gas-type appliance (such as a water heater or a clothes dryer) is present. Since gasoline is carcinogenic, wear fuel resistant gloves when there's a possibility of being exposed to fuel, and, if you spill any fuel on your skin, rinse it off immediately with soap and water. Mop up any spills immediately and do not store fuel-soaked rags where they could ignite. The fuel system is under constant pressure, so, if any fuel lines are to be disconnected, the fuel pressure in the system must be relieved first. When you perform any kind of work on the fuel system, wear safety glasses and have a Class B type fire extinguisher on hand.

1   If you smell fuel while driving or after the vehicle has been sitting in the sun, inspect the fuel system immediately.

2   Remove the fuel filler cap and inspect it for damage and corrosion. The gasket should have an unbroken sealing imprint. If the gasket is damaged or corroded, remove it and install a new one.

3   Inspect the fuel feed and return lines for cracks. Make sure that the threaded flare nut type connectors which secure the metal fuel lines to the fuel injection system and the banjo bolts which secure the banjo fittings to the in-line fuel filter are tight.

4   Since some components of the fuel system - the fuel tank and part of the fuel feed and return lines, for example - are underneath the vehicle, they can be inspected more easily with the vehicle raised on a hoist. If that's not possible, raise the vehicle and support it securely on jackstands.

5   With the vehicle raised and safely supported, inspect the fuel tank and filler neck for punctures, cracks and other damage. The connection between the filler neck and the tank is particularly critical. Sometimes a rubber filler neck will leak because of loose clamps or deteriorated rubber. These are problems a home mechanic can usually rectify.

❋❋ WARNING:

Do not, under any circumstances, try to repair a fuel tank (except rubber components). A welding torch or any open flame can easily cause fuel vapors inside the tank to explode.

6   Carefully check all rubber hoses and metal lines leading away from the fuel tank. Check for loose connections, deteriorated hoses, crimped lines and other damage. Carefully inspect the lines from the tank to the fuel injection system. Repair or replace damaged sections as necessary (see Chapter 4).

19 Interior ventilation filter replacement (every 30,000 miles [48,000 km] or 36 months)

▶ Refer to illustrations 19.1 and 19.2

1 Open the hood. Remove the pushpin fasteners from the filter cover on the right side of the cowl (see illustration).

2 Push the tab at the end of the filter to release it (see illustration).
3 Lift out the filter and clean or replace it.
4 Installation is the reverse of removal. Make sure that the air flow arrow points to the interior of the vehicle.

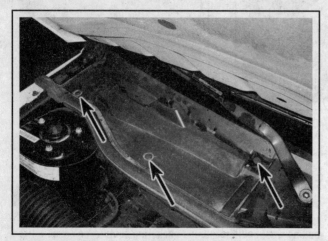

19.1 These plastic pushpin fasteners secure the cover over the cabin air filter

19.2 Press this tab to release the cabin air filter

20 Brake fluid change (every 30,000 miles [48,000 km] or 36 months)

❋❋ WARNING:

Brake fluid can harm your eyes and damage painted surfaces, so use extreme caution when handling or pouring it. Do not use brake fluid that has been standing open or is more than one year cld. Brake fluid absorbs moisture from the air. Excess moisture can cause a dangerous loss of braking effectiveness.

➡Note: Used brake fluid is considered a hazardous waste and must be disposed of in accordance with federal, state and local laws. DO NOT pour it into a sink, septic system, storm drain or on the ground.

1 At the specified intervals, the brake fluid should be drained and replaced. Since the brake fluid may drip or splash when pouring it, place plenty of rags around the master cylinder to protect any surrounding painted surfaces.

2 Before beginning work, purchase the specified brake fluid (see *Recommended lubricants and fluids* in this Chapter's Specifications).

3 Remove the cap from the fluid reservoir.
4 Using a hand suction pump or similar device, withdraw the fluid from the fluid reservoir.
5 Add new fluid to the reservoir until it rises to the base of the filler neck.
6 Bleed the brake system as described in Chapter 9 at all four brakes until new and uncontaminated fluid is expelled from the bleeder screw. Be sure to maintain the fluid level in the master cylinder as you perform the bleeding process. If you allow the master cylinder to run dry, air will enter the system.
7 Refill the reservoir with fluid and check the operation of the brakes. The pedal should feel solid when depressed, with no sponginess.

❋❋ WARNING:

Do not operate the vehicle if you are in doubt about the effectiveness of the brake system.

21 Drivebelt check and replacement (50,000 miles [80,000 km] or 60 months and every 15,000 miles [24,000 km] and 18 months thereafter)

CHECK

♦ **Refer to illustration 21.2**

✳✳ WARNING:

Before checking, adjusting or replacing a drivebelt, make sure the ignition key is not in the ignition lock cylinder.

1   The drivebelts are located at the front of the engine and play an important role in the operation of the vehicle and its components. Due

to their function and material makeup, belts are prone to failure after a period of time and should be inspected and adjusted periodically to prevent major damage. All models use a single serpentine belt; no adjustment is necessary because an automatic tensioner is used.

2   With the engine turned off, open the hood and locate the drivebelt(s) at the front of the engine. Use a flashlight to carefully check for a severed core, separation of the adhesive rubber on both sides of the core and for core separation from the belt side. Inspect the ribs for separation from the adhesive rubber and for cracking or separation of the ribs, torn or worn ribs or cracks in the inner ridges of the ribs (see illustration). Also check for fraying and glazing, which gives the belt a shiny appearance. Inspect both sides of the belt by twisting the belt to check the underside. Use your fingers to feel the belt where you can't see it. If any of the above conditions are evident, replace the belt(s).

➡**Note: The drivebelt inspection can be made easier by removing the under-vehicle splash shield.**

REPLACEMENT

➡**Note: Take the old belt with you when purchasing new ones in order to make a direct comparison for length, width and design.**

2.2L four-cylinder engine

♦ **Refer to illustrations 21.5 and 21.7**

3   Loosen the right front wheel lug nuts. Raise the vehicle and support it securely on jackstands. Remove the right front wheel.

4   Remove the right inner fender splash shield.

5   Using a breaker bar or ratchet, insert the end into the square hole on the tensioner (see illustration), and slowly rotate the drivebelt tensioner counterclockwise and remove the drivebelt from the pulleys.

6   Take the old belt to the parts store in order to make a direct comparison for length, width and design.

7   After replacing the drivebelt, make sure that it's properly routed (see illustration), and that it fits properly in the ribbed grooves in the pulleys. It is essential that the belt be properly centered.

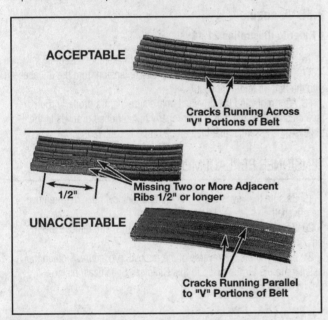

21.2 Check a multi-ribbed belt for signs like these - if the belt looks worn, replace it

21.5 Insert the end of a breaker bar or ratchet into the square hole on the tensioner, and slowly rotate tune drivebelt tensioner counterclockwise

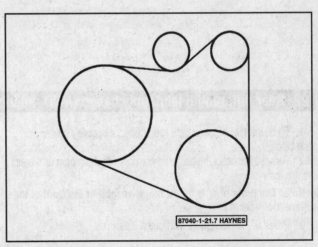

21.7 Drivebelt routing diagram - 2.2L four-cylinder engine

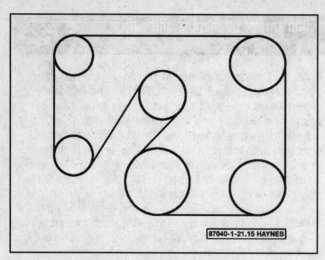

21.15 Drivebelt routing diagram - 3.0L V6 engine

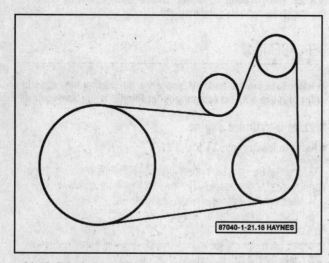

21.18 Drivebelt routing diagram - 3.5L V6 engine

3.0L V6 engine

▶ **Refer to illustration 21.15**

8   Refer to Chapter 4 and remove the air intake duct assembly.

9   Raise the vehicle and support it securely on jackstands.

10   Place a floor jack with a block of wood under the oil pan. Raise the engine just enough to take the weight off of the right engine mount.

11   Remove the two bolts that secure the mount to the engine bracket.

12   Remove the two nuts that attach the mount to the frame. Remove the mount.

13   Remove the engine mount bracket from the engine.

14   Turn the tensioner clockwise to release tension from the drivebelt. Slip the belt off and remove it.

15   After replacing a drivebelt, make sure that it's properly routed (see illustration), and that it fits in the ribbed grooves in the pulleys. It is essential that the belt be properly centered.

3.5L V6 engine

▶ **Refer to illustration 21.18**

16   Refer to Chapter 4 and remove the air intake duct assembly.

17   Turn the tensioner clockwise to release tension from the drivebelt. Slip the belt off and remove it.

18   After replacing the drivebelt, make sure that it's properly routed (see illustration), and that it fits properly in the ribbed grooves in the pulleys. It is essential that the belt be properly centered.

TENSIONER REPLACEMENT

19   Be sure the key is not in the ignition lock cylinder, then remove the drivebelt.

20   Remove the tensioner mounting fastener(s) and remove the tensioner.

21   Installation is the reverse of the removal procedure. Tighten the fasteners to the torque listed in this Chapter's Specifications.

22   Rear differential lubricant change (AWD models) (50,000 miles [80,000 km] or 72 months)

1   Raise the rear of the vehicle and support it securely on jackstands.

2   Remove the check/fill plug, then remove the drain plug and drain the lubricant.

➡**Note: The drain plug is below the driveshaft at the front of the differential housing.**

3   Reinstall the drain plug and tighten it securely.

4   Add new lubricant until it is even with the lower edge of the filler hole (see Section 4). See *Recommended lubricants and fluids* for the specified lubricant type.

5   Reinstall the check/fill plug and tighten it securely.

➡**Note: It may take some driving with sharp right and left turns to distribute the fluid evenly. Recheck the level after about 50 miles of driving.**

23 Fuel filter replacement (every 60,000 miles [96,000 km] or 72 months)

✳✳ WARNING:

Gasoline is extremely flammable, so take extra precautions when you work on any part of the fuel system. Don't smoke or allow open flames or bare light bulbs near the work area, and don't work in a garage where a gas-type appliance (such as a water heater or a clothes dryer) is present. Since gasoline is carcinogenic, wear fuel-resistant gloves when there's a possibility of being exposed to fuel, and, if you spill any fuel on your skin, rinse it off immediately with soap and water. Mop up any spills immediately and do not store fuel-soaked rags where they could ignite. The fuel system is under constant pressure, so, if any fuel lines are to be disconnected, the fuel pressure in the system must be relieved first. When you perform any kind of work on the fuel system, wear safety glasses and have a Class B type fire extinguisher on hand.

→Note: Only 2002 and 2003 models have external fuel filters. Later vehicles use fuel filters that are inside the fuel tank.

1   Raise the rear of the vehicle and support it securely on jackstands.

2   Disconnect the cable from the negative battery terminal (see Chapter 5, Section 1).

3   Refer to Chapter 4 and relieve the fuel system pressure.

4   Remove the fuel filter clamp screw and loosen the clamp from the left side of the fuel tank.

5   Place rags or a drain pan under the filter.

6   Disconnect the three quick-connect fuel lines from the filter (see Chapter 4). Remove the fuel filter.

7   Installation is the reverse of removal. Check for fuel leaks while the engine is running.

24 Cooling system servicing (draining, flushing and refilling) (at 100,000 miles [160,000 km] or 120 months and every 50,000 miles [80,500 km] or 60 months thereafter)

✳✳ WARNING 1:

Wait until the engine is completely cool before beginning this procedure.

✳✳ WARNING 2:

Do not allow engine coolant (antifreeze) to come in contact with your skin or painted surfaces of the vehicle. Rinse off spills immediately with plenty of water. Antifreeze is highly toxic if ingested. Never leave antifreeze lying around in an open container or in puddles on the floor; children and pets are attracted by its sweet smell and may drink it. Check with local authorities about disposing of used antifreeze. Many communities have collection centers which will see that antifreeze is disposed of safely.

1   Periodically, the cooling system should be drained, flushed and refilled to replenish the antifreeze mixture and prevent formation of rust and corrosion, which can impair the performance of the cooling system and cause engine damage. When the cooling system is serviced, all hoses and the radiator cap should be checked and replaced if necessary.

DRAINING

▶ Refer to illustration 24.4

2   Apply the parking brake and block the wheels. If the vehicle has just been driven, wait several hours to allow the engine to cool down before beginning this procedure.

3   Once the engine is completely cool, remove the coolant reservoir cap.

4   Move a large container under the radiator drain to catch the coolant. Use a flat-blade screwdriver to open the radiator drain plug

(see illustration).

5   On four-cylinder models, move the drain pan to the water pump area. Remove the drain plug from the bottom of the water pump.

6   While the coolant is draining, check the condition of the radiator hoses, heater hoses and clamps (refer to Section 11 if necessary).

7   Replace any damaged clamps or hoses (see Chapter 3).

FLUSHING

▶ Refer to illustration 24.10

8   Once the system is completely drained, remove the thermostat from the engine (see Chapter 3). Then reinstall the thermostat housing without the thermostat. This will allow the system to be flushed.

9   Reinstall the water pump drain plug, if removed and tighten the

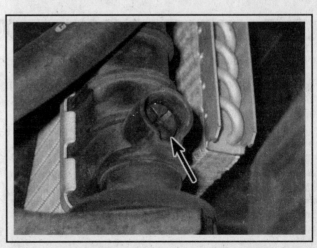

24.4 Use a screwdriver to loosen the radiator drain plug - it's on the right side of the vehicle

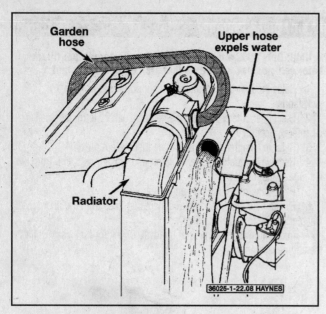

Garden hose
Upper hose expels water
Radiator

36025-1-22.08 HAYNES

24.10 With the thermostat removed, disconnect the upper radiator hose and flush the radiator and engine block with a garden hose

radiator drain plug. Turn the heating system controls to Hot, so that the heater core will be flushed at the same time as the rest of the cooling system.

10 Disconnect the upper radiator hose from the radiator. Place a garden hose in the upper radiator inlet, turn the water on and flush the system until the water runs clear out of the upper radiator hose (see illustration).

11 In severe cases of contamination or clogging of the radiator, remove the radiator (see Chapter 3) and have a radiator repair facility clean and repair it if necessary. Many deposits can be removed by the chemical action of a cleaner available at auto parts stores. Follow the procedure outlined in the manufacturer's instructions.

➡Note: When the coolant is regularly drained and the system refilled with the correct antifreeze/water mixture, there should be no need to use chemical cleaners or descalers.

12 After flushing, drain the radiator again to drain the water from the system. Replace the thermostat (see Chapter 3).

REFILLING

13 Close and tighten the radiator drain.

14 Place the heater temperature control in the maximum heat position.

15 Slowly add new coolant/water mixture to the reservoir up to the lower mark.

16 Leave the cap off and run the engine in a well-ventilated area until the thermostat opens (coolant will begin flowing through the radiator and the upper radiator hose will become hot; the engine cooling fan will turn on).

17 Turn the engine off and let it cool. Add more coolant mixture to bring the level back up to the HOT mark on the reservoir.

18 Squeeze the upper radiator hose to expel air, then add more coolant mixture if necessary. Replace the radiator cap.

19 Start the engine, allow it to reach normal operating temperature and check for leaks.

---

25 Spark plug check and replacement (every 100,000 miles [160,000 km] or 72 months)

⯈ Refer to illustrations 25.1, 25.8, 25.9, 25.10a and 25.10b

1 Spark plug replacement requires a spark plug socket that fits onto a ratchet. This socket is lined with a rubber grommet to protect the porcelain insulator of the spark plug and to hold the plug while you insert it into the spark plug hole (see illustration).

2 If you are replacing the plugs, purchase the new plugs and replace each plug one at a time.

➡Note: When buying new spark plugs, it's essential that you obtain the correct plugs for your specific vehicle. This information can be found in this Chapter's Specifications, on the Vehicle Emissions Control Information (VECI) label located on the underside of the hood or in the owner's manual. If these sources specify different plugs, purchase the spark plug type specified on the VECI label because that information is provided specifically for your engine.

3 Inspect each of the new plugs for defects. If there are any signs of cracks in the porcelain insulator of a plug, don't use it.

4 Remove the air intake duct assembly (see Chapter 4).

5 Disconnect any hoses or components that would interfere with access and move them out of the way. If you're working on a 2002 or 2003 3.0L V6 model, remove the intake manifold (see Chapter 2B).

6 Remove the bolts and detach each ignition coil or coil module from the spark plugs (see Chapter 5).

7 If compressed air is available, blow any dirt or foreign material away from the spark plug area before proceeding.

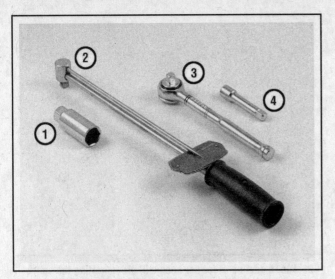

25.1 Tools required for changing spark plugs

1 **Spark plug socket** - This will have special padding inside to protect the spark plug's porcelain insulator
2 **Torque wrench** - Although not mandatory, using this tool is the best way to ensure the plugs are tightened properly
3 **Ratchet** - Standard hand tool to fit the spark plug socket
4 **Extension** - Depending on model and accessories, you may need special extensions and universal joints to reach one or more of the plugs

25.8 Use a ratchet and extension to remove the spark plugs

✳✳ WARNING:

Always wear eye protection when using compressed air!

8 Remove the spark plug (see illustration).
9 Whether you are replacing the plugs at this time or intend to re-use the old plugs, compare each old spark plug with those shown in the chart (see illustration) to determine the overall running condition of the engine.

A **normally worn** spark plug should have light tan or gray deposits on the firing tip.

A **carbon fouled** plug, identified by soft, sooty, black deposits, may indicate an improperly tuned vehicle. Check the air cleaner, ignition components and engine control system.

An **oil fouled** spark plug indicates an engine with worn piston rings and/or bad valve seals allowing excessive oil to enter the chamber.

This spark plug has been **left in the engine too long,** as evidenced by the extreme gap. Plugs with such an extreme gap can cause misfiring and stumbling accompanied by a noticeable lack of power.

A **physically damaged** spark plug may be evidence of severe detonation in that cylinder. Watch that cylinder carefully between services, as a continued detonation will not only damage the plug, but could also damage the engine.

A **bridged or almost bridged** spark plug, identified by a build-up between the electrodes caused by excessive carbon or oil build-up on the plug.

25.9 Inspect the spark plug to determine engine running conditions

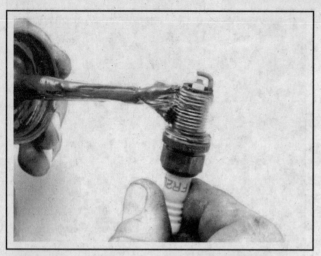

25.10a A light coat of anti-seize compound applied to the threads of the spark plugs will keep the threads in the cylinder head from being damaged the next time the plugs are removed

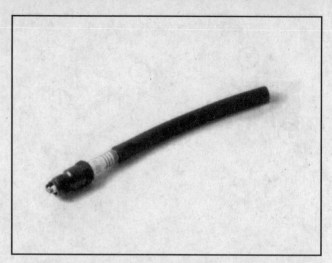

25.10b A section of rubber hose will aid in getting the spark plug threads started

10 Apply a small amount of anti-seize compound to the spark plug threads (see illustration). It's often difficult to insert spark plugs into their holes without cross-threading them. To avoid this possibility, fit a short piece of rubber hose over the end of the spark plug (see illustration). The flexible hose acts as a universal joint to help align the plug with the spark plug hole. Should the plug begin to cross-thread, the hose will slip on the spark plug, preventing thread damage. Tighten the plug to the torque listed in this Chapter's Specifications.

11 Attach the ignition coils or coil module to the new spark plugs.

12 Replace the rest of the components you removed.

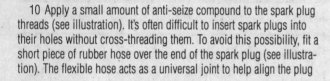

Specifications

Recommended lubricants and fluids

➡**Note: Listed here are manufacturer recommendations at the time this manual was written. Manufacturers occasionally upgrade their fluid and lubricant specifications, so check with your auto parts store for current recommendations.**

Engine oil type	API "certified for gasoline engines"
Viscosity	
Four-cylinder and 3.0L V6 models	SAE 5W-30
3.5L V6 models	SAE 5W-20
Fuel	Unleaded fuel, 87 octane or higher
Coolant	50/50 mixture of distilled water and DEX-COOL®
Brake and clutch fluid	DOT 3 brake fluid
Transaxle	
Manual	
2002 through 2006 models	Dexron® III or equivalent
2007 models	GM manual transmission fluid #88861800

Transaxle (continued)
    Automatic
        Four-cylinder models

Conventional transaxle models	Dexron® VI automatic transmission fluid or equivalent
VT25-E continuously variable	
transaxle	DEX-CVT fluid with DEX-CVT additive
3.0L V6 models	Dexron® VI automatic transmission fluid or equivalent
3.5L V6 models	ATF Z1 automatic transmission fluid
Transfer case (AWD models)	
2.2L and 3.0L V6 models	GM Versatrak® fluid or equivalent
3.5L V6 models	Synthetic axle lubricant GM #12378261 or equivalent
Rear differential (AWD models)	GM Versatrak® fluid or equivalent

Capacities

Engine oil (including filter)	
Four-cylinder engine	5.0 quarts (4.7 liters)
3.0L V6 engine	5.0 quarts (4.7 liters)
3.5L V6 engine	4.5 quarts (4.2 liters)
Coolant	
Four-cylinder engine	Up to 9 quarts (8.3 liters)
3.0L V6 engine	7.8 quarts (7.4 liters)
3.5L V6 engine	10.3 quarts (9.7 liters)
Automatic transaxle (drain and refill)	
Continuously variable transaxle	6.9 quarts (6.5 liters)
Four speed transaxle	7.0 quarts (6.6 liters)
Five speed transaxle	Up to 4.5 quarts (4.3 liters)
Manual transaxle	1.7 quarts (1.6 liters)
Transfer case (AWD models)	0.5 quart (0.5 liter)
Rear differential (AWD models)	0.8 quart (0.7 liter)

Ignition system

Spark plug type	
Four-cylinder engine	
2006 and earlier models	AC 41-105 or equivalent
2007 models	AC 41-103 or equivalent
Spark plug gap	0.043-inch (1.1 mm)
V6 engine	
2003 and earlier models	Saturn # 24425327
2004 and later models	
Standard spark plug	AC 41-629
Platinum plug spark plug	AC 41-800
Spark plug gap	0.040-inch (1.01 mm)
Engine firing order	
Four-cylinder engine	1-3-4-2
3.0L V6 engine	1-2-3-4-5-6
3.5L V6 engine	1-4-2-5-3-6

Brakes

Disc brake pad lining thickness (minimum)	1/16 inch (1.5 mm)

Torque specifications	Ft-lbs (unless otherwise indicated)	Nm

➡**Note: One foot-pound (ft-lb) of torque is equivalent to 12 inch-pounds (in-lbs) of torque. Torque values below approximately 15 ft-lbs are expressed in inch-pounds, since most foot-pound torque wrenches are not accurate at these smaller values.**

Automatic transaxle		
Pan bolts	67 in-lbs	7.5
Strainer bolts	96 in-lbs	11
Drivebelt tensioner mounting fastener(s)		
Four-cylinder engine	33	45
3.0L V6 engine	30	40
3.5L V6 engine	16	22
Spark plugs		
Four-cylinder engine	15	20
3.0L V6 engine	18	25
3.5L V6 engine	156 in-lbs	17.5
Wheel lug nuts	100	140

Section

Reference to other Chapters

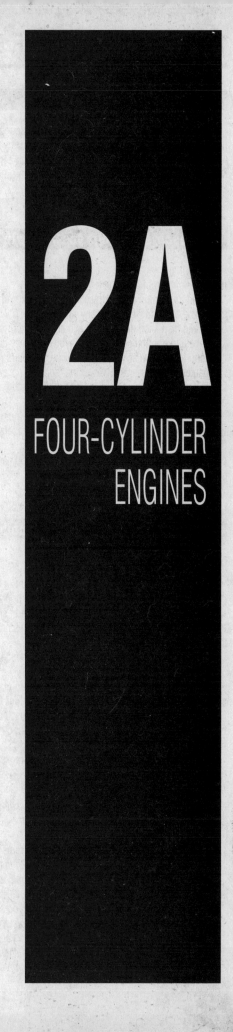

2A

FOUR-CYLINDER ENGINES

1 General information

This Part of Chapter 2 is devoted to in-vehicle repair procedures for the 2.2L DOHC (Double Overhead Camshaft) four-cylinder engine as well as removal of the balance shafts. Information concerning engine removal and installation and engine overhaul can be found in Part D of this Chapter.

These engines are equipped with a single timing chain to drive the camshafts. The balance shaft chain drives the two balance shafts and the water pump sprocket. The balance shaft chain is mounted directly behind the camshaft timing chain.

2 Repair operations possible with the engine in the vehicle

Many major repair operations can be accomplished without removing the engine from the vehicle.

Clean the engine compartment and the exterior of the engine with some type of degreaser before any work is done. It will make the job easier and help keep dirt out of the internal areas of the engine.

Depending on the components involved, it may be helpful to remove the hood to improve access to the engine as repairs are performed (refer to Chapter 11 if necessary). Cover the fenders to prevent damage to the paint. Special pads are available, but an old bedspread or blanket will also work.

If vacuum, exhaust, oil or coolant leaks develop, indicating a need for gasket or seal replacement, the repairs can generally be made with the engine in the vehicle. The intake and exhaust manifold gaskets, oil pan gasket, crankshaft oil seals and cylinder head gasket are all accessible with the engine in place.

Exterior engine components, such as the intake and exhaust manifolds, the oil pan, the oil pump, the water pump, the starter motor, the alternator and the fuel system components can be removed for repair with the engine in place.

Since the cylinder head can be removed without pulling the engine, camshaft and valve component servicing can also be accomplished with the engine in the vehicle. Replacement of the timing chain, balance shaft chain and sprockets is also possible with the engine in the vehicle. Balance shaft removal, however, will require removal of the engine.

In extreme cases caused by a lack of necessary equipment, repair or replacement of piston rings, pistons, connecting rods and rod bearings is possible with the engine in the vehicle. However, this practice is not recommended because of the cleaning and preparation work that must be done to the components involved.

3 Top Dead Center (TDC) for number one piston - locating

♦ **Refer to illustration 3.5**

1   Top Dead Center (TDC) is the highest point in the cylinder that each piston reaches as it travels up-and-down during crankshaft rotation. Each piston reaches TDC on the compression stroke and again on the exhaust stroke, but TDC generally refers to piston position on the compression stroke.

2   Positioning the piston(s) at TDC is an essential part of certain repair procedures discussed in this manual.

3   Before beginning this procedure, be sure to place the transmission in Neutral and apply the parking brake or block the rear wheels. Remove the spark plugs (see Chapter 1). Also disable the fuel system by unplugging the electrical connector in the wiring harness to the fuel injectors.

4   In order to bring any piston to TDC, the crankshaft must be turned using one of the methods outlined below. When looking at the front of the engine, normal crankshaft rotation is clockwise.

a) *The preferred method is to turn the crankshaft with a socket and ratchet attached to the bolt threaded into the front of the crankshaft.*

b) *A remote starter switch, which may save some time, can also be used. Follow the instructions included with the switch. Once the piston is close to TDC, use a socket and ratchet as described in the previous paragraph.*

c) *If an assistant is available to turn the ignition switch to the Start position in short bursts, you can get the piston close to TDC without a remote starter switch. Make sure your assistant is out of the vehicle, away from the ignition switch, then use a socket and ratchet as described in Paragraph a) to complete the procedure.*

5   Insert a compression gauge into the number one cylinder spark plug hole. Turn the crankshaft (see Step 4) until compression registers on the gauge, then turn it slowly until the TDC mark on the timing chain cover is aligned with the notch on the crankshaft pulley (see illustration).

6   After the number one piston has been positioned at TDC on the compression stroke, TDC for any of the remaining pistons can be located by turning the crankshaft and following the firing order. Divide the crankshaft pulley into two equal sections, with a chalk mark 180-degrees from the TDC mark. Rotating the engine past TDC no. 1 to the next mark will place the engine at TDC for cylinder no. 3.

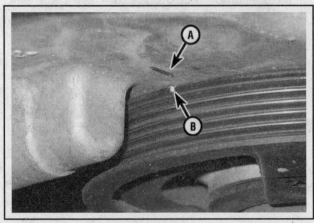

3.5 Timing marks - align the pointer on the engine front cover (A) with the notch in the crankshaft pulley (B)

4 Valve cover - removal and installation

REMOVAL

▶ Refer to illustration 4.8

1 Disconnect the cable from the negative battery terminal (see Chapter 5, Section 1).

2 Refer to Chapter 4 and remove the air intake duct assembly.

3 Remove the ignition coil assembly from the valve cover (see Chapter 5).

4 Disconnect the coolant hose from the fuel rail and the cylinder head. Move it aside.

✻✻ WARNING:

Don't loosen the hose clamps.

5 Detach the ground cable from the valve cover.

6 Refer to Chapter 4 and relieve the fuel system pressure.

7 Unscrew the fitting and detach the fuel line from the fuel rail (see Chapter 4). Position the line out of the way.

8 Remove the valve cover bolts (see illustration) then lift the valve cover off. Tap gently with a soft-face hammer, if necessary, to break the gasket seal.

INSTALLATION

▶ Refer to illustrations 4.10 and 4.11

9 Clean the gasket surfaces on the intake manifold, cylinder head and valve cover. Use a shop rag and brake system cleaner to wipe off all residue from the sealing surfaces.

10 Insert a new valve cover gasket into the grooved recess in the valve cover. Make sure the gasket is positioned properly in the groove (see illustration).

11 Install new O-rings and spark plug seals in the valve cover (see illustration).

12 The remainder of installation is the reverse of the removal Steps. Tighten the valve cover bolts evenly, starting with the center bolts and working outwards, to the torque listed in this Chapter's Specifications.

13 Reconnect the battery (see Chapter 5, Section 1).

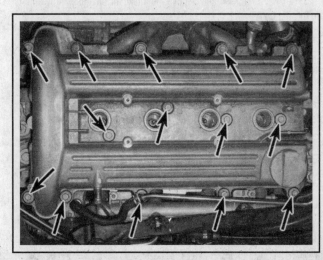

4.8 Location of the valve cover mounting bolts

4.10 Install the gasket into the grooved recess in the valve cover

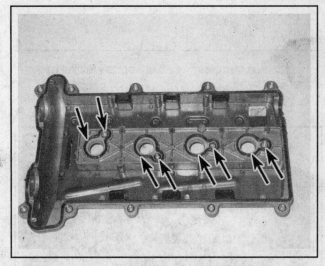

4.11 Be sure to change all the spark plug seals and O-rings in the valve cover

5 Intake manifold - removal and installation

✳✳ WARNING:

Wait until the engine is completely cool before beginning this procedure.

REMOVAL

1 Disconnect the cable from the negative battery terminal (see Chapter 5).

2 Refer to Chapter 4 and remove the intake air duct assembly and the throttle body.

3 Remove the mounting bolts from the PCM. Move the PCM aside.

4 Disconnect the fuel injector wiring harness from the intake manifold.

5 Disconnect the wiring from the MAP sensor (see Chapter 6).

6 Raise the vehicle and support it securely on jackstands. Unclip the wiring harness from the bottom of the intake manifold. You may then lower the vehicle if it will make manifold removal easier.

7 Remove the dipstick tube mounting bolt and position the dipstick to the side.

8 Disconnect the wiring bolt at the lower part of the manifold. Disconnect the EVAP purge hose.

9 Disconnect any vacuum hoses connected to the manifold, including the hose leading to the brake booster. Mark the hoses, if necessary, to ensure correct reassembly.

10 Remove the intake manifold mounting bolts and nuts.

11 Pull the manifold away and disconnect the brake vacuum hose by pressing the tab.

12 Lift the intake manifold from the engine compartment.

INSTALLATION

13 Remove the old gaskets from the intake manifold. Thoroughly clean the surfaces of the manifold and cylinder head. Install new intake manifold gaskets.

➡**Note: The manufacturer states that the intake manifold gaskets are not reusable.**

14 Install the manifold over the studs on the cylinder head. Install the bolts and nuts and tighten them finger-tight.

15 Tighten the bolts to the torque listed in this Chapter's Specifications, starting with the center bolts and working towards the ends.

16 The remainder of installation is the reverse of the removal steps.

17 Reconnect the battery (see Chapter 5, Section 1).

18 Run the engine and check for vacuum, coolant and fuel leaks.

6 Exhaust manifold - removal and installation

▶ **Refer to illustrations 6.3, 6.6 and 6.7**

REMOVAL

1 Disconnect the cable from the negative battery terminal (see Chapter 5).

2 Refer to Chapter 4 and remove the air intake duct assembly.

3 Remove the heat shield from the exhaust manifold (see illustration).

4 Disconnect the wiring from both of the oxygen sensors.

5 Raise the vehicle and support it securely on jackstands.

6 Remove the front section of exhaust pipe (see illustration). Disconnect the oxygen sensor wiring from the heat shield.

7 Remove the exhaust manifold mounting nuts and detach the exhaust pipe from the manifold (see illustration).

6.3 Location of the heat shield mounting bolts (typical)

6.6 Soak the exhaust pipe retaining nuts with penetrating oil, then remove them (viewed from above)

INSTALLATION

8   Using a scraper, thoroughly clean the mating surfaces on the cylinder head, manifold and exhaust pipe. Wipe the surfaces clean with a rag and brake system cleaner.

9   Check the mating surface with a precision straightedge to be sure that they are perfectly flat and not damaged in any way. A warped or damaged manifold may require machining or, if severe enough, replacement. Install the new gasket to the cylinder head studs and place the manifold on the cylinder head. Tighten the nuts evenly, working from the center outwards, to the torque listed in this Chapter's Specifications.

10 Connect the exhaust pipe to the manifold and tighten the nuts evenly to the torque listed in this Chapter's Specifications.

11 The remainder of installation is the reverse of the removal steps.

12 Reconnect the battery (see Chapter 5, Section 1).

13 Run the engine and check for exhaust leaks.

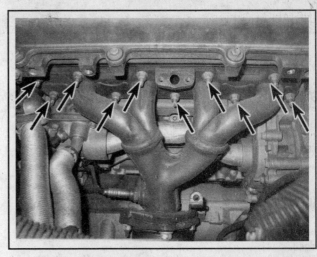

6.7 Exhaust manifold mounting nuts (typical)

7   Engine front cover - removal and installation

REMOVAL

▶ **Refer to illustrations 7.7a and 7.7b**

1   Disconnect the cable from the negative battery terminal (see Chapter 5, Section 1).

2   Loosen the right front wheel lug nuts, then raise the front of the vehicle and support it securely on jackstands. Remove the right front wheel.

3   Drain the engine oil (see Chapter 1).

4   Remove the drivebelt (see Chapter 1).

5   Remove the drivebelt tensioner from the front cover (see Chapter 1).

6   Remove the crankshaft pulley (see Section 10). Support the engine with an engine hoist or engine support fixture and remove the right engine mount (see Section 17).

7   Loosen the engine cover fasteners gradually and evenly, then remove the fasteners (see illustrations).

➡**Note: Draw a sketch of the engine cover and cover fasteners. Identify the location of all bolts for installation in their original locations.**

8   Remove the water pump bolt from the engine front cover (see illustration 7.7b).

9   Remove the front cover.

10 If the cover-to-block gasket is in good condition, leave it in place.

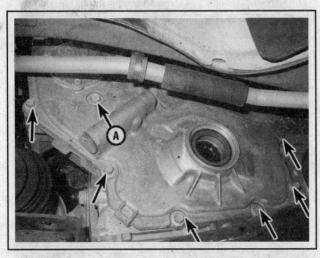

7.7a The engine cover mounting bolts can be accessed from below . . .

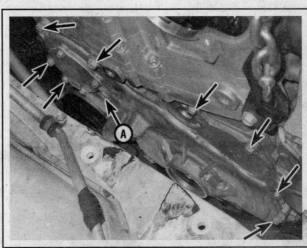

7.7b . . . and from above the engine compartment - don't forget the front cover/water pump bolt (A)

INSTALLATION

11 Inspect and clean all sealing surfaces of the engine front cover and the block.

> **✳✳ CAUTION:**
>
> **Be very careful when scraping on aluminum engine parts. Aluminum is soft and gouges easily. Severely gouged parts may require replacement.**

12 If necessary, replace the crankshaft front oil seal in the front cover (see Section 10).

13 Install a new gasket if necessary.

➡**Note: The cover gasket is reusable if it has not been damaged.**

14 Install the front cover and cover fasteners. Make sure the hub on the inner rotor is aligned with the flats on the crankshaft and the engine cover fasteners are in their original locations. Tighten the fasteners by hand until the cover is contacting the block around its entire periphery.

15 Install the long water pump bolt.

16 Tighten the bolts to the torque listed in this Chapter's Specifications.

17 Install the drivebelt tensioner, tightening the bolt to the torque listed in this Chapter's Specifications.

18 Install the crankshaft pulley (see Section 10) and the drivebelt (see Chapter 1).

19 Reinstall the remaining parts in the reverse order of removal.

20 Fill the crankcase with the recommended oil (see Chapter 1).

21 Reconnect the battery (see Chapter 5, Section 1).

22 Start the engine and check for leaks. Check all fluid levels.

8 Timing chain and sprockets - removal, inspection and installation

REMOVAL

> **✳✳ CAUTION ✳✳**
>
> **The timing system is complex. Severe engine damage will occur if you make any mistakes. Do not attempt this procedure unless you are highly experienced with this type of repair. If you are at all unsure of your abilities, consult an expert. Double-check all your work and be sure everything is correct before you attempt to start the engine.**

◆ **Refer to illustrations 8.8, 8.9, 8.10, 8.11a, 8.11b, 8.12, 8.14 and 8.15**

1 Disconnect the cable from the negative battery terminal (see Chapter 5). Remove the spark plugs (see Chapter 1).

2 Remove the valve cover (see Section 4). Using a wrench on the flats of the intake camshaft, rotate the engine (clockwise when facing the sprockets) to 60-degrees before TDC. This is achieved when the diamond-shaped spot on the intake sprocket is straight up (12 o'clock position).

3 Drain the engine oil (see Chapter 1).

4 Remove the drivebelt (see Chapter 1).

5 Remove the drivebelt tensioner from the front cover.

6 Remove the engine front cover (see Section 7).

7 Remove the valve cover (see Section 4).

8 Remove the timing chain tensioner (see illustration).

9 Remove the upper timing chain guide (see illustration).

10 Remove the exhaust camshaft sprocket bolt (see illustration). Be sure to discard the bolt and install a new bolt on reassembly.

11 Remove the adjustable timing chain guide (see illustrations).

12 Unscrew the access plug and remove the fixed timing chain guide upper mounting bolt (see illustration).

13 Remove the fixed timing chain guide lower mounting bolt and lift the guide from the engine block.

14 Remove the intake camshaft sprocket bolt (see illustration). Be sure to discard the bolt and install a new bolt on reassembly.

15 Remove the timing chain through the top of the cylinder head (see illustration).

16 Remove the timing chain drive sprocket and slide the timing chain oiling nozzle off the engine block.

8.8 Remove the timing chain tensioner from the cylinder head

8.9 Remove the upper timing chain guide mounting bolts

8.10 Use a wrench on the hex drive on the camshaft to prevent the camshaft from turning while loosening the sprocket bolt

8.11a Remove the adjustable timing chain guide mounting bolt . . .

8.11b . . . then lift the guide out through the top of the cylinder head

8.12 Access plug for the fixed timing chain guide upper mounting bolt

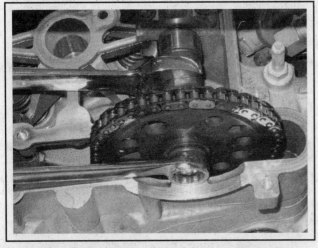

8.14 Use a wrench on the hex drive on the camshaft when loosening the camshaft sprocket bolt

8.15 Carefully remove the timing chain and the intake camshaft sprocket through the top of the cylinder head

8.23 The round dot (alignment mark) on the sprocket should be in the 5 o'clock position. When installing the chain, one of the silver plated links must be aligned with this dot

8.25 The copper link must align with the INT on the intake camshaft and the silver link with the EXH on the exhaust camshaft

INSPECTION

17 Clean all parts with clean solvent and dry with compressed air, if available.

18 Inspect the chain tensioner for excessive wear or other damage. Be sure to drain all the oil out of the chain tensioner if it is to be reused.

19 Inspect the timing chain guides for deep grooves, excessive wear, or other damage.

20 Inspect the timing chain for excessive wear or damage.

21 Inspect the crankshaft and camshaft sprockets for chipped or broken teeth, excessive wear, or damage.

22 Replace any component that is in questionable condition.

INSTALLATION

> ❋❋ **CAUTION** ❋❋
>
> **Before starting the engine, carefully rotate the crankshaft by hand through at least two full revolutions (use a socket and breaker bar on the crankshaft pulley centerbolt). If you feel any resistance, STOP! There is something wrong - most likely, valves are contacting the pistons. You must find the problem before proceeding. Check your work and see if any updated repair information is available.**

♦ **Refer to illustrations 8.23, 8.25, 8.29, 8.33a, 8.33b, 8.33c, 8.33d and 8.33e**

23 Before installing the timing chain, make sure the timing mark (round dot) on the crankshaft sprocket is pointing to the 5 o'clock position (see illustration).

24 Install the intake camshaft sprocket onto the camshaft. Be sure to install a new bolt. Tighten the intake camshaft sprocket bolt lightly, finger tight at this time.

> ❋❋ **CAUTION:**
>
> **Do not turn the camshaft more than 1/2 turn to avoid any valve/piston contact. The camshafts should be positioned correctly before the timing chain is installed.**

25 Install the timing chain by lowering it from the top through the

opening. Be sure the timing chain drops down around both sides of the cylinder block bosses. Be sure the bright colored link (copper) on the chain is aligned with the INT designation and diamond shape on the camshaft sprocket (see illustration).

➥**Note: The copper link will be installed at the intake camshaft sprocket (front) while the silver links will be installed at the crankshaft sprocket and the exhaust camshaft sprocket (rear).**

26 Drape the timing chain over the crankshaft sprocket and engage the plated link (silver) on the chain with the crankshaft sprocket timing mark located in the 5 o'clock position (see illustration 8.23).

27 Install the adjustable timing chain guide. Install the bolts and tighten them to the torque listed in this Chapter's Specifications.

28 Install the exhaust camshaft sprocket onto the camshaft. Be sure to install a new bolt. Be sure the plated link (silver) on the chain is aligned with the EXH designation and diamond shape (which should be pointing to the 10 o'clock position) on the camshaft sprocket (see illustration 8.25). Tighten the exhaust camshaft sprocket bolt lightly, finger tight at this time.

29 Install the fixed timing chain guide (see illustration). Tighten the bolts to the torque listed in this Chapter's Specifications.

30 Install the upper timing chain guide (see illustration 8.9). Tighten the bolts to the torque listed in this Chapter's Specifications.

31 Hold the intake camshaft with a wrench on the camshaft's hex to prevent it from turning, then tighten the intake camshaft bolt to the torque listed in this Chapter's Specifications.

32 Hold the exhaust camshaft with a wrench on the camshaft's hex to prevent it from turning, then tighten the exhaust camshaft bolt to the torque listed in this Chapter's Specifications.

33 Install the timing chain tensioner. The timing chain tensioner must be installed in its compressed state. Follow the steps to correctly compress the tensioner.

> ❋❋ **CAUTION:**
>
> **The timing chain tensioner must be installed in the compressed state. Do not install a tensioner in its released state. Damage to the tensioner and timing chain will occur.**

a) *Completely disassemble the tensioner and drain all the oil (see illustration). Inspect the tensioner body, the piston and all components for scoring or damage. If necessary, replace the tensioner with a new one.*

b) Install the tensioner piston into the vise with the flats seated in the jaws of the vice (see illustration).
c) Install the ratchet cylinder into the piston, aligning the groove with the locating pin (see illustration).
d) Drive the ratchet cylinder into the piston with a flat-bladed screwdriver. Rotate the ratchet cylinder clockwise when it reaches the bottom (see illustration). The ratchet cylinder should be locked into position.
e) The tensioner must measure 2.83 inches (72 mm) from end-to-end (see illustration).

34 Install the timing chain oiling nozzle. Tighten the bolt to the torque listed in this Chapter's Specifications. Using a tool with a plastic or rubber tip, strike a sharp blow to the tensioner at the chain end, this should release the tensioner against the chain.

35 Apply a small amount of RTV sealant to the threads and install the timing chain guide access plug. Tighten the bolt to the torque listed in this Chapter's Specifications.

36 Install the valve cover (see Section 4).

37 Install the engine front cover (see Section 7).

38 The remainder of installation is the reverse of the removal Steps. Install a new oil filter and refill the crankcase with oil (see Chapter 1).

39 Reconnect the battery (see Chapter 5, Section 1).

40 Run the engine and check for leaks.

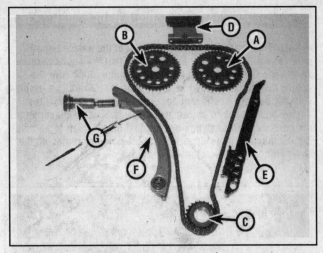

8.29 Timing chain component details

A	Intake camshaft sprocket	E	Fixed timing chain guide
B	Exhaust camshaft sprocket	F	Adjustable timing chain guide
C	Crankshaft sprocket		
D	Upper timing chain guide	G	Timing chain tensioner

8.33a Timing tensioner details

A Timing chain tensioner body
B Ratchet cylinder
C Spring adjuster
D Spring
E Piston

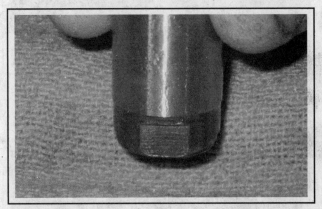

8.33b Install the piston with the flats locked into the jaws of the vise

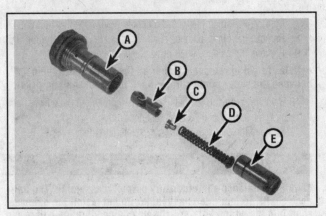

8.33c Align the groove in the ratchet cylinder with the pin in the piston

8.33d Using a flat-bladed screwdriver, drive the ratchet cylinder down to the bottom and rotate it clockwise to lock it into position

8.33e The tensioner should measure the correct length in its compressed state or it must be replaced with a new tensioner

9 Balance shaft chain and balance shafts - removal, inspection and installation

→Note: This procedure covers removal of the balance shaft chain and balance shafts, but take note that the shafts themselves can only be removed from the engine block after the engine has been removed from the vehicle. If there is a problem with the balance shafts that does warrant their removal, the engine would have to be removed anyway, since replacement of the balance shaft bushings is a job that must be left to an automotive machine shop. If you're just removing or replacing the chain, ignore the steps that don't apply.

REMOVAL

▶ Refer to illustrations 9.5, 9.6 and 9.9

1   Disconnect the cable from the negative battery terminal (see Chapter 5, Section 1).
2   Drain the engine oil (see Chapter 1).
3   Position the engine at TDC for cylinder number 1 (see Section 3).

✳✳ **CAUTION:**

Do not rotate the engine to find TDC number 1 when the timing chain is removed unless the engine has been rotated accidentally. If the engine is not positioned at TDC number 1, the camshafts must be removed to prevent damage to the valves (see Section 11).

4   Remove the timing chain, timing chain guides and sprockets (see Section 8).
5   Remove the balance shaft chain tensioner (see illustration).
6   Remove the adjustable balance shaft chain guide (see illustration).
7   Remove the small balance shaft chain guide (see illustration 9.6).
8   Remove the upper balance shaft chain guide (see illustration 9.6).
9   Remove the balance shaft drive chain (see illustration).

→Note: To aid in removal, gather all the slack in the chain between the water pump sprocket and the crankshaft sprocket.

10   If you're removing the balance shafts (engine removed from the vehicle), remove the balance shaft retainer bolts.
11   Remove the balance shafts from the engine block.

✳✳ **CAUTION:**

Mark each balance shaft to insure correct reassembly. The balance shafts are not interchangeable. Do not install the balance shaft into the wrong bore or extreme engine vibration will occur.

9.5 Location of the balance shaft chain tensioner mounting bolts

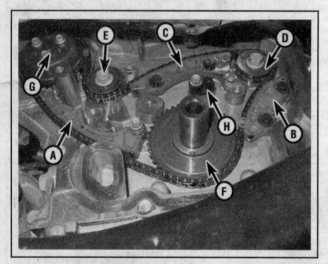

9.6 Balance shaft chain and guide details

A   Adjustable balance shaft chain guide
B   Small balance shaft chain guide
C   Upper balance shaft chain guide
D   Intake side (front) balance shaft sprocket
E   Exhaust side (rear) balance shaft sprocket
F   Crankshaft/balance shaft sprocket
G   Water pump sprocket
H   Timing chain oiling nozzle

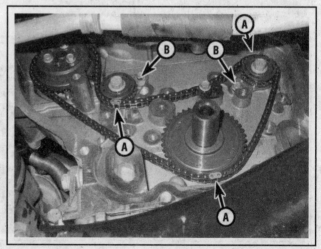

9.9 Balance shaft sprocket/chain alignment marks (A) and retainer bolts (B)

9.18 The timing mark (round dot) on the crankshaft sprocket should point to the 6 o'clock position (approximately)

9.20 With the arrow on the intake side balance shaft sprocket pointing up (and aligned with the cutout on the balance shaft retainer, not visible in this photo, but similar to the one shown in illustration 9.21a), install a drill bit into the hole to lock the sprocket in place

INSPECTION

12 Clean all parts with clean solvent and dry with compressed air, if available.

13 Inspect the chain tensioners for excessive wear or other damage.

14 Inspect the balance shaft chain guides for deep grooves, excessive wear, or other damage.

15 Inspect the balance shaft chain for excessive wear or damage.

16 Inspect the crankshaft and water pump sprockets for chipped or broken teeth, excessive wear, or damage.

17 Replace any component that is damaged.

INSTALLATION

▶ **Refer to illustrations 9.18, 9.20, 9.21a, 9.21b, 9.26a, 9.26b and 9.28**

18 Before installing the balance shaft chain, make sure the crankshaft timing mark (round dot) is pointing to the 6 o'clock position (see illustration).

✳✳ CAUTION:

Do not rotate the engine to find TDC number 1 after the timing chain has been removed unless the engine has been rotated accidentally. If the engine is not positioned at TDC number 1, the camshafts must be removed to prevent damage to the valves (see Section 11).

19 Install the balance shafts into the bores and tighten the balance shaft retainer bolts to the torque listed in this Chapter's Specifications.

20 Align the balance shaft sprockets before installing the balance shaft chain. Starting with the intake side balance shaft, place the alignment arrow pointing up, then temporarily install a drill bit into the alignment hole and the sprocket teeth to lock the balance shaft sprocket in place (see illustration).

21 Now position the exhaust side (rear) balance shaft sprocket with the arrow pointing down and aligned with the cutout in the retainer, then install a drill bit into the alignment hole to hold the sprocket (see illustrations).

22 Install the balance shaft chain onto the balance shaft/crankshaft sprocket and the balance shafts. Align the colored links with the align-

9.21a Location of the alignment notch for the sprocket arrow (A) and the alignment hole (B) on the exhaust side balance shaft sprocket

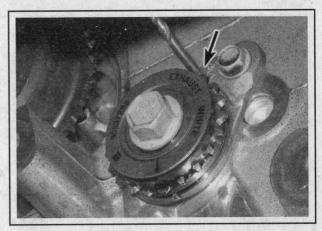

9.21b Install the drill into the exhaust balance shaft retainer to lock it into position

9.26a Rotate the plunger 90-degrees, align the holes in the body and piston . . .

9.26b . . . then insert a drill bit to retain the piston in the locked position

9.28 After the tensioner is installed and the bolts tightened, remove the drill bit

ment marks on each sprocket. Position the copper-colored link onto the intake side balance shaft, aligning the mark with the colored link at approximately the 12 o'clock position (see illustration 9.9).

➡Note: The copper link will be installed at the intake balance shaft sprocket (front) while the silver links will be installed at the crankshaft sprocket and the exhaust balance shaft sprocket (rear).

23 Working clockwise, position the second colored link (silver) on the crankshaft/balance shaft sprocket, aligning the mark on the sprocket with the colored link at the 6 o'clock position (see illustration 9.18).

24 Finally, pass the chain over the water pump sprocket, under the exhaust balance shaft sprocket and into position. Align the third colored link (silver) on the exhaust balance shaft sprocket, aligning the mark on the sprocket with the colored link at the 6 o'clock position.

25 Install the balance shaft chain guides (see illustration 9.6). Tighten the bolts to the torque listed in this Chapter's Specifications.

26 Reset the balance shaft chain tensioner. Turn the tensioner plunger 90-degrees in the bore and compress the tensioner plunger (see illustration). Rotate the plunger back to the original position at 12 o'clock and install a drill bit through the hole in the body into the plunger (see illustration).

27 Install the balance shaft chain tensioner and torque the bolts to the Specifications listed in this Chapter.

28 Remove the drill bit to release the plunger (see illustration).

29 Recheck all the balance shaft chain timing marks.

30 Install the timing chain (see Section 8) and all components removed previously.

31 Reconnect the battery (see Chapter 5, Section 1).

32 Install a new oil filter and refill the crankcase with oil (see Chapter 1).

33 Run the engine and check for leaks.

10 Crankshaft pulley and front oil seal - removal and installation

REMOVAL

▶ Refer to illustrations 10.4, 10.5 and 10.7

1 Disconnect the cable from the negative battery terminal (see Chapter 5, Section 1).

2 Remove the drivebelt (see Chapter 1).

3 Loosen the right front wheel lug nuts. Raise the vehicle and support it securely on jackstands. Remove the wheel.

4 Remove the splash shield (see illustration).

5 Use a breaker bar and socket to remove the crankshaft pulley center bolt (see illustration). Discard the bolt and obtain a new one for installation.

➡Note: It will be necessary to lock the pulley in position using a strap wrench or a large pin spanner. Be sure to wrap a length of old drivebelt around the pulley to protect it if you are using a strap wrench.

6 Slide the pulley off the nose of the crankshaft. If the pulley is stuck, use a puller that bolts to the three threaded holes in the pulley

10.4 Carefully pry out the plastic fasteners and remove the splash shield

10.5 A large pin spanner can be used to prevent the pulley from rotating while the bolt is loosened

10.7 Use a seal puller to remove the old crankshaft seal, taking care not to damage the crankshaft or the seal bore in the cover

hub. Additionally, a spacer, such as a deep socket that just fits into the hole in the pulley and bears on the crankshaft, will be required to avoid damage to the crankshaft.

7   Use a seal puller or a large screwdriver to remove the crankshaft front oil seal (see illustration).

8   Clean the seal bore and check it for nicks or gouges. Also examine the area of the hub that rides in the seal for signs of abnormal wear or scoring. For many popular engines, repair sleeves are available to restore a smooth finish to the sealing surface. Check with your auto parts store.

INSTALLATION

▶ **Refer to illustration 10.9**

9   Coat the lip of the new seal with clean engine oil and drive it into the bore with a seal driver or a socket slightly smaller in diameter than the seal (see illustration). The open side of the seal faces into the engine.

10   Using clean engine oil, lubricate the sealing surface of the hub. Install the crankshaft pulley. Install a new center bolt and tighten it to the torque listed in this Chapter's Specifications.

❋❋ CAUTION:

You must use a new pulley bolt.

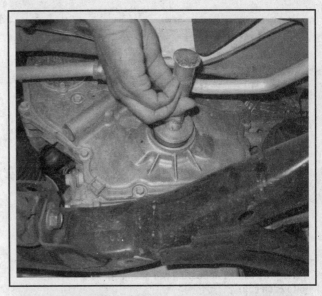

10.9 Driving the new front cover seal in with a seal driver

11   The remainder of the installation is the reverse of the removal procedure.

12   Reconnect the battery (see Chapter 5, Section 1).

---

11 Camshafts and hydraulic lash adjusters - removal, inspection and installation

❋❋ CAUTION:

New camshaft sprocket bolts must be purchased.

➡**Note: This is a difficult procedure, involving special tools. Read through the entire Section and obtain the necessary tools before beginning the procedure.**

REMOVAL

▶ **Refer to illustrations 11.5a and 11.5b**

1   Disconnect the cable from the negative battery terminal (see Chapter 5, Section 1).

2   Remove the valve cover (see Section 4).

3   Set the engine to TDC for cylinder number one (see Section 3),

11.5a Install a camshaft locking tool to hold the sprockets and timing chain in place - make sure the camshaft sprockets are locked properly and the tool is bolted to the cylinder head

11.5b The diamond-shaped hole on the intake camshaft should be in the 12 o'clock position

11.7a The camshaft bearing cap designations are stamped onto each cap

11.7b Note that the arrow on the cap faces the timing chain end of the engine

then turn the crankshaft counterclockwise until the engine is set at 60-degrees before TDC. At this point, the diamond-shaped hole on the intake camshaft should be in the 12 o'clock position.

✳✳ CAUTION:

Do not remove the camshafts with the engine at TDC or the valves could be damaged.

4   Remove the upper timing chain guide (see Section 8).
5   Install a special tool to secure the camshaft sprockets in position (see illustrations). This camshaft locking tool (jig) can be purchased through a dealership parts department or through specialty automotive tool suppliers.
6   Remove the camshaft sprocket bolts and slide the camshaft sprockets forward, then tighten the wingnuts to hold the sprockets securely.

Intake camshaft

▶ Refer to illustrations 11.7a, 11.7b, 11.8, 11.9 and 11.10

7   Each camshaft cap is marked with a number indicating its position (see illustrations). A little at a time, loosen each bearing cap bolt slowly and evenly, allowing the camshaft to lift from the cylinder head, parallel to the surface of the cylinder head.

✳✳ CAUTION:

The caps must be installed in their original locations. Keep all parts from each camshaft together; never mix parts from one camshaft with those for another.

8   Remove the rocker arms (see illustration).
9   Place the rocker arms in a suitable container, in order, so they can be reinstalled in their original positions (see illustration).

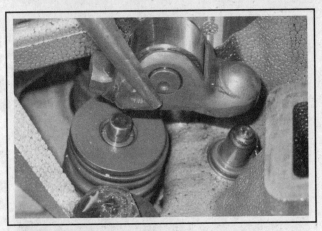

11.8 Remove each rocker arm . . .

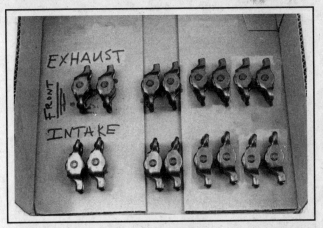

11.9 . . . and store them in an organized manner so they can be returned to their original locations

11.10 Pull the lash adjusters from their bores in the head and store them along with their corresponding rocker arms

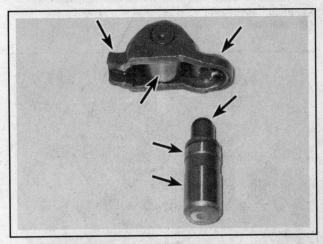

11.15 Check the rocker arms and lash adjusters for wear at the indicated points

10 Remove the hydraulic lash adjusters from their bores in the cylinder head (see illustration). Store these with their corresponding rocker arms so they can be reinstalled in their original locations.

Exhaust camshaft

11 Mark the exhaust bearing caps in the original positions and remove them from the cylinder head. Each camshaft cap is designated with a number (see illustrations 11.7a and 11.7b). Loosen each bearing cap nut slowly and evenly, allowing the camshaft to lift from the cylinder head, parallel to the surface of the cylinder head.

❋❋ CAUTION:

The camshaft bearing caps are numbered to identify the locations of the caps. The caps must be installed in their original locations. Keep all parts from each camshaft together; never mix parts from one camshaft with those for another.

12 Mark the positions of the rocker arms so they can be reinstalled in their original locations, then remove the rocker arms.

13 Place the rocker arms in a suitable container so they can be reinstalled in their original positions (see illustration 11.9).

14 Lift the hydraulic lash adjusters from their bores in the cylinder

head. Store these with their corresponding rocker arms so they can be reinstalled in their original locations (see illustration 11.10).

INSPECTION

▶ **Refer to illustrations 11.15, 11.18, 11.19, 11.20, 11.21 and 11.22**

15 Check each hydraulic lash adjuster for excessive wear, scoring, pitting, or an out-of-round condition (see illustration). Replace as necessary.

16 Measure the outside diameter of each adjuster at the top and bottom of the adjuster. Then take a second set of measurements at a right angle to the first. If any measurement is significantly different from the others, the adjuster is tapered or out of round and must be replaced. If the necessary equipment is available, measure the diameter of the lash adjuster and the inside diameter of the corresponding cylinder head bore. Subtract the diameter of the lash adjuster from the bore diameter to obtain the oil clearance. Compare the measurements obtained to those given in this Chapter's Specifications. If the adjusters or the cylinder head bores are excessively worn, new adjusters or a new cylinder head (or both) may be required. If the valve train is noisy, particularly if the noise persists after a cold start, you can suspect a faulty lash adjuster.

11.18 Check the cam lobes for pitting, excessive wear, and scoring. If scoring is excessive, as shown here, replace the camshaft

11.19 Measure each camshaft lobe height with a micrometer

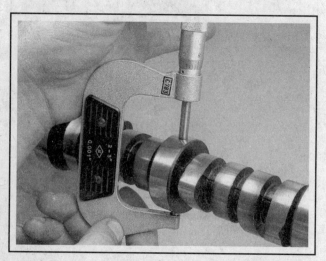

11.20 Measure each journal diameter with a micrometer. If any journal is less than the specified minimum, replace the camshaft

11.21 Lay a strip of Plastigage on each camshaft journal, in line with the camshaft

17 Inspect the rocker arms for signs of wear or damage. The areas of wear are: the tip that contacts the valve stem, the socket that contacts the lash adjuster and the roller that contacts the camshaft (see illustration 11.15).

18 Examine the camshaft lobes for scoring, pitting, galling (wear due to rubbing), and evidence of overheating (blue, discolored areas). Look for flaking of the hardened surface layer of each lobe (see illustration). If any such wear is evident, replace the camshaft.

19 Measure the lobe height of each cam lobe on the intake camshaft, and record your measurements (see illustration). Compare the measurements for excessive variation; if the lobe heights vary more than 0.005 inch (0.125 mm), replace the camshaft. Compare the lobe height measurements on the exhaust camshaft and follow the same procedure. Do not compare intake camshaft lobe heights with exhaust camshaft lobe heights, as they are different. Only compare intake lobes with intake lobes and exhaust lobes with exhaust lobes.

20 Inspect the camshaft bearing journals and the cylinder head bearing surfaces for pitting or excessive wear. If any such wear is evident,

replace the component concerned. Using a micrometer, measure the diameter of each camshaft bearing journal at several points (see illustration). If the diameter of any journal is less than specified, replace the camshaft.

21 To check the bearing journal oil clearance, remove the rocker arms and hydraulic lash adjusters (if not already done), use a suitable solvent and a clean lint-free rag to clean all bearing surfaces, then install the camshafts and bearing caps with a piece of Plastigage across each journal (see illustration). Tighten the bearing cap bolts to the specified torque. Don't rotate the camshafts.

22 Remove the bearing caps and measure the width of the flattened Plastigage with the Plastigage scale (see illustration). Scrape off the Plastigage with your fingernail or the edge of a credit card. Don't scratch or nick the journals or bearing caps.

23 If the oil clearance of any bearing is worn beyond the service limit, install a new camshaft and repeat the check. If the clearance is still excessive, replace the cylinder head.

24 To check camshaft endplay, remove the hydraulic lash adjust-

11.22 Compare the width of the crushed Plastigage to the scale on the package to determine the journal oil clearance

11.29 Camshaft and timing sprocket alignment details

ers, clean the bearing surfaces carefully, and install the camshafts and bearing caps. Tighten the bearing cap bolts to the specified torque, then measure the endplay using a dial indicator mounted on the cylinder head so that its tip bears on the camshaft end.

25 Lightly but firmly tap the camshaft fully toward the gauge, zero the gauge, then tap the camshaft fully away from the gauge and note the gauge reading. If the measured endplay is at or beyond the specified service limit, install a new camshaft thrust cap and repeat the check. If the clearance is still excessive, the camshaft or the cylinder head must be replaced.

INSTALLATION

▶ **Refer to illustration 11.29**

26 Lubricate the rocker arms and hydraulic lash adjusters with engine assembly lubricant or fresh engine oil. Install the adjusters into their original bores, then install the rocker arms in their correct locations.

27 Lubricate the camshafts with camshaft installation lubricant and install them in their correct locations. Position the camshafts with the slots in the end of the camshafts positioned as shown in illustration 11.29, align-

ing them with the slots in the camshaft sprockets.

28 Install the camshaft bearing caps in their correct locations, except for the front end and rear end bearing caps on each camshaft. Install the cap bolts and tighten by hand until snug. Tighten the bolts in four to five steps, starting with the center cap and working to the outside caps, to the torque listed in this Chapter's Specifications.

29 Slide the camshaft sprockets and timing chain along the guide pins toward the camshafts. Rotate the camshafts with an open-end wrench on the hex drive on each camshaft until the slots are aligned with the projections on the sprockets (see illustration). Install new bolts and tighten the camshaft sprockets to the torque listed in this Chapter's Specifications (see Section 8).

30 Remove the camshaft locking tool from the cylinder head. Then install the front and rear camshaft caps and tighten them to the torque listed in this Chapter's Specifications. Note that the rear cap on the intake camshaft is equipped with larger bolts and requires a different torque.

31 Install the upper timing chain guide (see Section 8). Rotate the engine by hand two revolutions - if you feel any resistance, stop and find out why.

32 The remainder of installation is the reverse of removal.

33 Reconnect the battery (see Chapter 5, Section 1).

12 Cylinder head - removal and installation

✳ CAUTION:

The engine must be completely cool when the head is removed. Failure to allow the engine to cool off could result in head warpage. New head bolts should be purchased ahead of time.

REMOVAL

1 Disconnect the cable from the negative battery terminal (see Chapter 5).

2 Wait until the engine is completely cool, then drain the cooling system (see Chapter 1).

3 Remove the drivebelt (see Chapter 1) and the drivebelt tensioner.

4 Remove the exhaust manifold (see Section 6).

5 Remove the intake manifold (see Section 5). Disconnect the coolant hose from the cylinder head.

6 Remove the timing chain (see Section 8).

7 Label and disconnect the electrical connectors from the cylinder head that will interfere with removal. Use tape and mark each connector to insure correct reassembly.

8 Remove the cylinder head bolts and discard them, following the reverse of the tightening sequence (see illustration 12.16). Loosen the

bolts in sequence 1/4-turn at a time. If the head is to be completely overhauled, refer to Section 11 for removal of the camshafts, rocker arms and hydraulic lash adjusters.

9   Use a prybar at the corners of the head-to-block mating surface to break the gasket seal. Do not pry between the cylinder head and engine block in the gasket sealing area.

10   Lift the cylinder head off the engine. If resistance is felt, place a wood block against the end and strike the wood block with a hammer. Store the cylinder head on wood blocks to prevent damage to the gasket sealing surfaces.

11   Remove the old cylinder head gasket. Before removing, note the correct orientation of the gasket for correct installation.

INSTALLATION

▶ **Refer to illustration 12.16**

12   The mating surfaces of the cylinder head and block must be perfectly clean when the head is installed. Use a gasket scraper to remove all traces of carbon and old gasket material, then clean the mating surfaces with brake system cleaner. If there's oil on the mating surfaces when the cylinder head is installed, the gasket may not seal correctly and leaks may develop. When working on the engine block, cover the open areas of the engine with shop rags to keep debris out during repair and reassembly. Use a vacuum cleaner to remove any debris that falls into the cylinders.

13   Check the engine block and cylinder head mating surfaces for nicks, deep scratches and other damage.

14   Use a tap of the correct size to chase the threads in the cylinder head bolt holes. Dirt, corrosion, sealant and damaged threads will affect torque readings.

15   Make sure the new gasket is located on the dowels in the block.

16   Carefully position the cylinder head on the engine block without disturbing the gasket. Install new cylinder head bolts and, following the recommended sequence (see illustration), tighten the bolts to the torque listed in this Chapter's Specifications. All the main cylinder head bolts (numbers 1 through 10) are tightened in the first step and second step.

The four smaller bolts located on the front of the cylinder head are the only ones tightened in the third step. Mark a stripe on each of the main cylinder head bolts to help keep track of the bolts that have been tightened the additional 155-degrees.

➡ **Note: The method used for the head bolt tightening procedure is referred to as a torque-angle method. A special torque angle gauge (available at most auto parts stores) is available to attach to a breaker bar and socket for better accuracy during the tightening procedure.**

17   Install the timing chain (see Section 8).

18   Install the exhaust manifold (see Section 6).

19   Install the intake manifold (see Section 5).

20   The remaining installation steps are the reverse of removal.

21   Reconnect the battery (see Chapter 5, Section 1).

22   Change the engine oil and filter and refill the cooling system (see Chapter 1), then start the engine and check carefully for oil and coolant leaks.

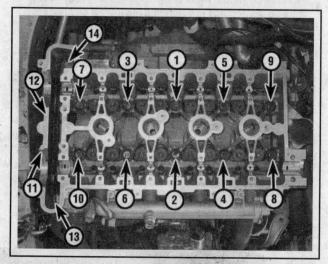

12.16 Cylinder head bolt tightening sequence

13 Oil pan - removal and installation

REMOVAL

1   Attach an engine support fixture of the type that mounts on top of the fenders and spans the engine compartment.

➡ **Note: These can be rented at most rental yards. Adjust the support to remove the weight from the right engine mount.**

2   Raise the vehicle and support it securely on jackstands.

3   Drain the engine oil.

4   Remove the right engine mount and its bracket. Raise the engine several inches for oil pan clearance.

5   Remove the lower air conditioning compressor mounting bolt (see Chapter 3). Loosen, but don't remove, the other compressor mounting bolts.

6   Remove the dipstick and the dipstick tube (the tube is bolted to the intake manifold).

7   Remove the oil pan bolts. Follow the reverse of the tightening sequence (see illustration 13.11).

8   Carefully remove the oil pan from the lower crankcase.

✳✳ CAUTION:

If the oil pan is difficult to separate from the lower crankcase, use a rubber mallet or a block of wood and a hammer to jar it loose. If it's stubborn and still won't come off, pry carefully on casting protrusions (not the mating surfaces!).

INSTALLATION

▶ **Refer to illustration 13.11**

9   Using a gasket scraper, thoroughly clean all old gasket material from the lower crankcase and oil pan. Remove residue and oil film with brake system cleaner.

10 Apply a 2 mm bead of RTV sealant to the perimeter of the oil pan, inboard of the bolt holes, and around the oil suction port. Allow the sealant to set-up before installing the oil pan to the engine (but be sure to install the pan within the time given by the sealant manufacturer).

11 Install the oil pan and bolts (see illustration). Follow the correct sequence and tighten the bolts to the torque listed in this Chapter's Specifications.

12 The remaining installation is the reverse of removal. Be sure to tighten the wheel lug nuts to the torque listed in the Chapter 1 Specifications.

13 Refill the engine with oil and install a new oil filter (see Chapter 1), then run the engine and check for leaks.

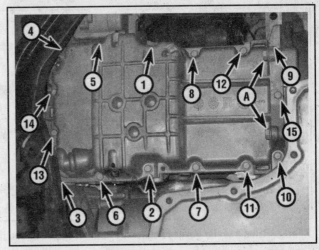

13.11 Oil pan bolt tightening sequence. Tighten the pan-to-transaxle bolts (A) until they're snug (but not too tight), then tighten the pan-to-block bolts in numerical order to the torque listed in this Chapter's Specifications, then tighten bolts (A) to the torque listed in this Chapter's Specifications

14 Oil pump - removal, inspection and installation

▶ **Refer to illustrations 14.5a and 14.5b**

1 Loosen the right-front wheel lug nuts, raise the front of the vehicle and support it securely on jackstands. Remove the right front wheel.

2 Remove the drivebelt (see Chapter 1).

3 Drain the engine oil (see Chapter 1).

4 Remove the engine front cover (see Section 7). On the front side of the engine cover, remove the four bolts retaining the round gerotor cover from the engine cover.

5 Working on the rear of the engine cover, loosen the oil pump cover screws a little at a time until they're all loose (see illustrations).

When all of the screws are loose, remove the cover.

INSPECTION

▶ **Refer to illustrations 14.8a, 14.8b, 14.8c and 14.10**

6 Note any identification marks on the rotors and withdraw the rotors from the pump body. If no marks can be seen, use a permanent marker and make your own to ensure that they will be installed correctly.

7 Thoroughly clean and dry the components.

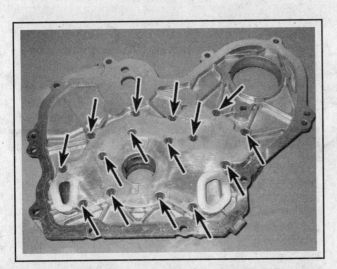

14.5a Location of the oil pump cover mounting screws

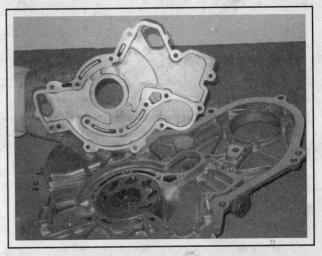

14.5b Lift the oil pump cover from the engine cover

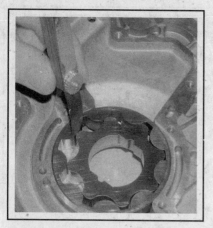

14.8a Using a feeler gauge to check the inner-to-outer rotor tip clearance . . .

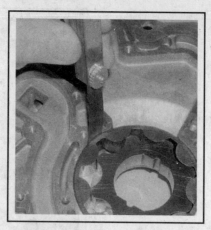

14.8b . . . and the outer rotor-to-housing clearance

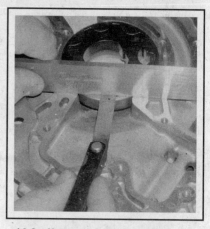

14.8c Use a straightedge and a feeler gauge to check the rotor-to-cover clearance

8   Inspect the rotors for obvious wear or damage. If either rotor, the pump body or the cover is scored or damaged, the complete oil pump assembly must be replaced. Also check the inner-to-outer rotor tip clearance, the outer rotor-to-housing clearance, and the rotor-to-cover side clearance (see illustrations).

9   If the oil pump components are in acceptable condition, dip the rotors in clean engine oil and install them into the pump body with any identification marks positioned as noted during disassembly.

10 Remove the oil pressure relief valve components from the front cover. Thoroughly clean and dry the components. Inspect the components for obvious wear or damage. Install them in the correct order (see illustration).

INSTALLATION

11 Install the rotors into the housing with the hub of the inner rotor facing the engine front cover. The inner rotor hub must be installed correctly or the engine front cover/gerotor cover will not fasten properly.

12 Install the oil pump cover and screws and tighten by hand until snug. Then tighten the screws gradually and evenly to the torque listed in this Chapter's Specifications. Install the oil pressure relief valve components.

13 Install the engine front cover (see Section 7).

14 Refer to Chapter 1 and fill the engine with fresh engine oil. Install a new oil filter.

15 Start the engine and check for leaks.

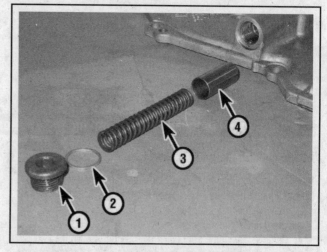

14.10 Oil pressure relief valve component details

1	Oil pressure relief valve plug	3	Spring
2	Sealing washer	4	Piston

16 Run the engine and make sure oil pressure comes up to normal quickly. If it doesn't, stop the engine and find out the cause. Severe engine damage can result from running an engine with insufficient oil pressure!

15 Flywheel/driveplate - removal and installation

REMOVAL

1   Raise the vehicle and support it securely on jackstands, then refer to Chapter 7 and remove the transaxle. If it's leaking, now would be a very good time to replace the front pump seal/O-ring (automatic transaxle only).

2   If you're working on a manual transaxle equipped vehicle, remove the pressure plate and clutch disc (see Chapter 8). Now is a good time to check/replace the clutch components.

3   Use a center punch or paint to make alignment marks on the flywheel/driveplate and crankshaft to ensure correct alignment during reinstallation.

4   Remove the bolts that secure the flywheel/driveplate to the crankshaft. If the crankshaft turns, wedge a screwdriver in the ring gear teeth to jam the flywheel. Discard the bolts; new ones should be used during installation.

5   Remove the flywheel/driveplate from the crankshaft. Since the flywheel is fairly heavy, be sure to support it while removing the last bolt.

If an automatic transmission-equipped vehicle has a spacer between the crankshaft and the driveplate, note which way it was installed.

INSTALLATION

6   Clean the flywheel to remove grease and oil. Inspect the surface for cracks, rivet grooves, burned areas and score marks. Light scoring can be removed with emery cloth. Check for cracked and broken ring gear teeth. Lay the flywheel on a flat surface and use a straightedge to check for warpage.

7   Clean and inspect the mating surfaces of the flywheel/driveplate and the crankshaft. If the crankshaft rear seal is leaking, replace the seal

before reinstalling the flywheel/driveplate (see Section 16).

8   Position the flywheel/driveplate against the crankshaft, installing the spacer if one was present originally. Be sure to align the mating marks made during removal. Note that some engines have an alignment dowel or staggered bolt holes to ensure correct installation. Before installing the new bolts, apply thread locking compound to the threads IF no thread locking compound is present.

9   Wedge a screwdriver in the ring gear teeth to keep the flywheel/driveplate from turning and tighten the bolts to the torque listed in this Chapter's Specifications. Work up to the final torque in three or four steps.

10   The remainder of installation is the reverse of the removal procedure.

16 Rear main oil seal - replacement

1   The one-piece rear main oil seal is pressed into the engine block and the crankcase reinforcement section. Remove the transaxle (see Chapter 7), the clutch components, if equipped (see Chapter 8) and the flywheel (see Section 15).

2   Pry out the old seal with a special seal removal tool or a flat-blade screwdriver.

❋❋ CAUTION:

To prevent an oil leak after the new seal is installed, be very careful not to scratch or otherwise damage the crankshaft sealing surface or the bore in the engine block.

3   Clean the crankshaft and seal bore in the block thoroughly and

de-grease these areas by wiping them with a rag soaked with brake system cleaner. Lubricate the lip of the new seal and the sealing surface of the crankshaft with engine oil.

4   Position the new seal onto the crankshaft. Make sure the edges of the new oil seal are not rolled over.

➡**Note: When installing the new seal, if so marked, the words THIS SIDE OUT on the seal must face out, toward the rear of the engine.**

Use a special rear main oil seal installation tool or a socket with the same diameter of the seal to drive the seal in place. Make sure the seal is driven in squarely; it must be flush along the entire circumference of the engine block and the crankcase reinforcement section.

5   The remainder of installation is the reverse of removal.

17 Powertrain mounts - check and replacement

CHECK

1   Engine mounts seldom require attention, but broken or deteriorated mounts should be replaced immediately or the added strain placed on the driveline components may cause damage or wear.

2   During the check, the engine must be raised slightly to remove the weight from the mounts.

3   Raise the vehicle and support it securely on jackstands, then position a jack under the engine oil pan. Place a large block of wood between the jack head and the oil pan, then carefully raise the engine just enough to take the weight off the mounts.

❋❋ WARNING:

DO NOT place any part of your body under the engine when it's supported only by a jack!

4   Check the mounts to see if the rubber is cracked, hardened or separated from the bushing in the center of the mount.

5   Check for relative movement between the mount and the engine

or frame (use a large screwdriver or prybar to attempt to move the mounts). If movement is noted, lower the engine and tighten the mount fasteners.

REPLACEMENT

◗ **Refer to illustration 17.9a, 17.9b and 17.9c**

6   Disconnect the negative battery cable from the battery (see Chapter 5). On all engines except the 2.0L, remove the engine air filter and housing (see Chapter 4).

7   Raise the vehicle and support it securely on jackstands.

8   Place a large block of wood between the jack head and the oil pan, then carefully raise the engine just enough to take the weight off the mounts.

❋❋ CAUTION:

Do not disconnect more than one mount at a time unless the engine will be removed from the vehicle.

17.9a Passenger-side engine mount upper mounting fasteners

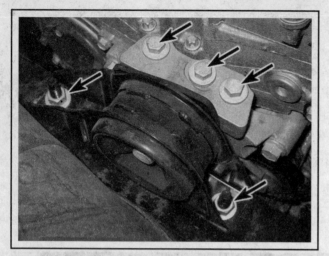

17.9b Front transaxle mount through-bolt

9   Remove the engine mount through-bolt/nuts and detach the mount from the chassis bracket (see illustrations).

10 Remove the fasteners holding the mount to the engine bracket.

11 Installation is the reverse of removal. Use thread-locking compound on the mount fasteners and be sure to tighten them securely.

12 The engine/transaxle assembly must be balanced in its weight distribution among the several powertrain mounts, before the mounting bolts are tightened. Loosen all the mount bolts, then shake the engine from side to side and front-to-rear as much as possible to settle it. The tighten all the mounts in this order: transmission mount-to-transmission bolts (rear first, then middle, then front); engine mount-to-bracket bolts (center first); shake the engine again front-to-rear; rear mount through-bolt; then front mount through-bolt.

13 Reconnect the battery (see Chapter 5, Section 1).

17.9c Rear transaxle mount-to-frame bolts

Specifications

General

Firing order	1-3-4-2
Compression ratio	10:1
Compression pressure	See Chapter 2D
Bore	3.385 to 3.386 inches (85.9 to 86.0 mm)
Stroke	3.727 inches (94.6 mm)
Displacement	134 cubic inches (2.2 liters)
Oil pressure	See Chapter 2D

FRONT OF VEHICLE

① ② ③ ④

1-3-4-2

87020-B-SPECS HAYNES

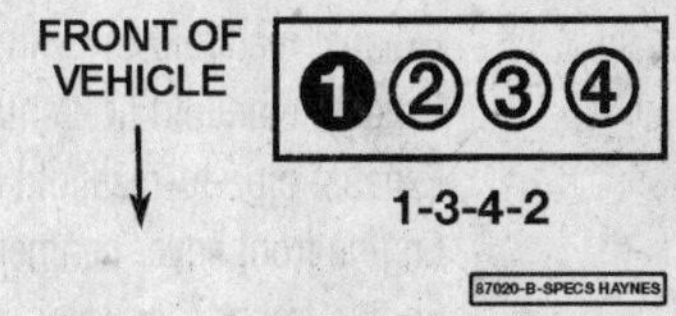

Cylinder locations and firing order

Timing chain tensioner

Timing chain tensioner compressed length	2.83 inches (72.0 mm)

Hydraulic lash adjuster

Lash adjuster diameter	0.4723 to 0.4728 inch (11.986 to 12.000 mm)
Lash adjuster-to-bore clearance	0.0005 to 0.0020 inch (0.013 to 0.051 mm)

Camshafts

Allowable lobe lift variation	0.005 inch (0.125 mm)
Endplay	0.0016 to 0.0057 inch (0.040 to 0.144 mm)
Journal diameter (all)	1.0604 to 1.0614 inches (26.935 to 26.960 mm)
Journal oil clearance	0.0015 to 0.0034 inch (0.040 to 0.086 mm)

Torque specifications

	Ft-lbs (unless otherwise indicated)	Nm

➡ **Note: One foot-pound (ft-lb) of torque is equivalent to 12 inch-pounds (in-lbs) of torque. Torque values below approximately 15 ft-lbs are expressed in inch-pounds, since most foot-pound torque wrenches are not accurate at these smaller values.**

	Ft-lbs (unless otherwise indicated)	Nm
Camshaft sprocket bolts*		
Step 1	63	85
Step 2	Tighten an additional 30-degrees	
Camshaft bearing cap bolts		
Intake camshaft rear cap bolts	18	24
All other camshaft cap bolts	89 in-lbs	10
Crankshaft pulley bolt*		
2002 and 2003 models		
Step 1	74	100
Step 2	Tighten an additional 75-degrees	
2004 and later models		
Step 1	74	100
Step 2	Tighten an additional 125-degrees	
Cylinder head bolts* (in sequence - see illustration 12.16)		
Step 1 - Central bolts (1 through 10)	22	30
Step 2 - Central bolts (1 through 10)	Tighten an additional 155-degrees	
Step 3 - Front bolts (11 through 14)	26	35
Drivebelt tensioner bolt	33	45
Flywheel/driveplate bolts		
Step 1	39	53
Step 2	Tighten an additional 25-degrees	

Torque specifications (continued)	Ft-lbs (unless otherwise indicated)	Nm

➡**Note: One foot-pound (ft-lb) of torque is equivalent to 12 inch-pounds (in-lbs) of torque. Torque values below approximately 15 ft-lbs are expressed in inch-pounds, since most foot-pound torque wrenches are not accurate at these smaller values.**

Exhaust manifold-to-cylinder head nuts	106 in-lbs	12
Exhaust manifold heat shield bolts	17	23
Exhaust pipe-to-manifold nuts	22	30
Engine front cover perimeter bolts	18	24
Engine front cover water pump bolt	18	24
Intake manifold bolts/nuts	89 in-lbs	10
Oil pump cover-to-engine front cover screws	53 in-lbs	6
Oil pump pressure relief valve plug	30	40
Oil pan-to-crankcase reinforcement bolts	18	24
Balance shaft chain tensioner	89 in-lbs	10
Balance shaft chain guides		
Adjustable balance shaft chain guide bolts	89 in-lbs	10
Small balance shaft chain guide bolts	89 in-lbs	10
Upper balance shaft guide bolts	89 in-lbs	10
Balance shaft retainer bolts	89 in-lbs	10
Timing chain tensioner	55	75
Timing chain guides		
Adjustable timing chain guide bolts	89 in-lbs	10
Fixed timing chain guide bolts	132 in-lbs	15
Upper timing chain guide bolts	89 in-lbs	10
Timing chain oiling nozzle bolt	89 in-lbs	10
Timing chain guide access hole plug	59	80
Valve cover bolts	89 in-lbs	10
Valve cover ground strap bolt	89 in-lbs	10
Water pump bolts	18	24
Water pump drain bolt	15	20

Bolt(s) must be replaced.

2B

3.0L V6 ENGINES

Section

Reference to other Chapters

1 General information

This Part of Chapter 2 is devoted to in-vehicle repair procedures for the 3.0L Double Over Head Cam (DOHC) V6 engine. This engine is equipped with two camshafts per cylinder head. All four camshaft sprockets are driven by one timing belt. This engine has aluminum cylinder heads, an iron block and two intake valves and two exhaust valves per cylinder. All information concerning engine removal and installation

can be found in Part D of this Chapter.

These engines are an interference design. In the event the timing belt breaks, the pistons will impact the valves and cause damage. The timing belt, tensioner and cylinder heads can be removed with the engine in the vehicle. It will be necessary to obtain special tools to perform certain repair operations on this engine.

2 Repair operations possible with the engine in the vehicle

Many major repair operations can be accomplished without removing the engine from the vehicle.

If possible, clean the engine compartment and the exterior of the engine with some type of pressure washer before any work is started. It will make the job easier and help keep dirt out of the internal areas of the engine.

It may help to remove the hood to improve access to the engine as repairs are performed (refer to Chapter 11 if necessary).

If vacuum, exhaust, oil or coolant leaks develop, indicating a need for gasket or seal replacement, the repairs can generally be made with the engine in the vehicle. The intake and exhaust manifold gaskets, timing cover gasket, oil pan gasket, crankshaft oil seals and cylinder head gaskets are all accessible with the engine in place.

Exterior engine components, such as the intake and exhaust manifolds, the oil pan, the water pump, the starter motor, the alternator and the fuel system components can be removed for repair with the engine in place.

Since the cylinder heads can be removed without pulling the engine, valve component servicing can also be accomplished with the engine in the vehicle. Replacement of the timing belt, camshaft sprockets and oil pump is also possible with the engine in the vehicle.

In extreme cases caused by a lack of necessary equipment, repair or replacement of piston rings, pistons, connecting rods and rod bearings is also possible with the engine in the vehicle. However, this practice is not recommended because of the cleaning and preparation work that must be done to the components involved.

3 Top Dead Center (TDC) for number one piston - locating

♦ **Refer to illustrations 3.1a and 3.1b**

Refer to Chapter 2, Part A for the TDC locating procedure.

➡**Note: To verify TDC number 1, remove the timing belt cover (see Section 7) and make sure the marks on the sprockets align with the marks on the engine/sprocket covers (see illustrations). At this point, number one cylinder is at TDC on the compression stroke.**

After the number one piston has been positioned at TDC on the compression stroke, TDC for any of the remaining pistons can be located by turning the crankshaft and following the firing order. Divide the crankshaft pulley into three equal sections, with chalk marks at 120-degree intervals (starting from the TDC mark). Rotating the engine past TDC no. 1 to the next mark will place the engine at TDC for cylinder no. 2.

3.1a When the engine is at TDC on the compression stroke for cylinder number one, the camshaft sprocket marks will be aligned with the cutouts on the rear timing belt covers (rear cylinder head shown)

3.1b Camshaft sprocket alignment marks - front cylinder head

4   Valve covers - removal and installation

REMOVAL

1   Disconnect the cable from the negative battery terminal (see Chapter 5, Section 1).

2   Remove the ignition coil pack(s) (see Chapter 5).

3   Remove the intake manifold (see Section 5).

4   Remove the oil filler tube.

5   If you're working on a front valve cover, disconnect the CMP sensor wiring from the sensor and the clip.

6   If you're working on the rear valve cover, position the knock sensor wiring away from the valve cover (see Chapter 6).

7   Loosen the valve cover bolts and remove the cover. If it's stuck, tap it with a hammer and block of wood.

➡️Note: The valve cover contains eight rubber O-rings that may stick to the surface of the cylinder head. Be sure to collect each O-ring and install it in the original location.

4.9a Install the rubber valve cover gasket into the groove in the valve cover . . .

INSTALLATION

▶ Refer to illustrations 4.9a, 4.9b, 4.10a and 4.10b

8   The mating surfaces of each cylinder head and valve cover must be perfectly clean when the valve covers are installed. Remove all traces of sealant, and clean the mating surfaces with brake system cleaner. If there's old sealant or oil on the mating surfaces when the valve cover is installed, oil leaks may develop.

9   Install the rubber valve cover gasket into the groove in the valve cover (see illustration). Also, install the rubber O-rings into the grooves around the valve cover bolts (see illustration).

10   Apply a bead of RTV sealant into the corners where the front camshaft bearing cap meets the cylinder head (see illustration), and around the housing seals at the rear (see illustration).

11   Carefully position the valve cover on the cylinder head and install the bolts.

➡️Note: Install the covers within five minutes of applying the RTV sealant.

Tighten the bolts to the torque listed in this Chapter's Specifications.

12   The remaining installation steps are the reverse of removal.

13   Reconnect the battery (see Chapter 5, Section 1).

14   Start the engine and check for oil leaks as the engine warms up.

4.9b . . . and install new O-rings around the valve cover bolt holes

4.10a Apply RTV sealant to the camshaft front bearing caps at the cylinder head . . .

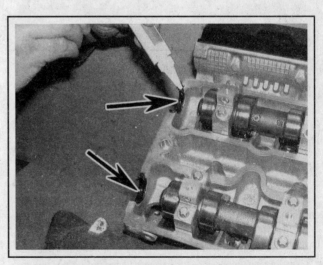

4.10b . . . and to the semi-circular cutouts on the rear of the cylinder head

5 Intake manifold - removal and installation

♦ **Refer to illustration 5.12**

1 Disconnect the cable from the negative battery terminal (see Chapter 5, Section 1).

2 Refer to Chapter 4 and remove the intake air duct. Remove the duct support bracket from the top of the engine.

3 Refer to Chapter 4 and relieve the fuel system pressure. Disconnect the fuel line at the quick-connect fitting.

4 Disconnect the wiring from the intake manifold. Secure the wiring out of the way.

5 Disconnect the EVAP purge solenoid and its hoses from the back of the manifold.

6 Disconnect the brake vacuum hose from the manifold.

7 Label and disconnect the other wiring from the intake manifold. Position the harnesses aside. Disconnect the PCV hose from the manifold.

8 Remove the throttle body coolant hose bracket bolts. Remove the throttle body mounting bolts and move the throttle body to the side. The coolant hoses can remain attached to it.

9 Remove the five upper manifold bolts. There is also a lower intake manifold bolt near the throttle body that must be removed. Lift off the upper section of the intake manifold.

10 Remove the bolts from the lower intake manifold adapter plate using the reverse of the tightening sequence (see illustration 5.12). Remove the lower intake manifold plate.

11 Clean all sealing surfaces thoroughly. Replace all of the lower intake manifold O-rings if any are damaged.

➡ **Note: Use thread locking compound on the lower intake manifold bolts.**

12 The remaining installation steps are the reverse of removal. Tighten all fasteners in the correct sequence to the torque values listed in this Chapter's Specifications (see illustration).

13 Reconnect the battery (see Chapter 5, Section 1), then start the engine and check carefully for leaks.

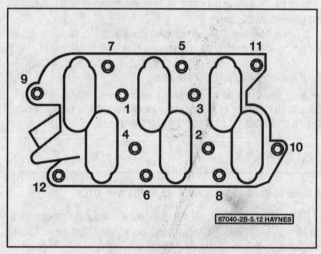

5.12 Tightening sequence for the lower intake manifold bolts

6 Exhaust manifolds - removal and installation

❊❊ **WARNING:**

Wait until the engine is completely cool before beginning this procedure.

REMOVAL

1 Disconnect the cable from the negative battery terminal (see Chapter 5, Section 1).

2 Raise the vehicle and support it securely on jackstands.

3 Remove the splash shield from below the engine compartment.

4 Working under the vehicle, apply penetrating oil to the exhaust pipe-to-manifold studs and nuts (they're usually corroded or rusty).

Front exhaust manifold

5 Disconnect the top oxygen sensor wiring.

6 Remove the bolt from the engine hoist bracket at the right front end of the engine.

7 Remove the dipstick tube.

8 Remove the four manifold mounting nuts that are accessible from the top.

9 Loosen the right front wheel lug nuts. Raise the vehicle and support it securely on jackstands. Remove the right front wheel and the inner fender splash shield.

10 Remove the front exhaust pipe.

11 Remove the drivebelt from the tensioner and allow it to hang in place.

12 Disconnect the air conditioning compressor wiring.

13 Remove the three compressor mounting bolts and use wire to hang the unit out of the way. Don't disconnect the refrigerant lines.

14 Remove the lower mounting nuts from the exhaust manifold, then detach the manifold from the cylinder head.

Rear exhaust manifold

15 Refer to Chapter 4 and remove the air intake duct assembly.

16 Remove the EVAP purge solenoid and set it aside for working clearance.

17 Raise the vehicle and support it securely on jackstands. Remove the middle exhaust manifold nut.

18 Disconnect the top oxygen sensor wiring.

19 Remove the front section of the exhaust pipe.

20 Refer to Chapter 10 and disconnect the stabilizer bar. It's not necessary to remove the bar completely as long as it can be turned for clearance.

21 Remove the exhaust manifold heat shield.

22 Remove the mounting nuts and remove the exhaust manifold.

23 Remove the mounting nuts from the exhaust manifold, then detach the manifold from the cylinder head.

INSTALLATION

24 Check the exhaust manifolds for cracks. Make sure the bolt threads are clean and undamaged. The exhaust manifold and cylinder head mating surfaces must be clean before the exhaust manifolds are reinstalled - use a gasket scraper to remove all carbon deposits.

25 Position a new gasket in place and slip the exhaust manifold over the studs on the cylinder head. Install the mounting nuts.

26 When tightening the mounting nuts, work from the center outwards, alternating between top and bottom rows. Tighten the bolts to the torque listed in this Chapter's Specifications.

27 The remaining installation steps are the reverse of removal. When reconnecting the EGR tube to the exhaust manifold, use a slight amount of anti-seize compound on the threads.

28 Reconnect the battery (see Chapter 5, Section 1).

29 Start the engine and check for leaks when the engine is cool and again when it's warm.

7 Timing belt cover - removal and installation

REMOVAL

1 Disconnect the cable from the negative battery terminal (see Chapter 5, Section 1).

2 Loosen the right wheel lug nuts. Raise the vehicle and support it securely on jackstands.

3 Remove the front wheel and the inner fender splash shield from the right side of the vehicle.

4 Refer to Chapter 4 and remove the intake air duct.

5 Attach an engine support fixture between the fenders and raise the engine slightly.

➡ **Note: As an alternative, you can place a floor jack and a block of wood under the oil pan to take the weight off of the right engine mount.**

6 Loosen the water pump pulley and idler pulley bolts. Leave the pulleys and the drivebelt on the vehicle at this time.

7 Remove the right engine mount, then the drivebelt (see Chapter 1).

Remove the engine mount bracket.

8 Remove the drivebelt idler pulley and the water pump.

9 Disconnect the harness connectors at the timing belt cover and position the wiring harness clear of the front cover.

10 Remove the drivebelt tensioner (see Chapter 1). Remove the crankshaft pulley (see Section 9).

11 Remove the timing belt cover mounting bolts. Remove the timing belt cover from the engine.

INSTALLATION

12 Clean the timing belt cover and the engine block. Inspect the timing belt cover for cracks and damage, replacing it if necessary.

13 Install the timing belt cover to the engine. Tighten the timing belt cover bolts to the torque listed in this Chapter's Specifications.

14 Install the remaining parts in the reverse order of removal.

15 Reconnect the battery (see Chapter 5, Section 1).

8 Timing belt and sprockets - removal, inspection and installation

❋❋ CAUTION ❋❋

The timing system is complex. Severe engine damage will occur if you make any mistakes. Do not attempt this procedure unless you are highly experienced with this type of repair. If you are at all unsure of your abilities, consult an expert. Double-check all your work and be sure everything is correct before you attempt to start the engine.

➡ **Note 1: Because this is an interference engine design, if the belt has broken, there will be damage to the valves and/or pistons. This will require removal of the cylinder heads.**

➡ **Note 2: The timing belt replacement procedure requires several special tools. The special tools are sold as a kit (J-42069) that includes two camshaft locking tools, a crankshaft locking** tool, a timing belt wedge and a camshaft timing sprocket gauge. Consult with a specialty tool distributor or dealership parts department for availability.

REMOVAL

◆ **Refer to illustrations 8.4, 8.5a, 8.5b, 8.6a, 8.6b, 8.7a, 8.7b, 8.8 and 8.10**

1 Disconnect the cable from the negative battery terminal (see Chapter 5, Section 1).

2 Remove the timing belt cover (see Section 7).

3 Set the engine to TDC for cylinder number one (see Section 3), then turn the crankshaft counterclockwise until the engine is set at 60-degrees before TDC. Remove the spark plugs (see Chapter 1).

8.4 Timing belt tool kit details

1	Timing sprocket gauge	4	Crankshaft locking tool
2	Camshaft sprocket	5	Camshaft sprocket
	locking tool		locking tool
3	Timing belt wedge		

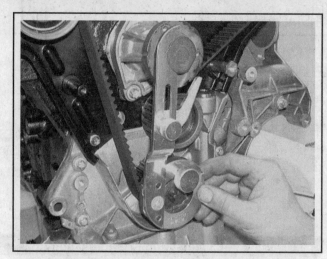

8.5a Install the crankshaft locking tool over the crankshaft sprocket flange, then turn the crankshaft clockwise until the tool contacts the water pump . . .

8.5b . . . then lock the tool in place by moving the lever arm against the water pump flange and tightening the thumbscrew

8.6a Install the camshaft sprocket locking tool between the two camshaft sprockets . . .

4   Install the crankshaft locking tool onto the crankshaft (see illustration).

5   Rotate the crankshaft clockwise approximately 60-degrees until the locking tool lever arm rests against the water pump pulley flange (see illustrations). Lock the tool in this position. The camshaft sprockets should align correctly (see illustrations 8.16a and 8.16b).

6   Install the special tools that lock the camshaft sprockets (see illustrations).

7   Loosen the timing belt tensioner (see illustrations).

8   Loosen the upper timing belt guide pulley (see illustration) and rotate it to release belt tension.

9   Remove the timing belt.

10   The camshaft sprockets can be removed at this point, if they are damaged, or to replace the oil seals (see illustration). Remove the keys from the shafts so they don't fall out and get lost.

❋❋ CAUTION:

Don't allow the camshaft(s) to turn. If the sprockets are removed, discard the bolts (new ones must be used on reassembly).

11   If it's worn or damaged, or if you're replacing the crankshaft front oil seal, the crankshaft sprocket can now be removed (see Section 9). If it won't come off by hand, carefully pry it off. Also remove the timing belt guide(s), noting how they are installed.

INSPECTION

12   Remove all dirt and oil from the timing belt area. Clean the teeth of the sprockets with brake system cleaner.

8.6b . . . and push the tool into position - the TOP mark must be up. Repeat this on the other set of camshafts

8.7a Loosen the timing belt tensioner bolt

8.7b Rotate the tensioner using an Allen key

8.8 Loosen the upper timing belt guide pulley

13 Inspect the sprocket teeth for wear and damage. Check the timing belt for any cracks or oil residue. Also check the camshaft for excessive endplay (see Section 10). Check the timing belt tensioner for smooth operation. Replace any worn parts with new ones.

14 Inspect the water pump (see Chapter 3).

INSTALLATION

▶ **Refer to illustrations 8.16a, 8.16b, 8.16c, 8.19, 8.21, 8.22, 8.23a, 8.23b, 8.24, 8.28 and 8.34**

✳ CAUTION ✳

Before starting the engine, carefully rotate the crankshaft by hand through at least two full revolutions (use a socket and breaker bar on the crankshaft pulley centerbolt). If you feel any resistance, STOP! There is something wrong - most likely, valves are contacting the pistons. You must find the problem before proceeding. Check your work and see if any updated repair information is available.

8.10 Use a wrench on the hex drive on the camshaft to prevent the camshaft from turning

8.16a Location of the number 1 and 2 camshaft timing marks (rear cylinder head)

8.16b Location of the number 3 and 4 camshaft timing marks (front cylinder head)

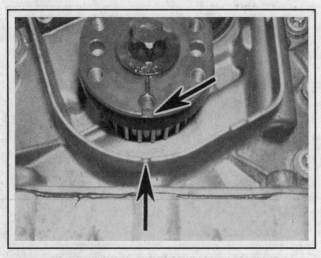

8.16c Align the crankshaft sprocket timing mark with the notch in the oil pump cover

8.19 Align the timing belt marks with the camshaft sprocket marks and the notches on the rear covers (number 1 and 2)

15 If any of the camshaft sprockets were removed, install them now with their keys and tighten the bolts to the torque listed in this Chapter's Specifications (see illustration 8.10).

※※ CAUTION:

Be sure to use new bolts.

16 Recheck the positions of the timing marks (see illustrations).
17 Remove the crankshaft locking tool.
18 Install the camshaft locking tools, if they were removed (see illustrations 8.6a and 8.6b).

➡ **Note: Be sure the timing marks are aligned properly (see illustrations 8.16a and 8.16b).**

19 Install the timing belt over the number 1 and 2 camshaft sprockets on the rear cylinder head, aligning the marks on the belt with the marks on the sprockets (see illustration).
20 Install the timing belt around the timing belt tensioner.

21 Install the timing belt under the upper timing belt guide pulley (see illustration).
22 Install the timing belt over the number 3 and 4 camshaft sprockets on the front cylinder head (see illustration). Align the timing belt marks with the sprocket timing marks and install the timing belt.
23 Install the timing belt around the crankshaft sprocket. Align the mark on the timing belt with the sprocket mark (see illustration). Install the timing belt wedge to prevent the timing belt from moving out of position (see illustration).
24 Rotate the crankshaft counterclockwise to gather the belt slack on the lower timing belt guide pulley side of the engine. Route the timing belt over the lower timing belt guide pulley (see illustration).
25 Remove the timing belt wedge.
26 Install the crankshaft locking tool again.
27 Remove the camshaft sprocket locking tools.
28 Install the timing belt gauge over number 3 and 4 camshaft sprockets (front) (see illustration).

➡ **Note: Some timing belt tool kits for these engines use a green "test belt" instead of the gauge shown in the photograph.**

8.21 Tighten the guide pulley bolt slightly, allowing it to move for adjustment purposes

8.22 Align the timing belt paint marks with the camshaft sprocket marks and the notches on the rear covers (number 3 and 4 on front cylinder head)

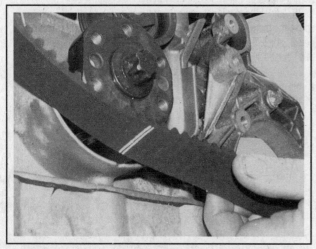

8.23a Install the timing belt around the crankshaft sprocket with the timing belt mark aligned with the sprocket mark

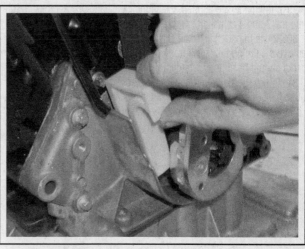

8.23b Install the timing belt wedge between the belt and the oil pump cover flange

8.24 Route the timing belt over the lower timing belt guide pulley

8.28 Make sure the timing sprocket gauge marks are aligned with the sprocket marks

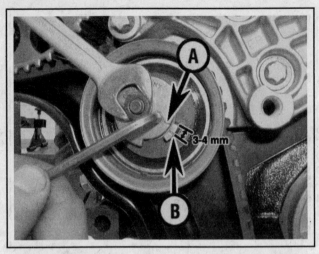

8.34 Adjust the tensioner center alignment mark (A) 1/8-inch (3 mm) above the mark on the spring loaded idler on the tensioner (B)

29 If the marks are aligned, install the camshaft sprocket locking tool onto the 3 and 4 camshaft sprockets (front).

30 Rotate the number 1 camshaft sprocket counterclockwise to remove the timing belt slack from the camshaft sprockets. The timing marks should be slightly retarded.

31 To tighten the timing belt tension around the camshaft sprockets, rotate the upper timing belt guide pulley counterclockwise until the nos. 1 and 2 cam sprocket timing marks are aligned.

32 Install the camshaft sprocket locking tool onto the 1 and 2 camshaft sprockets (rear) if the marks are aligned.

33 Tighten the upper timing belt guide pulley bolt to the torque listed in this Chapter's Specifications.

34 Adjust the tensioner center alignment mark 1/8-inch (3 mm) above the mark on the spring loaded idler on the tensioner (see illustration).

35 Remove the crankshaft locking tool and the camshaft sprocket locking tool.

❉❉ CAUTION:

Do not rotate the engine counterclockwise or the timing belt slack between the crankshaft sprocket and the tensioner will be altered, causing timing belt adjustment problems.

36 Rotate the engine 1-3/4 turns clockwise and install the crankshaft locking tool. Continue turning the crankshaft until number 1 TDC is located. Lock the tool against the water pump flange.

37 Recheck the camshaft sprocket marks and realign them if necessary. If they are aligned, continue with the next step.

38 Adjust the tensioner center alignment mark 1/8-inch (3 mm) above the mark on the spring loaded idler on the tensioner (see illustration 8.34). Tighten the timing belt tensioner bolt to the torque listed in this Chapter's Specifications.

39 Recheck the camshaft sprocket timing marks and the crankshaft sprocket marks.

40 Install the timing belt cover (see Section 7).

41 Reconnect the battery (see Chapter 5, Section 1).

9 Crankshaft pulley and front oil seal - removal and installation

REMOVAL

▶ **Refer to illustrations 9.8, 9.9a and 9.9b**

1 Disconnect the cable from the negative battery terminal (see Chapter 5, Section 1).

2 Loosen the right front wheel lug nuts. Raise the vehicle and support it securely on jackstands. Remove the wheel

3 Remove the inner fender splash shield from the passenger side of the vehicle.

4 Remove the crankshaft pulley bolts using the force from the drivebelt to prevent the engine from rotating.

➡**Note: If the engine rotates during bolt removal, lock the flywheel using a special tool to prevent engine rotation.**

5 Remove the drivebelt (see Chapter 1).

6 Unscrew the bolts and lift the balancer off.

7 Remove the timing belt (see Section 8).

8 Use a pin spanner (see illustration) to hold the crankshaft sprocket stationary, then remove the crankshaft center bolt.

9 Remove the crankshaft sprocket and the seal hub from the crankshaft (see illustrations).

10 Use a seal puller or a screwdriver to remove the crankshaft front oil seal. Be careful not to scratch the crankshaft.

11 Clean the seal bore and check it for nicks or gouges. Also examine the area of the hub that rides in the seal for signs of abnormal wear or scoring.

INSTALLATION

12 Coat the lip of the new seal with clean engine oil and drive it into the bore with a seal driver or a deep socket slightly smaller in diameter than the seal. The open side of the seal faces into the engine.

13 Lubricate the crankshaft seal hub with clean engine oil.

14 Install the crankshaft sprocket. Install the center bolt and tighten it to the torque listed in this Chapter's Specifications.

15 The remainder of installation is the reverse of removal.

16 Reconnect the battery (see Chapter 5, Section 1).

9.8 Here's a homemade pin spanner being used to immobilize the crankshaft sprocket

9.9a Remove the crankshaft sprocket . . .

9.9b . . . and the hub from the crankshaft

10 Camshafts and cam followers - removal, inspection and installation

REMOVAL

➡Note: The intake camshafts are marked A and the exhaust camshafts are marked E.

1   Disconnect the cable from the negative battery terminal (see Chapter 5, Section 1).

2   Set the engine to 60-degrees before TDC for cylinder no. 1.

✳✳ CAUTION:

Do not remove the camshafts with the engine at TDC number 1, or the valves could be damaged.

3   Remove the valve cover(s) (see Section 4).
4   Remove the timing belt (see Section 8).
5   Remove the camshaft sprockets (see illustration 8.10). Mark each camshaft sprocket to insure correct reassembly. Discard the bolts (new ones must be used on reassembly).

➡Note: Also mark the position of the camshaft dowels to the camshaft sprockets. This will insure accurate reassembly of the camshaft sprockets later.

6   Each camshaft cap is designated with a letter and a number, with corresponding number marks on the cylinder head.

✳✳ CAUTION:

The caps must be installed in their original locations. Keep all parts from each camshaft together; never mix parts from one camshaft with those for another.

Loosen each bearing cap bolt a little at a time, starting from the center bearing caps and working out, allowing the camshaft to lift from the cylinder head parallel to the surface of the cylinder head.

Front cylinder head camshafts and followers

▶ **Refer to illustrations 10.8 and 10.9**

7   The camshaft bearing caps on the front cylinder head are designated with an R, plus the number of the cap. Make note of the location of each camshaft bearing cap to insure correct reassembly. If no marks are present, or they are hard to see, make your own - the bearing caps must be reinstalled in their original positions.

8   Remove the camshaft from the cylinder head (see illustration). Be sure to remove the camshaft seal with the camshaft.

10.8 Lift the camshaft from the cylinder head

10.9 Lift the cam followers from their bores. A magnet or suction cup may be required to extract them

10.10 The letter and number designations are located on the same side of the camshaft housing

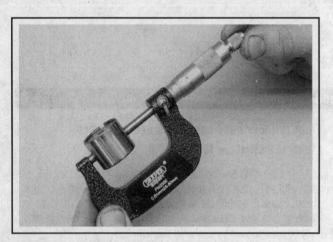

10.14 Measure the cam follower outside diameter at several points

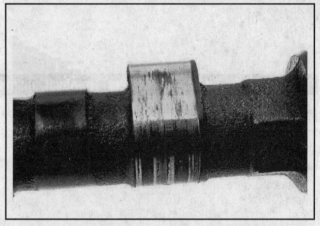

10.15 Check the cam lobes for pitting, excessive wear, and scoring. If scoring is excessive, as shown here, replace the camshaft

9   Obtain twelve small, clean containers, and number them 1 to 12. Remove each cam follower and place them in the containers (see illustration). Do not interchange the cam followers, or the rate of wear will be much increased. Store the followers right-side up to prevent the oil from draining out of the hydraulic lash adjuster mechanisms.

Rear cylinder head camshafts and followers

▶ Refer to illustration 10.10

10   The camshaft bearing caps on the rear cylinder head are designated with an L, plus the number of the cap (see illustration). Make note of the location of each camshaft bearing cap to insure correct reassembly. If no marks are present, or they are hard to see, make your own - the bearing caps must be reinstalled in their original positions.

11   Remove the camshaft from the cylinder head (see illustration 10.8). Be sure to remove the camshaft seal with the camshaft.

12   Obtain twelve small, clean containers, and number them 1 to 12. Remove each cam follower and place them in the containers (see illustration 10.9). Do not interchange the cam followers, or the rate of wear will be much increased. Store the followers right-side up to prevent the oil from draining out of the hydraulic lash adjuster mechanisms.

INSPECTION

▶ Refer to illustrations 10.14, 10.15, 10.16, 10.18, 10.19a and 10.19b

13   With the camshafts and cam followers removed, check each for signs of obvious wear (scoring, pitting, etc).

14   Measure the outside diameter of each cam follower - take measurements at the top and bottom of each cam follower, then a second set at right-angles to the first; if any measurement is significantly different from the others, the cam follower is tapered or out-of round and must be replaced (see illustration). If the necessary equipment is available, measure the inside diameter of the corresponding cylinder head bore, then subtract the diameter of the lifter from the inside diameter of the lifter bore to calculate the oil clearance. Check the specifications listed in this Chapter; if the cam followers or the cylinder head bores are excessively worn, new cam followers and/or a new cylinder head may be required.

15   Visually examine the camshaft lobes for score marks, pitting, galling (wear due to rubbing) and evidence of overheating (blue, discolored areas) (see illustration). Look for flaking away of the hardened

10.16 Measure the camshaft lobe height (greatest dimension) with a micrometer

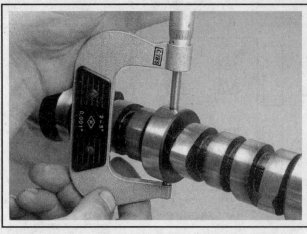

10.18 Measure each journal diameter with a micrometer. If any journal is less than the specified minimum, replace the camshaft

10.19a Lay a strip of Plastigage on each camshaft journal, in line with the camshaft

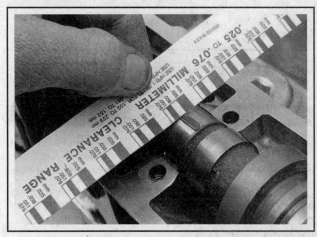

10.19b Compare the width of the crushed Plastigage to the scale on the package to determine the journal oil clearance

surface layer of each lobe. If any such signs are evident, replace the component concerned.

16 Measure the lobe height of each cam lobe on the intake camshaft, and record your measurements (see illustration). Compare the measurements for excessive variation; if the lobe heights vary more than 0.005 inch (0.125 mm), replace the camshaft. Compare the lobe height measurements on the exhaust camshaft and follow the same procedure. Do not compare intake camshaft lobe heights with exhaust camshaft lobe heights, as they are different. Only compare intake lobes with intake lobes and exhaust lobes with exhaust lobes.

17 Examine the camshaft bearing journals and the cylinder head bearing surfaces for signs of obvious wear or pitting. If any such signs are evident, consult an automotive machine shop for advice. Also check that the bearing oilways in the cylinder head are clear.

18 Using a micrometer, measure the diameter of each journal at several points (see illustration). If the diameter of any one journal is less than the specified value, replace the camshaft.

19 To check the bearing journal running clearance, use a suitable solvent and a clean lint-free rag to clean all bearing surfaces, then install the camshafts (without the cam followers) and bearing caps with a strip of Plastigage across each journal (see illustration). Tighten the

bearing cap bolts in the proper sequence (see Step 31) to the specified torque setting (do not rotate the camshafts), then remove the bearing caps and use the scale provided to measure the width of the compressed strips (see illustration). Scrape off the Plastigage with your fingernail or the edge of a credit card - don't scratch or nick the journals or bearing caps.

20 If the running clearance of any bearing is found to be worn to beyond the specified service limits, install a new camshaft and repeat the check; if the clearance is still excessive, the cylinder head must be replaced.

21 To check camshaft endplay, clean the bearing surfaces and install the camshafts (without the cam followers) and bearing caps. Tighten the bearing cap bolts to the specified torque, then measure the endplay using a dial indicator mounted on the cylinder head so that its tip bears on the camshaft right-hand end.

22 Tap the camshaft fully towards the gauge, zero the gauge, then tap the camshaft fully away from the gauge and note the gauge reading. If the endplay measured is found to be at or beyond the specified service limit, install a new camshaft and repeat the check; if the clearance is still excessive, the cylinder head must be replaced.

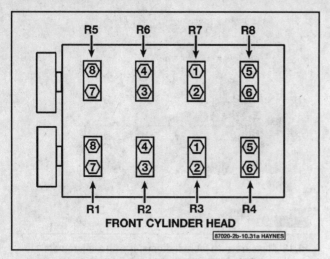

10.31a Camshaft bearing cap marks and tightening sequence for the front cylinder head

10.31b Camshaft bearing cap marks and tightening sequence for the rear cylinder head

INSTALLATION

23 Make sure the engine is positioned at 60-degrees before TDC for cylinder no. 1.

✳ CAUTION:

Do not install the camshafts with the engine at TDC number 1 or the valves and pistons will be damaged.

24 On reassembly, liberally oil the cylinder head cam follower bores and the cam followers. Carefully install the cam followers in the cylinder head, ensuring that each cam follower is reinstalled into its original bore, and is the correct way up.

25 It is highly recommended that new camshaft oil seals are installed, as a precaution against later failure.

26 Lubricate the camshaft journals and lobes with camshaft installation lubricant or clean engine oil.

Front cylinder head camshafts

27 Ensuring that each camshaft is in its original location, install the camshafts, locating the pin on the front of the exhaust camshaft at 12 o'clock and the pin on the intake camshaft at 7 o'clock. This position will allow the least spring tension on the valves and camshaft on initial installation.

Rear cylinder head camshafts

28 Ensuring that each camshaft is in its original location, install the camshafts, locating the pin on the front of the exhaust camshaft at 1 o'clock and the pin in the intake camshaft at 11 o'clock. This position will allow the least spring loaded tension on the valves and camshaft on initial installation.

Both cylinder head camshafts

♦ **Refer to illustrations 10.31a and 10.31b**

29 Apply a small amount of anaerobic sealant between the camshaft cap and the cylinder head on the front caps. This will prevent oil leaks.

30 Install each of the camshaft bearing caps to its previously-noted position, so that its numbered sides are aligned (see illustration 10.10).

31 Ensuring that each cap is kept square to the cylinder head as it is tightened down, tighten the camshaft bearing cap bolts slowly and a little at a time, in the proper sequence, until each cap touches the cylinder head (see illustrations). Tighten the camshaft caps to the torque listed in this Chapter's Specifications.

32 Wipe off all surplus sealant, so that none is left to find its way into any oilways. Follow the sealant manufacturer's instructions as to the time needed for curing.

33 Install the sprockets to the camshafts (see Section 8).

34 The remainder of the reassembly procedure, including installation of the timing belt, is as described in Section 8.

11 Cylinder heads - removal and installation

✳ CAUTION:

The engine must be completely cool when the cylinder heads are removed. Failure to allow the engine to cool off could result in cylinder head warpage.

➥**Note: Cylinder head removal is a difficult and time-consuming job requiring several special tools. Read through the procedure and obtain the necessary tools before beginning.**

REMOVAL

1 Disconnect the cable from the negative battery terminal (see Chapter 5, Section 1).

2 Drain the cooling system (see Chapter 1).

3 Remove the valve covers (see Section 4).

4 Remove the upper and lower intake manifolds and the intake manifold spacer (see Section 5).

5 Remove the coolant crossover housing (see Chapter 3).

11.24 Install the head gasket over the locating dowels

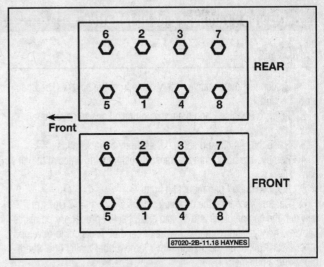

11.25 Cylinder head bolt tightening sequence

6 Remove the rear exhaust manifold (see Section 6). Disconnect the exhaust pipe from the front cylinder head.

7 Remove the timing belt (see Section 8).

8 Remove the camshaft sprockets and the rear timing belt cover (see Section 8).

9 Remove the upper radiator hose and the coolant extension housing (see Chapter 3).

10 Remove the exhaust camshafts (see Section 10).

11 Remove the dipstick tube.

12 Remove the PCM from its bracket.

13 Disconnect the ground wires from the heads.

14 Remove the rear engine lifting bracket.

15 Disconnect the oxygen sensor wiring and brackets.

16 Closely check the cylinder heads to make sure that all interfering hoses, wires and other components are removed.

17 Following the reverse of the tightening sequence (see illustration 11.25), use a breaker bar to remove the cylinder head bolts. Loosen the bolts 1/4-turn at a time.

18 Use a prybar at the corners of the cylinder head-to-engine block mating surface to break the cylinder head gasket seal. Do not pry between the cylinder head and engine block in the gasket sealing area.

19 Lift the cylinder head(s) off the engine. If the head is stuck, place a wood block against the end and strike the wood block with a hammer.

✳✳ **CAUTION:**

The cylinder heads are aluminum; store them on wood blocks to prevent damage to the gasket sealing surfaces.

20 Remove the cylinder head gasket(s). Before removing, note which gasket goes on which side (they are different and cannot be interchanged).

INSTALLATION

▶ **Refer to illustrations 11.24 and 11.25**

✳✳ **CAUTION:**

New cylinder head bolts must be used for reassembly. Failure to use new bolts may result in cylinder head gasket leakage and engine damage.

21 The mating surfaces of the cylinder heads and engine block must be perfectly clean when the cylinder heads are installed. Use a gasket scraper to remove all traces of carbon and old gasket material, then clean the mating surfaces with lacquer thinner or acetone. If there's oil on the mating surfaces when the cylinder heads are installed, the gaskets may not seal correctly and leaks may develop. When working on the engine block, cover the open areas of the engine with shop rags to keep debris out during repair and reassembly. Use a vacuum cleaner to remove any debris that falls into the cylinders.

✳✳ **CAUTION:**

Do not use abrasive wheels or sharp metal scrapers on the heads or block surface. Use a plastic scraper and chemical gasket remover, or the head gasket surfaces could have future leaks.

22 Check the engine block and cylinder head mating surfaces for nicks, deep scratches and other damage.

23 Use a tap of the correct size to chase the threads in the cylinder head bolt holes. Dirt, corrosion, sealant and damaged threads will affect torque readings.

24 Make sure the part numbers on the head gaskets face UP. Install the head gasket, locating the dowels in the alignment holes in the gaskets (see illustration).

25 Carefully position the cylinder heads on the engine block without disturbing the gaskets. Install the NEW cylinder head bolts. The cylinder head bolts are torque-to-yield design and they cannot be reused. Following the recommended sequence (see illustration), tighten the cylinder head bolts, in five steps, to the torque listed in this Chapter's Specifications.

➡**Note: The method used for the cylinder head bolt tightening procedure is referred to as "torque-angle" method. Follow the procedure exactly.**

Tighten the bolts in Step 1 using a torque wrench, then use a breaker bar and a torque-angle gauge for Steps 2 through 5.

26 The remaining installation steps are the reverse of removal.

27 Reconnect the battery (see Chapter 5, Section 1).

28 Change the engine oil and filter and refill the cooling system (see Chapter 1), then start the engine and check carefully for oil and coolant leaks.

12 Oil pan - removal and installation

REMOVAL

1   Disconnect the negative battery cable from the battery (see Chapter 5, Section 1).

2   Refer to Chapter 1 and drain the engine oil and remove the oil filter.

3   Raise the vehicle and support it securely on jackstands.

4   Remove the bolts from the transaxle bellhousing brace at the oil pan.

5   Remove the oil pan mounting bolts.

6   Carefully separate the oil pan from the engine block. Don't pry between the engine block and oil pan except at the proper pry points as damage to the sealing surfaces may result and oil leaks could develop. If necessary, dislodge the oil pan with a large rubber mallet or a wood block and a hammer.

INSTALLATION

◆ **Refer to illustrations 12.10a and 12.10b**

7   Use a gasket scraper or putty knife to remove all traces of old gasket material and sealant from the pan and engine block.

❋❋ CAUTION:

Be careful not to gouge the oil pan or block, or oil leaks could develop later.

8   Clean the mating surfaces with lacquer thinner or acetone. Make sure the bolt holes in the engine block are clean.

9   Install special alignment dowels (tool J-44715) into the designated holes (one forward and one rear) of the engine block reinforcement. These special tools allow the oil pan to remain aligned without sliding around.

10 Apply a 2 mm bead of RTV sealant to the flange of the oil pan, 3 mm from the inside edge. Apply a small amount of RTV sealant at the front and rear seams on the engine block, where the rear seal retainer and the oil pump meet the engine block (see illustrations).

11 Carefully position the oil pan against the engine block, then install the front bracket assembly and tighten the bolts finger tight. Install the bolts into the bellhousing brace/oil pan and tighten them finger tight. Apply thread locking compound to the threads of the oil pan bolts, then install them. Remove the alignment dowels and tighten the bolts to the torque listed in this Chapter's Specifications. Start at the center of the oil pan and work out toward the ends in a spiral pattern.

12 The remaining steps are the reverse of removal.

13 Install a new oil filter and fill the crankcase with oil (see Chapter 1).

14 Reconnect the battery (see Chapter 5, Section 1).

15 Start the engine and check carefully for oil leaks at the oil pan. Drive the vehicle and check again.

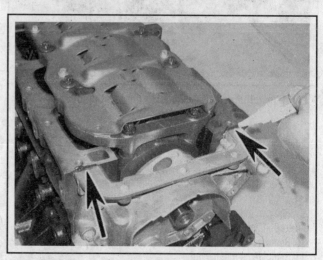

12.10a Apply a small amount of RTV sealant at the front and rear seams, where the oil pump meets the engine block . . .

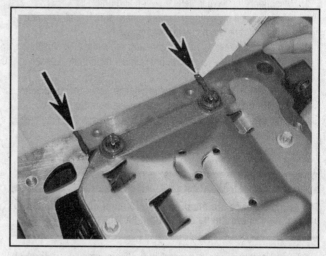

12.10b . . . and the rear seal retainer meets the engine block

13 Oil pump - removal, inspection and installation

REMOVAL

1   Disconnect the cable from the negative terminal of the battery (see Chapter 5, Section 1).

2   Raise the front of the vehicle and support it securely on jackstands.

3   Drain the engine oil (see Chapter 1).

4   Remove the drivebelt (see Chapter 1).

5   Remove the timing belt cover (see Section 7) and the timing belt (see Section 8).

6   Remove the rear timing belt cover.

7   Remove the air conditioning compressor and idler pulley bracket bolts. Tie the assembly out of the way with a piece of wire. Don't disconnect the refrigerant lines from the compressor.

13.13 Remove the oil pump cover from the oil pump housing

13.14a Note the locations of the rotor identification marks for correct reassembly - the rotor marks must face the same direction

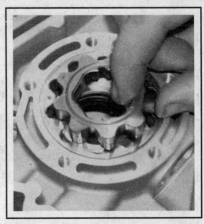

13.14b Lift the rotors from the oil pump housing for inspection

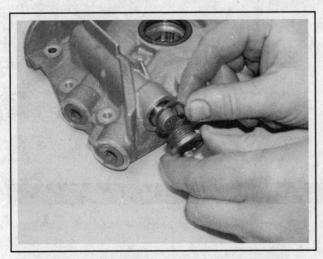

13.18a Remove the oil pressure relief valve components from the oil pump housing for inspection

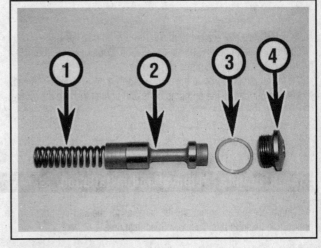

13.18b Oil pressure relief valve components

1   Spring
2   Plunger
3   Washer
4   Plug

8   Unbolt the alternator and move it out of the way, supporting it with a length of wire or rope.

9   Remove the oil pump suction tube. Discard the O-ring - it will have to be replaced.

10 Remove the crankshaft sprocket (see Section 9).

11 Remove the three oil pan-to-oil pump bolts.

12 Remove the main oil pump mounting bolts and separate the pump from the engine block.

INSPECTION

◆ **Refer to illustrations 13.13, 13.14a, 13.14b, 13.18a, 13.18b, 13.18c and 13.18d**

13 Working on the rear of the oil pump, loosen the oil pump cover screws a little at a time. Remove the oil pump cover (see illustration).

14 Note any identification marks on the rotors and withdraw the rotors from the pump body (see illustrations).

15 Thoroughly clean and dry the components.

16 Inspect the rotors for obvious wear or damage. If either rotor, the pump body or the cover is scored or damaged, the complete oil pump assembly must be replaced.

17 If the oil pump components are in acceptable condition, dip the rotors in clean engine oil and install them into the pump body with any identification marks positioned as noted during disassembly. Install the pump cover, tightening the screws securely.

18 Remove the oil pressure relief valve and oil control valve components from the oil pump body (see illustrations). Thoroughly clean and dry the components. Inspect the components for obvious wear or damage. Install them in the correct order (see illustrations).

INSTALLATION

19 Using a seal driver, install a new seal into the bore of the pump. Install a new gasket onto the engine block. Coat the oil pump side of the gasket with anaerobic sealant. Be careful to apply a thin layer of

13.18c Remove the oil pressure control valve components from the oil pump housing

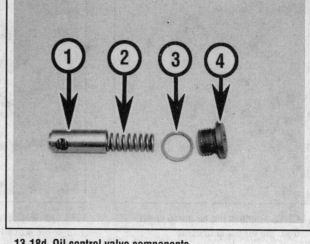

13.18d Oil control valve components

1	Plunger	3	Sealing washer
2	Spring	4	Plug

sealant and keep any sealant from entering the oil passageways.

20 Prime the oil pump prior to installation. Pour clean oil into the pick-up port and turn the pump by hand.

21 Install the oil pump to the engine. Apply a non-hardening thread-locking compound to the oil pump bolts and tighten them to the torque listed in this Chapter's Specifications.

22 The remainder of installation is the reverse of removal procedure.

23 Reconnect the battery (see Chapter 5, Section 1).

24 Install a new oil filter and fill the crankcase with oil (see Chapter 1). Start the engine and check for proper oil pressure and leaks.

14 Driveplate - removal and installation

This procedure is essentially the same as for the four-cylinder engine. Refer to Part A and follow the procedure outlined there. However, use the bolt torque listed in this Chapter's Specifications.

15 Rear main oil seal - replacement

This procedure is essentially the same as for the four-cylinder engine. Refer to Chapter 2, Part A and follow the procedure outlined there.

16 Engine mounts - check and replacement

This procedure is essentially the same as for the four-cylinder engine. Refer to Chapter 2, Part A and follow the procedure outlined there.

Specifications

General

Displacement	182 cubic inches (3.0 liters)
Bore and stroke	3.44 x 3.40 inches (86.0 x 85.0 mm)
Cylinder numbers (front to rear)	
Front cylinder head	2-4-6
Rear cylinder head	1-3-5
Firing order	1-2-3-4-5-6

```
┌─────────────────────┐
│  ①   ③   ⑤          │   FRONT OF
│                     │   VEHICLE
│  ②   ④   ⑥          │      ↓
└─────────────────────┘
      1-2-3-4-5-6
                        87020-B-SPECS HAYNES
```

Cylinder location and firing order

Camshaft and cam followers

Endplay	0.0016 to 0.0057 inch (0.040 to 0.144 mm)
Lobe lift (intake and exhaust)	Not available
Allowable lobe lift variation	0.005 inch (0.125 mm)
Journal diameter (all)	1.099 to 1.100 inches (27.939 to 27.960 mm)
Journal-to-bearing (oil) clearance	
Standard	0.0015 to 0.0020 inch (0.038 to 0.050 mm)
Service limit	0.002 inch maximum (0.05 mm)
Cam follower diameter	1.2976 to 1.2982 inches (32.959 to 32.975 mm)
Cam follower oil clearance	0.0010 to 0.0026 inch (0.025 to 0.066 mm)

Torque specifications

	Ft-lbs (unless otherwise indicated)	Nm

➡**Note: One foot-pound (ft-lb) of torque is equivalent to 12 inch-pounds (in-lbs) of torque. Torque values below approximately 15 ft-lbs are expressed in inch-pounds, since most foot-pound torque wrenches are not accurate at these smaller values.**

	Ft-lbs (unless otherwise indicated)	Nm
Camshaft sprocket bolts*		
Step 1	37	50
Step 2	Tighten an additional 60-degrees	
Step 3	Tighten an additional 15-degrees	
Camshaft cap bolts	71 in-lbs	8
Drivebelt tensioner bolts	18	24
Crankshaft sprocket bolt		
Step 1	184	249
Step 2	Tighten an additional 45-degrees	
Step 3	Tighten an additional 15-degrees	
Cylinder head bolts*		
Step 1	18	24
Step 2	Tighten an additional 90-degrees	
Step 3	Tighten an additional 90-degrees	
Step 4	Tighten an additional 90-degrees	
Step 5	Tighten an additional 15-degrees	
Crankshaft pulley bolts	15	20
Driveplate bolts		
Step 1	48	65
Step 2	Tighten an additional 30-degrees	
Step 3	Tighten an additional 15-degrees	
Engine lifting bracket bolts	71 in-lbs	8
Exhaust manifold-to-cylinder head nuts	15	20
Exhaust pipe-to-exhaust manifold nuts	25	34
Engine mount bracket bolts	41	56

Bolt(s) must be replaced.

➡**Note: One foot-pound (ft-lb) of torque is equivalent to 12 inch-pounds (in-lbs) of torque. Torque values below approximately 15 ft-lbs are expressed in inch-pounds, since most foot-pound torque wrenches are not accurate at these smaller values.**

Intake manifold		
Upper intake manifold bolts/nut	66 in-lbs	7.5
Lower intake manifold bolts	132 in-lbs	15
Oil pan-to-engine block bolts		
Front bracket-to-oil pan bolts	30	40
Transaxle bellhousing brace-to-oil pan bolts	48	65
Oil pan bolts	132 in-lbs	15
Oil pump-to-engine block mounting bolts	80 in-lbs	9
Oil pick-up tube bolts	71 in-lbs	8
Power steering pump pulley bolts	71 in-lbs	8
Timing belt cover bolts	71 in-lbs	8
Timing belt upper guide pulley bolt	30	40
Timing belt lower guide pulley bolt	30	40
Timing belt tensioner bolt	15	20
Valve cover bolts	71 in-lbs	8
Water pump pulley bolts	71 in-lbs	8

Bolt(s) must be replaced.

Notes

Notes

2C

3.5L V6 ENGINES

Section

Reference to other Chapters

1 General information

This Part of Chapter 2 is devoted to in-vehicle repair procedures for the 3.5L V6 engine. Since these procedures are based on the assumption that the engine is installed in the vehicle, many of the steps outlined in this Part of Chapter 2 will not apply if the engine has been removed.

A "RAHA" system (Rocker Arm Hydraulic Actuator) is used on all models. The RAHA system is nearly identical to the VTEC system which is Honda's design for Variable Valve Timing and Lift Electronic Control (V-TEC). Refer to Chapter 6 for additional information.

2 Repair operations possible with the engine in the vehicle

Many major repair operations can be accomplished without removing the engine from the vehicle.

Clean the engine compartment and the exterior of the engine with some type of degreaser before any work is done. It will make the job easier and help keep dirt out of the internal areas of the engine.

When working on the engine, cover the fenders to prevent damage to the paint. Special pads are available, but an old bedspread or blanket will also work.

If vacuum, exhaust, oil or coolant leaks develop, indicating a need for gasket or seal replacement, the repairs can generally be made with the engine in the vehicle. The intake and exhaust manifold gaskets, oil pan gasket, crankshaft front oil seal and cylinder head gaskets are all accessible with the engine in place.

Exterior engine components, such as the intake and exhaust manifolds, the oil pan, the oil pump, the water pump (see Chapter 3), the starter motor, the alternator, the ignition coils (see Chapter 5) and the fuel system components (see Chapter 4) can be removed for repair with the engine in place.

Since the cylinder heads can be removed without pulling the engine, valve component servicing can also be accomplished with the engine in the vehicle. Replacement of the camshafts, timing belt and sprockets is also possible with the engine in the vehicle.

In extreme cases caused by a lack of necessary equipment, repair or replacement of piston rings, pistons, connecting rods and rod bearings is possible with the engine in the vehicle. However, this practice is not recommended because of the cleaning and preparation work that must be done to the components involved.

3 Top Dead Center (TDC) for number one piston - locating

▶ Refer to illustrations 3.5 and 3.6

1 Top Dead Center (TDC) is the highest point in the cylinder that each piston reaches as it travels up-and-down during crankshaft rotation. Each piston reaches TDC on the compression stroke and again on the exhaust stroke, but TDC generally refers to piston position on the compression stroke.

2 Positioning the piston(s) at TDC is an essential part of certain repair procedures discussed in this manual.

3 Before beginning this procedure, be sure to place the transaxle in Neutral and apply the parking brake or block the rear wheels. Remove the ignition coils and the spark plugs, as this will make the crankshaft much easier to turn (see Chapter 1).

4 In order to bring any piston to TDC, the crankshaft must be turned using one of the methods outlined below. When looking at the front of the engine, normal crankshaft rotation is clockwise.

※※ WARNING:

If method b) or c) is used, disable the fuel system by removing the fuel pump relay from the underhood fuse block.

a) *The preferred method is to turn the crankshaft with a socket and ratchet attached to the bolt threaded into the front of the crankshaft.*

b) *A remote starter switch, which may save some time, can also be used. Follow the instructions included with the switch. Once the piston is close to TDC, use a socket and ratchet as described in the previous paragraph.*

c) *If an assistant is available to turn the ignition switch to the Start position in short bursts, you can get the piston close to TDC without a remote starter switch. Make sure your assistant is out of the vehicle, away from the ignition switch, then use a socket and ratchet as described in Paragraph a) to complete the procedure.*

5 Turn the crankshaft until the TDC notch on the crankshaft pulley is aligned with the pointer on the timing belt lower cover (see illustration).

6 Locate the camshaft sprocket timing mark on the front cylinder bank. Look through the hole in the timing belt cover to check that the camshaft sprocket timing mark is aligned with the mark on the cover (see illustration). If the no. 1 mark is not showing, rotate the crankshaft clockwise one revolution and realign the marks.

7 When the crankshaft pulley timing marks are aligned, and the "1" mark on the camshaft sprocket is aligned with its mark on the cover, the number one piston is at TDC on the compression stroke.

8 After the number one piston has been positioned at TDC on the compression stroke, TDC for any of the remaining pistons can be located by turning the crankshaft clockwise and following the firing order, aligning the cylinder number on the camshaft sprocket with the pointer on the timing belt cover (they're arranged in the firing order).

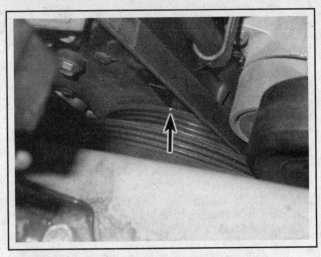

3.5 Align the TDC mark on the crankshaft pulley with the pointer

3.6 Position the inspection hole cover aside and check the alignment of the camshaft sprocket timing mark with the mark on the timing belt cover (there is an inspection hole on each cylinder bank) - the numeral 1 is visible when the number 1 piston is at TDC

4   Valve covers - removal and installation

REMOVAL

▶ **Refer to illustrations 4.11a and 4.11b**

. 1   Disconnect the cable from the negative terminal of the battery (see Chapter 5, Section 1).

2   Remove the ignition coils (see Chapter 5).

Left (front) valve cover

3   Remove the engine oil dipstick.

4   Remove the PCV valve and its bolt (see Chapter 6).

Right valve cover

5   Disconnect the wiring from the MAP sensor, the IAT sensor and the ECT sensor (see Chapter 6).

6   Disconnect the hose from the EVAP purge valve.

7   Refer to Section 6 and remove the intake manifold.

8   Disconnect the wiring from the fuel injectors.

Both valve covers

9   Remove the wiring bracket from the head. Make sure that all of the interfering wiring and hoses are disconnected.

10   Remove the ignition coils (see Chapter 5).

11   Remove the retaining bolts (see illustrations), then lift the valve cover off. If the cover is stuck to the head, bump the end with a block of wood and a hammer to jar it loose.

❊❊ CAUTION:

Don't pry at the cover-to-head joint or damage to the sealing surfaces may occur, leading to oil leaks after the cover is reinstalled.

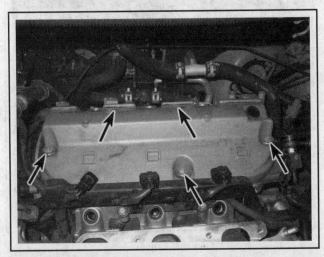

4.11a Valve cover retaining bolts (rear valve cover)

4.11b Valve cover retaining bolts (front valve cover)

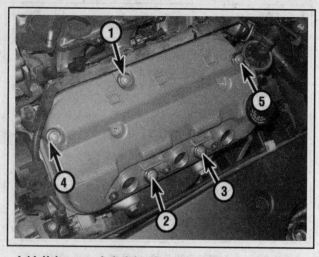

4.14 Valve cover bolt tightening sequence

12 Remove the original gasket and seal washers and clean the mating surfaces of the cylinder head and valve cover. If you removed the front valve cover, remove and inspect the PCV valve (see Chapter 1).

INSTALLATION

♦ **Refer to illustration 4.14**

13 Position a new gasket in the groove and install new sealing washers on the bolts. Also make sure to replace the spark plug seals.

14 Install the cover and tighten the bolts, a little at a time, to the torque listed in this Chapter's Specifications. Follow the correct torque sequence (see illustration).

15 Reinstall the remaining components.

16 Reconnect the battery. Refer to Chapter 5, Section 1.

17 Run the engine and check for oil leaks.

---

5 Valve clearance - check and adjustment

CHECK

1 The valve clearance generally does not need adjustment unless valvetrain components have been replaced, a valve job has been performed or if the valves are noisy.

2 The simplest check for proper valve adjustment is to listen carefully to the engine running with the hood open. If the valvetrain is noisy, adjustment is necessary.

3 The valve clearance must be checked and adjusted with the engine cold.

ADJUSTMENT

♦ **Refer to illustrations 5.6, 5.7 and 5.9**

4 Remove the valve covers (see Section 4).

5 Rotate the crankshaft clockwise and position the number one piston at TDC (see Section 3).

6 In this position, adjust the valves for cylinder number one (see illustration). There are four valves for each cylinder.

7 Starting with the intake valve, insert a feeler gauge of the correct thickness (see this Chapter's Specifications) between the valve stem and the rocker arm (see illustration). Withdraw it; you should feel a slight drag. If there's no drag or a heavy drag, loosen the adjuster nut and back off the adjuster screw. Carefully tighten the adjuster screw until you can feel a slight drag on the feeler gauge as you withdraw it.

8 Hold the adjuster screw with a screwdriver to keep it from turning and tighten the locknut. Recheck the clearance to make sure it hasn't changed. Repeat the procedure in this Step and the previous Step on the other intake valve, then on the two exhaust valves.

9 Rotate the crankshaft pulley clockwise until the number 4 on the camshaft sprocket is aligned with the pointer on the timing belt cover

(see illustration 3.6). Check and adjust the number 4 cylinder valves (see illustration).

10 Rotate the crankshaft pulley 120-degrees clockwise until the number 2 cylinder is at TDC. Check and adjust the number 2 cylinder valves.

11 Rotate the crankshaft pulley clockwise until the number "5" shows at the camshaft cover and adjust the number five cylinder valves.

12 Rotate the crankshaft pulley clockwise until the number "3" shows at the camshaft cover and adjust the number three cylinder valves.

13 Rotate the crankshaft pulley clockwise until the number "6" shows at the camshaft cover and adjust the number six cylinder valves.

14 Refer to Section 4 and install the valve covers.

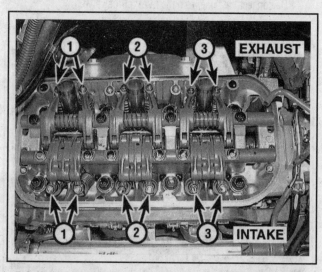

5.6 Valve layout for the rear cylinder head

5.7 Insert a feeler gauge between the valve stem and the rocker arm, loosen the locknut with a box end wrench and adjust the clearance with a screwdriver

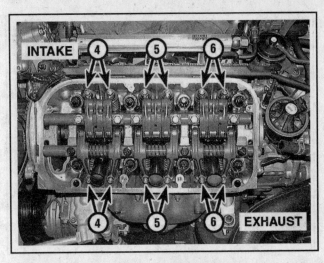

5.9 Valve layout for the front cylinder head

6 Intake manifold - removal and installation

✳✳ WARNING:

Wait until the engine is completely cool before beginning this procedure.

UPPER INTAKE MANIFOLD AND SPACER

▶ Refer to illustrations 6.9, 6.10, 6.11, 6.12a and 6.12b

1 If you're also going to be removing the lower intake manifold, relieve the fuel pressure (see Chapter 4).

2 Disconnect the cable from the negative terminal of the battery (see Chapter 5, Section 1).

3 Remove the breather hose and the air intake duct (see Chapter 4).

4 Disconnect the vacuum hoses and other connections from the throttle body.

5 Remove the throttle body (see Chapter 4).

6 Disconnect the brake booster hose and the PCV hoses from the intake manifold.

7 Remove the interfering engine harness connectors (IAT, IAC, MAP, EVAP canister, etc.) from their respective components. Label each connector with tape to insure correct reassembly. Remove the air outlet duct bracket.

8 Remove the intake manifold cover.

➡Note: Follow the reverse order of the tightening sequence (see illustration 6.12b).

9 Following the reverse of the tightening sequence (see illustration 6.11), remove the bolts and nuts and remove the manifold (see illustration).

10 Remove the spacer and gaskets (see illustration).

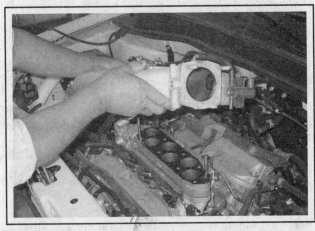

6.9 Lift the upper intake manifold from the engine . . .

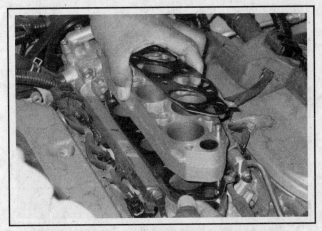

6.10 . . . then remove the spacer plate, if equipped

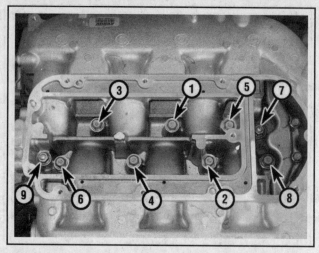

6.11 Upper intake manifold bolt tightening sequence

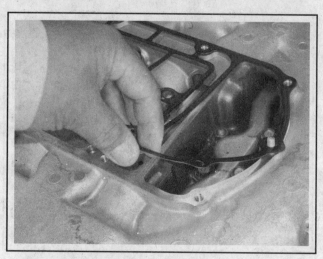

6.12a Install a new intake manifold cover gasket on the upper intake manifold

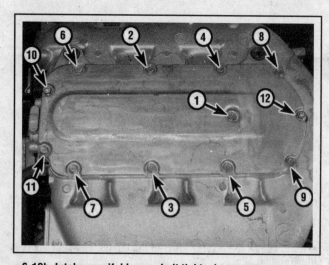

6.12b Intake manifold cover bolt tightening sequence

6.16 Location of the lower intake manifold mounting fasteners - the four corner nuts are hidden from view

11 To install the upper manifold, clean the mounting surfaces of the upper and lower manifold and remove all traces of the old gasket material or sealant. Install the new gasket over the studs on the lower manifold, then install the spacer (if removed) and upper intake manifold. Tighten the fasteners in sequence (see illustration) to the torque listed in this Chapter's Specifications.

12 Install the intake manifold cover and tighten the bolts in sequence (see illustrations) to the torque listed in this Chapter's Specifications.

13 The remainder of installation is the reverse of the removal procedure. Reconnect the battery (see Chapter 5, Section 1). Check the coolant level and add some, if necessary (see Chapter 1).

LOWER INTAKE MANIFOLDS

▶ **Refer to illustration 6.16**

14 Remove the upper intake manifold and the spacer plate (see Steps 1 through 10).

15 Remove the fuel rails and injectors from the lower intake mani-

folds (see Chapter 4).

16 Remove the mounting fasteners, then detach the two lower intake manifold sections from the cylinder heads (see illustration). If they are stuck, don't pry between the gasket mating surfaces or damage may result.

17 Carefully use a scraper to remove all traces of old gasket material and sealant from the manifold and cylinder heads, then clean the mating surfaces with brake system cleaner.

18 Install new gaskets, then position the lower manifolds on the cylinder heads. Make sure the gaskets and manifolds are aligned over the dowels in the cylinder heads and install the nuts/bolts.

19 Tighten the fasteners, a little at a time, to the torque listed in this Chapter's Specifications. Work from the center out towards the ends to avoid warping the manifolds.

20 Install the upper intake manifold.

21 The remainder of the installation is the reverse of the removal procedure. Check the coolant level and add some, if necessary (see Chapter 1). Run the engine and check for fuel, vacuum and coolant leaks.

7 Upper catalytic converters - removal and installation

❄❄ WARNING:

The engine must be completely cool before beginning this procedure.

➡Note: These models are not equipped with separate exhaust manifolds but instead use catalytic converter assemblies bolted directly to the cylinder heads.

REMOVAL

♦ **Refer to illustration 7.4**

1   Disconnect the cable from the negative terminal of the battery (see Chapter 5, Section 1).

2   Spray penetrating oil on the exhaust fasteners and allow it to soak in.

3   Block the rear wheels to prevent the vehicle from rolling. Set the parking brake and place the transaxle in Park. Raise the front of the vehicle and support it securely on jackstands. Remove the splash guard from below the engine compartment.

4   Disconnect the exhaust pipes from the catalytic converters (see illustration).

5   Disconnect the oxygen sensor wiring.

6   If you're working on a rear catalytic converter, remove its mounting bracket.

7   Remove the front air dam if working on a front converter. Refer to Chapter 3 and position the cooling fan/radiator assembly forward slightly to allow clearance for removing the front catalytic converter.

8   Remove the nuts retaining the converter to the cylinder head and remove it.

INSTALLATION

9   Use a scraper to remove any traces of old gasket material and carbon deposits from the manifold and cylinder head mating surfaces.

10   Position a new gasket over the cylinder head studs.

11   Install the catalytic converter and thread the mounting nuts into place. Tighten the nuts to the torque listed in this Chapter's Specifications in three equal steps.

12   Reinstall the remaining parts in the reverse order of removal. Apply engine oil to the studs and install the nuts.

13   Reconnect the battery. Refer to Chapter 5, Section 1.

14   Run the engine and check for exhaust leaks.

7.4 Remove the exhaust pipe-to-catalytic converter nuts (third nut not visible here)

8 Timing belt and sprockets - removal, inspection and installation

❄❄ CAUTION ❄❄

The timing system is complex. Severe engine damage will occur if you make any mistakes. Do not attempt this procedure unless you are highly experienced with this type of repair. If you are at all unsure of your abilities, consult an expert. Double-check all your work and be sure everything is correct before you attempt to start the engine.

REMOVAL

♦ **Refer to illustrations 8.7a, 8.7b, 8.8, 8.9a, 8.9b, 8.10, 8.11, 8.12, 8.13, 8.14, 8.15 and 8.16**

1   Disconnect the cable from the negative terminal of the battery (see Chapter 5, Section 1).

2   Place the transaxle in Park, apply the parking brake and block the rear wheels.

3   Remove the drivebelt (see Chapter 1).

4   Remove the spark plugs to make it easier to turn the crankshaft (see Chapter 1), then position the number one piston at TDC (see Section 3).

5   Loosen the lug nuts on the right front wheel. Raise the front of the vehicle and support it securely on jackstands. Remove the right front wheel.

6   Remove the right front inner fender splash shield.

7   Remove the upper timing belt covers (see illustrations).

8   If you intend to re-use the belt, mark the belt to indicate the direction of rotation (see illustration).

9   Make sure the timing marks are properly aligned (see illustrations).

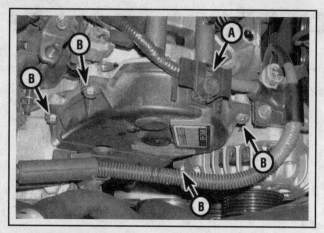

8.7a Detach the wiring harness from the retainer (A) and remove the bolts (B) from the upper timing belt cover (front cylinder bank)

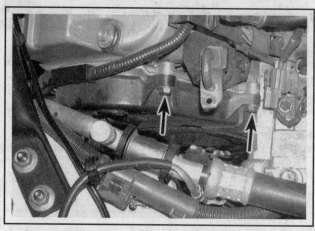

8.7b Remove the upper timing belt cover from the rear cylinder bank (arrows indicate two of the four bolts)

8.8 Mark the direction of rotation on the timing belt

8.9a Camshaft timing marks (front cylinder bank) - align the mark on the sprocket with the mark on the rear cover

8.9b Camshaft sprocket timing marks - rear cylinder bank

10 Wedge a large screwdriver into the driveplate ring gear teeth, then have an assistant unscrew the crankshaft pulley bolt (see illustration).

➡**Note 1: Access to the driveplate varies between models. Some have inspection covers that must be removed and others require the removal of the starter.**

➡**Note 2: When the crankshaft pulley bolt is loosened, the position of the timing marks on the crankshaft pulley and the camshafts may be disturbed. Check and align them again. Temporarily reinstall the crankshaft pulley bolt to turn the crankshaft.**

11 Remove the lower timing belt cover (see illustration).

12 Slip the timing belt guide plate off the crankshaft sprocket, noting how it's installed. Also note the alignment of the crankshaft sprocket timing marks (see illustration).

13 Obtain a long bolt of the proper size and thread pitch to fit into the threaded boss near the timing belt tensioner pulley. Bevel the threaded end somewhat with a file or grinder. Thread the bolt into the boss so that it pushes against the timing belt tensioner - the bolt is used to hold the tensioner in position (see illustration). Do not apply excessive force when tightening.

14 Remove the idler pulley bolt (see illustration), then remove the timing belt.

➡**Note: Discard the idler pulley bolt; a new one should be used upon installation.**

15 The camshaft sprockets can be removed at this point, if they are damaged or to replace the oil seals (see illustration). Remove the keys from the shafts so they don't fall out and get lost.

※※ **CAUTION:**

Don't allow the camshaft(s) to turn.

16 If it's worn or damaged, or if you're replacing the crankshaft front oil seal, the crankshaft sprocket can now be removed (see illustration). If it won't come off by hand, carefully pry it off.

➡**Note: Before removing the sprocket, remove the Crankshaft Position (CKP) sensor (see Chapter 6).**

INSPECTION

17 Inspect the sprocket teeth for wear and damage. Check the timing belt for any cracks or oil residue. Also check the camshaft for excessive endplay (see Section 11). Check the timing belt tensioner for smooth

8.10 Use a long ratchet or breaker bar to loosen the crankshaft pulley bolt, as it can be very tight

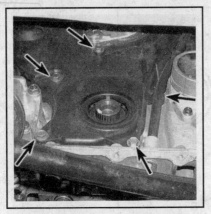

8.11 Remove the bolts and the lower timing belt cover (not all bolts are visible here)

8.12 Crankshaft sprocket timing marks

8.13 Thread a long bolt (A) into the boss as shown to hold the timing belt adjuster (B) in position

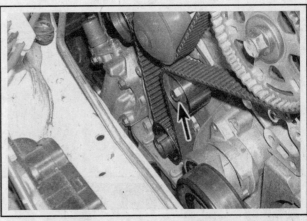

8.14 Loosen the timing belt idler, remove the idler pulley and the timing belt

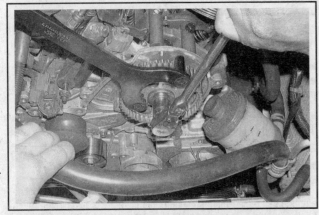

8.15 Use a two-pin spanner to prevent the camshaft from turning while you loosen the sprocket bolt

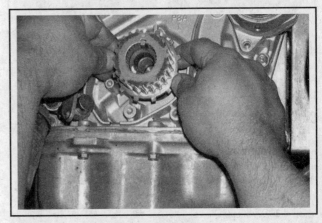

8.16 Remove the crankshaft sprocket

operation. Replace any worn parts with new ones.

18 Inspect the water pump (see Chapter 3).

➡**Note: Because of the work involved in getting at the water pump, it's a good idea to replace the water pump whenever the timing belt is removed.**

INSTALLATION

▶ **Refer to illustration 8.22**

19 Remove all dirt and oil from the timing belt area. Clean the teeth of the sprockets with brake system cleaner.

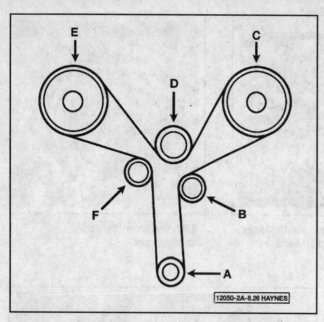

8.22 Timing belt routing

A   Crankshaft sprocket
B   Idler pulley
C   Camshaft sprocket (front cylinder bank)
D   Water pump pulley
E   Camshaft sprocket (rear cylinder bank)
F   Tensioner

8.32 Compress the tensioner by prying against the pulley (A) until the holes on the rod and tensioner body are in alignment, then insert a pin (B) with a diameter of 0.08 inch (2.0 mm), locking the tensioner in a retracted position

20 If any of the timing belt sprockets were removed, install them now with their keys and tighten the bolts to the torque listed in this Chapter's Specifications.

21 Install the idler pulley using a new bolt, but don't tighten the bolt yet (just finger-tight).

22 Recheck the position of the timing marks (see illustrations 8.9a, 8.9b and 8.12). Install the timing belt in a clockwise direction, starting at the crankshaft sprocket and tensioner pulley, then rear camshaft sprocket, water pump, front camshaft sprocket, and idler pulley (see illustration). If you're re-using the original belt, the arrow you made in

Step 9 should point in the normal direction of rotation.

➡**Note: If you're installing a new timing belt, or if the tensioner piston has extended and you're unable to install the original timing belt, remove the tensioner and compress the piston as described in Steps 31 through 33.**

23 Install the outer timing belt guide over the crankshaft sprocket with the concave side facing away from the belt.

24 Tighten the idler pulley bolt to the torque listed in this Chapter's Specifications. Remove the long bolt that was holding the tensioner pulley in position (see illustration 8.13).

25 Turn the crankshaft slowly six revolutions clockwise using a socket and breaker bar on the crankshaft pulley bolt to seat the belt, then return to TDC. Recheck the alignment of cam and crank sprocket timing marks.

✳✳ CAUTION:

If you feel any resistance, back up and recheck all timing marks. Do not force the crankshaft to turn or engine damage will occur! If you feel any resistance, STOP! There is something wrong - most likely valves are contacting the pistons. You must find the problem before proceeding. Check your work and see if any updated repair information is available.

26 Install the lower timing belt cover.

27 Install the crankshaft pulley, aligning the pulley keyway with the crankshaft key. Install the bolt and tighten it to the torque listed in this Chapter's Specifications. Use the method described in Step 10 to keep the crankshaft from turning.

28 Recheck the timing marks (see illustrations 8.9a, 8.9b and 8.12).

✳✳ CAUTION:

If the timing marks are not aligned exactly as shown, repeat the timing belt installation procedure. DO NOT start the engine until you're absolutely certain that the timing belt is installed correctly. Serious and costly engine damage could occur if the belt is installed incorrectly.

39 The remainder of the installation is the reverse of removal.

30 Run the engine and check for coolant or oil leaks.

➡**Note: If the CHECK ENGINE light comes on after starting the engine, have a dealer service department perform a crankshaft position variation learn procedure with a factory scan tool.**

TENSIONER RETRACTING/REPLACEMENT

▶ **Refer to illustration 8.32**

31 The belt tensioner does not normally need to be removed for a timing belt replacement procedure, but there are other engine procedures that require the tensioner be removed. Once removed, the tensioner piston will extend in length. The following Steps apply only if the tensioner has been removed from the engine.

32 Compress the tensioner in a press until you can insert a drill bit or other pin (0.080-inch or 2 mm diameter) into the tensioner to hold it in the retracted position (see illustration).

33 Install the tensioner, being careful not to dislodge the locating pin, and tighten the mounting bolts to the torque listed in this Chapter's Specifications. After completing the remainder of the timing belt installation procedure, remove the tensioner locating pin.

9 Crankshaft front oil seal - replacement

▶ Refer to illustrations 9.2 and 9.4

1 Remove the timing belt (see Section 8), the crankshaft position sensor (see Chapter 6) and the crankshaft sprocket (see Section 8).

2 Carefully pry the seal out of the engine with a screwdriver or seal removal tool (see illustration). Be careful not to scratch the housing bore or damage the crankshaft (if the crankshaft is scratched, the new seal will end up leaking).

3 Clean the oil seal bore and coat the outer edge of the new seal with a small amount of engine oil to ease installation. Also lubricate the seal lip.

4 Using a seal driver or a socket with an outside diameter slightly smaller than the outside diameter of the seal, carefully drive the new seal into place with a hammer (see illustration). Make sure it's installed squarely and driven in to the same depth as the original.

5 Reinstall the crankshaft sprocket and timing belt (see Section 8).

6 Run the engine and check for oil leaks at the front seal.

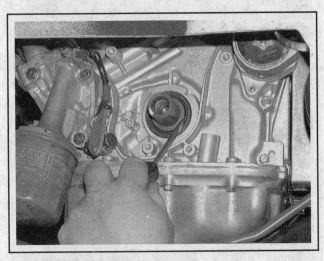

9.2 Carefully pry out the oil seal

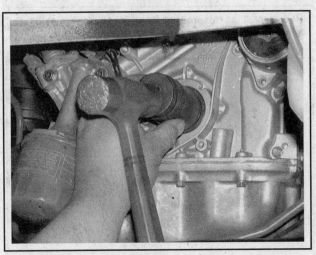

9.4 Lubricate the seal lip and tap the new crankshaft seal into place with a seal driver or a large socket and a hammer

10 Rocker arm assembly - removal, inspection and installation

REMOVAL

1 Remove the valve cover (see Section 4).

2 Completely loosen all of the valve adjusting locknuts and screws.

3 Loosen the rocker shaft mounting bolts 1/2-turn at a time, in the reverse of the tightening sequence, until the spring force is relieved (see illustrations 10.11a and 10.11b).

4 Lift the rocker arms and shaft assembly from the cylinder head. Do not remove the shaft mounting bolts; they will keep the rocker arm assembly components together.

INSPECTION

▶ Refer to illustrations 10.5, 10.6, 10.7 and 10.8

5 If you wish to disassemble and inspect the rocker arm assembly (a good idea as long as you have them off), remove the mounting bolts and slip the rocker arms and springs off the shafts (see illustration). Keep the parts in order so you can reassemble them in the same positions.

➡Note: Keep the rocker arms for each cylinder together by wrapping them with a heavy rubber band.

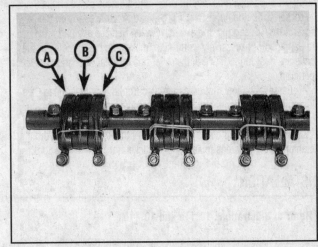

10.5 RAHA intake rocker arm components (note the rubber bands installed to hold the components together)

A Primary intake rocker arm
B Mid intake rocker arm
C Secondary intake rocker arm

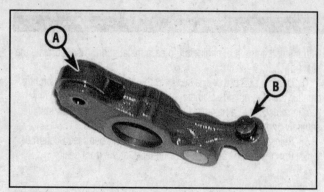

10.6 Inspect the rockers arms for wear and damage at the roller (A) and the valve stem end of the adjusters (B)

10.8 Check for smooth movement of the piston in each RAHA rocker arm

10.7 Push down on the plunger of each lost motion assembly - they should move smoothly

10.11a Rocker arm/shaft mounting bolts TIGHTENING sequence - front cylinder head

10.11b Rocker arm/shaft mounting bolts TIGHTENING sequence - rear cylinder head

6   Thoroughly clean the parts and inspect them for wear and damage. Check the rocker arm faces that contact the camshaft and the rocker arm tips (see illustration). Check the surfaces of the shafts that the rocker arms ride on, as well as the bearing surfaces inside the rocker arms, for scoring and excessive wear. Replace any parts that are damaged or excessively worn. Also, make sure the oil holes in the shafts are not plugged. Check the roller tips for wear and smoothness of operation.

7   Remove the lost motion assemblies from the cylinder head (see illustration), and clean them. Check for smoothness of plunger operation by pushing down gently with your finger.

8   Check the smoothness of operation of the Rocker Arm Hydraulic Actuator (RAHA) pistons in each intake rocker arm (see illustration).

INSTALLATION

▶ **Refer to illustrations 10.11a and 10.11b**

9   Lubricate all components with engine oil and reassemble the shafts. When installing the rocker arms, shafts and springs, note the markings and the difference between the left and right side parts.

10 Coat the wear surfaces of the rocker arms with camshaft installation lubricant and install the rocker arm assembly.

11 Tighten the rocker shaft (or bridge) mounting bolts a little at a time, following the recommended tightening sequence, to the torque listed in this Chapter's Specifications (see illustrations).

12 The remainder of installation is the reverse of removal.

13 Adjust the valve clearances (see Section 5).

14 Run the engine and check for oil leaks and proper operation.

11 Camshafts - removal, inspection and installation

✳✳ WARNING:

Wait until the engine is completely cool before beginning this procedure.

REMOVAL

▶ **Refer to illustrations 11.16 and 11.17**

1 If you're removing the camshaft from the rear cylinder head, relieve the fuel system pressure (see Chapter 4).

2 Remove the valve covers (see Section 4).

3 Remove the timing belt (see Section 8).

4 Remove the rocker arms/shafts as an assembly (see Section 10).

➡**Note: Refer to the Inspection procedures below and check camshaft endplay before removing the camshafts.**

5 Remove the camshaft sprockets (see Section 8).

6 Remove the battery (see Chapter 5).

7 Disconnect the wire harness retainers from the fuse block.

8 Release the plastic clips, lift the fuse block and move it to the rear.

9 Remove the battery tray.

Front camshaft

10 Refer to Chapter 1 and drain the coolant.

11 Remove the upper radiator hose.

12 Remove the EGR valve (see Chapter 6).

Rear camshaft

13 Remove the underhood fuse box or position it out of the way.

14 Disconnect the interfering engine wiring harness connectors. Move the harnesses aside.

15 Refer to Chapter 4 and disconnect the fuel supply line at the fuel rail.

Both camshafts

16 Remove the camshaft retainer plate and its O-ring (see illustration).

17 Carefully slide the camshaft out of the cylinder head, being careful not to nick the bearings as you withdraw it (see illustration).

INSPECTION

▶ **Refer to illustrations 11.20a and 11.20b**

18 Keeping careful track of the location of the components, remove the rocker arms and springs from the rocker shafts and bolt the bare rocker shafts to the cylinder head, tightening them to the torque listed in this Chapter's Specifications.

19 Mount a dial indicator so that it contacts the nose of the camshaft. Pry the camshaft forwards and back with a screwdriver (wrap the tip with tape to prevent damage to the camshaft). Record the movement of the dial indicator and compare it to this Chapter's Specifications. If the endplay is excessive, install a new retainer plate and check the endplay again. If the endplay is still excessive, the camshaft must be replaced.

20 Remove the retainer plate and slide the camshaft out of the head. Measure the journal diameters and lobe heights on each camshaft, comparing your measurements to this Chapter's Specifications. Check also for visual signs of wear, scoring, pitting or overheating.

➡**Note: The arrangement of lobes is different between the front and rear camshafts (see illustrations).**

11.16 Remove the bolts and the camshaft retainer plate

11.17 Pull the camshaft straight out of the cylinder head, taking care not to nick the journals or bearings

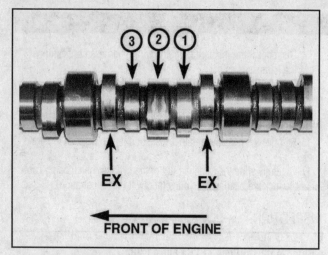

11.20a Arrangement of camshaft lobes on the left cylinder bank (front) camshaft

| 1 | Primary intake lobe | 3 | Secondary intakelobe |
| 2 | Mid intake lobe | | |

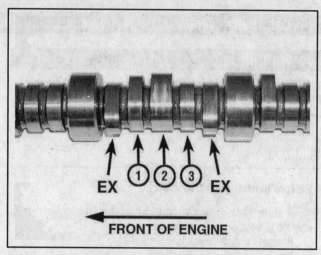

11.20b Arrangement of camshaft lobes on the right cylinder bank (rear) camshaft

| 1 | Primary intake lobe | 3 | Secondary intake lobe |
| 2 | Mid intake lobe | | |

INSTALLATION

▶ **Refer to illustration 11.21**

21 The camshaft oil seal should be replaced whenever a camshaft is removed or replaced. Remove the timing belt rear covers from each cylinder head to access the camshaft seals (see illustration).

22 Pry the old seal out with a screwdriver or seal removal tool.

23 Lubricate the lips with engine oil, then install a new camshaft oil seal by driving it in squarely with a seal installation tool to the same depth as the original seal. A socket of the appropriate size will also work.

24 Clean the camshaft thoroughly with solvent, then lubricate the journals and lobes with camshaft installation lubricant and carefully install the camshaft into the cylinder head.

25 Lubricate and install a new O-ring on the camshaft retainer plate. Install the retainer plate and tighten the bolts to the torque listed in this Chapter's Specifications.

26 Reinstall the remaining components in the reverse order of removal. Refer to Section 5 for the valve adjustment procedure. If the coolant was drained, refill the cooling system (see Chapter 1).

27 Run the engine at low speed for five minutes to allow the air to bleed from the lost motion assemblies, then check for leaks and

11.21 Remove the two bolts and the timing belt rear cover from each cylinder head

proper operation.

➡ **Note: There will be some tappet noise during the first few minutes of operation. If the noise continues, it may indicate a problem with one of the lost motion assemblies.**

12 Cylinder heads - removal and installation

✳✳ **WARNING:**

Allow the engine to cool completely before beginning this procedure.

REMOVAL

▶ **Refer to illustrations 12.7 and 12.12**

1 Relieve the fuel system pressure (see Chapter 4).

2 Disconnect the cable from the negative terminal of the battery

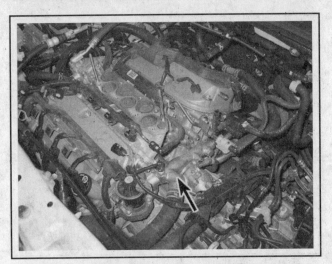

12.7 Remove the coolant passage mounting bolts from both cylinder heads - lightly tap the passage with a soft-faced hammer to break the gasket seal and remove the coolant passage

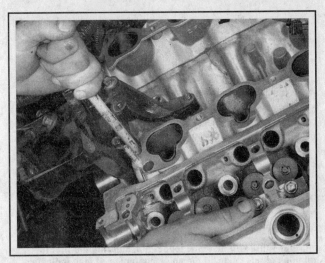

12.12 Pry up carefully on a casting protrusion

(see Chapter 5, Section 1).

3 Drain the cooling system (see Chapter 1).

4 Remove the upper intake manifold and spacer (see Section 6).

5 Remove the catalytic converter assemblies (see Section 7).

6 Remove the timing belt and the camshaft sprockets (see Section 8).

7 Remove the coolant passage from the cylinder heads (see illustration).

8 Remove the valve cover (see Section 4) and the rocker arms/shafts assembly (see Section 10).

9 Remove the fuel rails and injectors (see Chapter 4).

10 Remove the lower intake manifold(s) (see Section 6).

11 Using a socket and breaker bar, loosen the cylinder head bolts in 1/4-turn increments until they can be removed by hand. Loosen them in a sequence opposite that of the tightening sequence (see illustration 12.19)

12 Lift the cylinder head off the engine block. If the head is stuck, pry against an external casting protrusion (see illustration).

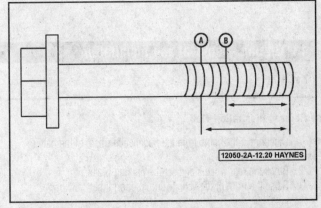

12.16 Measurement points for 12-point cylinder head bolts. Minimum diameter for either point is 0.42 inch (10.6 mm)

A   2.0 inches (50 mm)   *B   1.8 inches (45 mm)*

❋❋ CAUTION:

Don't pry between the head and block. The gasket surfaces may be damaged and leaks could result.

INSTALLATION

▶ **Refer to illustrations 12.16 and 12.19**

13 The mating surfaces of the cylinder heads and block must be perfectly clean when the heads are installed. Use a gasket scraper to remove all traces of carbon and old gasket material. Be careful not to gouge the soft aluminum. Clean the mating surfaces with lacquer thinner or acetone. If there's oil on the mating surfaces when the head is installed, the gasket may not seal correctly and leaks could develop. When working on the block, stuff the cylinders with clean shop rags to keep out debris. Use a vacuum cleaner to remove material that falls into the cylinders.

14 Check the block and head mating surfaces for nicks, deep scratches and other damage. If damage is slight, it can be removed with a file; if it's excessive, machining may be the only alternative.

15 Use a tap of the correct size to chase the threads in the head bolt holes, then clean the holes with compressed air - make sure that nothing remains in the holes.

❋❋ WARNING:

Wear eye protection when using compressed air!

16 Mount each bolt in a vise and run a die down the threads to remove corrosion and restore the threads. Dirt, corrosion, sealant and damaged threads will affect torque readings. If you're working on an engine with 12-point cylinder head bolts, measure the diameter of the bolts at the indicated areas (see illustration). Replace any bolt with a diameter less than the minimum allowable.

➡ **Note: It is suggested that new head bolts be used when the heads are installed, regardless of measurement or condition.**

17 Clean the oil-control orifices thoroughly and reinstall them with new O-rings. Position the new gaskets over the oil-control orifices and locating dowels in the block.

18 Carefully set the head on the block without disturbing the gasket.

19 Before installing the head bolts, apply a small amount of clean engine oil to the threads and under the bolt heads. Install the bolts and special washers and tighten them finger tight. Following the recommended sequence (see illustration), tighten the bolts to the torque listed in this Chapter's Specifications in three steps.

20 The remaining installation steps are the reverse of removal.

21 Reconnect the battery (see Chapter 5, Section 1).

22 Refill the cooling system, change the oil and filter (see Chapter 1), then run the engine and check for leaks. Run the engine at low speed for five minutes to allow the air to bleed from the lost motion assemblies, then check for leaks and proper operation.

➡️**Note: There will be some tappet noise during the first few minutes of operation. If the noise continues, it may indicate a problem with one of the lost motion assemblies.**

12.19 Cylinder head bolt TIGHTENING sequence

13 Oil pan - removal and installation

REMOVAL

▶ **Refer to illustration 13.6**

1 Disconnect the cable from the negative terminal of the battery (see Chapter 5, Section 1).

2 Block the rear wheels and set the parking brake.

3 Raise the front of the vehicle and support it securely on jackstands.

4 Drain the engine oil and remove the oil filter (see Chapter 1).

5 Unbolt the exhaust pipes from the upper catalytic converter assemblies (see Section 7) and from the rear portion of the exhaust system. Remove the front portion of the exhaust system along with its bracket.

6 Remove the torque converter cover (if equipped), then remove the bolts/nuts and lower the oil pan. If the pan is stuck, carefully pry at the tabs on the casting corners (see illustration). Don't damage the mating surfaces of the pan and block or oil leaks could develop.

INSTALLATION

7 Use a scraper to remove all traces of old sealant from the block and oil pan. Be careful not to gouge the soft aluminum surfaces. Clean the mating surfaces with brake system cleaner.

8 Make sure the threaded bolt holes in the block are clean.

9 Inspect the oil pump pick-up screen assembly for damage and a blocked strainer (see Section 14).

10 Apply a bead of gray RTV sealant to the mating surface of the oil pan.

➡️**Note: Install the oil pan within 4 minutes of sealant application.**

11 Carefully position the oil pan on the engine block and install

the bolts. Tighten the bolts a little at a time to the first torque listed in this Chapter's Specifications. Start with the center bolts and work out towards the ends, in a criss-cross pattern. Do the same procedure to the final torque. After the oil pan-to-block bolts have been tightened, tighten the pan-to-transaxle bolts to the torque listed in this Chapter's Specifications.

12 The remainder of installation is the reverse of removal. Be sure to add oil and install a new oil filter.

➡️**Note: Wait 30 minutes (to allow the sealant to cure) before adding oil.**

13 Reconnect the battery (see Chapter 5, Section 1).

14 Run the engine and check for oil pressure and leaks.

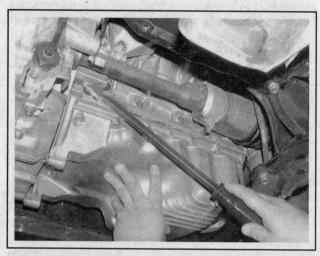

13.6 Use a prybar or screwdriver to pry the pan loose at the casting tabs - DO NOT pry on the gasket surface

14 Oil pump - removal, inspection and installation

REMOVAL

▶ **Refer to illustrations 14.4 and 14.5**

1 Remove the timing belt (see Section 8).
2 Remove the belt idler pulley
3 Remove the oil filter mount assembly.
4 Refer to Section 13 and remove the oil pan. Remove the oil pickup tube (see illustration).
5 Remove the bolts and detach the oil pump housing from the engine (see illustration). You may have to pry carefully between the main bearing cap and the pump housing with a screwdriver. Remove the oil transfer tube along with its O-rings.

INSPECTION

▶ **Refer to illustrations 14.6 and 14.7**

6 Use a Phillips screwdriver to remove the screws holding the pump cover to the rear of the housing (see illustration).
7 Lift the cover off and inspect the pump rotors (see illustration). If any wear or damage is evident, replace the pump. Check the rotor clearance with a feeler gauge and compare it to this Chapter's Specifications.
8 Use a scraper to remove any traces of old sealant from the pump body and engine block, being careful not to damage the delicate aluminum.

14.4 Oil pick-up screen bolt locations

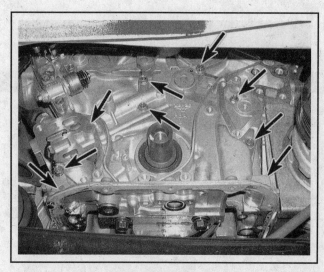

14.5 Oil pump housing bolt locations

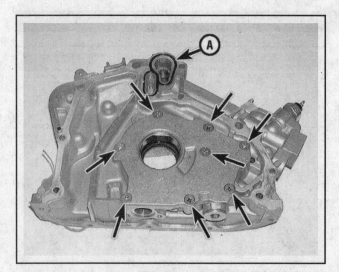

14.6 Remove the screws from the pump cover and replace the O-ring seal (A)

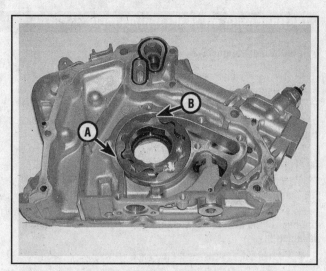

14.7 Inspect the condition of the rotors and the inside of the cover - with feeler gauges, measure the clearances at (A) (outer rotor-to-housing) and (B) (inner rotor-to-outer rotor). Also lay a straightedge across the face of the pump housing and measure the housing-to-rotor axial clearance

INSTALLATION

9   Replace the old crankshaft oil seal (see Section 9). Apply engine oil or multi-purpose grease to the seal lip.

10   Pack the pump cavities with petroleum jelly and install the cover. Apply non-hardening thread-locking compound to the threads and tighten the screws to the torque listed in this Chapter's Specifications following a criss-cross pattern.

11   Use acetone or lacquer thinner and a clean rag to remove all traces of oil from the gasket surfaces. Install the oil transfer tube with new O-rings.

12   Apply a bead of anaerobic sealant to the oil pump flange and the threads of the mounting bolts. Avoid using an excessive amount of sealant, especially around oil passages and bolt holes. Parts must be assembled within five minutes of sealant application, otherwise the material must be removed and reapplied. Wherever O-rings or rubber seals are employed, use new ones.

13   Engage the flat surfaces on the oil pump drive rotor with the matching flats on the crankshaft and slide the pump into place.

14   Install the pump mounting bolts in their original locations and tighten them to the torque listed in this Chapter's Specifications in a criss-cross pattern.

15   Using a new O-ring, install the oil pick-up tube/screen and tighten the fasteners to the torque listed in this Chapter's Specifications.

16   Reinstall the remaining parts in the reverse order of removal.

17   Wait 30 minutes to allow the sealant to cure, then add oil, start the engine and check for proper oil pressure and leaks.

18   Recheck the engine oil level after operating the engine.

15 Driveplate - removal and installation

1   Remove the transaxle (see Chapter 7).

2   Remove the bolts that secure the driveplate to the crankshaft.

3   Clean the driveplate and inspect the surface for cracks. Check for worn, cracked or broken ring-gear teeth. Lay it on a flat surface and use a straightedge to check for warpage.

4   Clean and inspect the mating surfaces of the driveplate and the crankshaft. If the crankshaft oil seal is leaking, replace it before reinstalling the driveplate (see Section 16).

5   Position the driveplate against the crankshaft. Install the washer plate.

6   Follow a criss-cross pattern and tighten the bolts in several stages to the torque listed in this Chapter's Specifications.

7   The remainder of installation is the reverse of the removal procedure.

16 Rear main oil seal - replacement

▶ Refer to illustration 16.2

1   Remove the driveplate (see Section 15).

2   The seal can be replaced without removing the oil pan or removing the seal retainer. However, the lip of the seal is quite stiff and it's possible to cock the seal in the retainer bore or damage it during installation. Pry out the old seal with a screwdriver (see illustration).

3   Apply multi-purpose grease to the crankshaft seal journal and the lip of the new seal, then carefully drive the new seal into place with a seal driver. The lip is stiff, so carefully work it onto the seal journal of the crankshaft. Don't rush it or you may damage the seal.

➡ Note: Drive the seal in squarely and only until it is flush with the back of the seal plate, no farther. Make sure the spring side is facing in.

4   The remaining steps are the reverse of removal.

16.2 Carefully pry the rear main seal out - don't damage the surface of the crankshaft or the new seal will leak

17 Powertrain mounts - check and replacement

CHECK

➡Note: There is only one engine mount used on these models. The other powertrain mounts are at the front and rear of the transaxle.

1 During the check, the engine must be raised slightly to remove the weight from the mounts.

2 Raise the vehicle and support it securely on jackstands, then position a floor jack under the engine oil pan. Place a large block of wood between the jack head and the oil pan, then carefully raise the engine just enough to take the weight off the mounts.

❋❋ WARNING:

DO NOT place any part of your body under the engine when it's supported only by a jack!

3 Check the mounts to see if the rubber is cracked, hardened or separated from the casing.

4 Check for relative movement between the mount plates and the engine or subframe. Use a large screwdriver or prybar to attempt to move the mounts. If movement is noted, lower the engine and tighten the mount fasteners.

REPLACEMENT

Engine mount

5 Raise the vehicle and support it securely on jackstands.

6 Use a floor jack with a block of wood under the oil pan to support the weight of the engine.

7 Unbolt the mount from the frame of the vehicle, then from the engine mount bracket.

8 Installation is the reverse of removal.

Front transaxle mount

9 Remove the battery (see Chapter 5).

10 Remove the three mounting bolts, then lift the underhood wiring junction block from the battery tray.

11 Remove the left headlight (see Chapter 12). Remove the battery tray bolt from behind the headlight.

12 Raise the vehicle and support it securely on jackstands. Remove the battery tray bolt from under the tray. Use a floor jack with a block of wood under the oil pan to support the weight of the engine.

13 Remove the upper side battery tray bolt and lift the tray out.

14 Disconnect the oxygen sensor wiring.

15 Remove the dipstick tube.

16 Refer to Chapter 5 and remove the starter.

17 Unbolt the mount from the frame.

18 Unbolt the mount bracket from the engine and remove the mount assembly from the vehicle.

19 Remove the nut and separate the mount from its bracket.

20 Installation is the reverse of removal.

Rear transaxle mount

21 Raise the vehicle and support it securely on jackstands. Use a floor jack with a block of wood under the oil pan to support the weight of the engine.

22 On AWD models, disconnect the stabilizer bar from its links (see Chapter 10). Rotate the stabilizer bar out of the way.

23 Remove the mount through-bolt.

24 Unbolt the mount from the frame and remove it.

25 Installation is the reverse of removal.

Final tightening, all mounts

26 To ensure maximum bushing life and prevent excessive noise and vibration, the vehicle should be level and the engine weight should be on the mounts during the final tightening stage.

➡Note: Use non-hardening thread locking compound on the nuts/bolts. Ensure that the bushings are not twisted or offset. If you have replaced more than one mount, or when you are installing the engine, tighten the mounts in the following order: front, rear, passenger-side and driver's-side.

Specifications

General

Cylinder numbers (timing belt end-to-transaxle end)

Rear (firewall) side	1-2-3
Front (radiator) side	4-5-6
Firing order	1-4-2-5-3-6
Bore	3.50 inches (89.0 mm)
Stroke	3.66 inches (93.0 mm)
Displacement	212 cubic inches (3.5 liters)

FRONT OF VEHICLE

1-4-2-5-3-6

42035-B-SPECS HAYNES

Cylinder locations

Valve adjustment

Intake	0.008 to 0.009 inch (0.20 to 0.22 mm)
Exhaust	0.011 to 0.013 inch (0.28 to 0.32 mm)

Camshaft and rocker arms

Camshaft bearing journal oil clearance

Standard	0.0020 to 0.0035 inch (0.050 to 0.089 mm)
Service limit	0.006 inch (0.15 mm)

Camshaft lobe height

Intake

Primary	1.3796 inches (35.041 mm)
Mid	1.4348 inches (36.445 mm)
Secondary	1.3891 inches (35.284 mm)
Exhaust	1.4302 inches (36.326 mm)

Camshaft endplay

Standard	0.002 to 0.008 inch (0.05 to 0.20 mm)
Service limit	0.008 inch (0.20 mm)
Camshaft runout limit (total indicator reading)	0.002 inch (0.04 mm)

Rocker arm-to-shaft oil clearance

Intake

Standard	0.001 to 0.0026 inch (0.026 to 0.067 mm)
Service limit	0.0026 inch (0.067 mm)

Exhaust

Standard	0.001 to 0.003 inch (0.026 to 0.077 mm)
Service limit	0.003 inch (0.077 mm)

Oil pump

Outer rotor-to-body clearance	0.004 to 0.007 inch (0.10 to 0.19 mm)
Outer rotor-to-inner rotor clearance	0.002 to 0.006 inch (0.05 to 0.15 mm)
Housing-to-rotor clearance	0.001 to 0.003 inch (0.02 to 0.07 mm)

Torque specifications

	Ft-lbs (unless otherwise indicated)	Nm

➡ **Note: One foot-pound (ft-lb) of torque is equivalent to 12 inch-pounds (in-lbs) of torque. Torque values below approximately 15 ft-lbs are expressed in inch-pounds, since most foot-pound torque wrenches are not accurate at these smaller values.**

	Ft-lbs	Nm
Camshaft thrust plate bolts	16	22
Camshaft sprocket bolts	67	91
Coolant passage		
Small bolts	104 in-lbs	11.5
Large bolts	16	22

Torque specifications (continued) Ft-lbs (unless otherwise indicated)   Nm

➡Note: One foot-pound (ft-lb) of torque is equivalent to 12 inch-pounds (in-lbs) of torque. Torque values below approximately 15 ft-lbs are expressed in inch-pounds, since most foot-pound torque wrenches are not accurate at these smaller values.

	Ft-lbs	Nm
Crankshaft pulley bolt		
Step 1	47	64
Step 2	Tighten an additional 60 degrees	
Crossmember bolts	40	54
Cylinder head bolts (in sequence - see illustration 12.25)		
If equipped with 6-point bolts		
Step 1	29	39
Step 2	51	69
Step 3	72	98
If using NEW 12-point bolts		
Step 1	21	28
Step 2	Tighten an additional 90-degrees	
Step 3	Tighten an additional 90-degrees	
Final step	Tighten an additional 90-degrees	
If using USED 12-point bolts		
Step 1	21	28
Step 2	Tighten an additional 90-degrees	
Final step	Tighten an additional 90-degrees	
Drivebelt tensioner bolt	19	26
Driveplate bolts	54	73
Exhaust manifold (catalytic converter) nuts	156 in-lbs	17.5
Intake manifold upper cover bolts		
Step 1	53 in-lbs	6
Step 2	106 in-lbs	12
Intake manifold-to-spacer fasteners		
Step 1	97 in-lbs	11
Step 2	16	22
Intake manifold-to-cylinder head fasteners	16	22
Oil pan bolts		
Step 1	53 in-lbs	6
Step 2	106 in-lbs	12
Oil pan-to-transaxle bolts	47	64
Oil pick-up screen mounting bolts	106 in-lbs	12
Oil pump housing mounting bolts	106 in-lbs	12
Oil pump cover screws	53 in-lbs	6
Rocker arm shaft bolts		
Step 1	106 in-lbs	12
Step 2	17	23
Timing belt adjuster bolt	19	26
Timing belt tensioner bolts	104 in-lbs	11.5
Timing belt idler pulley bolt	33	45
Timing belt cover bolts	106 in-lbs	12
Rear main oil seal retainer bolts	106 in-lbs	12
Valve adjuster nuts	168 in-lbs	19
Valve cover bolts		
Step 1	53 in-lbs	6
Step 2	106 in-lbs	12

NOTES

Section

Reference to other Chapters

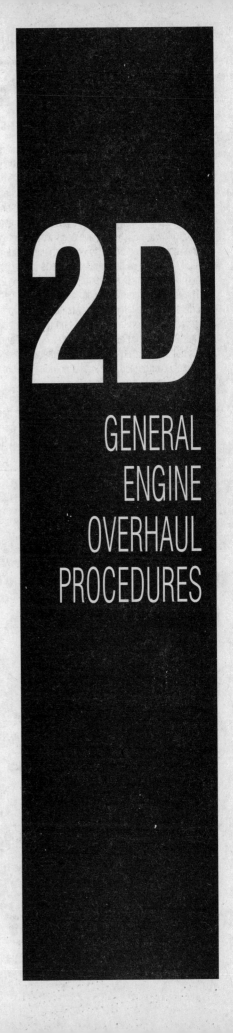

2D

GENERAL ENGINE OVERHAUL PROCEDURES

1 General information - engine overhaul

▶ **Refer to illustrations 1.1, 1.2, 1.3, 1.4, 1.5 and 1.6**

Included in this portion of Chapter 2 are general information and diagnostic testing procedures for determining the overall mechanical condition of your engine.

The information ranges from advice concerning preparation for an overhaul and the purchase of replacement parts and/or components to detailed, step-by-step procedures covering removal and installation.

The following Sections have been written to help you determine whether your engine needs to be overhauled and how to remove and install it once you've determined it needs to be rebuilt. For information concerning in-vehicle engine repair, see Chapter 2A or 2B.

The Specifications included in this Part are general in nature and include only those necessary for testing the oil pressure, checking the engine compression, and bottom-end torque specifications. Refer to Chapter 2A or 2B for additional engine Specifications.

It's not always easy to determine when, or if, an engine should be completely overhauled, because a number of factors must be considered.

High mileage is not necessarily an indication that an overhaul is needed, while low mileage doesn't preclude the need for an overhaul. Frequency of servicing is probably the most important consideration. An engine that's had regular and frequent oil and filter changes, as well as other required maintenance, will most likely give many thousands of miles of reliable service. Conversely, a neglected engine may require an overhaul very early in its service life.

Excessive oil consumption is an indication that piston rings, valve seals and/or valve guides are in need of attention. Make sure that oil leaks aren't responsible before deciding that the rings and/or guides are bad. Perform a cylinder compression check to determine the extent of the work required (see Section 3). Also check the vacuum readings under various conditions (see Section 4).

Check the oil pressure with a gauge installed in place of the oil pressure sending unit and compare it to this Chapter's Specifications (see Section 2). If it's extremely low, the bearings and/or oil pump are probably worn out.

Loss of power, rough running, knocking or metallic engine noises, excessive valve train noise and high fuel consumption rates may also point to the need for an overhaul, especially if they're all present at the same time. If a complete tune-up doesn't remedy the situation, major mechanical work is the only solution.

An engine overhaul involves restoring the internal parts to the specifications of a new engine. During an overhaul, the piston rings are replaced and the cylinder walls are reconditioned (rebored and/or honed) (see illustrations 1.1 and 1.2). If a rebore is done by an automotive machine shop, new oversize pistons will also be installed. The main

1.1 An engine block being bored - an engine rebuilder will use special machinery to recondition the cylinder bores

1.2 If the cylinders are bored, the machine shop will normally hone the engine on a machine like this

1.3 A crankshaft having a main bearing journal ground

1.4 A machinist checks for a bent connecting rod, using specialized equipment

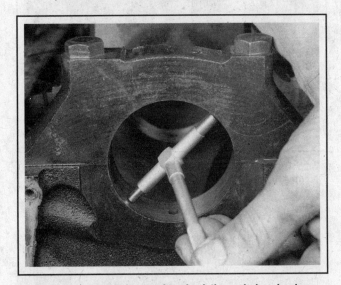

1.5 A bore gauge being used to check the main bearing bore

1.6 Uneven piston wear like this indicates a bent connecting rod

bearings and connecting rod bearings are generally replaced with new ones and, if necessary, the crankshaft may be reground to restore the journals (see illustration 1.3). Generally, the valves are serviced as well, since they're usually in less-than-perfect condition at this point. While the engine is being overhauled, other components, such as the starter and alternator, can be rebuilt as well. The end result should be a like-new engine that will give many trouble-free miles.

➡Note: Critical cooling system components such as the hoses, drivebelts, thermostat and water pump should be replaced with new parts when an engine is overhauled.

The radiator should be checked carefully to ensure that it isn't clogged or leaking (see Chapter 3). If you purchase a rebuilt engine or short block, some rebuilders will not warranty their engines unless the radiator has been professionally flushed. Also, we don't recommend overhauling the oil pump - always install a new one when an engine is rebuilt.

Overhauling the internal components on today's engines is a difficult and time-consuming task that requires a significant amount of specialty tools and is best left to a professional engine rebuilder (see illustrations 1.4, 1.5 and 1.6). A competent engine rebuilder will handle the inspection of your old parts and offer advice concerning the reconditioning or replacement of the original engine. Never purchase parts or have machine work done on other components until the block has been thoroughly inspected by a professional machine shop. As a general rule, time is the primary cost of an overhaul, especially since the vehicle may be tied up for a minimum of two weeks or more. Be aware that some engine builders only have the capability to rebuild the engine you bring them while other rebuilders have a large inventory of rebuilt exchange engines in stock. Also be aware that many machine shops could take as much as two weeks time to completely rebuild your engine depending on shop workload. Sometimes it makes more sense to simply exchange your engine for another engine that's already rebuilt to save time.

2   Oil pressure check

▶ **Refer to illustrations 2.2a and 2.2b**

1   Low engine oil pressure can be a sign of an engine in need of rebuilding. A low oil pressure indicator (often called an "idiot light") is not a test of the oiling system. Such indicators only come on when the oil pressure is dangerously low. Even a factory oil pressure gauge in the instrument panel is only a relative indication, although much better for driver information than a warning light. A better test is with a mechanical (not electrical) oil pressure gauge.

2   Locate the oil pressure sending unit on the engine block.

a) On the four-cylinder engine, it's on the front left side of the engine, near the bottom of the oil filter (see illustration).

b) On the 3.0L V6 engine, it's at the lower right (passenger's side) rear corner of the engine.

c) On the 3.5L V6 engine, it's on the oil pump housing behind the oil filter adapter (see illustration).

3   Unscrew and remove the oil pressure sending unit and screw in the hose for your oil pressure gauge. If necessary, install an adapter fitting. Use Teflon tape or thread sealant on the threads of the adapter and/or the fitting on the end of your gauge's hose.

4   Check the oil pressure with the engine running (normal operating temperature) at the specified engine speed, and compare it to this Chapter's Specifications. If it's extremely low, the bearings and/or oil pump are probably worn out.

2.2a On the four-cylinder engine, the oil pressure sending unit is located on the front left side of the engine, near the bottom of the oil filter

2.2b On the 3.5L V6 engine, the oil pressure sending unit is located on top of the oil pump housing

3   Cylinder compression check

▶ **Refer to illustration 3.6**

1   A compression check will tell you what mechanical condition the upper end of your engine (pistons, rings, valves, head gaskets) is in. Specifically, it can tell you if the compression is down due to leakage caused by worn piston rings, defective valves and seats or a blown head gasket.

➡ **Note: The engine must be at normal operating temperature and the battery must be fully charged for this check.**

2   Begin by cleaning the area around the ignition coils before you remove the spark plugs (compressed air should be used, if available).

The idea is to prevent dirt from getting into the cylinders as the compression check is being done.

3   Remove all of the spark plugs from the engine (see Chapter 1).

4   Block the throttle open. Remove the air intake duct from the throttle body (see Chapter 4) and use a wood dowel or something similar to block the throttle plate open.

❄❄ **CAUTION:**

Be certain that whatever is used to block the throttle open doesn't scratch the throttle body bore or get sucked into the intake manifold.

5   Disable the fuel system (see Chapter 4, Section 2).

6   Install a compression gauge in the spark plug hole (see illustration).

7   Crank the engine over at least seven compression strokes and watch the gauge. The compression should build up quickly in a healthy engine. Low compression on the first stroke, followed by gradually increasing pressure on successive strokes, indicates worn piston rings. A low compression reading on the first stroke, which doesn't build up during successive strokes, indicates leaking valves or a blown head gasket (a cracked head could also be the cause). Deposits on the undersides of the valve heads can also cause low compression. Record the highest gauge reading obtained.

8   Repeat the procedure for the remaining cylinders and compare the results to this Chapter's Specifications.

9   Add some engine oil (about three squirts from a plunger-type oil can) to each cylinder, through the spark plug hole, and repeat the test.

10 If the compression increases after the oil is added, the piston rings are definitely worn. If the compression doesn't increase significantly, the leakage is occurring at the valves or head gasket. Leakage past the valves may be caused by burned valve seats and/or faces or warped, cracked or bent valves.

11 If two adjacent cylinders have equally low compression, there's a strong possibility that the head gasket between them is blown. The appearance of coolant in the combustion chambers or the crankcase would verify this condition.

12 If one cylinder is slightly lower than the others, and the engine has a slightly rough idle, a worn lobe on the camshaft could be the cause.

3.6 Use a compression gauge with a threaded fitting for the spark plug hole, not the type that requires hand pressure to maintain the seal

13 If the compression is unusually high, the combustion chambers are probably coated with carbon deposits. If that's the case, the cylinder heads should be removed and decarbonized.

14 If compression is way down or varies greatly between cylinders, it would be a good idea to have a leak-down test performed by an automotive repair shop. This test will pinpoint exactly where the leakage is occurring and how severe it is.

4   Vacuum gauge diagnostic checks

▶ **Refer to illustrations 4.4 and 4.6**

1   A vacuum gauge provides inexpensive but valuable information about what is going on in the engine. You can check for worn rings or cylinder walls, leaking head or intake manifold gaskets, restricted exhaust, stuck or burned valves, weak valve springs, improper ignition or valve timing and ignition problems.

2   Unfortunately, vacuum gauge readings are easy to misinterpret, so they should be used in conjunction with other tests to confirm the diagnosis.

3   Both the absolute readings and the rate of needle movement are important for accurate interpretation. Most gauges measure vacuum in inches of mercury (in-Hg). The following references to vacuum assume the diagnosis is being performed at sea level. As elevation increases (or atmospheric pressure decreases), the reading will decrease. For every 1,000-foot increase in elevation above approximately 2000 feet, the gauge readings will decrease about one inch of mercury.

4   Connect the vacuum gauge directly to the intake manifold vacuum, not to ported (throttle body) vacuum (see illustration). Be sure no hoses are left disconnected during the test or false readings will result.

5   Before you begin the test, allow the engine to warm up completely. Block the wheels and set the parking brake. With the transmis-

4.4 A simple vacuum gauge can be handy in diagnosing engine condition and performance. Connect it to an intake manifold vacuum source, not a ported (throttle body) source

sion in Park, start the engine and allow it to run at normal idle speed.

6   Read the vacuum gauge; an average, healthy engine should normally produce about 17 to 22 in-Hg with a fairly steady needle (see illustration). Refer to the following vacuum gauge readings and what they indicate about the engine's condition:

7   A low steady reading usually indicates a leaking gasket between the intake manifold and cylinder head(s) or throttle body, a leaky vacuum hose, late ignition timing or incorrect camshaft timing. Check ignition timing with a timing light and eliminate all other possible causes, utilizing the tests provided in this Chapter before you remove the timing belt cover to check the timing marks.

8   If the reading is three to eight inches below normal and it fluctuates at that low reading, suspect an intake manifold gasket leak at an intake port or a faulty fuel injector.

9   If the needle has regular drops of about two-to-four inches at a steady rate, the valves are probably leaking. Perform a compression check or leak-down test to confirm this.

10   An irregular drop or down-flick of the needle can be caused by a sticking valve or an ignition misfire. Perform a compression check or leak-down test and read the spark plugs.

11   A rapid vibration of about four in-Hg variation at idle combined with exhaust smoke indicates worn valve guides. Perform a leak-down test to confirm this. If the rapid vibration occurs with an increase in engine speed, check for a leaking intake manifold gasket or head gasket, weak valve springs, burned valves or ignition misfire.

12   A slight fluctuation, say one inch up and down, may mean ignition problems. Check all the usual tune-up items and, if necessary, run the engine on an ignition analyzer.

13   If there is a large fluctuation, perform a compression or leak-down test to look for a weak or dead cylinder or a blown head gasket.

14   If the needle moves slowly through a wide range, check for a clogged PCV system, incorrect idle fuel mixture, throttle body or intake manifold gasket leaks.

15   Check for a slow return after revving the engine by quickly snapping the throttle open until the engine reaches about 2,500 rpm and let it shut. Normally the reading should drop to near zero, rise above normal idle reading (about 5 in-Hg over) and then return to the previous idle reading. If the vacuum returns slowly and doesn't peak when the throttle is snapped shut, the rings may be worn. If there is a long delay, look for a restricted exhaust system (often the muffler or catalytic converter). An easy way to check this is to temporarily disconnect the exhaust ahead of the suspected part and redo the test.

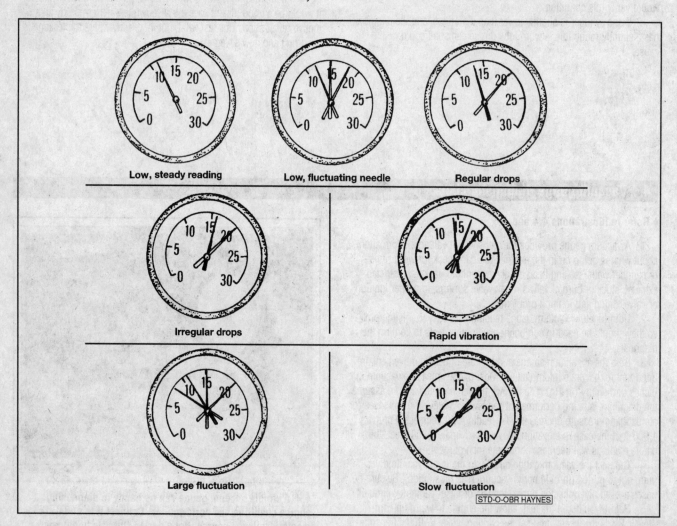

Low, steady reading
Low, fluctuating needle
Regular drops
Irregular drops
Rapid vibration
Large fluctuation
Slow fluctuation

STD-O-OBR HAYNES

4.6 Typical vacuum gauge readings

5   Engine rebuilding alternatives

The do-it-yourselfer is faced with a number of options when purchasing a rebuilt engine. The major considerations are cost, warranty, parts availability and the time required for the rebuilder to complete the project. The decision to replace the engine block, piston/connecting rod assemblies and crankshaft depends on the final inspection results of your engine. Only then can you make a cost effective decision whether to have your engine overhauled or simply purchase an exchange engine for your vehicle.

Some of the rebuilding alternatives include:

Individual parts - If the inspection procedures reveal that the engine block and most engine components are in reusable condition, purchasing individual parts and having a rebuilder rebuild your engine may be the most economical alternative. The block, crankshaft and piston/connecting rod assemblies should all be inspected carefully by a machine shop first.

Short block - A short block consists of an engine block with a crankshaft and piston/connecting rod assemblies already installed. All new bearings are incorporated and all clearances will be correct. The existing camshafts, valve train components, cylinder head and external

parts can be bolted to the short block with little or no machine shop work necessary.

Long block - A long block consists of a short block plus an oil pump, oil pan, cylinder head, valve cover, camshaft and valve train components, timing sprockets and belt or gears and timing cover. All components are installed with new bearings, seals and gaskets incorporated throughout. The installation of manifolds and external parts is all that's necessary.

Low mileage used engines - Some companies now offer low mileage used engines that are a very cost effective way to get your vehicle up and running again. These engines often come from vehicles that have been in totaled in accidents or come from other countries that have a higher vehicle turn over rate. A low mileage used engine also usually has a similar warranty like the newly remanufactured engines.

Give careful thought to which alternative is best for you and discuss the situation with local automotive machine shops, auto parts dealers and experienced rebuilders before ordering or purchasing replacement parts.

6   Engine removal - methods and precautions

▶ **Refer to illustrations 6.1, 6.2, and 6.3**

If you've decided that an engine must be removed for overhaul or major repair work, several preliminary steps should be taken. Read all removal and installation procedures carefully prior to committing to this job. These engines are removed by lowering the engine to the floor, along with the transaxle, then raising the vehicle sufficiently to slide the assembly out; this will require a vehicle hoist as well as an engine hoist.

Locating a suitable place to work is extremely important. Adequate work space, along with storage space for the vehicle, will be needed. If

a shop or garage isn't available, at the very least a flat, level, clean work surface made of concrete or asphalt is required.

Cleaning the engine compartment and engine before beginning the removal procedure will help keep tools clean and organized (see illustrations 6.1 and 6.2).

An engine hoist will also be necessary. Make sure the hoist is rated in excess of the combined weight of the engine and transaxle. Safety is of primary importance, considering the potential hazards involved in removing the engine from the vehicle.

If you're a novice at engine removal, get at least one helper. One person cannot easily do all the things you need to do to remove a big

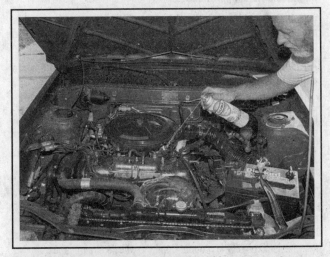

6.1 After tightly wrapping water-vulnerable components, use a spray cleaner on everything, with particular concentration on the greasiest areas, usually around the valve cover and lower edges of the block. If one section dries out, apply more cleaner

6.2 Depending on how dirty the engine is, let the cleaner soak in according to the directions and then hose off the grime and cleaner. Get the rinse water down into every area you can get at; then dry important components with a hair dryer or paper towels

heavy engine and transaxle assembly from the engine compartment. Also helpful is to seek advice and assistance from someone who's experienced in engine removal.

Plan the operation ahead of time. Arrange for or obtain all of the tools and equipment you'll need prior to beginning the job (see illustration 6.3). Some of the equipment necessary to perform engine removal and installation safely and with relative ease are (in addition to a vehicle hoist and an engine hoist) a heavy duty floor jack (preferably fitted with a transmission jack head adapter), complete sets of wrenches and sockets as described in the front of this manual, wooden blocks, plenty of rags and cleaning solvent for mopping up spilled oil, coolant and gasoline.

Plan for the vehicle to be out of use for quite a while. A machine shop can do the work that is beyond the scope of the home mechanic. Machine shops often have a busy schedule, so before removing the engine, consult the shop for an estimate of how long it will take to rebuild or repair the components that may need work.

6.3 Get an engine stand sturdy enough to firmly support the engine while you're working on it. Stay away from three-wheeled models; they have a tendency to tip over more easily, so get a four-wheeled unit

7   Engine - removal and installation

✳✳ WARNING 1:

Gasoline is extremely flammable, so take extra precautions when you work on any part of the fuel system. Don't smoke or allow open flames or bare light bulbs near the work area, and don't work in a garage where a gas-type appliance (such as a water heater or clothes dryer) is present. Since gasoline is carcinogenic, wear fuel-resistant gloves when there's a possibility of being exposed to fuel, and, if you spill any fuel on your skin, rinse it off immediately with soap and water. Mop up any spills immediately and do not store fuel-soaked rags where they could ignite. The fuel system is under constant pressure, so, if any fuel lines are to be disconnected, the fuel pressure in the system must be relieved first (see Chapter 4 for more information). When you perform any kind of work on the fuel system, wear safety glasses and have a Class B type fire extinguisher on hand.

✳✳ WARNING 2:

The engine must be completely cool before beginning this procedure.

➡Note 1: Engine removal on these models is a difficult job, especially for the do-it-yourself mechanic working at home. Because of the vehicle's design, the manufacturer states that the engine and transaxle have to be removed as a unit from the bottom of the vehicle - not the top. With a floor jack and

jackstands, the vehicle can't be raised high enough and supported safely enough for the engine/transaxle assembly to slide out from underneath. The manufacturer recommends that removal of the engine transaxle assembly only be performed on a frame-contact type vehicle hoist and using an adjustable engine cradle support table.

➡Note 2: Read through the entire Section before beginning this procedure. The engine and transaxle are removed as a unit from below, then separated outside the vehicle.

➡Note 3: Keep in mind that during this procedure you'll have to adjust the height of the vehicle to perform certain operations.

REMOVAL

▶ Refer to illustrations 7.16, 7.26, 7.29, 7.38a, 7.38b and 7.41

1   If you're working on a V6 model, take the vehicle to a properly equipped repair shop and have the air conditioning system evacuated.
2   Park the vehicle on a frame-contact type vehicle hoist, then engage the arms of the hoist with the jacking points of the vehicle. Raise the hoist arms until they contact the vehicle, but not so much that the wheels come off the ground. Point the wheels straight ahead.
3   Place the hood in the widest-open position.
4   Disconnect the cable from the negative battery terminal (see Chapter 5, Section 1).
5   Relieve the fuel system pressure (see Chapter 4), then disconnect

the cable from the negative terminal of the battery (see Chapter 5, Section 1).

6   Drain the engine oil and coolant (see Chapter 1).

7   Remove the engine cover (see Chapter 2A, 2B or 2C).

8   Remove the air filter housing and the air intake duct (see Chapter 4).

9   Remove the battery and the cover of the underhood fuse block (see Chapter 5).

10   Remove the inner fuse cover and remove the three fuse block mounting bolts that are with the fuses.

11   Remove the nut from the power steering and battery cable connection.

12   Use a screwdriver to release the tabs on the sides of the fuse block and lift it from the connectors.

13   Disconnect the side wiring and remove the underhood fuse block.

14   Remove the wiring clips on the side of the battery tray.

15   Remove the main connectors from the fuse block housing. Lay the positive battery cable over the engine so it can be removed along with the engine.

16   Follow all wiring harnesses from the engine and transaxle and disconnect the electrical connectors leading to the vehicle wiring harnesses. Make sure to label the connectors as you disconnect them (see illustration). Several can be laid over the engine to be removed with it. Disconnect the harnesses from the transaxle as well as the engine.

17   Remove the lower section of the underhood fuse block and the battery tray.

18   On 3.5L V6 models, remove the Powertrain Control Module (PCM) (see Chapter 6).

19   Clearly label and disconnect all vacuum lines, emissions hoses, and ground straps between the engine and the engine compartment. Masking tape and/or a touch up paint applicator work well for marking items. Take instant photos or sketch the locations of components and brackets.

20   Disconnect the fuel line from the fuel rail (see Chapter 4).

21   Drain the coolant (see Chapter 1). Disconnect the radiator hoses from the engine. Label and disconnect all other hoses such as the coolant reservoir hose and the heater hoses.

22   Remove the headlight housings (see Chapter 12). Tie the radiator assembly to the front upper frame support with wire.

23   If you're working on a V6 model, remove the drivebelt now (see Chapter 1).

24   Loosen the driveaxle/hub nuts (see Chapter 8) and the front

wheel lug nuts, then raise the vehicle on the hoist. Remove the front wheels.

25   Raise the vehicle and make sure it's secure on the hoist. Remove the inner fender splash shields.

✱✱ WARNING:

Tie the front of the body down to the hoist so the vehicle doesn't tilt back and fall off the hoist when the weight of the engine and transaxle is removed.

26   On automatic transaxle models, remove the driveplate inspection plate and remove the torque converter-to-flywheel bolts (see illustration).

➡Note: Some models aren't equipped with inspection plates. On these vehicles, the starter must be removed for access to these bolts.

27   If you're working on a four-cylinder model, remove the drivebelt now (see Chapter 1).

28   On V6 models, refer to Chapter 3 and remove the air conditioning compressor. On four-cylinder models, the compressor can be unbolted and secured out of the way, after the wiring is disconnected.

✱✱ WARNING:

On four-cylinder models, don't disconnect the refrigerant lines.

29   Remove the pushpin fasteners that attach the front air dam to the engine cradle. Disconnect the automatic transaxle cooling lines from the transaxle (see illustration).

30   Detach the exhaust pipe from the exhaust manifold/catalytic converter assemblies and from the rear portion of the exhaust system, then remove the front portion of the exhaust system (see Chapter 4).

31   On AWD models, refer to Chapter 8 and remove the driveshaft. The transfer case may also be removed at this time (see Chapter 7C).

32   Disconnect the shift cable(s) from the transaxle (see Chapter 7A or 7B). Disconnect the cable bracket.

33   Remove the pinch bolt from the intermediate shaft and steering gear input shaft connector (see Chapter 10). Be sure to paint a mark across the connector to insure correct alignment on reassembly.

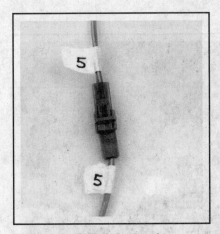

7.16 Label both ends of each wire or vacuum connection before disconnecting them

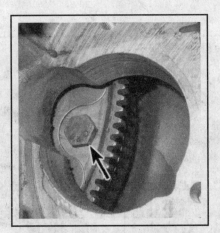

7.26 Remove the torque converter bolts (on this model they're accessed through the starter opening)

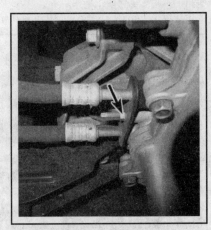

7.29 On automatic transaxle-equipped models, remove the nut and detach the transaxle cooler lines from the transaxle

34 Detach the tie-rod ends from the steering knuckle arms (see Chapter 10).

35 Detach the stabilizer bar links from the stabilizer bar (see Chapter 10).

36 Remove the front driveaxles (see Chapter 8).

37 On manual transaxle vehicles, refer to Chapter 8 and disconnect the hydraulic line from the clutch release cylinder (where the line connects to the transaxle).

38 Attach one end of an engine lifting sling or chain to the lift bracket (see illustration). Attach the other end of the sling or chain to a lift bracket bolted to the transaxle (see illustration). Be sure the positioning of the chain or sling will keep the engine and transaxle level.

➡Note: The sling or chain must be long enough to allow the engine hoist to lower the engine/transaxle assembly to the ground, without letting the hoist arm contact the vehicle.

39 Roll the hoist into position and attach the sling or chain to it. Take up the slack until there is slight tension on the hoist.

➡Note: Depending on the design of the engine hoist, it may be helpful to position the hoist from the side of the vehicle, so that when the engine/transaxle assembly is lowered, it will fit between the legs of the hoist.

40 Carefully mark the position of the subframe in relation to the vehicle chassis. Remove the right-side engine mount, remove the left-side mount-to-transaxle bolts, and unbolt the rest of the mounts from the subframe (see Chapter 2A).

41 Support the subframe with two floor jacks (one on each side) and remove the subframe mounting bolts (see illustration). Lower the subframe to the floor and remove it from under the vehicle.

42 Recheck to be sure nothing is still connecting the engine or transaxle to the vehicle. Label and disconnect anything remaining.

43 Slowly lower the engine/transaxle assembly to the floor.

44 Once the powertrain assembly is on the floor, disconnect the engine lifting hoist and raise the vehicle using the vehicle hoist until it clears the powertrain assembly.

45 Reconnect the chain or sling and raise the engine and transaxle. Support the engine with blocks of wood or another floor jack. Support the transaxle with another floor jack, preferably one with a transmission jack head adapter. At this point the transaxle can be unbolted and removed from the engine. Be very careful to ensure that the components are supported securely so they won't topple off their supports during disconnection.

46 Reconnect the lifting chain to the engine, then raise the engine and attach it to an engine stand.

INSTALLATION

47 Installation is the reverse of removal, noting the following points:

a) Check the engine/transaxle mounts. If they're worn or damaged, replace them.

b) Attach the transaxle to the engine following the procedure described in Chapter 7.

c) Align the subframe reference marks before tightening the bolts.

d) Tighten the subframe mounting bolts and bracket bolts to the torque listed in this Chapter's Specifications. Note the locations of the various size bolts (see illustration). Replace all the large subframe bolts with new ones.

e) On automatic transaxle-equipped models, use new O-rings on the transaxle cooler line fittings.

f) Add coolant, engine oil, power steering and transmission fluids (see Chapter 1).

g) Reconnect the negative battery cable (see Chapter 5, Section 1).

h) Run the engine and check for proper operation and leaks. Shut off the engine and recheck fluid levels.

7.38a Right-side engine lifting bracket (near power steering pump)

7.38b Left-side lifting bracket (on transaxle)

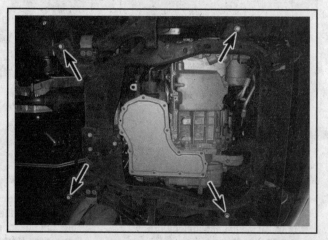

7.41 Location of the main subframe mounting bolts

8 Engine overhaul - disassembly sequence

1   It's much easier to disassemble the engine if it's mounted on a portable engine stand. A stand can often be rented quite cheaply from an equipment rental yard. Before the engine is mounted on a stand, the driveplate should be removed from the engine.

2   If a stand isn't available, it's possible to remove the external engine components with it blocked up on the floor. Be extra careful not to tip or drop the engine when working without a stand.

3   If you're going to obtain a rebuilt engine, all external components must come off first, to be transferred to the replacement engine. These components include:

> *Driveplate*
> *Ignition system components*
> *Emissions-related components*
> *Engine mounts and mount brackets*
> *Fuel injection components*
> *Intake/exhaust manifolds*
> *Oil filter*
> *Thermostat and housing assembly*
> *Water pump*

➡ **Note: When removing the external components from the engine, pay close attention to details that may be helpful or important during installation. Note the installed position of gaskets, seals, spacers, pins, brackets, washers, bolts and other small items.**

4   If you're going to obtain a short block (assembled engine block, crankshaft, pistons and connecting rods), then you should remove the timing belt, cylinder head, oil pan, oil pump pick-up tube, oil pump and water pump from your engine so that you can turn in your old short block to the rebuilder as a core. See *Engine rebuilding alternatives* for additional information regarding the different possibilities to be considered.

9 Pistons and connecting rods - removal and installation

REMOVAL

▶ **Refer to illustrations 9.1, 9.3 and 9.4**

➡ **Note: Prior to removing the piston/connecting rod assemblies, remove the cylinder head(s) and oil pan (see Chapter 2A, 2B or 2C).**

1   Use your fingernail to feel if a ridge has formed at the upper limit of ring travel (about 1/4-inch down from the top of each cylinder). If carbon deposits or cylinder wear have produced ridges, they must be completely removed with a special tool (see illustration). Follow the manufacturer's instructions provided with the tool. Failure to remove the ridges before attempting to remove the piston/connecting rod assemblies may result in piston breakage.

2   After the cylinder ridges have been removed, turn the engine so the crankshaft is facing up.

3   Before the connecting rods are removed, check the connecting rod endplay with feeler gauges. Slide them between the first connecting rod and the crankshaft throw until the play is removed (see illustration). Repeat this procedure for each connecting rod. The endplay is equal to the thickness of the feeler gauge(s). Check with an automotive machine shop for the endplay service limit (a typical endplay should measure between 0.005 to 0.015 inch [0.127 to 0.396 mm]). If the play exceeds the service limit, new connecting rods will be required. If new rods (or a new crankshaft) are installed, the endplay may fall under the minimum allowable. If it does, the rods will have to be machined to restore it. If necessary, consult an automotive machine shop for advice.

4   Check the connecting rods and caps for identification marks. If they aren't plainly marked, use paint or a marker (see illustration) to clearly identify each rod and cap (1, 2, 3, etc., depending on the cylinder they're associated with).

✳ CAUTION:

Do not use a punch and hammer to mark the connecting rods or they may be damaged.

9.1 Before you try to remove the pistons, use a ridge reamer to remove the raised material (ridge) from the top of the cylinders

9.3 Checking the connecting rod endplay (side clearance)

9.4 If the connecting rods or caps are not marked, use permanent ink or paint to mark the caps to the rods by cylinder number (for example, this would be number 4 cylinder connecting rod)

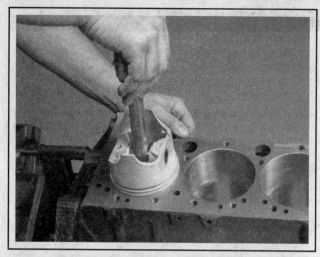

9.13 Install the piston ring into the cylinder, then push it down into position using a piston so the ring will be square in the cylinder

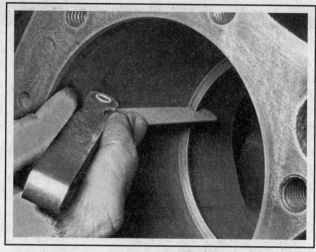

9.14 With the ring square in the cylinder, measure the ring end gap with a feeler gauge

9.15 If the ring end gap is too small, clamp a file in a vise as shown and file the piston ring ends - be sure to remove all raised material

5   Loosen each of the connecting rod cap bolts 1/2-turn at a time until they can be removed by hand.

➡**Note: If you're working on a four-cylinder engine or a 3.0L V6, new connecting rod cap bolts must be used when reassembling the engine. Save the old bolts for use when checking the connecting rod bearing oil clearance.**

6   Remove the number one connecting rod cap and bearing insert. Don't drop the bearing insert out of the cap.

7   Remove the bearing insert and push the connecting rod/piston assembly out through the top of the engine. Use a wooden or plastic hammer handle to push on the upper bearing surface in the connecting rod. If resistance is felt, double-check to make sure that all of the ridge was removed from the cylinder.

8   Repeat the procedure for the remaining cylinders.

9   After removal, reassemble the connecting rod caps and bearing inserts in their respective connecting rods and install the cap bolts finger tight. Leaving the old bearing inserts in place until reassembly will help prevent the connecting rod bearing surfaces from being accidentally nicked or gouged.

10   The pistons and connecting rods are now ready for inspection

and overhaul at an automotive machine shop.

➡**Note: If you remove the pistons from the connecting rods (not recommended for home mechanics) be sure to mark the orientation of the connecting rods prior to disassembly. All pistons have arrows or other marks that face toward the front of the engine. Four-cylinder connecting rods have bosses at the split that face to the rear. Connecting rods and rod caps on 3.0L V6 engines have bumps that face to the rear.**

PISTON RING INSTALLATION

◆ **Refer to illustrations 9.13, 9.14, 9.15, 9.19a, 9.19b and 9.22**

11   Before installing the new piston rings, the ring end gaps must be checked. It's assumed that the piston ring side clearance has been checked and verified correct.

12   Lay out the piston/connecting rod assemblies and the new ring sets so the ring sets will be matched with the same piston and cylinder during the end gap measurement and engine assembly.

13   Insert the top (number one) compression ring into the first cylinder and square it up with the cylinder walls by pushing it in with the top of the piston (see illustration). The ring should be near the bottom of the cylinder, at the lower limit of ring travel.

14   To measure the end gap, slip feeler gauges between the ends of the ring until a gauge equal to the gap width is found (see illustration). The feeler gauge should slide between the ring ends with a slight amount of drag. A typical ring gap should fall between 0.010 and 0.020 inch (0.25 to 0.50 mm) for compression rings and up to 0.030 inch (0.76 mm) for the oil ring steel rails. If the gap is larger or smaller than specified, double-check to make sure you have the correct rings before proceeding.

15   If the gap is too small, it must be enlarged or the ring ends may come in contact with each other during engine operation, which can cause serious damage to the engine. If necessary, increase the end gaps by filing the ring ends very carefully with a fine file. Mount the file in a vise equipped with soft jaws, slip the ring over the file with the ends contacting the file face and slowly move the ring to remove material from the ends. When performing this operation, file only by pushing the ring from the outside end of the file towards the vise (see illustration).

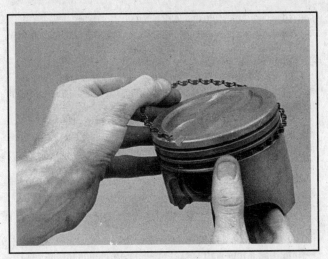

9.19a Installing the spacer/expander in the oil ring groove

9.19b DO NOT use a piston ring installation tool when installing the oil control side rails

16 Excess end gap isn't critical unless it's greater than 0.040 inch (1.01 mm). Again, double-check to make sure you have the correct ring type.

17 Repeat the procedure for each ring that will be installed in the first cylinder and for each ring in the remaining cylinders. Remember to keep rings, pistons and cylinders matched up.

18 Once the ring end gaps have been checked/corrected, the rings can be installed on the pistons.

19 The oil control ring (lowest one on the piston) is usually installed first. It's composed of three separate components. Slip the spacer/expander into the groove (see illustration). If an anti-rotation tang is used, make sure it's inserted into the drilled hole in the ring groove. Next, install the upper side rail in the same manner (see illustration). Don't use a piston ring installation tool on the oil ring side rails, as they may be damaged. Instead, place one end of the side rail into the groove between the spacer/expander and the ring land, hold it firmly in place and slide a finger around the piston while pushing the rail into the groove. Finally, install the lower side rail.

20 After the three oil ring components have been installed, check to make sure that both the upper and lower side rails can be rotated smoothly inside the ring grooves.

21 The number two (middle) compression ring is installed next. It's usually stamped with a mark which must face up, toward the top of the piston. Do not mix up the top and middle rings, as they have different cross-sections.

➡**Note: Always follow the instructions printed on the ring package or box - different manufacturers may require different approaches.**

22 Use a piston ring installation tool and make sure the identification mark is facing the top of the piston, then slip the ring into the middle groove on the piston (see illustration). Don't expand the ring any more than necessary to slide it over the piston.

23 Install the number one (top) compression ring in the same manner. Make sure the mark is facing up. Be careful not to confuse the number one and number two compression rings.

24 Repeat the procedure for the remaining pistons and rings.

INSTALLATION

25 Before installing the piston/connecting rod assemblies, the cyl-

9.22 Use a piston ring installation tool to install the number 2 and the number 1 (top) rings - be sure the directional mark on the piston ring(s) is facing toward the top of the piston

inder walls must be perfectly clean, the top edge of each cylinder bore must be chamfered, and the crankshaft must be in place.

26 Remove the cap from the end of the number one connecting rod (refer to the marks made during removal). Remove the original bearing inserts and wipe the bearing surfaces of the connecting rod and cap with a clean, lint-free cloth. They must be kept spotlessly clean.

Connecting rod bearing oil clearance check

▶ **Refer to illustrations 9.30, 9.35, 9.37 and 9.41**

27 Clean the back side of the new upper bearing insert, then lay it in place in the connecting rod.

28 Make sure the tab on the bearing fits into the recess in the rod. Don't hammer the bearing insert into place and be very careful not to nick or gouge the bearing face. Don't lubricate the bearing at this time.

29 Clean the back side of the other bearing insert and install it in the rod cap. Again, make sure the tab on the bearing fits into the recess in the cap, and don't apply any lubricant. It's critically important that the mating surfaces of the bearing and connecting rod are perfectly clean and oil-free when they're assembled.

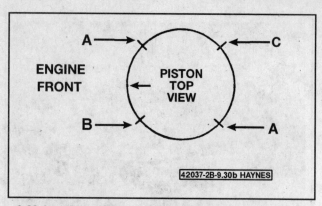

9.30 Locations of the piston ring end gaps

A   Oil ring side rail gaps
B   Top compression ring gap and oil ring spacer gap
C   Second compression ring gap

30 Position the piston ring gaps at the specified intervals around the piston as shown (see illustration).

31 Lubricate the piston and rings with clean engine oil and attach a piston ring compressor to the piston. Leave the skirt protruding about 1/4-inch to guide the piston into the cylinder. The rings must be compressed until they're flush with the piston.

32 Rotate the crankshaft until the number one connecting rod journal is at BDC (Bottom Dead Center) and apply a liberal coat of engine oil to the cylinder walls.

33 With the arrow or cavity mark on the top of the piston crown facing the front (timing belt or chain end) of the engine, gently insert the piston/connecting rod assembly into the number one cylinder bore and rest the bottom edge of the ring compressor on the engine block.

34 Tap the top edge of the ring compressor to make sure it's contacting the block around its entire circumference.

35 Gently tap on the top of the piston with the end of a hammer handle (see illustration) while guiding the end of the connecting rod into place on the crankshaft journal. The piston rings may try to pop out of the ring compressor just before entering the cylinder bore, so keep some downward pressure on the ring compressor. Work slowly, and if any resistance is felt as the piston enters the cylinder, stop immediately. Find out what's hanging up and fix it before proceeding. Do not force the piston into the cylinder - you might break a ring and/or the piston.

36 Once the piston/connecting rod assembly is installed, the connecting rod bearing oil clearance must be checked before the rod cap is permanently installed.

37 Cut a piece of the appropriate size Plastigage slightly shorter than the width of the connecting rod bearing and lay it in place on the number one connecting rod journal, parallel with the journal axis (see illustration).

38 Clean the connecting rod cap bearing face and install the rod cap. Make sure the mating mark on the cap is on the same side as the mark on the connecting rod (see illustration 9.4).

39 Install the old rod bolts at this time, and tighten them to the torque listed in this Chapter's Specifications.

➡**Note: Use a thin-wall socket to avoid erroneous torque readings that can result if the socket is wedged between the rod cap and the bolt. If the socket tends to wedge itself between the fastener and the cap, lift up on it slightly until it no longer contacts the cap.**

DO NOT rotate the crankshaft at any time during this operation.

40 Remove the fasteners and detach the rod cap, being very careful not to disturb the Plastigage. Discard the cap bolts at this time as they cannot be reused.

➡**Note: You MUST use new connecting rod bolts.**

41 Compare the width of the crushed Plastigage to the scale printed on the Plastigage envelope to obtain the oil clearance (see illustration). The connecting rod oil clearance is usually about 0.001 to 0.002 inch. Consult an automotive machine shop for the clearance specified for the rod bearings on your engine.

42 If the clearance is not as specified, the bearing inserts may be the wrong size (which means different ones will be required). Before deciding that different inserts are needed, make sure that no dirt or oil was between the bearing inserts and the connecting rod or cap when the clearance was measured. Also, recheck the journal diameter. If the Plastigage was wider at one end than the other, the journal may be tapered. If the clearance still exceeds the limit specified, the bearing will

9.35 Use a plastic or wooden hammer handle to push the piston into the cylinder

9.37 Place Plastigage on each connecting rod bearing journal parallel to the crankshaft centerline

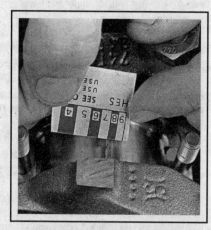

9.41 Use the scale on the Plastigage package to determine the bearing oil clearance - be sure to measure the widest part of the Plastigage and use the correct scale; it comes with both standard and metric scales

have to be replaced with an undersize bearing.

> ❊❊ **CAUTION:**
>
> **When installing a new crankshaft always use a standard size bearing.**

Final installation

43 Carefully scrape all traces of the Plastigage material off the rod journal and/or bearing face. Be very careful not to scratch the bearing - use your fingernail or the edge of a plastic card.

44 Make sure the bearing faces are perfectly clean, then apply a uniform layer of clean moly-base grease or engine assembly lube to both of them. You'll have to push the piston into the cylinder to expose the face of the bearing insert in the connecting rod.

45 Slide the connecting rod back into place on the journal, install the rod cap, install the bolts and tighten them to the torque listed in this Chapter's Specifications.

> ❊❊ **CAUTION:**
>
> **Install new connecting rod cap bolts on four-cylinder engines and 3.0L V6 engines. Do NOT reuse old bolts - they have stretched and cannot be reused.**

46 Repeat the entire procedure for the remaining pistons/connecting rods.

47 The important points to remember are:
  a) *Keep the back sides of the bearing inserts and the insides of the connecting rods and caps perfectly clean when assembling them.*
  b) *Make sure you have the correct piston/rod assembly for each cylinder.*
  c) *The mark on the piston must face the front (timing belt or chain end) of the engine.*
  d) *Lubricate the cylinder walls liberally with clean oil.*
  e) *Lubricate the bearing faces when installing the rod caps after the oil clearance has been checked.*

48 After all the piston/connecting rod assemblies have been correctly installed, rotate the crankshaft a number of times by hand to check for any obvious binding.

49 As a final step, check the connecting rod endplay again. On 3.0L V6 engines, make sure that the bumps on the connecting rods and rod caps are facing toward the rear.

50 Compare the measured endplay to the tolerance listed in this Chapter's Specifications to make sure it's acceptable. If it was correct before disassembly and the original crankshaft and rods were reinstalled, it should still be correct. If new rods or a new crankshaft were installed, the endplay may be inadequate. If so, the rods will have to be removed and taken to an automotive machine shop for resizing.

10 Crankshaft - removal and installation

REMOVAL

▶ **Refer to illustrations 10.1 and 10.3**

➡ **Note: The crankshaft can be removed only after the engine has been removed from the vehicle. It's assumed that the driveplate, crankshaft pulley, timing belt or chain, oil pan, oil pump body, oil filter and piston/connecting rod assemblies have already been removed. The rear main oil seal retainer must be unbolted and separated from the block before proceeding with crankshaft removal.**

1 Before the crankshaft is removed, measure the endplay. Mount a dial indicator with the indicator in line with the crankshaft and touching the end of the crankshaft as shown (see illustration).

2 Pry the crankshaft all the way to the rear and zero the dial indicator. Next, pry the crankshaft to the front as far as possible and check the reading on the dial indicator. The distance traveled is the endplay. A typical crankshaft endplay will fall between 0.003 to 0.010 inch (0.076 to 0.254 mm). If it is greater than that, check the crankshaft thrust surfaces for wear after it's removed. If no wear is evident, new main bearings should correct the endplay.

3 If a dial indicator isn't available, feeler gauges can be used. Gently pry the crankshaft all the way to the front of the engine. Slip feeler gauges between the crankshaft and the front face of the thrust bearing or washer to determine the clearance (see illustration).

4 Loosen the main bearing bolts 1/4-turn at a time each, until they can be removed by hand.

5 Gently tap the main bearing caps or bridge with a soft-face hammer. Pull the main bearing caps or bridge straight up and off the cylin-

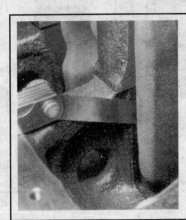

10.3 Checking crankshaft endplay with feeler gauges at the thrust bearing journal

10.1 Checking crankshaft endplay with a dial indicator

ENGINE BEARING ANALYSIS

Debris

Babbitt bearing embedded with debris from machinings

Microscopic detail of debris

Microscopic detail of gouges

Overplated copper alloy bearing gouged by cast iron debris

Aluminum bearing embedded with glass beads

Microscopic detail of glass beads

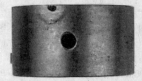

Damaged lining caused by dirt left on the bearing back

Misassembly

Result of a lower half assembled as an upper - blocking the oil flow

Excessive oil clearance is indicated by a short contact arc

Polished and oil-stained backs are a result of a poor fit in the housing bore

Result of a wrong, reversed, or shifted cap

Overloading

Damage from excessive idling which resulted in an oil film unable to support the load imposed

Damaged upper connecting rod bearings caused by engine lugging; the lower main bearings (not shown) were similarly affected

The damage shown in these upper and lower connecting rod bearings was caused by engine operation at a higher-than-rated speed under load

Misalignment

A poorly finished crankshaft caused the equally spaced scoring shown

A tapered housing bore caused the damage along one edge of this pair

A warped crankshaft caused this pattern of severe wear in the center, diminishing toward the ends

A bent connecting rod led to the damage in the "V" pattern

Corrosion

Microscopic detail of corrosion

Corrosion is an acid attack on the bearing lining generally caused by inadequate maintenance, extremely hot or cold operation, or inferior oils or fuels

Lubrication

Result of dry start: The bearings on the left, farthest from the oil pump, show more damage

Microscopic detail of cavitation

Example of cavitation - a surface erosion caused by pressure changes in the oil film

Result of a low oil supply or oil starvation

Severe wear as a result of inadequate oil clearance

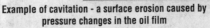

Damage from excessive thrust or insufficient axial clearance

Bearing affected by oil dilution caused by excessive blow-by or a rich mixture

der block. Try not to drop the bearing inserts if they come out with the caps.

6   Carefully lift the crankshaft out of the engine. It may be a good idea to have an assistant available, since the crankshaft is quite heavy and awkward to handle. With the bearing inserts in place inside the engine block and main bearing caps, reinstall the main bearing caps and tighten the bolts finger tight. Make sure you install the main bearing caps with the arrows facing the front (timing belt or chain end) of the engine.

INSTALLATION

7   Crankshaft installation is the first step in engine reassembly. It's assumed at this point that the engine block and crankshaft have been cleaned, inspected and repaired or reconditioned.

8   Position the engine block with the bottom facing up.

9   Remove the main bearing caps or bridge.

10   If they're still in place, remove the original bearing inserts from the block and from the main bearing caps. Wipe the bearing surfaces of the block and main bearing cap assembly with a clean, lint-free cloth. They must be kept spotlessly clean. This is critical for determining the correct bearing oil clearance.

Main bearing oil clearance check

◆ **Refer to illustrations 10.17, 10.19a, 10.19b, 10.19c and 10.21**

11   Without mixing them up, clean the back sides of the new upper main bearing inserts (with grooves and oil holes) and lay one in each main bearing saddle in the block. Each upper bearing has an oil groove and oil hole in it.

✳ CAUTION:

The oil holes in the block must line up with the oil holes in the upper bearing inserts.

The thrust washers must be installed in the correct positions. Clean the back sides of the lower main bearing inserts and lay them in the corresponding location in the main bearing cap assembly. Make sure the

10.17 Place the Plastigage onto the crankshaft bearing journal as shown

tab on the bearing insert fits into the recess in the block or main bearing cap assembly. The upper bearings with the oil holes are installed into the engine block while the lower bearings without the oil holes are installed in the main bearing caps.

✳ CAUTION:

DO NOT apply any lubrication at this time.

12   Clean the faces of the bearing inserts in the block and the crankshaft main bearing journals with a clean, lint-free cloth.

13   Check or clean the oil holes in the crankshaft, as any dirt here can go only one way - straight through the new bearings.

14   Once you're certain the crankshaft is clean, carefully lay it in position in the cylinder block.

15   Before the crankshaft can be permanently installed, the main bearing oil clearance must be checked.

16   Cut several strips of the appropriate size of Plastigage. They must be slightly shorter than the width of the main bearing journal.

17   Place one piece on each crankshaft main bearing journal, parallel with the journal axis as shown (see illustration).

18   Clean the faces of the bearing inserts in the main bearing caps. Hold the bearing inserts in place and install the assembly onto the crankshaft and cylinder block. DO NOT disturb the Plastigage. Make sure you install the main bearing caps with the arrows facing the front (timing belt or chain end) of the engine.

19   Apply clean engine oil to all bolt threads prior to installation, then install all bolts finger-tight. Tighten the main bearing cap bolts in the sequence shown (see illustrations) progressing in steps, to the torque listed in this Chapter's Specifications. DO NOT rotate the crankshaft at any time during this operation. On 3.0L engines, make sure that the bridge adjusting sleeves are loosened.

20   Remove the bolts in the reverse order of the tightening sequence and carefully lift the main bearing caps or bridge straight up and off the block. Do not disturb the Plastigage or rotate the crankshaft. If the main bearing caps are difficult to remove, tap them gently from side-to-side with a soft-face hammer to loosen it.

21   Compare the width of the crushed Plastigage on each journal to the scale printed on the Plastigage envelope to determine the main bearing oil clearance (see illustration). A typical main bearing oil clearance should fall between 0.0015 and 0.0023-inch. Check with an automotive machine shop for the oil clearance for your engine.

22   If the clearance is not as specified, the bearing inserts may be the wrong size (which means different ones will be required). Before deciding if different inserts are needed, make sure that no dirt or oil was between the bearing inserts and the cap or block when the clearance was measured. If the Plastigage was wider at one end than the other, the crankshaft journal may be tapered. If the clearance still exceeds the limit specified, the bearing insert(s) will have to be replaced with an undersize bearing insert(s).

✳ CAUTION:

When installing a new crankshaft, always install a standard bearing insert set.

23   Carefully scrape all traces of the Plastigage material off the main bearing journals and/or the bearing insert faces. Be sure to remove all residue from the oil holes. Use your fingernail or the edge of a plastic card - don't nick or scratch the bearing faces.

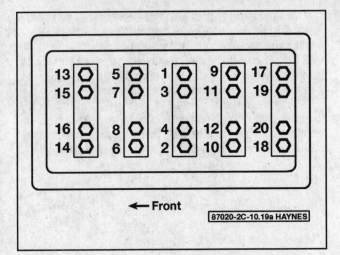

10.19a Main bearing cap bolt tightening sequence for four-cylinder engines

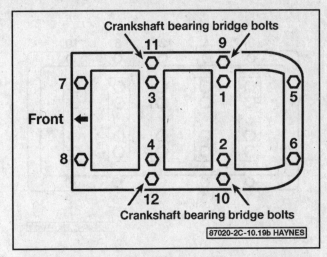

10.19b Main bearing cap bolt tightening sequence for 3.0L V6 engines

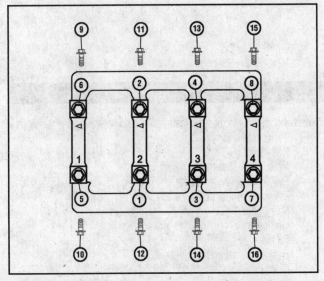

10.19c Main bearing cap bolt tightening sequence for 3.5L V6 engines

10.21 Use the scale on the Plastigage package to determine the bearing oil clearance - be sure to measure the widest part of the Plastigage and use the correct scale; it comes with both standard and metric scales

Final installation

▶ Refer to illustration 10.31

24 Carefully lift the crankshaft out of the cylinder block.

25 Clean the bearing insert faces in the cylinder block, then apply a thin, uniform layer of moly-base grease or engine assembly lube to each of the bearing surfaces. Be sure to coat the thrust faces as well as the journal face of the thrust bearing.

26 Make sure the crankshaft journals are clean, then lay the crankshaft back in place in the cylinder block.

27 Clean the bearing insert faces and apply the same lubricant to them. Clean the engine block thoroughly. The surfaces must be free of oil residue.

28 Assemble the main bearing caps or bridge and bearings and install each main bearing cap onto the crankshaft and cylinder block. Make sure the arrows face the front (timing belt or chain end)

of the engine.

➡Note: On 3.0L V6 engines, fill the side grooves with RTV sealant before installing the rear main bearing cap.

29 Prior to installation, apply clean engine oil to all bolt threads wiping off any excess, then install all bolts finger-tight.

30 Torque the main bearing cap bolts followed by the side bolts in the correct sequence.

➡Note: On 3.0L V6 engines, back off the crankshaft bearing bridge adjusting sleeves. With the bridge/bearing cap bolts loose, unscrew the sleeves until they don't contact the block. Tighten the main bearing cap bolts (in the correct sequence) to the torque listed in this Chapter's Specifications, then apply thread locking compound to the sleeves and tighten them to the torque listed in this Chapter's Specifications. Finally, install and tighten the outer crankshaft bearing bridge bolts to the torque listed in this Chapter's Specifications. Once all of the bridge/bearing cap bolts have been properly tightened, inject sealant into the grooves in the rear main bearing cap.

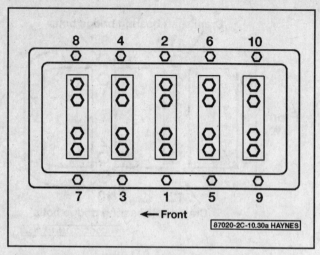

10.31 Lower crankcase perimeter bolt tightening sequence for four-cylinder engines

31 On four-cylinder engines, install the lower crankcase perimeter bolts and tighten them to the torque listed in this Chapter's Specifications in the proper sequence (see illustration).

32 Recheck crankshaft endplay with a feeler gauge or a dial indicator. The endplay should be correct if the crankshaft thrust faces aren't worn or damaged and if new bearings have been installed.

33 Rotate the crankshaft a number of times by hand to check for any obvious binding. It should rotate with a running torque of 50 in-lbs or less. If the running torque is too high, correct the problem at this time.

34 Install a new rear main oil seal (see Chapter 2A, 2B or 2C).

11 Engine overhaul - reassembly sequence

1 Before beginning engine reassembly, make sure you have all the necessary new parts, gaskets and seals as well as the following items on hand:

> *Common hand tools*
> *A 1/2-inch drive torque wrench*
> *New engine oil*
> *Gasket sealant*
> *Thread locking compound*

2 If you obtained a short block, it will be necessary to install the cylinder heads, the oil pump and pick-up tube, the oil pan, the water pump, the timing belt/chain and cover(s), and the valve cover(s) (see Chapter 2A, 2B or 2C). In order to save time and avoid problems, the external components must be installed in the following general order:

> *Thermostat and housing cover*
> *Water pump*
> *Intake and exhaust manifolds*
> *Fuel injection components*
> *Emission control components*
> *Spark plugs*
> *Ignition coils*
> *Oil filter*
> *Engine mounts and mount brackets*
> *Driveplate*

12 Initial start-up and break-in after overhaul

※※ WARNING:

Have a fire extinguisher handy when starting the engine for the first time.

1 Once the engine has been installed in the vehicle, double-check the engine oil and coolant levels.

2 With the spark plugs out of the engine and the ignition system and fuel pump disabled (see Section 3), crank the engine until oil pressure registers on the gauge or the light goes out.

3 Install the spark plugs and ignition coils, then restore the fuel pump function.

4 Start the engine. It may take a few moments for the fuel system to build up pressure, but the engine should start without a great deal of effort.

5 After the engine starts, it should be allowed to warm up to normal operating temperature. While the engine is warming up, make a thor-

ough check for fuel, oil and coolant leaks.

6   Shut the engine off and recheck the engine oil and coolant levels.

7   Drive the vehicle to an area with minimum traffic, accelerate from 30 to 50 mph, then allow the vehicle to slow to 30 mph with the throttle closed. Repeat the procedure 10 or 12 times. This will load the piston rings and cause them to seat properly against the cylinder walls. Check again for oil and coolant leaks.

8   Drive the vehicle gently for the first 500 miles (no sustained high speeds) and keep a constant check on the oil level. It is not unusual for an engine to use oil during the break-in period.

9   At approximately 500 to 600 miles, change the oil and filter.

10 For the next few hundred miles, drive the vehicle normally. Do not pamper it or abuse it.

11 After 2000 miles, change the oil and filter again and consider the engine broken in.

GLOSSARY

B

Backlash - The amount of play between two parts. Usually refers to how much one gear can be moved back and forth without moving the gear with which it's meshed.

Bearing Caps - The caps held in place by nuts or bolts which, in turn, hold the bearing surface. This space is for lubricating oil to enter.

Bearing clearance - The amount of space left between shaft and bearing surface. This space is for lubricating oil to enter.

Bearing crush - The additional height which is purposely manufactured into each bearing half to ensure complete contact of the bearing back with the housing bore when the engine is assembled.

Bearing knock - The noise created by movement of a part in a loose or worn bearing.

Blueprinting - Dismantling an engine and reassembling it to EXACT specifications.

Bore - An engine cylinder, or any cylindrical hole; also used to describe the process of enlarging or accurately refinishing a hole with a cutting tool, as to bore an engine cylinder. The bore size is the diameter of the hole.

Boring - Renewing the cylinders by cutting them out to a specified size. A boring bar is used to make the cut.

Bottom end - A term which refers collectively to the engine block, crankshaft, main bearings and the big ends of the connecting rods.

Break-in - The period of operation between installation of new or rebuilt parts and time in which parts are worn to the correct fit. Driving at reduced and varying speed for a specified mileage to permit parts to wear to the correct fit.

Bushing - A one-piece sleeve placed in a bore to serve as a bearing surface for shaft, piston pin, etc. Usually replaceable.

C

Camshaft - The shaft in the engine, on which a series of lobes are located for operating the valve mechanisms. The camshaft is driven by gears or sprockets and a timing chain. Usually referred to simply as the cam.

Carbon - Hard, or soft, black deposits found in combustion chamber, on plugs, under rings, on and under valve heads.

Cast iron - An alloy of iron and more than two percent carbon, used for engine blocks and heads because it's relatively inexpensive and easy to mold into complex shapes.

Chamfer - To bevel across (or a bevel on) the sharp edge of an object.

Chase - To repair damaged threads with a tap or die.

Combustion chamber - The space between the piston and the cylinder head, with the piston at top dead center, in which air-fuel mixture is burned.

Compression ratio - The relationship between cylinder volume (clearance volume) when the piston is at top dead center and cylinder volume when the piston is at bottom dead center.

Connecting rod - The rod that connects the crank on the crankshaft with the piston. Sometimes called a con rod.

Connecting rod cap - The part of the connecting rod assembly that attaches the rod to the crankpin.

Core plug - Soft metal plug used to plug the casting holes for the coolant passages in the block.

Crankcase - The lower part of the engine in which the crankshaft rotates; includes the lower section of the cylinder block and the oil pan.

Crank kit - A reground or reconditioned crankshaft and new main and connecting rod bearings.

Crankpin - The part of a crankshaft to which a connecting rod is attached.

Crankshaft - The main rotating member, or shaft, running the length of the crankcase, with offset throws to which the connecting rods are attached; changes the reciprocating motion of the pistons into rotating motion.

Cylinder sleeve - A replaceable sleeve, or liner, pressed into the cylinder block to form the cylinder bore.

D

Deburring - Removing the burrs (rough edges or areas) from a bearing.

Deglazer - A tool, rotated by an electric motor, used to remove glaze from cylinder walls so a new set of rings will seat.

E

Endplay - The amount of lengthwise movement between two parts. As applied to a crankshaft, the distance that the crankshaft can move forward and back in the cylinder block.

F

Face - A machinist's term that refers to removing metal from the end of a shaft or the face of a larger part, such as a flywheel.

Fatigue - A breakdown of material through a large number of loading and unloading cycles. The first signs are cracks followed shortly by breaks.

Feeler gauge - A thin strip of hardened steel, ground to an exact thickness, used to check clearances between parts.

Free height - The unloaded length or height of a spring.

Freeplay - The looseness in a linkage, or an assembly of parts, between the initial application of force and actual movement. Usually perceived as slop or slight delay.

Freeze plug - See Core plug.

G

Gallery - A large passage in the block that forms a reservoir for engine oil pressure.

Glaze - The very smooth, glassy finish that develops on cylinder walls while an engine is in service.

H

Heli-Coil - A rethreading device used when threads are worn or damaged. The device is installed in a retapped hole to reduce the thread size to the original size.

I

Installed height - The spring's measured length or height, as installed on the cylinder head. Installed height is measured from the spring seat to the underside of the spring retainer.

J

Journal - The surface of a rotating shaft which turns in a bearing.

K

Keeper - The split lock that holds the valve spring retainer in position on the valve stem.

Key - A small piece of metal inserted into matching grooves machined into two parts fitted together - such as a gear pressed onto a shaft - which prevents slippage between the two parts.

Knock - The heavy metallic engine sound, produced in the combustion chamber as a result of abnormal combustion - usually detonation. Knock is usually caused by a loose or worn bearing. Also referred to as detonation, pinging and spark knock. Connecting rod or main bearing knocks are created by too much oil clearance or insufficient lubrication.

L

Lands - The portions of metal between the piston ring grooves.

Lapping the valves - Grinding a valve face and its seat together with lapping compound.

Lash - The amount of free motion in a gear train, between gears, or in a mechanical assembly, that occurs before movement can begin. Usually refers to the lash in a valve train.

Lifter - The part that rides against the cam to transfer motion to the rest of the valve train.

M

Machining - The process of using a machine to remove metal from a metal part.

Main bearings - The plain, or babbitt, bearings that support the crankshaft.

Main bearing caps - The cast iron caps, bolted to the bottom of the block, that support the main bearings.

O

O.D. - Outside diameter.

Oil gallery - A pipe or drilled passageway in the engine used to carry engine oil from one area to another.

Oil ring - The lower ring, or rings, of a piston; designed to prevent excessive amounts of oil from working up the cylinder walls and into the combustion chamber. Also called an oil-control ring.

Oil seal - A seal which keeps oil from leaking out of a compartment. Usually refers to a dynamic seal around a rotating shaft or other moving part.

O-ring - A type of sealing ring made of a special rubberlike material; in use, the O-ring is compressed into a groove to provide the sealing action.

Overhaul - To completely disassemble a unit, clean and inspect all parts, reassemble it with the original or new parts and make all adjustments necessary for proper operation.

P

Pilot bearing - A small bearing installed in the center of the flywheel (or the rear end of the crankshaft) to support the front end of the input shaft of the transmission.

Pip mark - A little dot or indentation which indicates the top side of a compression ring.

Piston - The cylindrical part, attached to the connecting rod, that moves up and down in the cylinder as the crankshaft rotates. When the fuel charge is fired, the piston transfers the force of the explosion to the connecting rod, then to the crankshaft.

Piston pin (or wrist pin) - The cylindrical and usually hollow steel pin that passes through the piston. The piston pin fastens the piston to the upper end of the connecting rod.

Piston ring - The split ring fitted to the groove in a piston. The ring contacts the sides of the ring groove and also rubs against the cylinder wall, thus sealing space between piston and wall. There are two types of rings: Compression rings seal the compression pressure in the combustion chamber; oil rings scrape excessive oil off the cylinder wall.

Piston ring groove - The slots or grooves cut in piston heads to hold piston rings in position.

Piston skirt - The portion of the piston below the rings and the piston pin hole.

Plastigage - A thin strip of plastic thread, available in different sizes, used for measuring clearances. For example, a strip of plastigage is laid across a bearing journal and mashed as parts are assembled. Then parts are disassembled and the width of the strip is measured to determine clearance between journal and bearing. Commonly used to measure crankshaft main-bearing and connecting rod bearing clearances.

Press-fit - A tight fit between two parts that requires pressure to force the parts together. Also referred to as drive, or force, fit.

Prussian blue - A blue pigment; in solution, useful in determining the area of contact between two surfaces. Prussian blue is commonly used to determine the width and location of the contact area between the valve face and the valve seat.

R

Race (bearing) - The inner or outer ring that provides a contact surface for balls or rollers in bearing.

Ream - To size, enlarge or smooth a hole by using a round cutting tool with fluted edges.

Ring job - The process of reconditioning the cylinders and installing new rings.

Runout - Wobble. The amount a shaft rotates out-of-true.

S

Saddle - The upper main bearing seat.

Scored - Scratched or grooved, as a cylinder wall may be scored by abrasive particles moved up and down by the piston rings.

Scuffing - A type of wear in which there's a transfer of material between parts moving against each other; shows up as pits or grooves in the mating surfaces.

Seat - The surface upon which another part rests or seats. For example, the valve seat is the matched surface upon which the valve face rests. Also used to refer to wearing into a good fit; for example, piston rings seat after a few miles of driving.

Short block - An engine block complete with crankshaft and piston and, usually, camshaft assemblies.

Static balance - The balance of an object while it's stationary.

Step - The wear on the lower portion of a ring land caused by excessive side and back-clearance. The height of the step indicates the ring's extra side clearance and the length of the step projecting from the back wall of the groove represents the ring's back clearance.

Stroke - The distance the piston moves when traveling from top dead center to bottom dead center, or from bottom dead center to top dead center.

Stud - A metal rod with threads on both ends.

T

Tang - A lip on the end of a plain bearing used to align the bearing during assembly.

Tap - To cut threads in a hole. Also refers to the fluted tool used to cut threads.

Taper - A gradual reduction in the width of a shaft or hole; in an engine cylinder, taper usually takes the form of uneven wear, more pronounced at the top than at the bottom.

Throws - The offset portions of the crankshaft to which the connecting rods are affixed.

Thrust bearing - The main bearing that has thrust faces to prevent excessive endplay, or forward and backward movement of the crankshaft.

Thrust washer - A bronze or hardened steel washer placed between two moving parts. The washer prevents longitudinal movement and provides a bearing surface for thrust surfaces of parts.

Tolerance - The amount of variation permitted from an exact size of measurement. Actual amount from smallest acceptable dimension to largest acceptable dimension.

U

Umbrella - An oil deflector placed near the valve tip to throw oil from the valve stem area.

Undercut - A machined groove below the normal surface.

Undersize bearings - Smaller diameter bearings used with re-ground crankshaft journals.

V

Valve grinding - Refacing a valve in a valve-refacing machine.

Valve train - The valve-operating mechanism of an engine; includes all components from the camshaft to the valve.

Vibration damper - A cylindrical weight attached to the front of the crankshaft to minimize torsional vibration (the twist-untwist actions of the crankshaft caused by the cylinder firing impulses). Also called a harmonic balancer.

W

Water jacket - The spaces around the cylinders, between the inner and outer shells of the cylinder block or head, through which coolant circulates.

Web - A supporting structure across a cavity.

Woodruff key - A key with a radiused backside (viewed from the side).

Specifications

General

Displacement	
Four-cylinder engine	134 cubic inches (2.2 liters)
2002 and 2003 V6 engine	182 cubic inches (3.0 liters)
2004 and later V6 engine	212 cubic inches (3.5 liters)
Bore	
Four-cylinder engine	3.386 inches (86 mm)
3.0L V6 engine	3.386 inches (86 mm)
3.5L V6 engine	3.50 inches (90 mm)
Stroke	
Four-cylinder engine	3.727 inches (94.6 mm)
3.0L V6 engine	3.40 inches (85 mm)
3.5L V6 engine	3.66 inches (93 mm)
Cylinder compression pressure	135 to 163 psi (930 to 1,130 kPa)
Oil pressure at 178-degrees F (80-degrees C)	
Four-cylinder models at 1,000 rpm	50 to 80 psi (345 to 550 kPa)
3.0L V6 models at idle, minimum	22 psi (150 kPa)
3.5L V6 models	
At curb idle	10 psi (78 kPa)
At 3,000 rpm	71 psi (490 kPa)

Torque specifications	Ft-lbs (unless otherwise indicated)	Nm

➡**Note: One foot-pound (ft-lb) of torque is equivalent to 12 inch-pounds (in-lbs) of torque. Torque values below approximately 15 ft-lbs are expressed in inch-pounds, since most foot-pound torque wrenches are not accurate at these smaller values.**

Connecting rod bearing cap bolts		
Four cylinder models*		
Step 1	18	24
Step 2	Tighten an additional 100-degrees	
3.0L V6 models*		
Step 1	26	35
Step 2	Tighten an additional 45-degrees	
Step 3	Tighten an additional 15-degrees	
3.5L V6 models		
Step 1	168 in-lbs	19
Step 2	Tighten an additional 90-degrees	
Main bearing caps (see illustrations 10.19a, 10.19b and 10.19c)		
Four cylinder models*		
Step 1	15	20
Step 2	Tighten an additional 70-degrees	
Perimeter bolts	18	24

These bolts must be replaced with new ones whenever they have been loosened or removed.

Torque specifications (continued)	Ft-lbs (unless otherwise indicated)	Nm

➡**Note: One foot-pound (ft-lb) of torque is equivalent to 12 inch-pounds (in-lbs) of torque. Torque values below approximately 15 ft-lbs are expressed in inch-pounds, since most foot-pound torque wrenches are not accurate at these smaller values.**

Main bearing caps (see illustrations 10.19a, 10.19b and 10.19c) (continued)		
3.0L V6 models*		
Bolts 1 through 8		
Step 1	37	50
Step 2	Tighten an additional 60-degrees	
Step 3	Tighten an additional 15-degrees	
Bearing bridge adjusting sleeves	71 in-lbs	8
Bolts 9 through 12	15	20
3.5L V6 models		
Bottom bolts	54	73
Side bolts	36	49
Engine cradle bolts*	114	154

* These bolts must be replaced with new ones whenever they have been loosened or removed.

Notes

Section

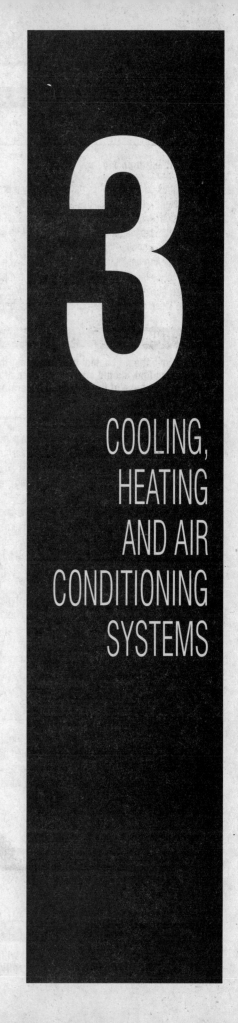

3

COOLING,
HEATING
AND AIR
CONDITIONING
SYSTEMS

1 General information

ENGINE COOLING SYSTEM

▶ **Refer to illustration 1.4**

All vehicles covered by this manual employ a pressurized engine cooling system with thermostatically controlled coolant circulation. The cooling system consists of a radiator, an expansion tank, a pressure cap (located on the expansion tank), a thermostat, one or two electric cooling fans and an impeller-type water pump.

The expansion tank functions somewhat differently than a conventional recovery tank. Designed to separate any trapped air in the coolant, it is pressurized by the radiator and has a pressure cap on top. The radiator on these models does not have a pressure cap.

✳✳ WARNING:

Unlike a conventional coolant recovery tank, the pressure cap on the expansion tank should never be opened after the engine has warmed up, because of the danger of severe burns caused by steam or scalding coolant.

The water pump mounted on the engine block pumps coolant through the engine. The coolant flows around each cylinder and toward the rear of the engine. Cast-in coolant passages direct coolant around the intake and exhaust ports, near the spark plug areas and in close proximity to the exhaust valve guides.

A wax-pellet type thermostat controls engine coolant temperature (see illustration). During warm up, the closed thermostat prevents coolant from circulating through the radiator. As the engine nears normal operating temperature, the thermostat opens and allows hot coolant to travel through the radiator, where it's cooled before returning to the engine.

The cooling system is sealed by a pressure-type cap on the coolant reservoir, which raises the boiling point of the coolant and increases the cooling efficiency of the radiator. If the system pressure exceeds the cap pressure relief value, the excess pressure in the system forces the spring-loaded valve inside the cap off its seat and allows the pressure to escape through the overflow tube.

ENGINE COOLING FANS

These models are equipped with either one (four-cylinder) or two (V6) electric cooling fans. The fans are controlled by relays and the main computer for the engine. The relays are located in the underhood fuse box. The computer uses information from various sensors and the air conditioning system to control the fan(s).

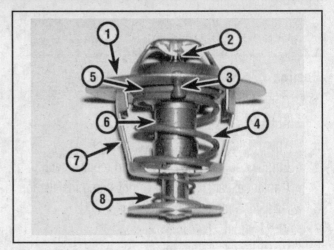

1.4 Typical thermostat

1 Flange	5 Valve seat
2 Piston	6 Valve
3 Jiggle pin	7 Frame
4 Main coil spring	8 Secondary coil spring

HEATING SYSTEM

A typical heating system consists of a blower fan and heater core located in a housing under the dash, the hoses connecting the heater core to the engine cooling system and the heater/air conditioning control head on the dashboard. Hot engine coolant is circulated through the heater core. When the heater mode is activated, a flap door in the housing opens to expose the heater core to the passenger compartment through air ducts. A fan switch on the control head activates the blower motor, which forces air through the core, heating the air.

AIR CONDITIONING SYSTEM

The air conditioning system consists of a condenser mounted in front of the radiator, an evaporator mounted adjacent to the heater core, a compressor mounted on the engine, a receiver-drier located near the condenser and the plumbing connecting all of the above components.

A blower fan forces the warmer air of the passenger compartment through the evaporator core (sort of a radiator-in-reverse), transferring the heat from the air to the refrigerant. The liquid refrigerant boils off into low pressure vapor, taking the heat with it when it leaves the evaporator.

2 Antifreeze - general information

▶ **Refer to illustration 2.5**

✳✳ WARNING:

Do not allow antifreeze to come in contact with your skin or painted surfaces of the vehicle. Rinse off spills immediately with plenty of water. Antifreeze is highly toxic if ingested. Never leave antifreeze lying around in an open container or in puddles on the floor; children and pets are attracted by its sweet smell and may drink it. Check with local authorities about disposing of used antifreeze. Many communities have collection centers which will see that antifreeze is disposed of safely. Never dump used antifreeze on the ground or pour it into drains.

❄ CAUTION:

Do not mix coolants of different colors. Doing so might damage the cooling system and/or the engine. Read the warning label in the engine compartment for additional information.

➡Note: Non-toxic antifreeze is now manufactured and available at local auto parts stores, but even this type must be disposed of properly.

The cooling system should be filled with a water/ethylene glycol based antifreeze solution, which will prevent freezing down to at least -20-degrees F (even lower in cold climates). It also provides protection against corrosion and increases the coolant boiling point. The engines in these vehicles have aluminum heads. The manufacturer recommends that the correct type of coolant be used and strongly urges that coolant types not be mixed (see the Chapter 1 Specifications).

Drain, flush and refill the cooling system at the intervals listed in the maintenance schedule (see Chapter 1).

Before adding antifreeze to the system, inspect all hose connections. Antifreeze can leak through very minute openings.

The exact mixture of antifreeze to water which you should use depends on the relative weather conditions. The mixture should contain at least 50-percent antifreeze, but should never contain more than 70-percent antifreeze. Consult the mixture ratio chart on the container before adding coolant.

➡Note: Premixed antifreeze, with water already added, is now commonly available at most auto parts stores. The percentage

2.5 Use a hydrometer (available at most auto parts stores) to test the condition of your coolant

is usually a 50/50 mix of antifreeze to water. Be sure to read the label on the antifreeze container closely to be certain that you are filling the cooling system with the proper mix of antifreeze and water.

Hydrometers are available at most auto parts stores to test the coolant (see illustration). Use antifreeze that meets factory specifications for engines with aluminum components (see Chapter 1).

3 Thermostat - check and replacement

CHECK

1 Before assuming the thermostat is to blame for a cooling system problem, check the coolant level, drivebelt tension (see Chapter 1) and temperature gauge operation.

2 If the engine seems to be taking a long time to warm up, based on heater output or temperature gauge operation, the thermostat is probably stuck open. Replace the thermostat with a new one.

3 If the engine runs hot, use your hand to check the temperature of the lower radiator hose. If the hose isn't hot, but the engine is, the thermostat is probably stuck closed, preventing the coolant inside the engine from escaping to the radiator. Replace the thermostat.

❄ CAUTION:

Don't drive the vehicle without a thermostat. The computer will stay in open loop and emissions and fuel economy will suffer.

4 If the lower radiator hose is hot, it means that the coolant is flowing and the thermostat is open. Consult the *Troubleshooting* Section at the front of this manual for cooling system diagnosis.

REPLACEMENT

❄ WARNING:

The engine must be completely cool before beginning this procedure.

5 Disconnect the cable from the negative battery terminal (see Chapter 5, Section 1).

6 Drain the cooling system (see Chapter 1). If the coolant is relatively new or in good condition (see Chapter 1), save it and reuse it. Read the **Warning** in Section 2.

3.7 Location of the water pump drain bolt (the water pump is on the firewall-side of the engine, at the timing chain end)

3.8 Remove the bolts securing the water pump pipe to the thermostat housing

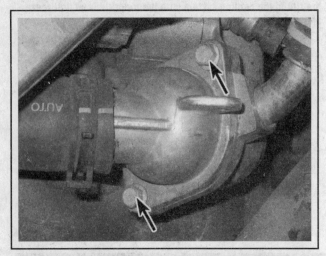

3.17 Remove the thermostat cover mounting bolts and separate the cover from the housing to access the thermostat

Four-cylinder engine

2006 and earlier models

♦ **Refer to illustrations 3.7 and 3.8**

➡**Note: The thermostat housing is located on the firewall-side of the engine.**

7   Remove the water pump drain bolt and drain the remaining coolant into a container (see illustration).

8   Remove the exhaust manifold heat shield (see Chapter 2A). Remove the bolts that hold the water pump pipe/thermostat housing cover to the thermostat housing (see illustration), then separate the cover from the housing and the water pipe from the water pump, using a twisting motion.

9   Remove the inner sleeve from the thermostat housing. Note the location of the notch on the lower section of the sleeve.

10 Note how the thermostat is installed (which end is facing out), then remove the thermostat.

11 Install the thermostat cartridge in the housing, aligning the dimple on the cartridge with the slot in the housing.

12 Install a new O-ring seal onto the water pipe.

13 Insert the water pipe into the water pump and swing the thermostat housing cover into place.

14 Install the bolts and tighten them to the torque listed in this Chapter's Specifications.

15 The remaining installation is the reverse of removal.

2007 models

♦ **Refer to illustrations 3.17, 3.18 and 3.19**

➡**Note: The thermostat housing is located at the left rear corner of the cylinder head.**

16 Loosen the hose clamps and detach the hoses from the fittings on the thermostat housing cover. If a hose sticks, grasp it near the end with a pair of adjustable pliers and twist it to break the seal, then pull it off. If the hose is old or if it has deteriorated, cut it off and install a new one. If the outer surface of the thermostat cover, which mates with the hose, is already corroded, pitted, or otherwise deteriorated, it might be damaged even more by hose removal. If it is, replace the thermostat cover.

17 Remove the fasteners and detach the thermostat cover (see illustration). If the cover is stuck, tap it with a soft-face hammer to jar it loose. Be prepared for some coolant to spill as the gasket seal is broken.

18 Note how it's installed, which end is facing out, then remove the thermostat (see illustration).

19 Install a new rubber gasket on the thermostat (see illustration) and install the thermostat in the housing, spring-end first.

20 Install the thermostat cover and bolts, then tighten the bolts to the torque listed in this Chapter's Specifications.

21 Reattach the radiator hose to the outlet pipe on the thermostat cover. Make sure that the hose clamp is tight. If it isn't, replace it.

22 The remaining installation is the reverse of the removal.

23 Refill the cooling system (see Chapter 1).

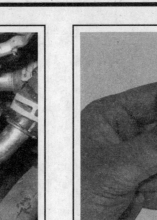

3.18 Remove the thermostat from the housing, noting how it is installed

3.19 Install a new rubber gasket around the perimeter of the thermostat

24 Reconnect the battery (see Chapter 5, Section 1).

25 Start the engine and allow it to reach normal operating temperature, then check for leaks and proper thermostat operation (as described in Steps 3 and 4).

V6 engines

2002 and 2003 models

▶ Refer to illustration 3.29

26 Refer to Chapter 2B and remove the intake manifold. It need not be completely removed from the engine compartment, however it must be raised for access to the thermostat housing.

27 Disconnect the radiator hose from the coolant pipe.

28 Remove the thermostat pipe along with its O-rings.

29 Unscrew the thermostat housing bolts, detach the housing and remove the O-ring (see illustration).

30 Install a new thermostat along with a new O-ring, tightening the housing bolts to the torque listed in this Chapter's Specifications. The remainder of installation is the reverse of removal.

2004 and later models

▶ Refer to illustrations 3.32, 3.34a and 3.34b

31 Refer to Chapter 5 and remove the battery.

32 Remove the bolts from the thermostat housing and pull the housing from the engine (see illustration). The radiator hose may be left attached if desired.

33 Remove the thermostat and the O-ring.

34 Install a new O-ring and position the new thermostat in the housing in exactly the same orientation (see illustrations).

35 Install the housing and tighten the bolts to the torque listed in this Chapter's Specifications.

36 The remainder of installation is the reverse of removal.

All models

37 Start the engine and allow it to reach normal operating temperature, then check for leaks and proper thermostat operation (as described in Steps 3 and 4).

3.29 The thermostat on 2003 and earlier V6 models is mounted on top of the engine

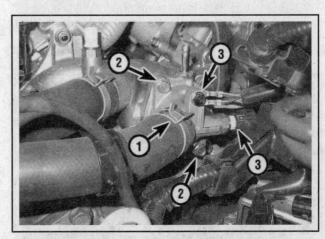

3.32 Location of the thermostat housing and cover and mounting details (2004 and later V6 engines)

1 *Lower radiator hose and clamp (use pliers to squeeze the clamp and slide it away from the thermostat housing)*
2 *Thermostat housing cover mounting bolts*
3 *Electrical connections (detach only if replacing the housing cover)*

3.34a On 2004 and later V6 models, the jiggle pin on the thermostat is at 12 o'clock . . .

3.34b . . . and the rubber tang on the seal is directly over the jiggle pin

4 Engine cooling fans - check and replacement

✳ WARNING:

To avoid possible injury or damage, DO NOT operate the engine with a damaged fan. Do not attempt to repair fan blades - replace a damaged fan with a new one.

CHECK

▶ **Refer to illustrations 4.1 and 4.3**

1   If the engine is getting hot (or overheating) and neither of the cooling fans are coming on, check their fuses first. If the fuses are okay, unplug the electrical connector for each fan motor and apply battery voltage to each one (see illustration). Use a fused jumper wire on termi-

nal A and another jumper wire going to ground on terminal B. If either fan motor doesn't come on, replace it.

✳ CAUTION:

Do not apply battery power to the harness side of the connector.

2   If the fan motors are okay, check the fan relay(s).
3   Locate the fan relays in the engine compartment fuse/relay box (see illustration).
4   Test the relays (see Chapter 12).
5   If the fuses, motors and relays are functional, check all wiring and connections to the fan motors. If no obvious problems are found, have the cooling fan system diagnosed by a dealer service department or repair shop with the proper diagnostic equipment.

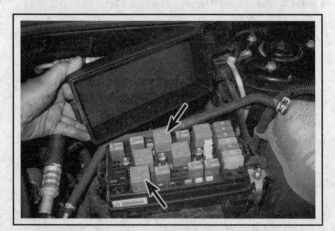

4.1 To test either fan motor, disconnect the electrical connector and use jumper wires to connect the fan directly to the battery and ground - if the fan still doesn't work, replace the motor

4.3 Release the tabs and remove the cover from the underhood fuse and relay box to access the cooling fan relays (check the underside of the cover for the relay locations on your model)

4.10 Plastic shroud (A) and left-side radiator mounting bracket (B)

4.12 Pull the radiator upward to detach it from the rubber mounts

REPLACEMENT

▶ Refer to illustrations 4.10, 4.12, 4.13a and 4.13b

✳✳ WARNING:

Wait until the engine is completely cool before beginning this procedure.

6 Refer to Chapter 11 and remove the front bumper cover.
7 Drain the engine coolant (see Chapter 1).
8 Disconnect the fan electrical connector. Unclip the transaxle cooler lines from the shroud.
9 Remove the air intake duct from the front top of the radiator.
10 Remove the plastic shroud and the air duct from the front of the air conditioning condenser by removing the two push-pins (see illustration).

11 Disconnect the radiator hoses from the radiator. Unclip the automatic transaxle cooler lines from the fan shroud.
12 Remove the upper condenser/radiator/fan module mounting brackets. Lift the assembly from its lower mounts and tilt the radiator assembly forward at the top (see illustration).
13 Unbolt the fan assembly from the radiator and lift it from its lower clips (see illustration). Pull the fan and shroud assembly out from between the radiator and the radiator support (see illustration).
14 To detach the fan blade from the motor, remove the motor shaft clip.
15 To detach the fan motor from the shroud, remove the mounting screws.
16 Installation is the reverse of removal. Fill the cooling system with the proper mixture of antifreeze and water (see Chapter 1) and check for leaks after the vehicle has reached normal operating temperature.

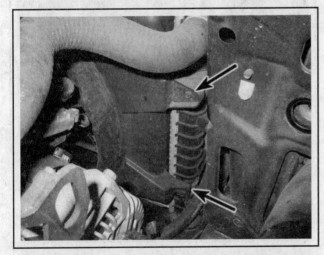

4.13a The fan/shroud assembly is retained by screws (top) and clips (bottom)

4.13b Pull the top of the radiator and condenser forward and remove the fan assembly, being careful not to nick the radiator core

5 Coolant expansion tank - removal and installation

▶ Refer to illustration 5.3

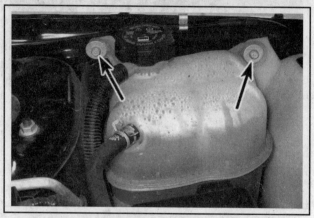

5.3 Coolant reservoir mounting bolts

❊❊ WARNING:

Wait until the engine is completely cool before beginning this procedure.

1   Carefully remove the pressure cap after the engine has completely cooled. Remove as much coolant as possible from the tank using a suction device. Alternatively, you can drain about half of the coolant from the system (see Chapter 1) before disconnecting the hoses. The coolant may be saved if it's in good condition.

2   Disconnect the upper hose from the tank and immediately plug it to prevent leakage. Check the hose for cracks or hardness and replace it if necessary.

3   Remove the two tank mounting bolts (see illustration).

4   Lift the tank and disconnect the low-level sensor.

5   Disconnect the hose from the bottom of the tank and plug it immediately.

6   Clean the inside of the tank with soapy water and a brush to remove any deposits. Inspect the tank carefully. If you find any damage, replace it.

7   Installation is the reverse of removal. Refill the cooling system (see Chapter 1).

6 Radiator - removal and installation

6.2 Automatic transaxle cooler line connections. Hold the fittings with a wrench while unscrewing the tube nuts

❊❊ WARNING:

Wait until the engine is completely cool before beginning this procedure.

REMOVAL

▶ Refer to illustrations 6.2, 6.3a and 6.3b

1   Disconnect the cable from the negative battery terminal (see Chapter 5, Section 1).

2   Disconnect the automatic transaxle cooler lines if so equipped (see illustration).

3   Refer to Section 4 and remove the radiator along with the fan(s), releasing the air conditioning condenser from the radiator clips as you do so (see illustrations).

4   Carefully lift out the radiator, being careful not to damage the fins on the radiator or air conditioning condenser.

5   Inspect the radiator for leaks and damage. If it needs repair, have a radiator shop or dealer service department perform the work, as special techniques are required.

6   Bugs and dirt can be removed from the radiator by spraying it with a garden hose nozzle from the back side. The radiator should be flushed out with a garden hose before installation.

7   Check the rubber mounts on the bottom of the radiator for wear or deterioration and replace them if necessary.

INSTALLATION

8   Installation is the reverse of the removal procedure. Carefully guide the radiator/fan assembly into position and make certain that the rubber mounts on the bottom are properly seated into the support. Attach the condenser to the radiator.

6.3a Release the clips from the condenser . . .

6.3b . . . and lift out the radiator

9   Tighten the radiator and air conditioning condenser bracket bolts securely.

10 After installation, fill the cooling system with the proper mixture of antifreeze and water (see Chapter 1).

11 Start the engine and check for leaks. Allow the engine to reach normal operating temperature, then recheck the coolant level and add more if required.

12 Check the transaxle fluid and add more as needed (see Chapter 1).

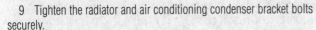

7   Water pump - check

◢ **Refer to illustration 7.3**

1   A failure in the water pump can cause serious engine damage due to overheating.

2   On four-cylinder engines the water pump is driven by the balance shaft chain. On 3.0L V6 engines, the water pump is driven by the serpentine drivebelt. On 3.5L V6 models, the water pump is driven by the timing belt. The water pump is located beneath the timing cover on all models. Water pump leaks are harder to detect with this design. Look for coolant coming out of the lower timing belt cover.

3   Water pumps are equipped with weep (or vent) holes (see illustration). If a failure occurs in the pump seal, coolant will leak from the hole. With the timing belt cover removed, use a flashlight and small mirror to find the hole on the water pump from underneath to check for leaks.

➡**Note: If there is coolant on any of the timing components or covers, consider it evidence of a severe leak.**

4   If the water pump shaft bearings fail, there may be a howling sound at the pump while it's running. Shaft wear can be felt with the drivebelt (3.0L V6 engine) or the timing belt (3.5L V6 engine) removed if the water pump pulley is rocked up and down.

5   Even a pump that exhibits no outward signs of a problem, such as noise or leakage, can still be due for replacement. Removal for close examination is the only sure way to tell. Sometimes the fins on the back of the impeller can erode to the point that cooling efficiency is hampered.

6   If the pump is defective, replace it with a new or rebuilt unit. It's considered normal practice to replace the water pump whenever the timing chain (four-cylinder engine) or timing belt (3.5L V6 engine) is replaced.

7.3 Typical weep hole on the underside of a water pump

8   Water pump - replacement

✳✳ WARNING:

Wait until the engine is completely cool before beginning this procedure.

1   Disconnect the cable from the negative battery terminal (see Chapter 5, Section 1).

2   Drain the cooling system (see Chapter 1). If the coolant is relatively new or in good condition, save it and reuse it. Read the Warning in Section 2.

FOUR-CYLINDER MODELS

▸ **Refer to illustrations 8.7, 8.13a, 8.13b, 8.15a and 8.15b**

3   Remove the air intake duct and the air filter housing (see Chapter 4).

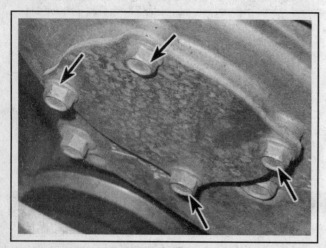

8.7   Remove the water pump cover bolts

4   Loosen the bolts of the right front wheel, raise the front of the vehicle and support it securely on jackstands. Remove the wheel.

5   Remove the right front inner wheel splash shield.

6   Remove the front exhaust manifold heat shield.

7   Remove the water pump access plate from the front cover (see illustration).

8   Remove the drain plug from the bottom of the water pump (see illustration 3.7).

9   Disconnect the electrical connector from the Engine Coolant Temperature (ECT) sensor.

10   Remove the bolts from the thermostat housing and its pipes.

11   Twist the coolant pipe out of the water pump and move the entire assembly toward the left of the vehicle. The hoses and thermostat cover can remain connected.

12   Remove the coolant pipe and its seals. Discard the seals.

13   Install a special holding tool onto the water pump (tool J-43651, available from specialty tool manufacturers and some dealer service departments). A tool can be fabricated if necessary (see illustrations). Be sure to lock the tool carefully, not allowing any sprocket movement. The bolts of the special tool will thread into the holes of the water pump sprocket that are not used for the sprocket bolts.

➡**Note: The water pump sprocket tool will lock the sprocket into position, allowing the balance shaft chain to remain in its timed state while the water pump is being replaced. If you're using a homemade tool like the one shown in the illustration, remove one of the sprocket-to-pump bolts before securing the tool to the engine front cover, as the tool will impede removal of one bolt.**

14   Remove the remaining water pump sprocket bolts.

15   Remove the two bolts from the front of the water pump and the two bolts from the rear, and remove the pump from the engine (see illustrations). If it's stuck, gently tap it with a soft-face hammer to break the seal.

16   Clean the bolt threads and the threaded holes in the engine and remove any corrosion or sealant. Clean the sealing surfaces. Remove the sealing ring from the water pump if the same pump is to be reused.

17   Install a new sealing ring into the groove of the pump. To install the new water pump, install a guide pin (threaded stud) into the water pump pulley to align the water pump sprocket with the water pump.

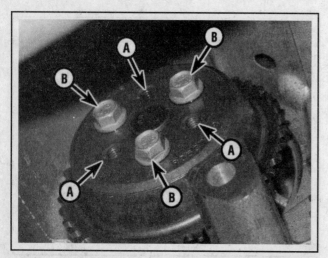

8.13a   Before installing the special tool onto the water pump sprocket, note the locations of the bolt holes for the sprocket tool (A) and the sprocket bolts (B)

8.13b   Remove one sprocket bolt, install the special tool and lock the sprocket tool into position before removing the other two sprocket bolts

8.15a Remove the two water pump bolts from the rear . . .

8.15b . . . and from the front

8.24a Removing the water pump bolts from a 3.0L V6 engine

18 Install the water pump mounting bolts and snug them up. Install two bolts into the water pump sprocket and tighten them loosely. Remove the sprocket holding tool and remove the guide pin. Install the third water pump sprocket bolt.

19 Tighten the four water pump mounting bolts and the water pump sprocket bolts to the torque listed in this Chapter's Specifications.

20 The remainder of installation is the reverse of removal. Lightly lubricate the new water pipe seals to ease installation.

21 Refill the cooling system (see Chapter 1). Run the engine and check for leaks.

V6 MODELS

▸ **Refer to illustrations 8.24a, 8.24b and 8.27**

❋❋ **CAUTION:**

If the water pump has been leaking coolant onto the timing belt, it will be necessary to replace the timing belt.

22 Remove the timing belt cover and inspect the belt (see Chapter 2).

➡**Note: Now is an excellent time to replace the timing belt.**

23 On 2004 and later models, remove the timing belt, the tensioner and the adjuster assembly (see Chapter 2C). If you're going to reuse the timing belt, be sure to paint alignment marks on the belt and on each sprocket before removing it.

24 Remove the water pump mounting bolts (see illustrations).

25 Carefully clean all sealing surfaces of the pump and the housing.

26 Compare the new pump to the old one to verify that they're identical.

27 Apply a thin film of RTV sealant to hold the new gasket in place (see illustration). Mate the pump to the block.

28 Install the pump bolts and tighten them to the torque listed in this Chapter's Specifications.

❋❋ **CAUTION:**

Don't over-tighten the bolts or the pump may become distorted.

29 Refill the cooling system (see Chapter 1). Run the engine and check for leaks.

8.24b 3.5L V6 water pump mounting bolts - one bottom bolt isn't visible in this photo

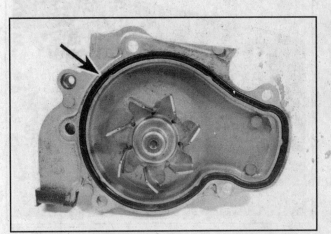

8.27 Apply a thin film of RTV sealant to the O-ring groove of the new pump, then carefully set a new O-ring in the groove - typical pump shown

9 Coolant temperature indicator - check

✳✳ WARNING:

Wait until the engine is completely cool before beginning this procedure.

1 The coolant temperature indicator system consists of the temperature gauge (on the dash), a sensor mounted on the engine and the vehicle's main computer. The Engine Coolant Temperature (ECT) sensor provides a signal to the Powertrain Control Module (PCM - the vehicle's computer) (see Chapter 6). The PCM controls the temperature gauge.

2 If the temperature gauge goes above normal and begins to read hot, check the coolant level in the system (see Chapter 1). Also, check that the coolant mixture is correct (see Section 2). Finally, refer to the *Troubleshooting* Section at the beginning of this book before assuming that the temperature indicator is faulty.

3 Start the engine and warm it up for 10 minutes. If the temperature gauge has not moved from the C position, check the wiring harness connections going to the instrument cluster.

4 If there is a problem with the ECT sensor, it is very likely that the CHECK ENGINE light will come on and the sensor or circuit will need repair (see Chapter 6). Due to the complexity of this system, further diagnosis and repair should be referred to a dealership service department or a qualified repair shop.

10 Blower motor resistor and blower motor - replacement

✳✳ WARNING:

The models covered by this manual are equipped with Supplemental Restraint systems (SRS), more commonly known as airbags. Always disable the airbag system before working in the vicinity of any airbag system component to avoid the possibility of accidental deployment of the airbag, which could cause personal injury (see Chapter 12).

BLOWER MOTOR RESISTOR

▶ **Refer to illustrations 10.1 and 10.3**

1 Working in the passenger compartment under the glove box, remove the two screws from the plastic lower panel and pull off the panel (see illustration).

2 Disconnect the electrical connector from the blower motor resistor. It's mounted near the blower assembly.

3 Remove the blower motor resistor mounting screws and remove the resistor from the blower housing (see illustration).

4 Installation is the reverse of removal.

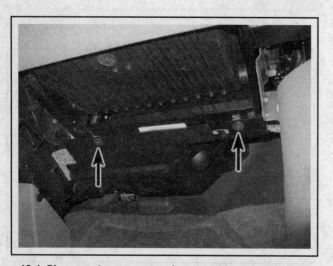

10.1 Blower motor access panel - remove the screws to remove the cover

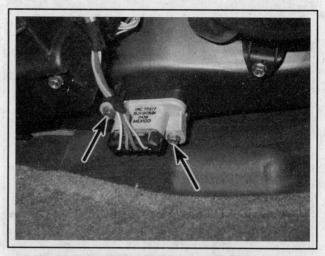

10.3 Mounting screws for the blower motor transistor

BLOWER MOTOR

▸ **Refer to illustration 10.7**

5   Working in the passenger compartment under the glove box, remove the two screws from the plastic lower panel and pull off the panel (see illustration 10.1).

6   Disconnect the blower motor electrical connector.

7   Remove the blower motor mounting screws, then remove the blower motor assembly (see illustration).

8   Remove the blower motor fan retaining clip and remove the blower fan from the motor.

9   Installation is the reverse of removal.

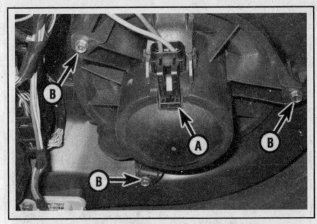

10.7 Disconnect the blower motor electrical connector (A) and remove the three mounting screws (B)

11 Heater/air conditioning control assembly - removal and installation

✳✳ WARNING:

The models covered by this manual are equipped with Supplemental Restraint Systems (SRS), more commonly known as airbags. Always disable the airbag system before working in the vicinity of any airbag system component to avoid the possibility of accidental deployment of the airbag, which could cause personal injury (see Chapter 12).

1   Disconnect the cable from the negative battery terminal (see Chapter 5, Section 1).

2   Refer to Chapter 11 and remove the trim bezel from around the shift lever.

3   Remove the screws from the small instrument panel center storage compartment, then slide it out.

4   Make sure that the two lower screws are removed and use a plastic trim tool or a screwdriver wrapped with electrical tape to pry the instrument panel center housing off. It has three clips on each side.

5   Disconnect all of the wiring from the rear of the unit.

6   Rotate the temperature selector knob fully counterclockwise. Release the retaining clips from the temperature cable and pull it from the rear of the knob.

➡**Note: Don't turn the knob or twist the cable while it's disconnected. They must stay in alignment until they're reconnected.**

7   Working from the rear of the unit, remove the four mounting screws from the heater control assembly and separate it from the housing.

8   Installation is the reverse of removal.

12 Heater core - replacement

▸ **Refer to illustration 12.3**

✳✳ WARNING:

The models covered by this manual are equipped with Supplemental Restraint Systems (SRS), more commonly known as airbags. Always disable the airbag system before working in the vicinity of any airbag system component to avoid the possibility of accidental deployment of the airbag, which could cause personal injury (see Chapter 12).

➡**Note: This is a time-consuming and complex procedure. Make sure that you have sufficient time as well as the proper equipment and parts before you begin.**

1   Disconnect the cable from the negative battery terminal (see Chapter 5, Section 1).

2   Drain the cooling system (see Chapter 1).

3   Disconnect the heater hoses from the heater core inlet and outlet pipes at the firewall (see illustration). Plug the heater core pipes to prevent coolant spillage when the heater housing is removed.

4   Remove the entire instrument panel (see Chapter 11).

12.3 Disconnect the heater hoses from inside the engine compartment

12.10a The heater core is behind a duct and a cover - removal requires extensive disassembly of the instrument panel, so allow plenty of time for this procedure

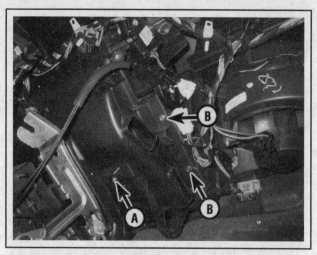

12.10b Remove the plastic duct from the front of the heater assembly by removing the screw from both sides (A) after first removing the shifter and its bracket - then remove the heater core cover screws (B)

MANUAL TRANSAXLE MODELS

5   Unbolt the shifter bracket and move the shifter assembly aside for access to the heater core.

➡**Note: On some models, it will be necessary to disconnect the shift cables from the shifter. Squeeze the retainers and lift them from the shifter.**

AUTOMATIC TRANSAXLE MODELS

6   Remove the control cable from the shifter.
7   Press the cable clip tabs and release the cable from the shifter.
8   Disconnect all wiring from the shift assembly.
9   Unbolt the shifter and set it aside in order to gain access to the heater core.

ALL MODELS

▶ **Refer to illustrations 12.10a and 12.10b**

10 Remove the large duct from the front of the heater unit (see illustrations).
11 Remove the heater core cover (see illustration 12.10b)
12 Remove the small plastic cover from the heater core pipes.
13 Remove the foam seal from the heater core pipes.
14 Remove the heater core by pulling on the end tanks.

➡**Note: Pull on the end tanks only. It will help to spray the pipes and the seal with a lubricant or soapy water first.**

15 Installation is the reverse of removal.
16 Reconnect the cable to the negative terminal of the battery (see Chapter 5, Section 1). Refill the cooling system (see Chapter 1).

13 Air conditioning and heating system - check and maintenance

▶ **Refer to illustration 13.1**

✳✳ WARNING:

The air conditioning system is under high pressure. Do not loosen any hose fittings or remove any components until after the system has been discharged by a dealer service department or service station. Always wear eye protection when disconnecting air conditioning system fittings.

1   The following maintenance checks should be performed on a regular basis to ensure the air conditioner continues to operate at peak efficiency.

   a) *Check the drivebelt. If it's worn or deteriorated, replace it (see Chapter 1).*

   b) *Check the system hoses. Look for cracks, bubbles, hard spots and deterioration. Inspect the hoses and all fittings for oil bubbles and seepage. If there's any evidence of wear, damage or leaks, replace the hose(s).*

   c) *Inspect the condenser fins for leaves, bugs and other debris. Use a fin comb or compressed air to clean the condenser.*

   d) *Make sure the system has the correct refrigerant charge.*

   e) *Check the evaporator housing drain tube for blockage (see illustration).*

2   It's a good idea to operate the system for about 10 minutes at least once a month, particularly during the winter. Long term non-use can cause hardening, and subsequent failure, of the seals.

3   Because of the complexity of the air conditioning system and the special equipment necessary to service it, in-depth troubleshooting and repairs are not included in this manual. However, simple checks and component replacement procedures are provided in this Chapter.

13.1 Look for the evaporator drain hose on the firewall - make sure it isn't clogged

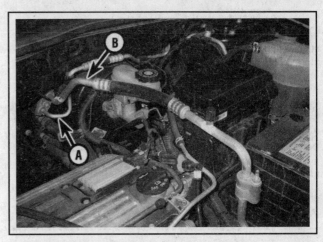

13.7 Evaporator inlet (A) and outlet (B) lines

13.8 Insert a thermometer into the center register, turn on the air conditioning system and wait for it to cool; depending on the humidity, the air should be 30 to 40-degrees cooler than theambient air

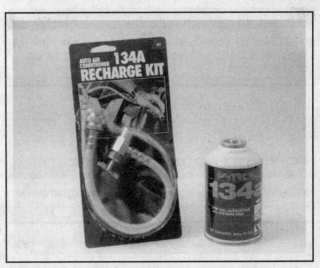

13.9 A basic charging kit for R-134a systems is available at most auto parts stores - it must say R-134a (not R-12) and so should the can of refrigerant

4   The most common cause of poor cooling is simply a low system refrigerant charge. If a noticeable drop in cool air output occurs, the following quick check will help you determine if the refrigerant level is low.

CHECKING THE REFRIGERANT CHARGE

▶ **Refer to illustrations 13.7 and 13.8**

5   Warm the engine up to normal operating temperature.

6   Place the air conditioning temperature selector at the coldest setting and the blower at the highest setting. Open the vehicle doors (to make sure the air conditioning system doesn't cycle off as soon as it cools the passenger compartment).

7   With the compressor engaged - the clutch will make an audible click and the center of the clutch will rotate - feel the evaporator inlet and outlet lines at the firewall (see illustration). The inlet (small diameter) line should feel warm and the outlet (large diameter) line should feel cold. If so, the system is properly charged.

8   Place a thermometer in the dashboard vent nearest the evaporator and operate the system until the indicated temperature is around 40 to 45-degrees F (see illustration). If the ambient (outside) air temperature is very high, say 110-degrees F, the duct air temperature may be as high as 60-degrees F, but generally the air conditioning is 30 to 40-degrees F cooler than the ambient air.

➡**Note: Humidity of the ambient air also affects the cooling capacity of the system. Higher ambient humidity lowers the effectiveness of the air conditioning system.**

ADDING REFRIGERANT

▶ **Refer to illustrations 13.9 and 13.12**

9   Buy an automotive charging kit at an auto parts store (see illustration). A charging kit includes a can of refrigerant, a tap valve and a short section of hose that can be attached between the tap valve and the

system low side service valve.

→Note: Leak detection kits with refrigerant dye, a UV light and special glasses are also available at most automotive supply stores. This kit can help you pinpoint leaks in your air conditioning system.

✳✳ CAUTION:

There are two types of refrigerant used in automotive systems; R-12 - which has been widely used on earlier models, and the more environmentally-friendly R-134a used in all models covered by this manual. These two refrigerants (and their appropriate refrigerant oils) are not compatible and must never be mixed or components will be damaged. Use only R-134a refrigerant in the models covered by this manual.

10 Hook up the charging kit by following the manufacturer's instructions.

✳✳ WARNING:

DO NOT hook the charging kit hose to the system high side! The fittings on the charging kit are designed to fit only on the low side of the system.

11 Back off the valve handle on the charging kit and screw the kit onto the refrigerant can, making sure first that the O-ring or rubber seal inside the threaded portion of the kit is in place.

✳✳ WARNING:

Wear protective eyewear when dealing with pressurized refrigerant cans.

12 Remove the dust cap from the low-side charging connection and attach the quick-connect fitting on the kit hose (see illustration).
13 Warm up the engine and turn on the air conditioner. Keep the charging kit hose away from the fan and other moving parts.

→Note: The compressor needs to be running in order to charge the system. However, if your system is very low on refrigerant, the compressor may turn off or not come on at all. If this happens, disconnect the A/C pressure switch electrical connector and use a jumper wire between the two terminals in the connector. This will keep the compressor running.

14 Turn the valve handle on the kit until the stem pierces the can, then back the handle out to release the refrigerant. You should be able to hear the rush of gas. Add refrigerant to the low side of the system until both the receiver-drier surface and the evaporator inlet pipe feel about the same temperature. Allow stabilization time between each addition.
15 If you have an accurate thermometer, place it in the center air conditioning vent and note the temperature of the air coming out of the vent. A fully-charged system which is working correctly should cool down to about 40-degrees F. Generally, an air conditioning system will put out air that is 30 to 40-degrees F cooler than the ambient air. For example, if the ambient (outside) air temperature is very high (over 100-degrees F), the temperature of air coming out of the registers should be 60 to 70-degrees F.
16 When the can is empty, turn the valve handle to the closed position and release the connection from the low-side port. Replace the dust cap.

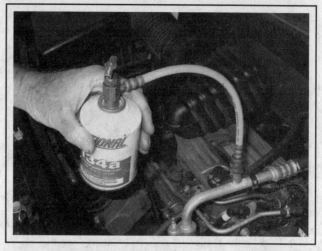

13.12 Add R-134a to the low-side port only - the procedure is easier if you wrap the can with a warm, wet towel to prevent icing

✳✳ CAUTION:

Never add more than one can of refrigerant to the system. If more refrigerant than that is required, the system should be evacuated and leak tested.

17 Remove the charging kit from the can and store the kit for future use with the piercing valve in the UP position, to prevent inadvertently piercing the can on the next use.

HEATING SYSTEMS

18 If the carpet under the heater core is damp, or if antifreeze vapor or steam is coming through the vents, the heater core is leaking. Remove it (see Section 12) and install a new unit (most radiator shops will not repair a leaking heater core).
19 If the air coming out of the heater vents isn't hot, the problem could stem from any of the following causes:

a) *The thermostat is stuck open, preventing the engine coolant from warming up enough to carry heat to the heater core. Replace the thermostat (see Section 3).*
b) *There is a blockage in the system, preventing the flow of coolant through the heater core. Feel both heater hoses at the firewall. They should be hot. If one of them is cold, there is an obstruction in one of the hoses or in the heater core, or the heater control valve is shut. Detach the hoses and back flush the heater core with a water hose. If the heater core is clear but circulation is impeded, remove the two hoses and flush them out with a water hose.*
c) *If flushing fails to remove the blockage from the heater core, the core must be replaced (see Section 12).*

ELIMINATING AIR CONDITIONING ODORS

20 Unpleasant odors that often develop in air conditioning systems are caused by the growth of a fungus, usually on the surface of the evaporator core. The warm, humid environment there is a perfect breeding ground for mildew to develop.

21 The evaporator core on most vehicles is difficult to access, and factory dealerships have a lengthy, expensive process for eliminating the fungus by opening up the evaporator case and using a powerful disinfectant and rinse on the core until the fungus is gone. You can service your own system at home, but it takes something much stronger than basic household germ-killers or deodorizers.

22 Aerosol disinfectants for automotive air conditioning systems are available in most auto parts stores, but remember when shopping for them that the most effective treatments are also the most expensive. The basic procedure for using these sprays is to start by running the system in the RECIRC mode for ten minutes with the blower on its highest speed. Use the highest heat mode to dry out the system and keep the compressor from engaging by disconnecting the wiring connector at the compressor (see Section 14).

23 Make sure that the disinfectant can comes with a long spray hose. Point the nozzle through the air recirculation door so that it protrudes inside the evaporator housing, then spray according to the manufacturer's recommendations. Try to cover the whole surface of the evaporator core, by aiming the spray up, down and sideways. Follow the manufacturer's recommendations for the length of spray and waiting time between applications.

24 Once the evaporator has been cleaned, the best way to prevent the mildew from coming back again is to make sure your evaporator housing drain tube is clear (see illustration 13.1).

14 Air conditioning compressor - removal and installation

✳✳ WARNING:

The air conditioning system is under high pressure. Do not loosen any hose fittings or remove any components until after the system has been discharged. Air conditioning refrigerant must be properly discharged into an EPA-approved recovery/recycling unit at a dealer service department or an automotive air conditioning repair facility. Always wear eye protection when disconnecting air conditioning system fittings.

➡Note: The receiver-drier should be replaced whenever the compressor is replaced.

REMOVAL

♦ Refer to illustrations 14.6 and 14.12

1 Have the air conditioning system refrigerant discharged and recovered by an air conditioning technician.
2 Disconnect the cable from the negative battery terminal (see Chapter 5, Section 1).
3 Remove the drivebelt (see Chapter 1).
4 Set the parking brake, block the rear wheels and raise the front of the vehicle, supporting it securely on jackstands.
5 Disconnect the compressor clutch electrical connector.

Four-cylinder models

6 Remove the bolt retaining the refrigerant lines to the compressor (see illustration).

2002 and 2003 V6 models

7 Refer to Chapter 6 and remove the interfering oxygen sensor from the exhaust manifold.

8 Loosen the hose retaining bolt about eight turns, then move the hose fitting forward and up to provide access. Seal all open connections to avoid contamination.

2004 and later V6 models

9 Remove the retaining bolt from the hose connector, pull the hose assembly free and discard the O-rings. Seal all open connections to avoid contamination.

10 Support the front of the subframe with a floor jack, then loosen the front subframe bolts.

➡Note: The manufacturer recommends that the subframe mounting bolts be replaced with new ones whenever they are loosened or removed.

11 Lower the engine assembly approximately one-half inch.

14.6 The air conditioning refrigerant lines are attached to the compressor with one bolt

All models

12 Remove the compressor mounting bolts (see illustration).
13 Remove the compressor.

INSTALLATION

14 The clutch may have to be transferred from the old compressor to the new unit.

15 If a new or rebuilt compressor is being installed, follow the directions supplied with the compressor to properly adjust the oil level before installing it.

16 Installation is the reverse of removal, using new O-rings where the line fittings attach to the compressor. Tighten the subframe mounting bolts to the torque listed in the Chapter 2 Specifications.

17 Reconnect the battery (see Chapter 5, Section 1).

18 Have the system evacuated, recharged and leak-tested by the shop that discharged it.

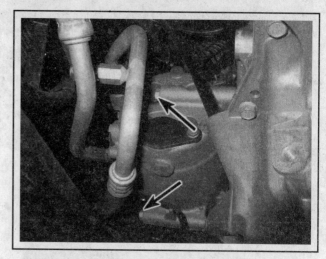

14.12 Compressor mounting bolts (two shown)

15 Air conditioning receiver-drier - removal and installation

♦ Refer to illustration 15.4

✳✳ WARNING:

The air conditioning system is under high pressure. Do not loosen any hose fittings or remove any components until after the system has been discharged. Air conditioning refrigerant must be properly discharged into an EPA-approved recovery/recycling unit at a dealer service department or an automotive air conditioning repair facility. Always wear eye protection when disconnecting air conditioning system fittings.

✳✳ CAUTION:

When replacing entire components, additional refrigerant oil must be added to them. Be sure to read the label on the container before adding any oil to the system; make sure it is compatible with the R-134a system.

1 Have the refrigerant discharged and recovered by an air conditioning technician.

2 Disconnect the cable from the negative battery terminal (see Chapter 5, Section 1).

3 Refer to Chapter 12 and remove the left headlight assembly.

4 Remove the receiver-drier nuts from the condenser and from the refrigerant lines (see illustration). Seal all open ports to avoid contamination.

✳✳ CAUTION:

Hold the condenser fitting with a large pair of pliers to avoid damage to the condenser. Treat the line with care.

5 Remove the mounting bolt and lift out the receiver-drier.

6 Installation is the reverse of removal. Be sure to install new seals onto the receiver-drier fittings. Apply a thin layer of refrigerant oil to the seals before installing them. If a new receiver-drier is being installed, add 2 ounces (60 ml) of fresh R-134a refrigerant oil. Assemble all connections with new O-rings, lightly lubricated with R-134a refrigerant oil.

7 Reconnect the battery (see Chapter 5, Section 1).

8 Have the system evacuated, charged and leak tested by the shop that discharged it.

15.4 The receiver/drier is mounted behind the left headlight (bumper cover removed for clarity)

A   Mounting nut   *B   Refrigerant line nuts*

16 Air conditioning condenser - removal and installation

❋❋ WARNING:

The air conditioning system is under high pressure. Do not loosen any hose fittings or remove any components until after the system has been discharged. Air conditioning refrigerant must be properly discharged into an EPA-approved recovery/recycling unit at a dealer service department or an automotive air conditioning repair facility. Always wear eye protection when disconnecting air conditioning system fittings.

❋❋ CAUTION:

When replacing entire components, additional refrigerant oil must be added to them. Be sure to read the label on the container before adding any oil to the system; make sure it is compatible with the R-134a system.

➡Note: The receiver-drier should be replaced whenever the condenser is replaced.

REMOVAL

▶ Refer to illustration 16.6

1   Have the refrigerant discharged and recovered by an air conditioning technician.

2   Disconnect the cable from the negative battery terminal (see Chapter 5, Section 1).

3   Refer to Chapter 11 and remove the front bumper cover.

4   On four-cylinder models, remove the plastic shroud and the air duct from the front of the air conditioning condenser by removing the two push-pins (see illustration 4.10).

5   Remove the two push-pins that secure the front air panel at the top front of the condenser. Remove the panel.

6   Disconnect the refrigerant lines from the condenser (see illustra-

tion). Cap all fittings on the condenser and lines to prevent entry of dirt or moisture.

7   Pull out on the upper retainers and lift the condenser from the vehicle (see illustration 6.3). Be careful not to damage any of the fins on it or the radiator.

INSTALLATION

8   Installation is the reverse of removal. Tighten the line fitting mounting bolts to the torque listed in this Chapter's Specifications. If a new condenser is being installed, add 1-1/6 ounces (35 ml) of fresh refrigerant oil. Assemble all connections with new O-rings, lightly lubricated with R-134a refrigerant oil.

9   Reconnect the battery (see Chapter 5, Section 1).

10 Have the system evacuated, charged and leak tested by the shop that discharged it.

16.6 Disconnect the refrigerant lines from the condenser (bumper cover removed for clarity)

Specifications

General

Radiator cap pressure rating	14 to 18 psi (93 to 123 kPa)
Thermostat rating (opening to fully open temperature range)	169 to 194-degrees F (76 to 90-degrees C)
Cooling system capacity	See Chapter 1
Refrigerant type	R-134a
Refrigerant capacity	Refer to HVAC specification tag

Torque specifications	Ft-lbs (unless otherwise indicated)	Nm

➡Note: One foot-pound (ft-lb) of torque is equivalent to 12 inch-pounds (in-lbs) of torque. Torque values below approximately 15 ft-lbs are expressed in inch-pounds, since most foot-pound torque wrenches are not accurate at these smaller values.

Condenser inlet and outlet bolts	86 in-lbs	9.5
Thermostat housing cover bolts		
Four-cylinder models	89 in-lbs	10
2002 and 2003 V6 models	15	20
2004 and later V6 models	106 in-lbs	12
Water pump bolts	106 in-lbs	12

Section

Reference to other Chapters

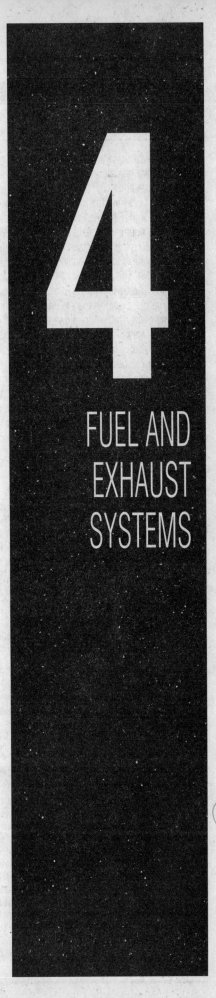

4

FUEL AND
EXHAUST
SYSTEMS

1 General information

AIR INDUCTION SYSTEM

The air induction system consists of the air filter assembly, the air intake duct, the resonator(s), the throttle body and the intake manifold.

The throttle body contains a throttle plate, which regulates the amount of air entering the intake manifold. The throttle body is also the location of the Throttle Position (TP) sensor, a potentiometer that monitors the opening angle of the throttle plate and sends a variable voltage signal to the Powertrain Control Module (PCM). On all models, the throttle plate is electronically controlled by the Powertrain Control Module (PCM). The Accelerator Pedal Position (APP) sensor relays the angle of the throttle link to the PCM, which processes this information and commands a small servo inside the throttle body to open or close the throttle plate. This setup allows the PCM to fine tune the position of the throttle plate in response to other inputs besides the position of the accelerator pedal, which means better fuel efficiency and lower emissions. The Accelerator Pedal Position (APP) sensor is located at the top of the accelerator pedal; there is no accelerator cable.

All of the air induction components (resonator, air filter housing, air intake duct and throttle body) are covered in this Chapter, except for the intake manifold, which is in Chapter 2. The information sensors such as the APP, Intake Air Temperature (IAT) and Mass Air Flow (MAF) sensors as well as the PCM are covered in Chapter 6.

FUEL SYSTEM

The fuel system consists of the fuel tank, an electric fuel pump (located in the fuel tank), the fuel rail and the fuel injectors. The fuel injection system is a multiport system, which means that the fuel injectors deliver fuel directly into the intake ports of the cylinders. Multiport systems provide much better control of the air/fuel mixture ratio than earlier fuel injection systems, and are therefore able to produce more power, better mileage and lower emissions.

All models are also equipped with a fuel pressure regulator (see Fuel pump and fuel lines below). The fuel pressure regulator is a part of a module in the fuel tank. On these models, the pressure regulator is simply spring-loaded; it is not vacuum-operated.

The fuel tank has two compartments and each compartment has its own module. The secondary fuel tank module on 2002 and 2003 models contains the fuel pressure regulator, the low-pressure siphon jet pump and a level sensor. The primary module on these vehicles contains the fuel pump, a fuel level sensor, the high-speed siphon jet pump and a strainer. On 2004 and later models, the arrangement is somewhat changed. The secondary fuel tank module contains only a fuel level sensor. All other components are in the primary fuel tank module. The siphon jet pumps are used only to supply fuel to the suction side of the main fuel pump.

The fuel pressure regulator cannot be replaced without replacing the entire secondary fuel tank module (2002 and 2003 models) or the primary fuel tank module (2004 and later models).

For more information about the fuel injection system, see Section 10. For more information about the PCM and the information sensors, refer to Chapter 6.

FUEL PUMP AND FUEL LINES

Fuel is circulated through metal lines located on the bottom of the vehicle from the fuel tank to the fuel injection system on the engine. On 2002 and 2003 models, the fuel flows to the body-mounted fuel filter. Some fuel is then returned to the secondary side of the fuel tank. 2004 and later models don't use a return line and the fuel filter is located in the primary fuel tank module. On these later models, the main fuel filter is replaced as a part of the primary fuel tank module. The main fuel pump on all models is a part of the primary fuel tank module.

EXHAUST SYSTEM

The exhaust system consists of the exhaust manifolds, the Y pipe that connects both manifolds (or converters) to the under-floor catalytic converter, the catalyst itself, the muffler and the tailpipe. The exhaust manifolds are covered in Chapter 2, and the catalytic converter is covered in Chapter 6.

2 Fuel pressure relief procedure

▶ **Refer to illustrations 2.2 and 2.4**

✳✳ WARNING:

Gasoline is extremely flammable, so take extra precautions when you work on any part of the fuel system. Don't smoke or allow open flames or bare light bulbs near the work area, and don't work in a garage where a gas-type appliance (such as a water heater or a clothes dryer) is present. Since gasoline is carcinogenic, wear fuel-resistant gloves when there's a possibility of being exposed to fuel, and, if you spill any fuel on your skin, rinse it off immediately with soap and water. Mop up any spills immediately and do not store fuel-soaked rags where they could ignite. The fuel system is under constant pressure, so, if any fuel lines are to be disconnected, the fuel pressure in the system must be relieved first. When you perform any kind of work on the fuel system, wear safety glasses and have a Class B type fire extinguisher on hand.

1 Because the pressure in the fuel system remains for some time after the ignition has been switched off, it must be relieved before any part of the fuel delivery system is worked on.

2 On most vehicles, the fuel pressure is relieved by removing a fuel pump fuse (which disables the fuel pump), then starting (or attempting to start) the engine (see illustration). However, the manufacturer doesn't recommend this method because it might set a Diagnostic Trouble Code (DTC). Instead, it recommends that you relieve system fuel pressure by draining off the residual fuel through the Schrader valve on the fuel rail (which is also used for measuring fuel pressure, as described in the next Section).

3 Remove the fuel filler cap to relieve any pressure built-up in the fuel tank.

4 The recommended setup for relieving fuel pressure (see illustration) is similar to the one that you'll need to measure fuel pressure in the next Section. Your fuel pressure relief setup must include a fuel pressure gauge with a hose and fitting suitable for connecting the gauge

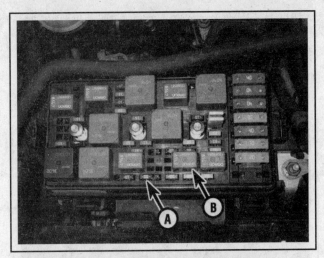

2.2 The fuel pump fuse (A) is located in the engine compartment fuse box; (B) is the fuel pump relay

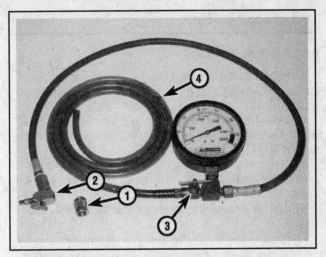

2.4 A typical fuel pressure gauge set up for relieving fuel pressure should include a screw-on adapter for the quick-release fitting (1), a quick-release fitting for connecting the gauge hose to the Schrader valve (2), a bleeder valve (3) and a bleeder hose (4) that's long enough to reach the container into which you're going to drain the fuel

to the Schrader valve-type test port on the fuel rail, and a bleeder valve so that you can drain off the excess fuel. You'll also need a container approved for storing fuel and a section of plastic tubing long enough to connect the bleeder valve to the container.

5 Disconnect the cable from the negative terminal of the battery (see Chapter 5, Section 1).

6 Locate the Schrader valve on the fuel rail, then unscrew the cap and connect the gauge (see illustration 3.3). Run the hose from the bleeder valve down to an approved container, then open the bleeder valve and let the excess fuel drain into the container. When the fuel ceases dribbling out, close the bleeder valve, disconnect and remove

your fuel pressure relief rig and screw the cap on the Schrader valve. The fuel pressure is now relieved. You may now open up the fuel system to service any component.

❊❊ WARNING:

This procedure merely relieves the pressure that the engine needs to run. But remember that fuel is still present in the system components, and take precautions accordingly before disconnecting any of them.

3   Fuel pump/fuel pressure - check

❊❊ WARNING:

Gasoline is extremely flammable, so take extra precautions when you work on any part of the fuel system. See the Warning in Section 2.

FUEL PUMP OPERATION CHECK

1 The fuel pump is located inside the fuel tank. Sit inside the vehicle with the windows closed, turn the ignition key to ON (not START) and listen for the sound made by the fuel pump as it's briefly turned on by the PCM when the key is turned to the On position (the sound will come from under the rear seat, because the fuel tank is located below

it). You will only hear the sound for a second or two, but that sound tells you that the pump is working. If you can't hear the pump, remove the fuel filler cap, then have an assistant turn the ignition switch to ON while you listen for the sound of the pump operating for a couple of seconds.

2 If the pump does not come on when the ignition key is turned to ON, check the fuel pump fuse and relay (both of which are located in the engine compartment fuse and relay box) (see illustration 2.2). If the fuse and relay are okay, check the wiring back to the fuel pump (see Section 5 if you need help locating the fuel pump electrical connector). If the fuse, relay and wiring are okay, the fuel pump is probably defective. If the pump runs continuously with the ignition key in its ON position, the Powertrain Control Module (PCM) is probably defective. Have the PCM checked by a dealer service department or other qualified repair shop.

FUEL PRESSURE CHECK

♦ **Refer to illustration 3.3**

3   To check the fuel pressure, locate the Schrader valve test port on the fuel rail, unscrew the cap and connect a fuel pressure gauge (see illustration).

4   Relieve the fuel pressure (see Section 2). After you have relieved the fuel pressure, make sure that the bleeder valve on your fuel pressure gauge is CLOSED.

5   Start the engine and allow it to idle. Note the gauge reading as soon as the pressure stabilizes, and compare it with the pressure listed in this Chapter's Specifications.

6   If the fuel pressure is not within specifications, check the following:

a)   *If you're working on a 2003 and earlier model, and the pressure is lower than specified, check for a restriction in the fuel system. To rule out the possibility of a clogged fuel filter, replace the filter (see Chapter 1).*

b)   *On 2004 and later models, if the pressure is lower than specified, check for a restriction in the fuel system (this includes the inlet strainer and the fuel filter). If no restrictions are found, replace the fuel pump module (see Section 5).*

c)   *If the fuel pressure is higher than specified, replace the fuel pump module (see Section 5).*

7   Turn off the engine. Verify that the fuel pressure loses no more than 8 psi for five minutes after the engine is turned off. If it does, the problem could be a leaky fuel injector, a fuel line leak, or a faulty check valve in the fuel pump module.

8   Relieve the fuel pressure (see Section 2), then disconnect the fuel pressure gauge. Mop up any spilled gasoline.

9   Start the engine and verify that there are no fuel leaks.

3.3 Locate the Schrader valve test port on the fuel rail, unscrew the cap and connect a fuel pressure gauge

4   Fuel lines and fittings - general information

❊❊ WARNING:

Gasoline is extremely flammable, so take extra precautions when you work on any part of the fuel system. See the Warning in Section 2.

1   Always relieve the fuel pressure before servicing fuel lines or fittings (see Section 2), then disconnect the cable from the negative battery terminal (see Chapter 5, Section 1) before proceeding.

2   The fuel supply line connects the fuel pump in the fuel tank to the fuel rail on the engine. The Evaporative Emission (EVAP) system lines connect the fuel tank to the EVAP canister and connect the canister to the intake manifold. All lines are secured to the underbody with small metal brackets that attach to the vehicle floorpan. The lines are attached to these metal brackets by plastic clips that are easy to detach from the brackets (see illustration).

3   Whenever you're working under the vehicle, be sure to inspect all fuel and evaporative emission lines for leaks, kinks, dents and other damage. Always replace a damaged fuel or EVAP line immediately. Leaking fuel and EVAP lines will result in loss of fuel and excessive air pollution (the leaking raw fuel emits unburned hydrocarbon vapors into the atmosphere).

4   If you find signs of dirt in the lines during disassembly, disconnect all lines and blow them out with compressed air. Inspect the fuel strainer on the fuel pump pick-up unit (see Sections 5 and 6) for damage and deterioration. Also inspect the fuel filter. On 2002 and 2003 models, it's attached to the side of the fuel tank. On later models, it's a part of the primary fuel tank module.

STEEL TUBING

5   Because fuel lines used on fuel-injected vehicles are under fairly high pressure, it is critical that they be replaced with lines of equivalent specification. If you have to replace a fuel or EVAP line, use only steel tubing that meets the manufacturer's specifications. Don't use copper or aluminum tubing to replace steel tubing. These materials cannot withstand normal vehicle vibration.

6   Some steel fuel lines have threaded fittings. When loosening these fittings to service or replace components:

a)   *Always hold the stationary fitting with a wrench while turning the tube nut (this will prevent the line from twisting).*

b)   *If you're going to replace one of these fittings, use original equipment parts or parts that meet original equipment standards.*

PLASTIC TUBING

7   Some fuel lines are plastic. If you have to replace these, use only the original equipment plastic tubing.

✳✳ CAUTION:

When removing or installing plastic fuel line tubing, be careful not to bend or twist it too much, which can damage it. And damaged fuel lines MUST be replaced! Also, be aware that the plastic fuel tubing is NOT heat resistant, so keep it away from excessive heat. Nor is it acid-proof, so don't wipe it off with a shop rag that has been used to wipe off battery electrolyte. If you accidentally spill or wipe electrolyte on plastic fuel tubing, replace the tubing.

FLEXIBLE HOSES

✳✳ WARNING:

Use only original equipment replacement hoses or their equivalent. Unapproved hoses might fail when subjected to the high operating pressures of the fuel system.

8   Don't route fuel hoses (or metal lines) within four inches of the exhaust system or within ten inches of the catalytic converter. Make sure that no rubber hoses are installed directly against the vehicle, particularly in places where there is any vibration. If allowed to touch some vibrating part of the vehicle, a hose can easily become chafed and it might start leaking. A good rule of thumb is to maintain a minimum of 1/4-inch clearance around a hose (or metal line) to prevent contact with the vehicle underbody.

DISCONNECTING AND RECONNECTING FUEL SYSTEM FITTINGS

9   The fittings in the fuel system consist of conventional spring-type hose clamps and quick-connect fittings. Quick-connect fittings are used to connect lines on the (high-pressure) supply side of the system, such as the connections at the fuel pump.

Conventional spring-type hose clamps

▶ **Refer to illustration 4.13**

10   Relieve the system fuel pressure (see Section 2), then disconnect the cable from the negative battery terminal (see Chapter 5, Section 1).
11   To disconnect a spring-type hose clamp, simply squeeze the two ends together with a pair of pliers to loosen the clamp, then slide the clamp away from the pipe to which the hose is attached.
12   If a spring-type hose clamp feels easy to squeeze open, or if it's obviously not clamping the hose tightly against the metal pipe to which the hose is connected, replace the clamp.
13   When installing spring-type hose clamps, make sure to slide the hose onto the pipe up to the second raised ridge on the pipe, then slide the hose clamp down the hose until it's centered between the two ridges (see illustration).
14   Reconnect the cable to the negative battery cable (see Chapter 5, Section 1).

4.13   Slide the hose onto the metal line up to the second raised ridge on the line or pipe (left arrow), then center the clamp between the two ridges

15   Start the engine and verify that no fuel is leaking out at the connection you just reconnected. If there's a leak, either the clamp is weak or it's not centered correctly between the two raised ridges on the metal line or pipe to which you connected the fuel hose. Or the hose itself is leaking because it's cracked or torn where the clamp squeezes down on it.

Quick-connect fittings

✳✳ CAUTION:

When disconnecting or reconnecting quick-connect fittings, be careful not to bend or twist them excessively, or they will be damaged and will have to be replaced. Also, be aware that the quick-connect fittings are NOT heat resistant, so keep them away from excessive heat. Nor are they acid-proof, so don't wipe them off with a shop rag that has been used to wipe off battery electrolyte. If you accidentally spill or wipe electrolyte on quick-connect fittings, replace them.

➡Note: You'll find quick-connect fittings like these on all models.

Plastic fittings

▶ **Refer to illustrations 4.19a, 4.19b and 4.23**

16   The following procedure shows how to disconnect and reconnect the quick-connect fittings at the fuel pump, but the procedure for disconnecting and reconnecting quick-connect fittings at the front of the fuel tank is identical. The second procedure here shows how to disconnect a typical quick-connect fitting at the fuel rail.
17   Relieve the system fuel pressure (see Section 2), then disconnect the cable from the negative battery terminal (see Chapter 5, Section 1).
18   To disconnect the fuel line quick-connect fittings at the fuel pump, you'll have to remove the fuel tank. To access the quick-connect fittings at the front of the fuel tank, raise the vehicle and place it securely on jackstands.
19   Holding the black side of the fitting with one hand, squeeze the

4.19a Squeeze these two retainer tangs . . .

4.19b . . . and pull the quick-connect fitting off the fuel pipe

4.23 Before reconnecting a quick-connect fitting, always inspect the condition of the retainer (A) and the O-ring inside the fitting (B)

retainer tabs on the white part of the fitting with your other hand to release the tabs, then pull the two halves of the fitting apart (see illustrations).

20 Inspect the contact surface of the line for dirt and damage.

21 Cover the disconnected ends of the fitting with plastic bags to keep out dirt and moisture.

22 Remove the old retainer from the fitting.

23 Inspect the O-ring inside the bore of the fitting. If it's cracked, torn or otherwise damaged, replace the fitting (see illustration).

24 Install a new retainer in the female side of the fitting. Be sure to align the locking pawls of the retainer with the grooves in the side of the connector.

25 Press the two halves of the quick-connect fitting together until both retainer tabs lock with a clicking sound.

26 Verify that the quick-connect fitting is correctly reconnected by trying to pull the two halves of the connector apart.

27 Reconnect the cable to the negative battery terminal (see Chapter 5, Section 1).

28 Turn the ignition key to the On position to pressurize the fuel system, then check for leaks.

Metal collar fittings

♦ Refer to illustrations 4.30 and 4.31

➡Note: These fittings require special tools that are available at auto parts stores.

29 Relieve the fuel system pressure (see Section 2).

30 Pull off the clip end of the retainer, then slide it off of the fitting (see illustration).

31 Using a fuel line separator tool of the proper size (available at most auto parts stores), insert it into the female side of the fitting, then push it into the fitting to release the locking tabs (see illustration). Pull the fitting apart.

32 Inspect the O-ring. If it's dried, cracked or worn, replace it.

33 Apply a few drops of clean engine oil to the male pipe end.

34 Push the fitting together until the tabs snap into place. Pull on the fitting to verify that it's securely connected.

35 Install the retainer, making sure it clips into place.

36 Turn the ignition key to the On position to pressurize the fuel system, then check for leaks.

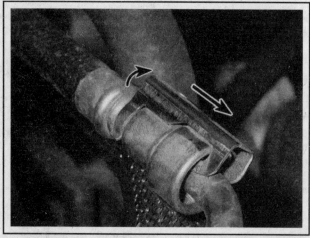

4.30 Pull the end of the retainer off the fuel line, then disengage the other end from the female side of the fitting

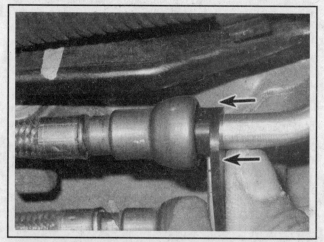

4.31 Push the fuel line separator into the fitting until it releases the locking tabs, then pull the two halves of the fitting apart

5 Fuel pump/fuel level sending unit modules - removal and installation

❋❋ WARNING:

Gasoline is extremely flammable, so take extra precautions when you work on any part of the fuel system. See the Warning in Section 2.

❋❋ CAUTION:

On 2004 and later models, the secondary fuel tank module should be removed before attempting to remove the primary module.

→Note: The primary fuel tank module is the one that contains the main fuel pump on all models.

1 Detach the cable from the negative battery terminal (see Chapter 5, Section 1). Relieve the fuel system pressure (see Section 2).
2 Refer to Section 7 and remove the fuel tank from the vehicle.

SECONDARY FUEL TANK MODULE, 2004 AND LATER MODELS

▶ Refer to illustrations 5.4, 5.5 and 5.6

3 Disconnect the EVAP hose quick-connect fitting on the top of the secondary fuel tank module (see Section 4).
4 Mark the position of the lock ring (see illustration).
5 Use a large pair of water pump pliers to remove the fuel tank module lock ring (see illustration). If it won't break loose, tap it with a hammer and a brass punch (to avoid sparks).
6 Disconnect electrical connector from the unit, then push down on the tab near the base of the module to release the suction port tube, then carefully pull the module out of the tank (see illustration).
7 Inspect the O-ring and replace it if it shows any sign of deterioration. Installation is the reverse of removal.

ALL OTHER FUEL TANK MODULES

▶ Refer to illustrations 5.8, 5.9, 5.10, 5.11 and 5.12

8 Disconnect all the electrical connectors from the module and pressure sensor (see illustration).

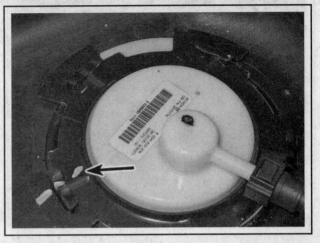

5.4 Mark the position of the lock ring

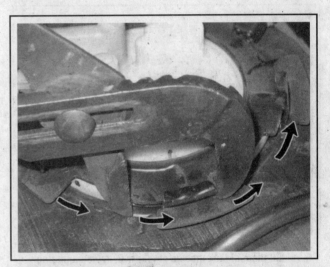

5.5 Use a large pair of water pump pliers to loosen and unscrew the fuel tank module locknut

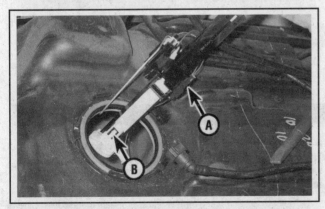

5.6 Disconnect the electrical connector (A), then push down on the tab near the base of the module to release the suction port tube (B)

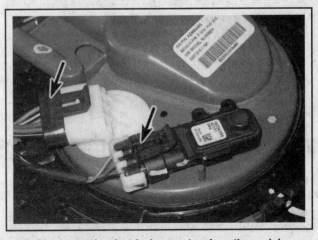

5.8 Disconnect the electrical connectors from the module and pressure sensor

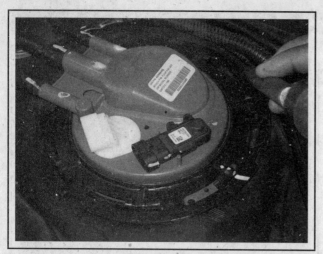

5.9 If the lock ring won't break loose with a pair of pliers, use a brass punch to drive the locking ring around

5.10 The lines must be released from the grooves on top of the tank

5.11 Lift the fuel tank module carefully to avoid damaging the fuel level sensor

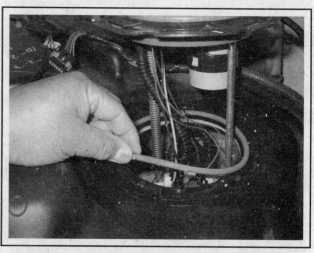

5.12 The module's O-ring must be undamaged - if it shows any sign of deterioration, replace it

9   Use a large pair of water pump pliers to remove the fuel tank module lock ring (see illustration 5.5). If it won't break loose, tap it with a hammer and a brass punch (to avoid sparks) (see illustration).

10 Release the lines from the top of the fuel tank (see illustration).

11 Carefully remove the module from the fuel tank (see illustration).

12 Inspect the O-ring and replace it if it shows any sign of deterioration (see illustration). Installation is the reverse of removal.

6   Fuel level sending unit - replacement

▶ Refer to illustrations 6.2 and 6.6

※※ WARNING:

Gasoline is extremely flammable, so take extra precautions when you work on any part of the fuel system. See the Warning in Section 2.

➥Note: The modules are serviced as complete assemblies. The only parts that can be replaced separately are the fuel level sensors. The primary and secondary level sending units are not interchangeable.

1   Refer to Section 5 and remove the appropriate module from the fuel tank.

2   Disconnect the wiring from the lower side of the top of the mod-

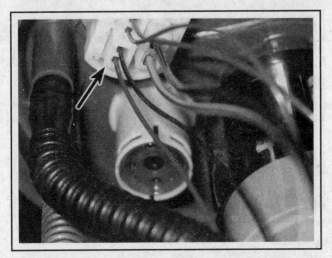

6.2 Disconnect the fuel level sensor from the base of the fuel tank module

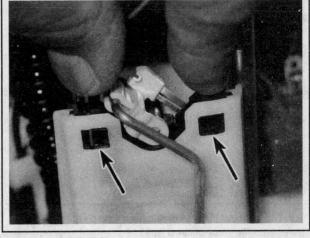

6.6 To replace the fuel level sensor, press the two levers to release these tabs

ule (see illustration).

➡**Note: The fuel pump is also connected to the top of the module. The fuel pump and the filter are replaced as part of the entire fuel tank module.**

2002 AND 2003 MODELS

3   If you're working on the secondary module, use a pointed tool to push on the silver connector and release the ground wire from the fuel pressure regulator.

4   Use a small screwdriver to release the clips securing the fuel level sender, then pull it straight down to remove it.
5   Installation is the reverse of removal.

2004 AND LATER MODELS

6   Push in on two retaining clips near the pivot of the float arm (see illustration).
7   Slide the level sensor up and off of the module.
8   Installation is the reverse of removal.

7   Fuel tank - removal and installation

◆ **Refer to illustrations 7.9 and 7.12**

※※ WARNING 1:

Gasoline is extremely flammable, so take extra precautions when you work on any part of the fuel system. See the Warning in Section 2.

※※ WARNING 2:

The following procedure is much easier to perform if the fuel tank is empty. The tank has no drain plug, so the fuel must be siphoned from the tank with a siphoning kit, which is available at most auto parts stores. NEVER try to start the siphoning action with your mouth!

1   Remove the fuel tank filler cap to relieve fuel tank pressure.

2   Relieve the fuel system pressure (see Section 2).
3   Disconnect the cable from the negative battery terminal (see Chapter 5, Section 1).
4   If the fuel tank is empty or nearly empty, it's not necessary to siphon the remaining fuel from the tank. But if there is a lot of fuel in the tank, obtain a siphon kit at an auto parts store and siphon out the remaining fuel.

※※ WARNING:

Always siphon fuel into an approved gasoline container.

5   Raise the rear of the vehicle and support it securely on jackstands.
6   Remove the rear section of the exhaust system.
7   On AWD models, remove the driveshaft (see Chapter 8).
8   Carefully clean around all of the vent hoses, squeeze the tabs and

7.9 The fuel tank fill hose uses a hose clamp - all other fittings are the quick-connect type

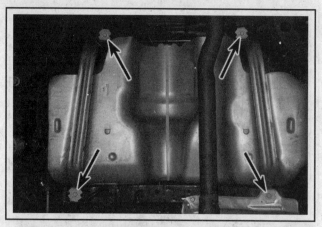

7.12 Fuel tank strap bolts

pull the connections apart.

9   Disconnect the filler hose from the tank (see illustration). Also detach the fuel hose(s) at the fitting(s) near the tank, and the EVAP hoses from the canister.

✳✳ WARNING:

Be sure to catch fuel spillage with rags. Dispose of the fuel-soaked rags in an approved container.

10 Disconnect the wiring harnesses from the fuel tank.

11 Support the fuel tank securely.

12 Remove the fuel tank retaining strap bolts (see illustration) and remove the straps.

13 Carefully lower the fuel tank.

14 If you're going to clean the fuel tank, refer to Section 8.

15 Installation is the reverse of removal. Be sure to tighten the fuel tank strap bolts securely.

16 Reconnect the cable to the negative battery terminal (see Chapter 5, Section 1), then start the engine and check for fuel leaks.

8   Fuel tank cleaning and repair - general information

1   The fuel tanks installed in these vehicles are made of plastic and are not repairable. If the fuel tank has been removed for cleaning, this is a job that should be left to a professional who has experience in this critical and potentially dangerous work. Even after cleaning and flushing of the fuel tank, explosive fumes can remain.

2   If the fuel tank is removed from the vehicle, it should not be placed in an area where sparks or open flames could ignite the fumes coming out of the tank. Be especially careful inside garages where a gas-type appliance is located because it could cause an explosion.

9   Air filter housing and ducts - removal and installation

FRESH AIR INTAKE DUCT

◆ Refer to illustration 9.2

1   Refer to Chapter 11 and remove the front bumper cover.

2   Remove the air intake bolts and lift off the duct (see illustration).

3   Installation is the reverse of removal.

AIR INTAKE DUCT (TO THROTTLE BODY)

Four-cylinder models

◆ Refer to illustrations 9.4 and 9.6

4   Disconnect the electrical connector from the IAT sensor (see illustration).

5   Disconnect the PCV fresh air hose from the valve cover.

6   Loosen the clamps at the air filter housing and the throttle body (see illustration).

7   Remove the air duct push-pin retainers from the support bracket and lift off the duct.

2002 and 2003 V6 models

8   Loosen the clamps at the air filter housing and the throttle body.

9   Remove the two mounting bolts from the duct and lift off the duct.

2004 and later V6 models

◆ Refer to illustration 9.10

10 Loosen the clamps at the air filter housing and the throttle body seal (see illustration).

11 Remove the mounting bolt near the air cleaner and lift off the duct.

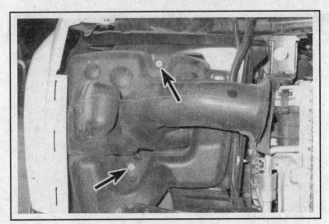

9.2 Fresh air intake duct mounting bolts

9.4 Disconnect the PCV valve hose at the valve cover (A) and the IAT sensor wiring (B)

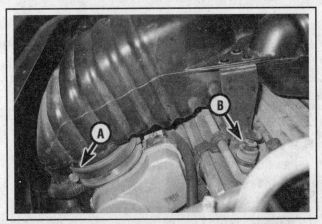

9.6 Throttle body clamp (A) and air duct bracket bolt (B)

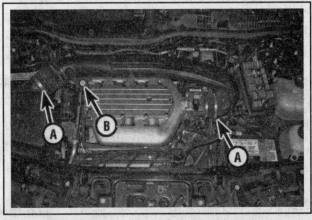

9.10 Air intake duct details - 2004 and later V6 models

A   Clamps   B   Mounting bolt

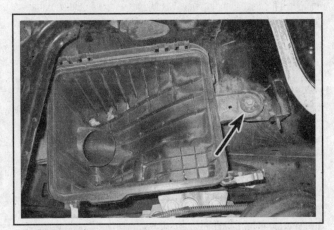

9.14a Air filter housing mounting bolt

9.14b Disengage the air filter housing from the body as you lift it off

AIR FILTER HOUSING

▶ Refer to illustrations 9.14a and 9.14b

12 Loosen the clamp and detach the duct from the air filter housing.

13 If you're working on a V6 model, disconnect the electrical connector from the MAF sensor (3.0L V6) or the IAT sensor (3.5L V6).

14 Remove the air filter housing mounting bolt and lift off the housing (see illustrations).

15 Installation is the reverse of removal.

10 Fuel injection system - general information

The Sequential Fuel Injection (SFI) system is a sequential multiport system. This means that there is a fuel injector in each intake port, and that these fuel injectors inject fuel into the intake ports in the cylinder firing order (1-4-2-5-3-6). The injectors are turned on and off by the Powertrain Control Module (PCM). When the engine is running, the PCM constantly monitors engine operating conditions with an array of information sensors, calculates the correct amount of fuel, then varies the interval of time during which the injectors are open. Sequential multiport systems provide better control of the air/fuel mixture ratio than earlier fuel injection systems, and are therefore able to produce more power, better mileage and lower emissions.

The SFI system consists of three sub-systems: air induction, electronic control and fuel delivery. The SFI system is also closely interrelated with PCM-controlled emission control systems. For additional information about the PCM, the information sensors and the emission control systems, refer to Chapter 6.

AIR INDUCTION SYSTEM

The air induction system consists of the resonator, the air filter assembly, the air intake ducts, the throttle body and the intake manifold. These models are equipped with an electronic throttle control system, which consists of the throttle body, two Throttle Position (TP) sensors, the Accelerator Pedal Position (APP) sensor and the Powertrain Control Module (PCM). The single-barrel, side-draft, cast aluminum electronic throttle body contains a throttle plate that regulates the amount of air entering the intake manifold. The throttle plate is opened and closed by the integral throttle actuator (an electric motor). The PCM-controlled throttle actuator opens and closes the throttle plate in response to the position of the accelerator pedal. The position (angle) of the accelerator pedal is determined by the Accelerator Pedal Position (APP) sensor, which is located at the top of the accelerator pedal. There is no cable because the APP sensor is an integral component of the accelerator pedal assembly. The throttle body is also the location of two Throttle Position (TP) sensors. A TP sensor is a potentiometer that monitors the opening angle of the throttle plate and sends a variable voltage signal to the Powertrain Control Module (PCM). Both TP sensors are integral components of the electronic throttle body and cannot be serviced separately. The throttle body is heated by engine coolant to prevent icing in cold weather.

A Manifold Absolute Pressure (MAP) sensor is located on top of the throttle body on 2004 and later V6 engines. On four-cylinder models, it's mounted on the intake manifold. The MAP sensor measures intake manifold pressure and vacuum and generates a variable voltage signal that's proportionate to the vacuum. The PCM uses this data to calculate the load on the engine. 2002 and 2003 V6 models use a Mass Air Flow (MAF) sensor instead of a MAP sensor. It's mounted to the outlet of the air filter housing. The MAF sensor measures the quantity of air being used by the engine.

Another information sensor, the Intake Air Temperature (IAT) sensor, is located in the air intake duct on four-cylinder engines. On 2004 and later V6 models, there are two IAT sensors. One is mounted in the air filter housing and the other is in the intake manifold near the throttle body. On 2002 and 2003 V6 engines, it's a part of the MAF sensor. The IAT sensor relays a voltage signal to the PCM that varies in accordance with the temperature of the incoming air in the manifold. The PCM uses this data to calculate how rich or lean the air/fuel mixture should be. All of the air induction components (resonator, air filter housing, air intake duct and throttle body) are covered in this Chapter, except for the intake manifold, which is covered in Chapter 2, and the information sensors, which are covered in Chapter 6.

These models are also equipped with an electronic idle control system. When the engine is idling, the PCM controls the idle speed by opening and closing the throttle plate as necessary in response to inputs from several information sensors, including the Engine Coolant Temperature (ECT) sensor, the Intake Air Temperature (IAT) sensor, the Manifold Absolute Pressure (MAP) sensor, the Power Steering Pressure (PSP) switch and the air conditioning ON switch.

ELECTRONIC CONTROL SYSTEM

For more information about the electronic control system (the PCM), its information sensors and output actuators, refer to Chapter 6.

FUEL DELIVERY SYSTEM

The fuel delivery system consists of the fuel pump, the fuel filter, the fuel pressure regulator, the fuel rail and fuel injectors and the lines and fittings that carry fuel between all of these components. Four-cylinder models are also equipped with a fuel pulsation damper that is bolted to the end of the fuel rail.

Fuel pump/fuel level sending unit module

The fuel pump module is an in-tank design; it cannot be removed from the top of the fuel tank without removing the tank. Fuel is drawn through a sock (or strainer) at the pump inlet and is then pumped into an integral fuel filter. On 2002 and 2003 models, the fuel filter is mounted to the side of the fuel tank. On later models, the filter is a part of the primary fuel pump module. After the pressurized fuel has been filtered, it's pumped through a supply line up to the fuel rail, which is located on top of the engine. Each of the two fuel pump modules also include a fuel level sending unit, which uses a float on the end of a float arm to operate a variable potentiometer, which sends a voltage signal to the PCM and to the fuel level gauge on the instrument cluster.

The fuel pressure is controlled by a regulator mounted in the secondary fuel tank module on 2002 and 2003 models. On later models, it's a part of the primary fuel tank module that includes the fuel pump. It's spring-loaded and not vacuum-controlled. When the fuel pressure rises beyond its normal operating range during deceleration or idle, the pressure regulator opens and fuel is diverted and dumped directly back into the fuel tank. A returnless system has one major advantage over a conventional fuel system with long supply and return lines. Because fuel isn't being pumped to the hot fuel rail on top of the engine, then returned to the fuel tank at an elevated temperature, there is less heat buildup of the fuel inside the tank, which means less fuel vapors inside the fuel tank. This in turn reduces the likelihood of leakage of evaporative emissions from the fuel tank, EVAP canister and EVAP hoses.

Fuel rail and fuel injector assembly (all models)

The fuel rail assembly is simply a single (four-cylinder) or pair (V6) of tubes bolted to the cylinder head (four-cylinder) or lower intake manifold (V6). The fuel rail houses the upper end of each fuel injector, and the lower end of each injector is inserted into the head or intake manifold. Each fuel injector is a solenoid-actuated, pintle-type design consisting of a solenoid, plunger, needle valve and housing. When the engine is running, there is always voltage on the hot side of each injector terminal. The PCM turns the injectors on and off by switching their ground paths on and off. When the ground path for an injector is closed by the PCM, current flows through the solenoid coil, the needle valve raises and pressurized fuel inside the injector housing squirts

out the nozzle. The quantity of fuel injected each time an injector opens is determined by the pulse width, which is the interval of time during which the valve is open.

11 Fuel injection system - check

▶ Refer to illustration 11.7

✳✳ WARNING:

Gasoline is extremely flammable, so take extra precautions when you work on any part of the fuel system. See the Warning in Section 2.

➡ **Note: The following procedure is based on the assumption that the fuel pump is working and the fuel pressure is adequate (see Section 3).**

1 Check all electrical connectors that are related to the system. Check the ground wire connections for tightness. Loose connectors and poor grounds can cause many problems that resemble more serious malfunctions.

2 Verify that the battery is fully charged. The Powertrain Control Module (PCM), information sensors and output actuators (the fuel injectors are output actuators) depend on a stable voltage supply in order to meter fuel correctly.

3 Inspect the air filter element (see Chapter 1). A dirty or partially blocked filter will severely impede performance.

4 Check all fuses related to the fuel system (see Chapter 12). If you find a blown fuse, replace it and see if it blows again. If it does, look for a wire shorted to ground in the circuit(s) protected by that fuse.

5 Check the air induction system between the throttle body and the intake manifold for air leaks, which will cause a lean air/fuel mixture ratio. When the mixture ratio becomes excessively lean, the engine will begin misfiring. Also inspect the condition of all vacuum hoses connected to the intake manifold and to the throttle body. A loose or broken vacuum hose will allow false (unmetered) air into the intake manifold.

6 Remove the air intake duct from the throttle body and look for dirt, carbon, varnish, or other residue in the throttle body, particularly around the throttle plate. If it's dirty, clean it with carb cleaner, a toothbrush and a clean shop towel.

7 With the engine running, place an automotive stethoscope against each injector, one at a time, and listen for a clicking sound that indicates operation (see illustration).

➡ **Note: This is a difficult task on V6 engines, especially on the rear cylinder bank.**

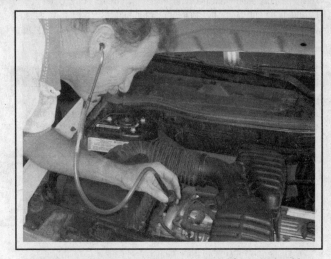

11.7 Use a stethoscope to listen to each injector; it should make a clicking sound that rises and falls with engine speed

✳✳ WARNING:

Stay clear of the drivebelt and any rotating components.

8 If you can hear the injectors operating, but the engine is misfiring, then the electrical circuits are functioning correctly, but the injectors might be dirty or clogged. Try a commercial injector cleaning product (available at auto parts stores). If cleaning the injectors doesn't help, the injectors probably need to be replaced.

9 If an injector is not operating (it makes no sound), remove any interfering components, disconnect the injector electrical connector and measure the resistance across the injector terminals with an ohmmeter. Compare your measurement with the resistance values of the other injectors. If the resistance of the non-operational injector is well outside the range of resistance of the other injectors, replace it.

10 If the injector is not operating, but the resistance reading is within the range of resistance of the other injectors, the PCM or the circuit between the PCM and the injector might be faulty.

12 Throttle body - inspection, removal and installation

❋❋ WARNING:

Wait until the engine is completely cool before beginning this procedure.

❋❋ CAUTION:

The manufacturer recommends that an idle-learn procedure be done any time the throttle body is removed on a 3.5L V6 engine. This is done to ensure that the idle is stable and that no Diagnostic Trouble Codes (DTCs) occur. Refer to Chapter 5, Section 1 for information on this procedure.

INSPECTION

1   Disconnect the air intake duct from the throttle body. Open the throttle plate and check the area for residue build-up. If it's dirty, clean it with solvent or carburetor cleaner. Make sure that the cleaner is safe for use with catalytic converters and oxygen sensors.

❋❋ CAUTION:

Don't clean the throttle motor with solvent. Also, don't use a metal brush to clean the bore of the throttle body - a special coating protects it. Instead, wipe the bore with a rag soaked with solvent.

REMOVAL AND INSTALLATION

▶ Refer to illustrations 12.8a, 12.8b and 12.8c

2   Disconnect the cable from the negative battery terminal (see Chapter 5, Section 1).

3   On V6 engines, pinch off the two coolant hoses to the throttle body. If you don't have tools suitable for doing this, drain the engine coolant until the level in the cooling system is lower than the throttle body (see Chapter 1).

4   Remove the air intake duct (see Section 9). It can simply be disconnected from the throttle body and moved aside on some models.

5   Disconnect the electrical connector from the throttle body. On 2004 and later V6 models, also disconnect the MAP sensor wiring.

6   Disconnect any remaining coolant or air hoses from the throttle body.

7   If you're working on a 2004 or later V6 model, remove the wiring harness bracket bolt from the throttle body.

8   Remove the throttle body mounting nuts or bolts and carefully lift off the throttle body (see illustrations). Discard the gasket; it should be replaced with a new one.

9   Cover the intake manifold opening with a clean shop towel.

10 Installation is the reverse of removal. Be sure to use a new gasket and tighten the throttle body fasteners to the torque listed in this Chapter's Specifications.

11 If you're working on a 2004 or later V6 model, perform the idle learn procedure (see Chapter 5, Section 1). If you're working on a four-cylinder or 2003 or earlier V6 model, turn the ignition key to the Run (not Start) position for one minute, without depressing the accelerator pedal; this is necessary for the PCM to "learn" the position of the throttle plate.

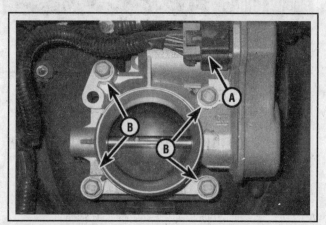

12.8a Throttle body mounting details (four-cylinder model shown, others similar)

A   Electrical connector   *B   Mounting bolts*

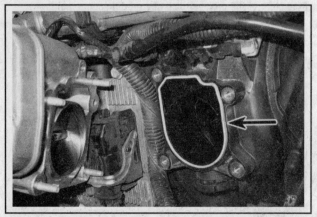

12.8b Remove the O-ring type throttle body gasket (four-cylinder engine). The manufacturer recommends replacing it with a new one regardless of its condition

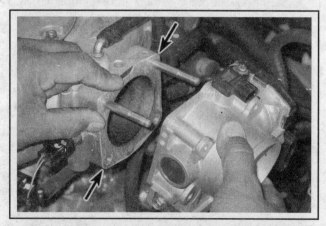

12.8c V6 models use a different type of gasket than the four-cylinder engine - if it sticks, carefully remove all traces of gasket material

13 Fuel pulsation damper (four-cylinder models) - removal and installation

✳✳ WARNING:

Gasoline is extremely flammable, so take extra precautions when you work on any part of the fuel system. See the Warning in Section 2.

➡Note: The damper is on the left (driver's) end of the fuel rail.

1 Relieve the system fuel pressure (see Section 2).

2 Disconnect the cable from the negative battery terminal (see Chapter 5, Section 1).

3 Refer to Section 9 and remove the air intake duct.

4 Remove the fuel pulsation damper bolts and pull it out of the fuel rail.

5 Inspect the O-rings and replace them if they're damaged.

6 Installation is the reverse of removal. Lubricate the O-rings with engine oil before installing them and tighten the bolts to the torque listed in this Chapter's Specifications.

7 Reconnect the cable to the negative battery terminal (see Chapter 5, Section 1).

8 Start the engine and check for leaks around the pulsation damper.

14 Fuel rail and injectors - removal and installation

✳✳ WARNING:

Gasoline is extremely flammable, so take extra precautions when you work on any part of the fuel system. See the Warning in Section 2.

1 Relieve the fuel system pressure (see Section 2).

2 Disconnect the cable from the negative battery terminal (see Chapter 5, Section 1).

3 Remove the engine cover.

4 Refer to Section 9 and remove the air intake duct. Place a clean shop towel over the open throttle body.

REMOVAL

Four-cylinder models

▶ **Refer to illustrations 14.9 and 14.10**

5 Clean the areas around the fuel injectors as best you can, using compressed air if it is available.

6 Unbolt the fuel line support bracket from the stud near the valve cover.

7 Disconnect the fuel line from the rail. Make sure to hold the fuel rail fitting with a back-up wrench to avoid damaging it. Also disconnect it from the quick-connect fitting (see Section 4).

8 Disconnect the wiring from the fuel injectors.

9 Remove the fuel rail mounting bolts and remove the fuel rail and its injectors as a single assembly (see illustration). If any of the injectors are difficult to extract from their bores, carefully pry them loose.

10 Release the fuel injector retaining clips (see illustration). Remove each injector from its bore in the fuel rail. Remove and discard the upper O-ring and the lower O-ring. Repeat this procedure for each injector.

➡Note: Even if you only removed the fuel rail assembly to replace a single injector or a leaking O-ring, it's a good idea to remove all of the injectors from the fuel rail and replace all of the O-rings at the same time. The isolator seal that fits at the bottom of each injector can also be replaced at this time.

2002 and 2003 (3.0L) V6 models

11 Disconnect the fuel line from the rail(s). Be sure to hold the fuel

14.9 To remove the fuel rail, set aside the coolant pipe (A), detach the harness clips (B), and remove the two mounting bolts (C)

14.10 To release an injector retainer, free it from the small lugs on each side of the injector and pull it off

rail fitting with a back-up wrench to avoid damaging it. Also disconnect it from the quick-connect fitting (see Section 4).

12 Refer to Chapter 2B and disconnect the intake manifold. It need not be completely removed. It can be raised and supported to provide access to the injectors.

13 Disconnect the wiring from the injectors.

14 Remove the fuel line support bracket bolts.

15 Remove the fuel rail mounting bolts.

16 Remove the front fuel rail with its injectors as an assembly, then remove the rear rail/injector assembly.

17 Release the fuel injector retaining clips. Remove each injector from its bore in the fuel rail. Remove and discard the upper O-ring and the lower O-ring. Repeat this procedure for each injector.

➡ **Note: Even if you only removed the fuel rail assembly to replace a single injector or a leaking O-ring, it's a good idea to remove all of the injectors from the fuel rail and replace all of the O-rings at the same time.**

14.19 To disconnect the electrical connector from a fuel injector, depress these two release tabs and pull off the connector

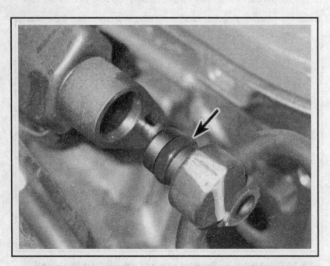

14.20b Remove and discard the old O-ring from the fuel rail crossover hose (3.5L V6 models)

2004 and later (3.5L) V6 models

▶ **Refer to illustrations 14.19, 14.20a, 14.20b, 14.21a, 14.21b and 14.22**

18 Refer to Chapter 2C and remove the upper intake manifold.

19 Disconnect the electrical connector from each injector (see illustration).

20 Disconnect the fuel supply line at the fitting near the end of the cylinder head (see illustrations). Remove the fuel line mounting bracket from the end of the cylinder head also.

21 Remove the four fuel rail bolts, then remove both fuel rails and their injectors as an assembly (see illustrations).

22 Release the fuel injector retaining clips (see illustration). Remove each injector from its bore in the fuel rail. Remove and discard the upper O-ring and the lower O-ring. Repeat this procedure for

14.20a To disconnect the crossover hose from the fuel rail (3.5L V6 models):

1 *Remove the fuel supply line bracket mounting nut and pull the bracket off the stud on the rear cylinder head*
2 *Remove the nut from the stud on the rear fuel rail and pull off the fitting*
3 *Disconnect the quick-connect fitting from the front fuel rail (see Section 4)*

14.21a To detach the fuel rail assembly from the intake manifold, remove the four mounting bolts: two on the front rail and two on the rear rail (3.5L V6 models)

each injector.

➡Note: Even if you only removed the fuel rail assembly to replace a single injector or a leaking O-ring, it's a good idea to remove all of the injectors from the fuel rail and replace all of the O-rings at the same time.

INSTALLATION

23 Coat the new upper O-rings with clean engine oil and slide them into place on each of the fuel injectors. Coat the new lower O-rings with clean engine oil and install them on the lower ends of the injectors.

14.21b Remove each fuel rail and its three injectors as a single assembly (3.5L V6 models)

24 Coat the outside surface of each upper O-ring with clean engine oil, then insert each injector into its bore in the fuel rail. Install the isolators with new seals on the injectors, if equipped.

25 Install the injectors and fuel rail assembly on the intake manifold. Tighten the fuel rail mounting bolts securely.

26 The remainder of installation is the reverse of removal.

27 Reconnect the cable to the negative battery terminal (see Chapter 5, Section 1).

28 Turn the ignition switch to ON (but don't operate the starter).This activates the fuel pump for about two seconds, which builds up fuel pressure in the fuel lines and the fuel rail. Repeat this step two or three times, then check the fuel lines, fuel rails and injectors for fuel leaks.

14.22 To remove an injector from the fuel rail, pull off the injector retainer, then carefully pull the injector straight out of its bore (3.5L V6 models)

15 Exhaust system servicing - general information

▶ Refer to illustration 15.1

⁕⁕ WARNING:

Inspect and repair exhaust system components only after enough time has elapsed after driving the vehicle to allow the system components to cool completely. Also, when working under the vehicle, make sure it is securely supported on jackstands.

1 The exhaust system consists of the exhaust manifolds, the catalytic converter, the muffler, the tailpipe and all connecting pipes, flanges and clamps. The exhaust system is isolated from the vehicle body and from chassis components by a series of rubber hangers (see illustration). Periodically inspect these hangers for cracks or other signs of deterioration, replacing them as necessary.

2 Conduct regular inspections of the exhaust system to keep it safe and quiet. Look for any damaged or bent parts, open seams, holes, loose connections, excessive corrosion or other defects which could allow exhaust fumes to enter the vehicle. Do not repair deteriorated

15.1 Most exhaust system hangers look like this one; to replace one of them, disengage it from the hook on the vehicle and from the hook on the exhaust bracket

exhaust system components; replace them with new parts.

3   If the exhaust system components are extremely corroded, or rusted together, you'll need welding equipment and a cutting torch to remove them. The convenient strategy at this point is to have a muffler repair shop remove the corroded sections with a cutting torch. If you want to save money by doing it yourself, but you don't have a welding outfit and cutting torch, simply cut off the old components with a hacksaw. If you have compressed air, there are special pneumatic cutting chisels (available from specialty tool manufacturers) that can also be used. If you decide to tackle the job at home, be sure to wear safety goggles to protect your eyes from metal chips and wear work gloves to protect your hands.

4   Here are some simple guidelines to follow when repairing the

exhaust system:

a) *Work from the back to the front when removing exhaust system components.*
b) *Apply penetrating oil to the exhaust system component fasteners to make them easier to remove.*
c) *Use new gaskets, hangers and clamps when installing exhaust systems components.*
d) *Apply anti-seize compound to the threads of all exhaust system fasteners during reassembly.*
e) *Be sure to allow sufficient clearance between newly installed parts and all points on the underbody to avoid overheating the floor pan and possibly damaging the interior carpet and insulation. Pay particularly close attention to the catalytic converter and heat shield.*

Specifications

Fuel system pressure (approximate)	48 to 60 psi (330 to 410 kPa)

Torque specifications

Note: One foot-pound (ft-lb) of torque is equivalent to 12 inch-pounds (in-lbs) of torque. Torque values below approximately 15 ft-lbs are expressed in inch-pounds, since most foot-pound torque wrenches are not accurate at these smaller values.

	Ft-lbs (unless otherwise indicated)	Nm
Fuel pulsation damper, four-cylinder models	44 in-lbs	5
Throttle body mounting bolts/nuts		
2002 and 2003 V6 models	66 in-lbs	7.5
All others	89 in-lbs	10

Section

Reference to other Chapters

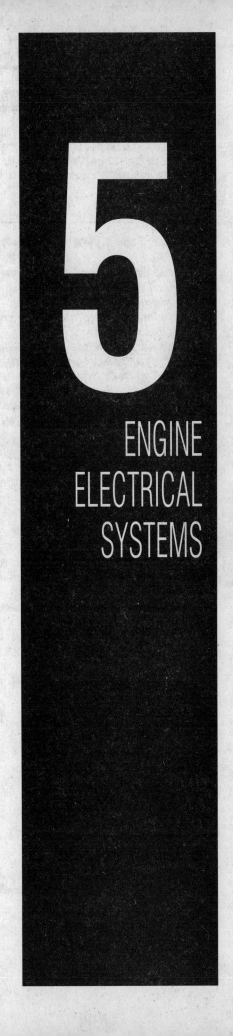

5

ENGINE
ELECTRICAL
SYSTEMS

---

1   General information, precautions and battery disconnection

The engine electrical systems include all ignition, charging and starting components. Because of their engine-related functions, these components are covered separately from body electrical devices such as the lights, the instruments, etc. (which you'll find in Chapter 12).

PRECAUTIONS

Always observe the following precautions when working on the electrical system:

a) *Be extremely careful when servicing engine electrical components. They are easily damaged if checked, connected or handled improperly.*
b) *Never leave the ignition switched on for long periods of time when the engine is not running.*
c) *Never disconnect the battery cables while the engine is running.*
d) *Maintain correct polarity when connecting battery cables from another vehicle during jump starting - see the "Booster battery (jump) starting" Section at the front of this manual.*
e) *Always disconnect the cable from the negative battery terminal before working on the electrical system, but read the following battery disconnection procedure first.*

It's also a good idea to review the safety-related information regarding the engine electrical systems located in the *Safety first!* Section at the front of this manual, before beginning any operation included in this Chapter.

BATTERY DISCONNECTION

Some systems on the vehicle require battery power to be available at all times, either to maintain continuous operation (alarm system, power door locks, etc.), or to maintain control unit memory (radio station presets, Powertrain Control Module and other control units). When the battery is disconnected, the power that maintains these systems is cut. So, before you disconnect the battery, please note that on a vehicle with power door locks, it's a wise precaution to remove the key from the ignition and to keep it with you, so that it does not get locked inside if the power door locks should engage accidentally when the battery is reconnected!

Devices known as "memory-savers" can be used to avoid some of these problems. Precise details vary according to the device used. The typical memory saver is plugged into the cigarette lighter and is connected to a spare battery. Then the vehicle battery can be disconnected from the electrical system. The memory saver will provide sufficient current to maintain audio unit security codes, PCM memory, etc. and will provide power to always hot circuits such as the clock and radio memory circuits.

✳✳ WARNING 1:

Some memory savers deliver a considerable amount of current in order to keep vehicle systems operational after the main battery is disconnected. If you're using a memory saver, make sure that the circuit concerned is actually open before servicing it.

✳✳ WARNING 2:

If you're going to work near any of the airbag system components, the battery MUST be disconnected and a memory saver must NOT be used. If a memory saver is used, power will be supplied to the airbag, which means that it could accidentally deploy and cause serious personal injury.

To disconnect the battery for service procedures requiring power to be cut from the vehicle, first remove the battery cover. Loosen the cable end bolt and disconnect the cable from the negative (black) battery terminal. Isolate the cable end to prevent it from coming into accidental contact with the battery terminal.

BATTERY RECONNECTION

After reconnecting the battery, you must enter the radio station presets (see your owner's manual)

POWERTRAIN CONTROL MODULE (PCM) IDLE LEARN PROCEDURE

Make sure that the PCM learns the engine idle characteristics after you perform either of the following procedures:
Replace, reset or update the PCM.

➡**Note: Erasing Diagnostic Trouble Codes (DTCs) does NOT require that you perform the idle learn procedure.**

Remove or replace the throttle body
1   Make sure that all electrical components (air conditioning system, lights, rear window defogger, sound system, etc.) are turned OFF.
2   Start the engine, bring it up to 3000 rpm and hold it there, with no load, in PARK or NEUTRAL, until the radiator fan comes on or until the engine coolant temperature reaches 194-degrees F.
3   Allow the engine to idle for at least five minutes with no load on it.

➡**Note: If the radiator fan comes on during this five-minute period, don't include the time during which the fan runs as part of the five minutes.**

---

2   Battery - emergency jump starting

Refer to the *Booster battery (jump) starting* procedure at the front of this manual.

3 Battery - check and replacement

✳ CAUTION:

Always disconnect the cable from the negative battery terminal FIRST and hook it up LAST or the battery may be shorted by the tool being used to loosen the cable clamps.

CHECK

▶ **Refer to illustrations 3.2 and 3.3**

1 Remove the battery cover. Disconnect the negative battery cable, then the positive cable from the battery.

2 Check the battery state of charge. Visually inspect the indicator eye on the top of the battery (if equipped with one); if the indicator eye is black in color charge the battery as described in Chapter 1. Next perform an open voltage circuit test using a digital voltmeter.

➡**Note: The battery's surface charge must be removed before accurate voltage measurements can be made. Turn on the high beams for ten seconds, then turn them off and let the vehicle stand for two minutes. With the engine and all accessories Off, touch the negative probe of the voltmeter to the negative terminal of the battery and the positive probe to the positive terminal of the battery (see illustration).**

The battery voltage should be 12.6 volts or slightly above. If the battery is less than the specified voltage, charge the battery before proceeding to the next test. Do not proceed with the battery load test unless the battery charge is correct.

3 Perform a battery load test. An accurate check of the battery condition can only be performed with a load tester (available at most auto parts stores). This test evaluates the ability of the battery to operate the starter and other accessories during periods of high current draw. Connect the load tester to the battery terminals (see illustration). Load test the battery according to the tool manufacturer's instructions. This tool increases the load demand (current draw) on the battery. Maintain the load on the battery for 15 seconds or less and observe that the battery voltage does not drop below 9.6 volts. If the battery condition is weak

or defective, the tool will indicate this condition immediately.

➡**Note: Cold temperatures will cause the minimum voltage reading to drop slightly. Follow the chart given in the manufacturer's instructions to compensate for cold climates. Minimum load voltage for freezing temperatures (32 degrees F) should be approximately 9.1 volts.**

REPLACEMENT

Battery

▶ **Refer to illustrations 3.4 and 3.5**

4 Disconnect the cable from the negative battery terminal first, then (and only then!) disconnect the cable from the positive battery terminal (see illustration).

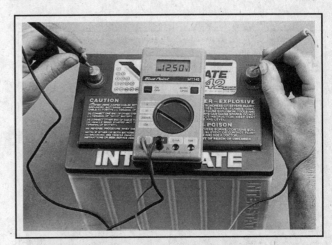

3.2 To test the open circuit voltage of the battery, touch the black probe of the voltmeter to the negative terminal and the red probe to the positive terminal of the battery; a fully charged battery should be at least 12.6 volts

3.3 Some battery load testers (like this one) are equipped with an ammeter that allows you to vary the amount of the load on the battery (less expensive testers only have a load switch that puts the battery under a fixed load)

3.4 Whenever you must disconnect the cables from the battery terminals, ALWAYS disconnect the cable from the negative terminal (1) FIRST, then disconnect the cable from the positive terminal (2)

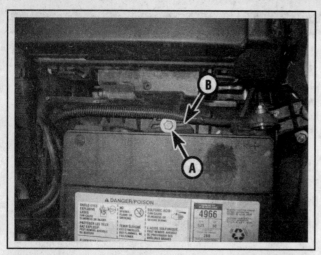

3.5 To detach the battery from the battery tray, remove the hold-down bolt (A) and hold-down bracket (B), then lift the battery out

3.12 Release the fuse box clips to position the assembly rearward - it doesn't need to be completely removed in order to remove the battery tray

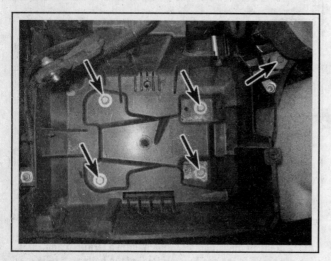

3.14 Battery tray mounting bolts

3.19 Battery tray support mounting bolts; a long extension and a ratchet is required to remove the lower bolt

5 Remove the battery hold-down clamp (see illustration).

6 Lift out the battery. Be careful - it's heavy.

➡ **Note: Battery straps and handlers are available at most auto parts stores for reasonable prices. They make it easier to remove and carry the battery.**

7 If you are replacing the battery, make sure you get one that's identical, with the same dimensions, amperage rating, cold cranking rating, etc.

8 Installation is the reverse of removal. Be sure to connect the positive cable first and the negative cable last (see Section 1).

Battery tray

▶ **Refer to illustrations 3.12 and 3.14**

9 While the battery is out, wipe off the plastic battery tray and inspect it for corrosion.

10 Disconnect all wiring harnesses from the tray assembly. Also disconnect air conditioning lines, etc.

11 Remove the cover from the underhood fuse box, then remove the three screws at the center of the fuse array.

12 Unclip the fuse box using a screwdriver (see illustration).

13 Carefully move the fuse box to the rear.

14 Remove the battery tray bolts (see illustration).

15 Lift the tray out while disconnecting the battery cooling duct and the drain tube.

16 Installation is the reverse of removal.

Battery tray support

▶ **Refer to illustration 3.19**

17 Remove the steel battery support tray if it's damaged due to corrosion or if it must be removed for access to components below it.

18 First remove the plastic battery tray (see Step 9).

19 Remove the three support mounting bolts. You'll need a ratchet with a long extension and a swivel socket to remove the lower one (see illustration).

20 Installation is the reverse of removal.

4   Battery cables - check and replacement

▶ **Refer to illustrations 4.4a and 4.4b**

1   Periodically inspect the entire length of each battery cable for damage, cracked or burned insulation and corrosion. Poor battery cable connections can cause starting problems and decreased engine performance.

2   Inspect the cable-to-terminal connections at the ends of the cables for cracks, loose wire strands and corrosion. The presence of white, fluffy deposits under the insulation at the cable terminal connection means that the cable is corroded and should be replaced. Also inspect the battery posts for distortion and corrosion. If they're corroded, clean them.

3   When removing the cables, always disconnect the cable from the negative battery terminal first and hook it up last, or you might accidentally short out the battery with the tool you're using to loosen the cable clamps. Even if you're only replacing the cable for the positive terminal, be sure to disconnect the negative cable from the battery first.

4   Disconnect the old cables from the battery, then trace each of them to their opposite ends and disconnect them (see illustrations). Be sure to note the routing of each cable before disconnecting it to ensure correct installation.

5   If you are replacing any of the old cables, take them with you when buying new cables. It is vitally important that you replace the cables with identical parts.

6   Clean the threads of the solenoid or ground connection with a wire brush to remove rust and corrosion. Apply a light coat of battery terminal corrosion inhibitor or petroleum jelly to the threads to prevent future corrosion.

7   Attach the cable to the solenoid or ground connection and tighten the mounting nut/bolt securely.

8   Before connecting a new cable to the battery, make sure that it reaches the battery post without having to be stretched.

9   Connect the cable to the positive battery terminal first, then connect the ground cable to the negative battery terminal (see Section 1).

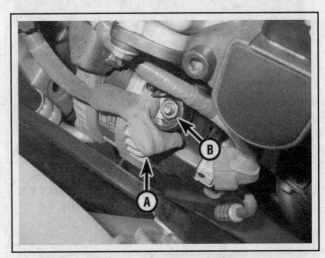

4.4a To detach the positive cable from the starter solenoid, raise the vehicle and place it securely on jackstands, then peel back the weather boot (A) and remove this nut (B)

4.4b To disconnect the positive battery cable from the alternator, peel back the rubber weather boot (A) and remove this nut (B)

5   Ignition system - general information

※※ **WARNING:**

Because of the high voltage generated by the ignition system, be extremely careful when performing any procedure involving ignition components.

1   The electronic ignition system consists of the Powertrain Control Module (PCM), the ignition switch, the battery, the individual ignition coils (2004 and later V6 models) or the coil pack (all other models) and the spark plugs.

2   The PCM alters ignition timing during warm-up, idle and warm running conditions. It controls ignition timing in accordance with the engine speed, the airflow or manifold absolute pressure and the engine coolant temperature. The PCM uses data from the Camshaft Position (Top Dead Center) [CMP (TDC)] sensors to determine ignition timing during start-ups, and anytime that the crank angle is abnormal. The PCM calculates engine speed based on the data that it receives from the Crankshaft Position (CKP) sensor. It uses a Manifold Absolute Pressure (MAP) sensor to determine manifold pressure or a Mass Air Flow (MAF) sensor to measure air flow. For more information about the CMP (TDC), CKP, MAF and MAP sensors, refer to Chapter 6.

6   Ignition system - check

▶ Refer to illustrations 6.4 and 6.5

➡Note 1: The ignition system components on these vehicles are difficult to diagnose. In the event of ignition system failure that you can't diagnose, have the vehicle tested at a dealer service department or other qualified auto repair facility.

6.4 You'll have to obtain a set of short spark plug wires to perform the spark test on four-cylinder or 2002 and 2003 3.0L V6 models; if the coil is delivering power to the plug, the tester will flash (four-cylinder engine shown)

6.5 To use a calibrated spark tester on a 3.5L V6 model, remove a coil and install the tester between the coil high-tension terminal and the spark plug. Crank the engine. If the coil is generating enough voltage to fire the plug, the tester will flash

➡Note 2: You'll need a calibrated spark tester for the following test. On four cylinder or 2002 and 2003 V6 models, you'll also need a set of short spark plug wires. The short wires are used to connect the ignition tester between the coil pack and the spark plugs. Spark testers are available at most auto supply stores.

1   If a malfunction occurs in the ignition system, do not immediately assume that any particular part is causing the problem. First, check the following items:

  a) Make sure that the cable clamps at the battery terminals are clean and tight.
  b) Test the condition of the battery (see Section 3). If it doesn't pass all the tests, replace it.
  c) Check the ignition coil or coil pack connections.
  d) Check any relevant fuses in the engine compartment fuse and relay box (see Chapter 12). If they're burned, determine the cause and repair the circuit.

FOUR-CYLINDER AND 2002 THROUGH 2003 V6 MODELS

2   If the engine turns over but won't start, verify that there is sufficient ignition voltage to fire the spark plugs as follows.
3   Remove the ignition coil pack (see Section 8).
4   Obtain a set of short test spark plug wires. Connect the spark plug wires between the coil pack and the spark plugs. Connect the calibrated spark tester between one of the spark plug wires and its spark plug in the engine (see illustration).

2004 AND LATER V6 MODELS

5   Check the ignition spark at the plugs. If the engine turns over but won't start, disconnect an ignition coil from a spark plug and attach a calibrated spark tester between the ignition coil high-tension terminal and the spark plug (see illustration).

ALL MODELS

6   Crank the engine and note whether or not the tester flashes.
7   If the tester flashes during cranking, the coil is delivering sufficient voltage to the spark plug to fire it. Repeat this test for each cylinder to verify that the other coils are OK.
8   If the tester doesn't flash, remove a coil from another cylinder and swap it for the one being tested (this applies to 2004 and later V6 models only). If the tester now flashes, you know that the original coil is bad. If the tester still doesn't flash, the PCM or wiring harness is probably defective. Have the PCM checked out by a dealer service department or other qualified repair shop (testing the PCM is beyond the scope of the do-it-yourselfer because it requires expensive special tools).
9   If the tester flashes during cranking but a misfire code (related to the cylinder being tested) has been stored, the spark plug could be fouled or defective.

7   Ignition control module (four-cylinder models) - replacement

♦ **Refer to illustrations 7.3 and 7.4**

1   Make sure that the ignition switch is Off.
2   Refer to Chapter 4 and remove the air intake duct and any interfering brackets, etc.
3   Disconnect the wiring from the ignition control module (see illustration).

4   Remove the three mounting screws and pull the module straight up (see illustration).
5   Transfer the interconnect from the old module to the new one. Make sure that the square end of the interconnect is aligned properly and that the rubber seal is in good condition - if it's not, replace it.
6   Installation is the reverse of removal.

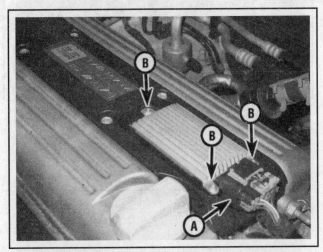

7.3 Disconnect the electrical connector (A) and remove the mounting screws (B) from the ignition control module (four-cylinder models)

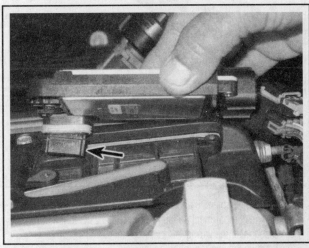

7.4 Pull the ignition control module straight up to remove it; to remove the interconnect, disconnect it from the module and plug it into the new module (four-cylinder models)

8   Ignition coils or coil pack - replacement

FOUR-CYLINDER MODELS

♦ **Refer to illustrations 8.2a, 8.2b and 8.3**

1   Refer to Section 7 and remove the ignition control module from the top of the coil pack.

2   Remove the four mounting bolts and pull the module from the spark plugs and valve cover (see illustrations).
3   Remove the three screws to remove the cover (see illustration).
4   If you're replacing the ignition coil pack, remove the four boots from the coil pack and inspect them for cracks, tears and deterioration, replacing them as necessary.

8.2a To detach the ignition coil pack (four-cylinder models) remove these four bolts

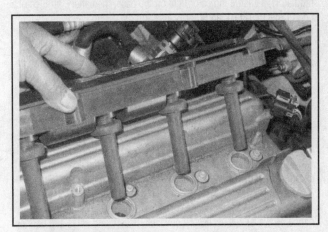

8.2b Pull the coil pack straight up to remove it (four-cylinder model)

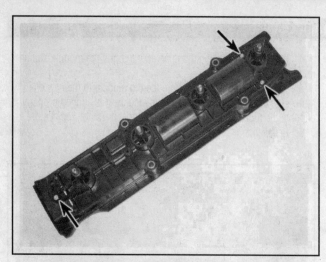

8.3 To remove the cover from the coil pack on four-cylinder models, remove these three screws

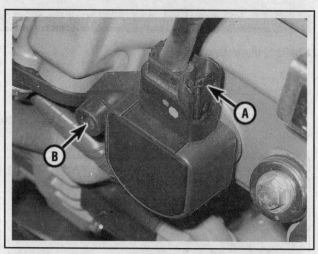

8.11 On 3.5L V6 models, press the tab (A) to disconnect the wiring, then remove the mounting screw (B)

2002 AND 2003 V6 MODELS

5 Refer to Chapter 2B and remove the intake manifold. It can be left in the engine compartment as long as there is access to the coil packs.
6 Disconnect the wiring harness from the coil pack(s).
7 Remove the two mounting bolts.
8 Remove the coil pack.

➡**Note: If the module is difficult to remove, bolts can be screwed into it for more leverage to aid in wiggling it free.**

9 Remove the gasket

2004 AND LATER V6 MODELS

▶ **Refer to illustration 8.11**

10 Remove the engine cover.
11 Disconnect the electrical connector and mounting bolt from the ignition coil (see illustration).
12 Remove the ignition coil from the spark plug.

ALL MODELS

13 Apply a little silicone dielectric compound to the inside of each boot before installing it.
14 Installation is the reverse of removal.

9 Charging system - general information and precautions

The charging system includes the alternator (with an integral voltage regulator), a charge indicator light on the dash, the battery, an Electrical Load Detector (ELD), an 80-amp fuse and the wiring connecting all of these components. The charging system supplies electrical power for the ignition system, the lights, the radio, etc. The alternator is driven by a drivebelt at one end of the engine. The alternator's voltage output is controlled by a conventional internal voltage regulator, which keeps charging output within a range of about 13.5 to 14.5 volts. The ELD, which is located in the engine compartment fuse and relay box, sends a variable voltage signal to the Powertrain Control Module (PCM) that varies in accordance with the total power demand imposed on the charging system by the electrical devices and systems in operation. The PCM uses this variable voltage signal to calculate the actual level of charging voltage needed and alters the charging voltage output accordingly.

The charging system doesn't ordinarily require periodic maintenance. However, the accessory drivebelt, battery and wires and connections should be inspected at the intervals outlined in Chapter 1.

The dashboard warning light should come on when the ignition key is turned to ON, but it should go off immediately after the engine is started. If it remains on, there is a malfunction in the charging system (see Section 10).

Be very careful when making electrical circuit connections to a vehicle equipped with an alternator and note the following:

a) *When reconnecting wires to the alternator from the battery, be sure to note the polarity.*
b) *Before using arc-welding equipment to repair any part of the vehicle, disconnect the wires from the alternator and the battery terminals.*
c) *Never start the engine with a battery charger connected.*
d) *Always disconnect both battery leads before using a battery charger.*
e) *The alternator is turned by an engine drivebelt that could cause serious injury if your hands, hair or clothes become entangled in it with the engine running.*
f) *Because the alternator is connected directly to the battery, it could arc or cause a fire if overloaded or shorted out.*
g) *Wrap a plastic bag over the alternator and secure it with rubber bands before steam cleaning the engine.*

10 Charging system - check

▶ **Refer to illustration 10.2**

1   If the charging system malfunctions, don't immediately assume that the alternator is causing the problem. First check the following items:

　　a) *Ensure that the battery cable connections at the battery are clean and tight.*
　　b) *If the battery is not a maintenance-free type, check the electrolyte level and specific gravity. If the electrolyte level is low, add clean, mineral-free tap water. If the specific gravity is low, charge the battery.*
　　c) *Check the alternator wiring and connections.*
　　d) *Check the drivebelt condition and tension (see Chapter 1).*
　　e) *Check the alternator mounting bolts for looseness.*
　　f) *Run the engine and check the alternator for abnormal noise.*

2   Use a voltmeter to check the battery voltage with the engine off. It should be at least 12.6 volts (see illustration).

3   Start the engine and check the battery voltage again. It should now be approximately 13.5 to 14.8 volts.

4   If the charging voltage reading is zero, inspect the condition of the fusible link that's located in the wire between the alternator and the starter solenoid terminals. If a fusible link is badly blown, it will be obvious that a meltdown has occurred. If a visual inspection is inconclusive, use a continuity tester or ohmmeter to determine whether there is continuity through the fusible link. If the fusible link is blown, replace the fusible link and the wire in which it's located as a single assembly (available at dealer parts departments). The correct size of the fusible link should be printed on the outside of the link. Make sure that you obtain the correct fusible link and wire for the application. After replacing the fusible link, check the charging voltage again.

5   If the voltage reading is more or less than the specified charging voltage, the voltage regulator is defective. Replace the alternator (the

10.2 To check charging voltage, hook up a multimeter to the battery terminals and note the indicated voltage with the engine running; it should be 13.8 to 14.8 volts

voltage regulator cannot be replaced separately).

6   The charging system (battery) light on the instrument cluster lights up when the ignition key is turned to ON, but it should go out when the engine starts.

7   If the charging system light stays on after the engine has been started, there is a problem with the charging system. Before replacing the alternator, check the battery condition, alternator belt tension and electrical cable connections.

8   If replacing the alternator doesn't restore voltage to the specified range, have the charging system tested by a dealer service department or other qualified repair shop.

11 Alternator - removal and installation

▶ **Refer to illustration 11.4**

1   Disconnect the cable from the negative battery terminal (see Section 1).

2   Remove the engine cover.

3   Remove the drivebelt (see Chapter 1).

4   Disconnect the battery cable and the other wiring connections from the alternator terminals (see illustration).

➡**Note: On 2004 and later V6 models, you will have to jack up the engine in order to get working room around the alternator (see Steps 15 and 16).**

FOUR-CYLINDER MODELS

▶ **Refer to illustration 11.6**

5   Refer to Chapter 4 and remove the air intake duct.

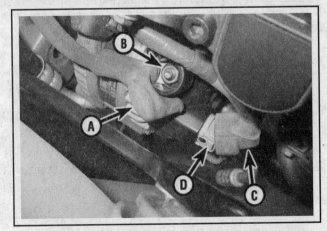

11.4 Typical alternator wiring - pull back the rubber boot (A) and disconnect the output cable (B), then peel back the other boot (C) and disconnect the control wiring (D)

11.6 To remove the alternator from a four-cylinder model, disconnect the wiring (A) and remove the mounting bolts (B) - lower bolt not visible here

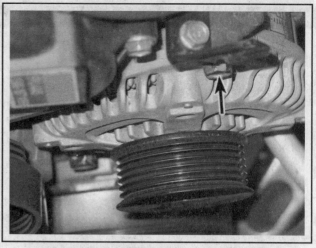

11.17a To detach the alternator from the upper mounting bracket, remove this bolt (3.5L V6)

6   Remove the alternator mounting bolts and lift it out (see illustration).

2002 AND 2003 V6 MODELS

7   Remove the drivebelt and its tensioner (see Chapter 1).
8   Raise the vehicle and support it securely on jackstands.
9   Remove the top alternator bolts.
10 Turn the front wheels fully to the right.
11 Remove the lower alternator mounting bolts and lower it carefully.

2004 AND LATER V6 MODELS

▶ **Refer to illustrations 11.17a and 11.17b**

12 Refer to Chapter 4 and remove the air filter housing.
13 Raise the vehicle and support it securely on jackstands.
14 Remove the drivebelt and tensioner (see Chapter 1).
15 Place a jack with a block of wood under the engine, support the engine's weight and remove the front engine mount bolt.
16 Jack up the engine enough to get clearance to the alternator.
17 Remove the alternator mounting bolts and maneuver it downward (see illustrations).

ALL MODELS

18 If you're replacing the alternator, take the old one with you when purchasing the replacement unit. Make sure that the new/rebuilt unit looks identical to the old alternator. Look at the electrical terminals on the backside of the alternator. They should be the same in number, size and location as the terminals on the old alternator. Finally, look at the identification numbers. They will be stamped into the housing or printed

11.17b To detach the alternator from the lower mounting bracket, remove this bolt (3.5L V6)

on a tag attached to the housing. Make sure that the I.D. numbers are the same on both alternators.

19 Many new/rebuilt alternators DO NOT have a pulley installed, so you might have to swap the pulley from the old unit to the new/rebuilt one. When buying an alternator, find out the store's policy regarding pulley swaps. Some stores perform this service free of charge. If your local auto parts store doesn't offer this service, you'll have to purchase a puller for removing the pulley and do it yourself.

20 Installation is the reverse of removal. Be sure to tighten the alternator mounting bolts securely.

21 Reconnect the cable to the negative terminal of the battery (see Section 1). Check the charging voltage (see Section 10) to verify that the alternator is operating correctly.

12 Starting system - general information and precautions

The starting system consists of the battery, the starter motor, the starter solenoid and the wires connecting them. The solenoid is mounted directly on the starter motor. The solenoid/starter motor assembly is installed on the front of the transaxle bellhousing.

When the ignition key is turned to the START position, the starter solenoid is actuated through the starter control circuit. The starter solenoid then connects the battery to the starter. The battery supplies the electrical energy to the starter motor, which does the actual work of cranking the engine.

The starter can only be operated when the shift lever is in the PARK or NEUTRAL position.

Always observe the following precautions when working on the starting system:

a) *Excessive cranking of the starter motor can overheat it and cause serious damage. Never operate the starter motor for more than 15 seconds at a time without pausing to allow it to cool for at least two minutes.*

b) *The starter is connected directly to the battery and could arc or cause a fire if mishandled, overloaded or shorted out.*

c) *Always detach the cable from the negative terminal of the battery before working on the starting system.*

13 Starter motor and circuit - check

▶ **Refer to illustrations 13.3 and 13.4**

1 If a malfunction occurs in the starting circuit, do not immediately assume that the starter is causing the problem. First, check the following items:

a) *Make sure the battery cable clamps, where they connect to the battery, are clean and tight.*

b) *Check the condition of the battery cables (see Section 4). Replace any defective battery cables with new parts.*

c) *Test the condition of the battery (see Section 3). If it does not pass all the tests, replace it with a new battery.*

d) *Check the starter solenoid wiring and connections. Refer to the wiring diagrams at the end of Chapter 12.*

e) *Check the starter mounting bolts for tightness.*

f) *Check the fuses in the engine compartment fuse and relay box (see Chapter 12). If they're burned, determine the cause and repair the circuit. Also, check the ignition switch circuit for correct operation (see the wiring diagrams at the end of Chapter 12).*

g) *Check the operation of the gear position switch (automatic transaxle) or clutch start circuit (manual transaxle). Make sure the shift lever is in PARK or NEUTRAL (automatic transaxle) or the clutch pedal is pressed (manual transaxle). Refer to Chapter 7 for the gear position switch check and adjustment procedure. Refer to the Chapter 12 wiring diagrams for the necessary circuit checks for the clutch activation system. These systems must operate correctly to provide battery voltage to the starter solenoid.*

h) *Check the operation of the starter cut relay. The starter cut relay is located in the fuse/relay box under the dash on the driver's side. Refer to Chapter 12 for the testing procedure.*

2 If the starter does not activate when the ignition switch is turned to the start position, check for battery voltage to the solenoid. This will determine if the solenoid is receiving the correct voltage signal from the ignition switch. Connect a voltmeter to the starter solenoid "S" terminal. Then note the indicated voltage when an assistant turns the ignition switch to the START position. It should be about the same as battery voltage. If there's no voltage at the S terminal, refer to the wiring diagrams at the end of Chapter 12 and check the starting system fuse(s). Also check the starter relay for correct operation if you're working on a 2004 or later V6 model. Refer to Chapter 12 for help with testing relays. If voltage is available but the starter motor doesn't engage and spin the driveplate, remove the starter from the engine (see Section 14) and bench test the starter (see Step 4).

3 If the starter turns over slowly, check the starter cranking voltage and the current draw from the battery. This test must be performed with the starter assembly on the engine. Crank the engine over (for 10 seconds or less) and observe the battery voltage. It should not drop below 8.5 volts. Also, observe the current draw using an ammeter (see illustration). It should not exceed 380 amps. If the starter motor exceeds these values, replace it. Several conditions might affect the starter's cranking power. The battery must be in good condition and the battery cold-cranking rating must not be under-rated for the application. Be sure to check the battery specifications carefully. The battery terminals and cables must be clean and not corroded. Also, in cases of extremely cold temperatures, make sure the battery and/or engine block is warmed before performing the tests.

13.3 To use an inductive ammeter, simply hold the ammeter over the positive or negative battery cable (whichever cable has better clearance)

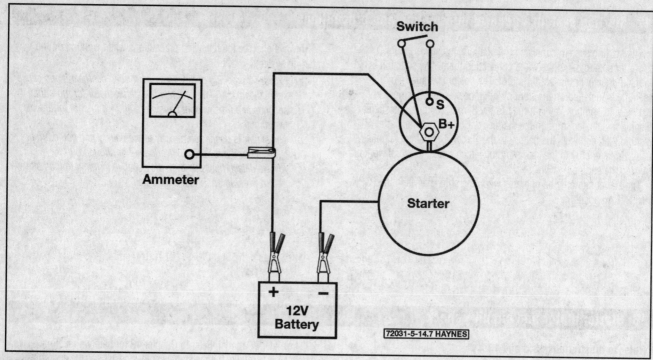

13.4 Starter motor bench testing details

4   If the starter is receiving voltage but does not activate, remove and check the starter/solenoid assembly on the bench. Most likely the solenoid is defective. In some rare cases, the engine may be seized so be sure to try and rotate the crankshaft pulley (see Chapter 2) before proceeding. With the starter/solenoid assembly mounted in a vise on the workbench, connect one jumper cable from the negative terminal (–) to the body of the starter (see illustration). Install another jumper cable from the positive terminal (+) on the battery to the B+ terminal on the starter. Install a starter switch and apply battery voltage to the solenoid S terminal (for 10 seconds or less) and observe the solenoid plunger, shift lever and overrunning clutch extend and rotate the pinion drive. If the pinion drive extends but does not rotate, the solenoid is operating but the starter motor is defective. If there is no movement but the solenoid clicks, the solenoid and/or the starter motor is defective. If the solenoid plunger extends and rotates the pinion drive, the starter/solenoid assembly is working properly.

14   Starter motor - removal and installation

⬧ **Refer to illustrations 14.3a, 14.3b and 14.4**

1   Detach the cable from the negative terminal of the battery (see Section 1).
2   On four-cylinder and 3.0L V6 models, raise the vehicle and support it securely on jackstands.
3   Disconnect the wiring from the starter (see illustrations).
4   Unscrew the starter mounting bolts, move aside any brackets and remove the starter (see illustration).
5   Manipulate the starter to clear the engine block and take it out of the bellhousing.
6   Installation is the reverse of removal. Be sure to tighten the starter mounting bolts to the torque listed in this Chapter's Specifications, then reconnect the cable to the negative terminal of the battery (see Section 1).

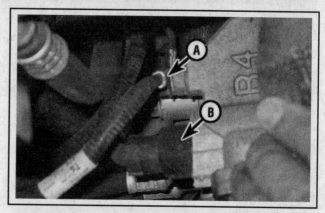

14.3a Disconnect the battery cable (A) and the solenoid wiring (B) from the starter (four-cylinder shown)

14.3b On 3.5L V6 models, peel back the rubber boot (A) and pull off the electrical connector (B), then peel back the rubber boot (C), remove the nut (D) and remove the starter cable

14.4 Upper (A) and lower (B) starter mounting bolts (3.5L V6 model)

Specifications

General

Battery voltage	
Engine off	12.6 volts
Engine running	13.5 to 14.5 volts

Torque specifications	Ft-lbs	Nm
Alternator mounting bolts		
Four-cylinder models	16	22
2002 and 2003 V6 models	26	35
2004 and later V6 models	33	45
Starter motor mounting bolts		
Four-cylinder models	30	40
2002 and 2003 V6 models	26	35
2004 and later V6 models	33	45

NOTES

6

EMISSIONS AND ENGINE CONTROL SYSTEMS

1 General information

▶ **Refer to illustration 1.4**

To prevent pollution of the atmosphere from incompletely burned and evaporating gases, and to maintain good driveability and fuel economy, a number of emission control systems are incorporated. They include the:

Catalytic converter
Evaporative Emissions Control(EVAP) system
Exhaust Gas Recirculation (EGR) system (2004 and later V6 models)
On-Board Diagnostic-II (OBD-II) system
Positive Crankcase Ventilation (PCV) system
Programmed Fuel Injection (PGM-FI) system (electronic engine control system)
Rocker Arm Hydraulic Actuator (RAHA) system (2004 and later V6 models)

Before assuming that an emissions control system is malfunctioning, check the fuel and ignition systems carefully. The diagnosis of some emission control devices requires specialized tools, equipment and training. If a procedure is beyond your ability, consult a dealer service department or other repair shop. Remember, the most frequent cause of emissions problems is simply a loose or broken wire or vacuum hose, so always check all hose and wiring connections first.

➡**Note: Because of a Federally mandated extended warranty which covers the emissions control system components, check with your dealer about warranty coverage before working on any emissions-related systems. Once the warranty has expired, you may wish to perform some of the component checks and/or replacement procedures in this Chapter to save money.**

Pay close attention to any special precautions outlined in this Chapter. It should be noted that the illustrations of the various systems might not exactly match the system installed on your vehicle because of annual changes made by the manufacturer during production and because of running changes made during a model year.

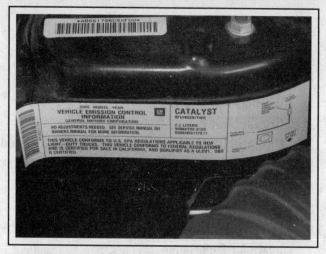

1.4 The Vehicle Emission Control Information (VECI) label is located in the engine compartment; the VECI label specifies the emission-control systems on your vehicle, and includes important tune-up specifications and a vacuum hose routing diagram

A Vehicle Emissions Control Information (VECI) label is attached to the underside of the hood (see illustration). This label specifies the important emissions systems on the vehicle and, where applicable, provides important tune-up or adjustment specifications. Part of the VECI label, the Vacuum Hose Routing Diagram, provides a vacuum hose schematic with emissions components identified. If there's a discrepancy between the information in this manual and the information on the VECI label, defer to the information on the VECI label. It contains the most up-to-date information about your vehicle, and might reflect some running change made to the vehicle after the manual was published.

2 On Board Diagnosis (OBD) system and trouble codes

SCAN TOOL INFORMATION

▶ **Refer to illustrations 2.1 and 2.2**

1   Hand-held scanners are handy for analyzing the engine management systems used on late-model vehicles. Because extracting the Diagnostic Trouble Codes (DTCs) from an engine management system is now the first step in troubleshooting many computer-controlled systems and components, even the most basic generic code readers are capable of accessing a computer's DTCs (see illustration). More powerful scan tools can also perform many of the diagnostics once associated with expensive factory scan tools. If you're planning to obtain a generic scan tool for your vehicle, make sure that it's compatible with OBD-II systems. If you don't plan to purchase a code reader or scan tool and don't have access to one, you can have the codes extracted by a dealer service department or by an independent repair shop.

2   With the advent of the Federally mandated emission control system known as On-Board Diagnostics-II (OBD-II), specially designed scanners were developed. Several tool manufacturers have released OBD-II scan tools for the home mechanic (see illustration).

➡**Note: An aftermarket generic scanner should work with any model covered by this manual. Before purchasing a generic scan tool, verify that it will work properly with the OBD-II system you want to scan. If necessary, of course, you can always have the codes extracted by a dealer service department or an independent repair shop with a professional scan tool. Some auto parts stores even provide this service.**

OBD SYSTEM GENERAL DESCRIPTION

3   All models are equipped with the second generation OBD-II system. This system consists of an on-board computer known as the Powertrain Control Module (PCM), and information sensors, which monitor various functions of the engine and send data to the PCM. This

2.1 Simple code readers are an economical way to extract trouble codes when the CHECK ENGINE light comes on

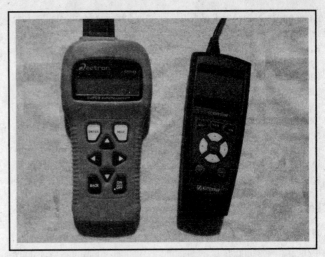

2.2 Scanners like these from Actron and AutoXray are powerful diagnostic aids - they can tell you just about anything that you want to know about your engine management system

system incorporates a series of diagnostic monitors that detect and identify fuel injection and emissions control systems faults and store the information in the computer memory. This updated system also tests sensors and output actuators, diagnoses drive cycles, freezes data and clears codes.

4 This powerful diagnostic computer must be accessed using an OBD-II scan tool, or OBD-II code reader, plugged into the 16-pin Data Link Connector (DLC) located under the driver's dash area. The PCM is located below the center of the instrument panel, mounted to the firewall. The PCM is the brain of the electronically controlled fuel and emissions system. It receives data from a number of sensors and other electronic components (switches, relays, etc.). Based on the information it receives, the PCM generates output signals to control various relays, solenoids (fuel injectors) and other actuators. The PCM is specifically calibrated to optimize the emissions, fuel economy and driveability of the vehicle.

5 It isn't a good idea to attempt diagnosis or replacement of the PCM or emission control components at home while the vehicle is under warranty. Because of a federally-mandated warranty which covers the emissions system components and because any owner-induced damage to the PCM, the sensors and/or the control devices may void this warranty, take the vehicle to a dealer service department if the PCM or a system component malfunctions.

INFORMATION SENSORS

6 **Accelerator Pedal Position (APP) sensor** - The APP sensor, which is part of the electronic throttle control system, is located at the accelerator pedal. All of these models are equipped with an Electronic Throttle Control (ETC) system, which uses an electronic throttle body - there is no accelerator cable. The throttle plate inside the throttle body is electronically controlled by the PCM. The APP sensor is a potentiometer that receives a constant voltage input from the PCM and sends back a voltage signal that varies in relation to the position (angle) of the accelerator pedal. As you press the accelerator pedal, the APP sensor alters its voltage signal to the PCM in proportion to the angle of the pedal, and the PCM commands a motor inside the throttle body to open or close the throttle plate accordingly. This system is also able to adjust the idle speed for all conditions.

7 **Camshaft Position (CMP) sensor** - The CMP sensor produces a signal that the PCM uses to identify the number 1 cylinder and to time the firing sequence of the fuel injectors.

8 **Crankshaft Position (CKP) sensor** - The CKP sensor produces a signal that the PCM uses to determine the position of the crankshaft. The CKP sensor is located behind the starter on four-cylinder models.

9 **Engine Coolant Temperature (ECT) sensor** - The ECT sensor is a thermistor (temperature-sensitive variable resistor) that sends a voltage signal to the PCM, which uses this data to determine the temperature of the engine coolant. The ECT sensor helps the PCM control the air/fuel mixture ratio and ignition timing, and it also helps the PCM determine when to turn the Exhaust Gas Recirculation (EGR) system on and off. 2004 and later V6 models have two ECT sensors.

10 **Fuel tank pressure sensor** - The fuel tank pressure sensor measures the fuel tank pressure when the PCM tests the EVAP system, and it's also used to control fuel tank pressure by signaling the EVAP system to purge the fuel tank vapors when the pressure becomes excessive.

11 **Input shaft (mainshaft) speed sensor** - The input shaft (or mainshaft) speed sensor is a magnetic pick-up coil located on the front of the transaxle.

12 **Intake Air Temperature (IAT) sensor** - The IAT sensor monitors the temperature of the air entering the engine and sends a signal to the PCM. On four-cylinder models, it's mounted in the intake air duct. On 2002 and 2003 V6 models, it's part of the MAF/IAT sensor in the outlet of the air filter housing. On 2004 and later V6 models, there is one near the throttle body in the intake manifold and another in the air filter housing.

13 **Knock sensor** - The knock sensor is a piezoelectric crystal that oscillates in proportion to engine vibration. The term piezoelectric refers to the property of certain crystals that produce a voltage when subjected to a mechanical stress. The oscillation of the piezoelectric crystal produces a voltage output that is monitored by the PCM, which retards the ignition timing when the oscillation exceeds a certain threshold. When the engine is operating normally, the knock sensor oscillates consistently and its voltage signal is steady. When detonation occurs, engine vibration increases, and the oscillation of the knock sensor exceeds a design threshold. Detonation is an uncontrolled explosion, after the

spark occurs at the spark plug, which spontaneously combusts the remaining air/fuel mixture, resulting in a pinging or slapping sound. If allowed to continue, the engine could be damaged.

14 **Manifold Absolute Pressure (MAP) sensor** - The MAP sensor monitors the pressure or vacuum downstream from the throttle plate, inside the intake manifold. The MAP sensor measures intake manifold pressure and vacuum on the absolute scale - from zero instead of from sea-level atmospheric pressure (14.7 psi). The MAP sensor converts the absolute pressure into a variable voltage signal that changes with the pressure. The PCM uses this data to determine engine load so that it can alter the ignition advance and fuel enrichment. 2002 and 2003 V6 models use a MAF/IAT sensor instead of a MAP sensor.

15 **Mass Air Flow/Intake Air Temperature (MAF/IAT) sensor** - The MAF/IAT sensor is used only on 2002 and 2003 V6 models. The MAF sensor is the means by which the PCM measures the amount of intake air drawn into the engine. It uses a hot-wire sensing element to measure the amount of air entering the engine. The wire is constantly maintained at a specified temperature above the ambient temperature of the incoming air by electrical current. As intake air passes through the MAF sensor and over the hot wire, it cools the wire, and the control system immediately corrects the temperature back to its constant value. The current required to maintain the constant value is used by the PCM to determine the amount of air flowing through the MAF sensor. The MAF sensor also includes an integral Intake Air Temperature (IAT) sensor. The two components cannot be serviced separately; if either sensor is defective, replace the MAF/IAT sensor.

16 **Output shaft (countershaft) speed sensor** - The output shaft (or countershaft) speed sensor is a magnetic pick-up coil, which is located on top of the transaxle. The output shaft speed sensor provides the Powertrain Control Module (PCM) with information about the rotational speed of the output shaft in the transmission. The PCM uses this information to control the torque converter and to calculate speed scheduling and the correct operating pressure for the transaxle.

17 **Oxygen sensors** - An oxygen sensor is a galvanic battery that generates a small variable voltage signal in proportion to the difference between the oxygen content in the exhaust stream and the oxygen content in the ambient air. The PCM uses the voltage signal from the upstream oxygen sensor to maintain a stoichiometric air/fuel ratio of 14.7:1 during cruise conditions by constantly adjusting the on-time of the fuel injectors. Four-cylinder engines use two oxygen sensors - one at the exhaust manifold and one in the exhaust pipe under the vehicle. V6 models have the same configuration, however they have two sensors for each bank of cylinders.

18 **Throttle Position (TP) sensor** - The TP sensor is a potentiometer that receives a constant voltage input from the PCM and sends back a voltage signal that varies in relation to the opening angle of the throttle plate inside the throttle body. This voltage signal tells the PCM the throttle position. The PCM uses this data, along with information from other sensors, to calculate injector pulse width (the interval of time during which an injector solenoid is energized by the PCM). The TP sensor is located on the throttle body (some models have two TP sensors). If the TP sensor is defective on any of these models, you must replace the throttle body. The TP sensor cannot be replaced separately.

19 **Transmission range switch** - The transmission range switch is located at the manual lever on the transaxle. The transmission range switch functions like a conventional Park/Neutral Position (PNP) switch: it prevents the engine from starting in any gear other than Park or Neutral, and it closes the circuit for the back-up lights when the shift lever is moved to Reverse. The PCM is able to determine the gear selected and is able to determine the correct position for the electronic pressure control system of the transaxle.

OUTPUT ACTUATORS

20 **EVAP canister purge valve** - The purge valve is normally closed, but when ordered to do so by the PCM, it allows the fuel vapors that are stored in the EVAP canister to be drawn into the intake manifold, where they're mixed with intake air, then burned along with the normal air/fuel mixture, under certain operating conditions. The purge valve also controls this vapor flow.

21 **EVAP canister vent shut valve** - The canister vent shut valve is normally open, but it closes and seals off the EVAP system for inspection and maintenance tests and for OBD-II leak and pressure tests.

22 **Exhaust Gas Recirculation (EGR) valve** - When the engine is put under a load (hard acceleration, passing, going up a steep hill, pulling a trailer, etc.), combustion chamber temperature increases. When combustion chamber temperature exceeds 2500 degrees, excessive amounts of oxides of nitrogen (NOx) are produced. NOx is a precursor of photochemical smog. When combined with hydrocarbons (HC), other reactive organic compounds (ROCs) and sunlight, it forms ozone, nitrogen dioxide, nitrogen nitrate and other nasty stuff. The PCM-controlled EGR valve allows exhaust gases to be recirculated back to the intake manifold where they dilute the incoming air/fuel mixture, which lowers the combustion chamber temperature and decreases the amount of NOx produced during high-load conditions. The EGR system is only used on 2004 and later V6 engines.

23 **Fuel injectors** - The fuel injectors, which spray a fine mist of fuel into the intake ports to mix with incoming air, are inductive coils under PCM control. For more information about the injectors, see Chapter 4.

24 **Ignition coils** - The ignition coils are under the control of the Powertrain Control Module (PCM). They are either individual (2004 and later V6 models) or are part of a coil pack assembly that is attached directly to the valve cover.

25 **Rocker arm oil control solenoid valve** - This solenoid valve allows oil to flow to the rocker arms at high engine speed to activate the high-lift rocker arms. This provides additional valve lift at times when the engine can utilize it. The rocker arm activation system is only used on 2004 and later V6 engines.

26 **Intake manifold runner control solenoid** - This solenoid controls vacuum which operates a valve in the intake manifold. When open, this shortens the path that the intake air takes when the engine speed is increased and provides a power increase. This system is only used on 2002 and 2003 V6 models.

OBTAINING AND CLEARING DIAGNOSTIC TROUBLE CODES (DTCS)

27 All models covered by this manual are equipped with on-board diagnostics. When the PCM recognizes a malfunction in a monitored emission control system, component or circuit, it turns on the Malfunction Indicator Light (MIL) on the dash. The PCM will continue to display the MIL until the problem is fixed and the Diagnostic Trouble Code (DTC) is cleared from the PCM's memory. You'll need a scan tool to access any DTCs stored in the PCM.

28 Before outputting any DTCs stored in the PCM, thoroughly inspect ALL electrical connectors and hoses. Make sure that all electrical connections are tight, clean and free of corrosion. And make sure that all hoses are correctly connected, fit tightly and are in good condition (no cracks or tears).

Accessing the DTCs

▶ **Refer to illustration 2.29**

29 On these models (all of which are equipped with On-Board Diagnostic II [OBD-II] systems), the Diagnostic Trouble Codes (DTCs) can only be accessed with a scan tool. Professional scan tools are expensive, but relatively inexpensive generic scan tools (see illustrations 2.1 and 2.2) are available at most auto parts stores. Simply plug the connector of the scan tool into the diagnostic connector (see illustration), which is located under the lower edge of the dash, just to the left of the steering column. Then follow the instructions included with the scan tool to extract the DTCs.

30 Once you have outputted all of the stored DTCs, look them up on the accompanying DTC chart.

31 After troubleshooting the source of each DTC, make any necessary repairs or replace the defective component(s).

Clearing the DTCs

32 Clear the DTCs with the scan tool in accordance with the instructions provided by the scan tool's manufacturer.

DIAGNOSTIC TROUBLE CODES

33 The accompanying tables are a list of the Diagnostic Trouble Codes (DTCs) that can be accessed by a do-it-yourselfer working at home (there are many, many more DTCs available to professional

2.29 The Data Link Connector (DLC) is located under the lower edge of the dash

mechanics with proprietary scan tools and software, but those codes cannot be accessed by a generic scan tool). If, after you have checked and repaired the connectors, wire harness and vacuum hoses (if applicable) for an emission-related system, component or circuit, the problem persists, have the vehicle checked by a dealer service department or other qualified repair shop.

OBD-II TROUBLE CODES

Code	Probable cause
P0030	HO2S heater control circuit (bank 1, sensor 1)
P0031	HO2S heater control circuit low (bank 1, sensor 1)
P0032	HO2S heater control circuit high (bank 1, sensor 1)
P0036	HO2S heater control circuit (bank 1 sensor 2)
P0037	HO2S heater control circuit low (bank 1, sensor 2)
P0038	HO2S heater control circuit high (bank 1, sensor 2
P0050	HO2S heater control circuit (bank 2, sensor 1)
P0051	HO2S heater control circuit low (bank 2, sensor 1)
P0052	HO2S heater control circuit high (bank 2, sensor 1)
P0056	HO2S heater control circuit (bank 2, sensor 2)
P0057	HO2S heater control circuit low (bank 2, sensor 2)
P0058	HO2S heater control circuit high (bank 2, sensor 2)
P0068	Throttle Position (TP) sensor inconsistent with Mass Air Flow (MAF) sensor
P0096	Intake Air Temperature (IAT) sensor 2 - circuit range/performance
P0097	Intake Air Temperature (IAT) sensor 2 circuit, low voltage

OBD-II TROUBLE CODES (CONTINUED)

Code	Probable cause
P0098	Intake Air Temperature (IAT) sensor 2 circuit, high voltage
P0101	Mass Air Flow (MAF) sensor circuit, range or performance problem
P0102	Mass Air Flow (MAF) sensor circuit, low voltage
P0103	Mass Air Flow (MAF) sensor circuit, high voltage
P0106	Manifold Absolute Pressure (MAP) or barometric pressure circuit, range or performance problem
P0107	Manifold Absolute Pressure (MAP) sensor circuit, low voltage
P0108	Manifold Absolute Pressure (MAP) sensor circuit, high voltage
P0112	Intake Air Temperature (IAT) sensor circuit, low voltage
P0113	Intake Air Temperature (IAT) sensor circuit, high voltage
P0116	Engine Coolant Temperature (ECT) sensor circuit, range or performance problem
P0117	Engine Coolant Temperature (ECT) sensor circuit, low voltage
P0118	Engine Coolant Temperature (ECT) sensor circuit, high voltage
P0120	Throttle position or pedal position sensor/switch circuit malfunction
P0121	Throttle position or pedal position sensor/switch circuit, range or performance problem
P0122	Throttle Position (TP) sensor circuit, low voltage
P0123	Throttle Position (TP) sensor circuit, high voltage
P0125	Engine Coolant Temperature (ECT) sensor, malfunction or slow response
P0128	Cooling system malfunction
P0130	O2 sensor circuit malfunction (bank 1, sensor 1)
P0131	O2 sensor circuit, low voltage (bank 1, sensor 1)
P0132	O2 sensor circuit, high voltage (bank 1, sensor 1)
P0133	O2 sensor circuit, slow response (bank 1, sensor 1)
P0134	O2 sensor circuit - no activity detected (bank 1, sensor 1)
P0135	O2 sensor heater circuit malfunction (bank 1, sensor 1)
P0136	O2 sensor circuit malfunction (bank 1, sensor 2)
P0137	O2 sensor circuit, low voltage (bank 1, sensor 2)
P0138	O2 sensor circuit, high voltage (bank 1, sensor 2)
P0139	O2 sensor circuit, slow response (bank 1, sensor 2)
P0140	O2 sensor circuit - no activity detected (bank 1, sensor 2)
P0141	O2 sensor heater circuit malfunction (bank 1, sensor 2)

Code	Probable cause
P0150	O2 sensor circuit malfunction (bank 2, sensor 1)
P0151	O2 sensor circuit, low voltage (bank 2, sensor 1)
P0152	O2 sensor circuit, high voltage (bank 2, sensor 1)
P0153	O2 sensor circuit, slow response (bank 2, sensor 1)
P0154	O2 sensor circuit - no activity detected (bank 2, sensor 1)
P0155	O2 sensor heater circuit malfunction (bank 2, sensor 1)
P0156	O2 sensor circuit malfunction (bank 2, sensor 2)
P0157	O2 sensor circuit, low voltage (bank 2, sensor 2)
P0158	O2 sensor circuit, high voltage (bank 2, sensor 2)
P0159	O2 sensor circuit, slow response (bank 2, sensor 2)
P0160	O2 sensor circuit - no activity detected (bank 2, sensor 2)
P0161	O2 sensor heater circuit malfunction (bank 2, sensor 2)
P0171	System too lean (bank 1)
P0172	System too rich (bank 1)
P0174	System too lean (bank 2)
P0175	System too rich (bank 2)
P0201	No. 1 injector circuit malfunction
P0202	No. 2 injector circuit malfunction
P0203	No. 3 injector circuit malfunction
P0204	No. 4 injector circuit malfunction
P0205	No. 5 injector circuit malfunction
P0206	No. 6 injector circuit malfunction
P0220	Throttle position or pedal position sensor/switch B circuit malfunction
P0221	Throttle position or pedal position sensor/switch B, range or performance problem
P0261	Cylinder no. 1 injector circuit, low
P0262	Cylinder no. 1 injector circuit, high
P0264	Cylinder no. 2 injector circuit, low
P0265	Cylinder no. 2 injector circuit, high
P0270	Cylinder no. 4 injector circuit, low
P0271	Cylinder no. 4 injector circuit, high
P0273	Cylinder no. 5 injector circuit, low

OBD-II TROUBLE CODES (CONTINUED)

Code	Probable cause
P0274	Cylinder no. 5 injector circuit, high
P0276	Cylinder no. 6 injector circuit, low
P0277	Cylinder no. 6 injector circuit, high
P0300	Random misfire detected
P0301	Cylinder no. 1 misfire detected
P0302	Cylinder no. 2 misfire detected
P0303	Cylinder no. 3 misfire detected
P0304	Cylinder no. 4 misfire detected
P0305	Cylinder no. 5 misfire detected
P0306	Cylinder no. 6 misfire detected
P0313	Misfire detected with low fuel
P0315	Crankshaft position system - variation not learned
P0318	Rough road sensor signal A - circuit malfunction
P0324	Knock control system error
P0325	Knock sensor circuit malfunction
P0326	Knock sensor no. 1 circuit, range or performance problem (bank 1 or single sensor)
P0327	Knock sensor no. 1 circuit, low input (bank 1 or single sensor)
P0328	Knock sensor no. 1 circuit, high input (bank 1 or single sensor)
P0332	Knock sensor no. 2 circuit, low input (bank 2)
P0333	Knock sensor no. 2 circuit, high input (bank 2)
P0335	Crankshaft Position (CKP) sensor A, no signal
P0336	Crankshaft Position (CKP) sensor A circuit - range or performance problem
P0337	Crankshaft Position (CKP) sensor A circuit - low input
P0340	Camshaft Position (CMP) sensor "A", circuit malfunction (bank 1)
P0341	Camshaft Position (CMP) sensor A, intermittent interruption
P0342	Camshaft Position (CMP) sensor "A", circuit - low input
P0343	Camshaft Position (CMP) sensor "A", circuit - high input
P0385	Crankshaft Position (CKP) sensor B, no signal
P0386	Crankshaft Position (CKP) sensor B circuit, range or performance problem
P0401	Exhaust Gas Recirculation (EGR) system, insufficient flow

Code	Probable cause
P0403	Exhaust Gas Recirculation (EGR) circuit malfunction
P0404	Exhaust Gas Recirculation (EGR) control circuit, range or performance problem
P0406	Exhaust Gas Recirculation (EGR) valve position sensor circuit, high voltage
P0420	Catalyst system efficiency below threshold (bank 1)
P0421	Warm-up catalyst efficiency below threshold (bank 1)
P0430	Catalyst system efficiency below threshold (front cylinder head)
P0431	Warm-up catalyst efficiency below threshold (bank 2)
P0440	Evaporative emission control (EVAP) system malfunction
P0442	Evaporative emission control (EVAP) system, small leak detected
P0443	Evaporative emission control (EVAP) canister purge valve, circuit malfunction
P0444	Evaporative emission control (EVAP) system, open purge control valve circuit
P0445	Evaporative emission control (EVAP) system, short in purge control valve circuit
P0446	Evaporative emission control (EVAP) system, vent control circuit malfunction
P0447	Evaporative emission control (EVAP) system, open vent control circuit
P0448	Evaporative emission control (EVAP) system, shorted vent control circuit
P0449	Evaporative emission control (EVAP) system, vent valve/solenoid circuit malfunction
P0451	Fuel Tank Pressure (FTP) sensor circuit, range or performance problem
P0452	Fuel Tank Pressure (FTP) sensor circuit, low voltage
P0453	Fuel Tank Pressure (FTP) sensor circuit, high voltage
P0454	Evaporative emission control (EVAP) system, pressure sensor intermittent
P0455	Evaporative emission control (EVAP) system, very large leak detected
P0496	Evaporative emission control (EVAP), high purge flow
P0498	Evaporative emission control (EVAP) canister vent shut valve control circuit, low voltage
P0499	Evaporative emission control (EVAP) canister vent shut valve control circuit, high voltage
P0506	Idle control system, rpm lower than expected
P0507	Idle control system, rpm higher than expected
P0601	Internal control module, memory check sum error
P0602	Powertrain Control Module (PCM) programming error
P0603	Powertrain Control Module (PCM), Keep Alive Memory (KAM) error
P0604	Internal control module, random access memory (RAM) error
P0605	Internal control module, read only memory (ROM) error

OBD-II TROUBLE CODES (CONTINUED)

Code	Probable cause
P0606	Powertrain Control Module (PCM) processor fault
P0607	Powertrain Control Module (PCM), internal circuit malfunction
P0607	Lost communication with Electronic Throttle Control System (ECTS)
P060D	Control Module Accelerator Pedal Position (APP) System Performance
P060E	Control Module Throttle Position (TP) System Performance
P0610	Control module - vehicle options error
P0628	Fuel pump control - circuit low
P0629	Fuel pump control - circuit high
P062F	Powertrain Control Module (PCM) internal control module Keep Alive Memory (KAM) error
P0630	VIN not programmed or mismatch
P0638	Throttle actuator control range/performance (bank 1)
P0641	Sensor reference voltage A malfunction
P0651	Sensor reference voltage B malfunction
P0685	Powertrain Control Module (PCM), power control circuit or internal circuit malfunction
P0688	Engine, control relay - short to positive

AUTOMATIC TRANSAXLE DIAGNOSTIC TROUBLE CODES

Code	Probable cause
P0700	Automatic transmission control system malfunction
P0701	Transmission control system, range or performance problem
P0710	Automatic Transmission Fluid (ATF) temperature sensor
P0711	ATF temperature sensor, range or performance problem
P0712	ATF temperature sensor, short circuit
P0713	ATF temperature sensor, open circuit
P0715	Input shaft (mainshaft) speed sensor
P0716	Input shaft (mainshaft) speed sensor, range or performance problem
P0717	Input shaft (mainshaft) speed sensor, no signal input
P0718	Input shaft (mainshaft) speed sensor, intermittent failure
P0720	Output shaft (countershaft) speed sensor
P0721	Output shaft (countershaft) speed sensor, range or performance problem

Code	Probable cause
P0722	Output shaft (countershaft) speed sensor, no signal input
P0723	Output shaft (countershaft) speed sensor, intermittent failure
P0730	Shift control system
P0731	1st gear, incorrect ratio
P0732	2nd gear, incorrect ratio
P0733	3rd gear, incorrect ratio
P0734	4th gear, incorrect ratio
P0735	5th gear, incorrect ratio
P0740	Lock-up control system
P0741	Torque converter clutch circuit, performance or stuck off
P0743	Torque converter clutch solenoid valve
P0746	Automatic transaxle clutch pressure control solenoid valve A, stuck off
P0747	Automatic transaxle clutch pressure control solenoid valve A, stuck on
P0748	Automatic transaxle clutch pressure control solenoid valve A
P0751	Shift solenoid valve A stuck off
P0752	Shift solenoid valve A stuck on
P0753	Shift solenoid valve A
P0756	Shift solenoid valve B stuck off
P0757	Shift solenoid valve B stuck on
P0758	Shift solenoid valve B
P0761	Shift solenoid valve C stuck off
P0762	Shift solenoid valve C stuck on
P0763	Shift solenoid valve C
P0766	Shift solenoid valve D, stuck off
P0767	Shift solenoid valve D, stuck on
P0776	Automatic transaxle clutch pressure control solenoid valve B, stuck off
P0777	Automatic transaxle clutch pressure control solenoid valve B, stuck on
P0778	Automatic transaxle clutch pressure control solenoid valve B
P0780	Shift control system or mechanical problem in hydraulic system
P0780	Shift control system
P0796	Automatic transaxle clutch pressure control solenoid valve C stuck off

AUTOMATIC TRANSAXLE DIAGNOSTIC TROUBLE CODES (CONTINUED)

Code	Probable cause
P0797	Automatic transaxle clutch pressure control solenoid valve C stuck on
P0798	Automatic transaxle clutch pressure control solenoid valve C
P0812	Transmission Range (TR) switch ATP R switch
P0815	Transmission gear selection switch upshift switch, short or stuck on
P0816	Transmission gear selection switch downshift switch, short or stuck on
P0842	2nd clutch transmission fluid pressure switch, short or stuck on
P0843	2nd clutch transmission fluid pressure switch, open or stuck off
P0845	Third clutch transaxle fluid pressure switch
P0847	3rd clutch transmission fluid pressure switch, shorted or stuck on
P0848	3rd clutch transmission fluid pressure switch, open or stuck off
P0872	4th clutch transmission fluid pressure switch, shorted or stuck on
P0873	4th clutch transmission fluid pressure switch, open or stuck off
P0957	Transmission gear selection switch, shorted or stuck on
P0958	Transmission gear selection switch, shorted or stuck off
P0962	Automatic transaxle clutch pressure control solenoid valve A, short
P0963	Automatic transaxle clutch pressure control solenoid valve A, open
P0966	Automatic transaxle clutch pressure control solenoid valve B, open or short
P0967	Automatic transaxle clutch pressure control solenoid valve B
P0970	Automatic transaxle clutch pressure control solenoid valve C, open or short
P0971	Automatic transaxle clutch pressure control solenoid valve C
P0973	Shift solenoid valve A, short
P0974	Shift solenoid valve A, open
P0976	Shift solenoid valve B, short
P0977	Shift solenoid valve B, open
P0979	Shift solenoid valve C, short
P0980	Shift solenoid valve C, open
P0982	Shift solenoid valve D, short
P0983	Shift solenoid valve D open

3   Accelerator Pedal Position (APP) sensor - replacement

▸ **Refer to illustration 3.1**

➥**Note:** The APP sensor is located at the top of the accelerator pedal and is an integral component of the accelerator pedal module (you cannot separate the APP sensor from the module). There is no accelerator cable.

1   Disconnect the electrical connector from the APP sensor (see illustration).

2   Remove the APP sensor module mounting bolts and remove the sensor module.

➥**Note:** The top bolt must be left in the sensor until it's removed from the vehicle. Make sure to place it in its hole before installing the sensor.

3   Installation is the reverse of removal.

3.1 To disconnect the electrical connector from the APP sensor, depress the lock tab and slide the lock out from the connector, then depress the release tab and pull the connector off the APP sensor

4   Camshaft Position (CMP) sensor - replacement.

➥**Note:** This procedure applies to V6 models only.

2002 AND 2003 (3.0L) V6 MODELS

▸ **Refer to illustration 4.1**

➥**Note:** The CMP sensor is located at the right (drivebelt) end of the front cylinder head.

1   Disconnect the CMP sensor electrical connector (see illustration).

2   Disconnect the knock sensor wiring for access to the CMP sensor mounting bolt, then remove the mounting bolt and CMP sensor.

3   Installation is the reverse of removal.

2004 AND LATER (3.5L) V6 MODELS

▸ **Refer to illustrations 4.6a, 4.6b and 4.7**

➥**Note:** The CMP sensor is located at the right (drivebelt) end of the front cylinder head, behind the timing belt rear cover.

4   Refer to Chapter 2C and remove the timing belt.

5   Remove the front camshaft sprocket.

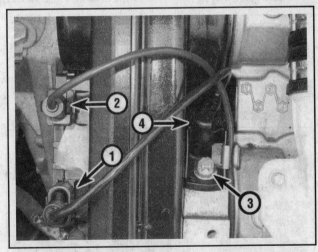

4.1 Camshaft Position (CMP) sensor removal details (3.0L V6 models):

1   *Disconnect the CMP sensor electrical connector*
2   *Disconnect the knock sensor No. 2 electrical connector, detach the lead from the clip and set it aside*
3   *Remove the CMP sensor retaining bolt*
4   *Remove the CMP sensor*

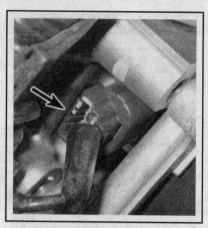

4.6a To disconnect the electrical connector from the CMP sensor, depress the release tab and pull off the connector

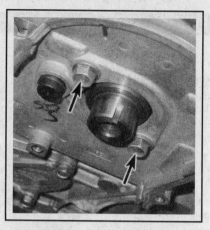

4.6b To detach the rear timing belt cover, remove these two bolts

4.7 To detach the CMP sensor from the rear timing belt cover, remove this mounting bolt

6   Disconnect the CMP wiring harness and remove the sprocket rear cover and its lower seal (see illustrations).

7   Remove the CMP sensor from the cover (see illustration).
8   Installation is the reverse of removal.

5   Crankshaft Position (CKP) sensor - replacement

FOUR-CYLINDER MODELS

▸ Refer to illustration 5.4

➡Note: The CKP sensor is behind the starter on these engines.

1   Raise the front of the vehicle and place it securely on jackstands.
2   Refer to Chapter 5 and remove the starter.
3   Disconnect the wiring from the CKP sensor.
4   Remove the mounting bolt and remove the CKP sensor (see illustration). Check the O-ring for deterioration.
5   Installation is the reverse of removal. Be sure to tighten the CKP sensor mounting bolt to the torque listed in this Chapter's Specifications.

2002 AND 2003 (3.0L) V6 MODELS

▸ Refer to illustration 5.7

➡Note: The CKP sensor is mounted near the transaxle on the front of the engine.

6   Raise the front of the vehicle and place it securely on jackstands.
7   Disconnect the wiring harness from the CKP sensor (see illustration).
8   Remove the CKP sensor mounting bolt and remove the sensor from the engine.
9   Installation is the reverse of removal. Replace the O-ring if necessary.

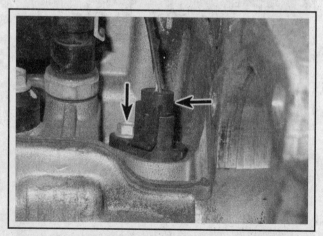

5.4 To remove the CKP sensor, disconnect the wiring and remove the sensor mounting bolt (four-cylinder models)

5.7 Removing the CKP sensor on a 3.0L V6 model

EMISSIONS AND ENGINE CONTROL SYSTEMS 6-15

5.11 Remove the two nuts that secure the shield for the CKP sensor wiring harness shield, then remove the shield (3.5L V6 models)

5.12 To remove the CKP sensor, remove the sensor mounting bolt (1), pull off the CKP sensor, depress the electrical connector release tab (2) and disconnect the connector from the sensor (3.5L V6 models)

2004 AND LATER (3.5L) V6 MODELS

♦ Refer to illustrations 5.11 and 5.12

➥Note: The CKP sensor is mounted under the timing belt cover near the front of the crankshaft.

10 Refer to Chapter 2C and remove the timing belt cover.
11 Remove the cover from the CKP wiring (see illustration).
12 Remove the CKP sensor (see illustration).
13 Installation is the reverse of removal. Perform the idle learning procedure to ensure that the idle remains stable (see Chapter 5, Section 1).

6   Engine Coolant Temperature (ECT) sensor - replacement

✳✳ WARNING:

Wait until the engine has cooled completely before beginning this procedure.

1 Remove the engine cover.
2 Drain the engine coolant (see Chapter 1).

➥Note: It is possible to replace the sensor without draining the coolant. If you don't drain the coolant, some coolant will run out of the coolant crossover when you remove the ECT sensor, so install the new sensor as quickly as possible.

FOUR-CYLINDER MODELS

♦ Refer to illustration 6.3

➥Note: The ECT sensor is at the rear of the engine near the transaxle end at the thermostat housing.

3 Disconnect the electrical connector from the ECT sensor (see illustration).

2002 AND 2003 (3.0L) V6 MODELS

➥Note: The ECT sensor is located on the coolant crossover, which is located at the left (driver's) end of the engine, between the cylinder heads.

4 Remove the battery (see Chapter 5).
5 Remove the cover from the fuse block and disconnect the power steering wire and the positive battery cable from the B+ terminal.
6 Disconnect all of the harnesses from the battery cooling box.
7 Loosen the fuse block connector mounting bolts.
8 Move the fuse block from its retainer and disconnect the wiring harness that supplies the front lights.

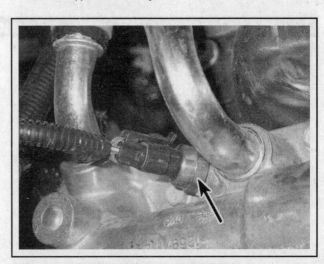

6.3 On four-cylinder engines, the ECT sensor is on the thermostat housing at the rear of the engine

6.11 ECT sensor location - 3.5L V6 engine

6.13 Always remove and discard the old ECT sensor O-ring and install a new O-ring when installing the sensor

9 Remove the battery cooling box.
10 Disconnect the electrical connector from the ECT sensor.

2004 AND LATER (3.5L) V6 MODELS

▶ **Refer to illustration 6.11**

➡Note: The ECT sensor is mounted at the left side of the front cylinder head in the pipe next to the thermostat housing.

11 Disconnect the electrical connector from the ECT sensor (see illustration).

ALL MODELS

▶ **Refer to illustration 6.13**

12 Unscrew the ECT sensor with a wrench (most deep sockets won't

fit over the ECT sensor).

✳✳ CAUTION:

If you're planning to reuse the old ECT sensor, handle it with care. Damage to the ECT sensor will adversely affect the operation of the PGM-FI system.

13 When installing the ECT sensor, apply some sealant to the threads if it's not designed to use an O-ring. If the sensor uses an O-ring instead of tapered threads, remove and discard the old ECT sensor O-ring (see illustration). Whether you're planning to reuse the old ECT sensor or install a new unit, be sure to use a new O-ring.
14 Installation is the reverse of removal. Be sure to tighten the ECT sensor to the torque listed in this Chapter's Specifications. Refill the cooling system (or, if you didn't drain the coolant, check the coolant level, adding as necessary) (see Chapter 1).

7 Intake Air Temperature (IAT) sensor - replacement

1 Remove the key from the ignition lock cylinder.

FOUR-CYLINDER MODELS

▶ **Refer to illustration 7.2**

➡Note: The IAT sensor is in the intake air duct.

2 Disconnect the electrical connector from the IAT sensor (see illustration).
3 Remove the sensor from the air duct.
4 Check the condition of the rubber grommet, replacing it if necessary.
5 Installation is the reverse of removal.

7.2 To remove the IAT sensor from a four-cylinder model, twist and pull it from the intake duct

7.10 To disconnect the electrical connector from the IAT sensor, depress this release tab and pull off the connector

7.11 The IAT sensor O-ring is countersunk into the intake manifold (3.5L V6 engine)

2002 AND 2003 V6 MODELS

6   The IAT sensor is an integral component of the Mass Air Flow (MAF) sensor. To replace the IAT sensor or the MAF sensor, refer to Section 10.

2004 AND LATER V6 MODELS

IAT sensor 1

➡**Note: This IAT sensor is located in the front side of the air filter housing.**

7   Disconnect the electrical connector from the IAT sensor. Remove the sensor from the air filter housing.

8   Check the condition of the rubber grommet, replacing it if necessary.
9   Installation is the reverse of removal.

IAT sensor 2

▶ **Refer to illustrations 7.10 and 7.11**

➡**Note: This sensor is mounted in the intake manifold next to the throttle body.**

10 Disconnect the wiring harness from the sensor (see illustration). Unscrew the sensor from the intake manifold
11 Remove and discard the old IAT sensor O-ring and install a new one (see illustration).
12 Installation is the reverse of removal. Tighten the sensor to the torque listed in this Chapter's Specifications.

---

8   Knock sensor - replacement

FOUR-CYLINDER MODELS

▶ **Refer to illustration 8.3**

➡**Note: This sensor is screwed into the side of the engine block on four cylinder engines.**

1   Disconnect the cable from the negative battery terminal (see Chapter 5, Section 1).
2   Raise the vehicle and support it securely on jackstands. Remove the starter motor (see Chapter 5).
3   Follow the lead from the knock sensor to its electrical connector, then disconnect the connector (see illustration).
4   Unscrew the knock sensor retaining bolt and detach the sensor from the engine block.
5   Installation is the reverse of removal. Be sure to tighten the knock sensor bolt to the torque listed in this Chapter's Specifications.

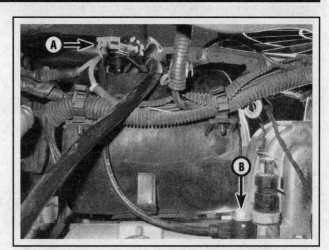

8.3 To remove the knock sensor from a four-cylinder model, disconnect the electrical connector (A) and remove the sensor mounting bolt (B) (shown from below)

8.14 To detach either of the knock sensors on a 3.0L V6 model, remove the retaining bolt

8.32 To disconnect the electrical connector from the knock sensor, depress this release button with the tip of a long slotted screwdriver and pull the connector straight up with a pair of long needle-nose pliers

8.33 You'll need to use a deep socket, a universal joint and an extension to unscrew the knock sensor. If you're unable to replace the knock sensor this way, remove the lower intake manifold

2002 AND 2003 V6 MODELS

Rear sensor

▶ Refer to illustration 8.14

➡Note: This sensor is screwed into the side of the engine block.

6   Disconnect the cable from the negative battery terminal (see Chapter 5, Section 1).

7   Loosen the lug nuts on the right front wheel. Raise the vehicle and support it securely on jackstands.

8   Follow the lead from the knock sensor to its electrical connector, then disconnect the connector.

➡Note: If you can't locate the electrical connector, you can wait to do this until after the sensor is unbolted from the engine block.

9   Remove the right inner fender splash shield.

10 Remove the drivebelt (see Chapter 1).

11 Remove the drivebelt tensioner bolts and remove the tensioner for access.

12 Disconnect the wiring from the alternator.

13 Remove the alternator mounting bolts and move the alternator aside for access to the knock sensor wiring harness.

14 Remove the knock sensor mounting bolt (see illustration) and free the sensor wiring from any clips.

15 Installation is the reverse of removal. Tighten the bolt to the torque listed in this Chapter's Specifications.

16 Be sure that the sensor wiring is attached exactly as it was, in order to avoid future damage.

Front sensor

➡Note: This sensor is screwed into the front side of the engine block.

17 Disconnect the cable from the negative battery terminal (see Chapter 5, Section 1).

18 Raise the vehicle and support it securely on jackstands.

19 Turn the wheels all the way to the right.

20 Follow the lead from the knock sensor to its electrical connector, then disconnect the connector (see illustration 4.1).

21 Disconnect the sensor wiring from the CMP sensor wiring clip.

22 Disconnect the sensor wiring from the other clip that is about 6 inches below the CMP wire clip.

23 Obtain a piece of strong twine or string about 4 feet long. Tie one end to the knock sensor wiring harness.

24 Tie the opposite end of the string to a solid engine part near the camshaft position (CMP) sensor.

25 Working under the vehicle, remove the sensor bolt (see illustration 8.14) and lower the sensor out.

26 Untie the string but leave it in place until you tie it to the wiring harness of the new sensor.

27 Pull the string from above to guide the sensor wiring around the air conditioning compressor bracket.

28 The remainder of installation is the reverse of removal. The sensor must be installed with the wiring pointing at the nine or ten o'clock position. Tighten the sensor bolt to the torque listed in this Chapter's Specifications.

2004 AND LATER V6 MODELS

▶ Refer to illustrations 8.32 and 8.33

➡Note: The knock sensor is located under the intake manifold, on top of the engine block.

29 Remove the intake manifold (see Chapter 2C).

30 Remove the fuel rail assembly (see Chapter 4).

31 The manufacturer recommends removing the injector base (the lower intake manifold) to access the knock sensor. However, with the right tools (a deep socket and a flexible extension) we have been able to access the knock sensor, so we recommend that you first try to replace the knock sensor without removing the lower intake manifold. If you're unable to do so, then remove the lower intake manifold (see Chapter 2C).

32 Disconnect the electrical connector from the knock sensor (see illustration).

33 Remove the knock sensor (see illustration).

34 Installation is the reverse of removal.

➡Note: Don't apply thread sealant to the sensor's threads.

Be sure to tighten the knock sensor to the torque listed in this Chapter's Specifications.

9 Manifold Absolute Pressure (MAP) sensor - replacement

FOUR-CYLINDER MODELS

▶ **Refer to illustration 9.2**

➡**Note: The MAP sensor is mounted in the intake manifold near the throttle body.**

1 Refer to Chapter 4 and remove the air intake duct.
2 Disconnect the electrical connector from the MAP sensor and remove the sensor (see illustration).
3 Remove the MAP sensor seal and replace it.
4 Installation is the reverse of removal.

2004 AND LATER V6 MODELS

▶ **Refer to illustration 9.6**

➡**Note 1: 2002 and 2003 V6 models use a MAF sensor instead of a MAP sensor.**

➡**Note 2: The MAP sensor is located on top of the throttle body.**

5 Remove the engine cover, if equipped.
6 Disconnect the electrical connector from the MAP sensor (see illustration). Remove the screw and detach the sensor from the throttle body.
7 Remove the old MAP sensor O-ring and discard it.
8 Installation is otherwise the reverse of removal. Be sure to use a new O-ring and tighten the MAP sensor screw securely.

9.2 The MAP sensor is mounted at the top of the intake manifold on four-cylinder models (throttle body removed for clarity)

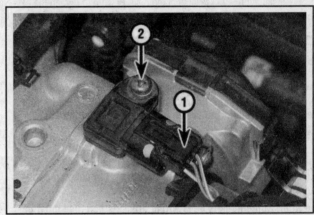

9.6 To disconnect the electrical connector from the MAP sensor, depress this release tab (1) and pull off the connector. To detach the MAP sensor from the throttle body, remove this screw (2)

10 Mass Air Flow/Intake Air Temperature (MAF/IAT) sensor - replacement

➡**Note: The MAF/IAT sensor, which is used only on 2002 and 2003 V6 models, is located at the air filter housing.**

1 Disconnect the electrical connector from the MAF/IAT sensor.
2 Disconnect the air intake tube from the sensor.

3 Remove the mounting nuts from the sensor and detach it from the air filter housing.
4 Installation is the reverse of removal.

11 Oxygen sensors - general precautions and replacement

GENERAL PRECAUTIONS

➡**Note: Because it is installed in the exhaust manifold or pipe, both of which contract when cool, an oxygen sensor might be very difficult to loosen when the engine is cold. Rather than risk damage to the sensor or its mounting threads, start and run the engine for a minute or two, then shut it off. Be careful not to burn yourself during the following procedure.**

1 Be particularly careful when servicing an oxygen sensor:
  a) *Oxygen sensors have a permanently attached pigtail and an elec-*
trical connector that cannot be removed. Damaging or removing the pigtail or electrical connector will render the sensor useless.
  b) *Keep grease, dirt and other contaminants away from the electrical connector and the louvered end of the sensor.*
  c) *Do not use cleaning solvents of any kind on an oxygen sensor.*
  d) *Oxygen sensors are extremely delicate. Do not drop a sensor, throw it around or handle it roughly.*
  e) *Make sure that the silicone boot on the sensor is installed in the correct position. Otherwise, the boot might melt and it might prevent the sensor from operating correctly.*

REPLACEMENT

Upstream oxygen sensors

▶ Refer to illustrations 11.3 and 11.4

➡Note: These sensors are in the upper section of the engine compartment, either in the exhaust pipe or screwed directly into the exhaust manifold(s).

2   Remove the engine cover (see Chapter 2A).

3   Disconnect the upstream oxygen sensor electrical connector (see illustration). Unclip it from any retainers.

4   Remove the upstream oxygen sensor (see illustration).

5   If you're going to install the old sensor, apply anti-seize compound to the threads of the sensor to facilitate future removal. If you're going to install a new oxygen sensor, it's not necessary to apply anti-seize compound to the threads; the threads on new sensors already have anti-seize compound on them.

6   Installation is the reverse of removal. Be sure to tighten the oxygen sensor securely.

Downstream oxygen sensors

▶ Refer to illustrations 11.8a and 11.8b

➡Note: On most models, these sensors are underneath the vehicle. On 2004 and later V6 models, they are at the bottom end of the catalytic converter at the lower part of the engine compartment.

7   Raise the vehicle and support it securely on jackstands.

8   Locate the downstream oxygen sensor (see illustrations), then trace the lead up to the electrical connector and disconnect the connector.

➡Note: Some models have wiring brackets that also must be removed.

9   On 2004 and later V6 models, disconnect the left transaxle mount and move it just enough for access (see Chapter 2C).

10   Unscrew the downstream oxygen sensor.

11   If you're going to install the old sensor, apply anti-seize compound to the threads of the sensor to facilitate future removal. If you're going to install a new oxygen sensor, it's not necessary to apply anti-

seize compound to the threads. The threads on new sensors already have anti-seize compound on them.

12   Installation is the reverse of removal. Be sure to tighten the oxygen sensor securely.

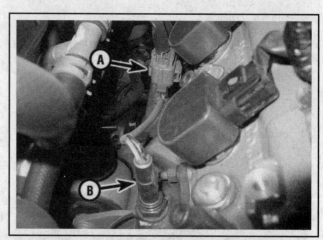

11.3 Upstream oxygen sensor electrical connector (A) and sensor (B) on a 3.5L V6 front cylinder head

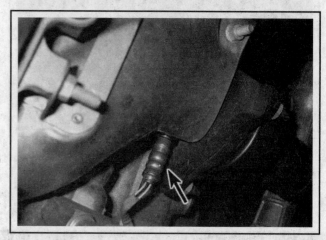

11.4 Four-cylinder upstream oxygen sensor

11.8a A special oxygen sensor socket is the best tool to remove these stubborn sensors - they have a slot to accommodate the wiring

11.8b Use a wrench to remove any sensor that doesn't have room for a socket

12 Transmission range switch - removal, installation and adjustment

➡Note 1: Refer to the "Vehicle Identification Numbers" at the front of this manual for information about transaxle identification.

➡Note 2: This switch is sometimes referred to as the Park/Neutral Position (PNP) switch.

REMOVAL

1 Place the shift lever in NEUTRAL.

VT25-E transaxle

2 Refer to Chapter 5 and remove the battery.
3 Remove the battery tray and the battery tray support (see Chapter 5).
4 Pry the end of the shift cable off of the ballstud on the transaxle range switch. Carefully use two screwdrivers to do this without twisting the end of the cable.
5 Disconnect the electrical connectors from the switch.
6 Remove the control lever nut and remove the lever.
7 Remove the two bolts and lift off the switch.

AF33-5 transaxle

▸ Refer to illustrations 12.11a, 12.11b and 12.12

8 Refer to Chapter 5 and remove the battery.
9 Remove the battery tray and the battery tray support (see Chapter 5).
10 Pry the end of the shift cable off of the ball stud on the transaxle range switch. Carefully use two screwdrivers to do this without twisting the end of the cable.
11 Disconnect the electrical connector from the switch (see illustrations).
12 Bend down the tabs on the lockwasher. Remove the shaft nut and washers (see illustration).
13 Remove the two bolts and lift off the switch. Note the position of the stud bolt.

4T45-E transaxle

14 Refer to Chapter 5 and remove the battery and battery tray.
15 Disconnect the end of the shift cable from the transaxle control lever.
16 Squeeze the tabs on the cable sheath and pull it out of its retaining bracket.
17 Remove the control lever nut and remove the lever.
18 Disconnect the electrical connector from the switch.
19 Remove the two screws and lift off the switch.

5-AT transaxle

▸ Refer to illustration 12.24

20 Loosen the lug nuts of the left front wheel.
21 Raise the vehicle and support it securely on jackstands.
22 Remove the left front wheel.
23 Remove the left front inner fender splash shield.

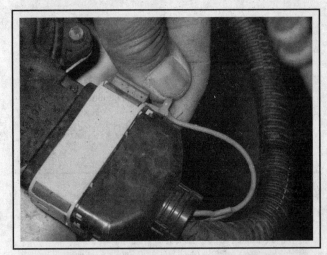

12.11a Pull out this safety clip from the transaxle range sensor electrical connector . . .

12.11b . . . then release the retainer - you can now disconnect the wiring connector

12.12 Hold the lever with a wrench while removing the lever nut from the transaxle range sensor

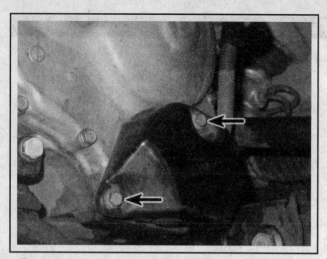

12.24 Remove the bolts and detach the cover from the transmission range switch

12.31 The transaxle range sensor must be correctly aligned during installation - new ones come with a special alignment tool that fits into the slot

24 Remove the cover from the transaxle control lever (see illustration).

25 Disconnect the wiring from the switch.

26 Remove the control lever nut and remove the lever.

27 Bend the tabs of the lockwasher down, then remove the control shaft nut.

28 Remove the two screws and lift off the switch.

INSTALLATION

VT25-E transaxle

▶ Refer to illustration 12.31

29 Make sure that the transaxle is in Neutral.

30 Put the new switch in place, aligning the flats on the switch with the flats on the shaft.

31 Install the switch, but leave the mounting fasteners snug until you verify that the engine will only start in Park and Neutral. If you have a switch alignment tool or if the replacement switch came with one, use it to align the switch following the instructions that came with the tool (see illustration).

32 Install the lever assembly. Tighten the nut to the torque listed in this Chapter's Specifications.

33 The remainder of installation is the reverse of removal. Replace any clips you removed with new ones.

34 Verify that the engine will only start in Park or Neutral.

35 Tighten the switch screws to the torque listed in this Chapter's Specifications.

AF33-5 transaxle

36 Install the switch and hand-tighten the fasteners.

37 Install the washers and the nut on the control shaft. Tighten the nut to the torque listed in this Chapter's Specifications.

38 Make sure that the control shaft lever is in Neutral. If you have a switch alignment tool or if the replacement switch came with one, use it to align the switch following the instructions that came with the tool (see illustration 12.31).

39 Install the switch, but leave the mounting fasteners snug until you verify that the engine will only start in Park and Neutral.

40 Verify that the engine will only start in Park or Neutral and tighten the switch screws to the torque listed in this Chapter's Specifications.

41 The remainder of installation is the reverse of removal.

4T45-E transaxles

42 Make sure the transaxle and the switch are both in the Neutral position.

43 Put the new switch in place, aligning the flats on the switch with the flats on the shaft.

44 Install the switch, but leave the mounting fasteners snug until you verify that the engine will only start in Park and Neutral. If you have a switch alignment tool or if the replacement switch came with one, use it to align the switch following the instructions that came with the tool (see illustration 12.31).

45 Verify that the engine will only start in Park or Neutral and tighten the switch screws to the torque listed in this Chapter's Specifications.

46 Install the nut on the control shaft. Tighten the nut to the torque listed in this Chapter's Specifications.

47 The remainder of installation is the reverse of removal.

5-AT transaxles

48 Make sure the transaxle and the switch are both in the Neutral position. The switch should click into Neutral and the hole in the control shaft should line up with the Neutral line.

49 Install the switch and snug the two fasteners.

50 Place the new lockwasher over the shaft. Align its pointer with the line on the switch.

51 Install the shaft nut while holding the flats on the end of the control shaft with a wrench. Tighten the nut to the torque listed in this Chapter's Specifications. Bend the tabs of the lockwasher up.

52 Tighten the switch mounting screws to the torque listed in this Chapter's Specifications.

53 The remainder of installation is the reverse of removal. Replace any clips you removed with new ones.

54 Verify that the engine will only start in Park or Neutral.

13 Transmission speed sensors - replacement

→Note 1: Refer to the "Vehicle Identification Numbers" at the front of this manual for information about transaxle identification.

VT25-E CONTINUOUSLY VARIABLE TRANSAXLE

1 The speed sensor assembly on these transaxles is located internally above the valve body. Service of these sensors should be left to a qualified shop.

AF33-5 TRANSAXLE

→Note: The speed sensors are located on top of the transaxle.

2 Refer to Chapter 5 and remove the battery.

3 Remove the cover from the fuse block, then disconnect the power steering wire and the positive battery cable from the B+ terminal.

4 Disconnect all of the harnesses from the battery cooling box.

5 Loosen the fuse block connector mounting bolts.

6 Move the fuse block from its retainer and disconnect the wiring harness that supplies the front lights.

7 Remove the battery cooling box.

8 Remove the battery tray bracket and the battery tray.

9 Remove the sensor mounting bolt and remove the sensor along with its O-ring.

10 Installation is the reverse of removal. Be sure to use a new O-ring and to tighten the sensor mounting bolt securely.

4T45-E TRANSAXLE

→Note: The Vehicle Speed Sensor (VSS) is mounted at the end of the transaxle.

11 Disconnect the cable from the negative battery terminal (see Chapter 5, Section 1).

12 Raise the vehicle and support it securely on jackstands.

13 Disconnect the wiring from the sensor.

14 Remove the stud and pull out the VSS. Remove and discard the O-ring.

15 Installation is the reverse of removal. Be sure to use a new O-ring and to tighten the sensor mounting bolt securely.

5-AT TRANSAXLE

→Note: The speed sensors are located on the front lower section of the transaxle.

16 Raise the vehicle and support it securely on jackstands.

17 Disconnect the wiring from the sensor.

18 Remove the sensor bolt and pull out the sensor.

19 Remove and discard the sensor O-ring.

20 Installation is the reverse of removal. Be sure to use a new O-ring and to tighten the sensor mounting bolt securely.

14 Powertrain Control Module (PCM) - removal and installation

GENERAL INFORMATION

1 The Powertrain Control Module (PCM) is the brain of the engine management system. It also controls a wide variety of other vehicle systems. In order to program the new PCM, the dealer needs the vehicle as well as the new PCM. If you're planning to replace the PCM with a new one, there is no point in trying to do so at home because you won't be able to program it yourself.

2 The PCM is located in the engine compartment on all models.

REMOVAL AND INSTALLATION

Four-cylinder models

♦ Refer to illustrations 14.5 and 14.6

3 Disconnect the cable from the negative terminal of the battery (see Chapter 5, Section 1).

4 Refer to Chapter 4 and remove the intake air duct.

5 Unplug the electrical connectors from the PCM (see illustration).

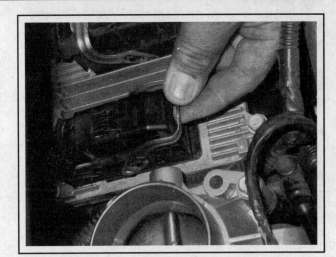

14.5 Swing open the locking levers, then unplug the electrical connectors from the PCM

6   Unscrew the mounting bolts and remove the PCM from the engine compartment (see illustration).

7   Installation is the reverse of removal.

2002 and 2003 V6 models

8   Refer to Chapter 5 and remove the battery. Make sure to record the radio station presets beforehand.

9   Remove the cover from the fuse block, then disconnect the power steering wire and the positive battery cable from the B+ terminal.

10 Disconnect all of the harnesses from the battery cooling box.

11 Loosen the fuse block connector mounting bolts.

12 Move the fuse block from its retainer and disconnect the wiring harness that supplies the front lights.

13 Remove the battery cooling box.

14 Unscrew the mounting bolts and remove the PCM from the engine compartment.

15 Installation is the reverse of removal.

2004 and later V6 models

16 Disconnect the cable from the negative battery terminal (see Chapter 5, Section 1).

17 Disconnect the wiring harnesses from the PCM.

14.6 PCM mounting bolts (four-cylinder model)a

18 Push in the retaining tab and slide the PCM forward to remove it.

19 Remove the PCM from its housing.

20 Installation is the reverse of removal.

15 Catalytic converter - description, check and replacement

➡**Note: Because of a Federally mandated extended warranty which covers emissions-related components like the catalytic converter, check with a dealer service department before replacing the converter at your own expense.**

DESCRIPTION

1   A catalytic converter (or catalyst) is an emission control device in the exhaust system that reduces certain pollutants in the exhaust gas stream. There are two types of converters: oxidation converters and reduction converters.

2   Oxidation converters contain a monolithic substrate (a ceramic honeycomb) coated with the semi-precious metals platinum and palladium. An oxidation catalyst reduces unburned hydrocarbons (HC) and carbon monoxide (CO) by adding oxygen to the exhaust stream as it passes through the substrate, which, in the presence of high temperature and the catalyst materials, converts the HC and CO to water vapor (H_2O) and carbon dioxide (CO_2).

3   Reduction converters contain a monolithic substrate coated with platinum and rhodium. A reduction catalyst reduces oxides of nitrogen (NOx) by removing oxygen, which in the presence of high temperature and the catalyst material produces nitrogen (N) and carbon dioxide (CO_2).

4   Catalytic converters that combine both types of catalysts in one assembly are known as "three-way catalysts" or TWCs. A TWC can reduce all three pollutants. All models covered by this manual are equipped with three-way catalysts.

CHECK

5   The test equipment for a catalytic converter (a dynamometer and a 5-gas analyzer) is expensive. If you suspect that the converter on your vehicle is malfunctioning, take it to a dealer or authorized emission

inspection facility for diagnosis.

6   Whenever you raise the vehicle to service underbody components, inspect the converter(s) for leaks, corrosion, dents and other damage. Carefully inspect the welds and/or flange bolts and nuts that attach the front and rear ends of the converter to the exhaust system. If you note any damage, replace the converter.

✳✳ WARNING:

Inspect catalytic converters only after enough time has elapsed after driving the vehicle to allow the system components to cool completely. Also, when working under the vehicle, make sure that it is securely supported on jackstands.

7   Although catalytic converters don't break too often, they can become restricted. The easiest way to check for a restricted converter is to use a vacuum gauge to diagnose the effect of a blocked exhaust on intake vacuum.

a) *Connect a vacuum gauge to any intake manifold vacuum source (any pipe on the intake manifold with a vacuum hose connected to it will provide the necessary intake manifold vacuum).*

b) *Warm the engine to operating temperature, place the transaxle in Park and apply the parking brake.*

c) *Note the vacuum reading at idle and write it down.*

d) *Quickly open the throttle to near its wide-open position and then quickly get off the throttle and allow it to close. Note the vacuum reading and write it down.*

e) *Do this test three more times, recording your measurement after each test.*

f) *If your fourth reading is more than one in-Hg lower than the reading that you noted at idle, the exhaust system might be restricted (the catalytic converter could be plugged, or an exhaust pipe or muffler could be restricted).*

REPLACEMENT

> **☀ WARNING:**
>
> Replace catalytic converters only after enough time has elapsed after driving the vehicle to allow the system components to cool completely. Also, when working under the vehicle, make sure it is securely supported on jackstands.

➥**Note 1: The following is a generalized procedure for most catalytic converters. The specifics vary among the engines used in these vehicles.**

➥**Note 2: Many exhaust specialist shops are able to replace catalytic converters at a lower cost than what you might pay for a new one from a dealer.**

8   Raise the vehicle and place it securely on jackstands.

9   Disconnect the electrical connector from the related oxygen sensor and remove the sensor (see Section 11).

10 Support the other sections of the exhaust system as necessary.

11 Remove the retaining nuts from the front and rear catalyst mounting flanges.

12 Remove the catalyst and pull off the gaskets.

13 Installation is the reverse of removal. Be sure to replace any rusted or damaged fasteners along with the gaskets.

---

16 Evaporative Emissions Control (EVAP) system - description and component replacement

GENERAL DESCRIPTION

1   The Evaporative Emissions Control (EVAP) system prevents fuel system vapors (which contain unburned hydrocarbons) from escaping into the atmosphere. On warm days, vapors trapped inside the fuel tank expand until the pressure reaches a certain threshold. Then the fuel vapors are routed from the fuel tank through the fuel vapor vent valve and the fuel vapor control valve to the EVAP canister, where they're stored temporarily until the next time the vehicle is operated. When the conditions are right (engine warmed up, vehicle up to speed, moderate or heavy load on the engine, etc.) the PCM opens the canister purge valve, which allows fuel vapors to be drawn from the canister into the intake manifold. Once in the intake manifold, the fuel vapors mix with incoming air before being drawn through the intake ports into the combustion chambers where they're burned up with the rest of the air/ fuel mixture. The EVAP system is complex and virtually impossible to troubleshoot without the right tools and training. However, the following description should give you a good idea of how it works:

2   The EVAP canister is located under the vehicle, near the fuel tank. The canister, which contains activated charcoal, is a repository for storing fuel vapors. You'll have to raise the vehicle to inspect or replace the canister, or any other part of the EVAP system, except for the canister purge valve (which is located in the engine compartment). But the canister is designed to be maintenance-free and should last the life of the vehicle. There are several other important components located on or near the canister: the canister filter, the canister vent shut valve, the two-way valve, the bypass solenoid valve and the fuel tank pressure sensor.

3   The EVAP canister filter is attached to the EVAP canister. When the canister is purged, fresh air is drawn through the filter before passing through the canister. The filter prevents dust and dirt particles from entering the EVAP canister and the EVAP system.

4   The canister vent shut valve is located on the top of the EVAP canister. The canister vent shut valve is normally closed, but it opens to allow fresh air from the filter to enter the EVAP canister when the canister is being purged.

5   The fuel tank pressure sensor is located on top of the fuel tank. It monitors the pressure inside the fuel tank, converts fuel tank absolute pressure into a variable voltage signal and transmits this data to the PCM.

6   The EVAP canister purge control solenoid valve regulates the flow of vapors being purged from the EVAP canister into the intake manifold. The canister purge valve is always closed when engine coolant temperature is low, which cuts off intake manifold vacuum to the EVAP canister. Above that threshold, the PCM opens or closes the purge solenoid valve in accordance with data from various information sensor inputs. The interval of time during which the purge valve is opened by the PCM is known as its "duty cycle." The purge valve is in the engine compartment.

GENERAL SYSTEM CHECKS

7   The most common symptom of a faulty EVAP system is a strong fuel odor (particularly during hot weather). If you smell fuel while driving or (more likely) right after you park the vehicle and turn off the engine, check the fuel filler cap first. Make sure that it's screwed onto the fuel filler neck all the way. If the odor persists, inspect all EVAP hose connections, both in the engine compartment and under the vehicle. You'll have to raise the vehicle and place it securely on jackstands to inspect most of the EVAP system, since it's located under the vehicle.

8   Be sure to inspect each hose attached to the canister for damage and leakage along its entire length. Repair or replace as necessary. Inspect the canister for damage and look for fuel leaking from the bottom. If fuel is leaking or the canister is otherwise damaged, replace it.

9   Poor idle, stalling, and poor driveability can be caused by a defective fuel vapor vent valve or canister purge valve, a damaged canister, cracked hoses, or hoses connected to the wrong tubes.

10 Fuel loss or fuel odor can be caused by fuel leaking from fuel lines or hoses, a cracked or damaged canister, or a defective vapor valve.

11 A complete test can only be done with a proprietary OBD-II scan tool, which will run a series of checks using the fuel tank pressure sensor and other output actuators to detect excessive pressure. A smoke machine is used to detect leaks. You'll have to take the vehicle to a dealer service department or other qualified repair shop to have the EVAP system professionally diagnosed.

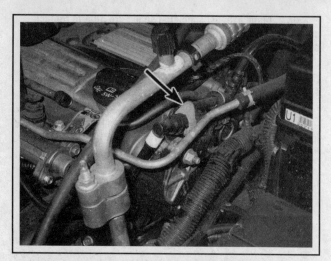

16.12 On four-cylinder models, the EVAP system purge control valve is at the top left of the engine

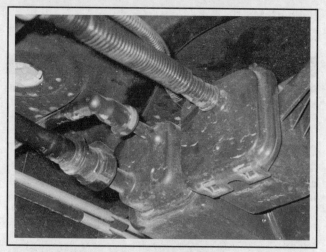

16.28 Disconnect the quick-connect fittings from the EVAP canister . . .

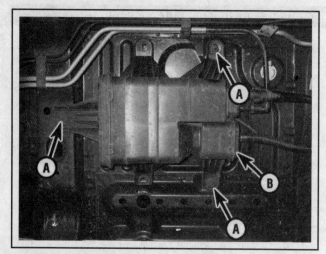

16.30 . . . then remove the fasteners (A) and lower the EVAP canister bracket (B is the canister air filter)

COMPONENT REPLACEMENT

EVAP purge control solenoid valve

Four-cylinder models

▶ Refer to illustration 16.12

➡Note: The valve is at the left side of the valve cover.

12 Refer to Chapter 4 and disconnect both quick-connect fittings from the valve (see illustration).
13 Disconnect the wiring harness from the valve.
14 Slide the valve from its bracket.
15 Installation is the reverse of removal.

2002 and 2003 V6 models

➡Note: The valve and its tube are at the top rear of the engine.

16 Refer to Chapter 4 and remove the intake air duct.
17 Disconnect the wiring harness from the valve.
18 Disconnect the purge line from the service port by pushing the release tab to the left then up. Pull the lines apart.
19 Pull the assembly from the two retainers on the engine.
20 Disconnect the vacuum hose from the valve and tube assembly.
21 Installation is the reverse of removal.

2004 and later V6 models

➡Note: The valve is at the lower left side of the engine.

22 Disconnect the wiring harness from the valve.
23 Disconnect both hoses.
24 Remove the purge valve along with its bracket from the engine.
25 Remove the valve from the bracket.
26 Installation is the reverse of removal.

EVAP canister

▶ Refer to illustrations 16.28 and 16.30

➡Note: The canister is mounted under the vehicle.

27 Raise the vehicle and support it securely on jackstands.
28 Disconnect the three lines from the canister (see illustration). See Chapter 4 for information on quick-connect fittings.
29 Disconnect the wiring from the canister.
30 Remove the canister bracket, lower the assembly and remove the canister from its bracket (see illustration).
31 Installation is the reverse of removal.

EVAP canister air filter

➡Note: The canister air filter is located under the vehicle attached to the canister.

32 Raise the vehicle and place it securely on jackstands.
33 On 2002 and 2003 models, remove the canister mounting bolts and pull the canister down a little.
34 Clean the road debris from the area, then carefully pry the filter cover off. Don't break the plastic tabs as you do so.
35 Pull out the filter.
36 Installation is the reverse of removal.

EVAP canister vent shut valve

➡ Note: The valve is mounted in the top of the canister.

37 Raise the vehicle and place it securely on jackstands.

38 Remove the canister from the vehicle (see Steps 28 through 30).

➡ Note: On 2002 and 2003 models, the canister only needs to be lowered enough for access to the valve on top of it.

39 Disconnect the wiring harness from the vent solenoid valve.

40 Twist the valve counterclockwise to remove it from the canister.

41 Installation is the reverse of removal.

Fuel Tank Pressure (FTP) sensor

42 Refer to Chapter 4, Section 7 for information about the fuel tank pressure sensor. The tank must at least be lowered enough to get access to the top of it.

---

17 Exhaust Gas Recirculation (EGR) system - description and component replacement

DESCRIPTION

➡ Note: The EGR system is used only on 2004 and later V6 models.

1 Oxides of nitrogen (or simply NOx) is a compound that is formed in the combustion chambers when the oxygen and nitrogen in the incoming air mix together. NOx is a natural byproduct of high combustion chamber temperatures. When NOx is emitted from the tailpipe, it mixes with reactive organic compounds (ROCs), hydrocarbons (HC) and sunlight to form ozone and photochemical smog. The EGR system reduces oxides of nitrogen by recirculating exhaust gases from the exhaust manifold, through the EGR valve and intake manifold, then back to the combustion chambers, where it mixes with the incoming air/fuel mixture before being consumed. These recirculated exhaust gases dilute the incoming air/fuel mixture, which cools the combustion chambers, thereby reducing NOx emissions.

2 The EGR system consists of the Powertrain Control Module (PCM), the EGR valve, the EGR valve position sensor and various other information sensors that the PCM uses to determine when to open the EGR valve. The degree to which the EGR valve is opened is referred to as "EGR valve lift." The PCM is programmed to produce the ideal EGR valve lift for varying operating conditions. The EGR valve position sen-sor, which is an integral part of the EGR valve, detects the amount of EGR valve lift and sends this information to the PCM. The PCM then compares it with the appropriate EGR valve lift for the operating conditions. The PCM increases current flow to the EGR valve to increase valve lift and reduces the current to reduce the amount of lift. If EGR flow is inappropriate to the operating conditions (idle, cold engine, etc.) the PCM simply cuts the current to the EGR valve and the valve closes.

EGR VALVE REPLACEMENT

▸ Refer to illustrations 17.3 and 17.5

➡ Note: The EGR valve is mounted near the coolant hose connections at the engine.

3 Disconnect the wiring harness from the EGR valve (see illustration).

4 Remove the two valve mounting bolts and lift off the EGR valve.

5 Remove the gasket and clean both gasket surfaces (see illustration).

6 Installation is the reverse of removal. Be sure to use a new EGR valve gasket, and tighten the EGR valve mounting nuts securely.

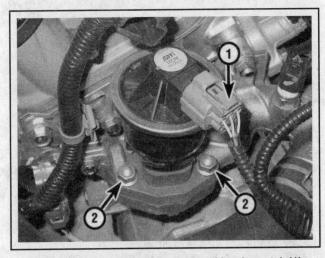

17.3 To remove the EGR valve, depress this release tab (1) and disconnect the electrical connector from the EGR valve, then remove these two mounting nuts (2)

17.5 Be sure to remove all traces of old gasket material with a gasket scraper, and be extremely careful not to scratch or gouge the surfaces

18 Positive Crankcase Ventilation (PCV) valve (2004 and later V6 models) - replacement

▶ **Refer to illustrations 18.2, 18.3 and 18.5**

1   The valve is mounted horizontally in the left end of the rear valve cover.

2   Disconnect and move aside any interfering hoses (see illustration).

3   Remove the mounting bolt (see illustration).

4   Remove the PCV valve.

5   Inspect the PCV valve O-ring for cracks, tears and other deterioration (see illustration). If it is worn or damaged, replace it.

6   Installation is the reverse of removal.

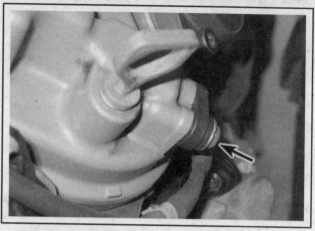

18.3 To remove the PCV valve, remove this bolt (2004 and later 3.5L V6 models)

18.2 To detach the MAF sensor wiring harness clips (1) from the bracket on the PCV fresh air inlet pipe, squeeze the split pins underneath and push the clips out of the bracket. Loosen and slide back the spring type hose clamps for the fresh air inlet pipe (2) and for the coolant pipe (3) (2004 and later 3.5L V6 models)

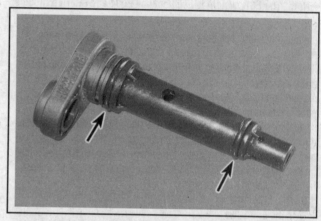

18.5 Remove and discard the two old PCV O-rings (2004 and later 3.5L V6 models)

19 Rocker Arm Hydraulic Actuator (RAHA) system - description and component replacement

DESCRIPTION

1   A low-lift, short-duration cam produces good torque, quick response, good fuel economy and low emissions at lower engine speeds, but can't deliver sufficient air/fuel mixture to the combustion chamber at higher engine speeds. A high-lift, long-duration cam produces good power at high engine speeds, but produces a ragged idle and poor driveability, wastes fuel and produces unacceptable emissions at lower engine speeds. That's why camshaft lobe profiles are always a compromise between economy and performance. The Saturn Rocker Arm Hydraulic Actuator (RAHA) system allows an engine to operate economically and make good power.

2   The RAHA system is used only on 2004 and later V6 models with the 3.5L engine. This Section is intended to familiarize you with how RAHA works and to show you how to replace the PCM-controlled components such as the RAHA solenoid valve and the RAHA oil control solenoid valve.

3   There are two cam lobes for each pair of intake valves on a RAHA engine. These primary and secondary lobe profiles differ in lift and duration: the secondary lobe has lower lift and less duration (it opens later and closes sooner), while the primary lobe has higher lift and more duration (opens sooner and closes later). Each lobe operates its own rocker arm, which in turn pushes on its own valve. At low speeds, the secondary camshaft lobe operates one intake valve and the primary cam

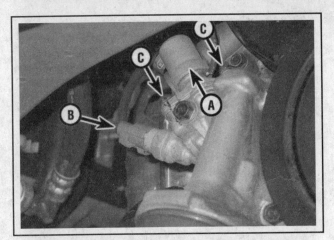

19.10a The RAHA solenoid valve (A) is located at the lower right rear corner of the engine, directly above the RAHA oil pressure switch (B). To detach the solenoid valve, remove the two mounting bolts (C)

19.10b To find the electrical connector for the RAHA solenoid valve, trace the electrical lead up to the connector. Depress the release tab (A) and pull the lower half of the connector out of the upper half

lobe operates the other valve. The low-lift, short-duration lobe produces good low-end torque and responsiveness.

4   When more power is needed at higher engine speeds, the PCM activates the solenoid valve, which allows higher oil pressure to a hydraulically-operated, spring-loaded pin inside the primary rocker arm. When hydraulic pressure overcomes spring pressure, the pin slides sideways and locks the secondary rocker arm to the primary rocker arm. The two rocker arms are both activated by the primary cam lobe; the secondary rocker arm no longer contacts its own camshaft lobe again until the system is disengaged. Both valves are now opened by the primary camshaft lobe with its higher lift and longer duration, increasing performance.

5   The PCM turns the solenoid valve on and off in accordance with engine rpm, vehicle speed, throttle opening angle, engine load and coolant temperature. Although diagnosis of the system is beyond the scope of the home mechanic, it's not difficult to replace the solenoid valve.

COMPONENT REPLACEMENT

RAHA solenoid valve

▶ Refer to illustrations 19.10a and 19.10b

➡Note: The RAHA solenoid valve is located at the lower right corner of the rear of the engine block at the upper end of the oil filter housing, above the RAHA oil pressure switch.

6   Loosen the lug nuts on the right front wheel.

7   Raise the front of the vehicle and place it securely on jackstands.

8   Remove the right front wheel.

9   Remove the right inner fender splash shield.

10   Locate the RAHA solenoid valve (see illustration), then trace the electrical lead up to the electrical connector (see illustration) and disconnect it.

11   Remove the three RAHA solenoid valve mounting bolts (see illustration 19.10a) and remove the solenoid valve.

12   Remove and discard the solenoid valve O-ring.

13   Installation is the reverse of removal. Be sure to use a new O-ring and tighten the solenoid valve mounting bolts to the torque listed in this Chapter's Specifications.

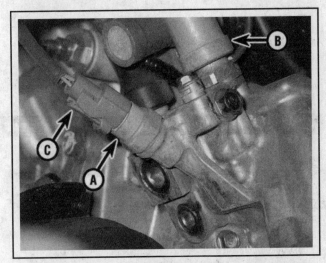

19.17 The RAHA oil pressure switch (A) is located below the RAHA solenoid valve (B). To disconnect the electrical connector from the oil pressure switch, depress the release tab (C) and pull off the connector

RAHA oil pressure switch

▶ Refer to illustrations 19.17 and 19.19

➡Note 1: The RAHA oil pressure switch is located at the lower right corner of the rear of the engine block, at the upper end of the oil filter housing, below the RAHA solenoid valve.

➡Note 2: The purpose of the oil pressure switch is to inform the PCM if the oil pressure in the system is in conformance with the PCM's instructions. If it's not, then a diagnostic trouble code will be stored.

14   Loosen the lug nuts on the right front wheel. Raise the front of the vehicle and place it securely on jackstands.

15   Remove the right front wheel.

16   Remove the right inner fender splash shield.

17   Disconnect the electrical connector from the RAHA oil pressure switch (see illustration).

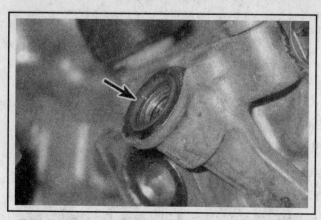

19.19 Always remove and discard the old RAHA oil pressure switch O-ring and install a new O-ring

18 Unscrew and remove the RAHA oil pressure switch.

19 Remove and discard the old oil pressure switch O-ring (see illustration).

20 Installation is the reverse of removal. Be sure to use a new O-ring and tighten the oil pressure switch to the torque listed in this Chapter's Specifications.

20 Intake Manifold Runner Control (IMRC) system - description and control solenoid replacement

DESCRIPTION

1 The Intake Manifold Runner Control (IMRC) system is used on 2002 and 2003 3.0L V6 models. The IMRC system consists of the vacuum control solenoid, the control diaphragms, the IMRC valve assembly inside the intake manifold and the vacuum hoses that supply the energy to operate the system. When commanded to do so by the Powertrain Control Module (PCM) at high engine speeds, the control actuator opens or closes the IMRC valves.

2 Basically, the control solenoid closes the IMRC valves at low speed and opens them at high speed. When the IMRC valves are closed, they increase the effective length of the intake runners, which improves torque at low speed. When the valves are open, they shorten the effective length of the intake runners, which improves power at high speed. When intake air is drawn into the cylinders at idle or at low engine speeds, less air is needed because the cylinders don't need to be filled so often or so quickly. So at low engine speeds, the air drawn into an engine with longer intake runners will have a higher velocity than one with shorter intake runners. However, at higher engine speeds, longer intake runners would prevent the cylinders from filling quickly enough and would therefore limit power. Most intake manifold designs are merely a compromise between the conflicting demands of low and high engine speeds.

IMRC CONTROL SOLENOID REPLACEMENT

▶ **Refer to illustration 20.4**

3 Remove the battery cover.

4 Disconnect the electrical connector from the IMRC control actuator (see illustration).

5 Disconnect the vacuum line from the number two cylinder bank diaphragm. Also disconnect the brake vacuum hose at the intake manifold.

6 Remove the actuator mounting screw, disconnect the two vacuum hoses and remove the actuator from the intake manifold.

7 Installation is the reverse of removal.

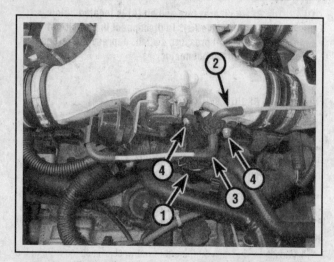

20.4 Intake Manifold Runner Control (IMRC) solenoid removal details

1 Electrical connector
2 Vacuum line port from cylinder head

Torque specifications	Ft-lbs (unless otherwise indicated)	Nm

→Note: One foot-pound (ft-lb) of torque is equivalent to 12 inch-pounds (in-lbs) of torque. Torque values below approximately 15 ft-lbs are expressed in inch-pounds, since most foot-pound torque wrenches are not accurate at these smaller values.

Crankshaft Position (CKP) sensor		
Four-cylinder models	89 in-lbs	10
2002 and 2003 V6 models	72 in-lbs	8
2004 and later V6 models	89 in-lbs	10
Engine Coolant Temperature (ECT) sensor		
Four-cylinder models	89 in-lbs	10
V6 models	156 in-lbs	17.5
Intake Air Temperature (IAT) sensor		
(2004 and later V6 models)	156 in-lbs	17.5
Intake Manifold Tuning (IMT) actuator		
mounting bolts	86 in-lbs	9.5
Knock sensor		
Four-cylinder models	18	24
2002 and 2003 V6 models	15	20
2004 and later V6 models	23	31
Manifold Absolute Pressure (MAP) sensor		
(2004 and later V6 models)	48 in-lbs	5.5
Positive Crankcase Ventilation (PCV) valve		
retaining bolt	104 in-lbs	11.5
Rocker Arm Hydraulic Actuator (RAHA) system		
RAHA oil pressure switch	192 in-lbs	21.5
RAHA solenoid valve mounting bolts	104 in-lbs	11.5
Transaxle range switch mounting screws		
VT25-E transaxle	96 in-lbs	11
AF33-5 transaxle	18	24
4T45-E transaxle	15	20
5-AT transaxle	108 in-lbs	12
Transaxle control shaft nut		
VT25-E transaxle	144 in-lbs	16
AF33-5 transaxle	62 in-lbs	7
4T45-E transaxle	26	35
5-AT transaxle, nut and locknut	108 in-lbs	12

NOTES

Section

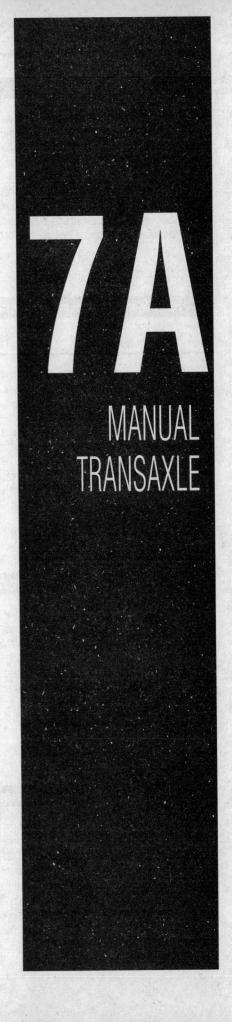

7A

MANUAL
TRANSAXLE

1 General information

The vehicles covered in this manual are equipped with either a 5-speed manual or an automatic transaxle. This Part of Chapter 7 contains information on the manual transaxle. Service procedures for the automatic transaxle are in Part B. Information on the transfer case used on AWD models is in Part C.

The transaxle is contained in a cast-aluminum casing bolted to the engine's left end, and consists of the gearbox and final drive differential. The transaxle unit type is stamped on a plate attached to the transaxle (see *Vehicle Identification Numbers* at the beginning of this manual).

TRANSAXLE OVERHAUL

Because of the complexity of the assembly, possible unavailability of replacement parts and special tools necessary, internal repair procedures for the transaxle are not recommended for the home mechanic. The bulk of the information in this Chapter is devoted to removal and installation procedures.

2 Shift lever - removal and installation

REMOVAL

1 Apply the Parking brake. Place the shift lever in Neutral.
2 Use a screwdriver wrapped with tape to pry off the side cover from the shift console.
3 Carefully pry up the bezel housing the power window switches.
4 Disconnect the wiring as you remove the bezel.
5 Use a flat-blade screwdriver on the adjusters to disconnect the shift cables from the adjusters.
6 Squeeze the cable retainers and pull the cables free.
7 Remove the four retaining nuts and lift the shifter assembly out.

INSTALLATION

8 Mount the shifter assembly and tighten the nuts securely.
9 Connect the cables to the shift lever assembly.
10 With the shifter in Neutral, adjust each cable by pushing the neutral lock clip. Move the shift handle so that each lock clip centers.
11 Push in the shift cable retainers to lock them in place.
12 Pull the shifter lock clip to its original position.
13 Reconnect the electrical connectors.
14 The remainder of installation is the reverse of removal.

3 Shift cables - removal and installation

1 Disconnect the shift cables from the bracket on the side of the transaxle by pulling (then discarding) the retaining clips.
2 Use two screwdrivers to evenly pry the cable ends from the balls on the transaxle levers. Take care to avoid forcing the ends to one side.
3 Disconnect the cables from the clip on the steering gear.
4 Refer to Section 2 and disconnect the cables from the shifter assembly.

5 Remove the cover from the right side of the console (see Chapter 11).
6 Pull the carpet back from the area where the cable passes through the firewall.
7 Pull the cable grommet out of the firewall and remove the cables.
8 Installation is the reverse of removal. Replace the clips you discarded. Make sure the grommet seats properly in the firewall.
9 Refer to Section 2 to adjust the cables.

4 Driveaxle oil seals - replacement

1 Oil leaks frequently occur due to wear of the driveaxle oil seals. Replacement of these seals is relatively easy, since the repair can be performed without removing the transaxle from the vehicle.
2 Driveaxle oil seals are located at the sides of the transaxle, where the driveaxles are attached. If leakage at the seal is suspected, raise the vehicle and support it securely on jackstands. If the seal is leaking, lubricant will be found on the sides of the transaxle and below the seals.
3 Refer to Chapter 8 and remove the driveaxle.
4 Use a screwdriver or prybar to carefully pry the oil seal out of the transaxle bore.

5 If the oil seal cannot be removed with a screwdriver or prybar, a special oil seal removal tool (available at auto parts stores) will be required.
6 Using a seal driver or a large deep socket (slightly smaller than the outside diameter of the seal) as a drift, install the new oil seal. Drive it into the bore squarely and make sure it's completely seated. Coat the seal lip with transaxle lubricant.
7 Install the driveaxle(s). Be careful not to damage the lip of the new seal as you slide the axles back into place.

5 Manual transaxle - removal and installation

REMOVAL

1 Disconnect the cable from the negative terminal of the battery (see Chapter 5).

2 Secure the top of the radiator to the core support frame using wire.

3 Refer to Section 3 and disconnect the shift cables from the transaxle.

4 Pull the retaining clip from the end of the clutch fluid line and remove the line from the transaxle.

5 Disconnect the two wiring harnesses (back-up lights and speed sensor) from the transaxle.

6 Support the engine from above with an engine support fixture or an engine hoist.

7 Loosen the front wheel lug nuts and the driveaxle/hub nuts. Raise the vehicle and support it securely on jackstands.

8 Remove the front wheels.

9 Remove the left inner fender splash shield.

10 Refer to Chapter 10 and disconnect the outer end of the steering tie-rod from the knuckle.

11 Disconnect the balljoints from the steering knuckles (see Chapter 10).

12 Disconnect the stabilizer bar from the links (see Chapter 10).

13 Refer to Chapter 8 and disconnect the steering gear from the intermediate shaft.

14 Remove the rear transaxle mount.

15 Remove the through-bolt from the front mount where it attaches to the subframe.

16 Disconnect the front air dam from the body of the vehicle but leave it connected to the subframe.

17 Place two floor jacks under the subframe and make sure that the subframe is supported solidly and balanced evenly.

18 With the help of an assistant, remove the subframe mounting bolts and slowly lower each jack a little at a time until the subframe is near the ground. Set the subframe aside.

19 Drain the fluid from the transaxle.

20 Refer to Chapter 8 and remove both driveaxles and the right inter-mediate shaft.

21 Remove the front transaxle mount. Unbolt the top transaxle mount.

22 Using the engine support fixture, lower the engine/transaxle assembly just enough to permit removing the transaxle.

23 Put a floor jack under the transaxle and secure them together so the transaxle can't fall.

24 Remove the engine/transaxle bolts that are on the engine side.

25 Remove the single transaxle-to-engine bolt.

26 Carefully pull the transaxle free of the alignment dowels and lower it, making sure that the input shaft doesn't get caught as it comes down.

27 When it's safely lowered, disconnect it from the jack.

INSTALLATION

28 Lubricate the input shaft with a light coat of high-temperature grease. Don't leave the transaxle in Neutral. With the transaxle secured to the jack, raise it into position behind the engine and carefully slide it forward, engaging the input shaft with the clutch. Rotate it to align the input shaft with the clutch splines. Do not use excessive force to install the transaxle - if the input shaft won't slide into place, readjust the angle of the transaxle or turn the input shaft so the splines engage properly with the clutch.

29 Once the transaxle is flush with the engine, install the transaxle-to-engine bolts. Tighten the bolts to the torque listed in this Chapter's Specifications.

✳✳ CAUTION:

Don't use the bolts to force the transaxle and engine together.

30 The remainder of installation of the transaxle is a reversal of the removal procedure, but note the following points:

a) Install **new** subframe mounting bolts and tighten them to the torque values listed in this Chapter's Specifications.

b) Tighten the driveaxle/hub nuts to the torque value listed in the Chapter 8 Specifications.

c) Tighten the wheel lug nuts to the torque listed in the Chapter 1 Specifications.

d) Fill the transaxle with the correct type and amount of transaxle fluid as described in Chapter 1.

6 Manual transaxle overhaul - general information

1 Overhauling a manual transaxle is a difficult job for the do-it-yourselfer. It involves the disassembly and reassembly of many small parts. Numerous clearances must be precisely measured and, if necessary, changed with select-fit spacers and snap-rings. As a result, if transaxle problems arise, it can be removed and installed by a competent do-it-yourselfer, but overhaul should be left to a transmission repair shop. Rebuilt transaxles may be available - check with your dealer parts department and auto parts stores. At any rate, the time and money involved in an overhaul is almost sure to exceed the cost of a rebuilt unit.

2 Nevertheless, it's not impossible for an inexperienced mechanic to rebuild a transaxle if the special tools are available and the job is done in a deliberate step-by-step manner so nothing is overlooked.

3 The tools necessary for an overhaul include internal and external snap-ring pliers, a bearing puller, a slide hammer, a set of pin punches, a dial indicator and possibly a hydraulic press. In addition, a large, sturdy workbench and a vise or transaxle stand will be required.

4 During disassembly of the transaxle, make careful notes of how each piece comes off, where it fits in relation to other pieces and what holds it in place.

5 Before taking the transaxle apart for repair, it will help if you have some idea what area of the transaxle is malfunctioning. Certain problems can be closely tied to specific areas in the transaxle, which can make component examination and replacement easier. Refer to the *Troubleshooting* Section at the front of this manual for information regarding possible sources of trouble.

7 Transaxle mount - replacement

1 Raise the vehicle and support it securely on jackstands. Insert a large screwdriver or prybar between the mount and the transaxle and pry up.

2 The transaxle should not move excessively away from the mount. If it does, replace the mount.

LEFT-END MOUNT

3 Raise the vehicle and support it securely on jackstands.

4 Remove the through-bolts from the front and rear transaxle mounts. Support the engine from below using a floor jack with a block of wood on it.

5 Refer to Chapter 5 and remove the battery, battery tray and tray support.

6 Disconnect the right and left upper engine mounts.

7 Using the jack, lower the engine enough to allow mount removal.

8 Unbolt the left transaxle mount from the left frame.

9 Installation is the reverse of removal.

SIDE MOUNTS

10 With the engine/transaxle supported with a jack and a block of wood, remove the nuts and bolts and remove the mount. It may be necessary to move the transaxle slightly to provide enough clearance to remove the mount.

11 Installation is the reverse of removal.

➡Note: Install all of the mount fasteners before tightening any of them.

Specifications

General

Transaxle oil type	See Chapter 1
Transaxle oil capacity	See Chapter 1

Torque specifications

	Ft-lbs (unless otherwise indicated)	Nm
Transaxle-to-engine mounting bolts	55	75
Engine/transaxle cradle bolts*	114	154

These bolts must be replaced with new ones whenever they have been loosened or removed.

Section

Reference to other Chapters

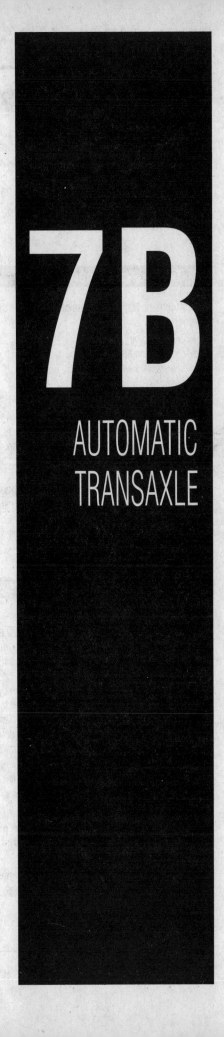

7B

AUTOMATIC TRANSAXLE

1 General information

All information on the automatic transaxle is included in this Part of Chapter 7. Information for the manual transaxle can be found in Part A of this Chapter, and information on the transfer case used on all-wheel drive models can be found in Part C.

Because of the complexity of the automatic transaxles and the specialized equipment necessary to perform most service operations, this Chapter contains only those procedures related to general diagnosis, routine maintenance, adjustment and removal and installation.

If the transaxle requires major repair work, it should be left to a dealer service department or an automotive or transmission repair shop. Once properly diagnosed you can, however, remove and install the transaxle yourself and save the expense, even if the repair work is done by a transmission shop.

2 Diagnosis - general

1 Automatic transaxle malfunctions may be caused by five general conditions:

a) *Poor engine performance*
b) *Improper adjustments*
c) *Hydraulic malfunctions*
d) *Mechanical malfunctions*
e) *Malfunctions in the computer or its signal network*

2 Diagnosis of these problems should always begin with a check of the easily repaired items: fluid level and condition (see Chapter 1), shift cable adjustment and shift lever installation. Next, perform a road test to determine if the problem has been corrected or if more diagnosis is necessary. If the problem persists after the preliminary tests and corrections are completed, additional diagnosis should be performed by a dealer service department or other qualified transmission repair shop. Refer to the Troubleshooting Section at the front of this manual for information on symptoms of transaxle problems.

PRELIMINARY CHECKS

3 Drive the vehicle to warm the transaxle to normal operating temperature.

4 Check the fluid level as described in Chapter 1:

a) *If the fluid level is unusually low, add enough fluid to bring the level within the designated area of the dipstick, then check for external leaks (see following).*
b) *If the fluid level is abnormally high, drain off the excess, then check the drained fluid for contamination by coolant. The presence of engine coolant in the automatic transmission fluid indicates that a failure has occurred in the internal radiator oil cooler walls that separate the coolant from the transmission fluid (see Chapter 3).*
c) *If the fluid is foaming, drain it and refill the transaxle, then check for coolant in the fluid, or a high fluid level.*

5 Check the engine idle speed.

➡**Note: If the engine is malfunctioning, do not proceed with the preliminary checks until it has been repaired and runs normally.**

6 Check and adjust the shift cable, if necessary (see Section 4).

7 If hard shifting is experienced, inspect the shift cable under the steering column and at the manual lever on the transaxle (see Section 4).

FLUID LEAK DIAGNOSIS

8 Most fluid leaks are easy to locate visually. Repair usually consists of replacing a seal or gasket. If a leak is difficult to find, the following procedure may help.

9 Identify the fluid. Make sure it's transmission fluid and not engine oil or brake fluid (automatic transmission fluid is a deep red color).

10 Try to pinpoint the source of the leak. Drive the vehicle several miles, then park it over a large sheet of cardboard. After a minute or two, you should be able to locate the leak by determining the source of the fluid dripping onto the cardboard.

11 Make a careful visual inspection of the suspected component and the area immediately around it. Pay particular attention to gasket mating surfaces. A mirror is often helpful for finding leaks in areas that are hard to see.

12 If the leak still cannot be found, clean the suspected area thoroughly with a degreaser or solvent, then dry it thoroughly.

13 Drive the vehicle for several miles at normal operating temperature and varying speeds. After driving the vehicle, visually inspect the suspected component again.

14 Once the leak has been located, the cause must be determined before it can be properly repaired. If a gasket is replaced but the sealing flange is bent, the new gasket will not stop the leak. The bent flange must be straightened.

15 Before attempting to repair a leak, check to make sure that the following conditions are corrected or they may cause another leak.

➡**Note: Some of the following conditions cannot be fixed without highly specialized tools and expertise. Such problems must be referred to a qualified transmission shop or a dealer service department.**

Gasket leaks

16 Check the pan periodically. Make sure the bolts are tight, no bolts are missing, the gasket is in good condition and the pan is flat (dents in the pan may indicate damage to the valve body inside).

17 If the pan gasket is leaking, the fluid level or the fluid pressure may be too high, the vent may be plugged, the pan bolts may be too tight, the pan sealing flange may be warped, the sealing surface of the transaxle housing may be damaged, the gasket may be damaged or the transaxle casting may be cracked or porous. If sealant instead of gasket material has been used to form a seal between the pan and the transaxle housing, it may be the wrong type of sealant.

Seal leaks

18 If a transaxle seal is leaking, the fluid level or pressure may be too high, the vent may be plugged, the seal bore may be damaged, the seal itself may be damaged or improperly installed, the surface of the shaft protruding through the seal may be damaged or a loose bearing may be causing excessive shaft movement.

19 Make sure the dipstick tube seal is in good condition and the tube is properly seated. Periodically check the area around the sensors for leakage. If transmission fluid is evident, check the seals for damage.

Case leaks

20 If the case itself appears to be leaking, the casting is porous and will have to be repaired or replaced.

21 Make sure the oil cooler hose fittings are tight and in good condition.

Fluid comes out vent pipe or fill tube

22 If this condition occurs the possible causes are, the transaxle is overfilled, there is coolant in the fluid, the case is porous, the dipstick is incorrect, the vent is plugged or the drain-back holes are plugged.

---

3   Shift lever - replacement

◆ **Refer to illustrations 3.3, 3.4 and 3.5**

1   Refer to Chapter 11 and remove the glove box, the center instrument panel bezel/storage compartment and the console.

2   Refer to Chapter 11 and remove the cover below the steering column.

3   Remove the shifter upper cover (see illustration).

4   Pry the rear cover from the shifter housing (see illustration).

5   Remove the side covers from the shifter housing (see illustration).

6   Carefully and evenly pry the end of the shift cable from the shifter assembly.

✲✲ CAUTION:

Use two screwdrivers to avoid twisting the cable end.

7   Remove the cable retaining clip and discard it. Lift the cable from the bracket.

8   Disconnect the park-lock cable from the shifter assembly.

9   Remove the cable retaining clip and discard it. Lift the cable from the bracket.

10 Rotate the bulb holder to remove it, then disconnect the rest of the wiring.

11 Remove the mounting nuts and remove the shifter assembly.

12 Installation is the reverse of removal. Be sure to replace the two clips you removed and discarded with new ones.

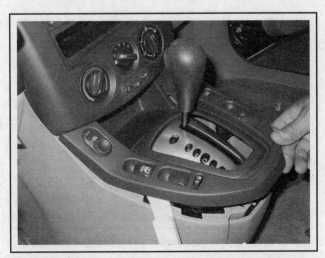

3.3 Carefully pry the top trim panel from the shifter using a plastic trim tool or a screwdriver wrapped with tape to avoid scratching it

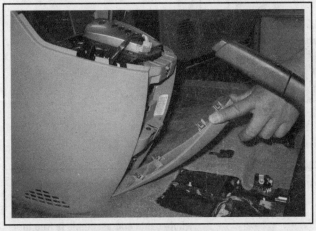

3.4 Carefully pry off the shifter rear panel

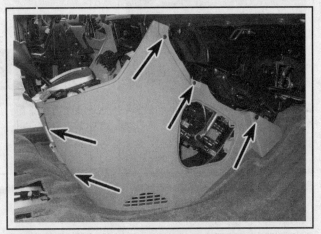

3.5 Each side panel is fastened with screws at the front and rear

4   Shift cable - replacement and adjustment

REPLACEMENT

♦ **Refer to illustrations 4.3 and 4.4**

➡**Note: On some models, the end of the shift cable is accessible without performing Steps 1 through 6.**

1   Refer to Chapter 5 and remove the battery, the battery tray and the tray support.

2   On models with VT25-E transaxles, raise the vehicle and support it securely on jackstands, then disconnect the cable from the steering gear.

3   Carefully and evenly pry the end of the shifter cable from the transaxle shift lever (see illustration).

❈❈ **CAUTION:**

Use a prying tool or two screwdrivers to avoid twisting the cable end.

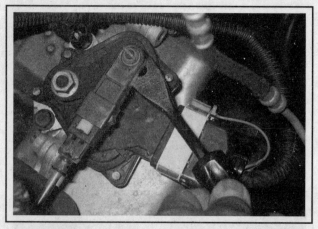

4.3   Carefully pry the cable end off of the transaxle shift lever

4   Remove the cable retaining clip and discard it (see illustration). Lift the cable from the bracket.

5   Perform Steps 1 through 5 in Section 3 to remove the console covers for access to the interior end of the shift cable.

6   Disconnect the cable from the shifter assembly using the same methods used on the transaxle end. Again, discard the cable clip.

7   Disconnect the cable from its retainer.

8   Release the cable grommet from the firewall and pull the cable through the hole.

9   Installation is the reverse of removal. Proceed to adjust the cable before connecting the cable to the bracket on the transaxle.

ADJUSTMENT

♦ **Refer to illustrations 4.12 and 4.14**

➡**Note: The adjustment portion of the cable is at the transaxle end on early models and at the shifter end on later models.**

10   Put the shifter into Neutral. Make sure that the transaxle is also in Neutral.

11   If not already done, pull the shift cable from the bracket by first squeezing the tabs of the clip (see illustration 4.5). The clip must be replaced with a new one.

12   Use a flat-blade screwdriver to release the tab under the protective sleeve over the adjustment lock (see illustration).

13   Slide the black tab outward.

14   Push the adjuster lock outward until the cable can move freely (see illustration).

15   Snap the cable back onto the bracket and install a new clip.

16   Snap the cable onto the ballstud of the transaxle shift lever.

17   Lock the shift cable adjustment tab.

18   Push the white tab in to lock the adjustment.

19   After installing any remaining components, apply the parking brake, lower the vehicle and operate the vehicle in each range to verify the adjustment is correct.

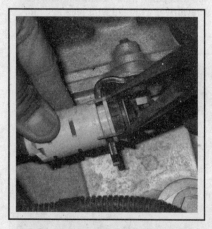

4.4   Pinch the cable retaining clip to release it - it should be replaced with a new one whenever it's removed

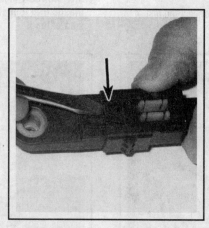

4.12   Release the tab and slide the sleeve

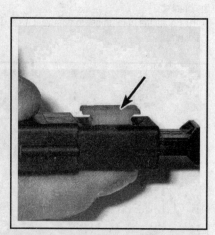

4.14   Push the white adjuster tab until it projects above the black sleeve - it's up enough when the whole cable end assembly is free to slide on the cable

5 Park/Lock cable - replacement and adjustment

▶ Refer to illustrations 5.4, 5.5 and 5.6

❋❋ WARNING:

These models are equipped with airbags. Always disable the airbag system before working in the vicinity of any airbag system component to avoid the possibility of accidental deployment of the airbag(s), which could cause personal injury (see Chapter 12).

1 Disconnect the cable from the negative terminal of the battery (see Chapter 5, Section 1).

2 Remove the steering column covers (see Chapter 11).

3 Remove the upper cover and the left side cover from the shifter housing (see Section 3).

4 Squeeze the retainer clip tabs and detach the Park/Lock cable from the shifter base (see illustration). Discard the retainer clip; a new one must be used on reassembly.

5 Detach the cable end from the Park/Lock lever on the shifter assembly (see illustration).

6 Remove the cable-tie (if equipped), then detach the Park/Lock cable from the ignition lock cylinder housing by disengaging the retaining fingers (see illustration).

7 Remove the cable, noting how it's routed.

8 Installation is the reverse of the removal procedure. Be sure to use a new retaining clip where the cable attaches to the shifter base, and a new end fitting where the cable attaches to the ignition lock cylinder housing.

9 Disengage the cable adjuster (at the shift lever end) and make sure the shifter lever is in the Park position (and the ignition lock cylinder should be in the Off position). Push the adjuster lock back into place.

10 Check the operation of the Park/Lock cable as follows.

a) With the shift lever in Park and the key in Lock, make sure the shifter lever cannot be moved to another position and the key can be removed.

b) With the key in Run and the shift lever in Neutral, make sure the key cannot be turned to Lock.

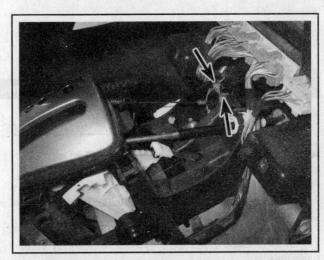

5.4 Squeeze the retainer clip to free the cable from the shifter base

5.6 The Park/Lock cable attaches to the underside of the ignition lock cylinder housing

5.5 Carefully pry the end of the Park/Lock cable from its post on the lever (pry towards the rear)

6 Auxiliary cooler - removal and installation

➡Note: This procedure applies only to models with a VT25-E transaxle. Other models use coolers that are integral parts of the radiator.

1 To gain access to the cooler, remove the front bumper cover (see Chapter 11).

2 Disconnect the lines from the cooler fittings.

3 Disconnect the lines from the radiator bracket.

4 Remove the air duct from the battery box.

5 Remove the plastic splash shield from the top front of the radiator assembly.

6 Remove the radiator assembly upper mounting brackets.

7 Release the condenser from the radiator.

8 Unclip the transaxle fluid cooler from the radiator and remove it.

9 Installation is the reverse of removal. Be sure to tighten all fasteners securely.

7 Automatic transaxle - removal and installation

REMOVAL

➡Note: If you're working on a vehicle with a 5-AT transaxle, have the air conditioning system evacuated by a shop that is properly equipped for this service.

1 If you're working on a vehicle with a 5-AT transaxle, refer to Chapter 4 and relieve the fuel pressure.

2 Refer to Chapter 5 and remove the battery.

3 Refer to Chapter 5, Section 3 and remove the battery tray and its support bracket.

4 Remove the air filter housing (see Chapter 4).

5 Disconnect the electrical connector for the transmission range sensor (see Chapter 6). Disconnect any other ground wires or wire retainers from the transaxle.

5-AT transaxle models

6 Disconnect all wiring from the engine compartment junction block.

7 Drain the cooling system (see Chapter 1).

8 Refer to Chapter 6 and remove the PCM.

9 Remove the air conditioning low pressure tube near the engine lift bracket.

10 Disconnect the air conditioning high-pressure switch wiring harness.

11 Disconnect the battery cable from the alternator.

12 Disconnect the tubes from the air conditioning compressor.

13 Remove the air conditioning tube that runs from the condenser to the compressor.

14 Remove the hose from the coolant reservoir.

15 Disconnect the radiator hoses from the engine.

16 Disconnect the two heater hoses from the engine.

17 Disconnect the fuel supply line from the engine.

18 Disconnect the EVAP hose from the engine.

19 Remove the flywheel inspection cover.

20 Remove the pushpin fasteners from the front fenders so that they are allowed to flex slightly.

21 Refer to Chapter 6 and remove the transmission range switch along with its bracket.

22 Remove the transaxle vent hose.

All models

▶ Refer to illustrations 7.30 and 7.35

23 Disconnect the shift cable from the transaxle shift lever (see Section 4). Disconnect the cable from the transaxle bracket.

24 Remove the headlight fasteners and attach the radiator to the core support so that it won't fall when the subframe is removed.

25 Attach an engine support fixture to the lifting hook at the transaxle end of the engine. If no hook is provided, use a bolt of the proper size and thread pitch to attach the support fixture chain to a hole at the end of the cylinder head.

➡Note: Engine support fixtures can be obtained at most equipment rental yards and some auto parts stores.

26 Loosen the front wheel lug nuts. Raise the vehicle and support it securely on jackstands.

27 Remove the wheels and the left inner fender splash shield.

28 Remove the pushpins that hold the front air dam to the subframe.

29 Drain the transaxle lubricant (see Chapter 1). Disconnect the interfering exhaust pipe on V6 models.

30 Disconnect the transaxle fluid cooler lines from the transaxle (see illustration). Seal the ends to prevent contamination.

31 Remove the transaxle-to-engine bolts that are accessible from above.

32 On AWD models, refer to Chapter 8 and remove the driveshaft. Mark its position on the transaxle so it can be installed properly.

33 Disconnect the lower stabilizer bar links. Detach the steering from the subframe by either unbolting the gear from the subframe or disconnecting the intermediate steering shaft (see Chapter 8).

34 Refer to Chapter 8 and disconnect the balljoints from the knuckles. Also disconnect the tie-rod ends from the knuckles.

35 With the engine supported from above, remove the transaxle mounts and the interfering brackets (see illustration).

36 Put two floor jacks under the subframe and make sure that the subframe is supported solidly and balanced evenly.

37 With the help of an assistant, remove the subframe mounting bolts and slowly lower each jack a little at a time until the subframe is near the ground. Set the subframe aside.

38 Disconnect the left driveaxle from the transaxle (see Chapter 8).

39 On FWD models, remove the right driveaxle and the intermediate shaft along with its support.

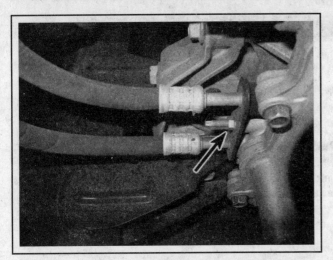

7.30 The transaxle cooler lines are secured by this stud and nut

7.35 The left transaxle mount is accessible after the battery support assembly has been removed - the front and rear transaxle mounts are visible

40 On AWD models, disconnect the right driveaxle from the transfer case (see Chapter 7C). Remove and discard the driveaxle O-ring.

41 Refer to Chapter 5 and remove the starter.

42 Working through the starter hole, paint an alignment mark on the driveplate and the torque converter. Rotate the engine clockwise and remove all of the torque converter-to-driveplate bolts.

43 On AWD models, refer to Chapter 7C and remove the transfer case. Remove the transfer case stub shaft from the transaxle if it didn't come out with the transfer case.

44 Support the transaxle with a jack - preferably a jack made for this purpose (available at most tool rental yards). Safety chains will help steady the transaxle on the jack.

45 Remove the remaining bolts securing the transaxle to the engine.

46 Move the transaxle to the side to disengage it completely from the engine block dowel pins and make sure the torque converter is detached from the driveplate. Lower the transaxle with the jack.

47 Remove the O-ring from the torque converter/differential and discard it.

INSTALLATION

48 Installation of the transaxle is a reversal of the removal procedure, but note the following points:

a) *As the torque converter is reinstalled, ensure that the drive tangs at the center of the torque converter hub engage with the recesses in the automatic transaxle fluid pump inner gear. This can be confirmed by turning the torque converter while pushing it towards the transaxle. If it isn't fully engaged, it will "clunk" into place.*

c) *Install all of the driveplate-to-torque converter nuts before tightening any of them.*

d) *Tighten the driveplate-to-torque converter nuts to the specified torque.*

e) *Tighten the transaxle mounting bolts to the specified torque.*

f) *Tighten the suspension crossmember mounting bolts to the torque values listed in this Chapter's Specifications.*

g) *Tighten the driveaxle/hub nuts to the torque value listed in the Chapter 8 Specifications.*

h) *Tighten the wheel lug nuts to the torque listed in the Chapter 1 Specifications.*

i) *Fill the transaxle with the correct type and amount of automatic transmission fluid as described in Chapter 1.*

j) *On completion, adjust the shift cable as described in Section 4.*

k) *After you've reconnected the battery, the Powertrain Control Module (PCM) must relearn its idle and fuel mixture trim strategy for optimum driveability and performance (see Chapter 5, Section 1 for this procedure).*

l) *Replace all O-rings discarded previously.*

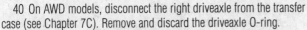

8 Automatic transaxle overhaul - general information

In the event of a problem occurring, it will be necessary to establish whether the fault is electrical, mechanical or hydraulic in nature, before repair work can be contemplated. Diagnosis requires detailed knowledge of the transaxle's operation and construction, as well as access to specialized test equipment, and so is deemed to be beyond the scope of this manual. It is therefore essential that problems with the automatic transaxle are referred to a dealer service department or other qualified repair facility for assessment.

Note that a faulty transaxle should not be removed before the vehicle has been diagnosed by a knowledgeable technician equipped with the proper tools, as troubleshooting must be performed with the transaxle installed in the vehicle.

Specifications

General

Fluid type and capacity   See Chapter 1

Torque specifications	Ft-lbs (unless otherwise indicated)	Nm

➡Note: One foot-pound (ft-lb) of torque is equivalent to 12 inch-pounds (in-lbs) of torque. Torque values below approximately 15 ft-lbs are expressed in inch-pounds, since most foot-pound torque wrenches are not accurate at these smaller values.

Engine/transaxle subframe bolts*	114	154
Torque converter-to-driveplate bolts		
All models except 5-AT	44	60
5-AT models	106 in-lbs	12
Transaxle-to-engine mounting bolts		
VT25-E and 4T45-E models	55	75
AF33-5 models	37	50
5-AT models	47	64

* These bolts must be replaced with new ones whenever they have been loosened or removed.

Section

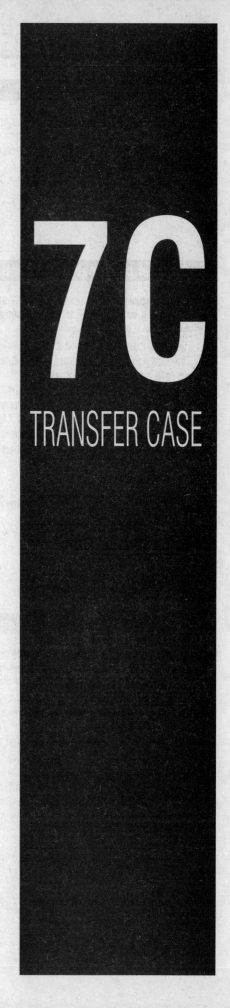

7C

TRANSFER CASE

1 General information

Due to the complexity of the transfer case covered in this manual and the need for specialized equipment to perform most service operations, this Chapter contains only routine maintenance and removal and installation procedures.

If the transfer case requires major repair work, it should be taken to a dealer service department or an automotive or transmission repair shop. You can, however, remove and install the transfer case yourself and save the expense of that labor, even if the repair work is done by a transmission shop.

2 Transfer case rear output shaft oil seal - replacement

➡**Note: This procedure applies only to NVG-900 transfer cases. The output shaft seal on MJ-8 transfer cases are not normally serviced.**

1 Raise the vehicle and support it securely on jackstands.

2 Drain the transfer case lubricant (see Chapter 1).

3 Remove the driveshaft (see Chapter 8).

4 Mark the relative positions of the pinion, nut and flange.

5 Use a beam- or dial-type inch-pound torque wrench to determine the torque required to rotate the pinion. Record it for use later.

6 Count the number of threads visible between the end of the nut and the end of the pinion shaft and record it for use later.

7 Remove the flange mounting nut using a chain wrench to hold the pinion flange while loosening the locknut.

8 Remove the companion flange; a small puller will be required for removal. The puller must be the type that has two bolts that screw into the companion flange.

9 Pry out the seal with a screwdriver or a seal removal tool. Don't damage the seal bore.

10 Lubricate the lips of the new seal with multi-purpose grease and tap it evenly into position with a seal installation tool or a large socket. Make sure it enters the housing squarely and is tapped into its full depth.

11 Align the mating marks made before disassembly and install the companion flange. If necessary, tighten the pinion nut to draw the flange into place.

12 Tighten the nut carefully until the original number of threads are exposed and the marks are aligned.

13 Measure the torque required to rotate the pinion and tighten the nut in small increments until it matches the figure recorded in Step 5.

14 Connect the driveshaft, add the specified lubricant to the transfer case (see Chapter 1) and lower the vehicle.

3 Transfer case driveaxle oil seal (right side) - removal and installation

➡**Note: This seal is only found on NVG-900 transfer cases. The front driveaxles used with MJ-8 transfer cases are connected directly to the transaxle - the transfer case directs power only to the rear wheels on these models.**

1 Remove the wheel cover or hub cap. Break the hub nut loose with a socket and large breaker bar.

2 Loosen the right-front wheel lug nuts, raise the vehicle and support it securely on jackstands. Remove the wheel.

3 Remove the right driveaxle and intermediate shaft (see Chapter 8).

4 Remove the exhaust crossover pipe if necessary for access.

5 Remove the stub shaft. If it's necessary to use a puller to extract the stub shaft, remove the retaining ring from the shaft. It must be replaced with a new one.

6 Carefully pry out the oil seal with a seal removal tool or a large screwdriver; make sure you don't scratch the seal bore.

7 Using a seal installer or a large deep socket as a drift, install the new oil seal. Drive it into the bore squarely and make sure it's completely seated.

8 Lubricate the lip of the new seal with multi-purpose grease, then install a new dust shield.

9 Install the intermediate shaft and driveaxle (see Chapter 8).

10 The remainder of installation is the reverse of removal. Check the transfer case lubricant level and add some, if necessary, to bring it to the appropriate level (see Chapter 1).

4   Transfer case - removal and installation

NVG-900 TRANSFER CASE

1   Loosen the right-front wheel lug nuts. Raise the front of the vehicle and support it securely on jackstands. Remove the wheel.
2   Unbolt the driveshaft center bearing. Unbolt the front portion of the driveshaft (see Chapter 8) and flex/compress the driveshaft to disconnect it from the transfer case. Suspend it from a piece of wire (don't let it hang).
3   Remove the right driveaxle and intermediate shaft (see Chapter 8).
4   Unbolt the steering gear from the engine/transaxle subframe for access.
5   Disconnect the transfer case mount.
6   Remove the transfer case brace.
7   Disconnect the transfer case vent hose.
8   Remove the transfer case mounting bolts and pull it from transaxle.
9   Installation is the reverse of removal, noting the following points:

a) Install all of the bolts hand tight. After they're in place, tighten them to the torque values listed in this Chapter's Specifications.
b) Tighten the driveshaft fasteners to the torque listed in the Chapter 8 Specifications.
c) Refill the transfer case with the proper type and amount of fluid (see Chapter 1).
d) Tighten the wheel lug nuts to the torque listed in the Chapter 1 Specifications.

MJ-8 TRANSFER CASE

10 Raise the vehicle and support it securely on jackstands.
11 Unbolt the front portion of the driveshaft (see Chapter 8) and suspend it from a piece of wire (don't let it hang from the center support bearing). Mark the components so they can be installed in the same position.
12 Remove the exhaust crossover pipe for access.
13 Disconnect the transfer case vent tube.
14 Remove the mounting bolts and keep them in order; they're different lengths. Lift the transfer case off of the transaxle.
15 Remove the four bolts securing the crossmember and remove the crossmember.
16 Remove the alternator (see Chapter 5).
17 Remove the six bolts securing the transfer case bracket to the engine block.
18 Working on the right side of the transfer case, remove the three transfer case mounting bolts.
19 Working on the left side, remove the final mounting bolt, then remove the transfer case from the vehicle.
20 Installation is the reverse of removal, noting the following points:

a) Tighten the exhaust system fasteners to the torque listed in the Chapter 4 Specifications.
b) Tighten the driveshaft fasteners to the torque listed in Chapter 8 Specifications
c) Tighten the transfer case fasteners to the torque listed in this Chapter's Specifications.
d) Refill the transfer case with the proper type and amount of fluid (see Chapter 1).
e) Tighten the wheel lug nuts to the torque listed in the Chapter 1 Specifications.

Specifications

Transfer case fluid type   See Chapter 1

Torque specifications

	Ft-lbs (unless otherwise indicated)	Nm
Transfer case-to-transaxle bolts/nuts		
NVG-900 transaxle	44	60
MJ-8 transaxle	38	52
Transfer case bracket-to-engine block		
mounting bolts, NVG-900	44	60

NOTES

Section

8

CLUTCH AND DRIVELINE

1   General information

The information in this Chapter deals with the components from the rear of the engine to the drive wheels, except for the transaxle, which is dealt with in the previous Chapter.

Since nearly all the procedures covered in this Chapter involve working under the vehicle, make sure it's securely supported on sturdy jackstands or on a hoist where the vehicle can be easily raised and lowered.

2   Clutch - description and check

1   All vehicles with a manual transaxle have a single dry plate, diaphragm spring-type clutch. The clutch disc has a splined hub which allows it to slide along the splines of the transaxle input shaft. The clutch and pressure plate are held in contact by spring pressure exerted by the diaphragm in the pressure plate.

2   The clutch release system is operated by hydraulic pressure. The hydraulic release system consists of the clutch pedal, a master cylinder, a reservoir, an actuator (or slave) cylinder (part of the release bearing assembly) and the hydraulic line connecting the two components. Some models have a remote fluid reservoir; on other models, a hose from the brake fluid reservoir supplies the clutch master cylinder.

3   When the clutch pedal is depressed, a pushrod pushes against brake fluid inside the master cylinder, applying hydraulic pressure to the release cylinder, which pushes the release bearing against the diaphragm fingers of the clutch pressure plate.

4   Terminology can be a problem when discussing the clutch components because common names are in some cases different from those used by the manufacturer. For example, the driven plate is also called the clutch plate or disc, the clutch release bearing is sometimes called a throwout bearing.

5   Unless you're replacing components with obvious damage, do these preliminary checks to diagnose clutch problems:

a) *The first check should be of the fluid level in the clutch master cylinder. If the fluid level is low, add fluid as necessary and inspect the hydraulic system for leaks. If the master cylinder reservoir is dry, bleed the system as described in Section 4 and recheck the clutch operation.*

b) *To check clutch spin-down time, run the engine at normal idle speed with the transaxle in Neutral (clutch pedal up - engaged). Disengage the clutch (pedal down), wait several seconds and shift the transaxle into Reverse. No grinding noise should be heard. A grinding noise would most likely indicate a bad pressure plate or clutch disc.*

c) *To check for complete clutch release, run the engine (with the parking brake applied to prevent vehicle movement) and hold the clutch pedal approximately 1/2-inch from the floor. Shift the transaxle between 1st gear and Reverse several times. If the shift is rough, component failure is indicated.*

d) *Visually inspect the pivot bushing at the top of the clutch pedal to make sure there's no binding or excessive play.*

3   Clutch master cylinder - removal and installation

REMOVAL

1   Working under the dashboard, disconnect the clutch master cylinder pushrod from the pedal.

2   Place some rags under the clutch master cylinder. On models that share the brake fluid reservoir, gently but securely pinch-off the clutch fluid supply hose, then detach the hose from the clutch master cylinder.

3   Place more rags under the master cylinder. Disconnect the pressure line from the master cylinder using a small pick on the left side to release the clip. Pull the line straight out and seal the open end of the line.

4   Remove the mounting nuts and detach the cylinder from the firewall. On models with a separate reservoir, slide the reservoir up and out of its mounting bracket and remove it along with the master cylinder.

✳✳ CAUTION:

Don't allow brake fluid to come into contact with the paint, as it will damage the finish. If you do spill fluid on the paint, wash it off immediately with plenty of water.

INSTALLATION

5   Place the master cylinder in position on the firewall and install the nuts. On models with a separate reservoir, slide the reservoir into its mounting bracket.

6   Tighten the master cylinder mounting nuts to the torque listed in this Chapter's Specifications.

7   Connect the pressure line fitting to the clutch master cylinder.

8   On models that share the brake fluid reservoir, attach the feed hose to the clutch master cylinder.

9   Working under the dash, connect the pushrod to the clutch pedal.

10   Fill the reservoir with brake fluid conforming to DOT 3 specifications and bleed the clutch system as outlined in Section 4.

4   Clutch hydraulic system - bleeding

➡**Note: The bleed screw is located in the clutch fluid line, where it connects to the transaxle.**

1   Bleed the hydraulic system whenever any part of the system has been removed or the fluid level has fallen so low that air has been drawn into the master cylinder. The bleeding procedure is very similar to bleeding a brake system.

2   Fill the master cylinder reservoir with new brake fluid conforming to DOT 3 specifications.

✳✳ CAUTION:

Do not re-use any of the fluid coming from the system during the bleeding operation or use fluid which has been inside an open container for an extended period of time.

3   Attach a hose to the bleed screw. It's best to put the other end into a jar of clean brake fluid, but at least point the hose toward a container or rags.

4   Have an assistant operate the clutch pedal about 5 times.

5   Now have your assistant pump the pedal rapidly 10 times without allowing the pedal to reach the top of its travel.

6   Repeat Steps 4 and 5 several times.

7   With the pedal in the up position, open the bleed screw.

8   Have your assistant push the pedal to the floor at a normal speed. Tighten the bleed screw and release the pedal, allowing it to return to its stop. If necessary, pull the pedal back up.

9   Continue Steps 7 and 8 until all air is evacuated from the system, indicated by a solid stream of fluid being ejected from the bleeder valve each time with no air bubbles. Keep a close watch on the fluid level inside the master cylinder reservoir - if the level drops too far, air will get into the system and you'll have to start all over again.

➡**Note: Wash the area with water to remove any excess brake fluid.**

10   Check the fluid level again, and add some, if necessary, to bring it to the appropriate level. Check carefully for proper operation before placing the vehicle into normal service.

5   Clutch components - removal, inspection and installation

✳✳ WARNING:

Dust produced by clutch wear is hazardous to your health. DO NOT blow it out with compressed air and DO NOT inhale it. DO NOT use gasoline or petroleum-based solvents to remove the dust. Brake system cleaner should be used to flush the dust into a drain pan. After the clutch components are wiped clean with a rag, dispose of the contaminated rags and cleaner in a covered, marked container.

REMOVAL

▶ **Refer to illustration 5.5**

1   Access to the clutch components is normally accomplished by removing the transaxle, leaving the engine in the vehicle. If the engine is being removed for major overhaul, check the clutch for wear and replace worn components as necessary. However, the relatively low cost of the clutch components compared to the time and trouble spent gaining access to them warrants their replacement anytime the engine or transaxle is removed, unless they are new or in near-perfect condition. The following procedures are based on the assumption the engine will stay in place.

2   Remove the transaxle from the vehicle (see Chapter 7, Part A). Support the engine while the transaxle is out. Preferably, an engine support fixture or a hoist should be used to support it from above.

3   Remove the clutch actuator cylinder (see Section 6).

4   To support the clutch disc during removal, install a clutch alignment tool through the clutch disc hub.

5   Carefully inspect the flywheel and pressure plate for indexing marks. The marks are usually an X, an O or a white letter. If they cannot be found, scribe or paint marks yourself so the pressure plate and the flywheel will be in the same alignment during installation (see illustration).

6   Turning each bolt a little at a time, loosen the pressure plate-to-flywheel bolts. Work in a criss-cross pattern until all spring pressure is relieved. Then hold the pressure plate securely and completely remove the bolts, followed by the pressure plate and clutch disc.

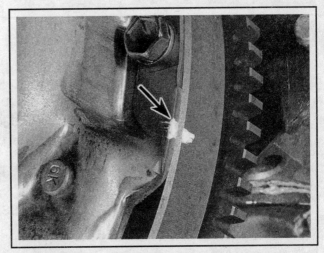

5.5 Mark the relationship of the pressure plate to the flywheel (if you're planning to re-use the old pressure plate)

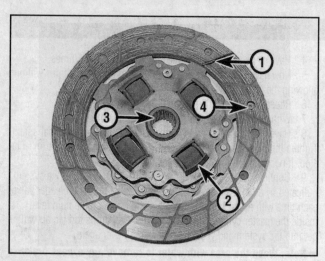

5.9 The clutch disc

1 **Lining** - *this will wear down in use*
2 **Springs or dampers** - *check for cracking and deformation*
3 **Splined hub** - *the splines must not be worn and should slide smoothly on the transaxle input shaft splines*
4 **Rivets** - *these secure the lining and will damage the flywheel or pressure plate if allowed to contact the surfaces*

INSPECTION

▶ **Refer to illustrations 5.9, 5.11a and 5.11b**

7 Ordinarily, when a problem occurs in the clutch, it can be attributed to wear of the clutch driven plate assembly (clutch disc). However, all components should be inspected at this time.

8 Inspect the flywheel for cracks, heat checking, grooves and other obvious defects. If the imperfections are slight, a machine shop can machine the surface flat and smooth, which is highly recommended regardless of the surface appearance. Refer to Chapter 2 for the flywheel removal and installation procedure.

9 Inspect the lining on the clutch disc. There should be at least 1/16-inch of lining above the rivet heads. Check for loose rivets, distortion, cracks, broken springs and other obvious damage (see illustration). As mentioned above, ordinarily the clutch disc is routinely replaced, so if in doubt about the condition, replace it with a new one.

10 The actuator cylinder may also be replaced along with the clutch disc (see Section 6).

11 Check the machined surfaces and the diaphragm spring fingers of the pressure plate (see illustrations). If the surface is grooved or otherwise damaged, replace the pressure plate. Also check for obvious damage, distortion, cracking, etc. Light glazing can be removed with emery cloth or sandpaper. If a new pressure plate is required, new and re-manufactured units are available.

INSTALLATION

▶ **Refer to illustration 5.14**

12 Install the flywheel if it was removed (see Chapter 2).

13 Before installation, clean the flywheel and pressure plate machined surfaces with brake cleaner. It's important that no oil or grease is on these surfaces or the lining of the clutch disc. Handle the parts only with clean hands.

14 Position the clutch disc and pressure plate against the flywheel with the clutch held in place with an alignment tool (see illustration). Make sure the disc is installed properly (most replacement clutch discs will be marked "flywheel side" or something similar - if not marked, install the clutch disc with the damper springs toward the transaxle).

15 Tighten the pressure plate-to-flywheel bolts only finger tight, working around the pressure plate.

16 Center the clutch disc by ensuring the alignment tool extends through the splined hub and completely into the crankshaft. Wiggle the tool up, down or side-to-side as needed to center the disc. Tighten the pressure plate-to-flywheel bolts a little at a time, working in a criss-cross pattern to prevent distorting the cover. After all of the bolts are snug, tighten them to the torque listed in this Chapter's Specifications. Remove the alignment tool.

17 Lubricate the face of the release bearing with a light film of high-temperature grease.

18 Install the clutch actuator cylinder (see Section 6).

19 Install the transaxle and all components removed previously.

NORMAL FINGER WEAR

EXCESSIVE WEAR

EXCESSIVE FINGER WEAR

BROKEN OR BENT FINGERS

5.11a Replace the pressure plate if excessive wear or damage are noted

5.11b Inspect the pressure plate surface for excessive score marks, cracks and signs of overheating

5.14 Center the clutch disc in the pressure plate with a clutch alignment tool

6 Clutch actuator cylinder - removal, inspection and installation

♦ **Refer to illustration 6.2**

✳ WARNING:

Dust produced by clutch wear is hazardous to your health. DO NOT blow it out with compressed air and DO NOT inhale it. DO NOT use gasoline or petroleum-based solvents to remove the dust. Brake system cleaner should be used to flush the dust into a drain pan. After the clutch components are wiped clean with a rag, dispose of the contaminated rags and cleaner in a covered, marked container.

REMOVAL

1 Remove the transaxle (see Chapter 7A).
2 Unbolt the actuator cylinder from the transaxle (see illustration).

INSPECTION

3 Wipe off the bearing with a clean rag and inspect it for damage, wear and cracks. Don't immerse the bearing in solvent - it's sealed for life and immersion in solvent will ruin it.
4 Hold the center of the bearing and rotate the outer portion while applying force. If the bearing doesn't turn smoothly or if it's noisy or rough, replace it.
➡**Note: Considering the difficulty involved with replacing the actuator cylinder, we recommend replacing it whenever the clutch components are replaced.**

5 Spin the bearing. There should be a slight amount of drag. If there's no drag at all, replace it.

INSTALLATION

6 Lightly lubricate the inside diameter of the actuator cylinder bearing with high-temperature grease.
7 Install the actuator cylinder onto the transaxle and tighten the bolts to the torque listed in this Chapter's Specifications.
8 Lubricate the face of the release bearing with a light film of high-temperature grease.
9 The remainder of installation is the reverse of removal.

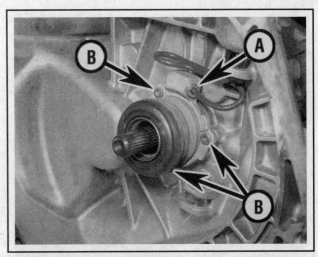

6.2 Clutch actuator cylinder details

A   Clutch hydraulic line fitting
B   Clutch release cylinder mounting fasteners

7 Driveaxles - removal and installation

FRONT

Removal

▶ **Refer to illustrations 7.1 and 7.9**

1   Remove the wheel cover or hub cap. Break the driveaxle/hub nut loose with a socket and large breaker bar (see illustration).

➡**Note: If the opening in the wheel is too small to accommodate your socket, wait until after the wheel is removed to loosen the nut. You can prevent the brake disc from turning by inserting a long punch into a disc cooling vane and letting it come to rest against the caliper mounting bracket.**

2   Loosen the wheel lug nuts, raise the vehicle and support it securely on jackstands. Remove the wheel.

3   Separate the lower control arm from the steering knuckle (see Chapter 10).

4   Refer to Chapter 10 and disconnect the tie-rod end from the steering knuckle.

5   Disconnect the stabilizer bar from the link at each end (see Chapter 10).

6   Remove the driveaxle/hub nut from the axle and discard it.

7   Swing the knuckle/hub assembly out (away from the vehicle) until the end of the driveaxle is free of the hub.

➡**Note: If the driveaxle splines stick in the hub, tap on the end of the driveaxle with a plastic hammer.**

Support the outer end of the driveaxle with a piece of wire to avoid unnecessary strain on the inner CV joint.

8   If you're removing the right driveaxle, carefully pry the inner CV joint off the intermediate shaft using a large screwdriver or prybar positioned between the CV joint housing and the intermediate shaft bearing support.

9   If you're removing the left driveaxle, pry the inner CV joint out of the transaxle using a large screwdriver or prybar positioned between the transaxle and the CV joint housing (see illustration). Be careful not to damage the differential seal.

10 Support the CV joints and carefully remove the driveaxle from the vehicle.

Installation

11 Pry the old spring clip from the inner end of the driveaxle (left side) or outer end of the intermediate shaft (right side) and install a new one. Lubricate the differential or intermediate shaft seal with multi-purpose grease and raise the driveaxle into position while supporting the CV joints.

➡**Note: Position the spring clip with the opening facing down; this will ease insertion of the driveaxle and prevent damage to the clip.**

12 Push the splined end of the inner CV joint into the differential side gear (left side) or onto the intermediate shaft (right side) and make sure the spring clip locks in its groove.

13 Apply a light coat of multi-purpose grease to the outer CV joint splines, pull out on the steering knuckle assembly and install the stub axle into the hub.

14 Insert the balljoint stud into the steering knuckle and tighten the bolt to the torque listed in the Chapter 10 Specifications. Install a new cotter pin. Also reconnect the tie-rod ends and the stabilizer bar links (see Chapter 10).

15 Install a *new* driveaxle/hub nut. Tighten the hub nut securely, but don't try to tighten it to the actual torque specification until you've lowered the vehicle to the ground.

➡**Note: If your socket won't fit through the opening in the wheel, tighten the driveaxle/hub nut now, using the technique described in Step 1 to prevent the brake disc from turning.**

16 Grasp the inner CV joint housing (not the driveaxle) and pull out to make sure the driveaxle has seated securely in the transaxle or on the intermediate shaft.

17 Install the wheel and lug nuts, then lower the vehicle. Tighten the lug nuts to the torque listed in the Chapter 1 Specifications.

18 Tighten the driveaxle/hub nut to the torque listed in this Chapter's Specifications.

INTERMEDIATE SHAFT

Removal

19 Remove the right driveaxle (see Steps 1 through 10).

20 Remove the O-ring seal from the intermediate shaft.

21 Unscrew the bolts from the intermediate shaft bearing retainer.

22 Pull the intermediate shaft from the transaxle.

7.1 Loosen the driveaxle/hub nut with a long breaker bar

7.9 Carefully pry the inner end of the driveaxle from the transaxle

Installation

23 Lubricate the lips of the transaxle seal with multi-purpose grease. Carefully guide the intermediate shaft into the transaxle side gear, then install the mounting nuts for the bearing support.

24 Tighten the nuts to the torque listed in this Chapter's Specifications. Make sure that the shaft is positively engaged into the transaxle.

25 Put the O-ring on the shaft.

26 Put a new wheel-retaining clip on the shaft.

27 The remainder of installation is the reverse of removal.

REAR (AWD MODELS)

Removal

28 Remove the wheel cover or hub cap. Break the driveaxle/hub nut loose with a socket and large breaker bar (see illustration 7.1).

29 Block the front wheels to prevent the vehicle from rolling. Loosen the wheel lug nuts, raise the rear of the vehicle and support it securely on jackstands. Remove the wheel.

30 Disconnect the stabilizer bar link from the lower control arm.

31 Support the lower control arm with a floor jack.

32 Disconnect the lower shock absorber from the control arm.

33 Remove the through-bolt from the lower toe-link arm.

34 Loosen the lower suspension rubber bumper nut.

35 Remove the outer through-bolt from the lower control arm.

36 Lower the floor jack and remove the coil spring.

37 Loosen the through-bolt in the upper control arm where it attaches to the steering knuckle.

38 Use a brass punch or a block of wood with a hammer to break the end of the driveaxle loose from the wheel hub. Remove the nut and discard it.

✳✳ CAUTION:

The manufacturer recommends that all suspension nuts and cotter pins be replaced with new ones any time they are removed.

---

39 Pull the lower part of the hub assembly up and out so that it comes away from the driveaxle. Secure it with wire or rope.

40 Pry the driveaxle out of the differential. Remove the retaining ring - it will have to be replaced with a new one.

Installation

41 Pry the old spring clip from the inner end of the driveaxle and install a new one.

42 Apply a light film of grease to the area on the inner CV joint stub shaft where the seal rides, then insert the splined end of the inner CV joint into the differential. Make sure the spring clip locks in its groove.

➡️**Note: Position the spring clip with the opening facing down; this will ease insertion of the driveaxle and prevent damage to the clip.**

43 Apply a light film of grease to the outer CV joint splines and insert the outer end of the driveaxle into the hub.

44 Install the coil spring (see Chapter 10).

45 Reconnect the rear suspension components following the procedures in Chapter 10.

46 Install a new driveaxle/hub nut. Tighten the hub nut securely, but don't try to tighten it to the actual torque specification until you've lowered the vehicle to the ground.

47 Install the wheel and lug nuts, then lower the vehicle. Tighten the lug nuts to the torque listed in the Chapter 1 Specifications.

48 Tighten the driveaxle/hub nut to the torque listed in this Chapter's Specifications. Install the wheel cover or hub cap.

---

8   Driveaxle boot - replacement

➡️**Note 1: If the CV joints are worn, indicating the need for an overhaul (usually due to torn boots), explore all options before beginning the job. Complete rebuilt driveaxles are available on an exchange basis, which eliminates much time and work.**

➡️**Note 2: Some auto parts stores carry split-type replacement boots, which can be installed without removing the driveaxle from the vehicle. This is a convenient alternative; however, the driveaxle should be removed and the CV joint disassembled and cleaned to ensure the joint is free from contaminants such as moisture and dirt which will accelerate CV joint wear.**

➡️**Note 3: These procedures apply to rear driveaxle boots as well as those used on the front of the vehicle.**

1   Remove the driveaxle from the vehicle (see Section 7).

2   Mount the driveaxle in a vise. The jaws of the vise should be lined with wood or rags to prevent damage to the driveaxle.

INNER CV JOINT AND BOOT

▶ **Refer to illustrations 8.3, 8.4, 8.5, 8.6a, 8.6b, 8.7, 8.11, 8.14, 8.16, 8.17a, 8.17b, 8.17c, 8.17d and 8.17e**

Removal

3   Remove the boot clamps (see illustration).

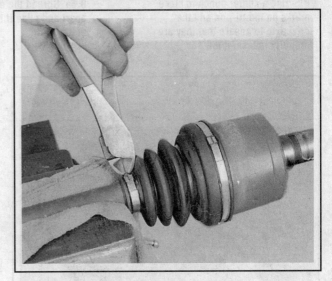

8.3 Cut off the boot clamps and discard them

8.4 Mark the relationship of the tri-pod assembly to the outer race

4   Pull the boot back from the inner CV joint and slide the joint housing off. Be sure to mark the relationship of the tri-pod to the outer race (see illustration).

5   Use a center punch to mark the tri-pod and axleshaft to ensure that they are reassembled properly (see illustration).

6   Spread the ends of the stop-ring apart, slide it towards the center of the shaft, then remove the retainer clip from the end of the axleshaft (see illustrations).

7   Use a hammer and a brass punch to drive the tri-pod joint from the driveaxle (see illustration).

8   Remove the stop-ring from the axleshaft and discard it.

Inspection

9   Clean the old grease from the outer race and the tri-pod bearing assembly. Carefully disassemble each section of the tri-pod assembly, one at a time so as not to mix up the parts, and clean the needle bearings with solvent.

10 Inspect the rollers, tri-pod, bearings and outer race for scoring, pitting or other signs of abnormal wear, which will warrant the replacement of the inner CV joint.

8.5 Use a center punch to place marks on the tri-pod and the driveaxle to ensure that they are properly reassembled

8.6a Spread the ends of the stop-ring apart and slide it towards the center of the shaft . . .

8.6b . . . then slide the tri-pod assembly back and remove the retainer clip

8.7 Drive the tri-pod joint from the axleshaft with a brass punch and hammer - make sure you don't damage the bearing surfaces or the splines on the shaft

8.11 Wrap the splined area of the axleshaft with tape to prevent damage to the boot(s) when installing it

Reassembly

11 Slide the clamps and boot onto the axleshaft. It's a good idea to wrap the axleshaft splines with tape to prevent damaging the boot (see illustration).

12 Install a new stop-ring on the axleshaft, but don't seat it in its groove; position it on the shaft past the groove.

13 Place the tri-pod on the shaft (making sure the marks are aligned) and install a new bearing retainer clip. Now slide the tri-pod up against the retainer clip and seat the stop-ring in its groove.

14 Apply CV joint grease to the tri-pod assembly, the inside of the joint housing and the inside of the boot (see illustration).

15 Slide the boot into place.

16 Position the CV joint mid-way through its travel, then equalize the pressure in the boot (see illustration).

17 Tighten the boot clamps (see illustrations).

18 Install the driveaxle assembly (see Section 8).

8.14 Pack the outer race with CV joint grease and slide it over the tri-pod assembly - make sure the match marks on the CV joint housing and tri-pod line up

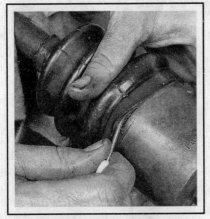

8.16 Equalize the pressure inside the boot by inserting a small, dull screwdriver between the boot and the outer race

8.17a To install new fold-over type clamps, bend the tang down . . .

8.17b . . . and flatten the tabs to hold it in place

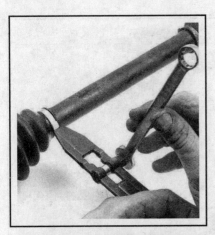

8.17c To install band-type clamps, you'll need a special tool; install the band with its end pointing in the direction of axle rotation and tighten it securely, then pivot the tool up 90-degrees and tap the center of the clip with a center punch . . .

8.17d . . . then bend the end of the clamp back over the clip and cut off the excess

8.17e If you're installing crimp-type boot clamps, you'll need a pair of special crimping pliers (available at most auto parts stores)

OUTER CV JOINT AND BOOT

▶ **Refer to illustrations 8.20, 8.25a, 8.25b and 8.25c**

Removal

19 Remove the boot clamps (see illustration 8.3).

20 Strike the edge of the CV joint housing sharply with a soft-face hammer to dislodge the outer CV joint from the axleshaft (see illustration). Remove and discard the bearing retainer clip from the axleshaft.

21 Slide the outer CV joint boot off the axleshaft.

Inspection

22 Thoroughly clean all components with solvent until the old CV grease is completely removed. Inspect the bearing surfaces of the inner tri-pods and housings for cracks, pitting, scoring, and other signs of wear. If any part of the outer CV joint is worn, you must replace the entire driveaxle assembly (inner CV joint, axleshaft and outer CV joint).

Reassembly

23 Slide a new sealing boot clamp and sealing boot onto the axleshaft. It's a good idea to wrap the axleshaft splines with tape to prevent damaging the boot (see illustration 8.11).

24 Place a new bearing retainer clip onto the axleshaft.

25 Place half the grease provided in the sealing boot kit into the outer CV joint assembly housing (see illustration). Put the remaining grease into the sealing boot (see illustrations).

26 Align the splines on the axleshaft with the splines on the outer CV joint assembly and gently drive the CV joint onto the axleshaft using a soft-faced hammer until the CV joint is seated to the axleshaft.

27 Position the CV joint mid-way through its travel, then equalize the pressure in the boot (see illustration 8.16).

28 Tighten the boot clamps (see illustrations 8.17a through 8.17e).

29 Install the driveaxle as outlined in Section 7.

8.20 Strike the edge of the CV joint housing sharply with a soft-faced hammer to dislodge the CV joint from the shaft

8.25a Pack the outer CV joint assembly with CV grease . . .

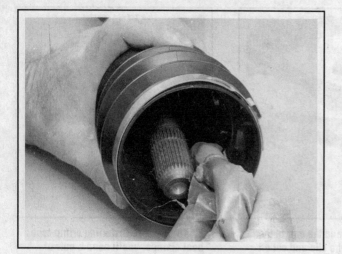

8.25b . . . then apply grease to the inside of the boot . . .

8.25c . . . until the level is up to the end of the axle

9   Driveshaft (AWD models) - removal and installation

REMOVAL

▶ Refer to illustrations 9.2, 9.4, 9.5 and 9.6

➡ **Note: The manufacturer recommends replacing driveshaft fasteners with new ones when installing the driveshaft.**

1   Raise the vehicle and support it securely on jackstands. Place the shift selector lever in Neutral.

2   Use chalk or a scribe to index the relationship of the driveshaft to the differential pinion yoke and the flange at the transfer case (see illustration).

3   Remove the driveshaft loop.

4   Disconnect the rear U-joint of the driveshaft from the rear differential assembly (see illustration).

5   Remove the front constant velocity joint bolts from the transfer case (see illustration).

6   Remove the mounting bolts from the center support bearing (see illustration).

7   With help from an assistant, carefully pull the driveshaft rearward so it disengages from the transfer case. Remove the driveshaft from the vehicle.

INSTALLATION

8   Installation is the reverse of removal. Make sure the marks you made previously are aligned. Tighten the fasteners to the torques listed in this Chapter's Specifications.

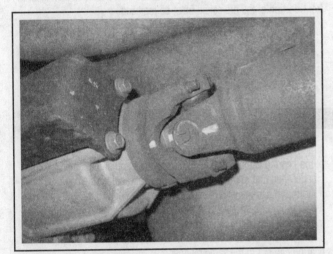

9.2 Mark the relationship of the driveshaft to the differential pinion yoke - also mark the other end of the driveshaft to the transfer case flange

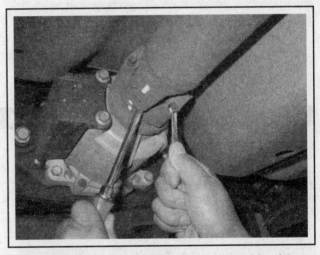

9.4 Immobilize the driveshaft by placing a screwdriver into the universal joint while loosening the bolts

9.5 Remove the bolts securing the driveshaft to the transaxle/transfer case

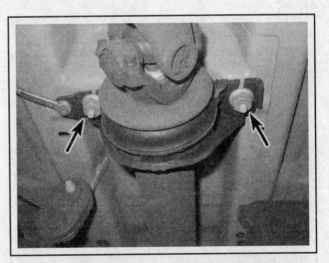

9.6 Remove the nuts securing the center support bearing

10 Driveshaft universal and constant velocity joints (AWD models) - general information and check

UNIVERSAL JOINTS

1   Universal joints are mechanical couplings which connect two rotating components that meet each other at different angles.

2   These joints are composed of a yoke on each side connected by a crosspiece called a trunnion. Cups at each end of the trunnion contain needle bearings which provide smooth transfer of the torque load. Snap-rings, either inside or outside of the bearing cups, hold the assembly together.

3   Wear in the needle roller bearings is characterized by vibration in the driveline, noise during acceleration, and in extreme cases of lack of lubrication, metallic squeaking and ultimately grating and shrieking sounds as the bearings disintegrate.

4   It is easy to check if the needle bearings are worn with the driveshaft in position, by trying to turn the shaft with one hand, the other hand holding the rear differential pinion flange when the rear universal joint is being checked, and the front half coupling when the front universal joint is being checked. Any movement between the driveshaft and the front half couplings, and around the rear half couplings, is indicative of considerable wear. Another method of checking for universal joint wear is to use a prybar inserted into the gap between the universal joint and the driveshaft or flange. Leave the vehicle in gear and try to pry the joint both radially and axially. Any looseness should be apparent with this method. A final test for wear is to attempt to lift the shaft and note any movement between the yokes of the joints.

5   If any of the above conditions exist, replace the universal joints with new ones.

CONSTANT VELOCITY JOINT

6   The constant velocity joint on the forward end of the driveshaft is not serviceable. If the joint wears out or the boot becomes damaged, the front portion of the driveshaft must be replaced.

11 Universal joints (AWD models) - replacement

▶ **Refer to illustrations 11.2a, 11.2b, 11.4a, 11.4b and 11.9**

➡**Note: A press or large vise will be required for this procedure. It may be advisable to take the driveshaft to a local dealer service department, service station or machine shop where the universal joints can be replaced for you, normally at a reasonable charge.**

1   Remove the driveshaft as outlined in Section 9.

2   Use a small pair of pliers to remove the snap-rings from the spider (see illustrations).

3   Supporting the driveshaft, place it in position on a workbench equipped with a vise.

4   Place a piece of pipe or a large socket, having an inside diameter slightly larger than the outside diameter of the bearing caps, over one of the bearing caps. Position a socket with an outside diameter slightly smaller than that of the opposite bearing cap against the cap (see illustration) and use the vise or press to force the bearing cap out (inside the pipe or large socket). Use the vise or large pliers to work the bearing cap the rest of the way out (see illustration).

5   Transfer the sockets to the other side and press the opposite bearing cap out in the same manner.

6   Pack the new universal joint bearings with grease. Ordinarily, specific instructions for lubrication will be included with the universal joint servicing kit and should be followed carefully.

7   Position the spider in the yoke and partially install one bearing cap in the yoke.

11.2a A pair of needle-nose pliers can be used to remove the universal joint snap-rings

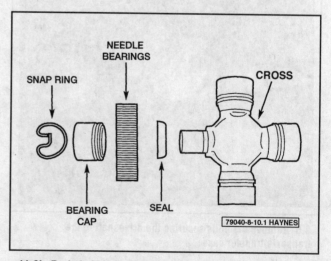

11.2b Exploded view of an outer snap-ring type U-joint

11.4a To press the universal joint out of the driveshaft yoke, set it up in a vise with the small socket pushing the joint and bearing cap into the large socket

11.4b Locking pliers can be used to remove the bearing caps from the yoke

8   Start the spider into the bearing cap, then partially install the other cap. Align the spider and press the bearing caps into position, being careful not to damage the dust seals.

9   Install the snap-rings. If difficulty is encountered in seating the snap-rings, strike the driveshaft yoke sharply with a hammer. This will spring the yoke ears slightly and allow the snap-rings to seat in the groove (see illustration).

10 Install the grease fitting and fill the joint with grease. Be careful not to overfill the joint, as this could blow out the grease seals.

11 Install the driveshaft (see Section 9).

11.9 If the snap-ring will not seat in the groove, strike the yoke with a brass hammer - this will relieve the tension that has set up in the yoke and slightly spring the yoke ears (this should also be done if the joint feels tight when assembled)

12 Driveshaft center support bearing (AWD models) - replacement

1   Remove the driveshaft (see Section 10).

2   Mark the relationship of the front portion of the driveshaft to the rear portion of the driveshaft (it's best to make the mark on the slip yoke). Disassemble the U-joint between the front half of the driveshaft and the center support bearing (see Section 11).

3   Remove the snap-ring from the end of the rear half of the driveshaft.

4   If you have access to a hydraulic press (one tall enough to accommodate the shaft) and the necessary fixtures, press the yoke off the driveshaft, then press the driveshaft out of the center support bearing. Reverse this operation to install the new bearing.

5   If you do not have the necessary equipment, take the shaft to an automotive machine shop or other qualified repair facility to have the old bearing pressed off and the new one pressed on.

13 Rear driveaxle oil seals (AWD models) - replacement

1   Raise the rear of the vehicle and support it securely on jackstands. Place the transaxle in Neutral with the parking brake off. Block the front wheels to prevent the vehicle from rolling.

2   Remove the driveaxle(s) (see Section 7).

3   Carefully pry out the driveaxle oil seal with a seal removal tool or a large screwdriver. Be careful not to damage or scratch the seal bore.

4   Using a seal installer or a large deep socket as a drift, install the new oil seal. Drive it into the bore squarely and make sure it's completely seated.

5   Lubricate the lip of the new seal with multi-purpose grease, then install the driveaxle. Be careful not to damage the lip of the new seal.

6   Check the differential lubricant level and add some, if necessary, to bring it to the appropriate level (see Chapter 1).

14 Rear differential assembly (AWD models) - removal and installation

REMOVAL

1   Raise the rear of the vehicle and support it securely on jackstands. Block the front wheels to prevent the vehicle from rolling.

2   Remove the driveshaft (see Section 9).

3   Remove the driveaxles (see Section 7).

4   Remove the rear section of the exhaust system.

5   Place a floor jack under the differential assembly and tie the assembly securely using wire or a similar method.

6   Remove the rear assembly support bracket.

7   Remove both side mount through-bolts. The nuts and bolts should be discarded and replaced with new ones when reinstalling the differential.

8   Carefully remove the differential.

INSTALLATION

9   Installation is the reverse of removal, noting the following points:

a) *Don't tighten any of the mounting fasteners until all of them have been installed.*

b) *Tighten all fasteners to the torque listed in this Chapter's specifications.*

15 Clutch pedal position switch - replacement

1   Disconnect the electrical connector from the clutch pedal position switch.

2   Carefully pry the switch from its bracket.

3   Installation is the reverse of removal.

Specifications

Clutch fluid type	See Chapter 1

Torque specifications   Ft-lbs (unless otherwise indicated)   Nm

➡ Note: One foot-pound (ft-lb) of torque is equivalent to 12 inch-pounds (in-lbs) of torque. Torque values below approximately 15 ft-lbs are expressed in inch-pounds, since most foot-pound torque wrenches are not accurate at these smaller values.

Clutch

	Ft-lbs	Nm
Clutch master cylinder mounting nuts	17	23
Clutch pressure plate-to-flywheel bolts	18	24
Clutch actuator cylinder mounting bolts	89 in-lbs	10

Driveaxles

	Ft-lbs	Nm
Driveaxle/hub nut*		
Front	151	205
Rear (AWD models)		
Step 1	63	85
Step 2	Tighten an additional 36-degrees	
Intermediate shaft bearing bracket nuts	37	50
* Nut must be replaced		

Driveshaft (AWD models)

	Ft-lbs	Nm
Center bearing mounting nuts	19	26
Driveshaft-to-transfer case bolts	19	26
Driveshaft-to-rear differential bolts	37	50

Rear differential assembly (AWD models)

	Ft-lbs	Nm
Rear bracket-to-body bolts	66	89
Rear bracket-to-differential bolts	92	125
Differential side mounting bolts	92	125

NOTES

Section

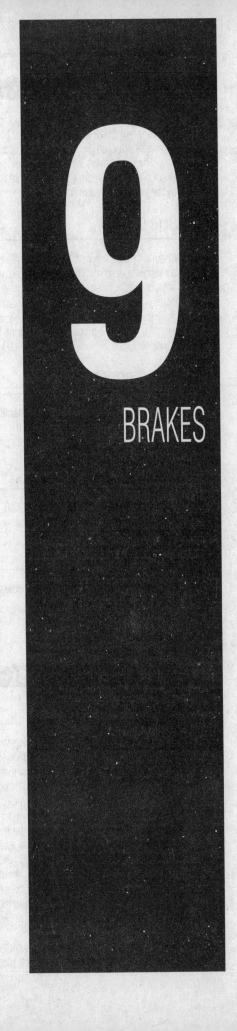

9

BRAKES

1 General information

The vehicles covered by this manual are equipped with hydraulically operated front and rear brake systems. The front brakes are disc type and the rear brakes are drum type. Both the front and rear brakes are self adjusting. The disc brakes automatically compensate for pad wear, while the drum brakes incorporate an adjustment mechanism that is activated by the parking brake mechanism.

HYDRAULIC SYSTEM

The hydraulic system consists of two separate circuits. The master cylinder has separate reservoir chambers for the two circuits and, in the event of a leak or failure in one hydraulic circuit, the other circuit will remain operative. A dual proportioning valve near the master cylinder provides brake balance between the front and rear brakes on vehicles not equipped with ABS. The proportioning is done by the ABS modulator on ABS models.

POWER BRAKE BOOSTER

The power brake booster, utilizing engine manifold vacuum and atmospheric pressure to provide assistance to the hydraulically operated brakes, is mounted on the firewall in the engine compartment.

PARKING BRAKE

The parking brake operates the rear brakes only, through cable actuation. It's activated by a lever mounted in the center console.

SERVICE

After completing any operation involving disassembly of any part of the brake system, always test drive the vehicle to check for proper braking performance before resuming normal driving. When testing the brakes, perform the tests on a clean, dry, flat surface. Conditions other than these can lead to inaccurate test results.

Test the brakes at various speeds with both light and heavy pedal pressure. The vehicle should stop evenly without pulling to one side or the other. Avoid locking the brakes, because this slides the tires and diminishes braking efficiency and control of the vehicle.

Tires, vehicle load and wheel alignment are factors which also affect braking performance.

PRECAUTIONS

There are some general cautions and warnings involving the brake system on this vehicle:

a) *Use only brake fluid conforming to DOT 3 specifications.*

b) *The brake pads and linings contain fibers that are hazardous to your health if inhaled. Whenever you work on brake system components, clean all parts with brake system cleaner. Do not allow the fine dust to become airborne. Also, wear an approved filtering mask.*

c) *Safety should be paramount whenever any servicing of the brake components is performed. Do not use parts or fasteners that are not in perfect condition, and be sure that all clearances and torque specifications are adhered to. If you are at all unsure about a certain procedure, seek professional advice. Upon completion of any brake system work, test the brakes carefully in a controlled area before putting the vehicle into normal service. If a problem is suspected in the brake system, don't drive the vehicle until it's fixed.*

2 Anti-lock Brake System (ABS) - general information

GENERAL INFORMATION

1   The anti-lock brake system is designed to maintain vehicle steerability, directional stability and optimum deceleration under severe braking conditions on most road surfaces. It does so by monitoring the rotational speed of each wheel and controlling the brake line pressure to each wheel during braking. This prevents the wheels from locking up.

2   The ABS system has three main components - the wheel speed sensors, the electronic control unit (ECU) and the hydraulic unit. Four wheel speed sensors - one at each wheel - send a variable voltage signal to the control unit, which monitors these signals, compares them to its program and determines whether a wheel is about to lock up. When a wheel is about to lock up, the control unit signals the hydraulic unit to reduce hydraulic pressure (or not increase it further) at that wheel's brake caliper. Pressure modulation is handled by electrically-operated solenoid valves.

3   If a problem develops within the system, an "ABS" warning light will glow on the dashboard. Sometimes, a visual inspection of the ABS system can help you locate the problem. Carefully inspect the ABS wiring harness. Pay particularly close attention to the harness and connections near each wheel. Look for signs of chafing and other damage caused by incorrectly routed wires. If a wheel sensor harness is damaged, the sensor must be replaced.

❋ WARNING:

Do NOT try to repair an ABS wiring harness. The ABS system is sensitive to even the smallest changes in resistance. Repairing the harness could alter resistance values and cause the system to malfunction. If the ABS wiring harness is damaged in any way, it must be replaced.

❋ CAUTION:

Make sure the ignition is turned off before unplugging or reattaching any electrical connections.

DIAGNOSIS AND REPAIR

4   If a dashboard warning light comes on and stays on while the vehicle is in operation, the ABS system requires attention. Although special electronic ABS diagnostic testing tools are necessary to properly diagnose the system, you can perform a few preliminary checks before taking the vehicle to a dealer service department.

 a) *Check the brake fluid level in the reservoir.*
 b) *Verify that the computer electrical connectors are securely connected.*
 c) *Check the electrical connectors at the hydraulic control unit.*
 d) *Check the fuses.*
 e) *Follow the wiring harness to each wheel and verify that all connections are secure and that the wiring is undamaged.*

5   If the above preliminary checks do not rectify the problem, the vehicle should be diagnosed by a dealer service department or other qualified repair shop. Due to the complex nature of this system, all actual repair work must be done by a qualified automotive technician.

WHEEL SPEED SENSOR - REPLACEMENT

6   Loosen the wheel lug nuts. Raise the vehicle and support it securely on jackstands.
7   Remove the wheel.
8   If you're working on a front sensor, refer to Section 5 and remove the brake disc. The sensor is located behind the hub on the steering knuckle. If you're working on a rear sensor, remove the brake shoes (see Section 6). The sensor is located behind the hub on the knuckle.
9   Disconnect the wiring harness from the speed sensor.
10 Remove the mounting bolt and remove the wheel speed sensor.
11 Installation is the reverse of removal.

3   Disc brake pads - replacement

▶ **Refer to illustrations 3.5 and 3.6a through 3.6k**

✳✳ WARNING:

Disc brake pads must be replaced on both front wheels at the same time - never replace the pads on only one wheel. Also, the dust created by the brake system is harmful to your health. Never blow it out with compressed air and don't inhale any of it. An approved filtering mask should be worn when working on the brakes. Do not, under any circumstances, use petroleum-based solvents to clean brake parts. Use brake system cleaner only!

1   Remove the cap from the brake fluid reservoir.
2   Loosen the wheel lug nuts, raise the end of the vehicle you're working on and support it securely on jackstands. Block the wheels at the opposite end.
3   Remove the wheels. Work on one brake assembly at a time, using the assembled brake for reference if necessary.
4   Inspect the brake disc carefully as outlined in Section 5. If machining is necessary, follow the information in that Section to remove the disc, at which time the pads can be removed as well.
5   Push the piston back into its bore to provide room for the new brake pads. A C-clamp can be used to accomplish this (see illustration). As the piston is depressed to the bottom of the caliper bore, the fluid in the master cylinder will rise. Make sure that it doesn't overflow. If necessary, siphon off some of the fluid.
6   Follow the accompanying photos (illustrations 3.6a through 3.6k), for the actual pad replacement procedure. Be sure to stay in order and read the caption under each illustration.
7   After the job has been completed, firmly depress the brake pedal a few times to bring the pads into contact with the disc. Check the level of the brake fluid, adding some if necessary. Check the operation of the brakes carefully before placing the vehicle into normal service.

3.5 Before removing the caliper, slowly compress the piston in the caliper bore using a large C-clamp between the outer brake pad and the back of the caliper

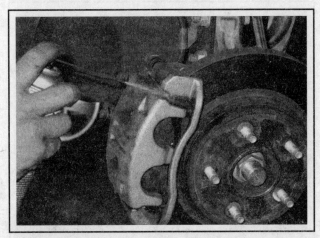

3.6a Always wash the brake assembly with brake cleaner before disassembling anything

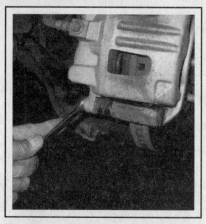

3.6b Remove the lower caliper bolt
- to detach the caliper completely,
remove both caliper bolts but don't
let the caliper hang by the brake hose

3.6c Swing the caliper up and secure
it with a piece of wire; don't allow it
to hang by the hose

3.6d Remove the inner brake pad . . .

3.6e . . . and the outer pad

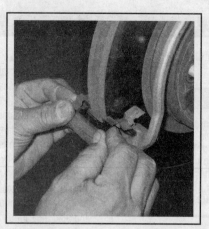

3.6f Remove the support plates;
make sure they're not worn and are a
tight fit. If necessary, replace them

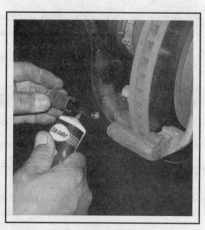

3.6g Lubricate the sliding pins
with high temperature grease after
cleaning them. Replace any damaged
rubber boots

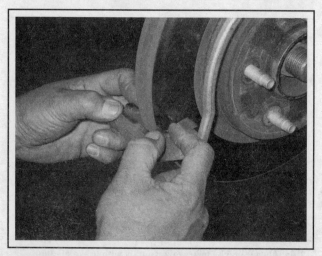

3.6h Replace the cleaned support plates

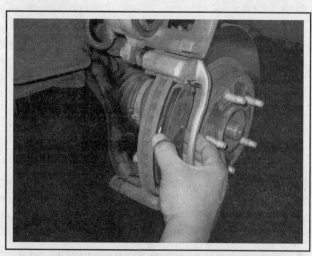

3.6i Install the new outer pad . . .

3.6j . . . and the new inner pad

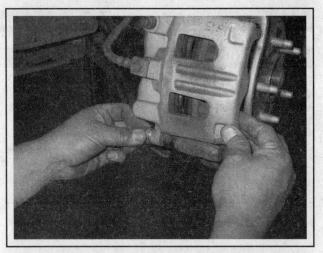

3.6k Install the sliding pins, then swing the caliper into place, replace the bolt and tighten both bolts to the torque listed in this Chapter's Specifications. If you have difficulty sliding the caliper assembly over the disc, push the piston farther into the bore using the C-clamp

4 Disc brake caliper - removal and installation

※※ WARNING:

Dust created by the brake system is harmful to your health. Never blow it out with compressed air and don't inhale any of it. An approved filtering mask should be worn when working on the brakes. Do not, under any circumstances, use petroleum-based solvents to clean brake parts. Use brake system cleaner only.

➡Note: If replacement is indicated (usually because of fluid leakage), it is recommended that the calipers be replaced, not overhauled. New and factory-rebuilt units are available, which makes this job quite easy. Always replace the calipers in pairs - never replace just one of them.

REMOVAL

▶ Refer to illustration 4.2

1 Loosen - but don't remove - the lug nuts on the front wheels. Raise the front of the vehicle and place it securely on jackstands. Remove the front wheels.

2 Disconnect the brake line from the caliper and plug it to keep contaminants out of the brake system and to prevent losing any more brake fluid than is necessary.

➡Note: If you're simply removing the caliper for access to other components, don't disconnect the hose.

3 Remove the caliper guide pin bolts.
4 Detach the caliper from its mounting bracket.

INSTALLATION

5 Install the caliper by reversing the removal procedure. Remember to replace the copper sealing washers on each side of the brake line fitting with new ones. Tighten the caliper guide pin bolts and the brake line banjo fitting bolt to the torque listed in this Chapter's Specifications.

6 Bleed the brake system (see Section 10).

7 Install the wheels and lug nuts and lower the vehicle. Tighten the wheel lug nuts to the torque listed in the Chapter 1 Specifications.

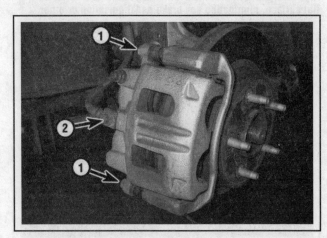

4.2 Brake caliper details:

1 Brake caliper mounting bolts
2 Brake line banjo fitting bolt

5 Brake disc - inspection, removal and installation

※※ WARNING:

The dust created by the brake system is harmful to your health. Never blow it out with compressed air and don't inhale any of it. An approved filtering mask should be worn when working on the brakes. Do not, under any circumstances, use petroleum-based solvents to clean brake parts. Use brake system cleaner only!

INSPECTION

▶ Refer to illustrations 5.3, 5.4, 5.5a, 5.5b, 5.6a and 5.6b

1   Loosen the wheel lug nuts, raise the vehicle and support it securely on jackstands. Remove the wheel and install the lug nuts to hold the disc in place against the hub flange.

➡**Note: If the lug nuts don't contact the disc when screwed on all the way, install washers under them.**

2   Remove the brake caliper (see Section 4). It isn't necessary to disconnect the brake hose. Suspend the caliper/bracket out of the way with a piece of wire.

3   Remove the two caliper mounting bracket-to-steering knuckle fasteners (see illustration) and remove the bracket.

4   Visually inspect the disc surface for score marks and other damage. Light scratches and shallow grooves are normal after use and may not always be detrimental to brake operation, but deep scoring requires disc refinishing by an automotive machine shop. Be sure to check both sides of the disc (see illustration). If pulsating has been noticed during application of the brakes, suspect disc runout.

5   To check disc runout, install the lug nuts to secure the disc to the hub, using washers if necessary. Place a dial indicator at a point about 1/2-inch from the outer edge of the disc (see illustration). Set the indicator to zero and turn the disc. The indicator reading should not exceed the specified allowable runout limit. If it does, the disc should be refinished by an automotive machine shop.

➡**Note: Some professionals recommend resurfacing the discs when replacing brake pads regardless of the dial indicator reading, as this will impart a smooth finish and ensure a perfectly flat surface, eliminating any brake pedal pulsation or other** undesirable symptoms. At the very least, if you elect not to have the discs resurfaced, remove the glaze from the surface with emery cloth or sandpaper, using a swirling motion (see illustration).

6   It's absolutely critical that the disc not be machined to a thickness under the specified minimum thickness. The minimum (or discard) thickness is cast or stamped into the disc. The disc thickness can be checked with a micrometer (see illustrations).

REMOVAL

7   Mark the disc in relation to the hub so that it can be installed in its original position on the hub, then remove the disc. If the disc has never been removed, there may be wave washers on the wheel studs securing it to the hub flange. Simply cut them off and discard them. If the disc is stuck to the hub, use a mallet to knock it loose. Penetrating oil applied around the disc's hub will also help (but don't let any oil get onto the disc friction surface; clean the disc with brake cleaner after you're done).

INSTALLATION

8   Clean the inner opening in the disc, and the area of the hub on which it seats. Remove any rust with fine emery paper before reinstalling the disc.

9   Place the disc in position over the threaded studs, aligning the mark made in Step 7.

10   Install the caliper mounting bracket and caliper, tightening the bolts to the torque values listed in this Chapter's Specifications.

➡**Note: The caliper mounting bracket bolts are of a special self-locking design; do not attempt to clean the threaded holes with a tap, or the threads of the bolt with a die.**

11   Install the wheel and lug nuts, then lower the vehicle to the ground. Tighten the lug nuts to the torque listed in the Chapter 1 Specifications. Depress the brake pedal a few times to bring the brake pads into contact with the disc. Bleeding won't be necessary unless the brake hose was disconnected from the caliper. Check the operation of the brakes carefully before driving the vehicle.

5.3 Brake caliper bracket mounting bolts - when the bracket is removed, the disc can slide off

5.4 The brake pads on this vehicle were obviously neglected, as they wore down completely and cut deep grooves into the disc - wear this severe means the disc must be replaced

5.5a use a dial indicator to check disc runout; if the reading exceeds the limit, the disc must be machined or replaced

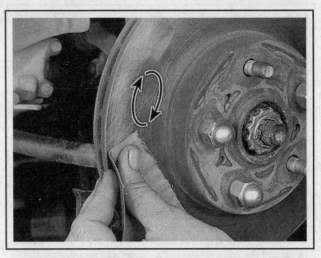

5.5b Using a swirling motion, remove the glaze from the disc surface with sandpaper or emery cloth

5.6a The minimum wear dimension is cast into the rear of the disc

5.6b Use a micrometer or dial calipers to measure disc thickness

6 Drum brake shoes - replacement

▶ Refer to illustrations 6.4a through 6.4w

✳✳ WARNING:

Drum brake shoes must be replaced on both wheels at the same time - never replace the shoes on only one wheel. Also, the dust created by the brake system is harmful to your health. Never blow it out with compressed air and don't inhale any of it. An approved filtering mask should be worn when working on the brakes. Do not, under any circumstances, use petroleum-based solvents to clean brake parts. Use brake system cleaner only!

1 Loosen the wheel lug nuts, raise the rear of the vehicle and support it securely on jackstands. Block the front wheels to keep the vehicle from rolling.

2 Release the parking brake.

3 Remove the wheel.

➡Note: All four rear brake shoes must be replaced at the same time, but to avoid mixing up parts, work on only one brake assembly at a time.

6.4a If the brake drum has never been removed, you'll have to pull off the drum retainer clip - it can be discarded

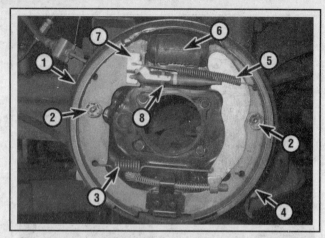

6.4b Rear brake shoe details

1	Leading shoe	5	Upper return spring
2	Shoe retainer and spring	6	Wheel cylinder
3	Lower return spring	7	Adjuster lever
4	Trailing shoe	8	Star-wheel assembly

6.4c Before removing anything, clean the brake assembly with brake cleaner and allow it to drip dry into a pan - DO NOT USE COMPRESSED AIR TO BLOW BRAKE DUST FROM PARTS!

6.4d Unhook the lower spring and remove it

6.4e The upper spring can now be removed from the adjuster lever - note how it engages

4   Follow the accompanying illustrations for the brake shoe replacement procedure (see illustrations 6.4a through 6.4w). Be sure to stay in order and read the caption under each illustration.

➡Note: If the brake drum cannot be easily removed, make sure the parking brake is completely released. If the drum still cannot be pulled off, the brake shoes will have to be retracted. This is done by first removing the plug from the backing plate. With the plug removed, push the lever off the adjuster star wheel with a narrow screwdriver while turning the adjuster wheel with another screwdriver, moving the shoes away from the drum (see illustration 6.4w). The drum should now come off.

5   Before reinstalling the drum, it should be checked for cracks, score marks, deep scratches and hard spots, which will appear as small discolored areas. If the hard spots cannot be removed with fine emery cloth or if any of the other conditions listed above exist, the drum must be taken to an automotive machine shop to have it resurfaced.

➡Note: Professionals recommend resurfacing the drums each time a brake job is done. Resurfacing will eliminate the possi-

bility of out-of-round drums. If the drums are worn so much that they can't be resurfaced without exceeding the maximum allowable diameter (stamped into the drum), then new drums will be required. At the very least, if you elect not to have the drums resurfaced, remove the glaze from the surface with emery cloth using a swirling motion.

6   Install the brake drum on the axle flange. Pump the brake pedal a couple of times, then turn the drum and listen for the sound of the shoes rubbing. If they are, turn the adjuster star wheel until the shoes stop rubbing.

7   Install the wheel and lug nuts, then lower the vehicle. Tighten the lug nuts to the torque listed in the Chapter 1 Specifications.

8   Make a number of forward and reverse stops and operate the parking brake to adjust the brakes until satisfactory pedal action is obtained.

9   Check the operation of the brakes carefully before driving the vehicle.

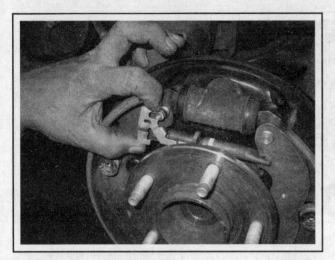

6.4f Remove the adjuster lever

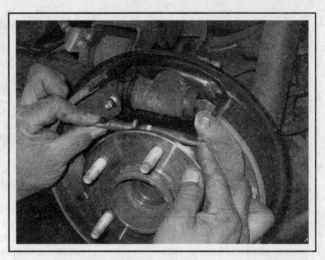

6.4g Remove the star-wheel assembly

6.4h Depress the front shoe retainer and turn it to remove it

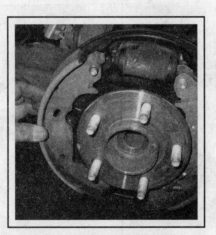

6.4i Remove the front brake shoe

6.4j Remove the rear shoe retainer and allow the shoe to come free

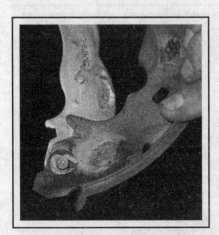

6.4k Pry open the clip to disconnect the parking brake lever from the rear shoe

6.4l Lubricate the backing plate contact points after thoroughly cleaning it

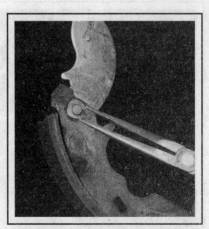

6.4m Crimp the clip to attach the new rear shoe to the parking brake lever

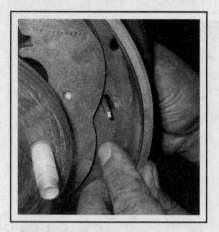

6.4n Install the pin through the backing plate and the rear shoe

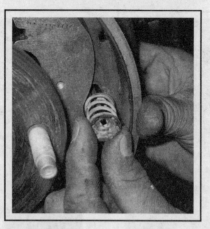

6.4o Install the spring and the retainer to the pin

6.4p Use the special tool to compress the spring and engage the retainer

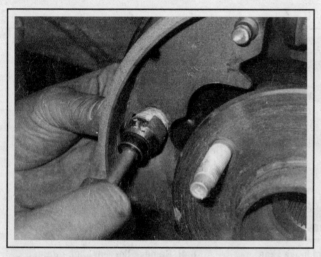

6.4q Perform the same procedure on the front brake shoe

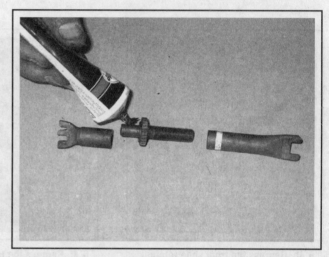

6.4r Clean the star-wheel adjuster and lubricate it lightly

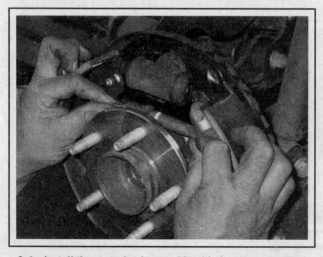

6.4s Install the star-wheel assembly with the star to the front

6.4t Install the adjuster lever

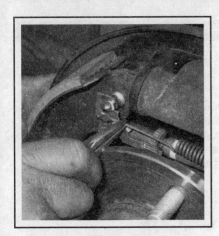

6.4u Install the upper spring, hooking it into the adjuster

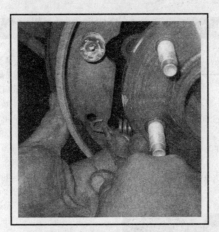

6.4v Install the lower spring

6.4w Adjust the star-wheel to give a very light drag when the brake drum is turned

7 Wheel cylinder - removal and installation

➡Note: If replacement is indicated (usually because of fluid leakage or sticky operation), it is recommended that the wheel cylinders be replaced, not overhauled. Always replace the wheel cylinders in pairs - never replace just one of them.

REMOVAL

♦ Refer to illustration 7.5

1   Block the front wheels to keep the vehicle from rolling. Loosen the rear wheel lug nuts, raise the rear of the vehicle and support it securely on jackstands.

2   Remove the wheel.

3   Remove the brake shoes (see Section 6).

4   Remove all dirt and foreign material from around the wheel cylinder.

5   At the rear of the backing plate, unscrew the brake line fitting, using a flare-nut wrench, if available (see illustration). Don't pull the brake line away from the wheel cylinder (it could become kinked).

6   Remove the wheel cylinder mounting bolts and detach the wheel cylinder from the backing plate.

INSTALLATION

7   Put the wheel cylinder in position, then connect the brake line fitting finger tight. Install the wheel cylinder mounting bolts and tighten them to the torque listed in this Chapter's Specifications. Tighten the brake line fitting securely.

8   Install the brake shoes (see Section 6).

9   Install the brake drum on the hub flange, then install the wheel and lug nuts.

10 Bleed the brake system as outlined in Section 10.

11 Lower the vehicle to the ground, then tighten the lug nuts to the torque listed in the Chapter 1 Specifications. Check the operation of the brakes carefully before driving the vehicle in traffic.

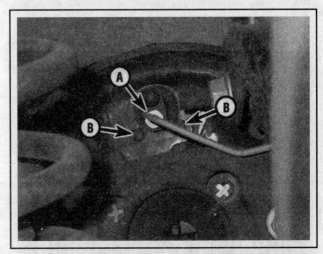

7.5 Brake line fitting (A) and wheel cylinder bolts (B)

8 Master cylinder - removal and installation

REMOVAL

▶ **Refer to illustration 8.6**

1   The master cylinder is located in the engine compartment, mounted to the power brake booster.

2   Disconnect the cable from the negative terminal of the battery (see Chapter 5, Section 1).

3   Remove as much fluid as you can from the reservoir with a syringe, such as an old turkey baster.

❋❋ WARNING 1:

If a baster is used, never again use it for the preparation of food.

❋❋ WARNING 2:

Don't depress the brake pedal until the reservoir has been refilled, otherwise air may be introduced into the brake hydraulic system.

4   On later models with manual transaxles, disconnect the clutch fluid hose from the brake master cylinder reservoir. Plug the line or wrap it with a plastic bag.

❋❋ CAUTION:

Brake fluid will damage paint. Cover all pained surfaces around the work area and be careful not to spill fluid during this procedure.

5   Place rags under the fluid fittings and prepare caps or plastic bags to cover the ends of the lines once they are disconnected. Loosen the fittings at the ends of the brake lines where they enter the master cylinder. To prevent rounding off the corners on these nuts, the use of a flare-nut wrench, which wraps around the nut, is preferred. Pull the brake lines slightly away from the master cylinder and plug the ends to prevent contamination.

6   Disconnect the electrical connector at the brake fluid level switch on the master cylinder reservoir (you must pull back the locking tab of the connector before removing it), then remove the nuts attaching the master cylinder to the power booster (see illustration). Pull the master cylinder off the studs and out of the engine compartment. Again, be careful not to spill the fluid as this is done.

7   If a new master cylinder is being installed, drive out the two retaining pins that hold the reservoir to the master cylinder body. Transfer the reservoir to the new master cylinder.

➡**Note: Be sure to install new seals when transferring the reservoir. If the same master cylinder is to be installed, check the condition of the master cylinder-to-booster seal for damage or hardness, replacing it if necessary.**

INSTALLATION

▶ **Refer to illustration 8.9**

8   Bench bleed the new master cylinder before installing it. Mount the master cylinder in a vise, with the jaws of the vise clamping on the mounting flange.

9   Attach a pair of master cylinder bleeder tubes to the outlet ports of the master cylinder (see illustration).

10 Fill the reservoir with brake fluid of the recommended type (see Chapter 1).

11 Slowly push the pistons into the master cylinder (a large Phillips screwdriver can be used for this) - air will be expelled from the pressure chambers and into the reservoir. Because the tubes are submerged in fluid, air can't be drawn back into the master cylinder when you release the pistons.

12 Repeat the procedure until no more air bubbles are present.

13 Remove the bleed tubes, one at a time, and install plugs in the open ports to prevent fluid leakage and air from entering. Install the reservoir cap.

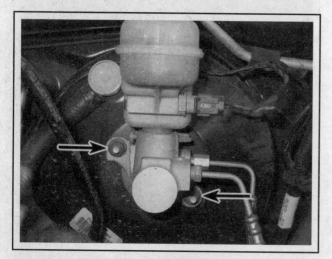

8.6 Brake master cylinder mounting nuts

8.9 The best way to bleed air from the master cylinder before installing it is with a pair of bleeder tubes that direct fluid into the reservoir during bleeding (typical unit shown)

14 Install the master cylinder over the studs on the power brake booster and tighten the attaching nuts only finger tight at this time.

➡Note: Be sure to install a new O-ring onto the sleeve of the master cylinder.

15 Thread the brake line fittings into the master cylinder by hand until you know they are started straight. Since the master cylinder is still a bit loose, it can be moved slightly in order for the fittings to thread in easily. Do not strip the threads as the fittings are tightened.

16 Tighten the mounting nuts to the torque listed in this Chapter's Specifications, then tighten the brake line fittings securely.

17 Connect the brake fluid switch electrical connector.

18 On models with manual transaxles, connect the fluid hose from the clutch master cylinder.

19 Fill the master cylinder reservoir with fluid. To bleed the cylinder on the vehicle, have an assistant depress the brake pedal and hold the pedal to the floor. Loosen the fitting to allow air and fluid to escape, then close the fitting. Repeat this procedure on both fittings until the fluid is clear of air bubbles.

❋❋ CAUTION:

Have plenty of rags on hand to catch the fluid - brake fluid will ruin painted surfaces. After the bleeding procedure is com- pleted, rinse the area under the master cylinder with clean water.

Bleed the remainder of the brake system as described in Section 10.

➡Note: On manual transaxle models without a separate clutch fluid reservoir, check the operation of the clutch. If the reservoir hose was plugged after it was disconnected, and an exces- sive amount of fluid was not lost, the clutch hydraulic system shouldn't require bleeding. If, however, the clutch does not dis- engage properly, bleed the clutch hydraulic system as described in Chapter 8.

20 Test the operation of the brake system carefully before placing the vehicle into normal service.

❋❋ WARNING:

Do not operate the vehicle if you are in doubt about the effec- tiveness of the brake system. It is possible for air to become trapped in the anti-lock brake system hydraulic control unit, so, if the pedal continues to feel spongy after repeated bleedings or the BRAKE or ANTI-LOCK light stays on, have the vehicle towed to a dealer service department or other qualified shop to be bled with the aid of a scan tool.

9   Brake hoses and lines - inspection and replacement

1   About every six months, with the vehicle raised and placed securely on jackstands, the flexible hoses which connect the steel brake lines with the front and rear brake assemblies should be inspected for cracks, chafing of the outer cover, leaks, blisters and other dam- age. These are important and vulnerable parts of the brake system and inspection should be complete. A light and mirror will be needed for a thorough check. If a hose exhibits any of the above defects, replace it with a new one.

FLEXIBLE HOSES

⬥ Refer to illustrations 9.3a, 9.3b and 9.3c

2   Clean all dirt away from the ends of the hose.

3   To disconnect a brake hose from the brake line, unscrew the metal tube nut with a flare nut wrench, then remove the U-clip from the female fitting at the bracket and remove the hose from the bracket (see illustrations).

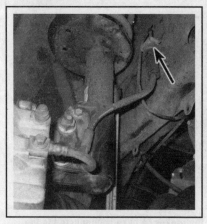

9.3a Front brake hose connection to the steel brake tubing

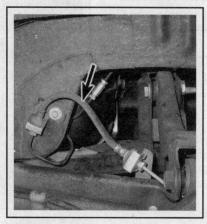

9.3b Rear brake hose

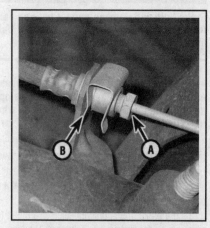

9.3c The steel bracket will hold the hose while the fitting nut (A) is loosened; to remove the hose from the bracket, remove the clip (B)

4   Disconnect the hose from the caliper, discarding the sealing washers on either side of the fitting.

5   Using new sealing washers, attach the new brake hose to the caliper or wheel cylinder.

6   To reattach a brake hose to the metal line, insert the end of the hose through the frame bracket, make sure the hose isn't twisted, then attach the metal line by tightening the tube nut fitting securely. Install the U-clip at the frame bracket.

7   Carefully check to make sure the suspension or steering components don't make contact with the hose. Have an assistant push down on the vehicle and also turn the steering wheel lock-to-lock during inspection.

8   Bleed the brake system (see Section 10).

METAL BRAKE LINES

9   When replacing brake lines, be sure to use the correct parts. Don't use copper tubing for any brake system components. Purchase steel brake lines from a dealer parts department or auto parts store.

10 Prefabricated brake line, with the tube ends already flared and fittings installed, is available at auto parts stores and dealer parts departments. These lines can be bent to the proper shapes using a tubing bender.

11 When installing the new line, make sure it's well supported in the brackets and has plenty of clearance between moving or hot components.

12 After installation, check the master cylinder fluid level and add fluid as necessary. Bleed the brake system as outlined in Section 10 and test the brakes carefully before placing the vehicle into normal operation.

10 Brake hydraulic system - bleeding

▶ Refer to illustration 10.8

✳✳ WARNING 1:

If air has found its way into the hydraulic control unit, the system must be bled with the use of a scan tool. If the brake pedal feels spongy even after bleeding the brakes, or the ABS light on the instrument panel does not go off, or if you have any doubts whatsoever about the effectiveness of the brake system, have the vehicle towed to a dealer service department or other repair shop equipped with the necessary tools for bleeding the system.

✳✳ WARNING 2:

Wear eye protection when bleeding the brake system. If the fluid comes in contact with your eyes, immediately rinse them with water and seek medical attention.

✳✳ CAUTION:

Brake fluid will damage paint. Cover all pained surfaces around the work area and be careful not to spill fluid during this procedure.

➡Note: Bleeding the brake system is necessary to remove any air that's trapped in the system when it's opened during removal and installation of a hose, line, caliper, wheel cylinder or master cylinder.

1   It will probably be necessary to bleed the system at all four brakes if air has entered the system due to a low fluid level, or if the brake lines have been disconnected at the master cylinder.

2   If a brake line was disconnected only at a wheel, then only that caliper or wheel cylinder must be bled.

3   If a brake line is disconnected at a fitting located between the master cylinder and any of the brakes, that part of the system served by the disconnected line must be bled, beginning with the fitting closest to the master cylinder and then working downstream, bleeding each fitting of each component as described in Step 19 of Section 8. This includes the proportioning valve or the ABS modulator assembly.

4   Remove any residual vacuum (or hydraulic pressure) from the brake power booster by applying the brake several times with the engine off.

5   Remove the master cylinder reservoir cap and fill the reservoir with brake fluid. Reinstall the cap.

➡Note: Check the fluid level often during the bleeding operation and add fluid as necessary to prevent the fluid level from falling low enough to allow air bubbles into the master cylinder.

6   Have an assistant on hand, as well as a supply of new brake fluid, an empty clear plastic container, a length of plastic, rubber or vinyl tubing to fit over the bleeder valve and a wrench to open and close the bleeder valve.

7   Working at the right rear wheel, loosen the bleeder screw slightly, then tighten it to a point where it's snug but can still be loosened quickly and easily.

8   Place one end of the tubing over the bleeder screw fitting and submerge the other end in brake fluid in the container (see illustration).

10.8 When bleeding the brakes, a hose is connected to the bleed screw at the caliper or wheel cylinder and submerged in brake fluid - air will be seen as bubbles in the tube and container (all air must be expelled before moving to the next wheel)

9   Have your assistant slowly depress the brake pedal and hold it in the depressed position.

10   While the pedal is held depressed, open the bleeder screw just enough to allow a flow of fluid to leave the valve. Watch for air bubbles to exit the submerged end of the tube. When the fluid flow slows after a couple of seconds, tighten the screw and have your assistant release the pedal.

11   Repeat Steps 9 and 10 until no more air is seen leaving the tube, then tighten the bleeder screw and proceed to the left front wheel, the left rear wheel and the right front wheel, in that order, and perform the same procedure. Be sure to check the fluid in the master cylinder reservoir frequently.

12   Never use old brake fluid. It contains moisture that can boil, rendering the brake system inoperative.

13   Refill the master cylinder with fluid at the end of the operation.

14   Check the operation of the brakes. The pedal should feel solid when depressed, with no sponginess. If necessary, repeat the entire process.

※※ WARNING:

Do not operate the vehicle if you are in doubt about the effectiveness of the brake system. It is possible for air to become trapped in the anti-lock brake system hydraulic control unit, so, if the pedal continues to feel spongy after repeated bleedings or the BRAKE or ANTI-LOCK light stays on, have the vehicle towed to a dealer service department or other qualified shop to be bled with the aid of a scan tool.

11   Power brake booster - removal and installation

※※ WARNING:

The ABS hydraulic control unit, if equipped, must be moved aside in order to remove the power brake booster. It's important to note that if the ABS hydraulic control unit is removed, and the hydraulic lines are detached from it (opening the circuit), then air can be introduced into the system. If air has found its way into the hydraulic control unit, the system must be bled with the use of a specialized scan tool. If the brake pedal feels "spongy" even after bleeding the brakes, or the ABS light or BRAKE warning light on the instrument panel stays on, or if you have any doubts whatsoever about the effectiveness of the brake system, have the vehicle towed to a dealer service department or other qualified repair shop equipped with this tool.

➡Note: The power brake booster is not serviceable. If it has failed, replace it with a new or rebuilt unit.

OPERATING CHECK

1   Depress the brake pedal several times with the engine off and make sure that there is no change in the pedal reserve distance.

2   Depress the pedal and start the engine. If the pedal goes down slightly, operation is normal.

AIRTIGHTNESS CHECK

3   Start the engine and turn it off after one or two minutes. Depress the brake pedal several times slowly. If the pedal goes down farther the first time but gradually rises after the second or third depression, the booster is airtight.

4   Depress the brake pedal while the engine is running, then stop the engine with the pedal depressed. If there is no change in the pedal reserve travel after holding the pedal for 30 seconds, the booster is airtight.

REMOVAL AND INSTALLATION

※※ CAUTION:

Brake fluid will damage paint. Cover all pained surfaces around the work area and be careful not to spill fluid during this procedure.

5   The power brake booster is not rebuildable. If a problem develops, it must be replaced with a new one.

6   Disconnect the cable from the negative terminal of the battery (see Chapter 5, Section 1).

7   Disconnect the vacuum hose check valve where it attaches to the power brake booster.

8   Unbolt the underhood electrical center and set it aside.

9   Refer to Chapter 5 and remove the battery.

10   Refer to Chapter 5, Section 3 and remove the battery tray assembly.

11   When the engine is completely cool, disconnect the hose from the coolant reservoir.

※※ WARNING:

The engine must be completely cool before disconnecting the hose.

12   Disconnect the sensor wiring harness from the master cylinder.

13   Remove the master cylinder mounting nuts, carefully pull it from its studs and position it aside. Don't disconnect the brake lines.

14   Disconnect any wiring harnesses from the booster.

15   On automatic transaxle-equipped models, move the transaxle control module out of the way.

11.23 This clip secures the brake booster pushrod to the pedal

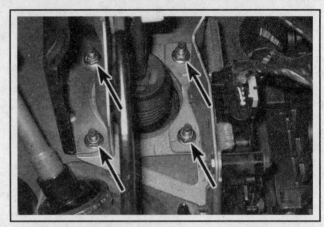

11.25 Brake booster mounting nuts

ABS-equipped models

16 Clean the areas around the ABS module fittings.

17 Disconnect the wiring from the module.

18 Put rags under the module to catch any spilled brake fluid.

19 Disconnect all of the hydraulic lines from the module. Make notes of their locations to help in assembly. Seal all openings to prevent contamination.

20 Loosen the ABS modulator mounting nuts and pull the unit from its bracket.

21 Remove the mounting bracket.

All models

▶ **Refer to illustrations 11.23 and 11.25**

22 Remove the plastic cover from beneath the steering wheel. It's secured by screws and clips.

23 Working under the instrument panel, remove the clip from the brake booster pushrod (see illustration).

24 Remove the foam insulator from the brake pedal assembly.

25 Remove the four brake booster nuts (see illustration).

26 Pull the brake booster forward and toward the center of the engine compartment to remove it. Pull out the foam washer if it didn't come out with the booster.

27 Installation is the reverse of removal. Before installing the new booster, lubricate the pushrod pin on the brake pedal arm with multi-purpose grease. Connect the pushrod to the brake pedal and install the clip.

28 Bleed the brakes (see Section 10).

29 Test the operation of the brakes thoroughly before placing the vehicle into normal service. Refer to the **Warning** at the beginning of this Section.

12 Parking brake - adjustment

▶ **Refer to illustrations 12.4**

1 The parking brake lever, when properly adjusted, should travel three to five clicks. If it travels less than specified, there's a chance the parking brake might not be releasing completely and might be dragging on the drum or disc. If the lever can be pulled more than specified, the parking brake may not hold adequately on an incline, allowing the car to roll.

2 Block the front wheels, raise the rear of the vehicle and support it securely on jackstands. Remove the rear wheels and install a few lug nuts to keep the drums in position. Place the transaxle in Neutral.

3 Refer to Chapter 11 and remove the console covers for access to the parking brake handle assembly.

4 With the parking brake lever released fully, loosen the nut on the adjuster rod (see illustration).

5 With the vehicle in Neutral, the rear shoe-to-drum clearance should be adjusted for the minimum clearance without significant drag (see Section 6).

6 Release and apply the parking brakes several times, then raise the lever three clicks. One or both rear drums should not rotate except

with great difficulty. With the lever raised one more click, the rear drums should both be locked. If not, perform the rear drum and parking cable procedure again.

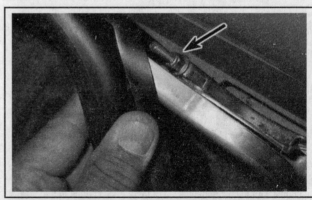

12.4 The parking brake can be adjusted by peeling back the rubber boot of the handle and turning this nut

13 Brake light switch - replacement

▶ **Refer to illustration 13.2**

1 The brake light switch is located at the top of the brake pedal bracket.

2 Disconnect the wiring connector(s) from the switch (see illustration).

3 Depress the brake pedal, then compress the switch's lock tabs. Rotate the switch counterclockwise while pulling and remove the switch.

4 To install the new switch, first make sure that the pedal is all the way at the top of its travel. Rotate the switch clockwise while inserting it into the mounting bracket, then connect the electrical connector(s). The switch should be fully seated against the pedal when the pedal is fully released.

5 Apply the brake pedal, release the pedal and verify that the brake lights go off when the pedal is released.

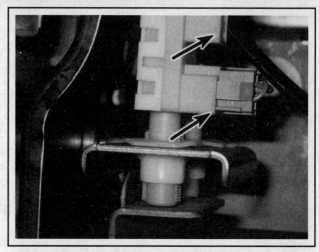

13.2 Disconnect the wiring connector(s) from the brake light switch, then turn it counterclockwise, press the lock tabs and pull the switch out

Specifications

General

Brake fluid type	See Chapter 1

Disc brakes

Brake pad minimum thickness	See Chapter 1
Disc lateral runout limit	0.002 inch (0.05 mm)
Disc minimum thickness	Cast into disc
Parallelism (thickness variation) limit	0.001 inch (0.025 mm)

Drum brakes

Maximum drum diameter	Cast into drum
Shoe lining minimum thickness	See Chapter 1

Torque specifications

	Ft-lbs (unless otherwise indicated)	Nm

➡**Note: One foot-pound (ft-lb) of torque is equivalent to 12 inch-pounds (in-lbs) of torque. Torque values below approximately 15 ft-lbs are expressed in inch-pounds, since most foot-pound torque wrenches are not accurate at these smaller values.**

	Ft-lbs	Nm
Brake hose banjo fitting bolt	32	43
Caliper guide pin bolts	32	43
Caliper mounting bracket bolts	136	184
Master cylinder mounting nuts	18	24
Power brake booster mounting nuts	18	24
Wheel cylinder mounting bolts	132 in-lbs	15
Wheel lug nuts	See Chapter 1	

Notes

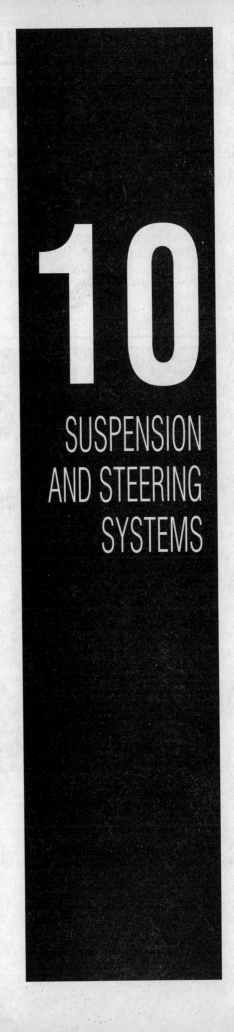

10

SUSPENSION AND STEERING SYSTEMS

Section

Reference to other Chapters

1 General information

▶ **Refer to illustrations 1.1 and 1.2**

The front suspension is a MacPherson strut design. The upper end of each strut is attached to the vehicle's body strut support. The lower ends of the struts are connected to the upper ends of the steering knuckles. The steering knuckles are attached to balljoints mounted on the outer ends of the suspension control arms (see illustration).

The rear suspension uses coil springs and shock absorbers (see illustration). Knuckles are used to mount the hubs and brake assemblies; the knuckles are located by four suspension arms.

The electrically power-assisted rack-and-pinion steering gear, which is located behind the engine/transaxle assembly, is mounted on the engine cradle. The steering gear actuates the tie-rods, which are attached to the steering knuckles. The steering column is designed to collapse in the event of an accident.

Frequently, when working on the suspension or steering system components, you may come across fasteners that seem impossible to loosen. These fasteners on the underside of the vehicle are continually subjected to water, road grime, mud, etc., and can become rusted or frozen, making them extremely difficult to remove. In order to unscrew these stubborn fasteners without damaging them (or other components), be sure to use lots of penetrating oil and allow it to soak in for a while. Using a wire brush to clean exposed threads will also ease removal of the nut or bolt and prevent damage to the threads. Sometimes a sharp

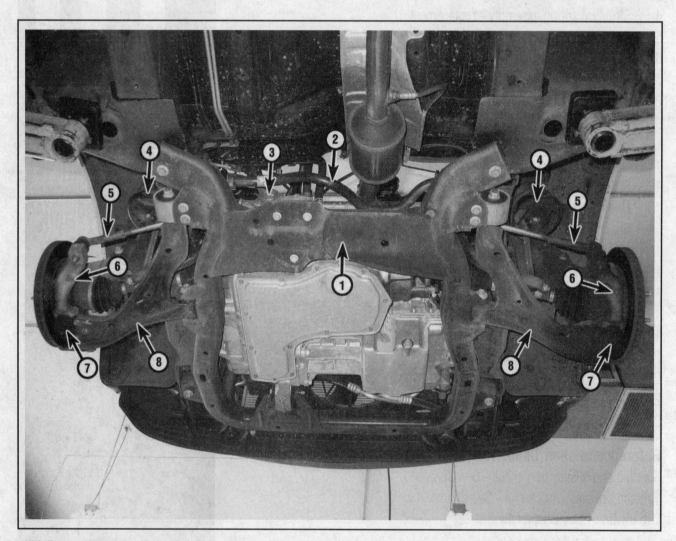

1.1 Front suspension and steering components

1	Subframe (cradle)	4	Strut/coil spring assembly	7	Balljoint
2	Stabilizer bar	5	Tie-rod end	8	Control arm
3	Steering gear	6	Steering knuckle		

blow with a hammer and punch will break the bond between nut and bolt threads, but care must be taken to prevent the punch from slipping off the fastener and ruining the threads. Heating the stuck fastener and surrounding area with a torch sometimes helps too, but isn't recommended because of the obvious dangers associated with fire. Long breaker bars and extension, or cheater, pipes will increase leverage, but never use an extension pipe on a ratchet - the ratcheting mechanism could be damaged. Sometimes tightening the nut or bolt first will help to break it loose. Fasteners that require drastic measures to remove should always be replaced with new ones.

Since most of the procedures dealt with in this Chapter involve jacking up the vehicle and working underneath it, a good pair of jackstands will be needed. A hydraulic floor jack is the preferred type of jack to lift the vehicle, and it can also be used to support certain components during various operations.

1.2 Rear suspension components

1 Rear hub and knuckle	4 Stabilizer bar	7 Upper control arm
2 Coil spring	5 Trailing arm	8 Toe link
3 Shock absorber	6 Lower control arm	

2 Stabilizer bar and bushings (front) - removal and installation

◆ **Refer to illustrations 2.4 and 2.6**

1 Loosen the front wheel lug nuts, then raise the front of the vehicle and support it securely on jackstands.

2 Remove the front wheels.

3 On four-cylinder models, remove the front section of the exhaust pipe.

4 Disconnect the stabilizer bar links from the bar (see illustration). If the ballstud turns with the nut, hold the stud with a Torx or Allen wrench, as applicable.

5 Disconnect the left tie-rod end from the steering knuckle (see Section 18).

→ **Note: The manufacturer recommends that these nuts be replaced with new ones whenever they are removed.**

6 Detach both stabilizer bar bushing retainers from the subframe (see illustration).

7 Slide the stabilizer bar out the left wheel well.

8 While the stabilizer bar is detached, slide off the retainer bush-ings and inspect them. If they're cracked, worn or deteriorated, replace them.

9 Clean the bushing area of the stabilizer bar with a stiff wire brush to remove any rust or dirt.

10 Lubricate the inside and outside of the new bushings with vegetable oil (used in cooking) to simplify reassembly.

❋❋ CAUTION:

Don't use petroleum or mineral-based lubricants or brake fluid - they will lead to deterioration of the bushings.

11 Install the links, tightening the link nuts to the torque listed in this Chapter's Specifications.

12 Install the retainers and bolts, tightening the bolts to the torque listed in this Chapter's Specifications.

13 Install the wheel and lug nuts, then lower the vehicle. Tighten the lug nuts to the torque listed in the Chapter 1 Specifications.

2.4 To detach the stabilizer bar link from the bar, remove the lower nut; if you're removing the strut (or replacing the link), remove the upper nut

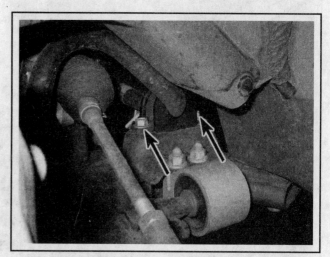

2.6 Bushing retainer bolts

3 Strut assembly (front) - removal, inspection and installation

REMOVAL

◆ **Refer to illustrations 3.4 and 3.5**

1 Loosen the wheel lug nuts, raise the vehicle and support it securely on jackstands. Remove the wheel. Support the control arm with a floor jack.

2 Unbolt the brake hose bracket from the strut.

3 Disconnect the upper end of the stabilizer bar link from the strut.

4 Mark the exact position of the strut to the steering knuckle (see illustration). Remove the strut-to-knuckle bolts and nuts.

→ **Note: The manufacturer recommends that the nuts and bolts be replaced with new ones when they are removed.**

5 Support the strut and spring assembly with one hand (or have an assistant hold it) and remove the three strut-to-shock tower fasteners (see illustration). Remove the strut assembly out from the fenderwell.

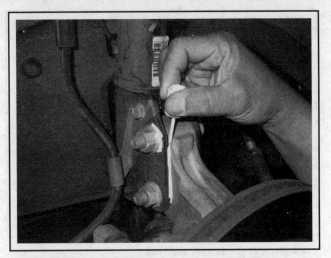

3.4 Mark the exact position of each strut on the steering knuckle before loosening the bolts

3.5 Strut upper mounting fasteners

INSPECTION

6   Check the strut body for leaking fluid, dents, cracks and other obvious damage that would warrant repair or replacement.

7   Check the coil spring for chips or cracks in the spring coating (this can cause premature spring failure due to corrosion). Inspect the spring seat for cuts, hardness and general deterioration.

8   If any undesirable conditions exist, proceed to the strut disassembly procedure (see Section 4).

INSTALLATION

9   Guide the strut assembly up into the fenderwell and insert the upper mounting studs through the holes in the shock tower. Once the studs protrude from the shock tower, install the nuts and bolt so the strut won't fall back through. This is most easily accomplished with the help of an assistant, as the strut is quite heavy and awkward.

10   Slide the steering knuckle into the strut flange and insert the two bolts. Install the nuts, match the position of the strut to the steering knuckle that was previously marked and tighten them to the torque listed in this Chapter's Specifications.

11   Reattach the brake hose bracket and the stabilizer bar link.

12   Install the wheel and lug nuts, then lower the vehicle and tighten the lug nuts to the torque listed in the Chapter 1 Specifications.

13   Tighten the three upper mounting nuts to the torque listed in this Chapter's Specifications.

14   It's a good idea to have the front wheel alignment checked and adjusted, if necessary, after this job has been performed.

---

4   Strut/coil spring assembly - replacement

1   If the struts or coil springs exhibit the telltale signs of wear (leaking fluid, loss of damping capability, chipped, sagging or cracked coil springs) explore all options before beginning any work. The strut/shock absorber assemblies are not serviceable and must be replaced if a problem develops. However, strut assemblies complete with springs may be available on an exchange basis, which eliminates much time and work. Whichever route you choose to take, check on the cost and availability of parts before disassembling your vehicle.

❊❊ WARNING:

Disassembling a strut is potentially dangerous and utmost attention must be directed to the job, or serious injury may result.

Use only a high-quality spring compressor and carefully follow the manufacturer's instructions furnished with the tool. After removing the coil spring from the strut assembly, set it aside in a safe, isolated area.

DISASSEMBLY

◆ Refer to illustrations 4.3, 4.4, 4.5, 4.6 and 4.7

2   Remove the strut and spring assembly (see Section 3). Mount the strut assembly in a vise. Line the vise jaws with wood or rags to prevent

4.3 Install the spring compressor in accordance with the tool manufacturer's instructions and compress the spring until all force is relieved from the upper spring seat

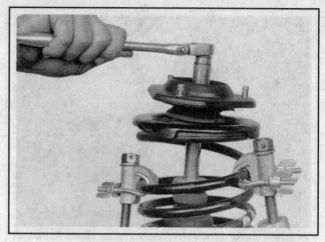

4.4 Remove the damper shaft nut

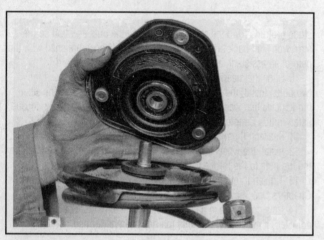

4.5 Lift the top mount assembly off the damper shaft; don't handle the plastic part - the bearing could fall apart (typical unit shown)

4.6 Remove the spring seat from the damper shaft (typical unit shown)

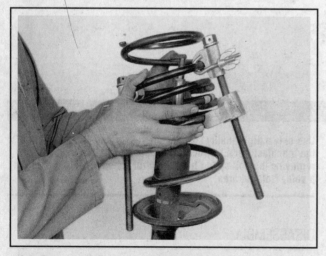

4.7 Remove the compressed spring assembly - keep the ends of the spring pointed away from your body

damage to the unit. Don't tighten the vise excessively.

3 Following the tool manufacturer's instructions, install the spring compressor (which can be obtained at most auto parts stores or equipment yards on a daily rental basis) on the spring and compress it sufficiently to relieve all force from the upper spring seat (see illustration). This can be verified by wiggling the spring.

4 Loosen the damper shaft nut (see illustration).

5 Remove the nut and suspension support (see illustration). Inspect the bearing in the suspension support for smooth operation. If it doesn't turn smoothly, replace the suspension support. Check the rubber portion of the suspension support for cracking and general deterioration. If there is any separation of the rubber, replace it.

6 Remove the top mount assembly from the damper shaft (see illustration). Remove the upper spring seat. Check the spring seat for cracking; replace it if necessary.

7 Carefully lift the compressed spring from the assembly (see illustration) and set it in a safe place.

✳✳ WARNING:

Never place your head near the end of the spring!

8   Remove the dust boot. Slide the rubber bumper off the damper shaft.

9   Check the lower insulator for wear, cracking and hardness and replace it if necessary.

REASSEMBLY

▶ **Refer to illustration 4.11**

10 If the lower insulator is being replaced, set it into position with the dropped portion seated in the lowest part of the seat. Replace the dust boot. Extend the damper rod to its full length and install the rubber bumper.

➡**Note: The spring end locating tab must be 180-degrees from the knuckle mounting bracket.**

11 Carefully place the coil spring onto the lower insulator, with the end of the spring resting in the lowest part of the insulator and against the rotation tab (see illustration).

12 Install the upper spring seat onto the shaft. Align its flat with the knuckle mounting bracket.

13 Install the top mount with its flat 180 degrees from the flat on the upper spring seat. This will align it with the rotation tab of the upper spring seat.

4.11 When installing the spring, make sure the end fits against the locating tab (typical unit shown)

14 Install the damper nut.

15 Remove the spring compressor tool. Tighten the shaft nut to the torque listed in this Chapter's Specifications.

---

5   Control arm (front) - removal, inspection and installation

REMOVAL

▶ **Refer to illustration 5.3**

1   Loosen the wheel lug nuts on the side to be dismantled, raise the front of the vehicle, support it securely on jackstands and remove the wheel.

2   Remove the cotter pin, loosen the balljoint nut and separate the balljoint from the steering knuckle before removing the nut (see Section 6). If possible, use a screw-type balljoint separator rather than a wedge or "pickle fork" tool to avoid damaging the rubber boot.

3   Remove the bolts that attach the rear of the control arm to the engine cradle (see illustration).

4   Remove the bolt and nut that attach the front of the control arm to the engine cradle.

5   Remove the control arm.

INSPECTION AND BUSHING REPLACEMENT

6   Make sure the control arm is straight. If it's bent, replace it. Do not attempt to straighten a bent control arm.

7   Inspect the bushings. If they're cracked, torn or worn, replace them.

8   To replace the rear bushing, remove the nut and slide the bushing off its post. When installing the new bushing, tighten the nut to the torque listed in this Chapter's Specifications.

9   If the front pivot bushing is in need of replacement, take the control arm to an automotive machine shop to have the old bushing pressed out and the new bushing pressed in.

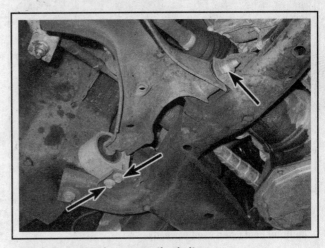

5.3 Lower control arm mounting bolts

INSTALLATION

10 Installation is the reverse of removal. Be sure to tighten all fasteners to the torque listed in this Chapter's Specifications.

➡**Note 1: The manufacturer recommends that the control arm mounting bolts be replaced with new ones when they are removed.**

➡**Note 2: Before tightening the control arm front pivot bolt, raise the outer end of the control arm with a floor jack to simulate normal ride height.**

➡**Note 3: Be sure to use a new cotter pin on the balljoint stud nut. If necessary, tighten the balljoint nut a little more to align the hole in the ballstud with the slots in the nut - don't loosen the nut to achieve this alignment.**

11 Install the wheel and lug nuts, lower the vehicle and tighten the lug nuts to the torque listed in the Chapter 1 Specifications.

12 It's a good idea to have the front wheel alignment checked, and if necessary, adjusted after this job has been performed.

6   Balljoints - replacement

1 Loosen the wheel lug nuts, raise the vehicle and support it securely on jackstands. Remove the wheel.

➡**Note: If you're going to remove the balljoint using a puller (as described in Steps 4 through 6), loosen the driveaxle/hub nut before raising the vehicle (see Chapter 8).**

PICKLEFORK/WEDGE METHOD

❋❋ CAUTION:

The following procedure is the quickest way to detach a balljoint from the steering knuckle, but it will very likely damage the balljoint boot. If you want to save the boot, proceed to Step 4.

2 Remove the cotter pin from the balljoint stud and loosen the nut a few turns (but don't remove it yet).

3 Separate the balljoint from the steering knuckle by hammering in a picklefork-type balljoint wedge. Remove the balljoint stud nut.

PULLER METHOD

▶ **Refer to illustrations 6.5a and 6.5b**

4 Remove the cotter pin from the balljoint stud and loosen the nut a few turns (but don't remove it yet).

5 Install a special puller and pop the balljoint stud from the steering knuckle (see illustration). Because of driveaxle interference, a special puller is needed that works from below the balljoint. If the special puller isn't available, try striking the steering knuckle near the side of the balljoint with a hammer while pulling the balljoint out (see illustration). The impact may break the balljoint loose. If these methods don't work, remove the driveaxle first.

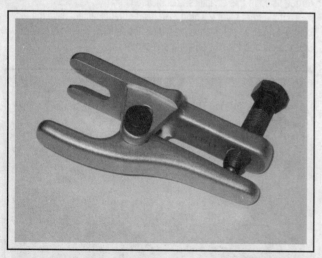

6.5a A balljoint separator tool like this one is available at most automotive parts stores and will not damage the balljoint boot when used correctly

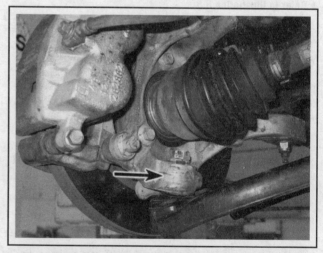

6.5b Strike the knuckle sharply with a hammer at this spot to try to pop the balljoint loose; there is little clearance above the balljoint for a typical puller - special pullers that avoid having to remove the driveaxle are available at auto parts stores

6   Remove the nut and pull the balljoint stud out of the steering knuckle.

ALL MODELS

▶ Refer to illustration 6.8

7   Refer to Section 5 and remove the control arm.

➡Note: The control arm can be left on the vehicle, but it's more difficult to drill out the rivets in that position.

8   Drill out the balljoint rivets (see illustration). Begin with a 5/16-inch (8 mm) starter hole and complete each with a 31/64-inch (12 mm) drill bit. Remove all drilling debris.

9   Install the new balljoint using the supplied bolts. Make sure to put the bolt heads on top and the nuts below. Tighten the bolts to the torque listed in this Chapter's Specifications.

10   The remainder of the installation is the reverse of removal. Tighten the balljoint-to-knuckle nuts and the control arm bolts to the torques listed in this Chapter's Specifications.

➡Note: Before tightening the control arm front pivot bolt, raise the outer end of the control arm with a floor jack to simulate normal ride height.

Be sure to use a new cotter pin. If necessary, tighten the balljoint nut a little more to align the hole in the ballstud with the slots in the nut - don't loosen the nut to achieve this alignment.

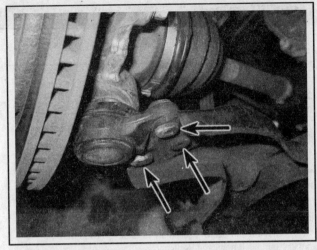

6.8 These large rivets must be drilled out to remove the old balljoint

11   Install the wheel and lug nuts, lower the vehicle and tighten the lug nuts to the torque listed in the Chapter 1 Specifications.

12   It's a good idea to have the front wheel alignment checked, and if necessary, adjusted after this job has been performed.

7   Hub and bearing assembly (front) - removal and installation

▶ Refer to illustration 7.7

❊❊ WARNING:

Dust created by the brake system is harmful to your health. Never blow it out with compressed air and don't inhale any of it. Do not, under any circumstances, use petroleum-based solvents to clean brake parts. Use brake system cleaner only.

1   Loosen the driveaxle/hub nut (see Chapter 8).

2   Loosen the wheel lug nuts, raise the vehicle and support it securely on jackstands. Remove the wheel.

3   Refer to Chapter 9 and remove the brake disc.

4   Disconnect the wheel speed sensor electrical connector and unclip the harness from the bracket (vehicles equipped with ABS).

5   Remove the driveaxle/hub nut.

6   Use wire to support the driveaxle (don't let it hang by the inner CV joint after the hub and bearing has been removed).

7   Remove the three hub mounting bolts (see illustration).

8   Remove the hub and bearing unit. If it's stuck to the driveaxle, tap the driveaxle end with a hammer and a block of wood to avoid damaging the threads.

9   Installation is the reverse of removal. The manufacturer recommends that the hub mounting bolts be replaced with new ones when they are removed. Tighten the bolts to the torque listed in this Chapter's Specifications.

7.7 Front hub-to-knuckle mounting bolts

8 Steering knuckle - removal and installation

REMOVAL

1 Loosen the driveaxle/hub nut (see Chapter 8). Loosen the wheel lug nuts, raise the vehicle and support it securely on jackstands. Remove the wheel.

2 Mark the exact position of the strut to the steering knuckle (see illustration 3.4).

3 Loosen, but do not remove, the strut-to-steering knuckle bolts.

➡**Note: The manufacturer recommends that the nuts and bolts be replaced with new ones whenever they are removed.**

4 Separate the tie-rod end from the steering knuckle arm (see Section 18).

5 If the hub and bearing assembly is to be removed from the knuckle, remove it now (see Section 7).

6 Disconnect the balljoint from the steering knuckle (see Section 6).

7 Push the driveaxle from the hub. Support the end of the driveaxle with a piece of wire.

8 Separate the steering knuckle from the strut.

INSTALLATION

9 Guide the knuckle and hub assembly into position, inserting the driveaxle into the hub.

10 Push the knuckle into the strut flange and install the bolts and nuts, but don't tighten them yet.

11 Connect the balljoint to the steering knuckle and tighten the nut to the torque listed in this Chapter's Specifications. Install a new cotter pin. If necessary, tighten the balljoint nut a little more to align the hole in the ballstud with the slots in the nut - don't loosen the nut to achieve this alignment.

12 Attach the tie-rod end to the steering knuckle arm (see Section 18). Tighten the strut bolt nuts, the balljoint-to-control arm bolt and nuts and the tie-rod nut to the torque values listed in this Chapter's Specifications. Replace all cotter pins with new ones.

13 Place the brake disc on the hub and install the caliper and wheel speed sensor as outlined in Chapter 9.

14 Install a new driveaxle/hub nut and tighten it securely (final tightening will be carried out when the vehicle is lowered).

15 Install the wheel and lug nuts, lower the vehicle and tighten the lug nuts to the torque listed in the Chapter 1 Specifications.

16 Tighten the driveaxle/hub nut to the torque listed in the Chapter 8 Specifications.

9 Stabilizer bar and bushings (rear) - removal and installation

▶ **Refer to illustrations 9.2 and 9.3**

1 Raise the rear of the vehicle and support it securely on jackstands.

2 Disconnect the stabilizer bar links from the bar (see illustration).

If the ballstud turns with the nut, use a Torx or Allen wrench, as applicable, to hold the stud.

3 Unbolt the stabilizer bar bushing retainers (see illustration). Remove the two retainer brackets from the body, if necessary.

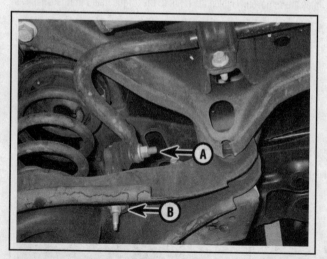

9.2 The rear stabilizer bar attachment to the link (A) and link attachment to the control arm (B)

9.3 Rear stabilizer bar bushing retainers

4   The stabilizer bar can now be removed from the vehicle. Remove the bushings from the stabilizer bar, noting their positions and orientation.

5   Check the bushings for wear, hardness, distortion, cracking and other signs of deterioration, replacing them if necessary. Check the stabilizer bar links as described in Section 2.

6   Using a wire brush, clean the areas of the bar where the bushings ride. Lubricate the inside and outside of the new bushings with vegetable oil (used in cooking).

❊❊ CAUTION:

Don't use petroleum or mineral-based lubricants or brake fluid - they will lead to deterioration of the bushings.

7   Installation is the reverse of removal. Tighten the links and the bushing retainer fasteners to the torques listed in this Chapter's Specifications.

10 Shock absorber (rear) - replacement

▸ Refer to illustrations 10.2, 10.4a and 10.4b

➡Note: When removing/replacing any rear suspension arms, move the suspension to its normal ride-height angle and position, then fully tighten the bolts.

1   Loosen the rear wheel lug nuts, raise the rear of the vehicle and support it securely on jackstands. Remove the wheel.

2   Remove the inner fender splash shield (see illustration).

3   Slightly raise the outer end of the lower control arm with a floor jack so it can't move downward when the shock absorber mounting bolts are removed.

❊❊ WARNING:

The jack must support the lower control arm until the shock absorber is reinstalled.

4   Remove the upper and lower shock absorber mounting bolts and remove the shock absorber (see illustrations).

5   Installation is the reverse of removal.

10.2 The upper shock absorber mounts are behind the inner fender splash shields - remove the pushpin fasteners

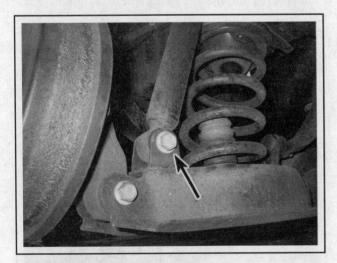

10.4a Shock absorber lower mounting bolt

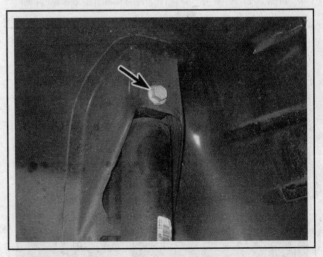

10.4b Shock absorber upper mounting bolt

11 Coil spring (rear) - removal and installation

1 Loosen the rear wheel lug nuts, raise the rear of the vehicle and support it securely on jackstands. Remove the wheel.

2 Refer to Section 9 and disconnect the stabilizer bar link from the lower control arm.

3 Unbolt the bracket at the front of the trailing arm from the body (see illustration 12.9).

4 Slightly raise the outer end of the control arm with a floor jack so it can't move downward when the shock absorber mounting bolt is removed (see illustration).

5 Remove the lower shock absorber mounting bolt (see illustration 10.4a).

6 Loosen the inner through-bolt at the lower control arm pivot.

7 Remove the outer through-bolt from the lower control arm.

8 Slowly and carefully lower the jack until the coil spring extends fully.

9 Installation is the reverse of removal. Make sure that the spring insulators are properly installed on the spring before putting the spring into place.

10 Tighten all fasteners to the torque values listed in this Chapter's Specifications.

12 Suspension arms (rear) - removal and installation

➡Note: Some of the bolts used on these components were enlarged during production. Make sure to check the bolt sizes so you can use the correct torque when tightening them.

1 Loosen the rear wheel lug nuts, raise the rear of the vehicle and support it securely on jackstands. Remove the rear wheel.

TOE LINK

▶ Refer to illustration 12.3

2 Mark the positions of the inner bolt heads or cam adjusters to the subframe prior to loosening any bolts.

➡Note: The inner mounting holes are slotted. Nuts with adjuster cams (for alignment purposes) are available at dealer parts departments.

3 Remove the inner and outer pivot bolts (see illustration). Remove the toe link.

4 Installation is the reverse of removal. Install the bolts with their heads facing forward.

5 Align the bolt heads or adjuster cams with the marks made in Step 2. Make sure that all the adjusters, if present, are in the same positions as when you marked them.

6 Before tightening the mounting bolts, raise the outer end of the lower control arm with a floor jack to simulate normal ride height.

7 Tighten the bolts to the torque values listed in this Chapter's Specifications.

8 It's a good idea to have the wheel alignment checked and, if necessary, adjusted.

TRAILING ARM

▶ Refer to illustrations 12.9 and 12.11

9 Remove the three mounting bolts from the trailing arm-to-body bracket (see illustration).

10 Unbolt the parking brake cable clip from the trailing arm.

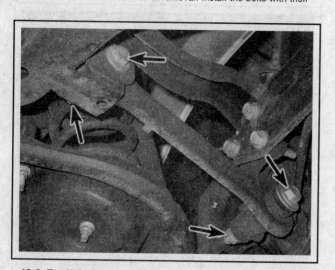

12.3 Toe link pivot nuts and bolts

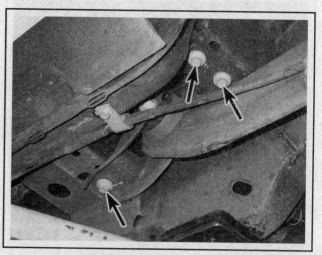

12.9 Trailing arm-to-body bolts

11 Remove the three bolts securing the arm to the knuckle and lift off the arm (see illustration).

12 If necessary, remove the through-bolt and separate the bracket from the trailing arm.

13 Installation is the reverse of removal. Install all of the mounting bolts finger tight before tightening any of them. Tighten all of the fasteners to the torques listed in this Chapter's Specifications. It's a good idea to have the wheel alignment checked and, if necessary, adjusted.

UPPER CONTROL ARM

▶ **Refer to illustrations 12.15 and 12.17**

14 Unbolt the trailing arm bracket from the body (see illustration 12.9).

15 Mark the position of the cam adjuster on the inner end of the upper control arm (see illustration).

16 Disconnect the ABS wiring from the upper control arm.

17 Remove the through-bolt from each end of the upper control arm pivot (see illustration). Lift out the arm.

18 To install the arm, first loosely install the bolt at each end.

19 After the adjuster marks are aligned, raise the lower control arm to simulate normal ride height, then tighten the fasteners to the torque listed in this Chapter's Specifications.

20 The remainder of installation is the reverse of removal. It's a good idea to have the wheel alignment checked and, if necessary, adjusted.

LOWER CONTROL ARM

▶ **Refer to illustration 12.26**

21 Refer to Section 9 and disconnect the stabilizer bar link from the lower control arm.

22 Unbolt the trailing arm bracket from the body (see illustration 12.9).

23 Position a floor jack under the outer end of the control arm and raise it slightly.

24 Remove the shock absorber lower mounting bolt.

25 Remove the bumper mounting nut at the center of the bottom of the spring.

26 Loosen the lower control arm inner pivot bolt (see illustration), remove the outer bolt and slowly lower the arm, allowing the coil spring to extend.

27 Remove the spring and its lower bumper.

28 Remove the arm inner bolt and lift out the arm.

29 Installation is the reverse of removal. Raise the lower control arm to simulate normal ride height, then tighten the fasteners to the torque listed in this Chapter's Specifications.

30 Have the wheel alignment checked by a dealer service department or an alignment shop.

12.11 Trailing arm-to-knuckle bolts

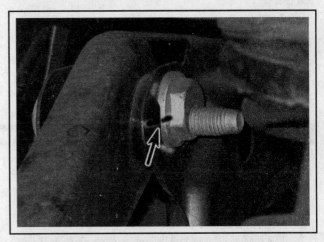

12.15 Mark the position of the cam adjuster on the inner pivot bolt of the upper control arm

12.17 Upper control arm pivot bolts

12.26 Lower control arm-to-rear knuckle bolt/nut (A) and inner pivot bolt/nut (B)

13 Hub and bearing assembly (rear) - removal and installation

♦ **Refer to illustration 13.6**

1 On AWD models, loosen the rear driveaxle/hub nut.

2 Loosen the wheel lug nuts, raise the vehicle and support it securely on jackstands. Remove the wheel.

3 Refer to Chapter 9 and remove the brake drum.

4 On AWD models, remove the driveaxle spindle nut. Use wire to support the end of the driveaxle.

5 Disconnect the wheel speed sensor on models equipped with ABS.

6 Remove the four hub mounting bolts (see illustration), then guide the hub and bearing out from the brake assembly.

7 Installation is the reverse of removal. After all four bolts have been installed, tighten them to the torque listed in this Chapter's Specifications.

8 On AWD models, install a new driveaxle/hub nut and tighten it securely (final tightening will be carried out after the vehicle has been lowered).

9 Install the brake drum and the wheel. Lower the vehicle and tighten the lug nuts to the torque listed in the Chapter 1 Specifications.

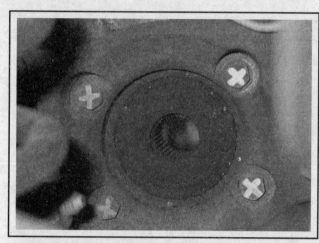

13.6 The rear hub is attached to the knuckle by four bolts

14 Suspension knuckle (rear) - removal and installation

1 Refer to Section 13 and remove the hub and bearing assembly.

2 Support the brake assembly securely using wire.

3 Unbolt the knuckle from the upper and lower control arms.

4 Remove the knuckle bolts from the trailing arm and the toe link.

5 Separate the knuckle from the other components and lift it out.

6 Installation is the reverse of removal, however, install all of the mounting bolts finger tight.

7 When the components are all connected, lower the vehicle and tighten the fasteners to the torques listed in this Chapter's Specifications. Tighten them in the following order: lower control arm, upper control arm, toe link and the trailing arm.

15 Steering system - general information

All models are equipped with rack-and-pinion steering. The steering gear is bolted to the subframe and operates the steering knuckles via tie-rods. The inner ends of the tie-rods are protected by rubber boots that should be inspected periodically for secure attachment, tears and leaking lubricant.

The power assist system consists of a torque sensor which is in the steering column, an electric power-assist motor (also in the steering column housing) and the Power Steering Control Module (PSCM). The PSCM gets inputs from the torque sensor as well as other sources and instructs the electric motor to apply the proper amount of assist to the steering system. If the PSCM detect a problem in the system, it will turn on a warning light on the instrument panel. System troubles must be diagnosed and repaired by a specialized repair shop.

The steering wheel operates the steering shaft, which actuates the steering gear through universal joints. Looseness in the steering can be caused by wear in the steering shaft universal joints, the steering gear, the tie-rod ends or loose retaining bolts.

16 Steering wheel - removal and installation

✳✳ WARNING:

The models covered by this manual are equipped with Supplemental Restraint Systems (SRS), more commonly known as airbags. Always disable the airbag system before working in the vicinity of any airbag system component to avoid the possibility of accidental deployment of the airbag(s), which could cause personal injury (see Chapter 12).

REMOVAL

1 Turn the steering wheel so that the wheels are pointing straight ahead. Turn the ignition key to Off, then disconnect the cable from the negative terminal of the battery (see Chapter 5, Section 1). Wait at least two minutes for the airbag system to lose power.

2002 and 2003 models

2 Refer to Chapter 11 and remove the upper steering column cover.
3 Turn the steering wheel for access to two of the triangle-shape holes in its rear.
4 Put a flat-blade screwdriver through one of the holes and twist it while gently pulling on the corner of the steering wheel center/airbag. The airbag should release.
5 Repeat this procedure for the other three triangle-shape holes, turning the steering wheel as necessary for access. After the airbag has been removed, straighten-out the steering wheel.

2004 and 2005 four-cylinder models

▶ Refer to illustrations 16.7a, 16.7b and 16.7c

6 Turn the steering wheel for access to one of the triangle-shape holes in its rear.
7 Put a flat-blade screwdriver through one of the holes and twist it while gently pulling on the corner of the steering wheel center/airbag. The airbag should release (see illustrations).

➡Note: Some models have two holes and retainers (one per side); others have four retainers (two per side).

8 Repeat this procedure on the other retainer(s), turning the steering wheel as necessary for access. After the airbag has been removed, straighten-out the steering wheel.

2005 V6 models

9 Turn the steering wheel for access to one of the three holes in its rear.
10 Put two flat-blade screwdrivers into the hole and push them toward the rear of the vehicle at the same time.

➡Note: Special tool J44298 is available to make this job easier. This should release the clips.

11 Repeat this procedure on the two other retainers, turning the steering wheel as necessary for access. After the airbag has been removed, straighten-out the steering wheel.

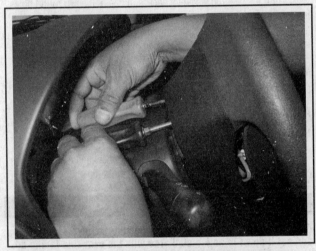

16.7a Flat-blade screwdrivers will release the airbag module clips (2004 and 2005 four-cylinder model shown)

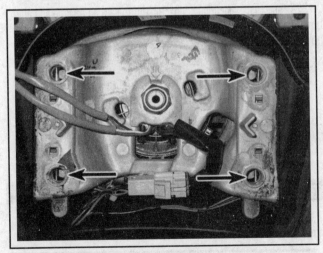

16.7b The airbag clip retaining springs . . .

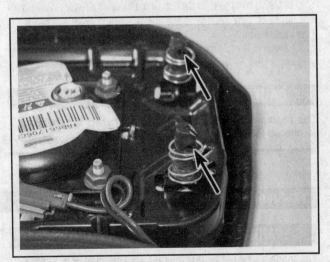

16.7c . . . engage these prongs on the airbag module (2004 and 2005 four-cylinder model shown)

16.15 Remove the airbag module carefully and disconnect the electrical connectors

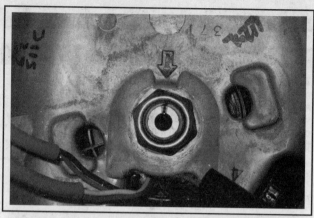

16.16 If there are no marks present, mark the steering wheel so it can be reinstalled in the same position on the shaft

2006 and later models

12 Turn the steering wheel for access to one of the two round holes in its rear.

13 Use a blunt tool to push in on the clip in the hole. This will release the retainer.

14 Repeat this procedure on the other retainer, turning the steering wheel as necessary for access. After the airbag has been removed, straighten-out the steering wheel.

All models

♦ **Refer to illustrations 16.15 and 16.16**

15 Pull the airbag module off the steering wheel and disconnect the electrical connector for the module (see illustration).

✳✳ WARNING:

Carry the airbag module with the trim side facing away from you and set it down in an isolated area with the trim side facing up.

16 Remove the steering wheel retaining nut, then mark the relationship of the steering shaft to the hub (if marks don't already exist or don't line up) to simplify installation and ensure steering wheel alignment (see illustration).

17 Use a puller to disconnect the steering wheel from the shaft or wiggle the steering wheel while pulling on it forcefully.

✳✳ CAUTION:

Don't hammer on the shaft or the steering wheel in an attempt to remove the wheel.

18 If it's necessary to remove the airbag clockspring, disengage the retaining fingers, detach the clockspring from the steering column and disconnect the electrical connectors.

INSTALLATION

➡**Note: Steps 20 and 21 need not be done if you're sure the airbag clockspring hasn't been rotated after steering wheel removal.**

19 Make sure that the front wheels are facing straight ahead.

20 Turn the hub of the clockspring counterclockwise by hand until it becomes harder to turn the cable (don't apply too much force). Rotate it clockwise and count the turns until the same resistance is met.

21 Rotate the clockspring back half that number of turns to center it. Install the clockspring, making sure its hub doesn't rotate in relation to the housing.

22 To install the steering wheel, align the mark on the hub with the mark on the shaft and slip the wheel onto the shaft. Install the nut and tighten it to the torque listed in this Chapter's Specifications.

➡**Note: If a new clockspring was installed, remove the yellow alignment tab through the opening in the steering wheel.**

23 Plug in the electrical connectors for the airbag module and any other connectors. Make sure the connector locks are pushed back into position for the module.

24 Install the airbag module and make sure all of the retainers are snapped securely.

25 Connect the negative battery cable (see Chapter 5, Section 1).

17 Steering column - removal and installation

✳✳ WARNING:

The models covered by this manual are equipped with Supplemental Restraint Systems (SRS), more commonly known as airbags. Always disable the airbag system before working in the vicinity of any airbag system component to avoid the possibility of accidental deployment of the airbag(s), which could cause personal injury (see Chapter 12).

➡**Note: If a new column is being installed, you must take the vehicle to a dealer to have them program the new electronic power steering controller that is in the column.**

REMOVAL

♦ **Refer to illustrations 17.11, 17.12, 17.13 and 17.14**

1 Park the vehicle with the wheels pointing straight ahead. Disconnect the cable from the negative terminal of the battery (see Chapter 5, Section 1).

2 Remove the steering wheel (see Section 16) and the steering column covers (see Chapter 11).

3 Unsnap the airbag clockspring electrical connectors at their connections below the steering column. Disconnect the airbag electrical connectors from the instrument panel harness.

4 Use a flat-blade screwdriver to release the clips from the airbag clockspring and slide it from the steering column (see Section 16).

5 Carefully pry the bezel from the lock cylinder.

6 Remove the multi-function switches (see Chapter 12).

7 Disconnect the electrical connectors from the ignition switch assembly.

8 Release the lock tabs on the park/lock cable end and remove it from the ignition lock cylinder housing.

9 Remove the two bolts from the lock cylinder housing. Remove the housing and slide the multi-function switch bracket from the column.

10 Refer to Chapter 11 and remove the driver's knee bolster trim panel. It's secured with two screws and clips.

11 Disconnect the electrical connectors from the power steering controller (see illustration).

12 Remove the through-bolt from the lower part of the steering column (see illustration).

13 Mark the relationship of the steering shaft U-joint to the intermediate shaft, then remove the pinch bolt (see illustration).

14 Remove the steering column upper mounting fasteners (see illustration), lower the column and pull it to the rear, making sure nothing is still connected. Separate the intermediate shaft from the steering shaft and remove the column.

17.11 Disconnect the electrical connectors from the electric power steering unit

17.12 Steering column lower through-bolt

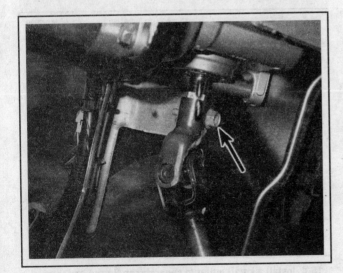

17.13 Upper steering shaft pinch bolt

17.14 Steering column upper mounting bolts

INSTALLATION

15 Guide the steering column into position, align the marks and connect the intermediate shaft, then install the three mounting bolts, but don't tighten them yet.

➡ **Note: The manufacturer recommends that a new pinch bolt be installed whenever it is removed. Tighten the pinch bolt to the torque values listed in this Chapter's Specifications.**

16 Slide the multi-function switch housing back onto the column, making sure that the lock tab is fully seated.

17 Install the ignition switch assembly and hand tighten the bolts so that there is a 1/8-inch gap at each end. Gradually and evenly tighten both bolts until you reach the torque listed in this Chapter's Specifications.

18 Tighten the left upper column mounting bolt to the torque listed in this Chapter's Specifications.

19 Tighten the lower column mounting through-bolt to the torque listed in this Chapter's Specifications.

20 Actuate the tilt lever and move the column up and down several times, finally setting it at its top position.

21 Tighten the top right column mounting bolt to the same torque as the other top bolt.

22 The remainder of installation is the reverse of removal.

18 Tie-rod ends - removal and installation

REMOVAL

▶ **Refer to illustrations 18.2 and 18.4**

1 Loosen the wheel lug nuts. Raise the front of the vehicle, support it securely on jackstands, block the rear wheels and set the parking brake. Remove the front wheel.

2 Hold the tie-rod with a pair of locking pliers or wrench and loosen the jam nut enough to mark the position of the tie-rod end in relation to the threads (see illustration).

3 Remove the cotter pin and loosen the nut on the tie-rod end stud.

4 Disconnect the tie-rod from the steering knuckle arm with a puller (see illustration). Remove the nut and separate the tie-rod.

5 Unscrew the tie-rod end from the tie-rod.

INSTALLATION

6 Thread the tie-rod end on to the marked position and insert the tie-rod stud into the steering knuckle arm. Tighten the jam nut securely.

7 Install the castle nut on the stud and tighten it to the torque listed in this Chapter's Specifications. Install a new cotter pin. If necessary, tighten the balljoint nut a little more to align the hole in the ballstud with the slots in the nut - don't loosen the nut to achieve this alignment.

8 Install the wheel and lug nuts. Lower the vehicle and tighten the lug nuts to the torque listed in the Chapter 1 Specifications.

9 Have the wheel alignment checked and, if necessary, adjusted.

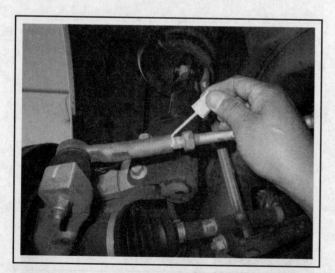

18.2 Back off the jam nut and mark the exposed threads to ensure that the new tie-rod end is threaded on the same number of turns

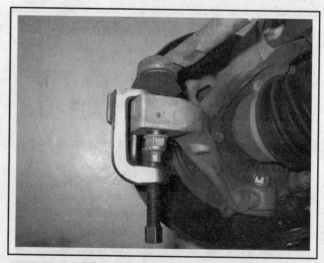

18.4 Install a small puller to separate the tie-rod end from the steering knuckle

19 Steering gear boots - replacement

▶ **Refer to illustration 19.3**

➡**Note: The steering gear can be left in place to perform this job, however it may be easier to remove it and replace the boots on a workbench.**

1   Loosen the lug nuts, raise the vehicle and support it securely on jackstands. Remove the wheel.

2   Remove the tie-rod end and jam nut (see Section 18).

3   Remove the steering gear boot clamps (see illustration) and slide off the boot.

4   Before installing the new boot, wrap the threads and serrations on the end of the steering rod with a layer of tape so the small end of the new boot isn't damaged. Apply grease from the supplied grease packet to the tie-rod in the area where the boot seats, and to the inner end of the inside of the boot.

5   Slide the new boot into position on the steering gear until it seats in the groove on the housing and the groove in the steering rod. Install the clamps.

6   Remove the tape and install the tie-rod end (see Section 18).

7   Install the wheel and lug nuts. Lower the vehicle and tighten the lug nuts to the torque listed in the Chapter 1 Specifications.

8   Have the wheel alignment checked and, if necessary, adjusted.

19.3 Remove the outer clamp from the steering gear boot with a pair of pliers; the inner clamp must be cut or pried off

20 Steering gear - removal and installation

✳✳ WARNING:

Make sure the steering shaft is not turned while the steering gear is removed or you could damage the clockspring for the airbag system. To prevent the shaft from turning, place the ignition key in the lock position or thread the seat belt through the steering wheel and clip it into place. Don't turn the front wheels.

REMOVAL

▶ **Refer to illustrations 20.2 and 20.6**

1   Park the vehicle with the front wheels pointing straight ahead.

Loosen the front wheel lug nuts, raise the front of the vehicle and support it securely on jackstands. Apply the parking brake and remove the wheels.

2   Mark the relationship of the intermediate shaft to the steering shaft U-joint and remove the pinch bolt (see illustration).

3   Separate the tie-rod ends from the steering knuckles (see Section 18).

4   Detach the links from the ends of the stabilizer bar.

5   On models equipped with a CVT automatic transaxle, unclip the shift cable from the steering gear.

6   Remove the steering gear mounting bolts (see illustration).

7   Separate the intermediate shaft U-joint from the steering gear input shaft, then remove the steering gear assembly out the right side of the vehicle.

20.2 Steering intermediate shaft pinch bolt

20.6 Left-side steering gear mounting bolt

INSTALLATION

8 Raise the steering gear into position and connect the intermediate shaft U-joint to the steering input shaft, aligning the marks.

9 Install the steering gear mounting bolts and tighten them to the torque listed in this Chapter's Specifications.

10 Connect the tie-rod ends to the steering knuckle arms (see Section 18).

11 The remainder of installation is the reverse of removal. Be sure to tighten all of the fasteners to the torques listed in this Chapter's Specifications.

12 Have the wheel alignment checked and, if necessary, adjusted.

21 Subframe/cradle - removal and installation

▶ **Refer to illustration 21.14**

1 Disconnect the cable from the negative battery terminal (see Chapter 5, Section 1).

2 Loosen the front wheel lug nuts, raise the front of the vehicle and support it securely on jackstands. Remove both front wheels.

➡**Note: The jackstands must be behind the front suspension subframe, not supporting the vehicle by the subframe.**

3 Use wire to tie the upper part of the radiator/condenser assembly to the front upper body structure.

4 Remove the plastic side splash shields.

5 Disconnect the front air dam from the subframe.

6 Unbolt the front and rear transaxle mounts from the subframe.

7 Remove the stabilizer bar bracket mounting bolts.

8 Disconnect the balljoints from the knuckles (see Section 6).

9 Remove the steering gear mounting bolts and use wire to tie the gear to the exhaust system.

10 Inspect the subframe for any hose, line or harness brackets that may be attached and detach them.

11 Support the engine from above using an engine hoist or equivalent (see Chapter 2C).

✳✳ WARNING:

DO NOT place any part of your body under the engine when it's supported only by a hoist or other lifting device.

12 Remove the frame brace if you're working on a V6 model.

13 Using two floor jacks, support the subframe. Position one jack on each side of the subframe, midway between the front and rear mounting points.

14 With the jacks sufficiently supporting the subframe, remove the fasteners securing the subframe brackets and the subframe (see illustration).

➡**Note: The manufacturer states that the subframe bolts should be replaced with new ones whenever they are removed.**

15 With the use of an assistant to steady the subframe, carefully lower the jacks until the subframe is sufficiently resting on the ground.

16 Remove the control arms if necessary.

INSTALLATION

17 Installation is the reverse of removal. Install new subframe mounting bolts and tighten them to the torque listed in this Chapter's Specifications.

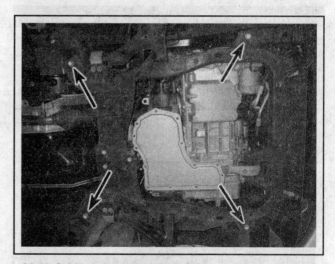

21.14 Subframe/cradle mounting bolts

22 Wheels and tires - general information

▶ **Refer to illustration 22.1**

1 All vehicles covered by this manual are equipped with metric-sized fiberglass or steel belted radial tires (see illustration). Use of other size or type of tires may affect the ride and handling of the vehicle.

Don't mix different types of tires, such as radials and bias belted, on the same vehicle as handling may be seriously affected. It's recommended that tires be replaced in pairs on the same axle, but if only one tire is being replaced, be sure it's the same size, structure and tread design as the other.

2   Because tire pressure has a substantial effect on handling and wear, the pressure on all tires should be checked at least once a month or before any extended trips (see Chapter 1).

3   Wheels must be replaced if they are bent, dented, leak air, have elongated bolt holes, are heavily rusted, out of vertical symmetry or if the lug nuts won't stay tight. Wheel repairs that use welding or peening are not recommended.

4   Tire and wheel balance is important in the overall handling, braking and performance of the vehicle. Unbalanced wheels can adversely affect handling and ride characteristics as well as tire life. Whenever a tire is installed on a wheel, the tire and wheel should be balanced by a shop with the proper equipment.

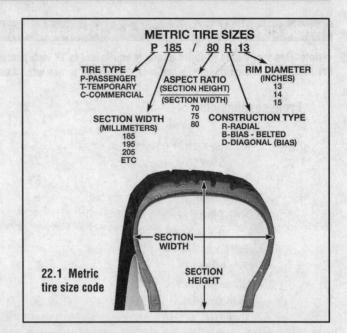

22.1 Metric tire size code

23 Wheel alignment - general information

▶ Refer to illustration 23.1

A wheel alignment refers to the adjustments made to the wheels so they are in proper angular relationship to the suspension and the ground. Wheels that are out of proper alignment not only affect vehicle control, but also increase tire wear. The alignment angles normally measured are camber, caster and toe-in (see illustration).

Getting the proper wheel alignment is a very exacting process, one in which complicated and expensive machines are necessary to perform the job properly. Because of this, you should have a technician with the proper equipment perform these tasks. We will, however, use this space to give you a basic idea of what is involved with a wheel alignment so you can better understand the process and deal intelligently with the shop that does the work.

Toe-in is the turning in of the wheels. The purpose of a toe specification is to ensure parallel rolling of the wheels. In a vehicle with zero toe-in, the distance between the front edges of the wheels will be the same as the distance between the rear edges of the wheels. The actual amount of toe-in is normally only a fraction of an inch. On the front end, toe-in is controlled by the tie-rod end position on the tie-rod. On the rear end, it's controlled by a cam at the inner end of the toe link. Incorrect toe-in will cause the tires to wear improperly by making them scrub against the road surface.

Camber is the tilting of the wheels from vertical when viewed from one end of the vehicle. When the wheels tilt out at the top, the camber is said to be positive (+). When the wheels tilt in at the top the camber is negative (-). The amount of tilt is measured in degrees from vertical and this measurement is called the camber angle. This angle affects the amount of tire tread which contacts the road and compensates for changes in the suspension geometry when the vehicle is cornering or traveling over an undulating surface. On the front end, camber is adjusted by altering the position of the steering knuckle in the suspension strut. On the rear end, it's adjusted by altering the position of the upper control arm on the subframe.

Caster is the tilting of the front steering axis from the vertical. A tilt toward the rear is positive caster and a tilt toward the front is negative caster. Too little caster will make the front end wander, while too much caster can make the steering effort higher. Caster is not adjustable on these vehicles; if it isn't within specification, check for bent suspension components.

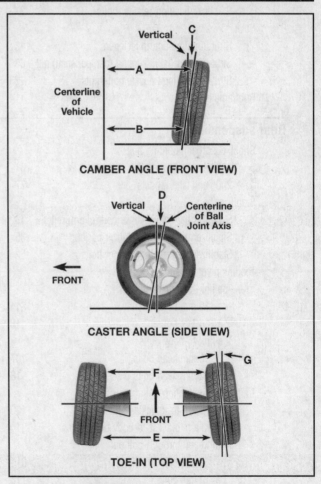

23.1 Camber, caster and toe-in angles

A minus B = C (degrees camber)
D = caster (expressed in degrees)

E minus F = toe-in (measured in inches)
G = toe-in (expressed in degrees)

Torque specifications	Ft-lbs (unless otherwise indicated)	Nm

➡ Note: One foot-pound (ft-lb) of torque is equivalent to 12 inch-pounds (in-lbs) of torque. Torque values below approximately 15 ft-lbs are expressed in inch-pounds, since most foot-pound torque wrenches are not accurate at these smaller values.

Front suspension

Balljoint		
Balljoint-to-steering knuckle nut		
Silver cup-shape balljoints	44	60
Black flat balljoints	30	40
Balljoint-to-control arm nuts and bolts	50	68
Hub/wheel bearing assembly mounting bolts	96	130
Control arm-to-subframe bolts		
Front bolts	148	201
Rear bolts	52	71
Control arm rear bushing nut		
Prior to casting no. 4A133A	90	122
Casting no. 4A133A and later	110	149
Stabilizer bar		
Stabilizer bar link nuts	48	65
Stabilizer bushing/retainer bolts	37	50
Strut		
Strut upper mounting fasteners	18	24
Strut-to-suspension support (damper shaft) nut	63	85
Strut-to-steering knuckle bolts/nuts	133	180
Subframe bolts	114	154

Rear suspension

Shock absorber mounting bolts		
2004 and earlier models	81	110
2005 and later models	77	104
Stabilizer bar		
Stabilizer bar link-to-lower control arm nut	132 in-lbs	15
Stabilizer bar link-to-stabilizer bar nut	35	47
Stabilizer bar bushing/retainer bolts	52	71
Toe link pivot bolts		
Toe link-to-knuckle bolts		
12 mm bolts	81	110
14 mm bolts	118	160
Toe link-to-body bolts		
15 mm head bolts	107	145
22 mm head bolts	118	160
Trailing arm mounting bolts		
Trailing arm-to-knuckle bolts	100	136
Trailing arm bracket-to-body bolts	81	110
Trailing arm through-bolt nut		
12 mm bolt	81	110
14 mm bolt	118	160

Torque specifications (continued)	Ft-lbs (unless otherwise indicated)	Nm

➡**Note: One foot-pound (ft-lb) of torque is equivalent to 12 inch-pounds (in-lbs) of torque. Torque values below approximately 15 ft-lbs are expressed in inch-pounds, since most foot-pound torque wrenches are not accurate at these smaller values.**

Rear suspension (continued)

	Ft-lbs	Nm
Control arm pivot bolts		
Upper control arm		
To knuckle	118	160
To suspension support		
12 mm bolt	81	110
14 mm bolt	118	160
Lower control arm	81	110
Hub/wheel bearing mounting bolts	62	84
Driveaxle/hub nut (AWD models)	See Chapter 8	

Steering system

	Ft-lbs	Nm
Steering column mounting bolts	18	24
Steering gear mounting bolts	81	110
Steering shaft universal joint pinch bolt	25	34
Steering wheel nut	30	40
Tie-rod end-to-steering knuckle nut		
Step 1	18	24
Step 2	Tighten an additional 90-degrees	
Wheel lug nuts	See Chapter 1	

Notes

Section

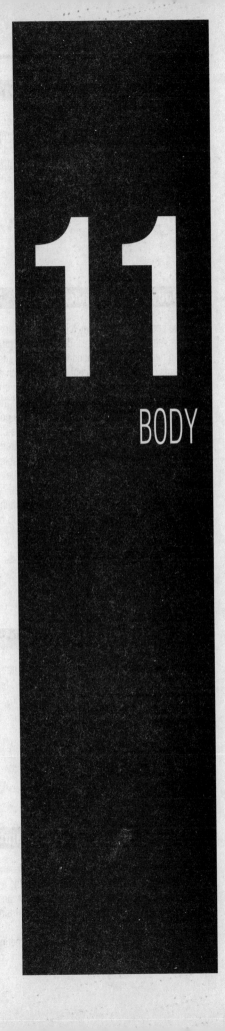

11

BODY

1 General information

These models feature a unibody layout, using a floor pan with integral side frame rails which support the body components, front and rear suspension systems and other mechanical components.

Certain components are particularly vulnerable to accident damage and can be unbolted and repaired or replaced. Among these parts are the body moldings, bumpers, front fenders, the hood and trunk lid, doors and all glass.

Only general body maintenance practices and body panel repair procedures within the scope of the do-it-yourselfer are included in this Chapter.

2 Body - maintenance

1 The condition of your vehicle's body is very important, because the resale value depends a great deal on it. It's much more difficult to repair a neglected or damaged body than it is to repair mechanical components. The hidden areas of the body, such as the wheel wells, the frame and the engine compartment, are equally important, although they don't require as frequent attention as the rest of the body.

2 Once a year, or every 12,000 miles, it's a good idea to have the underside of the body steam-cleaned. All traces of dirt and oil will be removed and the area can then be inspected carefully for rust, damaged brake lines, frayed electrical wires, damaged cables and other problems.

3 At the same time, clean the engine and the engine compartment with a steam cleaner or water-soluble degreaser.

4 The wheel wells should be given close attention, since undercoating can peel away and stones and dirt thrown up by the tires can cause the paint to chip and flake, allowing rust to set in. If rust is found, clean down to the bare metal and apply an anti-rust paint.

5 The body should be washed about once a week. Wet the vehicle thoroughly to soften the dirt, and then wash it down with a soft sponge and plenty of clean soapy water. If the surplus dirt is not washed off very carefully, it can wear down the paint.

6 Spots of tar or asphalt thrown up from the road should be removed with a cloth soaked in kerosene. Scented lamp oil is available in most hardware stores and the smell is easier to work with than straight kerosene.

7 Once every six months, wax the body and chrome trim. If chrome cleaner is used to remove rust from any of the vehicle's plated parts, remember that the cleaner also removes part of the chrome, so use it sparingly. On any plated parts where chrome cleaner is used, use a good paste wax over the plating for extra protection.

3 Vinyl trim - maintenance

Don't clean vinyl trim with detergents, caustic soap or petroleum-based cleaners. Plain soap and water works just fine, with a soft brush to clean dirt that may be ingrained. Wash the vinyl as frequently as the rest of the vehicle.

After cleaning, application of a high quality rubber and vinyl protectant will help prevent oxidation and cracks. The protectant can also be applied to weather stripping, vacuum lines and rubber hoses, which often fail as a result of chemical degradation, and to the tires.

4 Upholstery and carpets - maintenance

1 Every three months, remove the floormats and clean the interior of the vehicle (more frequently if necessary). Use a stiff whisk broom to brush the carpeting and loosen dirt and dust, and then vacuum the upholstery and carpets thoroughly, especially along seams and crevices.

2 Dirt and stains can be removed from carpeting with basic household or automotive carpet shampoos available in spray cans. Follow the directions and vacuum again, then use a stiff brush to bring back the nap of the carpet.

3 Most interiors have cloth or vinyl upholstery, either of which can be cleaned and maintained with a number of material-specific cleaners or shampoos available in auto supply stores. Follow the directions on the product for usage, and always spot-test any upholstery cleaner on an inconspicuous area (bottom edge of a backseat cushion) to ensure

that it doesn't cause a color shift in the material.

4   After cleaning, vinyl upholstery should be treated with a protectant.

➡Note: Make sure the protectant container indicates the product can be used on seats - some products may make a seat too slippery.

❋❋ CAUTION:

Do not use protectant on steering wheels.

5   Leather upholstery requires special care. It should be cleaned regularly with saddlesoap or leather cleaner. Never use alcohol, gasoline, nail polish remover or thinner to clean leather upholstery.

6   After cleaning, regularly treat leather upholstery with a leather conditioner, rubbed in with a soft cotton cloth. Never use car wax on leather upholstery.

7   In areas where the interior of the vehicle is subject to bright sunlight, cover leather seating areas of the seats with a sheet if the vehicle is to be left out for any length of time.

5   Body repair - minor damage

FLEXIBLE PLASTIC BODY PANELS (FRONT AND REAR BUMPER FASCIAS, DOORS, FENDERS, QUARTER PANELS)

The following repair procedures are for minor scratches and gouges. Repair of more serious damage should be left to a dealer service department or qualified auto body shop. Below is a list of the equipment and materials necessary to perform the following repair procedures on plastic body panels. Although a specific brand of material may be mentioned, it should be noted that equivalent products from other manufacturers may be used instead.

Wax, grease and silicone removing solvent
Cloth-backed body tape
Sanding discs
Drill motor with three-inch disc holder
Hand sanding block
Rubber squeegees
Sandpaper
Non-porous mixing palette
Wood paddle or putty knife
Curved-tooth body file
Flexible parts repair material

1   Remove the damaged panel, if necessary or desirable. In most cases, repairs can be carried out with the panel installed.

2   Clean the area(s) to be repaired with a wax, grease and silicone removing solvent applied with a water-dampened cloth.

3   If the damage is structural, that is, if it extends through the panel, clean the backside of the panel area to be repaired as well. Wipe dry.

4   Sand the rear surface about 1-1/2 inches beyond the break.

5   Cut two pieces of fiberglass cloth large enough to overlap the break by about 1-1/2 inches. Cut only to the required length.

6   Mix the adhesive from the repair kit according to the instructions included with the kit, and apply a layer of the mixture approximately 1/8-inch thick on the backside of the panel. Overlap the break by at least 1-1/2 inches.

7   Apply one piece of fiberglass cloth to the adhesive and cover the cloth with additional adhesive. Apply a second piece of fiberglass cloth to the adhesive and immediately cover the cloth with additional adhesive in sufficient quantity to fill the weave.

8   Allow the repair to cure for 20 to 30 minutes at 60-degrees to 80-degrees F.

9   If necessary, trim the excess repair material at the edge.

10   Remove all of the paint film over and around the area(s) to be repaired. The repair material should not overlap the painted surface.

11   With a drill motor and a sanding disc (or a rotary file), cut a V

along the break line approximately 1/2-inch wide. Remove all dust and loose particles from the repair area.

12   Mix and apply the repair material. Apply a light coat first over the damaged area; then continue applying material until it reaches a level slightly higher than the surrounding finish.

13   Cure the mixture for 20 to 30 minutes at 60-degrees to 80-degrees F.

14   Roughly establish the contour of the area being repaired with a body file. If low areas or pits remain, mix and apply additional adhesive.

15   Block sand the damaged area with sandpaper to establish the actual contour of the surrounding surface.

16   If desired, the repaired area can be temporarily protected with several light coats of primer. Because of the special paints and techniques required for flexible body panels, it is recommended that the vehicle be taken to a paint shop for completion of the body repair.

STEEL BODY PANELS (HOOD, LIFTGATE, TOP)

◆ See photo sequence

Repair of minor scratches

17   If the scratch is superficial and does not penetrate to the metal of the body, repair is very simple. Lightly rub the scratched area with a fine rubbing compound to remove loose paint and built up wax. Rinse the area with clean water.

18   Apply touch-up paint to the scratch, using a small brush. Continue to apply thin layers of paint until the surface of the paint in the scratch is level with the surrounding paint. Allow the new paint at least two weeks to harden, and then blend it into the surrounding paint by rubbing with a very fine rubbing compound. Finally, apply a coat of wax to the scratch area.

19   If the scratch has penetrated the paint and exposed the metal of the body, causing the metal to rust, a different repair technique is required. Remove all loose rust from the bottom of the scratch with a pocket knife, and then apply rust inhibiting paint to prevent the formation of rust in the future. Using a rubber or nylon applicator, coat the scratched area with glaze-type filler. If required, the filler can be mixed with thinner to provide a very thin paste, which is ideal for filling narrow scratches. Before the glaze filler in the scratch hardens, wrap a piece of smooth cotton cloth around the tip of a finger. Dip the cloth in thinner and then quickly wipe it along the surface of the scratch. This will ensure that the surface of the filler is slightly hollow. The scratch can now be painted over as described earlier in this Section.

These photos illustrate a method of repairing simple dents. They are intended to supplement Body repair - minor damage in this Chapter and should not be used as the sole instructions for body repair on these vehicles.

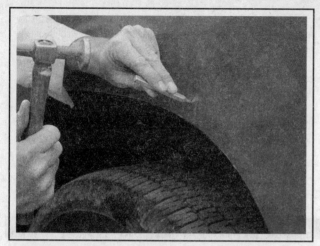

1 If you can't access the backside of the body panel to hammer out the dent, pull it out with a slide-hammer-type dent puller. In the deepest portion of the dent or along the crease line, drill or punch hole(s) at least one inch apart . . .

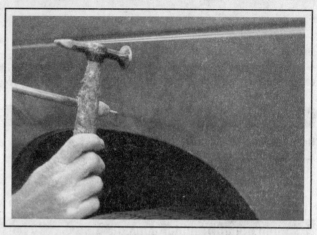

2 . . . then screw the slide-hammer into the hole and operate it. Tap with a hammer near the edge of the dent to help 'pop' the metal back to its original shape. When you're finished, the dent area should be close to its original contour and about 1/8-inch below the surface of the surrounding metal

3 Using coarse-grit sandpaper, remove the paint down to the bare metal. Hand sanding works fine, but the disc sander shown here makes the job faster. Use finer (about 320-grit) sandpaper to feather-edge the paint at least one inch around the dent area

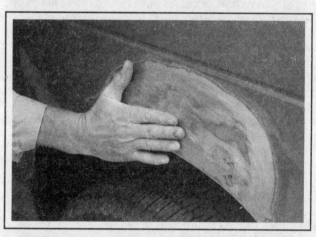

4 When the paint is removed, touch will probably be more helpful than sight for telling if the metal is straight. Hammer down the high spots or raise the low spots as necessary. Clean the repair area with wax/silicone remover

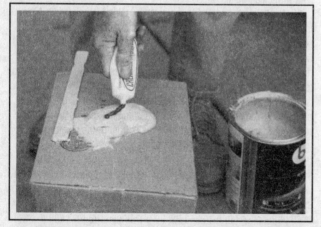

5 Following label instructions, mix up a batch of plastic filler and hardener. The ratio of filler to hardener is critical, and, if you mix it incorrectly, it will either not cure properly or cure too quickly (you won't have time to file and sand it into shape)

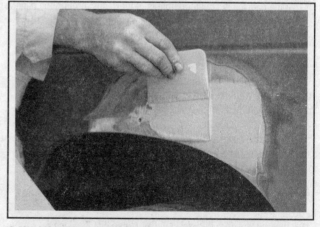

6 Working quickly so the filler doesn't harden, use a plastic applicator to press the body filler firmly into the metal, assuring it bonds completely. Work the filler until it matches the original contour and is slightly above the surrounding metal

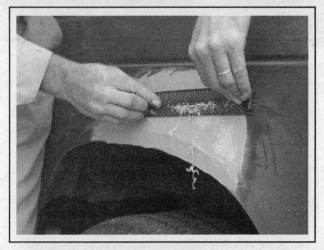

7 Let the filler harden until you can just dent it with your fingernail. Use a body file or Surform tool (shown here) to rough-shape the filler

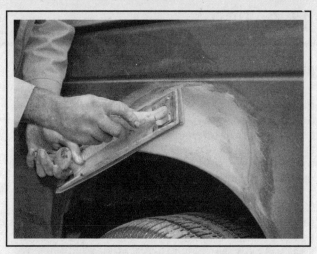

8 Use coarse-grit sandpaper and a sanding board or block to work the filler down until it's smooth and even. Work down to finer grits of sandpaper - always using a board or block - ending up with 360 or 400 grit

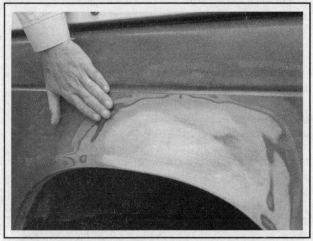

9 You shouldn't be able to feel any ridge at the transition from the filler to the bare metal or from the bare metal to the old paint. As soon as the repair is flat and uniform, remove the dust and mask off the adjacent panels or trim pieces

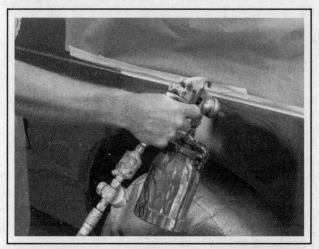

10 Apply several layers of primer to the area. Don't spray the primer on too heavy, so it sags or runs, and make sure each coat is dry before you spray on the next one. A professional-type spray gun is being used here, but aerosol spray primer is available inexpensively from auto parts stores

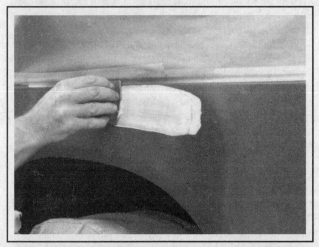

11 The primer will help reveal imperfections or scratches. Fill these with glazing compound. Follow the label instructions and sand it with 360 or 400-grit sandpaper until it's smooth. Repeat the glazing, sanding and respraying until the primer reveals a perfectly smooth surface

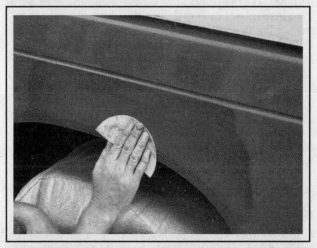

12 Finish sand the primer with very fine sandpaper (400 or 600-grit) to remove the primer overspray. Clean the area with water and allow it to dry. Use a tack rag to remove any dust, then apply the finish coat. Don't attempt to rub out or wax the repair area until the paint has dried completely (at least two weeks)

Repair of dents

20 When repairing dents, the first job is to pull the dent out until the affected area is as close as possible to its original shape. There is no point in trying to restore the original shape completely as the metal in the damaged area will have stretched on impact and cannot be restored to its original contours. It is better to bring the level of the dent up to a point that is about 1/8-inch below the level of the surrounding metal. In cases where the dent is very shallow, it is not worth trying to pull it out at all.

21 If the back side of the dent is accessible, it can be hammered out gently from behind using a soft-face hammer. While doing this, hold a block of wood firmly against the opposite side of the metal to absorb the hammer blows and prevent the metal from being stretched.

22 If the dent is in a section of the body that has double layers, or some other factor makes it inaccessible from behind, a different technique is required. Drill several small holes through the metal inside the damaged area, particularly in the deeper sections. Screw long, self-tapping screws into the holes just enough for them to get a good grip in the metal. Now the dent can be pulled out by pulling on the protruding heads of the screws with locking pliers.

23 The next stage of repair is the removal of paint from the damaged area and from an inch or so of the surrounding metal. This is easily done with a wire brush or sanding disk in a drill motor, although it can be done just as effectively by hand with sandpaper. To complete the preparation for filling, score the surface of the bare metal with a screwdriver or the tang of a file or drill small holes in the affected area. This will provide a good grip for the filler material. To complete the repair, see the Section on filling and painting.

Repair of rust holes or gashes

24 Remove all paint from the affected area and from an inch or so of the surrounding metal using a sanding disk or wire brush mounted in a drill motor. If these are not available, a few sheets of sandpaper will do the job just as effectively.

25 With the paint removed, you will be able to determine the severity of the corrosion and decide whether to replace the whole panel, if possible, or repair the affected area. New body panels are not as expensive as most people think and it is often quicker to install a new panel than to repair large areas of rust.

26 Remove all trim pieces from the affected area except those which will act as a guide to the original shape of the damaged body, such as headlight shells, etc. Using metal snips or a hacksaw blade, remove all loose metal and any other metal that is badly affected by rust. Hammer the edges of the hole in to create a slight depression for the filler material.

27 Wire brush the affected area to remove the powdery rust from the surface of the metal. If the back of the rusted area is accessible, treat it with rust inhibiting paint.

28 Before filling is done, block the hole in some way. This can be done with sheet metal riveted or screwed into place, or by stuffing the hole with wire mesh.

29 Once the hole is blocked off, the affected area can be filled and painted. See the following subsection on filling and painting.

Filling and painting

30 Many types of body fillers are available, but generally speaking, body repair kits which contain filler paste and a tube of resin hardener are best for this type of repair work. A wide, flexible plastic or nylon applicator will be necessary for imparting a smooth and contoured finish to the surface of the filler material. Mix up a small amount of filler on a clean piece of wood or cardboard (use the hardener sparingly). Follow the manufacturer's instructions on the package, otherwise the filler will set incorrectly.

31 Using the applicator, apply the filler paste to the prepared area. Draw the applicator across the surface of the filler to achieve the desired contour and to level the filler surface. As soon as a contour that approximates the original one is achieved, stop working the paste. If you continue, the paste will begin to stick to the applicator. Continue to add thin layers of paste at 20-minute intervals until the level of the filler is just above the surrounding metal.

32 Once the filler has hardened, the excess can be removed with a body file. From then on, progressively finer grades of sandpaper should be used, starting with a 180-grit paper and finishing with 600-grit wet-or-dry paper. Always wrap the sandpaper around a flat rubber or wooden block, otherwise the surface of the filler will not be completely flat. During the sanding of the filler surface, the wet-or-dry paper should be periodically rinsed in water. This will ensure that a very smooth finish is produced in the final stage.

33 At this point, the repair area should be surrounded by a ring of bare metal, which in turn should be encircled by the finely feathered edge of good paint. Rinse the repair area with clean water until all of the dust produced by the sanding operation is gone.

34 Spray the entire area with a light coat of primer. This will reveal any imperfections in the surface of the filler. Repair the imperfections with fresh filler paste or glaze filler and once more smooth the surface with sandpaper. Repeat this spray-and-repair procedure until you are satisfied that the surface of the filler and the feathered edge of the paint are perfect. Rinse the area with clean water and allow it to dry completely.

35 The repair area is now ready for painting. Spray painting must be carried out in a warm, dry, windless and dust free atmosphere. These conditions can be created if you have access to a large indoor work area, but if you are forced to work in the open, you will have to pick the day very carefully. If you are working indoors, dousing the floor in the work area with water will help settle the dust that would otherwise be in the air. If the repair area is confined to one body panel, mask off the surrounding panels. This will help minimize the effects of a slight mismatch in paint color. Trim pieces such as chrome strips, door handles, etc., will also need to be masked off or removed. Use masking tape and several thickness of newspaper for the masking operations.

36 Before spraying, shake the paint can thoroughly, and then spray a test area until the spray-painting technique is mastered. Cover the repair area with a thick coat of primer. The thickness should be built up using several thin layers of primer rather than one thick one. Using 600-grit wet-or-dry sandpaper, rub down the surface of the primer until it is very smooth. While doing this, the work area should be thoroughly rinsed with water and the wet-or-dry sandpaper periodically rinsed as well. Allow the primer to dry before spraying additional coats.

37 Spray on the top coat, again building up the thickness by using several thin layers of paint. Begin spraying in the center of the repair area and then, using a circular motion, work out until the whole repair area and about two inches of the surrounding original paint is covered. Remove all masking material 10 to 15 minutes after spraying on the final coat of paint. Allow the new paint at least two weeks to harden, then use a very fine rubbing compound to blend the edges of the new paint into the existing paint. Finally, apply a coat of wax.

6 Body repair - major damage

1 Major damage must be repaired by an auto body shop specifically equipped to perform unibody repairs. These shops have the specialized equipment required to do the job properly.
2 If the damage is extensive, the body must be checked for proper alignment or the vehicle's handling characteristics may be adversely affected and other components may wear at an accelerated rate.

3 Due to the fact that some of the major body components (hood, fenders, doors, etc.) are separate and replaceable units, any seriously damaged components should be replaced rather than repaired. Sometimes the components can be found in a wrecking yard that specializes in used vehicle components, often at considerable savings over the cost of new parts.

7 Hinges and locks - maintenance

Once every 3000 miles, or every three months, the hinges and latch assemblies on the doors, hood and trunk should be given a few drops of light oil or lock lubricant. The door latch strikers should also be lubricated with a thin coat of grease to reduce wear and ensure free movement. Lubricate the door and trunk locks with spray-on graphite lubricant.

8 Windshield and fixed glass - replacement

Replacement of the windshield and fixed glass requires the use of special fast-setting adhesive/caulk materials and some specialized tools and techniques. These operations should be left to a dealer service department or a shop specializing in glass work.

9 Hood - removal, installation and adjustment

➡Note: The hood is awkward to remove and install; at least two people should perform this procedure.

REMOVAL AND INSTALLATION

▶ Refer to illustrations 9.2 and 9.3

1 Open the hood, then place blankets or pads over the fenders and cowl area of the body. This will protect the body and paint as the hood is lifted off.
2 Make marks around the hood hinge to ensure proper alignment during installation (see illustration).
3 Have an assistant support one side of the hood. Take turns removing the hinge-to-hood bolts and lift off the hood (see illustration).
4 Installation is the reverse of removal. Align the hinge bolts with the marks made in Step 2.

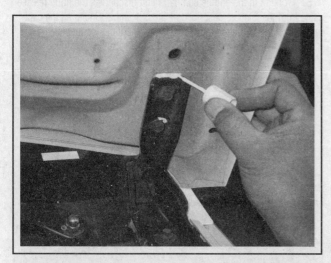
9.2 Draw alignment marks around the hood hinges to ensure proper alignment of the hood when it's reinstalled

9.3 Support the hood with your shoulder while removing the hood bolts

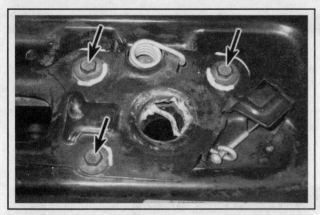

9.7 To adjust the hood latch horizontally or vertically, loosen these bolts

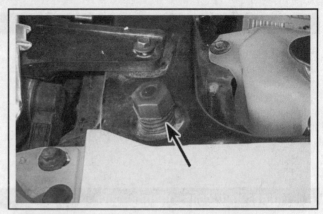

9.8 To adjust the vertical height of the leading edge of the hood so that it's flush with the fenders, turn each edge cushion (arrow indicates one) clockwise (to lower the hood) or counterclockwise (to raise the hood)

ADJUSTMENT

▶ **Refer to illustrations 9.7 and 9.8**

5   Fore-and-aft and side-to-side adjustment of the hood is done by moving the hinges after loosening the hinge-to-body bolts.

6   Loosen the bolts and move the hood into correct alignment. Move it only a little at a time. Tighten the hinge bolts and carefully lower the hood to check the position.

7   If necessary after installation, the entire hood latch assembly can be adjusted from side-to-side on the radiator support so the hood closes properly (see illustration). Scribe a line or mark around the hood latch mounting bolts to provide a reference point, then loosen them and reposition the latch assembly, as necessary. Following adjustment, retighten the mounting bolts.

8   Finally, adjust the hood bumpers on the radiator support so the hood, when closed, is flush with the fenders (see illustration).

9   The hood latch assembly, as well as the hinges, should be periodically lubricated with white, lithium-base grease to prevent binding and wear.

10 Hood latch and release cable - removal and installation

LATCH

▶ **Refer to illustration 10.1**

1   Open the hood and scribe a line around the latch to aid alignment when installing, then remove the retaining bolts securing the hood latch to the radiator support (see illustration). Remove the latch.

2   Disconnect the hood release cable by disengaging the cable from the latch.

3   Installation is the reverse of removal.

CABLE

▶ **Refer to illustration 10.4**

4   Working in the passenger compartment, release the cable from the retainer and slide the end out of the handle (see illustration).

5   Working in the engine compartment, disconnect the hood release cable from the latch as described in Steps 1 and 2. Unclip all the cable retaining clips on the radiator support and the inner fenderwell.

6   The remainder of the installation is the reverse of removal.

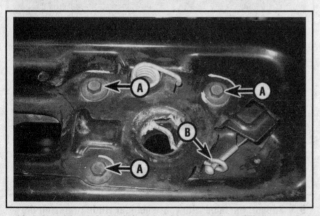

10.1 Hood latch bolts (A) and cable attachment (B)

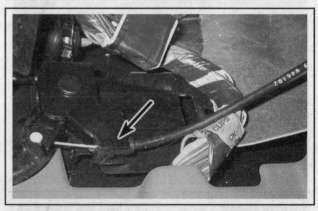

10.4 Pull the cable out of the retainer, then slide the end out of the handle

11 Bumper covers - removal and installation

FRONT BUMPER COVER

2005 and earlier models

▶ **Refer to illustrations 11.3a, 11.3b, 11.4, 11.6, 11.7, 11.8a, 11.8b and 11.8c**

1   Apply the parking brake, raise the vehicle and support it securely on jackstands.

2   Refer to Chapter 12 and remove the headlights and parking lights.

3   Remove the screws and pushpins from the front air dam and lift it off (see illustrations).

➡**Note: Use a small screwdriver to pop the center button up on the plastic fasteners, but do not try to remove the center buttons. They stay in the fastener.**

4   Unclip the front inner fender splash shields from the bumper cover (see illustration). Pull the liners to the rear or remove them completely.

5   Disconnect the fog lights (if so equipped).

6   Unbolt the bumper cover from the lower front part of each fender (see illustration).

7   Remove the retainers from the top and the bottom of the bumper cover (see illustration).

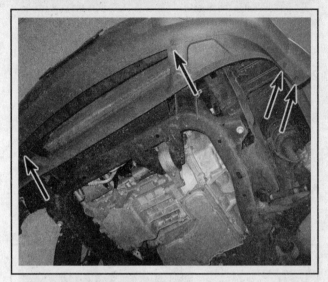

11.3a Remove the air dam fasteners . . .

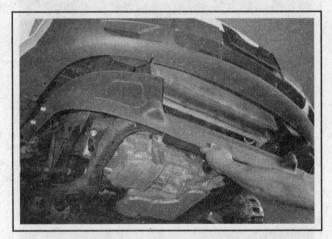

11.3b . . . and separate the air dam from the bumper cover

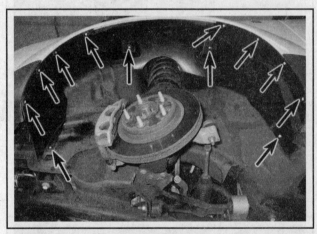

11.4 The front inner fender splash shields are retained by plastic pushpin fasteners - pry the heads out and remove them

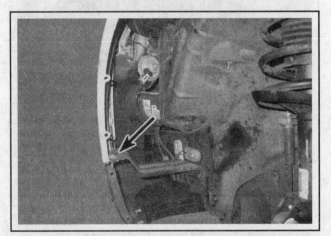

11.6 The bumper cover-to-fender screws are accessible when the inner fender splash shields are removed

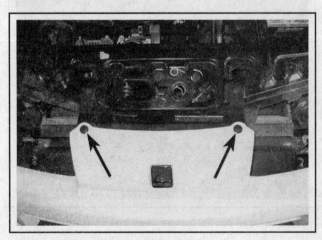

11.7 Bumper cover top mounting fasteners

8 Pull the bumper cover forward to release the lock tabs from the fenders, then lift off the cover (see illustrations).

9 Installation is the reverse of removal. Make sure the tabs (if equipped) on the back of the bumper cover fit into the corresponding clips on the body before installing the fasteners. An assistant is helpful at this point.

2006 and later models

10 Refer to Chapter 12 and remove the headlights.

Standard models

11 Remove the upper grille.
12 Remove the hood stop bumpers.
13 Remove the upper bumper support.

All models

14 Remove the fasteners from the lower air dam and lift it off.

15 Remove the two pushpins from the front of each wheel well liner.
16 Pull the bumper cover forward to release it as you lift it off.
17 Installation is the reverse of removal.

REAR BUMPER COVER

2005 and earlier models

▸ **Refer to illustrations 11.18, 11.19, 11.20 and 11.21**

18 Remove the inner fender splash shields (see illustration).
19 Open the liftgate and remove the pushpin fasteners from the top of the bumper cover (see illustration).

➡**Note: Use a small screwdriver to pop the center button up on the plastic fasteners, but do not try to remove the center buttons. They stay in the fastener.**

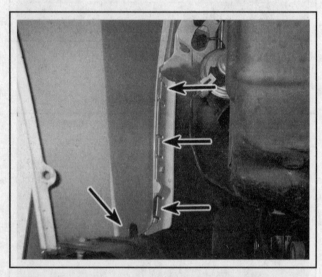

11.8a The ends of the bumper cover are attached with clips

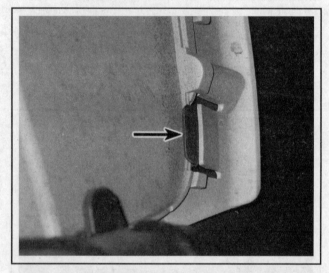

11.8b Release the bumper cover end clips . . .

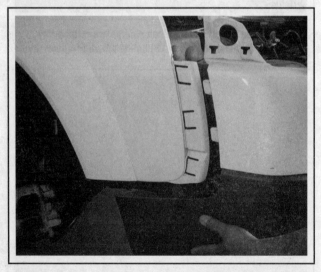

11.8c . . . and pull the bumper cover free

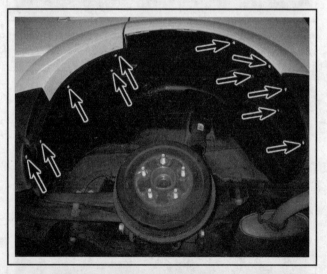

11.18 The rear inner fender splash shields are attached with plastic pushpins - pry the heads out and remove them

20 Detach the fasteners securing the bottom of the bumper cover (see illustration).

21 Unclip each end of the bumper cover from the body by working through the wheel wells to reach the tabs (see illustration).

22 Pull the bumper cover out and away from the vehicle.

23 Installation is the reverse of removal.

2006 and later models

24 Open the liftgate and remove the six pushpin fasteners from the top of the bumper cover.

25 Remove the four fasteners from the bottom.

26 Remove the two fasteners at each end of the bumper cover inside the wheel wells.

27 Pull the bumper cover out and away from the vehicle.

28 Installation is the reverse of removal.

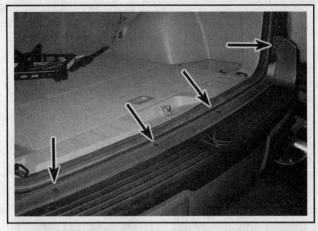

11.19 Rear bumper cover upper mounting fasteners

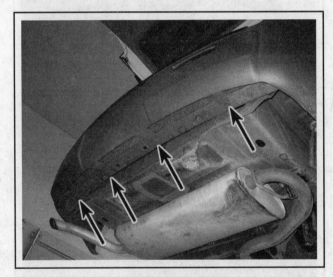

11.20 Rear bumper cover lower mounting fasteners

11.21 Remove the inner fender splash shield for access to the clips at the ends of the rear bumper cover

12 Front fender - removal and installation

♦ **Refer to illustrations 12.4, 12.5, 12.6a, 12.6b, 12.7a, 12.7b and 12.10**

1 Loosen the front wheel lug nuts. Raise the vehicle, support it securely on jackstands and remove the front wheel.

2 Open the hood.

3 Detach the inner fenderwell push pins, then remove the inner fender splash shield (see illustration 11.4).

4 Remove the pushpin at the front of the rocker molding (see illustration).

5 Pull the molding forward and remove the fender lower mounting bolts (see illustration).

6 Remove the triangular windshield filler/mirror panel by removing the screw and sliding it up (see illustrations).

7 Remove the side marker light housing (see illustrations).

8 Remove the two bolts under the ends of the front bumper cover.

9 If necessary, remove the antenna mast (see Chapter 12).

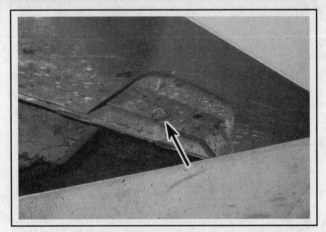

12.4 Remove this pushpin at the front of the rocker molding

10 Remove the fasteners along the top edge of the fender (see illustration).

11 Detach the fender from the bumper cover, then lift off the fender. It's a good idea to have an assistant support the fender while it's being moved away from the vehicle to prevent damage to the surrounding body panels.

12 Installation is the reverse of removal. Check the alignment of the fender to the hood and front edge of the door before final tightening of the fender fasteners.

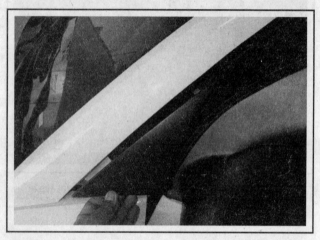

12.5 Pull the molding forward and remove the fender lower mounting bolts

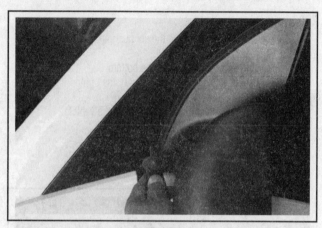

12.6a Remove the trim panel screw . . .

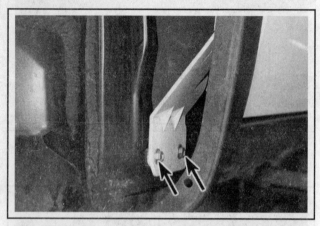

12.6b . . . then lift the panel upward

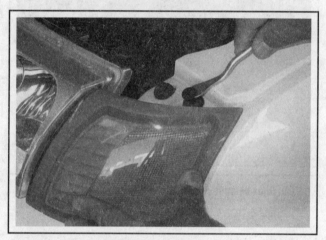

12.7a Remove the push pin . . .

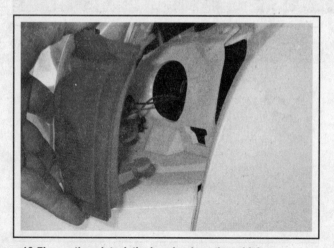

12.7b . . . then detach the housing from the vehicle

12.10 Remove the fender upper mounting fasteners

13 Radiator grille - removal and installation

2005 AND EARLIER MODELS

1 Refer to Section 11 and remove the front bumper cover.
2 Release the retaining clips and pull the grille to the rear.
3 Installation is the reverse of removal.

2006 AND LATER MODELS

4 Remove the hood stop bumper screws and pull up the grille.
5 Installation is the reverse of removal.

14 Cowl covers - removal and installation

♦ **Refer to illustrations 14.4a and 14.4b**

1 Remove the wiper arms (see Chapter 12). Make sure the wipers are in the parked position and note the locations of the blades on the windshield.
2 Remove the push pin fasteners securing the cowl cover.

➡**Note: Use a small screwdriver to pop the center button up on the plastic fasteners, but do not try to remove the center buttons. They stay in the fastener.**

3 Remove the right cowl cover.
4 Lift the left grille and disconnect the washer hose (see illustrations).
5 Installation is the reverse of removal.

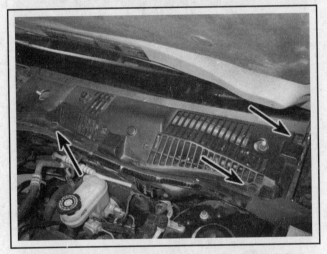

14.4a Remove the pushpin fasteners, then lift off the left cowl cover

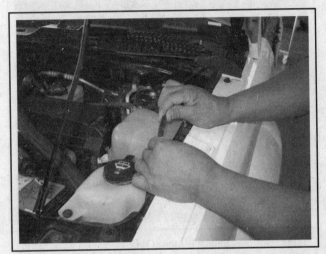

14.4b Disconnect the washer hose to remove the left section of the cowl cover

15 Door trim panels - removal and installation

※※ **WARNING:**

The models covered by this manual are equipped with Supplemental Restraint systems (SRS), more commonly known as airbags. Always disarm the airbag system before working in the vicinity of any airbag system component to avoid the possibility of accidental deployment of the airbag, which could cause personal injury (see Chapter 12).

※※ **CAUTION:**

Wear gloves when working inside the door openings to protect against sharp metal edges.

FRONT AND REAR DOORS

♦ **Refer to illustrations 15.2, 15.3a, 15.3b, 15.3c, 15.5a, 15.5b, 15.6, 15.8, 15.9, 15.10a, 15.10b and 15.12**

1 Disconnect the cable from the negative battery terminal (see Chapter 5, Section 1).
2 Pry off the screw cover from the inside release handle cover and remove the screw (see illustration).
3 Slide the handle forward and out. Disengage the two rods and set the clips aside (see illustrations).
4 Disconnect the power window wiring if so equipped.
5 Use a plastic trim tool or a screwdriver wrapped with tape to pry

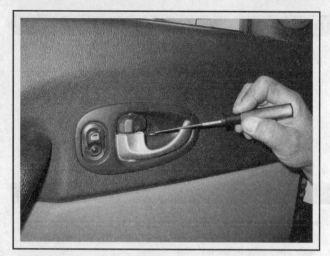

15.2 Pry off the small cover from the door latch handle, then remove the screw under it

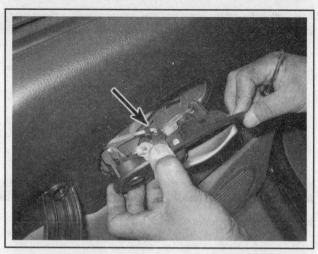

15.3a Carefully pull out the door release handle and detach the upper rod . . .

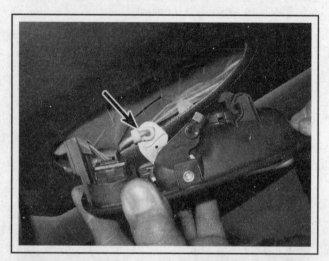

15.3b . . . then detach the lower rod

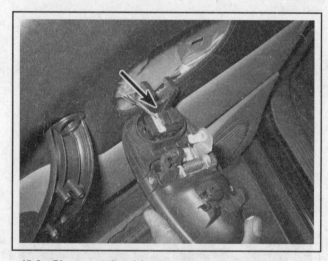

15.3c Disconnect the wiring

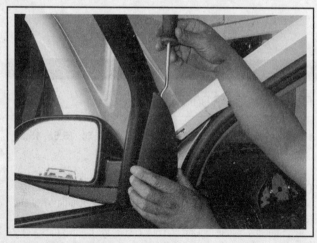

15.5a Pry off the mirror cover - be careful to avoid scratching the trim

off the triangular panel at the top of the front doors (see illustration), then disconnect the speaker wiring (see illustration).

6 Remove the screw at the top of the door panel (see illustration).

7 If the vehicle has manual windows, use a special handle removal tool to remove the retaining clip from the handle, then pull the handle from its shaft.

8 Remove the cover from the pull-handle (see illustration). It has a tab near the bottom that must be released.

9 Remove the screws behind the pull-handle cover (see illustration).

10 Remove the fasteners at the bottom edge of the panel (see illustration). Later models also have pushpin fasteners at the rear edge that must be removed (see illustration).

➡**Note: Use a small screwdriver to pop the center button up on the plastic fasteners, but do not try to remove the center buttons - they stay in the fastener.**

11 Carefully pull the panel upward until the clips disengage.

15.5b Disconnect the speaker wiring

15.6 There is a screw under the mirror trim panel

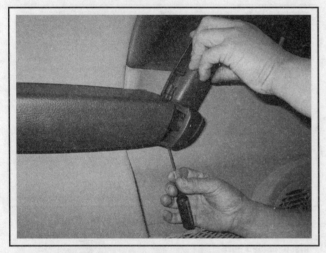

15.8 Pry the cover from the door pull handle

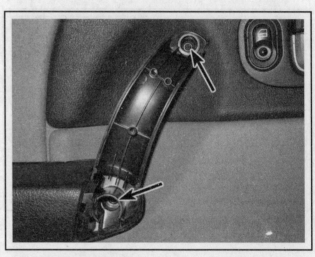

15.9 Remove the two handle screws

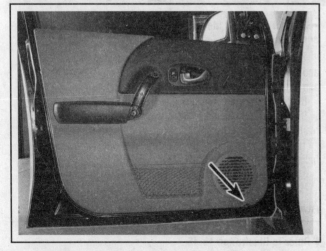

15.10a There are door panel screws at the lower edge of the door . . .

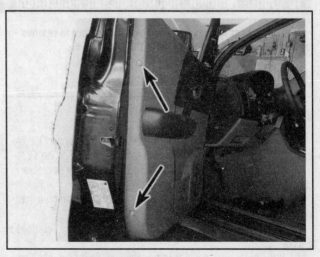

15.10b . . . and at the rear

12 For access to the door outside handle or the door window regulator inside the door, raise the window fully, then carefully peel back the plastic watershield (see illustration).

13 Installation is the reverse of removal.

LIFTGATE

▶ **Refer to illustrations 15.14 and 15.15**

14 Open the liftgate and remove the pushpin fasteners and the screws at the handle (see illustration).

➡**Note: Use a small screwdriver to pop the center button up on the plastic fasteners, but do not try to remove the center buttons. They stay in the fastener.**

15 Pull on the bottom part of the trim panel to disengage the lower retaining clips (see illustration).

16 Reach under the panel and disconnect the wiring harnesses.

17 Pry the panel off from the top and remove it.

18 Installation is the reverse of removal.

15.12 Carefully peel back the plastic watershield

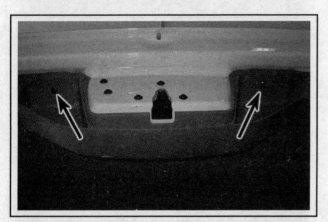

15.14 Remove these screws from the liftgate trim panel

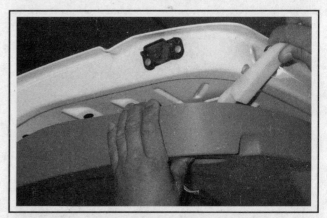

15.15 Pry outward starting at the bottom of the panel; the courtesy lights have been previously pried out and disconnected here

16 Door - removal, installation and adjustment

➡**Note: The door is heavy and somewhat awkward to remove - at least two people should perform this procedure.**

REMOVAL AND INSTALLATION

▶ **Refer to illustration 16.8**

1 Raise the window completely in the door and disconnect the cable from the negative battery terminal (see Chapter 5, Section 1).

2 Open the door all the way and support it with a jack or blocks covered with rags to prevent damaging the outer surface.

3 Remove the fender (see Section 12) if you're working on a front door and must replace the hinges.

4 Remove the inner door trim panel and watershield as described in Section 15.

5 If the outer door panel is to be removed, do it now (see Section 17).

6 Disconnect all electrical connections, ground wires and harness retaining clips from inside the door.

➡**Note: It is a good idea to label all connections to aid the reassembly process.**

7 From the door side, detach the rubber conduit between the body and the door. Then, pull the wiring harness through the conduit hole and remove it from the door.

8 Unbolt the door stop strut (see illustration).

9 Mark around the door hinges with a pen or a scribe to facilitate realignment during reassembly.

10 With an assistant holding the door, remove the hinge-to-door bolts and lift off the door.

11 Installation is the reverse of removal.

ADJUSTMENT

▶ **Refer to illustration 16.15**

12 Having proper door-to-body alignment is a critical part of a well-functioning door assembly. First check the door hinge pins for excessive play. Fully open the door and lift up and down on the door without

lifting the body. If a door has 1/16-inch or more excessive play, the hinges should be replaced.

13 Door-to-body alignment adjustments are made by loosening the hinge-to-body bolts or hinge-to-door bolts and moving the door. Proper body alignment is achieved when the top of the doors are parallel with the roof section, the front door is flush with the fender, the rear door is flush with the rear quarter panel and the bottom of the doors are aligned with the lower rocker panel. If these goals can't be reached by adjusting the hinge-to-body or hinge-to-door bolts, body alignment shims may

have to be purchased and inserted behind the hinges to achieve correct alignment.

14 To adjust the door-closed position, scribe a line or mark around the striker plate to provide a reference point, then check that the door latch is contacting the center of the latch striker. If not, adjust the up and down position first.

15 Finally adjust the latch striker sideways position, so that the door panel is flush with the center pillar or rear quarter panel and provides positive engagement with the latch mechanism (see illustration).

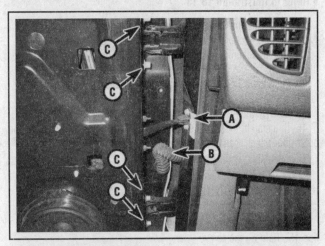

16.8 Door mounting details

A Door stop strut
B Wiring harness rubber conduit
C Hinge-to-door mounting bolts

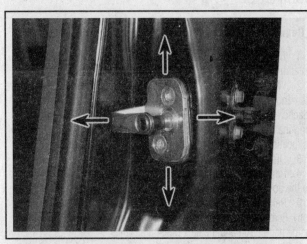

16.15 Adjust the door lock striker by loosening the mounting screws and gently tapping the striker in the desired direction

17 Door outer panel - removal and installation

▶ **Refer to illustrations 17.3 and 17.4**

1 For front doors, use a plastic trim tool or a screwdriver wrapped with tape to remove the cover from the inside of the door mirror. Remove the mirror, disconnecting the wiring harness as you do so (see Section 21).

2 Pull the outside door handle and remove the pushpin fastener. Move the handle forward to remove it (see Section 18).

3 Remove the screw from the rear of the outer glass seal strip.

Carefully pry the seal strip up at the rear and work forward to remove it (see illustration).

4 Remove the fasteners from the rear of the outer door panel and lift it off (see illustration).

5 Installation is the reverse of removal. Make sure to tighten the fasteners snug and in the correct sequence to avoid distortion. The top-most rear screw must be tightened first. Next tighten the topmost front screw, then the one next to it. Work your way back around in order to the upper rear screw.

17.3 Remove the screw from the rear of the front door upper trim, then gently pry it up starting from the rear

17.4 The outer door panel is light but can be easily scratched if dropped - get an assistant to help

18 Door latch, lock cylinder and handles - removal and installation

✳✳ CAUTION:

Wear gloves when working inside the door openings to protect against cuts from sharp metal edges.

DOOR LATCH

▶ **Refer to illustrations 18.2 and 18.5**

1 Raise the window, then remove the door trim panel and watershield (see Section 15).
2 Working through the large access hole, disengage the rods from the handle and lock cylinder (see illustration). All door lock rods are attached by plastic clips. The plastic clips can be removed by unsnapping the portion engaging the connecting rod and pulling the rod out of its locating hole.
3 Disconnect the electrical connectors at the latch.
4 Release the inside handle rod and the lock rod from the guides on the door.
5 Remove the screws securing the latch to the door (see illustration). Remove the latch assembly through the door opening with the inside handle rod and the lock rod still attached.
6 After the latch is removed, disconnect the two rods from the latch.
7 Installation is the reverse of removal.

OUTSIDE HANDLE

▶ **Refer to illustration 18.8**

8 While pulling the handle, remove the pushpin from the bottom of

the handle (see illustration).
9 Slide the handle forward to disengage it.
10 Installation is the reverse of removal.

DOOR LOCK CYLINDER

▶ **Refer to illustration 18.13**

11 Make sure that the window is in the up position.
12 Refer to Section 17 and remove the outer door panel.
13 Pull the retaining clip from the rear of the door lock cylinder (see illustration).
14 Push the lock into the door and remove the lock rod from the latch.
15 Remove the lock cylinder.
16 To install it, first make sure that the lock is correctly placed on the outer door panel, then install the retaining clip.
17 Installation is the reverse of removal.

INSIDE DOOR HANDLE

18 Pry off the screw cover at the center of the handle trim (see Section 15). Remove the screw.
19 Slide the handle assembly forward while pulling it out of the door panel.
20 Disconnect both rods from the latch.
21 If the vehicle has power windows, disconnect the wiring harness from the rear of the handle.
22 Installation is the reverse of removal.

18.2 The actuating rods are attached with plastic lips - snap them off of the rods, then pull the rods out of the holes in the clips

18.5 Latch mounting screws

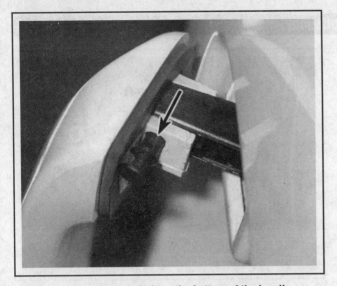

18.8 Remove the pushpin from the bottom of the handle

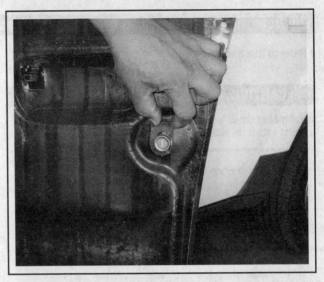

18.13 The outer door panel must be removed before the lock retaining clip can be removed

19 Door window glass - removal and installation

✳✳ CAUTION:

Wear gloves when working inside the door openings to protect against cuts from sharp metal edges.

DOOR GLASS

▶ **Refer to illustration 19.4**

1   Remove the door trim panel and the plastic watershield (see Section 15).

2   Remove the top outer seal from the top of the door by first removing the screw at its rear. Gently pry the seal upward, starting at the rear (see Section 17).

3   On rear doors, remove the door speaker for access.

4   Position the window so the bottom glass bolts are accessible through the openings in the door structure (see illustration). Remove the bolts.

5   On rear windows only, pull the window out of the regulator guide plate.

6   Slide the glass down and out of the side guide channels.

7   Pull the window through the upper opening, sliding it to the outside as you do so.

8   Installation is the reverse of removal.

LIFTGATE, WINDSHIELD AND QUARTER WINDOW GLASS

9   Replacement of these glass pieces requires the use of special fast-setting urethane adhesive materials, some specialized tools and techniques. These operations should be left to a dealer service department or a shop specializing in glass work.

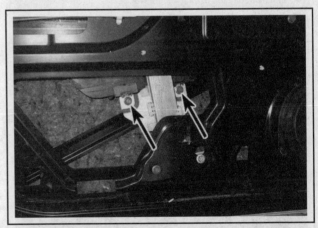

19.4 The window must be raised somewhat to access the glass mounting bolts; it may be necessary to temporarily install the power window switch

20 Door window glass regulator - removal and installation

♦ Refer to illustration 20.3

✳✳ CAUTION:

Wear gloves when working inside the door openings to protect against cuts from sharp metal edges.

1   Remove the window glass (see Section 19).
2   Disconnect the electrical connector from the window regulator motor on vehicles so equipped.
3   Remove the two bolts that go through conventional holes (see illustration).
4   Loosen (only) the bolts that go through keyhole-shaped holes.
5   Remove the regulator through the bottom access hole in the door.
6   Installation is the reverse of removal. Lubricate the rollers and wear points on the regulator with white grease before installation.

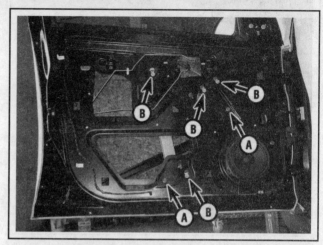

20.3 Remove the two bolts that go through conventional holes (A), then partially loosen the bolts that go through the keyhole-shaped holes (B)

21 Mirrors - removal and installation

OUTSIDE MIRRORS

♦ Refer to illustration 21.3

1   Pry the upper corner of the trim panel out until its retaining clip disengages (see illustration 15.5).
2   Slide the panel up to disengage it from the door panel.
3   Disconnect the electrical connector from the mirror, then remove the three mirror retaining bolts and detach the mirror from the vehicle (see illustration).
4   Installation is the reverse of removal.

INSIDE MIRROR

♦ Refer to illustration 21.7

5   Disconnect the electrical connector from the mirror, if equipped.
6   Remove the setscrew located at the base of the mirror stalk.
7   Slide the mirror upwards to remove it from its mount (see illustration).
8   If the mount plate itself has come off the windshield, adhesive kits are available at auto parts stores to resecure it. Follow the instructions included with the kit. Be sure to position the flanged part of the mount away from the glass and the narrower part pointing up.

21.3 Outside mirror fasteners

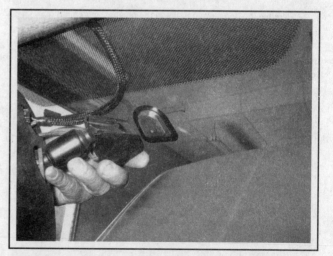

21.7 Remove the mirror set screw, then lift the mirror carefully upwards

22 Liftgate - removal, installation and adjustment

➡Note: The liftgate is heavy and awkward to remove - at least two people should perform this procedure.

REMOVAL AND INSTALLATION

▸ Refer to illustrations 22.4, 22.7 and 22.8

1 Disconnect the cable from the negative battery terminal (see Chapter 5, Section 1).
2 Open the liftgate and support it securely.
3 Firmly grasp the interior roof trim panel that is attached nearest the top of the liftgate and pull it free.
4 Disconnect the two wiring harness connectors at the top rear of the roof (see illustration).
5 Disconnect the washer hose.
6 Release the grommet and pull the hose and the wiring harnesses out of the upper jamb.
7 With an assistant holding the liftgate, disconnect the support struts by prying out the small clips, then pulling the struts from their ballstuds (see illustration).
8 With an assistant holding the liftgate, remove the hinge-to-body bolts and lift the liftgate off (see illustration).

➡Note: Draw a reference line around the hinges on the body before removing the bolts.

9 Installation is the reverse of removal.

ADJUSTMENT

10 Having proper liftgate-to-body alignment is a critical part of a well-functioning liftgate assembly. First check the liftgate hinge pins for excessive play. Fully open the liftgate and lift up and down on the liftgate without lifting the body. If a liftgate has 1/8-inch or more excessive play, the hinges should be replaced.
11 Liftgate-to-body alignment adjustments are made by loosen-

ing the hinge-to-body bolts or hinge-to-liftgate bolts and moving the liftgate. Proper body alignment is achieved when the top of the liftgate is parallel with the roof section and the sides of the liftgate are flush with the rear quarter panels and the bottom of the liftgate is aligned with the lower liftgate sill. If these goals can't be reached by adjusting the hinge-to-body or hinge-to-liftgate bolts, body alignment shims may have to be purchased and inserted behind the hinges to achieve correct alignment.
12 To adjust the liftgate-closed position, scribe a line or mark around the striker plate to provide a reference point, then check that the liftgate latch is contacting the center of the latch striker. If not, adjust the up and down position first.
13 Finally adjust the latch striker sideways position, so that the liftgate panel is flush with the rear quarter panel and provides positive engagement with the latch mechanism.

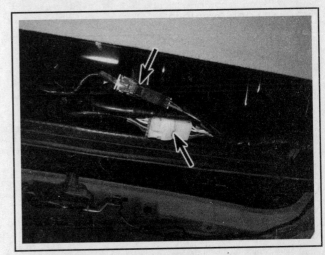

22.4 Disconnect the liftgate wiring harness connectors under the rear roof trim panel

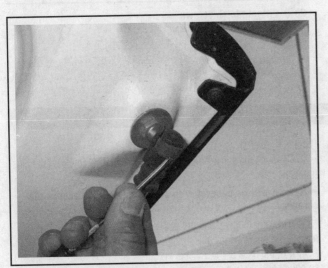

22.7 Use a small screwdriver to release the clip, then pull the liftgate support strut off its ballstud

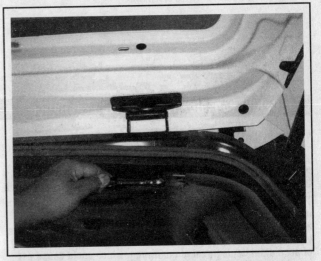

22.8 Have an assistant standing ready as you detach the liftgate hinges

23 Liftgate latch, lock cylinder and handle - removal and installation

LIFTGATE LATCH

▶ **Refer to illustrations 23.3 and 23.5**

1   Disconnect the cable from the negative battery terminal (see Chapter 5, Section 1).

2   Open the liftgate and remove the door trim panel and watershield as described in Section 15.

3   Disconnect the electrical connector from the latch, then disconnect the handle rod from the crank (see illustration).

4   Remove the lock cylinder (see Step 11).

5   Unbolt and remove the latch along with the two rods attached to it (see illustration).

6   Disconnect the lock cylinder rod and the crank rod from the latch.

7   Installation is the reverse of removal.

LIFTGATE LOCK CYLINDER

8   Open the liftgate and remove the door trim panel and watershield as described in Section 15.

9   Working through the large access hole, use a small tool to press in on the lock cylinder release button. It's on the bottom of the outer handle assembly.

10 Pull the lock cylinder out of the handle assembly and disconnect the rod from its lever.

11 Installation is the reverse of removal.

LIFTGATE OUTSIDE HANDLE

12 Open the liftgate and remove the door trim panel and watershield as described in Section 15.

13 Remove the lock cylinder.

14 Disconnect the outside handle rod from the handle.

15 Remove the two handle mounting screws and detach the handle from the liftgate (see illustration 23.3)

16 Installation is the reverse of removal.

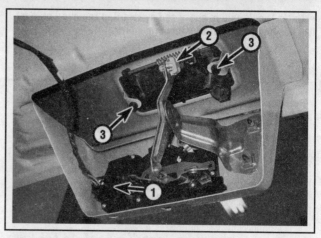

23.3 Liftgate latch and outside handle details;

1   *Liftgate latch electrical connector*
2   *Liftgate outside handle rod*
3   *Liftgate outside handle mounting fasteners*

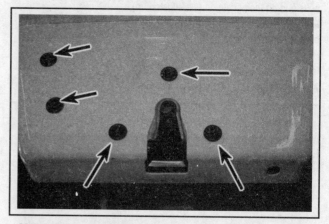

23.5 Liftgate latch screws

24 Center console - removal and installation

▶ **Refer to illustrations 24.2 and 24.5**

✳✳ WARNING:

The models covered by this manual are equipped with Supplemental Restraint Systems (SRS), more commonly known as airbags. Always disable the airbag system before working in the vicinity of any airbag system component to avoid the possibility of accidental deployment of the airbag, which could cause personal injury (see Chapter 12).

1   Disconnect the cable from the negative battery terminal (see Chapter 5, Section 1).

2   Remove the screws from the lower sides of the console (see illustration).

➡**Note: It will be necessary to adjust the seats to access the screws.**

3   On early models, pull out the liner from the cup holder and remove the screw beneath it.

4   Lift the back of the console and disconnect the wiring harness (if so equipped).

5   Remove the console from the floor. The upper section can be separated from the lower if necessary (see illustration).

6   Installation is the reverse of removal.

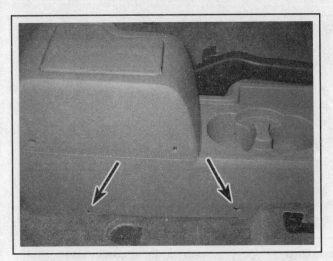

24.2 Remove the lower screws and lift the console (seats removed for clarity) - disconnect any wiring as you remove it (right side shown, left side similar)

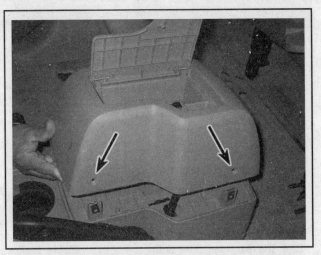

24.5 The upper section can be removed from the main part after removing two screws from each side - disconnect the wiring as you remove it

25 Dashboard trim panels - removal and installation

❋❋ WARNING:

Models covered by this manual are equipped with a Supplemental Restraint System (SRS), more commonly known as airbags. Always disable the airbag system before working in the vicinity of any airbag system component to avoid the possibility of accidental deployment of the airbag, which could cause personal injury (see Chapter 12).

1 These panels provide access to various instrument panel mounting screws. Some of the covers use fasteners and others are easily pried off with a screwdriver wrapped with tape or a plastic automotive trim removal stick. If you're going to remove the entire instrument panel, remove all of the covers.

2 Disconnect the cable from the negative terminal of the battery (see Chapter 5, Section 1).

SHIFTER CONSOLE BEZEL

▶ **Refer to illustrations 25.4 and 25.5**

3 Place the shifter into Neutral.

4 Use a plastic trim tool or a screwdriver wrapped with tape to pry up at the front of the bezel (see illustration). Work toward the rear two clips until the bezel is detached.

5 Lift the bezel and disconnect the wiring (see illustration).

6 Installation is the reverse of removal.

25.4 Use a soft tool to pry up the console top bezel

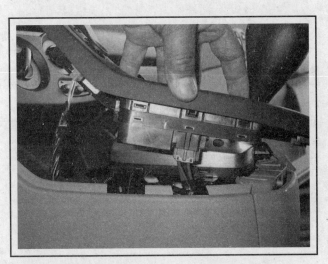

25.5 Disconnect the wiring as you remove the shifter console top bezel

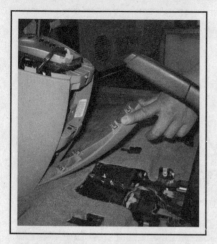

25.8 The rear cover of the shifter
console can be carefully pried off

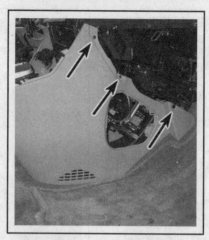

25.11a Shifter console cover
side fasteners

25.11b Shifter console cover
rear fasteners

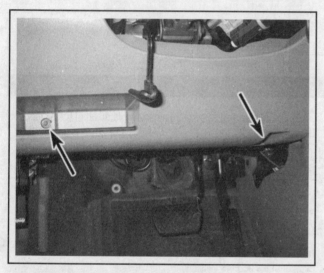

25.13 Remove the fasteners securing the driver's
knee bolster

25.16 Pry the glove box pivots inward

SHIFTER CONSOLE SIDE AND REAR COVERS

▶ **Refer to illustrations 25.8, 25.11a and 25.11b**

7   Refer to Section 24 and remove the center console.
8   Pull off the cover from the rear of the shifter console (see illustration).
9   Remove the shifter console bezel (see Steps 3 through 5).
10 Remove the glove box (see Steps 16 and 17) and the driver's knee bolster (see Steps 13 and 14).
11 Remove the screws from the side trim panels as well as the push-pin fasteners (see illustrations).
12 Installation is the reverse of removal.

DRIVER'S KNEE BOLSTER

▶ **Refer to illustration 25.13**

13 Remove the two screws (see illustration).
14 Pull the panel rearward to detach its clips.
15 Installation is the reverse of removal.

GLOVE BOX

▶ **Refer to illustrations 25.16 and 25.17**

16 Open the glove box and pry out the pivot pins (see illustration).

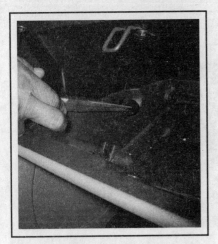

25.17 Twist the glove box stops to remove them

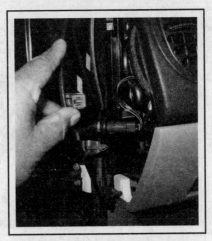

25.20 Disconnect the wiring as you remove the instrument panel end cover

25.21 Push the centers of the fasteners in with a pointed tool, then remove the fasteners

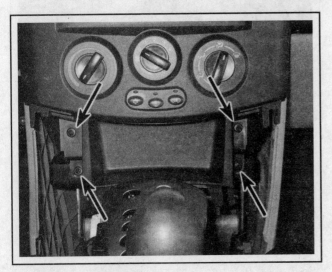

25.25 Remove these screws . . .

25.26 . . . then pull the bottom of the center bezel out to remove it

17 Twist the two door stop pins to remove them (see illustration). Remove the glove box.
18 Installation is the reverse of removal.

INSTRUMENT PANEL END COVERS

▶ **Refer to illustrations 25.20 and 25.21**

19 Remove the driver's knee bolster (see Steps 13 and 14).
20 Remove the left end cover by pulling it to disengage the clips (see illustration).
21 Open the glove box and remove the fasteners at the right end cover to remove it (see illustration).

22 Disconnect the door switches from the covers and remove them.
23 Installation is the reverse of removal.

CENTER PANEL BEZEL

▶ **Refer to illustrations 25.25 and 25.26**

24 Remove the shifter console bezel (see Steps 3 through 5).
25 Remove the center storage bin from the bezel (see illustration).
26 Use a plastic trim tool or a screwdriver wrapped with tape to pull the bottom of the bezel rearward to unclip it. Work your way toward the top until all the clips are detached (see illustration).
27 Disconnect the wiring and the cable from the back of the bezel.

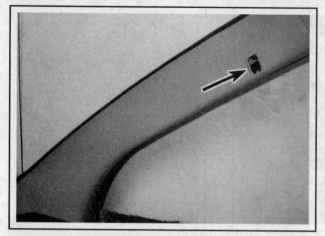

25.31 The windshield pillar cover retaining screw is under this plastic cover

25.34 Remove the instrument cluster bezel screws

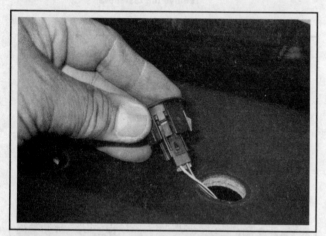

25.44 Pull the light sensor from the top of the instrument panel, then disconnect the electrical connector

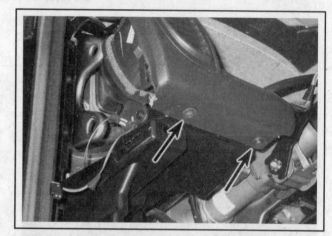

25.45a Remove the fasteners securing the left side . . .

28 Installation is the reverse of removal.
29 Make sure to center the temp control knob by inserting the centering tab into the slot in the shaft.
30 Center the temp door by lining up the lug on its cable with the center of the detent spring. When both centering procedures have been done, snap the temp cable onto the temp knob shaft.

WINDSHIELD PILLAR COVERS

▶ **Refer to illustration 25.31**

31 Pry off the screw covers and remove the screws (see illustration).
32 Gently but firmly pull the covers from the pillars.
33 Installation is the reverse of removal.

INSTRUMENT CLUSTER BEZEL

▶ **Refer to illustration 25.34**

34 Lower the steering column and remove the mounting screws from the bezel (see illustration).
35 Pull the bezel rearward to unclip it.

36 Installation is the reverse of removal.

UPPER PANEL COVER

▶ **Refer to illustrations 25.44, 25.45a, 25.45b, 25.45c, 25.45d and 25.45e**

37 Remove the driver's knee bolster (see Steps 13 and 14).
38 Remove both instrument panel end covers (see Steps 19 through 22).
39 Remove the shifter console bezel (see Steps 3 through 5).
40 Remove the center panel bezel (see Steps 24 through 27).
41 Refer to Section 26 and remove the steering column covers.
42 Remove the instrument cluster bezel (see Steps 34 and 35).
43 Working in the right end of the instrument panel, remove the screw from the air register. Remove the air register.
44 If your vehicle is equipped with a light sensor in the top of the instrument panel, use a plastic trim tool or a screwdriver wrapped with tape to pry it up (see illustration). Disconnect the electrical connector from the sensor and remove it.
45 Pry the plastic covers from the instrument panel fasteners, then remove all of the bolts and screws (see illustrations).
46 Carefully lift the upper instrument panel through one of the doors.

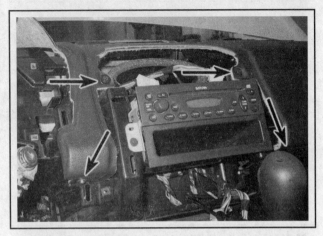

25.45b . . . at the center . . .

25.45c . . . and at the right lower edge of the upper panel cover

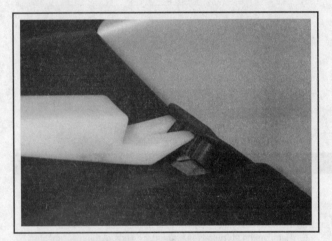

25.45d Pry up the covers from the top of the instrument panel . . .

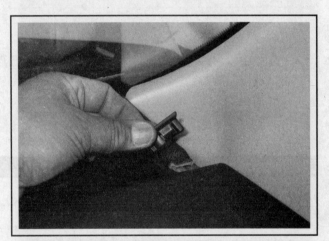

25.45e . . . then lift them off and remove the screws under them

26 Steering column covers - removal and installation

▶ Refer to illustrations 26.2 and 26.3

✳✳ WARNING:

Models covered by this manual are equipped with a Supplemental Restraint System (SRS), more commonly known as airbags. Always disable the airbag system before working in the vicinity of any airbag system component to avoid the possibility of accidental deployment of the airbag, which could cause personal injury (see Chapter 12).

1   Disconnect the cable from the negative terminal of the battery (see Chapter 5, Section 1).

2   Remove the screws from the bottom of the lower cover (see illustration).

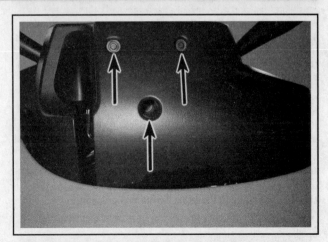

26.2 The steering column cover screws are accessible from the bottom

3   Pry the upper cover up until it unclips from the lower cover (see illustration).

4   Pry the ignition switch bezel out of the lower cover. Remove the covers.

5   Installation is the reverse of the removal procedure.

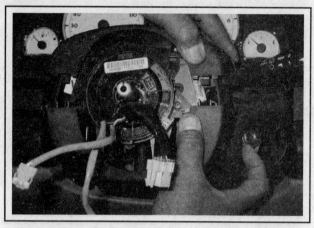

26.3 Separate the steering column covers after removing the screws

27 Instrument panel - removal and installation

▶ Refer to illustrations 27.11a, 27.11b, 27.11c, 27.13a, 27.13b, 27.13c, 27.13d, 27.13e and 27.13f

✳✳ WARNING:

Models covered by this manual are equipped with a Supplemental Restraint System (SRS), more commonly known as airbags. Always disable the airbag system before working in the vicinity of any airbag system component to avoid the possibility of accidental deployment of the airbag, which could cause personal injury (see Chapter 12).

➡ Note 1: This is a difficult procedure for the home mechanic. There are many hidden fasteners, difficult angles to work in and many electrical connectors to tag and disconnect/connect. We recommend that this procedure be done only by an experienced do-it-yourselfer.

➡ Note 2: During removal of the instrument panel, make careful notes of how each piece comes off, where it fits in relation to other pieces and what holds it in place. If you note how each part is installed before removing it, getting the instrument panel back together again will be much easier.

➡ Note 3: It is not mandatory, but it is suggested to remove both front seats to allow additional working space and lessen the chance of damage to the seats during this procedure.

1   Disconnect the cable from the negative battery terminal (see Chapter 5, Section 1).

2   Remove the instrument panel upper cover and the glove box (see Section 25)

3   Remove the instrument cluster and the radio (see Chapter 12).

4   Refer to Section 24 and remove the center storage console.

5   Remove the shifter console side covers (see Section 25).

6   Remove the air outlets that are at the ends of the instrument panel.

7   Unclip the instrument cluster wiring from the instrument panel and disconnect the radio ground wire.

8   Working at the right end of the panel, disconnect the large wiring harnesses from the body control module.

9   Remove the diagnostic link connector by releasing its retaining tabs and pushing it through the instrument panel.

10 Pry out the kick panels/door thresholds.

11 Disconnect the electrical connector for the passenger airbag module, then remove the two bolts securing the passenger airbag module (see illustrations). Remove the airbag.

12 Several electrical connectors and ground wires must be disconnected in order to remove the instrument panel. Most are designed so that they will only fit on the matching connector, but if there is any doubt, mark the connectors with masking tape and a marking pen before disconnecting them.

13 Remove all of the fasteners holding the instrument panel to the body (see illustrations). Once all are removed, lift the panel, then pull it away from the windshield and take it out through the driver's door opening (see illustration).

➡ Note: This is a two-person job.

14 Installation is the reverse of removal. Make sure that there is an insulator at each matching point where the instrument panel attaches to the support. Install the mounting screws and tighten them starting from the middle and working outward.

27.11a Pull out the airbag orange safety clip, then disconnect the electrical connector

27.11b Remove the two bolts securing the passenger airbag module . . .

27.11c . . . then release the tabs securing the airbag

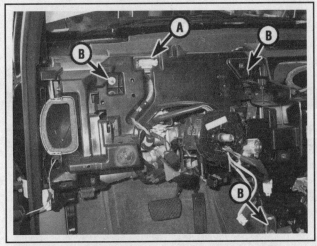

27.13a Release the wiring harness (A), then remove the mounting fasteners from the left side of the instrument panel (B)

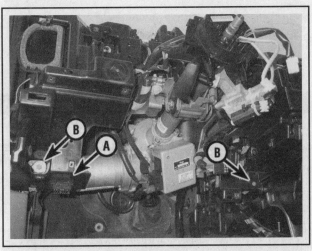

27.13b Disconnect the ALDL connector (A), then remove the fasteners from the bottom of the instrument panel (B)

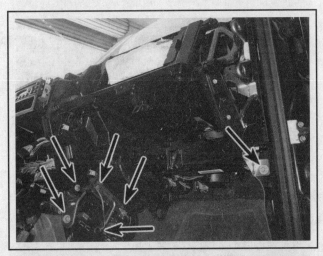

27.13c Working on the lower right hand side, remove these fasteners from the instrument panel

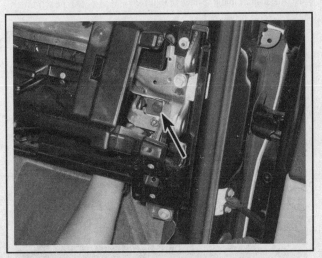

27.13d There is a concealed stud at the lower right of the panel that must be removed from below

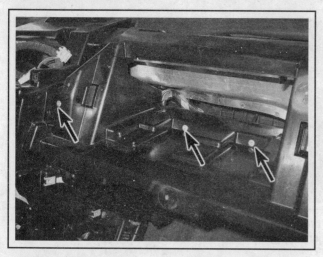

27.13e Remove the remaining upper mounting fasteners . . .

27.13f . . . then have an assistant help you guide the panel out the door opening

28 Seats - removal and installation

FRONT SEAT

▶ **Refer to illustrations 28.1a, 28.1b and 28.2**

1 Slide the seat forward and use a screwdriver to push the tab of the quick-disconnect to release the shoulder belt from the seat (see illustrations).

2 Remove the mounting bolts at the rear of the seats (see illustration).

3 Slide the seat to the rear and disconnect the wiring.

4 Disengage the front seat mount hooks from the floor and lift out the seat.

5 Installation is the reverse of removal.

REAR SEAT

▶ **Refer to illustrations 28.7 and 28.8**

6 Remove the cargo area carpet.

7 Remove the seat mounting bolts that are under the cover (see illustration).

8 Remove the two bolts that are under the seat cushion at the front (see illustration).

9 Lift out the seat. Installation is the reverse of removal.

28.1a Pull the seat hinge cover slightly open for access to the belt release

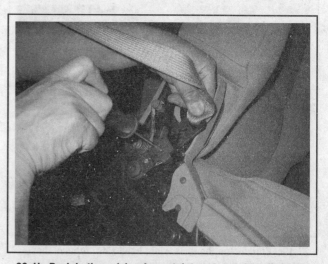

28.1b Push in the quick-release tab to remove the seat belt

28.2 The front seats are retained by bolts at the rear - pull the seat rearward to disengage the front clips

28.7 The mounting bolts of the rear seat are under the cargo area carpet

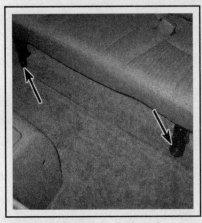

28.8 Remove the seat cushion mounting fasteners

Notes

Section

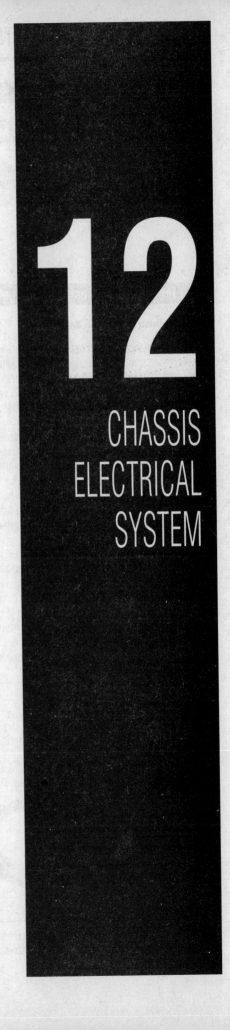

12

CHASSIS ELECTRICAL SYSTEM

1 General information

The electrical system is a 12-volt, negative ground type. Power for the lights and all electrical accessories is supplied by a lead/acid-type battery, which is charged by the alternator.

This Chapter covers repair and service procedures for the various electrical components not associated with the engine. Information on the battery, alternator and starter motor can be found in Chapter 5.

It should be noted that when portions of the electrical system are serviced, the cable should be disconnected from the negative battery terminal to prevent electrical shorts and/or fires.

2 Electrical troubleshooting - general information

▶ **Refer to illustrations 2.5a and 2.5b**

A typical electrical circuit consists of an electrical component, any switches, relays, motors, fuses, fusible links or circuit breakers related to that component and the wiring and connectors that link the component to both the battery and the chassis. To help you pinpoint an electrical circuit problem, wiring diagrams are included at the end of this Chapter.

Before tackling any troublesome electrical circuit, first study the appropriate wiring diagrams to get a complete understanding of what makes up that individual circuit. For instance, noting whether other components related to the circuit are operating correctly can often narrow down potential causes of trouble. If several components or circuits fail at one time, chances are the problem is in a fuse or ground connection, because several circuits are often routed through the same fuse and ground connections.

Electrical problems usually stem from simple causes, such as loose or corroded connections, a blown fuse, a melted fusible link or a failed relay. Visually inspect the condition of all fuses, wires and connections in a problem circuit before troubleshooting the circuit.

If test equipment and instruments are going to be utilized, use the diagrams to plan ahead of time where you will make the necessary connections in order to accurately pinpoint the trouble spot.

The basic tools needed for electrical troubleshooting include a circuit tester or voltmeter (a 12-volt bulb with a set of test leads can also be used), a continuity tester, which includes a bulb, battery and set of test leads, and a jumper wire, preferably with a circuit breaker incorporated, which can be used to bypass electrical components (see illustrations). Before attempting to locate a problem with test instruments, use the wiring diagram(s) to decide where to make the connections.

VOLTAGE CHECKS

▶ **Refer to illustration 2.6**

Voltage checks should be performed if a circuit is not functioning properly. Connect one lead of a circuit tester to either the negative battery terminal or a known good ground. Connect the other lead to a connector in the circuit being tested, preferably nearest to the battery or fuse (see illustration). If the bulb of the tester lights, voltage is present, which means that the part of the circuit between the connector and the battery is problem free. Continue checking the rest of the circuit in the same fashion. When you reach a point at which no voltage is present, the problem lies between that point and the last test point with voltage. Most of the time the problem can be traced to a loose connection.

➡**Note: Keep in mind that some circuits receive voltage only when the ignition key is in the Accessory or Run position.**

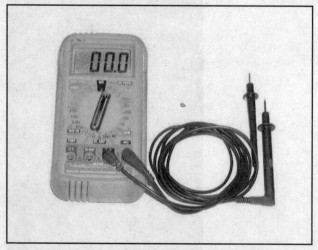

2.5a The most useful tool for electrical troubleshooting is a digital multimeter that can check volts, amps, and test continuity

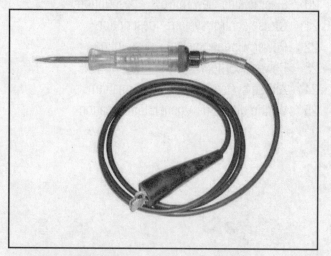

2.5b A simple test light is a very handy tool for testing voltage

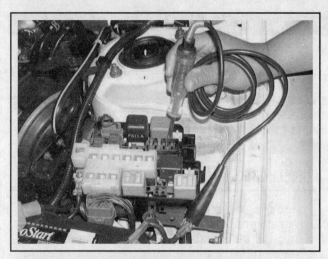

2.6 In use, a basic test light's lead is clipped to a known good ground, then the pointed probe can test connectors, wires or electrical sockets - if the bulb lights, the circuit being tested has battery voltage

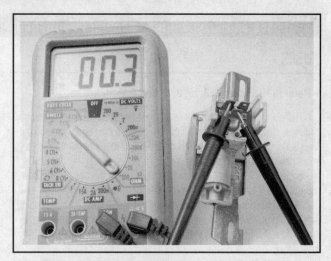

2.9 With a multimeter set to the ohm scale, resistance can be checked across two terminals - when checking for continuity, a low reading indicates continuity, a high reading or infinity indicates lack of continuity

FINDING A SHORT

One method of finding shorts in a live circuit is to remove the fuse and connect a test light in place of the fuse terminals (fabricate two jumper wires with small spade terminals, plug the jumper wires into the fuse box and connect the test light). There should be voltage present in the circuit. Move the suspected wiring harness from side-to-side while watching the test light. If the bulb goes off, there is a short to ground somewhere in that area, probably where the insulation has rubbed through.

GROUND CHECK

Perform a ground test to check whether a component is properly grounded. Disconnect the battery and connect one lead of a continuity tester or multimeter (set to the ohm scale), to a known good ground. Connect the other lead to the wire or ground connection being tested. If the resistance is low (less than 5 ohms), the ground is good. If the bulb on a self-powered test light does not go on, the ground is not good.

CONTINUITY CHECK

▶ **Refer to illustration 2.9**

A continuity check is done to determine if there are any breaks in a circuit - if it is passing electricity properly. With the circuit off (no power in the circuit), a self-powered continuity tester or multimeter can be used to check the circuit. Connect the test leads to both ends of the circuit (or to the power end and a good ground), and if the test light comes on the circuit is passing current properly (see illustration). If the resistance is low (less than 5 ohms), there is continuity; if the reading is 10,000 ohms or higher, there is a break somewhere in the circuit. The same procedure can be used to test a switch, by connecting the continuity tester to the switch terminals. With the switch turned On, the test light should come on (or low resistance should be indicated on a meter).

FINDING AN OPEN CIRCUIT

When diagnosing for possible open circuits, it is often difficult to locate them by sight because the connectors hide oxidation or terminal misalignment. Merely wiggling a connector on a sensor or in the wiring harness may correct the open circuit condition. Remember this when an open circuit is indicated when troubleshooting a circuit. Intermittent problems may also be caused by oxidized or loose connections.

Electrical troubleshooting is simple if you keep in mind that all electrical circuits are basically electricity running from the battery, through the wires, switches, relays, fuses and fusible links to each electrical component (light bulb, motor, etc.) and to ground, from which it is passed back to the battery. Any electrical problem is an interruption in the flow of electricity to and from the battery.

CONNECTORS

Most electrical connections on these vehicles are made with multi-wire plastic connectors. The mating halves of many connectors are secured with locking clips molded into the plastic connector shells. The mating halves of large connectors, such as some of those under the instrument panel, are held together by a bolt through the center of the connector.

To separate a connector with locking clips, use a small screwdriver to pry the clips apart carefully, then separate the connector halves. Pull only on the shell - never pull on the wiring harness as you may damage the individual wires and terminals inside the connectors. Look at the connector closely before trying to separate the halves. Often the locking clips are engaged in a way that is not immediately clear. Additionally, many connectors have more than one set of clips.

Each pair of connector terminals has a male half and a female half. When you look at the end view of a connector in a diagram, be sure to understand whether the view shows the harness side or the component side of the connector. Connector halves are mirror images of each other, and a terminal shown on the right side end-view of one half will be on the left side end view of the other half.

3 Fuses and fusible links - general information

FUSES

♦ **Refer to illustrations 3.1a, 3.1b and 3.3**

The electrical circuits of the vehicle are protected by a combination of fuses, circuit breakers and fusible links. Fuse blocks are located in the passenger's side of the shifter console and in the engine compartment near the battery (see illustrations).

Each of the fuses is designed to protect a specific circuit, and the various circuits are identified on the fuse panel cover.

Miniaturized fuses are employed in the fuse blocks. These compact fuses, with blade terminal design, allow fingertip removal and replacement. If an electrical component fails, always check the fuse first. The best way to check a fuse is with a test light. Check for power at the exposed terminal tips of each fuse. If power is present on one side of the fuse but not the other, the fuse is blown. A blown fuse can also be confirmed by visually inspecting it (see illustration).

Be sure to replace blown fuses with the correct type. Fuses of different ratings are physically interchangeable, but only fuses of the proper rating should be used. Replacing a fuse with one of a higher or lower value than specified is not recommended. Each electrical circuit needs a specific amount of protection. The amperage value of each fuse is molded into the fuse body.

If the replacement fuse immediately fails, don't replace it again until the cause of the problem is isolated and corrected. In most cases, this will be a short circuit in the wiring caused by a broken or deteriorated wire.

FUSIBLE LINKS

Some circuits are protected by fusible links. The links are used in circuits that are not ordinarily fused, such as the high-current side of the charging or starting circuits. Conventional inline fusible links, such as those used in the starter cable, are characterized by a bulge in the cable. Newer cartridge-type fusible links, which are similar in appearance to a large cartridge-type fuse, are located in their own fusible link block in the engine compartment fuse and relay box (see illustration 3.1a). After disconnecting the cable from the negative battery terminal, simply remove the fusible link and replace it with a unit of the same amperage.

3.1a The engine compartment fuse and relay box is located at the left side of the engine compartment. There's a guide on the bottom of the cover

3.1b There's also a fuse box inside the vehicle at the right end of the shifter console, behind a small access door that has a fuse guide on it

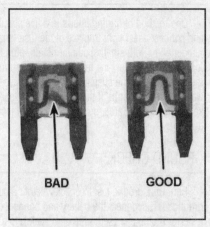

3.3 When a fuse blows, the element between the terminals melts

4 Circuit breakers - general information

Circuit breakers protect certain circuits, such as the power windows or heated seats. Depending on the vehicle's accessories, there might be circuit breakers in or near either of the fuse and relay boxes.

Some circuit breakers reset automatically, so an electrical overload in a circuit breaker-protected system will cause the circuit to fail momentarily, then come back on. If the circuit does not come back on, check it immediately.

For a basic check, pull the circuit breaker up out of its socket on the fuse panel, but just far enough to probe with a voltmeter. The breaker should still contact the sockets.

With the voltmeter negative lead on a good chassis ground, touch each end prong of the circuit breaker with the positive meter probe. There should be battery voltage at each end. If there is battery voltage only at one end, the circuit breaker must be replaced.

Some circuit breakers must be reset manually and others are automatically reset.

5 Relays - general information and testing

GENERAL INFORMATION

1   Several electrical accessories in the vehicle, such as the fuel injection system, horns, starter, and fog lamps use relays to transmit the electrical signal to the component. Relays use a low-current circuit (the control circuit) to open and close a high-current circuit (the power circuit). If the relay is defective, that component will not operate properly. Most relays are mounted in the engine compartment fuse/relay box, with some specialized relays located above the interior fuse box in the dash (see illustrations 3.1a and 3.1b). If a faulty relay is suspected, it can be removed and tested using the procedure below or by a dealer service department or a repair shop. Defective relays must be replaced as a unit.

TESTING

▶ **Refer to illustrations 5.2a and 5.2b**

2   Most of the relays used in these vehicles are of a type often called "ISO" relays, which refers to the International Standards Organization. The terminals of ISO relays are numbered to indicate their usual circuit connections and functions. There are two basic layouts of terminals on the relays used in these vehicles (see illustrations).

3   Refer to the wiring diagram for the circuit to determine the proper connections for the relay you're testing. If you can't determine the correct connection from the wiring diagrams, however, you may be able to determine the test connections from the information that follows.

4   Two of the terminals are the relay control circuit and connect to the relay coil. The other relay terminals are the power circuit. When the relay is energized, the coil creates a magnetic field that closes the larger contacts of the power circuit to provide power to the circuit loads.

5   Terminals 85 and 86 are normally the control circuit. If the relay contains a diode, terminal 86 must be connected to battery positive (B+) voltage and terminal 85 to ground. If the relay contains a resistor, terminals 85 and 86 can be connected in either direction with respect to B+ and ground.

6   Terminal 30 is normally connected to the battery voltage (B+) source for the circuit loads. Terminal 87 is connected to the circuit leading to the component being powered. If the relay has several alternate terminals for load or ground connections, they usually are numbered 87A, 87B, 87C, and so on.

7   Use an ohmmeter to check continuity through the relay control coil.

   a) *Connect the meter according to the polarity shown in illustration 5.2a for one check; then reverse the ohmmeter leads and check continuity in the other direction.*

   b) *If the relay contains a resistor, resistance will be indicated on the meter, and should be the same value with the ohmmeter in either direction.*

   c) *If the relay contains a diode, resistance should be higher with the ohmmeter in the forward polarity direction than with the meter leads reversed.*

   d) *If the ohmmeter shows infinite resistance in both directions, replace the relay.*

8   Remove the relay from the vehicle and use the ohmmeter to check for continuity between the relay power circuit terminals. There should be no continuity between terminal 30 and 87 with the relay de-energized.

9   Connect a fused jumper wire to terminal 86 and the positive battery terminal. Connect another jumper wire between terminal 85 and ground. When the connections are made, the relay should click.

10 With the jumper wires connected, check for continuity between the power circuit terminals. Now, there should be continuity between terminals 30 and 87.

11 If the relay fails any of the above tests, replace it.

B+   **B+**   **B+**   **B+**

86   30   86   30

87A   87A

85   87   85   87

Relay with   **Relay with**
internal resistor   **internal diode**

5.2a Typical ISO relay designs, terminal numbering and circuit connections

85 87
Control   Power
circuits   circuits
86 30
9632218
U.S.A.

5.2b Most relays are marked on the outside to easily identify the control circuits and the power circuits (four terminal type shown)

6 Turn signal and hazard flasher relay - check and replacement

CHECK

1   When the turn signal and hazard flasher relay is functioning properly, you can hear an audible click when it's operating.

2   If the turn signals fail on one side or the other and the flasher unit does not make its characteristic clicking sound, or if a bulb on one side of the vehicle flashes much faster than normal but the bulb at the other end of the vehicle (on the same side) doesn't light at all, a turn signal bulb is probably faulty.

3   If both turn signals fail to blink, the problem might be a blown fuse, a faulty flasher unit, a defective switch or a loose or open connection. If a quick check of the fuse box indicates that the turn signal fuse has blown, check the wiring for a short before installing a new fuse.

REPLACEMENT

▶ **Refer to illustration 6.5**

4   Refer to Chapter 11 and remove the center bezel of the instru-

ment panel. The panel must be pulled back far enough for access to the flasher.

5   Disconnect the electrical connector from the flasher unit (see illustration). Remove the unit from the panel.

6   Make sure that the replacement unit is identical to the original. Compare the old one to a new one before buying it.

7   Installation is the reverse of removal.

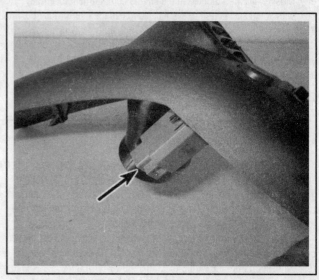

6.5 The turn signal and hazard flasher relay is located behind the hazard switch in the center instrument panel bezel

7 Ignition key lock cylinder, housing and switch - replacement

1   Disconnect the cable from the negative terminal of the battery (see Chapter 5, Section 1).

2   Remove the upper and lower steering column covers (see Chapter 11).

3   Release the retaining tabs of the park lock cable and disconnect it from the lock cylinder housing.

KEY LOCK CYLINDER

▶ **Refer to illustration 7.5**

4   Insert the ignition key into the lock cylinder and turn it to the Run position.

5   Insert a pick or other small tool into the hole in the back of the lock cylinder housing and push it in to depress the release button (see

illustration). Pull the lock cylinder out of the housing.

6   To install the lock cylinder, make sure the ignition switch is still in the Run position. If it isn't, rotate it to the Run position with a screwdriver or needle-nose pliers. The lock cylinder won't fit all the way into the bore if the switch is in any other position.

7.5 With the key turned to the RUN position, insert a thin tool into this hole in the lock cylinder housing and depress the release button

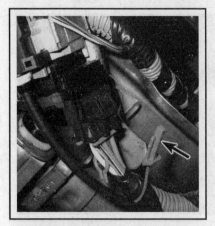

7.11 Pull out the safety clip, then unplug the main electrical connector from the ignition switch

7.12 Ignition switch housing

A   *Housing mounting screw (one of two shown)*
B   *Park/Lock cable*

7.14 Ignition switch-to-housing screws

7   Insert the lock cylinder into the housing, making sure it engages with the switch and clicks into place.

8   Verify that the ignition switch operates correctly in the Off, Acc, Run and Start positions.

HOUSING AND SWITCH

Removal

▶ **Refer to illustrations 7.11, 7.12 and 7.14**

9   Refer to Chapter 10 and remove the steering wheel.

10 Refer to Section 8 and remove both multi-function switches. The wiring doesn't have to be disconnected.

11 Detach the two electrical connectors from the ignition switch (see illustration).

12 Remove the two ignition switch housing screws (see illustration). Insert the key and turn it to the Accessory position.

13 Slide the entire assembly off of the steering column.

14 Remove the ignition switch screws from the housing and separate the ignition switch (see illustration).

Installation

15 Turn the ignition switch to ACC, then place it into the housing. Tighten the ignition switch screws securely.

16 Put the lock cylinder housing onto the steering column and mate it to the multi-function lever bracket, then install the bolts. Make sure the lock tab on the lock cylinder housing engages with its slot in the steering column, then tighten the bolts securely.

17 Tighten the lower mounting bolt, then the upper mounting bolt, but only until they are seated firmly.

18 Finally, tighten the lower bolt, followed by the upper bolt, to the torque listed in this Chapter's Specifications.

19 The remainder of the installation procedure is the reverse of removal.

8   Multi-function switches - replacement

▶ **Refer to illustrations 8.3 and 8.4**

✳✳ WARNING:

The models covered by this manual are equipped with Supplemental Restraint Systems (SRS), more commonly known as airbags. Always disable the airbag system before working in the vicinity of any airbag system components to avoid the possibility of accidental deployment of the airbag(s), which could cause personal injury (see Section 24).

➡**Note:** The multi-function switches (also referred to as combination switches or steering column switches) are two separate switch units connected to a central housing known as the switch bracket, which encircles the steering column. The switches can be replaced separately.

1   Disconnect the cable from the negative terminal of the battery (see Chapter 5, Section 1).

2   Remove the upper and lower steering column covers (see Chapter 11).

3   Push in the lock tabs and pull the switch from its housing (see illustration).

4   Disconnect the wiring from the switch (see illustration).

5   Installation is the reverse of removal. Make sure that the switch snaps securely into place.

8.3 To detach either multi-function switch, push in on these two tabs and pull the switch out

8.4 Disconnect the electrical connectors from the multi-function switches after they're pulled out

9 Instrument panel switches - replacement

✳✳ WARNING:

The models covered by this manual are equipped with Supplemental Restraint Systems (SRS), more commonly known as airbags. Always disable the airbag system before working in the vicinity of any airbag system component to avoid the possibility of accidental deployment of the airbag(s), which could cause personal injury (see Section 24).

SWITCHES IN THE CENTER OF THE INSTRUMENT PANEL

♦ Refer to illustration 9.2

➡Note: These include the panel dimmer, the fog light switch and the hazard switch.

1 Refer to Chapter 11 and remove the center instrument panel bezel, pulling it out far enough to access the switches from the rear.
2 Disconnect the electrical connector from the switch and remove it from the bezel (see illustration).
3 Installation is the reverse of the removal procedure.

SWITCHES ON THE SHIFTER CONSOLE

♦ Refer to illustration 9.5

➡Note: These include the power window switches, heated seat switches, footwell light switches and the power mirror switches.

4 Refer to Chapter 11 and remove the shifter console bezel, pulling it upward enough to access the switches.
5 Disconnect the electrical connector from the switch and remove it from the bezel (see illustration).
6 Installation is the reverse of removal.

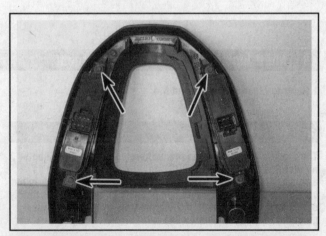

9.2 The center instrument panel bezel has several switches (depending on models and options) that are typically retained by screws

9.5 Power window switches mounted in the shifter console are attached by screws - others are retained directly to the panel by clips

10 Instrument cluster - removal and installation

▶ Refer to illustration 10.3

❊❊ WARNING:

The models covered by this manual are equipped with Supplemental Restraint Systems (SRS), more commonly known as airbags. Always disable the airbag system before working in the vicinity of any airbag system component to avoid the possibility of accidental deployment of the airbag(s), which could cause personal injury (see Section 24).

1 Disconnect the cable from the negative battery terminal (see Chapter 5, Section 1).
2 Remove the instrument cluster trim panel (see Chapter 11).
3 Remove the cluster mounting screws (see illustration) and pull the instrument cluster towards the steering wheel.
4 Installation is the reverse of removal.

10.3 To detach the instrument cluster, remove these four mounting screws (upper screws not visible in this photo; vicinity given)

11 Radio and speakers - removal and installation

❊❊ WARNING:

The models covered by this manual are equipped with Supplemental Restraint Systems (SRS), more commonly known as airbags. Always disable the airbag system before working in the vicinity of any airbag system component to avoid the possibility of accidental deployment of the airbag(s), which could cause personal injury (see Section 24).

RADIO

▶ Refer to illustration 11.3

1 Disconnect the cable from the negative battery terminal (see Chapter 5, Section 1).

2 Remove the center trim panel (see Chapter 11).
3 Remove the radio mounting screws and pull the radio from the instrument panel (see illustration).
4 Disconnect the electrical connector and the antenna cable from the back of the radio.
5 Installation is the reverse of removal.

SPEAKERS

Lower door speakers

▶ Refer to illustration 11.7

6 Remove the door trim panel (see Chapter 11).
7 Remove the speaker mounting screws (see illustration), remove the speaker from the door, then disconnect the electrical connector.
8 Installation is the reverse of removal.

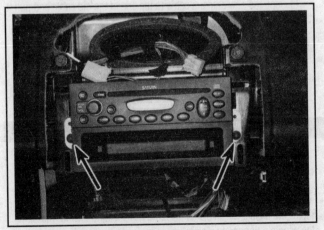

11.3 To detach the radio unit from the instrument panel, remove these screws

11.7 To remove a door speaker, remove the speaker mounting screws and disconnect the electrical connector

11.9 Pry the trim panel/speaker mount outward at the top, then slide it up to remove it

11.12 Twist the tweeter speakers to remove them

Upper front door speakers

▶ **Refer to illustrations 11.9 and 11.12**

➡**Note: The tweeters are located in the front doors.**

9   Pull off the upper speaker panel, starting at the top (see illustration).
10 Lift it to slide the lower tabs out of the door panel.
11 Disconnect the electrical connector.
12 Twist the speaker to remove it from the panel (see illustration).
13 Installation is the reverse of removal.

Rear speakers

14 Remove the carpet retaining trim piece.
15 Remove the pillar trim.
16 Remove the rear upper trim molding.
17 Remove the rear floor storage bin.
18 Remove the cargo hooks.
19 Pull the quarter trim panel out, disengaging its retaining clips.
20 Remove the speaker mounting screws, then remove the speaker and disconnect the electrical connector.
21 Installation is the reverse of removal.

12 Antenna - replacement

1   Unscrew the antenna mast from the mounting base.

ANTENNA MOUNTING BASE

2   Unscrew the antenna mast.
3   Refer to Chapter 11 and remove the fender.
4   Pry off the antenna mast bezel trim.
5   Disconnect the antenna base lead from the main antenna cable.
6   Remove the antenna base mounting nuts and remove the base from the fender.
7   Installation is the reverse of removal.

ANTENNA CABLE

8   Remove the radio and disconnect the antenna cable from it (see Section 11).
9   Remove the right inner fender splash shield
10 Disconnect the antenna cable from the antenna base.
11 Tape the new antenna cable to the end of the old cable and pull it through the firewall.
12 Installation is otherwise the reverse of removal. Make sure that the cable is routed correctly and that all clips are installed.

13 Wiper motor - check and replacement

WIPER MOTOR CIRCUIT CHECK

➡**Note: Refer to the wiring diagrams for the following checks. When checking for voltage, probe a grounded 12-volt test light to each terminal at a connector until it lights; this verifies voltage (power) at the terminal. If the following checks fail to locate the problem, have the system diagnosed by a dealer service department or other properly equipped repair facility.**

1   If the wipers work slowly, make sure that the battery is in good condition and has a strong charge (see Chapter 5). If the battery is in good condition, remove the wiper motor (see below) and operate the wiper arms by hand. Check for binding linkage and pivots. Lubricate or repair the linkage or pivots as necessary. Reinstall the wiper motor. If the wipers still operate slowly, check for loose or corroded connections, especially the ground connection. If all connections look OK, replace the motor.

2   If the wipers fail to operate when activated, check the fuse in the driver's side interior fuse panel. If the fuse is OK, connect a jumper wire between the wiper motor's ground terminal and ground, then retest. If the motor works now, repair the ground connection. If the motor still doesn't work, turn the wiper switch to the HI position and check for voltage at the motor.

➡**Note: The cowl cover will have to be removed (see Chapter 11) to access the wiper motor electrical connector.**

3   If there's voltage at the connector, remove the motor and check it off the vehicle with fused jumper wires from the battery. If the motor now works, check for binding linkage (see Step 1). If the motor still doesn't work, replace it. If there's no voltage to the motor, check for voltage at the wiper control relays. If there's voltage at the wiper control relays and no voltage at the wiper motor, have the switch tested. If the switch is OK, the wiper control relay is probably bad. See Section 5 for relay testing.

4   If the interval (delay) function is inoperative, check the continuity of all the wiring between the switch and wiper control module.

5   If the wipers stop at the position they're in when the switch is turned off (fail to park), check for voltage at the park feed wire of the wiper motor connector when the wiper switch is OFF but the ignition is ON. If no voltage is present, check for an open circuit between the wiper motor and the fuse panel.

REPLACEMENT

Windshield wiper motor

▶ **Refer to illustrations 13.6 and 13.9**

6   Remove the wiper arm nuts and mark the relationship of the wiper arms to their shafts (see illustration). Remove both wiper arms.

7   Remove the plastic cowl cover (see Chapter 11).

8   Disconnect the electrical connector from the wiper motor.

9   Remove the three windshield wiper motor and link assembly mounting bolts (see illustration) and remove the wiper motor and link assembly.

10 Using a screwdriver, carefully pry the link rod from the pivot pin on the motor's crank arm.

11 Remove the nut and washer that secures the crank arm to the motor shaft.

12 Mark the relationship of the crank arm to the motor shaft and remove the crank arm.

13 Remove the two motor mounting bolts and remove the motor from its mounting bracket.

14 Installation is the reverse of removal.

Rear wiper motor

▶ **Refer to illustration 13.18**

15 Flip open the cap covering the rear wiper arm retaining nut and remove the nut.

16 Mark the relationship of the rear wiper arm to the motor shaft, then remove the arm.

17 Remove the trim panel from the rear hatch (see Chapter 11).

18 Remove the rear wiper motor mounting bolts (see illustration) and remove the motor and bracket.

19 Disconnect the electrical connector from the motor.

20 Installation is the reverse of removal.

13.6 Mark the positions of the wiper arms on their shafts before removing them; the arms can usually be wiggled off - don't try to pry them off

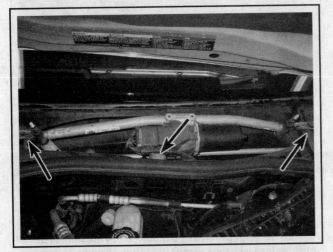

13.9 Wiper assembly mounting bolts

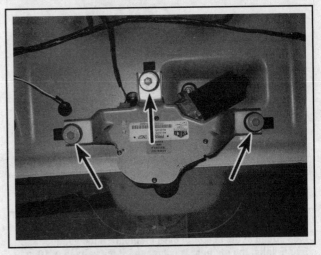

13.18 Rear wiper motor mounting bolts

14 Rear window defogger - check and repair

1 The rear window defogger consists of a number of horizontal elements baked onto the glass surface.

2 Small breaks in the element can be repaired without removing the rear window.

CHECK

▶ **Refer to illustrations 14.4, 14.5 and 14.7**

3 Turn the ignition switch and defogger system switches to the ON position. Using a voltmeter, place the positive probe against the defogger grid positive terminal and the negative probe against the ground terminal. If battery voltage is not indicated, check the fuse, defogger switch and related wiring. If voltage is indicated, but all or part of the defogger doesn't heat, proceed with the following tests.

4 When measuring voltage during the next two tests, wrap a piece of aluminum foil around the tip of the voltmeter positive probe and press the foil against the heating element with your finger (see illustration). Place the negative probe on the defogger grid ground terminal.

5 Check the voltage at the center of each heating element (see illustration). If the voltage is 5 or 6-volts, the element is okay (there is no break). If the voltage is zero, the element is broken between the center of the element and the positive end. If the voltage is 10 to 12-volts, the element is broken between the center of the element and ground. Check each heating element.

6 Connect the negative lead to a good body ground. The reading should stay the same. If it doesn't, the ground connection is bad.

7 To find the break, place the voltmeter negative probe against the defogger ground terminal. Place the voltmeter positive probe with the foil strip against the heating element at the positive terminal end and slide it toward the negative terminal end. The point at which the voltmeter deflects from several volts to zero is the point at which the heating element is broken (see illustration).

REPAIR

▶ **Refer to illustration 14.13**

8 Repair the break in the element using a repair kit specifically recommended for this purpose, available at most auto parts stores. Included in this kit is plastic conductive epoxy.

9 Prior to repairing a break, turn off the system and allow it to cool off for a few minutes.

10 Lightly buff the element area with fine steel wool, then clean it thoroughly with rubbing alcohol.

11 Use masking tape to mask off the area being repaired.

12 Thoroughly mix the epoxy, following the instructions provided

14.4 When measuring the voltage at the rear window defogger grid, wrap a piece of aluminum foil around the positive probe of the voltmeter and press the foil against the wire with your finger

14.5 To determine if a heating element has broken, check the voltage at the center of each element - if the voltage is 5 or 6-volts, the element is unbroken - if the voltage is 10 or 12-volts, the element is broken between the center and the ground side - if there is no voltage, the element is broken between the center and the positive side

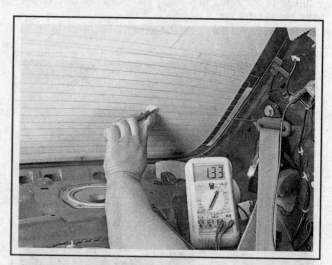

14.7 To find the break, place the voltmeter negative lead against the defogger ground terminal, place the voltmeter positive lead with the foil strip against the heating element at the positive terminal end and slide it toward the negative terminal end - the point at which the voltmeter reading changes abruptly is the point at which the element is broken

with the repair kit.

13 Apply the epoxy material to the slit in the masking tape, overlapping the undamaged area about 3/4-inch on either end (see illustration).

14 Allow the repair to cure for 24 hours before removing the tape and using the system.

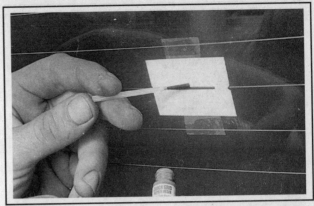

14.13 To use a defogger repair kit, apply masking tape to the inside of the window at the damaged area, then brush on the special conductive coating

15 Headlight bulbs - replacement

▶ Refer to illustration 15.3

※※ WARNING:

Gas-filled bulbs are under pressure and may shatter if the surface is scratched or the bulb is dropped. Wear eye protection and handle the bulbs carefully, grasping only the base whenever possible. Do not touch the surface of the bulb with your fingers because the oil from your skin could cause it to overheat and fail prematurely. If you do touch the bulb surface, clean it with rubbing alcohol.

1 Refer to Section 16 and remove the headlight housing.

2 Disconnect the electrical connector from the bulb holder assembly.

3 Rotate the bulb holder counterclockwise to remove it from the housing (see illustration).

4 Without touching the bulb glass with your bare fingers, insert the new bulb assembly into the headlight housing. Twist it clockwise to lock it in place, then plug in the electrical connector.

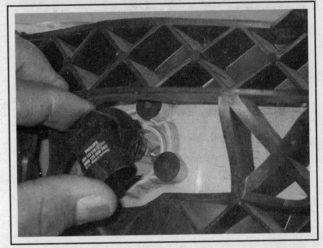

15.3 To remove the headlight bulb holder from the headlight housing, rotate the bulb holder counterclockwise and pull it out

16 Headlight housing - replacement

▶ Refer to illustrations 16.2, 16.3a, 16.3b and 16.4

※※ WARNING:

These vehicles are equipped with gas-filled headlight bulbs that are under pressure and may shatter if the surface is damaged or the bulb is dropped. Wear eye protection and handle the bulbs carefully, grasping only the base whenever possible. Do not touch the surface of the bulb with your fingers because the oil

from your skin could cause it to overheat and fail prematurely. If you do touch the bulb surface, clean it with rubbing alcohol.

1 Disconnect the cable from the negative battery terminal (see Chapter 5, Section 1).

2 Remove the upper headlight mounting bolts (see illustration). On 2002 through 2005 models, remove the side marker light housings (see Section 19).

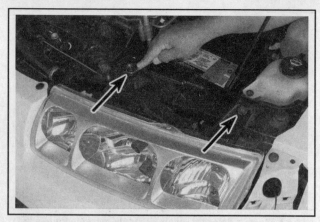

16.2 Headlight housing mounting bolts

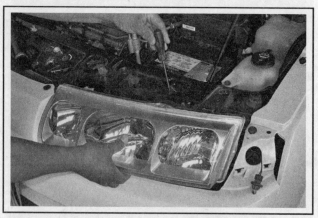

16.3a Use a long screwdriver to release the headlight assembly tab

16.3b The headlight assembly retaining tab

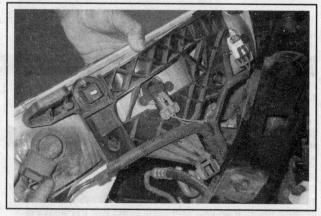

16.4 Pull the headlight assembly out and disconnect the electrical connectors

3   Disengage the headlight assembly lower retainer by pushing down the tab with a screwdriver (see illustrations).

4   Maneuver the housing out of the support structure (see illustration).

5   Disconnect the electrical connectors from the bulb holders.

6   Installation is the reverse of removal.

7   Check the headlight adjustment (see Section 17).

17 Headlights - adjustment

◆ Refer to illustrations 17.2 and 17.5

➥Note 1: The headlights must be aimed correctly. If adjusted incorrectly they could blind the driver of an oncoming vehicle and cause a serious accident or seriously reduce your ability to see the road. The headlights should be checked for proper aim every 12 months and any time a new headlight is installed or front-end bodywork is performed. It should be emphasized that the following procedure is only an interim step, which will provide temporary adjustment until a properly equipped shop can adjust the headlights.

➥Note 2: There are no horizontal adjustment screws on any of the models covered in this manual.

1   There are several methods of adjusting the headlights. The simplest method requires masking tape, a blank wall and a level floor.

2   Position masking tape vertically on the wall in reference to the vehicle centerline and the centerlines of both headlights (see illustration).

3   Position a horizontal tape line in reference to the centerline of all the headlights.

➥Note: It may be easier to position the tape on the wall with the vehicle parked only a few inches away.

4   Adjustment should be made with the vehicle parked 25 feet from the wall, sitting level, the gas tank half-full and no unusually heavy load in the vehicle.

5   Starting with the low beam adjustment, position the high intensity zone so it is two inches below the horizontal line. Make the adjustment by turning the vertical adjusting screw to raise or lower the beam (see illustration).

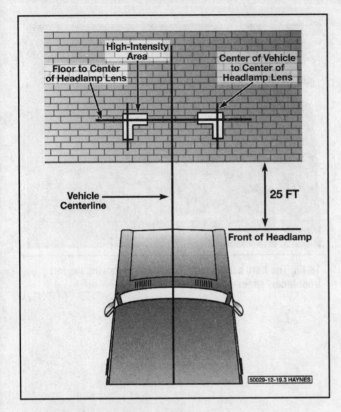

17.2 Headlight adjustment details

17.5 Headlight vertical adjuster screw

6   With the high beams on, the high intensity zone should be vertically centered with the exact center just below the horizontal line.

➡**Note: It may not be possible to position the headlight aim exactly for both high and low beams. If a compromise must be made, keep in mind that the low beams are the most used and have the greatest effect on driver safety.**

7   Have the headlights adjusted by a dealer service department or service station at the earliest opportunity.

18 Horn - check and replacement

❋❋ **WARNING:**

The models covered by this manual are equipped with Supplemental Restraint Systems (SRS), more commonly known as airbags. Always disable the airbag system before working in the vicinity of any airbag system components to avoid the possibility of accidental deployment of the airbag(s), which could cause personal injury (see Section 24).

CHECK

➡**Note: Check the fuses before beginning electrical diagnosis.**

1   Disconnect the electrical connector from the horn.

2   To test the horn, connect battery voltage to the horn terminal with a jumper wire. If the horn doesn't sound, replace it.

3   If the horn does sound, check for voltage at the terminal when the horn button is depressed. If there's voltage at the terminal, check for a bad ground at the horn.

4   If there's no voltage at the horn, check the relay (see Section 5).

➡**Note: The horn relay is located in the underhood fuse/relay box.**

5   If the relay is OK, check for voltage to the relay power and control circuits. If either of the circuits is not receiving voltage, inspect the wiring between the relay and the fuse panel.

6   If both relay circuits are receiving voltage, depress the horn button and check the circuit from the relay to the horn pad for continuity to ground. If there's no continuity, check the circuit for an open. If there's no open circuit, replace the horn pad.

➡**Note: The horn pad is an integral component of the driver's airbag module. See Chapter 10, "Steering wheel - removal and installation", for the replacement procedure.**

7   If there's continuity to ground through the horn button, check for an open or short in the circuit from the relay to the horn.

18.8a Remove the left headlight housing to access the horn

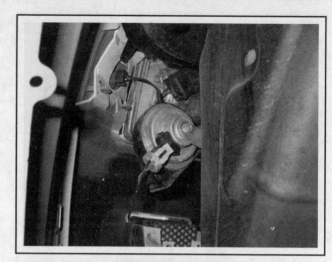

18.8b The horn can also be reached by removing the left front inner fender splash shield

REPLACEMENT

‣ Refer to illustrations 18.8a and 18.8b

8 Refer to Section 16 and remove the left headlight housing (see illustrations).
9 Disconnect the horn wiring and remove the horn.
10 Installation is the reverse of removal.

19 Bulb replacement

EXTERIOR LIGHT BULBS

Side marker light bulbs (2002 through 2005 models)

‣ Refer to illustrations 19.1a, 19.1b and 19.2

1 Remove the side marker housing (see illustrations).
2 Remove the bulb holder from the housing (see illustration).
3 Remove the bulb from the holder.
4 Installation is the reverse of removal.

Front turn signal/parking light bulbs

‣ Refer to illustrations 19.6 and 19.7

5 Remove the headlight housing (see Section 16).
6 Turn the bulb holder counterclockwise and remove it from the headlight housing (see illustration).
7 Pull the bulb straight out of the holder to remove it (see illustration).
8 Installation is the reverse of removal.

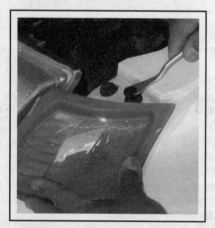

19.1a Pry out this pushpin to release the top of the side marker light housing

19.1b Lift the housing upward, then outward, to disengage the clips

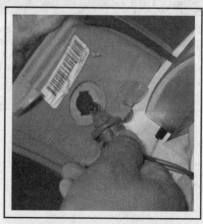

19.2 Turn the bulb socket to remove it from the housing

19.6 Twist the turn signal/parking light bulb holder counterclockwise to remove it from the headlight housing

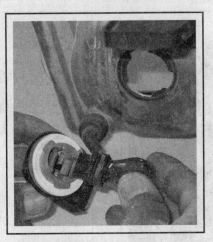

19.7 Pull the parking light bulb straight out of its socket

19.13 The washer jet can be removed before removing the light assembly

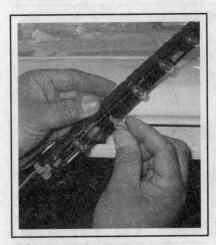

19.16 The center high-mounted brake light bulbs are individually replaceable

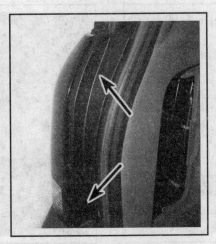

19.19 Taillight housing screws

19.20 Pull the housing rearward to release it

Fog lamp bulbs

9   Raise the front of the vehicle and place it securely on jackstands.

10 If you're working on a 2006 or 2007 model, remove the fender inner liner/splash shield (see Chapter 11). On 2005 and earlier models, reach up through the opening in the bottom of the front bumper cover for access to the bulb.

11 Disconnect the electrical connector from the fog lamp bulb holder. Turn the fog lamp bulb holder counterclockwise and pull it out of the fog lamp housing.

12 Installation is the reverse of removal.

Center high-mounted brake light

▶ Refer to illustrations 19.13 and 19.16

➡Note: The center high-mounted brake light bulb is located in the upper edge of the rear hatch.

13 Pull out the washer jet and disconnect the washer hose (see illustration).

14 Remove the two screws from the light housing and pull it away from the liftgate.

15 Disconnect the electrical connector from the assembly and remove it.

16 Depress the tabs and detach the lens from the bulb assembly. The individual bulbs can be replaced (see illustration).

17 Installation is the reverse of removal.

Rear brake/tail, turn signal, brake and back-up light bulbs

▶ Refer to illustrations 19.19, 19.20 and 19.21

18 Open the liftgate.

19 Remove the taillight screws (see illustration).

20 Pull the light assembly to the rear to disengage the outer clips (see illustration).

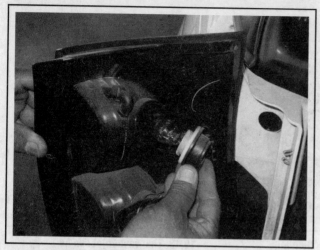

19.21 Turn the bulb sockets counterclockwise to remove them

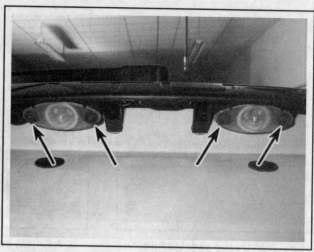

19.24 License plate light lens screws

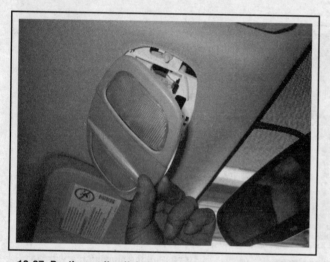

19.27 Pry the reading light lens down from the front edge only

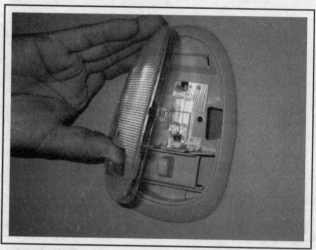

19.30 The cargo light lens can usually be removed by hand. If necessary, carefully pry it off with a small screwdriver

21 Turn the bulb holder counterclockwise and remove it from the housing (see illustration).

22 Remove the bulb from its holder.

23 Installation is the reverse of removal.

License plate light bulbs

▶ **Refer to illustration 19.24**

24 Remove the license plate light housing screws (see illustration) and remove the license plate light housing from its bezel.

25 Pull the bulb from its socket.

26 Installation is the reverse of removal.

INTERIOR LIGHT BULBS

Reading light bulbs

▶ **Refer to illustration 19.27**

27 Remove the lens from the reading light housing by prying at the

front with a small screwdriver (see illustration).

28 Pull the bulb straight out of its socket.

29 Installation is the reverse of removal.

Cargo and dome light bulb

▶ **Refer to illustration 19.30**

30 Remove the lens from the light housing (see illustration).

31 Remove the bulb from the terminals.

32 Installation is the reverse of removal.

Instrument cluster light bulbs

▶ **Refer to illustration 19.34a and 19.34b**

33 Remove the instrument cluster (see Section 10).

34 Turn the bulb socket using a small screwdriver, then remove it from the instrument cluster (see illustrations).

➡ **Note: It's best to replace all bulbs if one has failed.**

35 Installation is the reverse of removal.

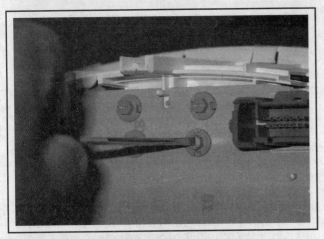

19.34a Rotate the bulb holder to release it . . .

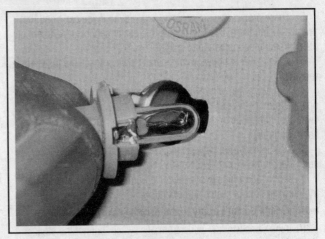

19.34b . . . then remove the bulb and holder

20 Electric side view mirrors - description

1 Most electric side view mirrors use two motors to move the glass; one for up and down adjustments and one for left-right adjustments.

2 The control switch has a selector portion that sends voltage to the left or right side mirror. With the ignition ON but the engine OFF, roll down the windows and operate the mirror control switch through all functions (LEFT-RIGHT and UP-DOWN) for both the left and right side mirrors.

3 Listen carefully for the sound of the electric motors running in the mirrors.

4 If the motors can be heard but the mirror glass doesn't move, there's a problem with the drive mechanism inside the mirror.

5 If the mirrors do not operate and no sound comes from the mir-

rors, check the fuse (see Section 3).

6 If the fuse is OK, remove the mirror control switch. Have the switch continuity checked by a dealership service department or other qualified automobile repair facility.

7 Make sure the mirror is properly grounded.

8 If the mirror still doesn't work, remove the mirror and check the wires at the mirror for voltage.

9 If there's not voltage in each switch position, check the circuit between the mirror and control switch for opens and shorts.

10 If there's voltage, remove the mirror and test it off the vehicle with jumper wires. Replace the mirror if it fails this test.

21 Cruise control system - description

These models have an electrically controlled throttle body - there is no accelerator cable. The accelerator pedal communicates with the throttle body through the Powertrain Control Module (PCM) (see Chapters 4 and 6 for more information about the electronic throttle control

system). The PCM also controls the cruise control system, which is an integral function of the electronic throttle control system. If the system malfunctions, take it to a dealer service department or other qualified repair shop for further diagnosis.

22 Power window system - description

1 The power window system operates electric motors, mounted in the doors, which lower and raise the windows. The system consists of the control switches, relays, motors, regulators, glass mechanisms and associated wiring.

2 The power windows can be lowered and raised from the master control switch by the driver or by remote switches located at the individual windows. Each window has a separate motor that is reversible. The position of the control switch determines the polarity and therefore the direction of operation.

3 The circuit is protected by a fuse. Each motor is also equipped with an internal circuit breaker; this prevents one stuck window from disabling the whole system.

4 The power window system will only operate when the ignition switch is ON. In addition, many models have a window lockout switch at the master control switch that, when activated, disables the switches at the rear windows and, sometimes, the switch at the passenger's window also. Always check these items before troubleshooting a window problem.

5   These procedures are general in nature, so if you can't find the problem using them, take the vehicle to a dealer service department or other properly equipped repair facility.

6   If the power windows won't operate, always check the fuses and relay first.

7   If only the rear windows are inoperative, or if the windows only operate from the master control switch, check the rear window lockout switch for continuity in the unlocked position. Replace it if it doesn't have continuity.

8   Check the wiring between the switches and fuse panel for continuity. Repair the wiring, if necessary.

9   If only one window is inoperative from the master control switch, try the other control switch at the window.

➡**Note: This doesn't apply to the driver's door window.**

10   If the same window works from one switch, but not the other, check the switch for continuity. Have the switch checked at a dealer service department or other qualified automobile repair facility.

11   If the switch tests OK, check for a short or open in the circuit between the affected switch and the window motor.

12   If one window is inoperative from both switches, remove the trim panel from the affected door and check for voltage at the switch and at the motor while the switch is operated.

13   If voltage is reaching the motor, disconnect the glass from the regulator (see Chapter 11). Move the window up and down by hand while checking for binding and damage. Also check for binding and damage to the regulator. If the regulator is not damaged and the window moves up and down smoothly, replace the motor. If there's binding or damage, lubricate, repair or replace parts, as necessary.

14   If voltage isn't reaching the motor, check the wiring in the circuit for continuity between the switches and motors. You'll need to consult the wiring diagram for the vehicle. If the circuit is equipped with a relay, check that the relay is grounded properly and receiving voltage.

23   Power door lock system - description

1   A power door lock system operates the door lock actuators mounted in each door. The system consists of the switches, actuators, the Body Control Module (BCM) and associated wiring. Diagnosis can usually be limited to simple checks of the wiring connections and actuators for minor faults that can be easily repaired.

2   Power door lock systems are operated by bi-directional solenoids located in the doors. The lock switches have two operating positions: Lock and Unlock. When activated, the switch sends a ground signal to the door lock control unit to lock or unlock the doors. Depending on which way the switch is activated, the control unit reverses polarity to the solenoids, allowing the two sides of the circuit to be used alternately as the feed (positive) and ground side.

3   Some vehicles may have an anti-theft system incorporated into the power locks. If you are unable to locate the trouble using the following general Steps, consult a dealer service department or other qualified repair shop.

4   Always check the circuit protection first. Some vehicles use a combination of circuit breakers and fuses.

5   Operate the door lock switches in both directions (Lock and Unlock) with the engine off. Listen for the click of the solenoids operating.

6   Test the switches for continuity. Remove the switches and have them checked by a dealer service department or other qualified automobile repair facility.

7   Check the wiring between the switches, control unit and solenoids for continuity. Repair the wiring if there's no continuity.

8   Check for a bad ground at the switches or the control unit.

9   If all but one lock solenoid operate, remove the trim panel from the affected door (see Chapter 11) and check for voltage at the solenoid while the lock switch is operated. One of the wires should have voltage in the Lock position; the other should have voltage in the Unlock position.

10   If the inoperative solenoid is receiving voltage, replace the solenoid.

11   If the inoperative solenoid isn't receiving voltage, check the relay for an open or short in the wire between the lock solenoid and the control unit.

➡**Note: It's common for wires to break in the section of harness that goes between the body and door because opening and closing the door fatigues and eventually breaks the wires.**

24   Airbag system - general information

All models are equipped with a Supplemental Restraint System (SRS), more commonly known as the airbag system. The airbag system is designed to protect the driver and the front seat passenger from serious injury in the event of a head-on or frontal collision. It consists of the impact sensors, a driver's airbag module in the center of the steering wheel, a passenger's airbag module in the glove box area of the instrument panel and a sensing/diagnostic module mounted under the center console. Some models are also equipped with side-curtain airbags and seat belt pre-tensioners.

AIRBAG MODULES

Driver's airbag

The airbag inflator module contains a housing incorporating the cushion (airbag) and inflator unit, mounted in the center of the steering wheel The inflator assembly is mounted on the back of the housing over a hole through which gas is expelled, inflating the bag almost instantaneously when an electrical signal is sent from the system. A spiral cable, or "clockspring" assembly on the steering column under the steering wheel carries this signal to the module. This clockspring can transmit an electrical signal regardless of steering wheel position. The igniter in the airbag converts the electrical signal to heat and ignites the powder, which inflates the bag.

Passenger's airbag

The airbag is mounted inside the right side of the instrument panel, in the vicinity of the glove box compartment. It's similar in design to the driver's airbag, except that it's larger than the steering wheel unit. The trim cover (on the side of the instrument panel that faces toward the passenger) is textured and colored to match the instrument panel and has a molded seam that splits open when the bag inflates.

Side curtain airbags

In addition to the side-impact airbags, extra side-impact protection is also provided by side-curtain airbags on some models. These are long airbags that, in the event of a side impact, come out of the headliner at each side of the car and come down between the side windows and the seats. They are designed to protect the heads of both front seat and rear seat passengers.

SENSING AND DIAGNOSTIC MODULE

The sensing and diagnostic module supplies the current to the airbag system in the event of the collision, even if battery power is cut off. It checks this system every time the vehicle is started, causing the "AIR BAG" light to go on then off, if the system is operating properly. If there is a fault in the system, the light will go on and stay on, flash, or the dash will make a beeping sound. If this happens, the vehicle should be taken to your dealer immediately for service. This module is mounted under the center console. There is also a roll-over sensor located directly behind it on later models.

SEAT BELT PRE-TENSIONERS

Some models are equipped with pyrotechnic (explosive) units in the front seat belt retracting mechanisms. During an impact that would trigger the airbag system, the airbag control unit also triggers the seat belt retractors. When the pyrotechnic charges go off, they accelerate the retractors to instantly take up any slack in the seat belt system to more fully prepare the driver and front seat passenger for impact.

The airbag system should be disabled any time work is done to or around the seats.

✳✳ WARNING:

Never strike the pillars or floorpan with a hammer or use an impact-driver tool in these areas unless the system is disabled.

DISARMING THE SYSTEM AND OTHER PRECAUTIONS

✳✳ WARNING:

Failure to follow these precautions could result in accidental deployment of the airbag and personal injury.

Whenever working in the vicinity of the steering wheel, steering column or any of the other SRS system components, the system must be disarmed.

To disarm the airbag system:

a) *Point the wheels straight ahead and turn the key to the Lock position.*
b) *Disconnect the cable from the negative battery terminal.*
c) *Wait at least two minutes for the back-up power supply to be depleted.*

Whenever handling an airbag module:

Always keep the airbag opening (the trim side) pointed away from your body. Never place the airbag module on a bench or other surface with the airbag opening facing the surface. Always place the airbag module in a safe location with the airbag opening facing up.

Never measure the resistance of any SRS component. An ohmmeter has a built-in battery supply that could accidentally deploy the airbag.

Never use electrical welding equipment on a vehicle equipped with an airbag without first disconnecting the electrical connector for each airbag.

Never dispose of a live airbag module. Return it to a dealer service department or other qualified repair shop for safe deployment and disposal.

COMPONENT REMOVAL AND INSTALLATION

Driver's side airbag module and spiral cable

Refer to Chapter 10, *Steering wheel - removal and installation*, for the driver's side airbag module and spiral cable removal and installation procedures.

Other airbag modules

We don't recommend removing any of the other airbag modules. These jobs are best left to a professional. Should you ever have to remove the instrument panel, you'll have to disconnect the electrical connector for the passenger airbag module and remove the fasteners that secure the passenger airbag module to the instrument panel reinforcement bracket.

25 Wiring diagrams - general information

Since it isn't possible to include all wiring diagrams for every year covered by this manual, the following diagrams are those that are typical and most commonly needed.

Prior to troubleshooting any circuits, check the fuse and circuit breakers (if equipped) to make sure they're in good condition. Make sure the battery is properly charged and check the cable connections (see Chapter 1).

When checking a circuit, make sure that all connectors are clean, with no broken or loose terminals. When unplugging a connector, do not pull on the wires - pull only on the connector housings.

Torque specifications	Ft-lbs (unless otherwise indicated)	Nm

➡ **Note: One foot-pound (ft-lb) of torque is equivalent to 12 inch-pounds (in-lbs) of torque. Torque values below approximately 15 ft-lbs are expressed in inch-pounds, since most foot-pound torque wrenches are not accurate at these smaller values.**

Lock cylinder housing to multi-function switch bracket bolts	71 in-lbs	8

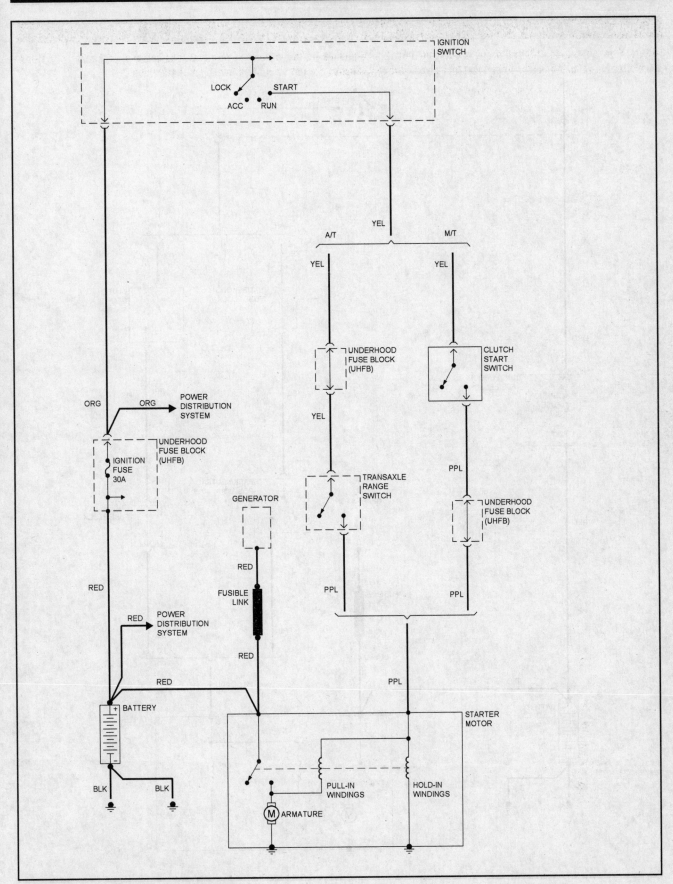

Starting system - 2002 and 2003 models (all)

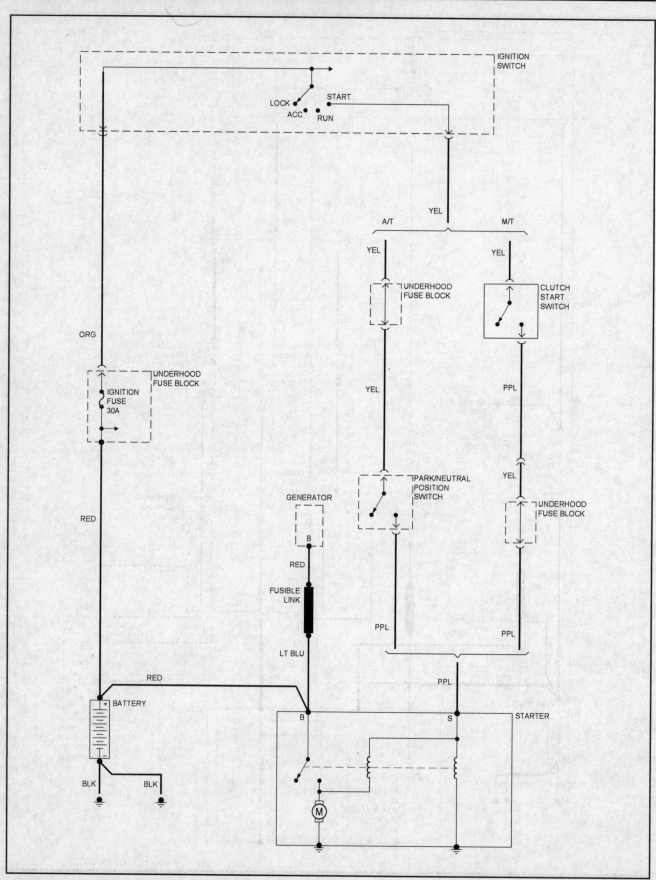

Starting system - 2004 and later four-cylinder models

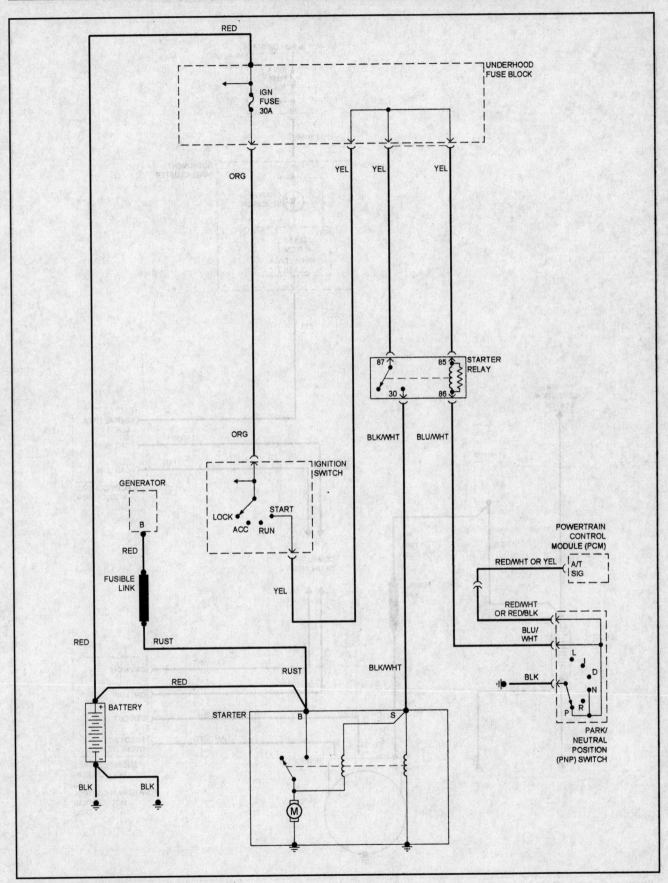

Starting system - 2004 and later V6 models

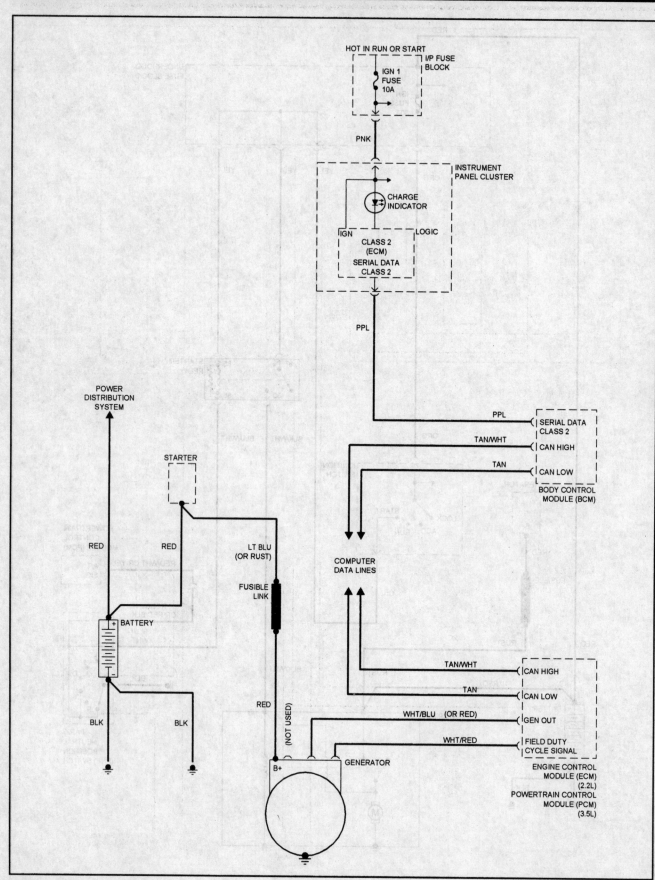

Charging system - all models

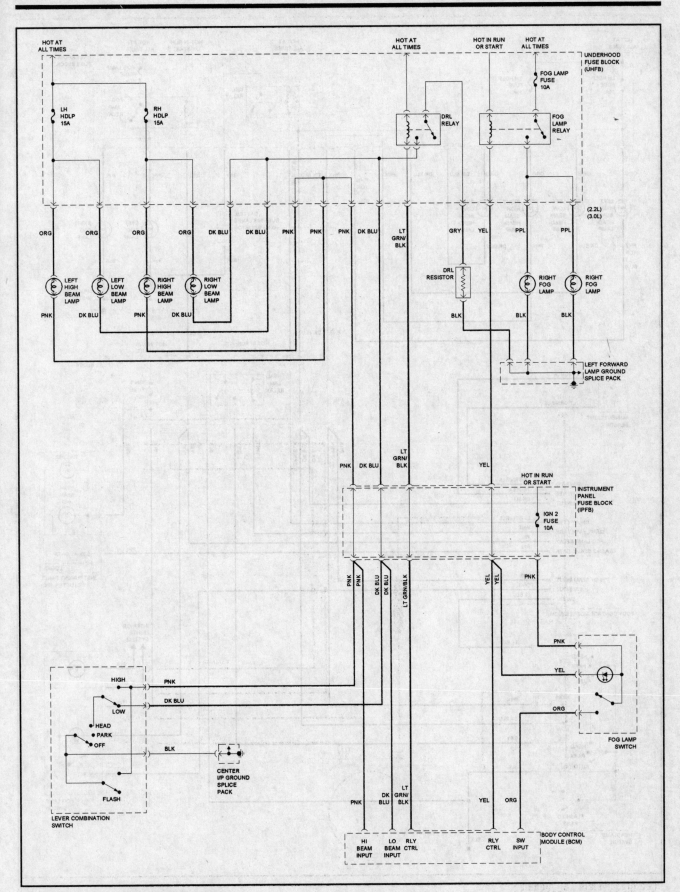

Headlight system - 2002 and 2003 models

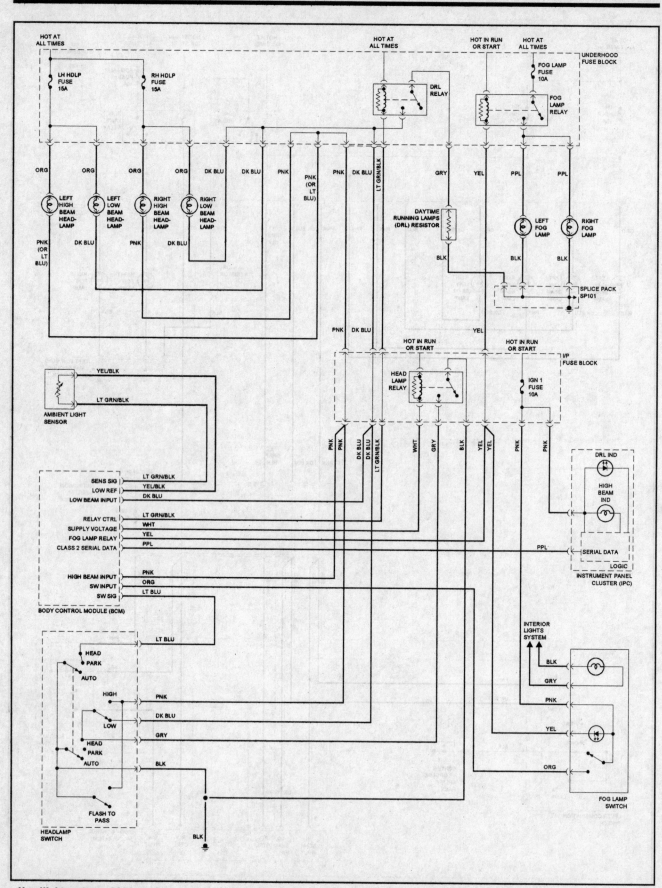

Headlight system - 2004 and later models (with Autolamps)

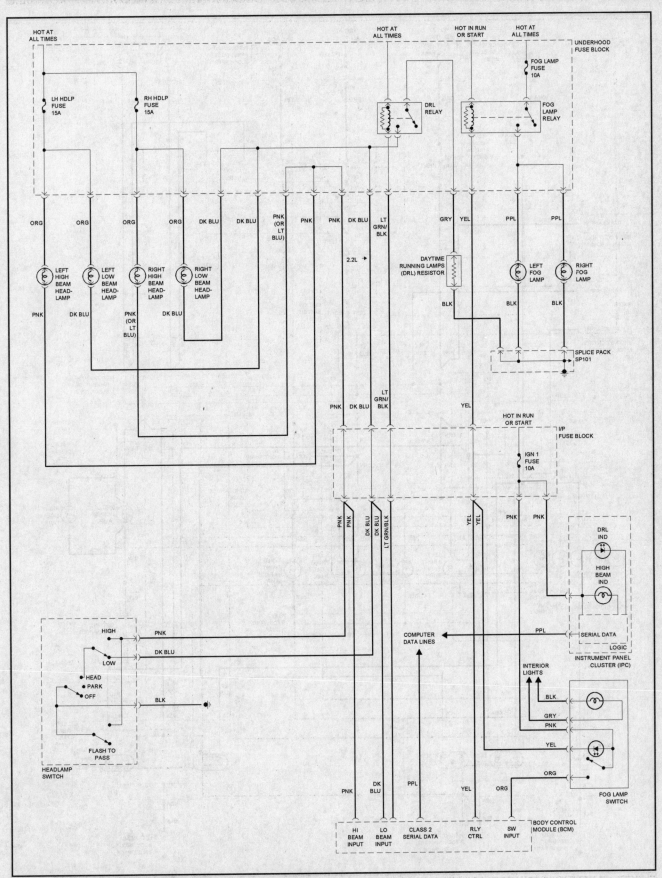

Headlight system - 2004 and later models (without Autolamps)

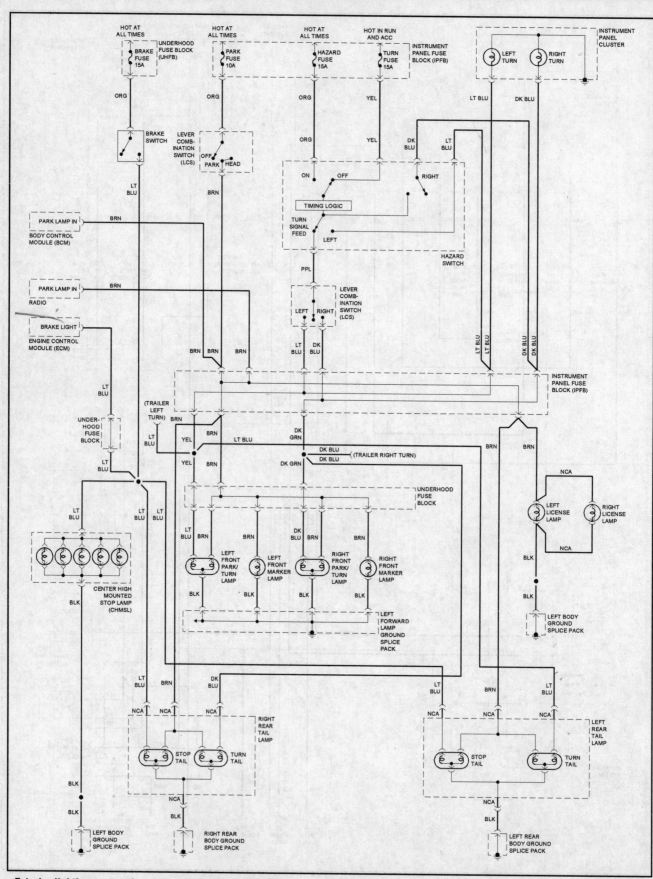

Exterior lighting system (except headlights) - 2002 models

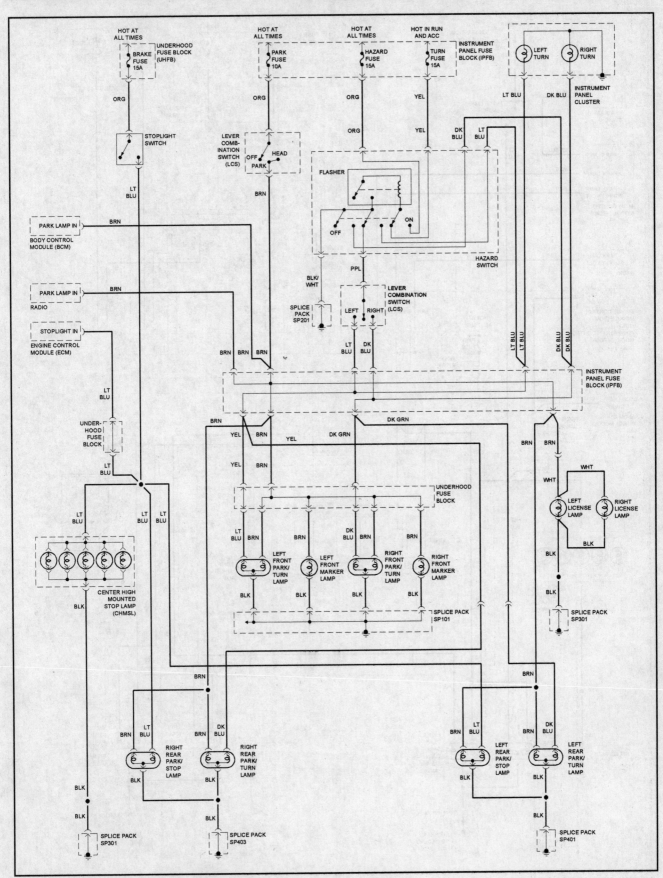

Exterior lighting system (except headlights) - 2003 models

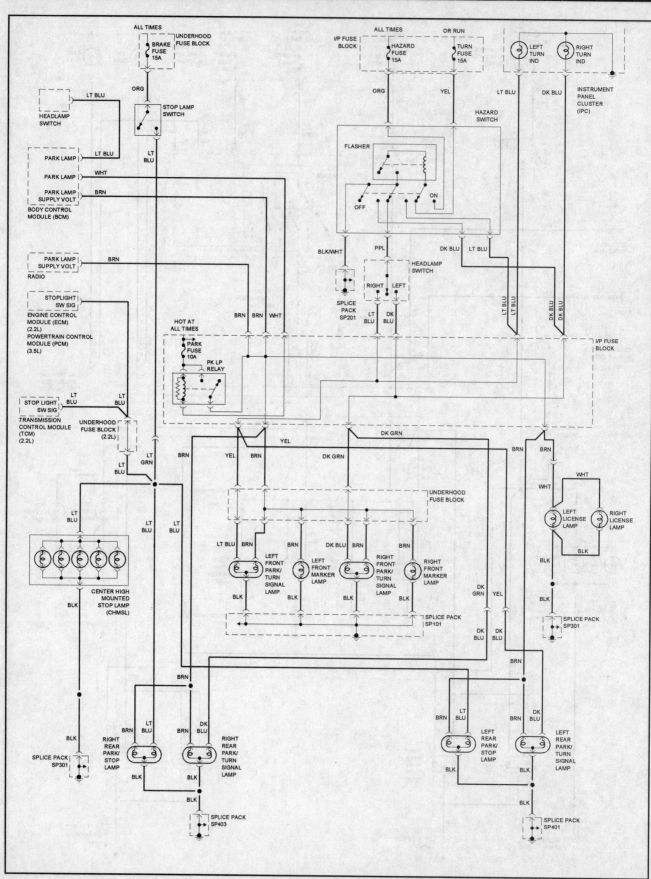

Exterior lighting system (except headlights) - 2004 and 2005 models (with Autolamps)

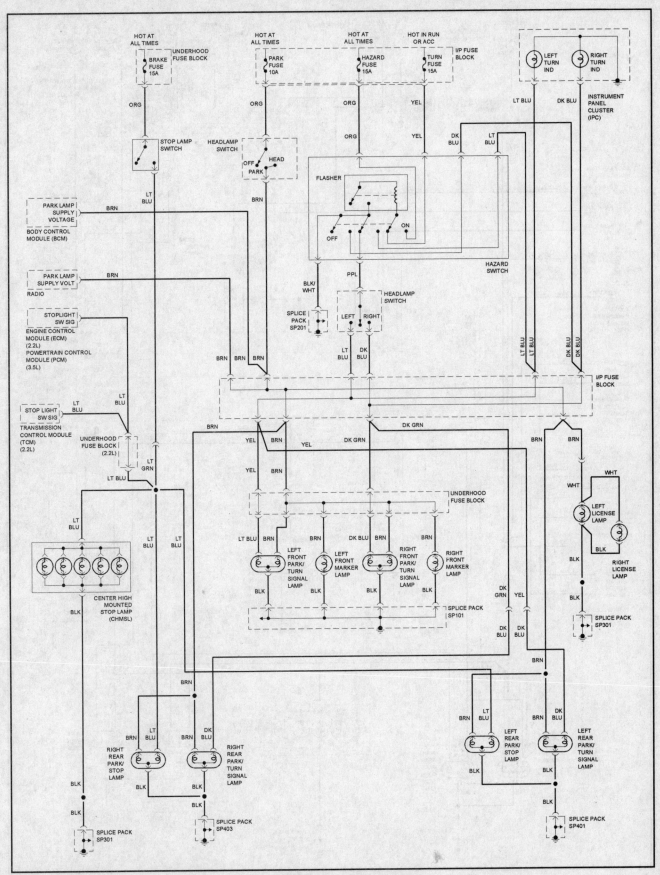

Exterior lighting system (except headlights) - 2004 and 2005 models (without Autolamps)

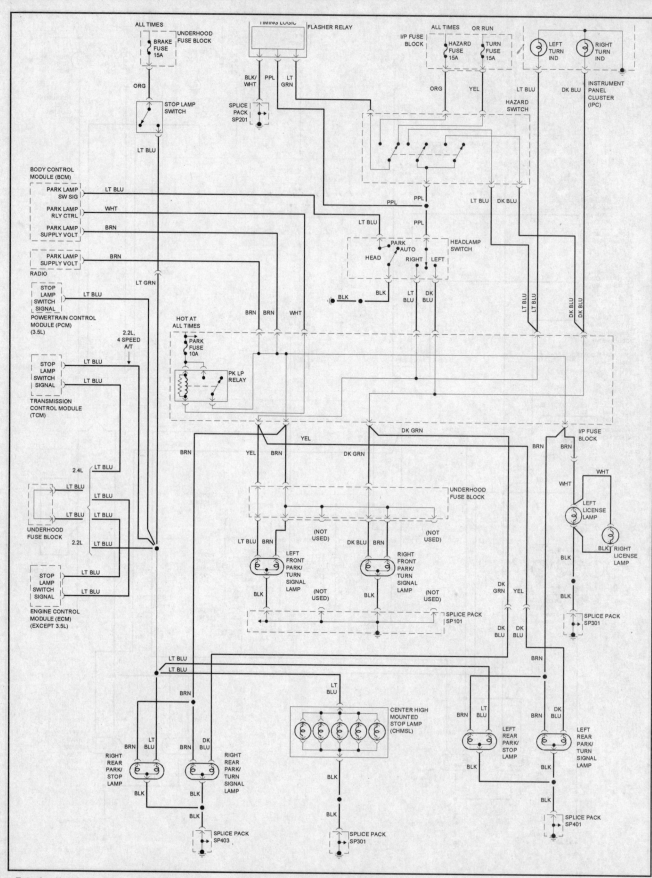

Exterior lighting system (except headlights) - 2006 and later models (with Autolamps)

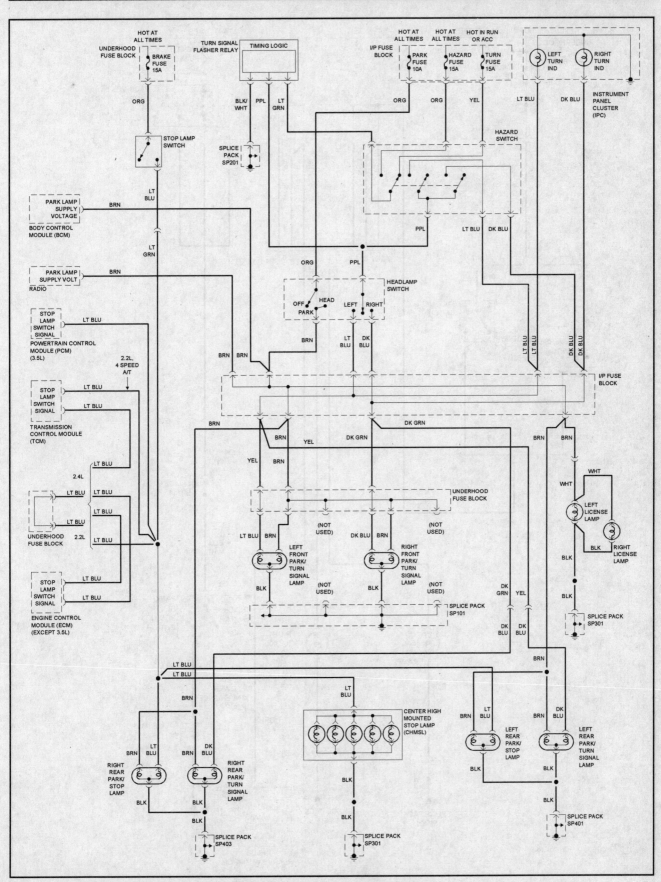

Exterior lighting system (except headlights) - 2006 and later models (without Autolamps)

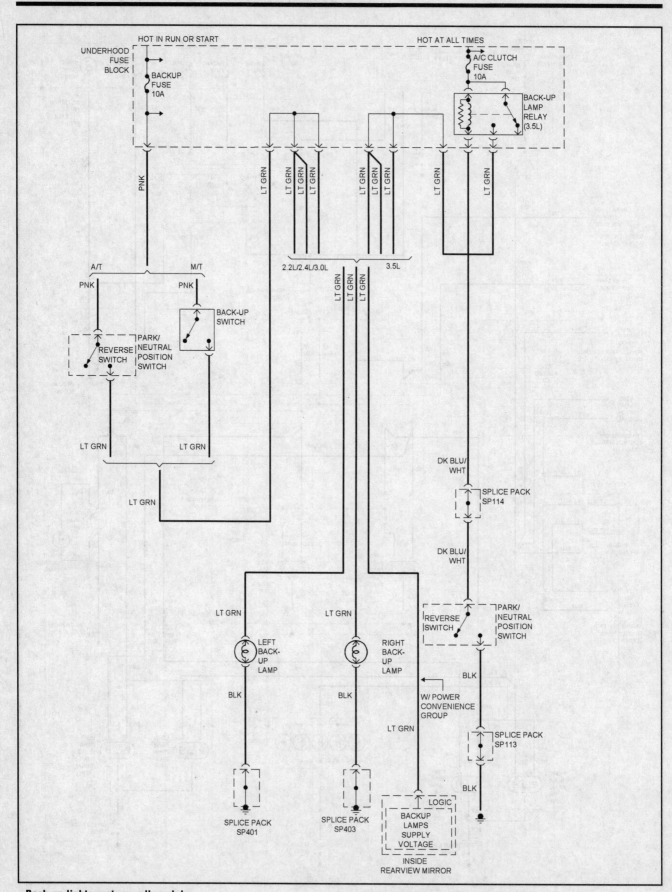

Back-up lights system - all models

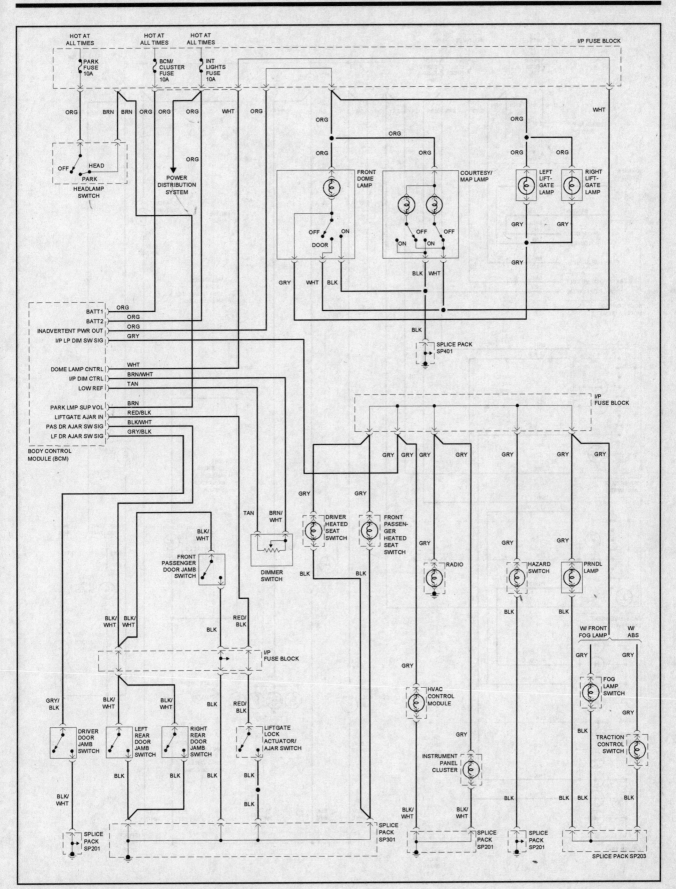

Interior lighting system - 2002 through 2005 models

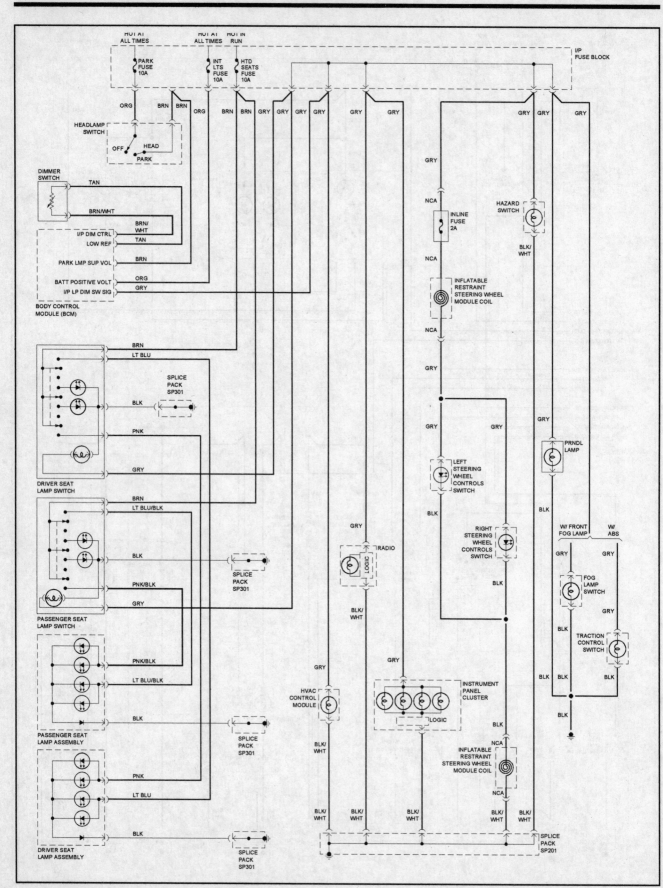

Interior lighting system - 2006 and later (Red Line models)

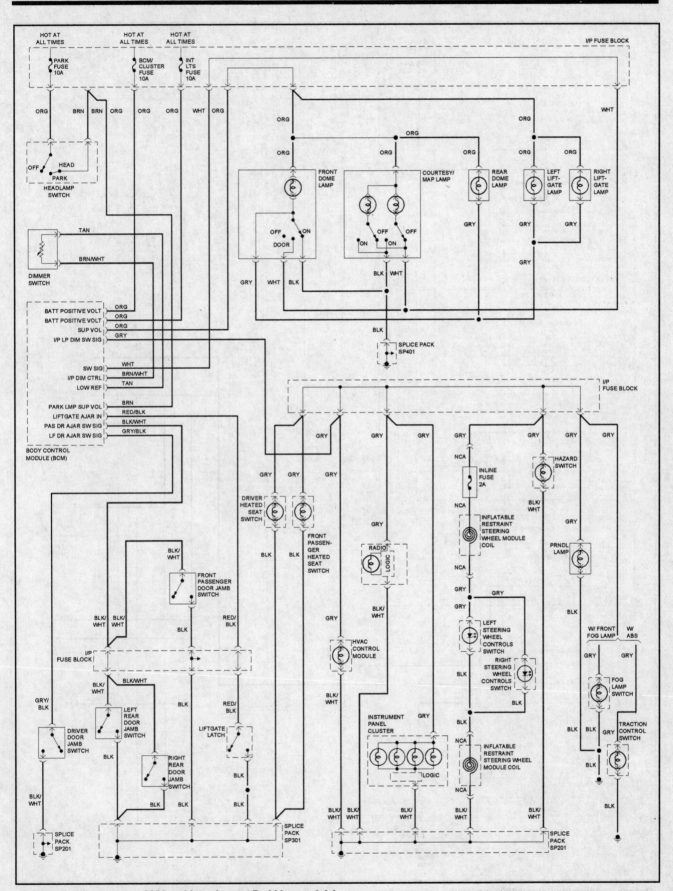

Interior lighting system - 2006 and later (except Red Line models)

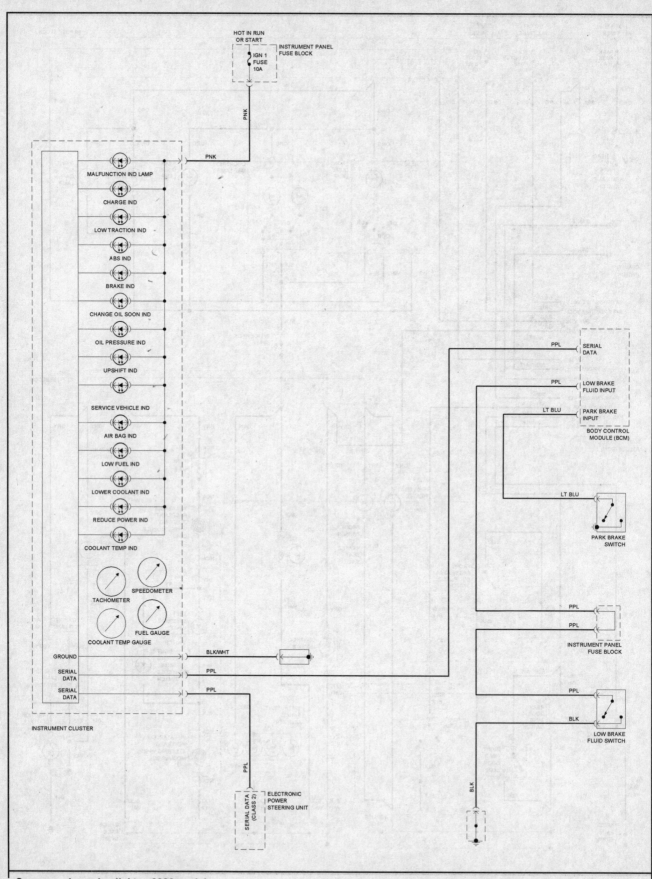

Gauges and warning lights - 2002 models

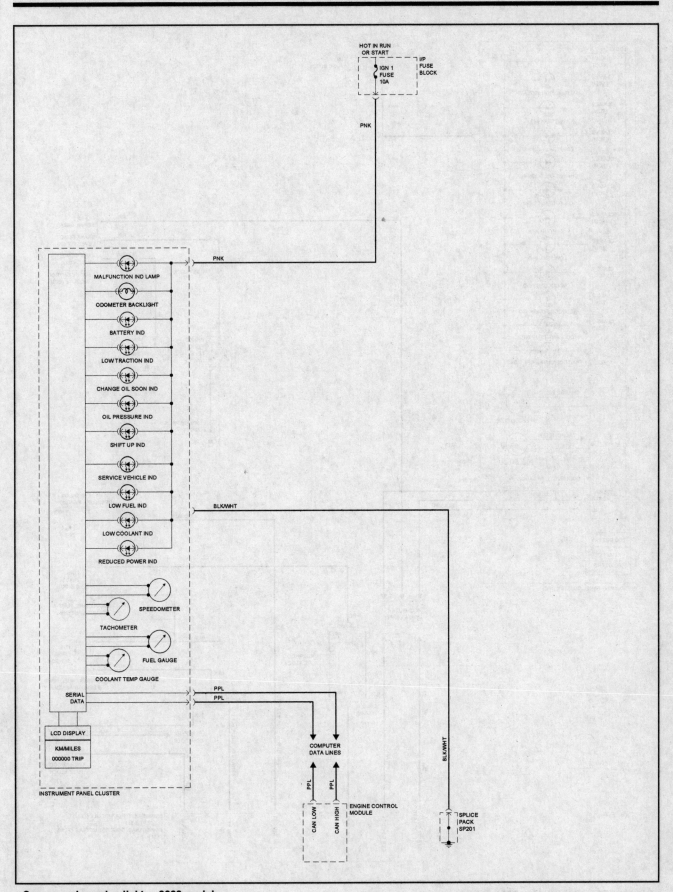

Gauges and warning lights - 2003 models

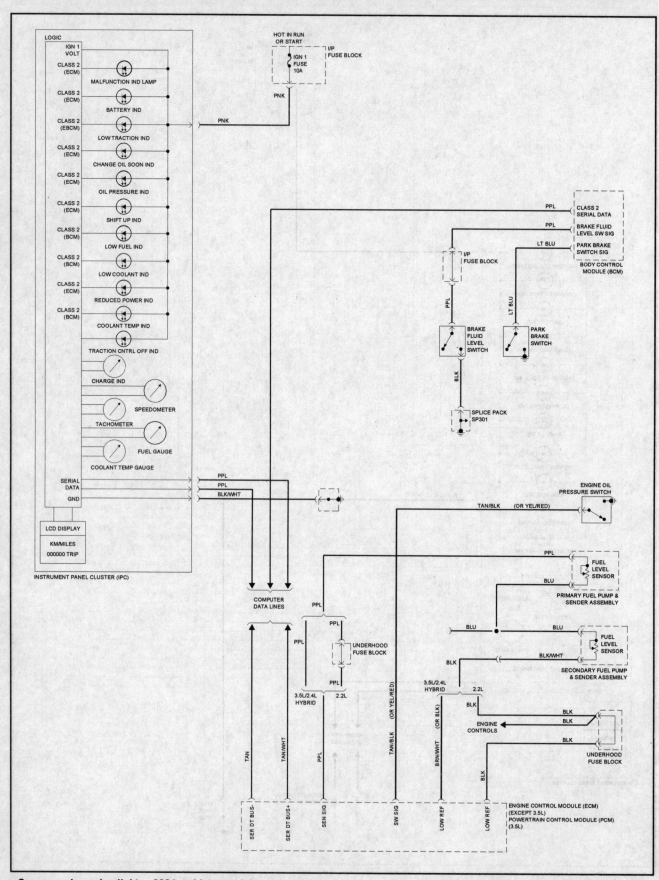

Gauges and warning lights - 2004 and later models

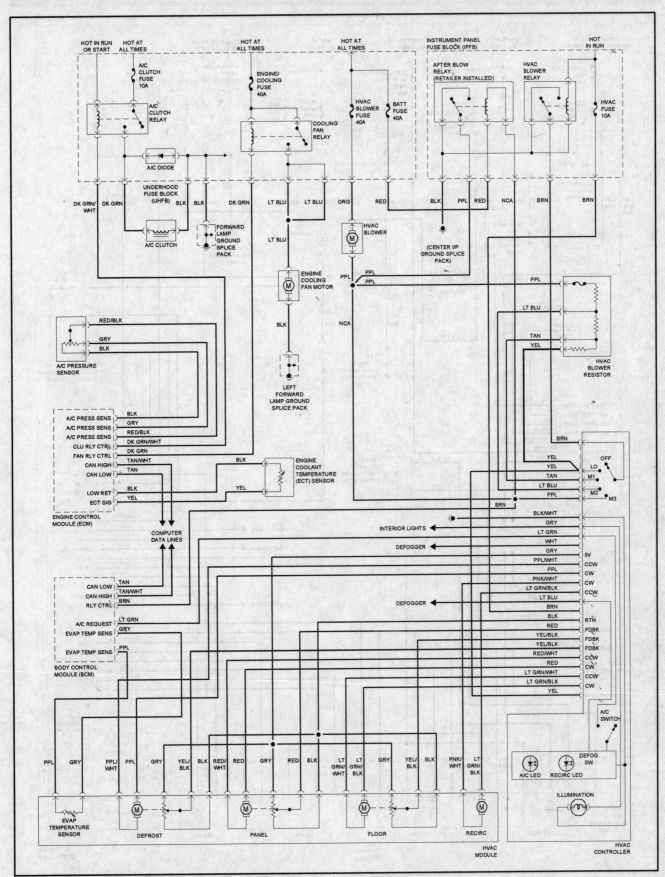

Air conditioning and engine cooling fan system - 2002 four-cylinder models (early production)

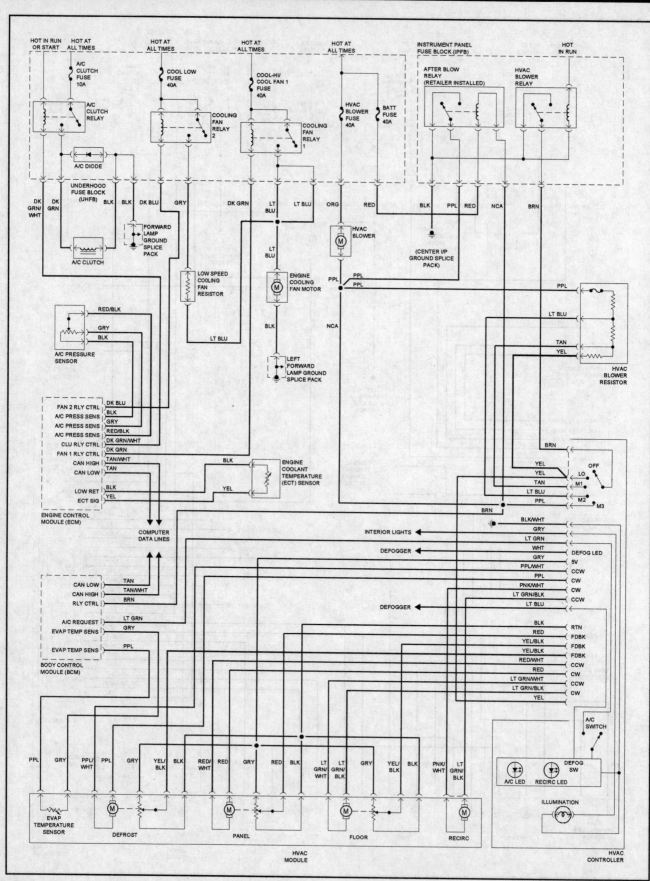

Air conditioning and engine cooling fan system - 2002 four-cylinder models (late production)

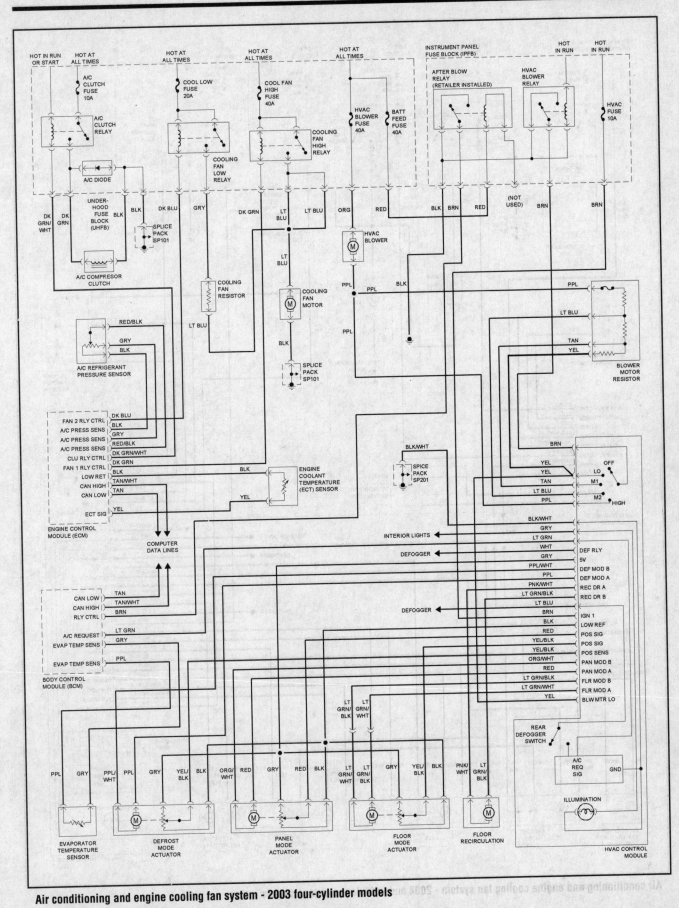

Air conditioning and engine cooling fan system - 2003 four-cylinder models

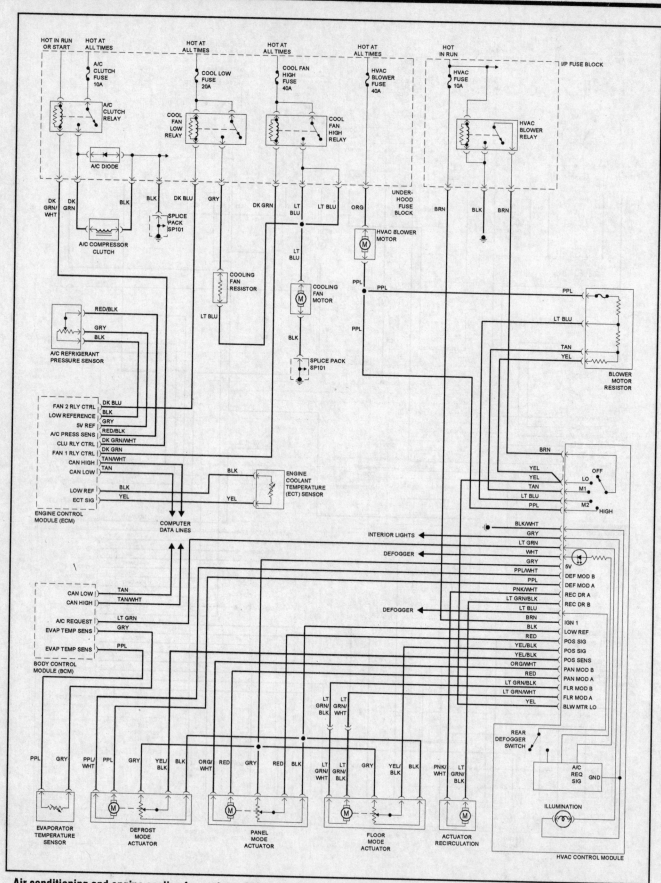

Air conditioning and engine cooling fan system - 2004 and 2005 four-cylinder models

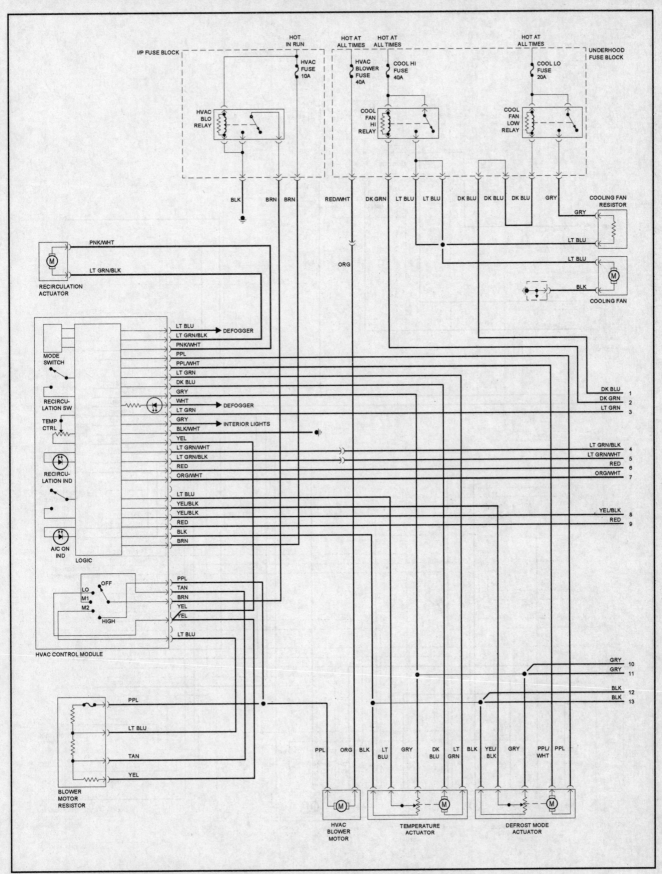

Air conditioning and engine cooling fan system - 2006 and later four-cylinder models (1 of 2)

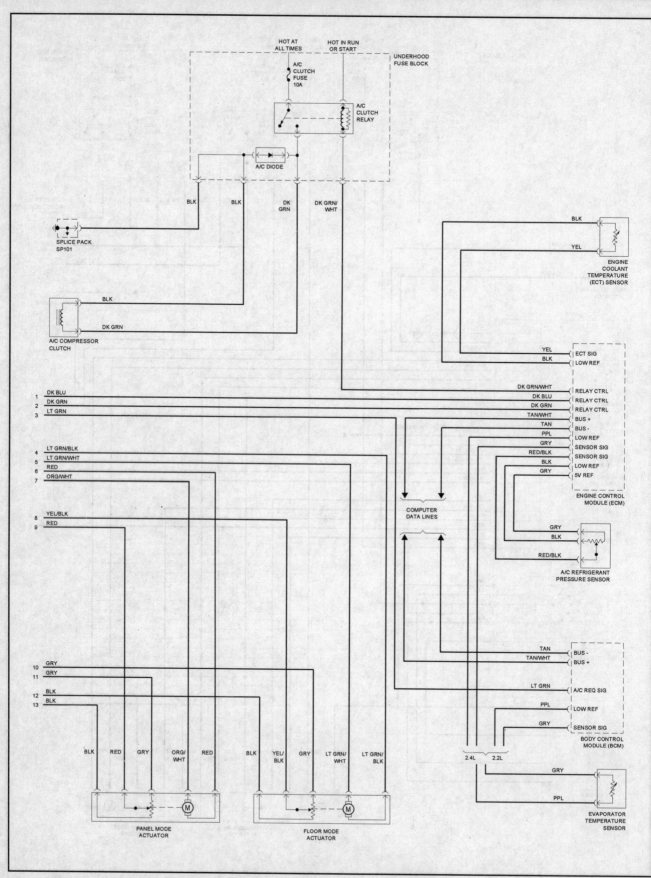

Air conditioning and engine cooling fan system - 2006 and later four-cylinder models (2 of 2)

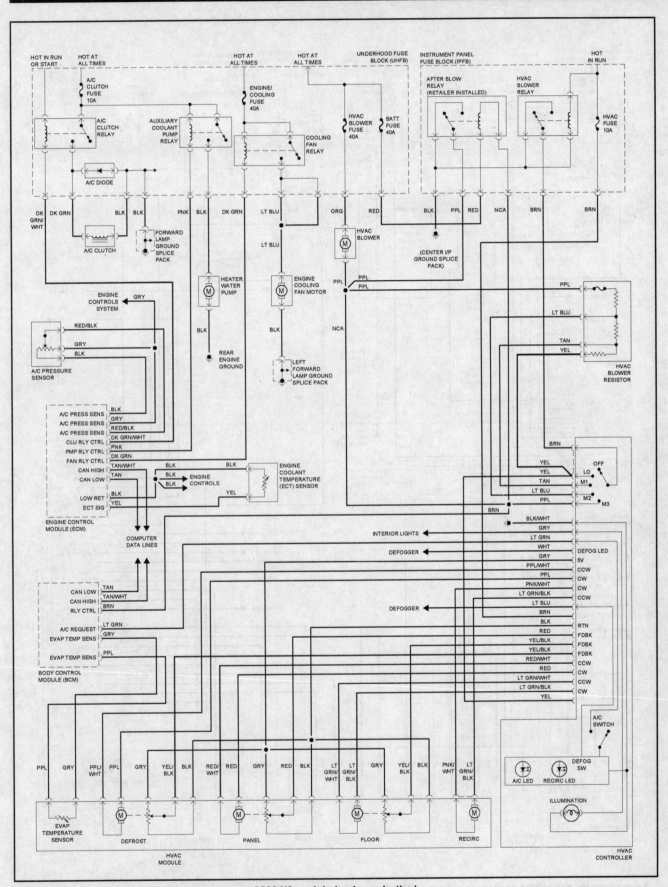

Air conditioning and engine cooling fan system - 2002 V6 models (early production)

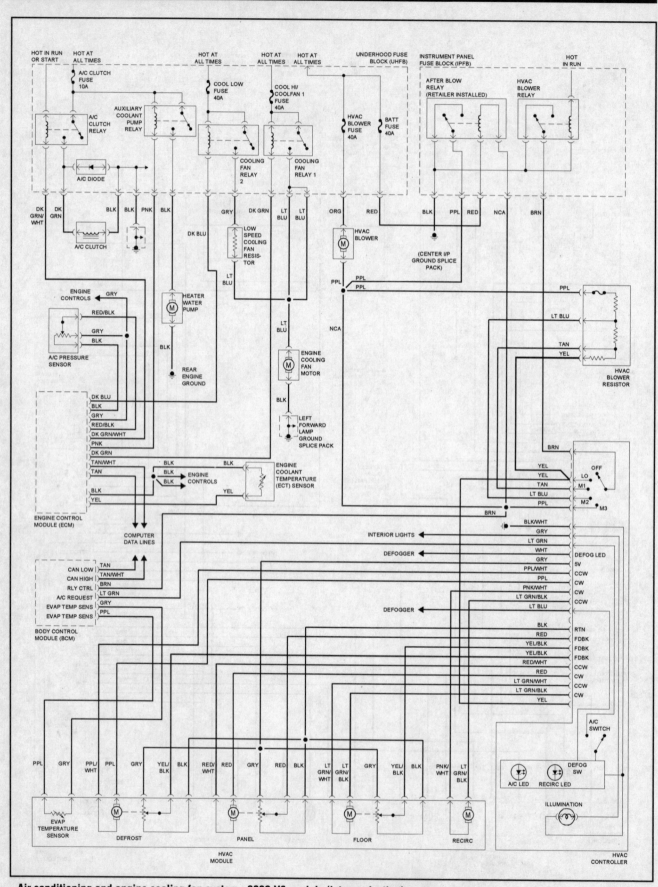

Air conditioning and engine cooling fan system - 2002 V6 models (late production)

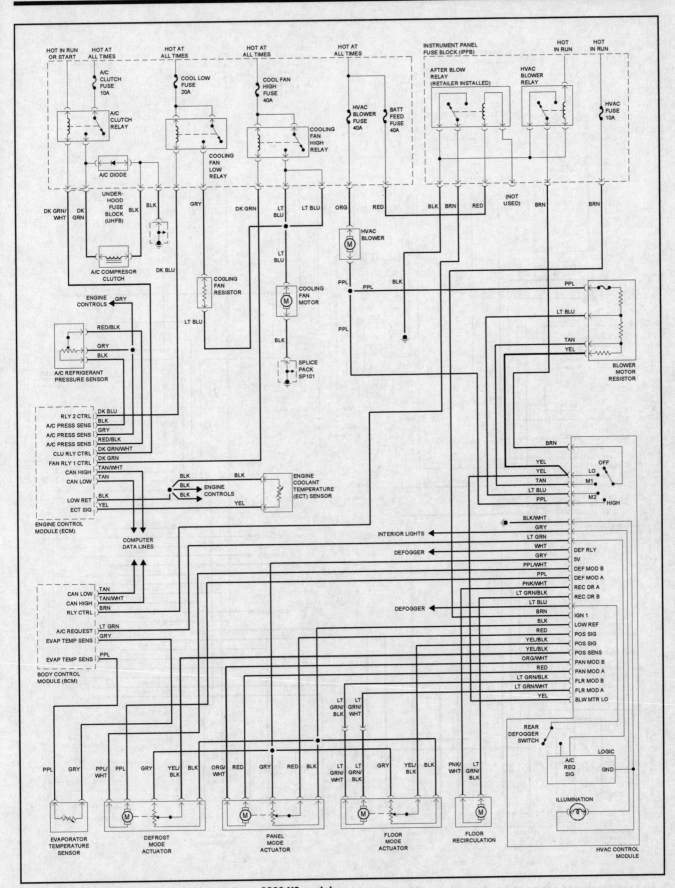

Air conditioning and engine cooling fan system - 2003 V6 models

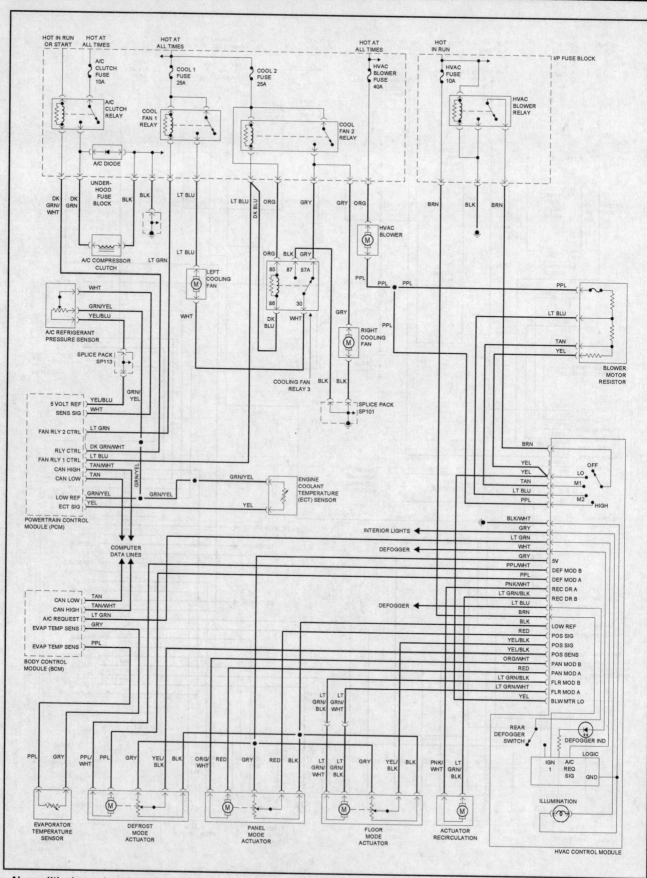

Air conditioning and engine cooling fan system - 2004 and 2005 V6 models

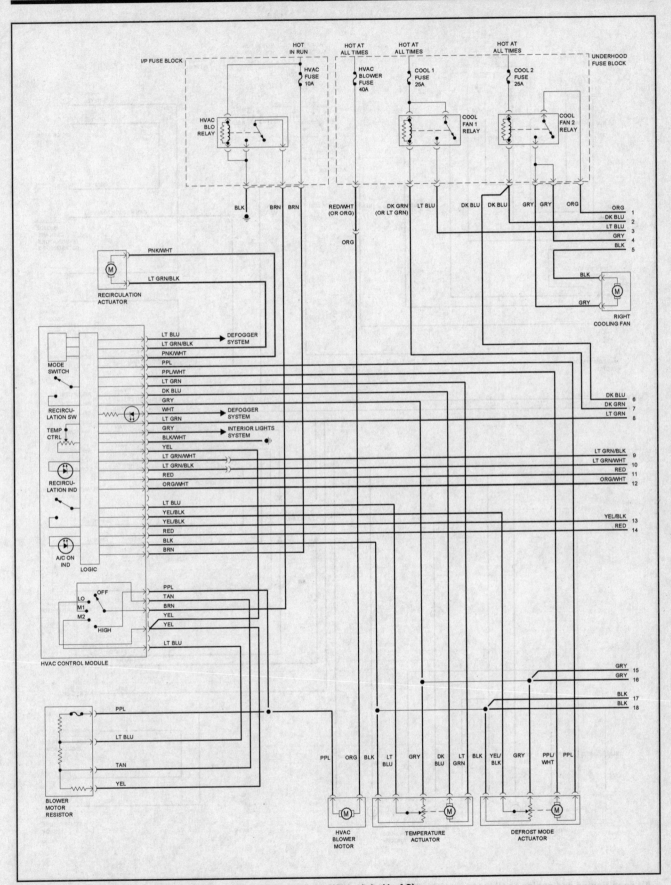

Air conditioning and engine cooling fan system - 2006 and later V6 models (1 of 2)

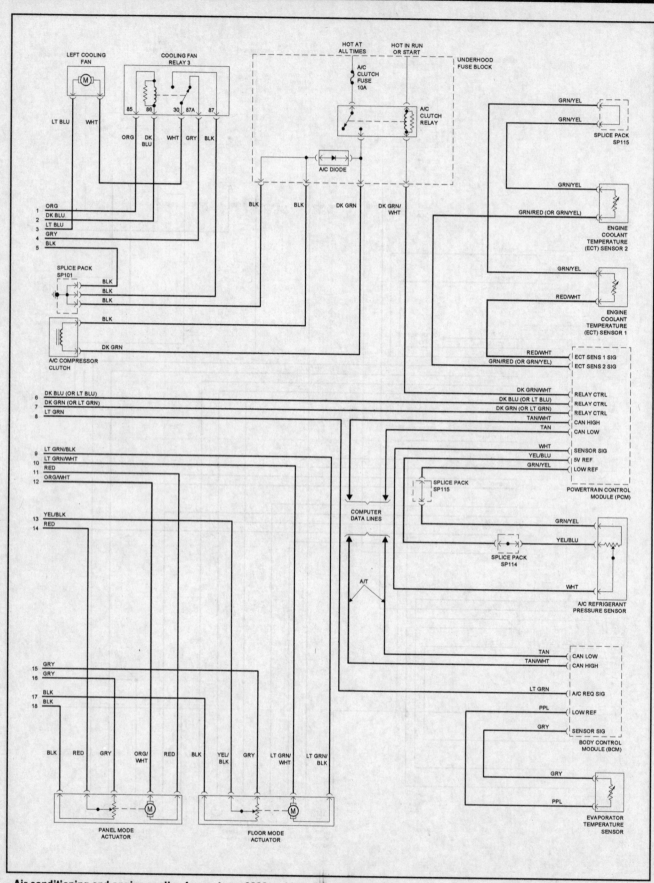

Air conditioning and engine cooling fan system - 2006 and later V6 models (2 of 2)

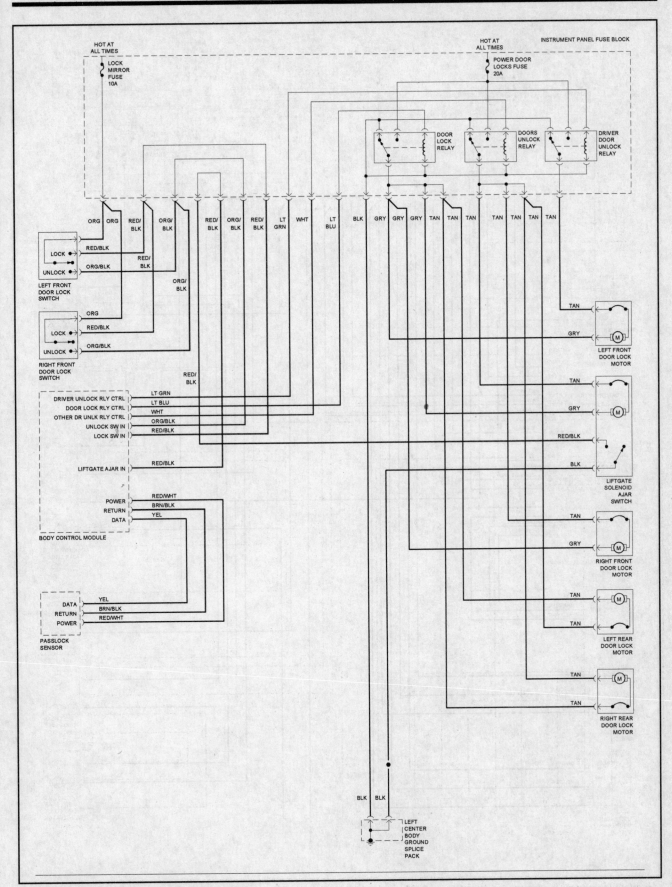

Power door lock system - 2002 and 2003 models

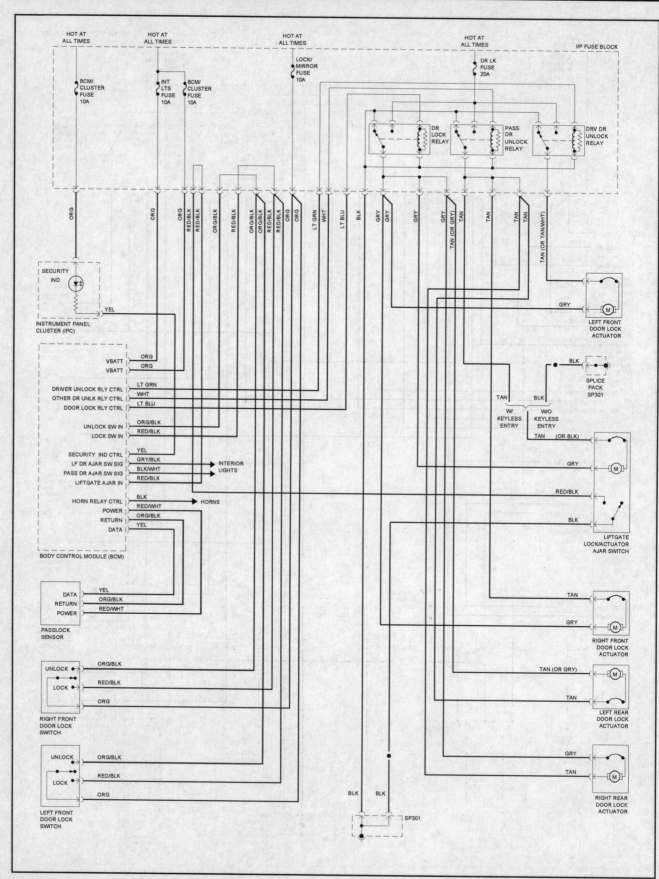

Power door lock system - 2004 and later models

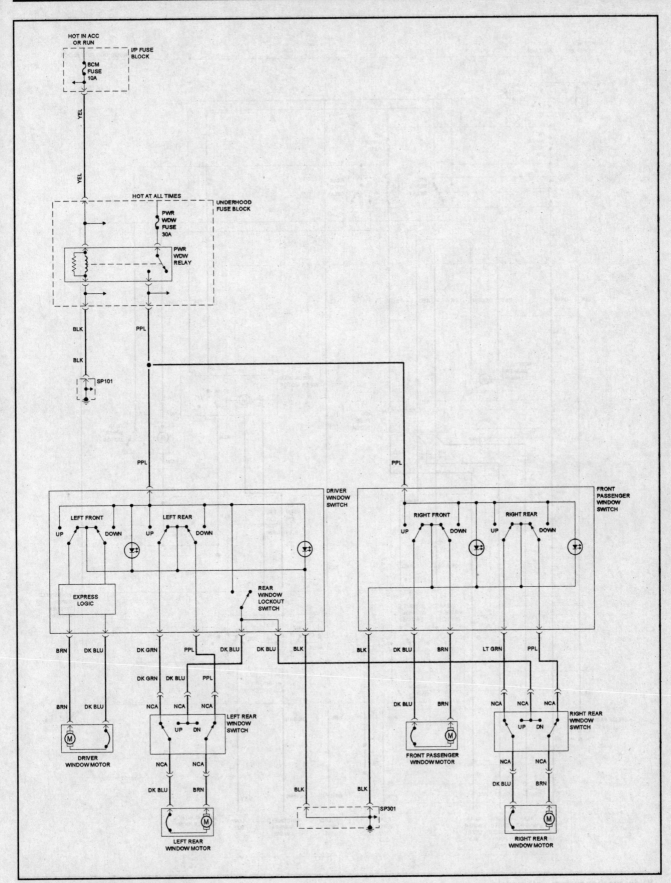

Power window system - all models

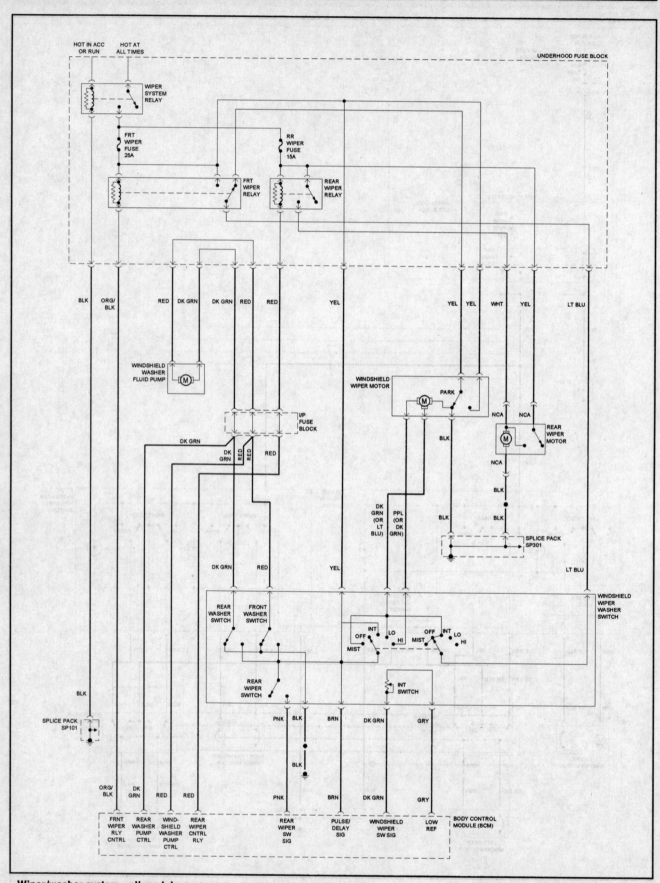

Wiper/washer system - all models

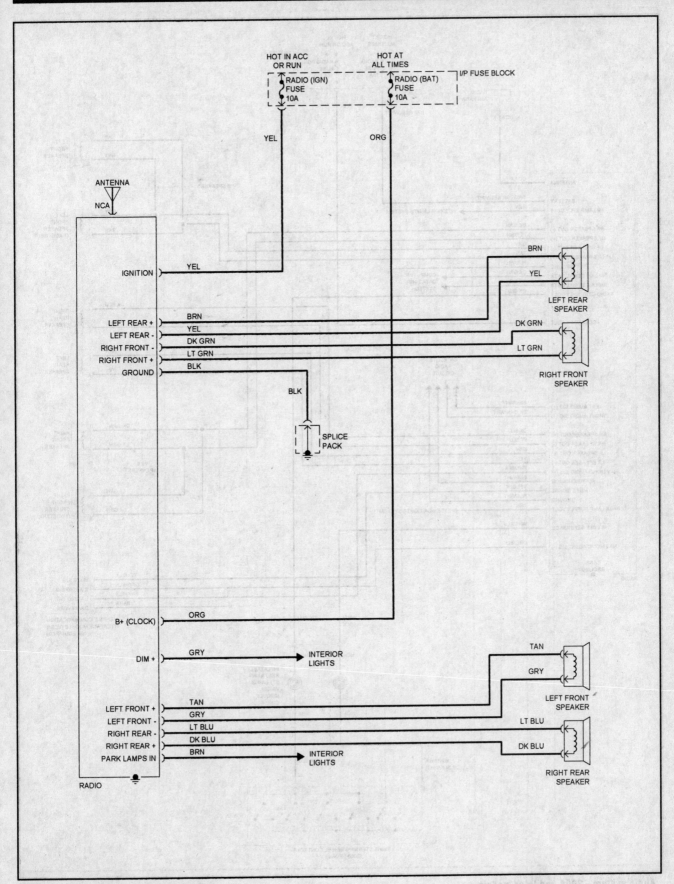

Audio system - 2002 and 2003 models

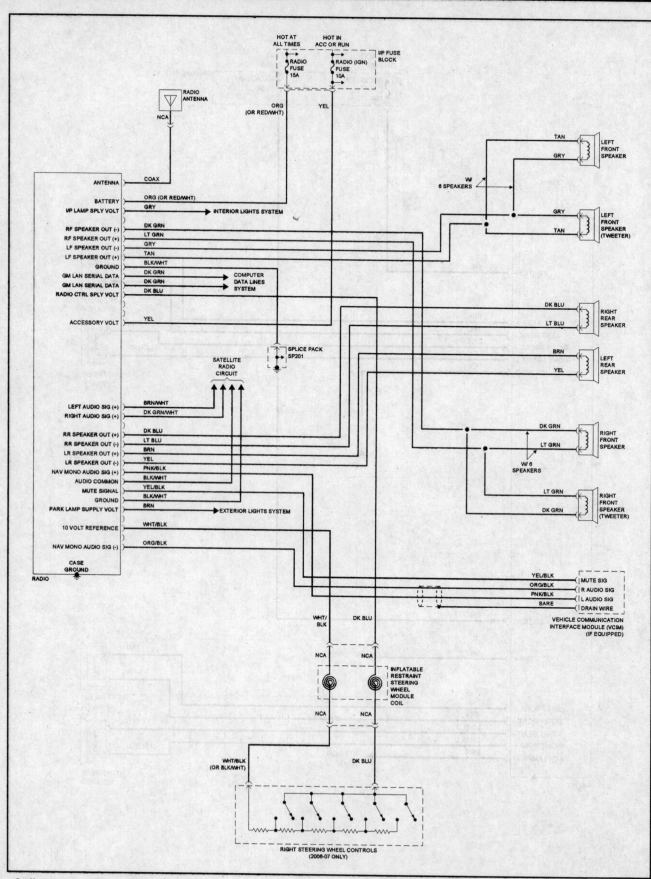

Audio system - 2004 and later models

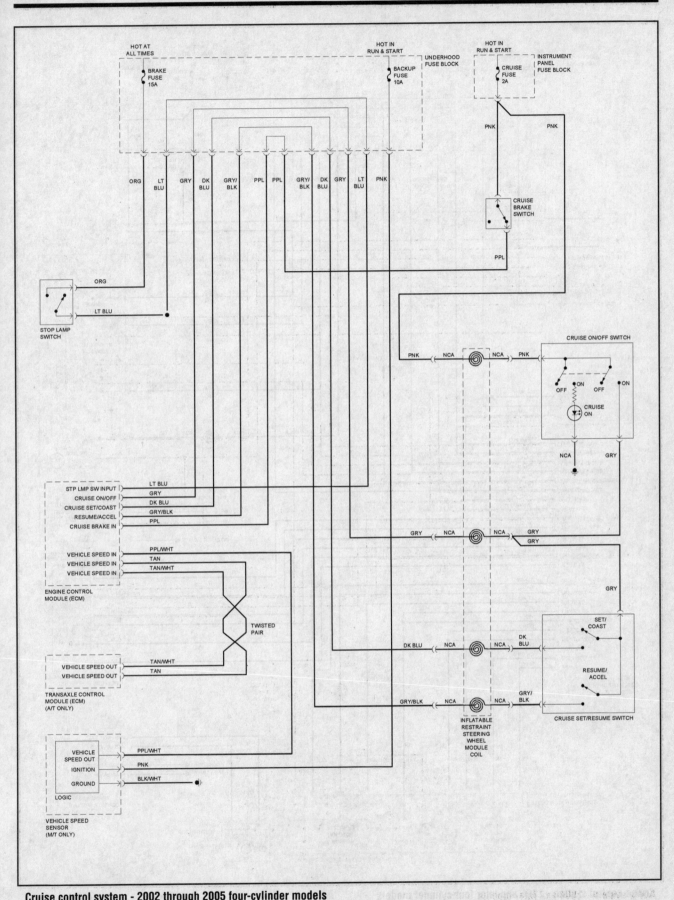

Cruise control system - 2002 through 2005 four-cylinder models

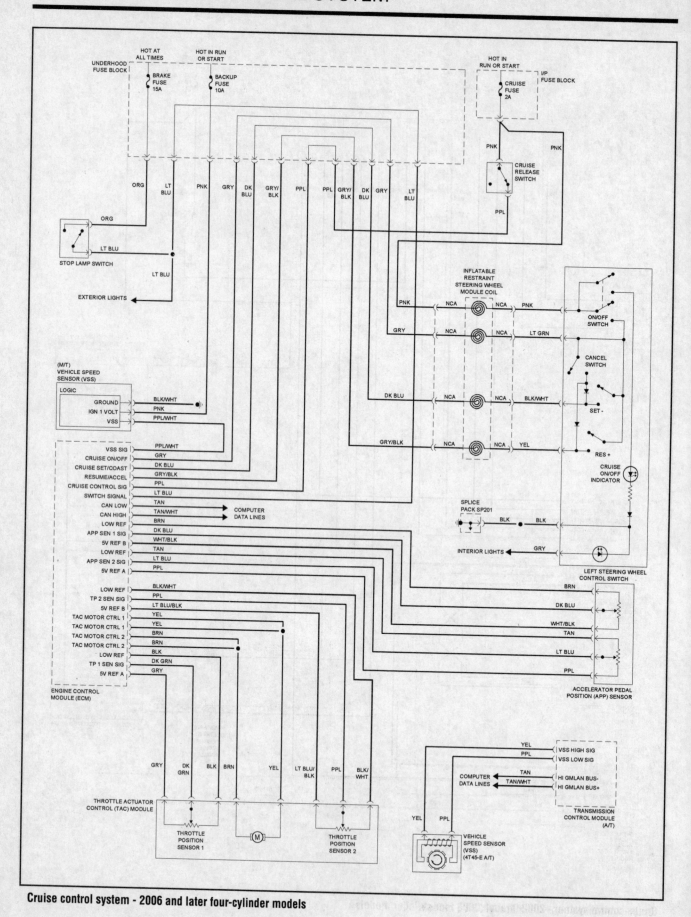

Cruise control system - 2006 and later four-cylinder models

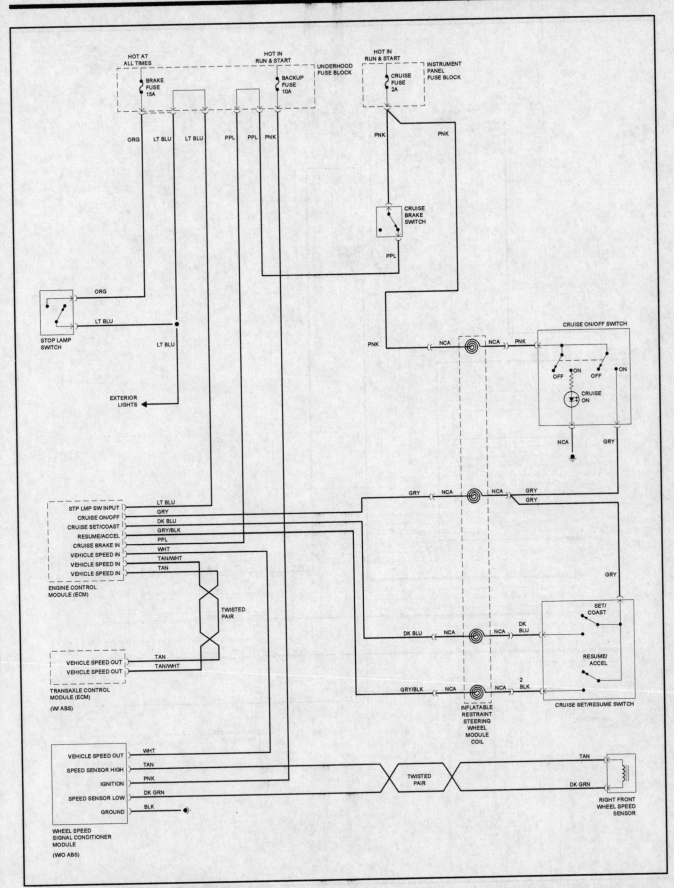

Cruise control system - 2002 and 2003 V6 models

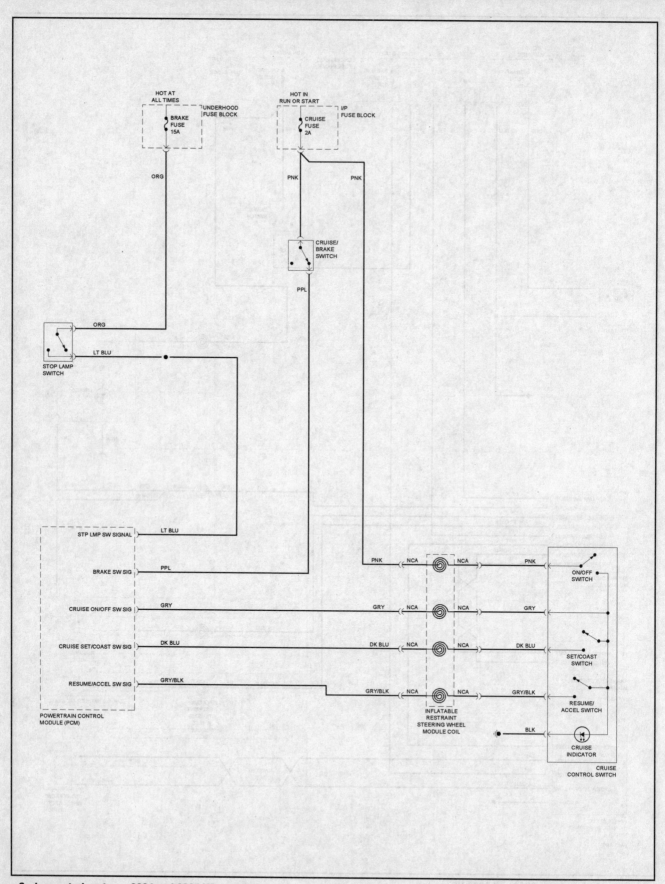

Cruise control system - 2004 and 2005 V6 models

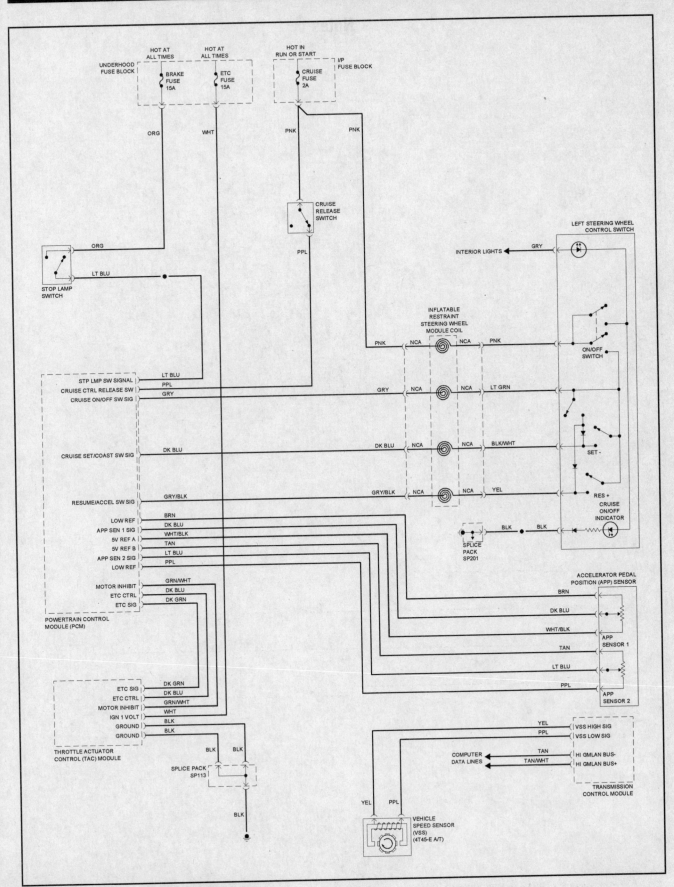

Cruise control system - 2006 and later V6 models

Notes

GLOSSARY

AIR/FUEL RATIO: The ratio of air-to-gasoline by weight in the fuel mixture drawn into the engine.

AIR INJECTION: One method of reducing harmful exhaust emissions by injecting air into each of the exhaust ports of an engine. The fresh air entering the hot exhaust manifold causes any remaining fuel to be burned before it can exit the tailpipe.

ALTERNATOR: A device used for converting mechanical energy into electrical energy.

AMMETER: An instrument, calibrated in amperes, used to measure the flow of an electrical current in a circuit. Ammeters are always connected in series with the circuit being tested.

AMPERE: The rate of flow of electrical current present when one volt of electrical pressure is applied against one ohm of electrical resistance.

ANALOG COMPUTER: Any microprocessor that uses similar (analogous) electrical signals to make its calculations.

ARMATURE: A laminated, soft iron core wrapped by a wire that converts electrical energy to mechanical energy as in a motor or relay. When rotated in a magnetic field, it changes mechanical energy into electrical energy as in a generator.

ATMOSPHERIC PRESSURE: The pressure on the Earth's surface caused by the weight of the air in the atmosphere. At sea level, this pressure is 14.7 psi at 32°F (101 kPa at 0°C).

ATOMIZATION: The breaking down of a liquid into a fine mist that can be suspended in air.

AXIAL PLAY: Movement parallel to a shaft or bearing bore.

BACKFIRE: The sudden combustion of gases in the intake or exhaust system that results in a loud explosion.

BACKLASH: The clearance or play between two parts, such as meshed gears.

BACKPRESSURE: Restrictions in the exhaust system that slow the exit of exhaust gases from the combustion chamber.

BAKELITE: A heat resistant, plastic insulator material commonly used in printed circuit boards and transistorized components.

BALL BEARING: A bearing made up of hardened inner and outer races between which hardened steel balls roll.

BALLAST RESISTOR: A resistor in the primary ignition circuit that lowers voltage after the engine is started to reduce wear on ignition components.

BEARING: A friction reducing, supportive device usually located between a stationary part and a moving part.

BIMETAL TEMPERATURE SENSOR: Any sensor or switch made of two dissimilar types of metal that bend when heated or cooled due to the different expansion rates of the alloys. These types of sensors usually function as an on/off switch.

BLOWBY: Combustion gases, composed of water vapor and unburned fuel, that leak past the piston rings into the crankcase during normal engine operation. These gases are removed by the PCV system to prevent the buildup of harmful acids in the crankcase.

BRAKE PAD: A brake shoe and lining assembly used with disc brakes.

BRAKE SHOE: The backing for the brake lining. The term is, however, usually applied to the assembly of the brake backing and lining.

BUSHING: A liner, usually removable, for a bearing; an anti-friction liner used in place of a bearing.

CALIPER: A hydraulically activated device in a disc brake system, which is mounted straddling the brake rotor (disc). The caliper contains at least one piston and two brake pads. Hydraulic pressure on the piston(s) forces the pads against the rotor.

CAMSHAFT: A shaft in the engine on which are the lobes (cams) which operate the valves. The camshaft is driven by the crankshaft, via a belt, chain or gears, at one half the crankshaft speed.

CAPACITOR: A device which stores an electrical charge.

CARBON MONOXIDE (CO): A colorless, odorless gas given off as a normal byproduct of combustion. It is poisonous and extremely dangerous in confined areas, building up slowly to toxic levels without warning if adequate ventilation is not available.

CARBURETOR: A device, usually mounted on the intake manifold of an engine, which mixes the air and fuel in the proper proportion to allow even combustion.

CATALYTIC CONVERTER: A device installed in the exhaust system, like a muffler, that converts harmful byproducts of combustion into carbon dioxide and water vapor by means of a heat-producing chemical reaction.

CENTRIFUGAL ADVANCE: A mechanical method of advancing the spark timing by using flyweights in the distributor that react to centrifugal force generated by the distributor shaft rotation.

CHECK VALVE: Any one-way valve installed to permit the flow of air, fuel or vacuum in one direction only.

CHOKE: A device, usually a moveable valve, placed in the intake path of a carburetor to restrict the flow of air.

CIRCUIT: Any unbroken path through which an electrical current can flow. Also used to describe fuel flow in some instances.

CIRCUIT BREAKER: A switch which protects an electrical circuit from overload by opening the circuit when the current flow exceeds a predetermined level. Some circuit breakers must be reset manually, while most reset automatically.

COIL (IGNITION): A transformer in the ignition circuit which steps up the voltage provided to the spark plugs.

COMBINATION MANIFOLD: An assembly which includes both the intake and exhaust manifolds in one casting.

COMBINATION VALVE: A device used in some fuel systems that routes fuel vapors to a charcoal storage canister instead of venting them into the atmosphere. The valve relieves fuel tank pressure and allows fresh air into the tank as the fuel level drops to prevent a vapor lock situation.

COMPRESSION RATIO: The comparison of the total volume of the cylinder and combustion chamber with the piston at BDC and the piston at TDC.

CONDENSER: 1. An electrical device which acts to store an electrical charge, preventing voltage surges. 2. A radiator-like device in the air conditioning system in which refrigerant gas condenses into a liquid, giving off heat.

CONDUCTOR: Any material through which an electrical current can be transmitted easily.

CONTINUITY: Continuous or complete circuit. Can be checked with an ohmmeter.

COUNTERSHAFT: An intermediate shaft which is rotated by a mainshaft and transmits, in turn, that rotation to a working part.

CRANKCASE: The lower part of an engine in which the crankshaft and related parts operate.

CRANKSHAFT: The main driving shaft of an engine which receives reciprocating motion from the pistons and converts it to rotary motion.

CYLINDER: In an engine, the round hole in the engine block in which the piston(s) ride.

CYLINDER BLOCK: The main structural member of an engine in which is found the cylinders, crankshaft and other principal parts.

CYLINDER HEAD: The detachable portion of the engine, usually fastened to the top of the cylinder block and containing all or most of the combustion chambers. On overhead valve engines, it contains the valves and their operating parts. On overhead cam engines, it contains the camshaft as well.

DEAD CENTER: The extreme top or bottom of the piston stroke.

DETONATION: An unwanted explosion of the air/fuel mixture in the combustion chamber caused by excess heat and compression, advanced timing, or an overly lean mixture. Also referred to as "ping".

DIAPHRAGM: A thin, flexible wall separating two cavities, such as in a vacuum advance unit.

DIESELING: A condition in which hot spots in the combustion chamber cause the engine to run on after the key is turned off.

DIFFERENTIAL: A geared assembly which allows the transmission of motion between drive axles, giving one axle the ability to turn faster than the other.

DIODE: An electrical device that will allow current to flow in one direction only.

DISC BRAKE: A hydraulic braking assembly consisting of a brake disc, or rotor, mounted on an axle, and a caliper assembly containing, usually two brake pads which are activated by hydraulic pressure. The pads are forced against the sides of the disc, creating friction which slows the vehicle.

DISTRIBUTOR: A mechanically driven device on an engine which is responsible for electrically firing the spark plug at a predetermined point of the piston stroke.

DOWEL PIN: A pin, inserted in mating holes in two different parts allowing those parts to maintain a fixed relationship.

DRUM BRAKE: A braking system which consists of two brake shoes and one or two wheel cylinders, mounted on a fixed backing plate, and a brake drum, mounted on an axle, which revolves around the assembly.

DWELL: The rate, measured in degrees of shaft rotation, at which an electrical circuit cycles on and off.

ELECTRONIC CONTROL UNIT (ECU): Ignition module, module, amplifier or igniter. See Module for definition.

ELECTRONIC IGNITION: A system in which the timing and firing of the spark plugs is controlled by an electronic control unit, usually called a module. These systems have no points or condenser.

END-PLAY: The measured amount of axial movement in a shaft.

ENGINE: A device that converts heat into mechanical energy.

EXHAUST MANIFOLD: A set of cast passages or pipes which conduct exhaust gases from the engine.

FEELER GAUGE: A blade, usually metal, or precisely predetermined thickness, used to measure the clearance between two parts.

FIRING ORDER: The order in which combustion occurs in the cylinders of an engine. Also the order in which spark is distributed to the plugs by the distributor.

FLOODING: The presence of too much fuel in the intake manifold and combustion chamber which prevents the air/fuel mixture from firing, thereby causing a no-start situation.

FLYWHEEL: A disc shaped part bolted to the rear end of the crankshaft. Around the outer perimeter is affixed the ring gear. The starter drive engages the ring gear, turning the flywheel, which rotates the crankshaft, imparting the initial starting motion to the engine.

FOOT POUND (ft. lbs. or sometimes, ft.lb.): The amount of energy or work needed to raise an item weighing one pound, a distance of one foot.

FUSE: A protective device in a circuit which prevents circuit overload by breaking the circuit when a specific amperage is present. The device is constructed around a strip or wire of a lower amperage rating than the circuit it is designed to protect. When an amperage higher than that stamped on the fuse is present in the circuit, the strip or wire melts, opening the circuit.

GEAR RATIO: The ratio between the number of teeth on meshing gears.

GENERATOR: A device which converts mechanical energy into electrical energy.

HEAT RANGE: The measure of a spark plug's ability to dissipate heat from its firing end. The higher the heat range, the hotter the plug fires.

HUB: The center part of a wheel or gear.

HYDROCARBON (HC): Any chemical compound made up of hydrogen and carbon. A major pollutant formed by the engine as a byproduct of combustion.

HYDROMETER: An instrument used to measure the specific gravity of a solution.

INCH POUND (inch lbs.; sometimes in.lb. or in. lbs.): One twelfth of a foot pound.

INDUCTION: A means of transferring electrical energy in the form of a magnetic field. Principle used in the ignition coil to increase voltage.

INJECTOR: A device which receives metered fuel under relatively low pressure and is activated to inject the fuel into the engine under relatively high pressure at a predetermined time.

INPUT SHAFT: The shaft to which torque is applied, usually carrying the driving gear or gears.

INTAKE MANIFOLD: A casting of passages or pipes used to conduct air or a fuel/air mixture to the cylinders.

JOURNAL: The bearing surface within which a shaft operates.

KEY: A small block usually fitted in a notch between a shaft and a hub to prevent slippage of the two parts.

MANIFOLD: A casting of passages or set of pipes which connect the cylinders to an inlet or outlet source.

MANIFOLD VACUUM: Low pressure in an engine intake manifold formed just below the throttle plates. Manifold vacuum is highest at idle and drops under acceleration.

MASTER CYLINDER: The primary fluid pressurizing device in a hydraulic system. In automotive use, it is found in brake and hydraulic clutch systems and is pedal activated, either directly or, in a power brake system, through the power booster.

MODULE: Electronic control unit, amplifier or igniter of solid state or integrated design which controls the current flow in the ignition primary circuit based on input from the pick-up coil. When the module opens the primary circuit, high secondary voltage is induced in the coil.

NEEDLE BEARING: A bearing which consists of a number (usually a large number) of long, thin rollers.

OHM: (Ω) The unit used to measure the resistance of conductor-to-electrical flow. One ohm is the amount of resistance that limits current flow to one ampere in a circuit with one volt of pressure.

OHMMETER: An instrument used for measuring the resistance, in ohms, in an electrical circuit.

OUTPUT SHAFT: The shaft which transmits torque from a device, such as a transmission.

OVERDRIVE: A gear assembly which produces more shaft revolutions than that transmitted to it.

OVERHEAD CAMSHAFT (OHC): An engine configuration in which the camshaft is mounted on top of the cylinder head and operates the valve either directly or by means of rocker arms.

OVERHEAD VALVE (OHV): An engine configuration in which all of the valves are located in the cylinder head and the camshaft is located in the cylinder block. The camshaft operates the valves via lifters and pushrods.

OXIDES OF NITROGEN (NOx): Chemical compounds of nitrogen produced as a byproduct of combustion. They combine with hydrocarbons to produce smog.

OXYGEN SENSOR: Use with the feedback system to sense the presence of oxygen in the exhaust gas and signal the computer which can reference the voltage signal to an air/fuel ratio.

PINION: The smaller of two meshing gears.

PISTON RING: An open-ended ring with fits into a groove on the outer diameter of the piston. Its chief function is to form a seal between the piston and cylinder wall. Most automotive pistons have three rings: two for compression sealing; one for oil sealing.

PRELOAD: A predetermined load placed on a bearing during assembly or by adjustment.

PRIMARY CIRCUIT: the low voltage side of the ignition system which consists of the ignition switch, ballast resistor or resistance wire, bypass, coil, electronic control unit and pick-up coil as well as the connecting wires and harnesses.

PRESS FIT: The mating of two parts under pressure, due to the inner diameter of one being smaller than the outer diameter of the other, or vice versa; an interference fit.

RACE: The surface on the inner or outer ring of a bearing on which the balls, needles or rollers move.

REGULATOR: A device which maintains the amperage and/or voltage levels of a circuit at predetermined values.

RELAY: A switch which automatically opens and/or closes a circuit.

RESISTANCE: The opposition to the flow of current through a circuit or electrical device, and is measured in ohms. Resistance is equal to the voltage divided by the amperage.

RESISTOR: A device, usually made of wire, which offers a preset amount of resistance in an electrical circuit.

RING GEAR: The name given to a ring-shaped gear attached to a differential case, or affixed to a flywheel or as part of a planetary gear set.

ROLLER BEARING: A bearing made up of hardened inner and outer races between which hardened steel rollers move.

ROTOR: 1. The disc-shaped part of a disc brake assembly, upon which the brake pads bear; also called, brake disc. 2. The device

mounted atop the distributor shaft, which passes current to the distributor cap tower contacts.

SECONDARY CIRCUIT: The high voltage side of the ignition system, usually above 20,000 volts. The secondary includes the ignition coil, coil wire, distributor cap and rotor, spark plug wires and spark plugs.

SENDING UNIT: A mechanical, electrical, hydraulic or electromagnetic device which transmits information to a gauge.

SENSOR: Any device designed to measure engine operating conditions or ambient pressures and temperatures. Usually electronic in nature and designed to send a voltage signal to an on-board computer, some sensors may operate as a simple on/off switch or they may provide a variable voltage signal (like a potentiometer) as conditions or measured parameters change.

SHIM: Spacers of precise, predetermined thickness used between parts to establish a proper working relationship.

SLAVE CYLINDER: In automotive use, a device in the hydraulic clutch system which is activated by hydraulic force, disengaging the clutch.

SOLENOID: A coil used to produce a magnetic field, the effect of which is to produce work.

SPARK PLUG: A device screwed into the combustion chamber of a spark ignition engine. The basic construction is a conductive core inside of a ceramic insulator, mounted in an outer conductive base. An electrical charge from the spark plug wire travels along the conductive core and jumps a preset air gap to a grounding point or points at the end of the conductive base. The resultant spark ignites the fuel/air mixture in the combustion chamber.

SPLINES: Ridges machined or cast onto the outer diameter of a shaft or inner diameter of a bore to enable parts to mate without rotation.

TACHOMETER: A device used to measure the rotary speed of an engine, shaft, gear, etc., usually in rotations per minute.

THERMOSTAT: A valve, located in the cooling system of an engine, which is closed when cold and opens gradually in response to engine heating, controlling the temperature of the coolant and rate of coolant flow.

TOP DEAD CENTER (TDC): The point at which the piston reaches the top of its travel on the compression stroke.

TORQUE: The twisting force applied to an object.

TORQUE CONVERTER: A turbine used to transmit power from a driving member to a driven member via hydraulic action, providing changes in drive ratio and torque. In automotive use, it links the driveplate at the rear of the engine to the automatic transmission.

TRANSDUCER: A device used to change a force into an electrical signal.

TRANSISTOR: A semi-conductor component which can be actuated by a small voltage to perform an electrical switching function.

TUNE-UP: A regular maintenance function, usually associated with the replacement and adjustment of parts and components in the electrical and fuel systems of a vehicle for the purpose of attaining optimum performance.

TURBOCHARGER: An exhaust driven pump which compresses intake air and forces it into the combustion chambers at higher than atmospheric pressures. The increased air pressure allows more fuel to be burned and results in increased horsepower being produced.

VACUUM ADVANCE: A device which advances the ignition timing in response to increased engine vacuum.

VACUUM GAUGE: An instrument used to measure the presence of vacuum in a chamber.

VALVE: A device which control the pressure, direction of flow or rate of flow of a liquid or gas.

VALVE CLEARANCE: The measured gap between the end of the valve stem and the rocker arm, cam lobe or follower that activates the valve.

VISCOSITY: The rating of a liquid's internal resistance to flow.

VOLTMETER: An instrument used for measuring electrical force in units called volts. Voltmeters are always connected parallel with the circuit being tested.

WHEEL CYLINDER: Found in the automotive drum brake assembly, it is a device, actuated by hydraulic pressure, which, through internal pistons, pushes the brake shoes outward against the drums.

Notes

MASTER INDEX

A